Economic Policy Options for a Prosperous Nigeria

Economic Policy Options for a Prosperous Nigeria

Edited by

Paul Collier
Chukwuma C. Soludo
and
Catherine Pattillo

palgrave
macmillan

First published 2008 by
PALGRAVE MACMILLAN
Houndmills, Basingstoke, Hampshire RG21 6XS and
175 Fifth Avenue, New York, N.Y. 10010
Companies and representatives throughout the world

PALGRAVE MACMILLAN is the global academic imprint of the Palgrave Macmillan division of St. Martin's Press, LLC and of Palgrave Macmillan Ltd. Macmillan® is a registered trademark in the United States, United Kingdom and other countries. Palgrave is a registered trademark in the European Union and other countries.

ISBN 978-0-230-54273-0 ISBN 978-0-230-58319-1 (eBook)
DOI 10.1057/9780230583191

A catalogue record for this book is available from the British Library.

A catalog record for this book is available from the Library of Congress.

10 9 8 7 6 5 4 3 2 1
17 16 15 14 13 12 11 10 09 08

Contents

List of Tables

List of Figures

Preface

In 2002, I mooted the idea for this book in a conversation with Professor Paul Collier. I envisioned a collaborative project that would bring together colleagues from Nigeria, Oxford and Washington to produce a work that would provide viable policy options for Nigerian decision-makers. We assigned topics of policy relevance to different authors from Nigeria, Oxford and Washington to research upon. This was before I came into government in 2003, first as the Economic Advisor to the President of the Federal Republic of Nigeria, and latterly as Governor of the Central Bank.

More recently, we were able to revive the idea by inviting the authors of the assigned topics from Oxford and Washington to a two-day workshop that took place on 23–24 October 2006 at the Central Bank of Nigeria in Abuja. Papers were presented on issues ranging from oil and the macroeconomic framework to monetary policy, trade and macroeconomic volatility, private investment, poverty and income distribution, fiscal federalism and public services delivery.

Each chapter has been subjected to a process of criticism and peer review. Authors were held to a high standard of analytical rigour, aware of the fact that African governments have grown weary of outsiders preaching at them and prescribing solutions with scant regard to evidence and analysis. We are persuaded that policy has to be informed by knowledge and evidence if it is to be favourably received by leaders and articulate publics alike. In our opinion, the best way to convince leaders and citizens in Africa, as elsewhere, is to present the evidence of scientific analysis and to let 'the facts speak for themselves'. This is what this book has sought to do.

A major finding that comes out is the fact that Nigeria's performance since independence has been rather disappointing despite considerable inflows of revenues from oil. The Nigerian experience provides telling confirmation of the role of waste and corruption in undermining growth rather than the classical 'Dutch disease' syndrome that is often associated with natural resource endowment.

Perhaps nowhere have the structural weaknesses of the Nigerian economy been more glaring than in agriculture and manufacturing. Ever since the discovery of oil, agricultural exports have dwindled over the decades, appearing to recover only in recent times. The challenge for policy in the years ahead is to deploy agrarian strategies that would boost peasant production while giving increasing attention to large-scale agricultural holdings. The lessons of the Green Revolution in Asia need to be taken on board. With the rise of India and China and the US Africa Growth and Opportunities Act (AGOA), there is an expanding global market for agricultural export. Diversification of exports, in addition to increasing value-added in terms of processing and semi-processing of such products, would change the revenue base positively while creating an avenue for increased employment opportunities in the country.

The manufacturing sector has not fared any better. Once thriving industries – notably textiles – have virtually disappeared; massive capacity under-utilization has also severely afflicted others. The challenges facing this sector have to do with the country's poor investment climate, skilled labour shortages, limited access to finance and absence of adequate physical infrastructure. These constraints have continued to erode the job-creating potentials of the nation's manufacturing sector, negatively affecting its international competitiveness and export performance. The key to reversing this downward secular trend lies in the provision of an incentive package for the manufacturing sector to make it more export oriented, creating firm-level efficiency, reducing transaction costs and minimizing risks and uncertainties in the business environment.

When we cast a glance at the infrastructure sector, the same dismal picture stares us in the face. Nigeria's railways, for example, have been virtually dormant for decades; its roads and highways remain in a state of massive disrepair. Water and electricity are way below the minimum needs of the country's expanding population and of the demands of mega-cities such as Lagos, Port Harcourt, Ibadan, Kano, Onitsha and Aba. Although succeeding governments have committed significant resources (in terms of budgetary allocation) to the needs of the infrastructure sector, many such schemes have fallen victim to corruption and rent-seeking behaviour. Several of the recent initiatives to address the infrastructure deficit are welcome. These include the US$8 billion Lagos–Kano–Abuja railway project and the private–public partnership in infrastructure development.

With regard to the power sector, one would note that current economic reforms promise encouraging results. The Energy Reform Act, which permits privatization of the national company and private sector participation in the sector as well as the establishment of the Energy Regulatory Commission, is commendable. What is needed is careful planning on a national scale, innovative financing approaches and an effective monitoring and regulatory regime for the sector to thrive in the years ahead. Coming to grips with this one sector alone and providing a steady power supply would considerably boost national GDP and would radically improve economic performance across the nation.

In considering the case of infrastructure, we must not forget the role and importance of ports development and the customs practices. The examples of Singapore and Hong Kong point to the fact that the development of port facilities could play a significant role in a nation's economic growth. Nigeria has a considerable stretch of coastline with enormous potential for the development of ports and harbours. Sea transportation is of particular significance because it offers an important avenue for linking the country with the rest of the world, thereby contributing to its international competitiveness. The country's ports have consistently failed to support effectively the external trade needs of the country, while a substantial component of the country's import business has consistently been diverted to neighbouring ports with significant losses in terms of revenues to the government. Nigeria has all it takes to provide world-class ports facilities and practices that would out-compete any other port in West Africa. With appropriate reforms, there is no reason why importers should not clear customs in less than 24 hours. However, the benefits from ports and tariff reforms may prove of limited benefit unless attention is also paid to the factors determining the internal costs of production.

Equally problematic has been the incidence of poverty. Although the incidence of poverty has fallen from 65.7 per cent in 1996 to 54 per cent in 2004, it is still considered relatively high. Empirical evidence suggests that, although the high level of poverty is incontestable, the issue of absolute poverty in the country has tended to be overemphasized. Using three measures of poverty – the head count, poverty gap and an index of poverty severity – Nigeria remains on a rather high poverty scale compared with some less resourceful African countries such as Uganda, Tanzania and Rwanda. National distribution of poverty is, however, concentrated more in the rural areas, and the severity is higher in the northern states. For the areas under consideration, economic distance is a factor in the incidence of poverty, explaining why a large proportion of poor people are concentrated in the rural areas. Major causes of household poverty are the size of household and the educational attainment of the head of household. Although schemes such as the National Poverty Eradication Programme, sponsored by the Federal Government, may have some impact, micro-level interventions for poverty reduction should be the domain of the state and local governments. In the long run, what would be most critical is a policy mix that boosts employment generation, enhances rapid industrialization, develops export-oriented trade and promotes accelerated growth. Promoting universal access and qualitative education is critical to the long-term solution to poverty, and programmes to enhance the productivity of peasant agriculture in the short to medium term would also help.

There is also the issue of human capital, skills and basic education. Over the last decades, Nigeria has witnessed a troubling decrease in child school enrolment, scoring lower than countries with far fewer economic resources. Evidence shows that rapid growth of basic primary education is positively correlated with labour and non-labour market outcomes. It is also an established fact that women with the highest rates of universal primary education (UPE) exposure are also more likely to delay their first marriage and have fewer children than otherwise. Given these potentials, there is a strong case for increased investment in a universal primary education programme.

Turning to the issue of public financial management, we are faced with the abiding challenge of evolving a framework of fiscal federalism that actually works. The contending issues have centred on questions of equity, revenue sharing and the neglect of natural resource-producing areas. To ensure a better framework for fiscal federalism, it would be necessary to set up an independent intergovernmental committee to promote a more effective framework for fiscal discipline and fiscal policy coordination and to ensure transparency of the budgetary process. The system of expenditure controls remains weak, and a situation whereby state and local governments have opportunities to waste public funds on projects that are at best questionable cannot be sustained for long. State governments should follow a cue from the Federal Government and enact the Fiscal Responsibility Acts for the respective states. There is also a need to decentralize tax administration in the country so as to enhance the fiscal and extractive capacity of the state. Competition and peer pressure based on increased mentoring from the federal level, including performance-based grants/transfers, would also prove effective. It would be essential to develop a framework for regular measuring of performance, disseminating good practices and encouraging peer learning.

Central to meeting the poverty challenge is the imperative of effective social services delivery, especially to the poor. Evidence from a survey of the revenue and expenditure profile of the Federation and its units shows critical challenges in the area of services delivery. Using five major performance measures – health, education, roads, potable water and sanitation – a rather dismal picture is revealed across all levels of government. In our view, resources may not necessarily be the chief binding constraint to public service delivery, as is sometimes claimed. Rather, institutions and leadership matter the most. Through a skilful combination of enhanced spending efficiency, increased internal revenue generation and judicious application of incentives/sanctions, leaderships can make a difference. In addition, there is the need to promote healthy competition among the tiers of government through benchmarking/marching grants and improvement in monitoring capacity.

During the recent past, Nigeria has been lauded for its significant achievements in economic reform under the administration of President Olusegun Obasanjo. Under the National Economic Empowerment and Development Strategy (NEEDS) framework, a successful programme of economic liberalization has been put in place; inflation is coming down; significant privatization gains have been recorded; the banking sector has undergone an internationally acclaimed consolidation; growth is looking up; and the country is no longer a debtor nation, having settled its accounts with the Paris Club in a buy-back of its US$30 billion debt and also having exited the London Club. Owing to the reforms, Nigeria has also been de-listed by the Financial Action Task

Force (FATF) from its list of non-compliant countries, and it has been given its first-ever sovereign credit rating of a BB minus. The challenge, going forward, is to build on these achievements and to sustain the reforms way into the future.

With the current prospects looking brighter for global oil prices, it is imperative that the present opportunity be judiciously utilized in order to avoid the mistakes of the past. Avoiding these errors would require that society must go through the difficult process of changing the incentives and restraints that face individuals. In this case, certain critical decisions would have to be taken with respect to current savings and consumption, asset composition decisions and the type of investments – structures or equipment – that the country can embark upon. One proposal is that Nigeria has got to invest its oil windfall and feed on incomes that are generated from those investments rather than the oil proceeds themselves, which characterizes the current case. There is an alternative proposal to carefully target the spending of the oil resources (which is a depletable resource) only on investments that enhance the long-term growth potentials of the country such as education and infrastructure. The point here is that the debate on the best use for revenues from depletable resources should begin. Currently, there is no coherent strategy, and much of the current oil revenues go into current consumption or are simply wasted.

Further, the country would need to consolidate on a fiscal process that is consistent with the needs of the domestic economy, in line with the goals of the new macroeconomic directions. In this case, a fiscal rule that imposes a constraint on government's fiscal behaviour would be an appropriate measure. This would also call for conditions that guarantee a better informed society in terms of fiscal constitution. The role of the Central Bank would, in this regard, be critical because of its dual role as a key component of a fiscal constitution and also the key authority on economic issues that ordinary citizens can trust.

Another critical challenge that Nigeria's economic managers have to face is that of evolving an effective monetary strategy, given a regime of fiscal dominance emanating from excess oil revenue. Although steps have been taken to establish the foundations for effective macroeconomic management – stronger political commitment to economic reform, evident commitment to fiscal responsibility and financial sector reforms – more needs to be done to put in place a more robust monetary policy regime. Clearly, the independence of the Central Bank would be critical.

Equally vital is the need to preserve macroeconomic stability. For several years, the Nigerian economy had the unenviable reputation of being among the most volatile in the world. There are different sources for such volatility: the terms of trade, monetary, revenue, expenditure and real exchange rate volatility. Volatility in major economic indicators reduces the country's growth potentials and complicates internal macroeconomic balancing problems. Terms-of-trade volatility complicates exchange rate management, reduces investment decisions and productivity; revenue volatility confounds budget planning and execution; expenditure volatility undermines the quality of public investment and services and amplifies monetary and real exchange rate volatility.

Clearly, a sustained reduction in volatility will make a big contribution to the country's long-term growth. Among the remedies to be considered are stability in budgetary spending and real exchange rate stability through establishment of a fiscal rule that has a legal–constitutional backing. This makes the Fiscal Responsibility Act critical. Second, oil revenue hedging or swapping with financial assets would be a preferred choice because it has far-reaching implications: it would broaden the revenue base and also help to control revenue volatility. Similarly, stability of the terms of trade through export diversification would avoid real exchange rate appreciation. In the longer term, it is imperative to take financial sector reforms to a higher level so as to deepen financial sector development. In this regard, the vigorous implementation of the proposed Financial System Strategy 2020 (FSS 2020) aimed at making Nigeria Africa's financial hub by the year 2020 is encouraged.

Nigeria's ambition is to be among the developed market economies within the next two decades. To do so, it would have to reform its financial sector, enhance agricultural productivity, accelerate industrialization, modernize the education system, invest massively in human capital and technical skills development, and, above all, deepen its international competitiveness while finding a niche within the integrated global marketplace.

Within the West African sub-region, Nigeria largely underwrites the process of integration within the Economic Community of West African States (ECOWAS). One of the pressing policy challenges is the objective of attaining a single currency within the English-speaking West African States, plus Guinea. It goes without saying that much would depend on what happens in Nigeria. A stable macroeconomic environment in Nigeria is a necessary condition for making the monetary union project more acceptable to other countries in the region. Thus, continued reforms to strengthen the effectiveness of monetary policy, institutional steps to bolster Central Bank independence and movement towards an inflation-targeting regime are critical measures. Convergence may prove to be a slow and painstaking process, given the economic disparities among the partner countries.

Ultimately, the prospects for Africa's largest nation will hinge largely on the capacity of its government to sustain the path of reform and to build on the foundations that have been laid in the recent past. Careful attention has to be given to the promotion of macroeconomic stability, taking control of the 'economic fundamentals', enhancing agricultural productivity, expanding and diversifying exports, accelerating industrialization, investing in human capital, getting rid of corruption, strengthening economic and political governance and building enduring institutions. Particular attention must be given to building the physical infrastructure base, boosting incentives to enhance savings and investments and creating a foundation for enduring growth.

CHUKWUMA C. SOLUDO
Governor, Central Bank of Nigeria

Acknowledgements

Studies done for this book were financed in part by the U.K. Department for International Development in Nigeria through its Policy and Knowledge facility. We would also like to thank the Research Committee of the World Bank for funding.

Introduction: Towards Evidence-based Policy

Paul Collier, Catherine Pattillo and Chukwuma C. Soludo

Economic policy choices profoundly affect the lives of ordinary people. Nigeria is fortunate to have huge opportunities: oil provides large public resources; Nigerians succeed the world over as entrepreneurs; Lagos is a superbly located big city that could rival the exporting cities of Asia. The choice of economic policies determines whether these opportunities are harnessed or dissipated. Nigerians are poor today because of mistaken choices over the past thirty years. Since 2003 the society has begun to correct past mistakes, but policy reform is a continuous process and despite some remarkable successes many issues remain to be addressed. Choices tend to go wrong if they are founded on hunches, special interests, beliefs or textbooks. They need to be based on evidence. The purpose of this book is to show that there is already plenty of evidence from Nigerian experience that can inform policy discussion. In a democracy, economic policy ultimately rests upon popular understanding of the issues. In the vacuum created by a lack of hard evidence, rogue nostrums thrive and confuse. Hence, this book is written not for an audience of technocrats but for all who wish to engage with policy choices.

The book is the result of collaboration between the Central Bank of Nigeria and the Centre for the Study of African Economies at Oxford University. In addition to people at these institutions it draws on a wide range of Nigerian and international scholars from a range of universities and international institutions. These include: the Nigerian Ministry of Finance; the University of Agriculture at Abeokuta, Akwa Ibom State University of Technology, Harvard University, the Universities of Ibadan, Indiana-Purdue at Indianapolis, Nottingham, Olabisi Onabanjo, Sussex, Technology at Akure, and Toronto; the Graduate Institute of International Studies; the African Institute for Applied Economics; the African Economic Research Consortium; the West African Monetary Institute; the IMF and the World Bank. All authors write entirely in an individual capacity and are indeed entirely free to disagree with each other. Evidence-based policy-making is a continuous process that Nigerian society will need to develop. The book covers a wide range of policy issues so that future discussion on them can be better grounded. When evidence is properly analysed it highlights problems and often suggests a range of options that might help to address them. We have, however, avoided 'recommendations' or 'lessons'. Evidence and analysis provide people with the basis to think for themselves about effective solutions. But evidence places limits on what can credibly be proposed: some apparent remedies rest on myths which the evidence in this book explodes.

The book is organized into four themes: macroeconomic management; fiscal management within a federal system; the policy climate for private activity; and the well-being of households, which is the key consequence of the other three sets of policies. Macroeconomic management is a vital issue in Nigerian economic policy. Nigeria is exposed to large external shocks and until recently mismanagement often amplified them: the Nigerian economy has been one of the most volatile in the world with profound consequences for investment and poverty. The system of fiscal management is the transmission mechanism from oil revenues to livelihoods: it determines how public money is spent. The quality of fiscal management depends upon both its design and its implementation. In Nigeria both have to be understood within the context of the federal system. While the system of fiscal management determines the delivery of public services such as health and education, the policy climate for private activity shapes how the vast majority of Nigerians earn their living. We show that in many respects economic policies have made earning a living unnecessarily difficult. The well-being of households, dependent upon the delivery of public services and the ability to earn an income, is the consequence of the three areas of policy choice. In the absence of hard evidence, powerful myths have built up about what has happened. This book confronts these myths with evidence derived from thorough analyses both of a new national survey of households and of a key initiative to improve service delivery. These four themes do not exhaust the range of economic policies and their consequences, but they are at the core of the economic issues that Nigerian society will confront and resolve.

Section I covers macroeconomic management. Oil revenues are central to Nigerian macroeconomic management because they are large and volatile and so all of the chapters in this section place oil centre-stage. Nigerian oil revenues constitute a huge opportunity for rapid growth and development, but harnessing these opportunities is not easy and depends upon both fiscal and monetary strategies. The chapters focus on growth strategies, fiscal strategies, monetary policies and the trade regime. The chapter on binding constraints to growth by Kwakwa, Adenikinju, Mousley and Owusu-Gyamfi provides a big-picture look at many of the issues dealt with in more detail in other chapters in the book. While Nigeria's growth performance since 2000 has strengthened, it needs to grow much faster to put a sizeable dent in poverty. Kwakwa and her co-authors argue that the prospects for sustaining high growth are better than in past oil booms, but that it makes sense, given limited government capacity and political will, to focus first on the most binding constraints. They rule out some potential suspects and zero in on bad infrastructure and a predatory business environment. Both reduce efficiency, and the consequent reduction in the return on investment weakens the incentive to invest. Business people cannot operate efficiently and maintain and upgrade their capital in a risky environment where changing tax, trade, licensing and regulation policies create uncertainties and opportunities for corruption. Poor management of the oil revenue cycle creates macroeconomic risk. In turn, this increases the uncertainty of investment and so makes banks reluctant to commit to long-term financing.

Making the most of oil revenues depends partly upon long-term decisions that shape the structure of the economy and partly upon short-term decisions that ride the tiger of volatility, with chapters focusing on both the long-run and short-run decisions. The chapter by Collier sets the scene. Globally over the past half-century in oil-exporting economies high oil prices have tended to generate a few years of growth followed by longer and more severe periods of decline. Democracy has not been enough to protect oil exporters from this failure to harness oil into sustained growth unless checks and balances are particularly robust. An unbalanced democracy, with intense electoral competition for the acquisition of power but weak checks and balances on how power is used, is particularly dysfunctional in oil economies. The chapter then outlines the three key public decisions on saving out of oil revenue which determine whether oil is transformed into sustained growth. Since this transformation depends upon getting these decisions right *continuously*, there is a good case for enshrining these principles of sound stewardship of depleting resources constitutionally so that any proposed departure from them is fully debated. The Fiscal Responsibility Bill is a key step in this direction. In effect, oil-exporting countries can benefit from having a *fiscal constitution*.

The chapters by Addison (see www.csae.ox.ac.uk/books) and by Sala-i-Martin and Subramanian address the fiscal choices posed by oil. Addison focuses on the short-term problem of volatility, Sala-i-Martin and Subramanian on the long-term problem of building and maintaining accountability of government to citizens. Addison shows that the Nigerian economy has been quite exceptionally volatile. This inevitably intensifies poverty as households are forced to cope with crises by running down the assets on which they depend for income. It also discourages investment as firms and banks avoid financing fixed investment by loans because of the risk of a crash. Thus, severe macroeconomic volatility – of the terms of trade, revenues, the overall fiscal balance, and the real exchange rate – has lowered growth. Sala-i-Martin and Subramanian show how damaging oil revenues have tended to be for the accountability of government. Essentially, the argument is 'no representation without taxation'. With oil revenues governments do not need to tax non-oil activities and without taxation households and firms are not provoked into scrutiny of government. To overcome this problem Sala-i-Martin and Subramanian suggest the simple and radical solution that some of the oil revenues could be distributed directly to households, with non-oil activity taxed more heavily to meet the resulting shortfall in revenue. Other oil exporters have indeed used some of their oil revenues to finance direct transfers to households. For example, the Mexican government pays money to parents as long as children attend primary school, a scheme which has been shown to be effective both in raising enrolment and in reducing poverty.

Another two chapters in this section focus on the complementary actions in monetary policy. Debrun, Masson and Pattillo consider the long-run challenge of how to commit credibly to low inflation, while Adam and Goderis consider the short-run problem of how to respond to a sudden surge in oil revenues. Debrun, Masson and Pattillo compare two long-term strategies for building confidence by 'tying the policy-maker's hands'. While clearly not the only options, both strategies have become common in developed countries. One is regional monetary union and the other is greater independence for the Central Bank of Nigeria. Regional monetary union, such as the one that Nigeria proposes to join in 2009, has historically been problematic. Nigeria's large fiscal deficits, arising from excessive spending on socially useless projects combined with inefficient and corrupt tax collection, created large financing needs that would have translated into higher inflation for a regional central bank. While fiscal policy is now greatly improved, the chapter models an estimate of long-run sustainable oil revenue and finds that further improvements would be needed before the region would benefit from the monetary union. The alternative is to strengthen the independence of the Central Bank of Nigeria and then move gradually to an inflation-targeting regime such as has been adopted in South Africa. This could increase the population's confidence in the commitment to low inflation. In addition to the direct benefit of lower inflation it could also make the monetary union project more acceptable to the other countries in the region, and more sustainable, since Nigeria's representatives at the regional central bank would be better able to resist financing pressures.

Adam and Goderis offer new insight on the question of the efficient management of surges in oil revenue. The innovation in their model is portfolio effects: the private sector can hold either naira or foreign currency, and the demand for naira depends on expected inflation or depreciation. They suggest that when the government chooses to save part of the revenue windfall this changes the path of government financing and opens the way for a more interventionist exchange rate policy. In this situation, intervention closely aligns the sales of foreign exchange with the extra spending warranted by the surge in oil prices, thereby insulating domestic financial markets from excessive exchange rate and inflation volatility. In their simulations of this scenario, the nominal exchange rate still appreciates but by less than under a pure float where the central bank would be selling all the foreign exchange exactly at a time when the private sector wants to hold more naira given the lower expected inflation (lower government financing) and the economic boom. In this context, it may therefore be neither necessary nor appropriate to sterilize the resulting injection of domestic currency. Since the demand for currency is higher, if the government increases its debt to sterilize the monetary injection this may undermine the process of building confidence in the currency. Indeed, debt repurchase may be a useful commitment mechanism, locking the government in to lower future financing needs and further increasing the demand for currency as a result of lower expected inflation.

Alaba, Adenikinju and Collier focus on how options for trade policy might affect the climate for private activity. They describe Nigeria's present restrictions on imports and consider the likely consequences of switching to the ECOWAS common external tariff, something currently planned for 2009. There are three distinct effects. In the short run tariffs would be reduced since the ECOWAS tariffs are lower than Nigeria's current tariffs. This would benefit most Nigerians since current tariffs are very high and have been identified by the Economic and Financial Crimes Commission as an epicentre of corruption. Paradoxically, although the Ministry of Finance directly gains some revenue from tariffs, this has been fully offset by the loss due to the appreciation in the exchange rate induced by the tariffs and the consequent reduction in the naira revenue from oil. The only difference between these offsetting effects is that the gain from tariffs is shown on the ministry's books whereas the loss (when the currency appreciates) is not calculated and so is unreported: the Ministry of Finance generates no net revenue from tariffs. The main effect of Nigeria's trade restrictions is likely to be on jobs. The manufacturing survey finds that, whereas firms rate competition from imports right at the bottom of the list of problems, the difficulties in accessing imported inputs are an important constraint. Customs restrictions both raise the cost of imported inputs and inflict delays. Accession to the ECOWAS trade rules would also remove all tariff restrictions on other members. This would shift some activities to Nigeria while others would move to neighbouring countries. The net effect would depend upon Nigeria's relative competitiveness. Judging by comparable surveys of manufacturing elsewhere in West Africa, Nigeria is considerably less competitive than its neighbours and so industry would be likely to relocate out of Nigeria unless the policy climate is rapidly improved. In the longer run, the ECOWAS common tariff might well prevent Nigeria from reducing its tariffs to the low levels that probably best suit the economy and that the government might wish to adopt. Other governments do not have oil revenues and so indeed have net revenue gains from tariffs. Unlike Nigeria they may therefore need to keep tariffs relatively high. This is particularly important for the potential development of Lagos as an export platform into world markets. All export platforms depend upon being able to import semi-processed inputs duty free, whereas ECOWAS imposes a 10 per cent tariff on them. Such a major competitive disadvantage would be liable to close off opportunities for penetrating global markets.

The section also includes a chapter by Mailafia which looks at lessons for Nigeria from the fast-growing Asian economies. These countries' success has been attributed to a set of well-coordinated policies and responses by businesses, farmers and households. These include investments in agriculture and technological advancement, stabilizing population growth, a focus on education and training, promotion of exports, and investments in infrastructure. In this environment savings and investment rates by households and firms were very high; productivity increased; and, even in countries that inherited ethno-religious diversities such as Singapore, the leadership helped forge a commitment to distribute the benefits of growth to all the citizens. Mailafia looks at how Nigeria measures up on policies that ushered in the East Asian 'miracle'. While Nigeria's oil-based economy poses additional policy challenges, some aspects of the Asian recipe are clearly relevant for the country.

Section II covers budgetary financial management within a federal system. Okogu and Osafo-Kwaako look at the federal government's challenges in delinking expenditures from volatile oil-based revenues in the short run and trying to make sure the use of oil resources is sustainable in the long term so that future generations of Nigerians will benefit. Ajakaiye focuses on how, in a federal system, fiscal policy must be coordinated to achieve these objectives. Okogu and Osafo-Kwaako explain some of the progress in fiscal policy management achieved under the NEEDS, starting with the well-known oil-price based fiscal rule, and better medium-term fiscal planning. Less well known are steps that have instituted a due process mechanism in public procurement, including reference to international prices and publication of public tenders so that there is competitive costing and less patronage in government contracts. Monthly publication of federal, state and local government shares of revenue from the federation account has for the first time allowed citizens to challenge government on how much is being received and whether it is reaching the intended beneficiaries. Signing on to the international Extractive Industries Transparency Initiative (EITI) means that oil and gas companies also have to be open on what revenues are paid to the government – financial and physical audits have revealed poor government record-keeping on revenues and systemic loss of crude oil before it reached export metering terminals. The challenge in sustaining and deepening the reforms is locking them in through legislation – elevating the importance of the National Assembly's role in guaranteeing a fiscal policy constitution for management of oil revenues.

Ajakaiye identifies threats to fiscal policy coordination commonly experienced in a federal system. Fiscal policy is more complicated in a federal system when revenue is exogenous and volatile, compromising implementation of budget plans; when states have different economic cycles so that some are booming when others are in recession and borrowing of subnational governments is not controlled; when there is a mismatch between spending responsibilities and resource allocation at a specific level of government, or spending responsibilities are vague; when capacity is weak so that there are weak 'links in the chain'. In Nigeria the autonomy of state governments with respect to control of public funds blunts effective fiscal policy coordination. Ajakaiye makes several proposals for improving fiscal policy coordination. For example, he suggests that any Fiscal Responsibility Law should impose reasonably hard budget constraints on state and local governments, including prohibitions on borrowing.

Stevens and Freinkman (see www.csae.ox.ac.uk/books) present a benchmarking study of Nigerian public financial management at the federal and state levels. There have recently been some dramatic improvements. For example, the recent introduction of competitive tendering in procurement has already saved over $750 million. The quality of financial management depends partly upon the design of the system and partly on its implementation. Globally, the design of financial management has improved enormously over recent decades as governments have shifted from measuring annual spending on capital projects to the performance of service delivery over a three-year horizon. The question shifts to 'How well are children learning?' rather than 'How many schools are being built?' Nigeria's budget system has remained frozen as it was inherited at independence and so is now radically behind international best practice. Meanwhile, the implementation of the inherited system has gradually deteriorated. Stevens and Freinkman show that, while remarkable improvements have been made at the federal level, the situation in the states is highly variable: some states have vigorously reformed and others are lagging. In a federal system this is fundamentally a choice at state level.

Ekpo and Englama set out the principles that underlay the design of Nigeria's federal system and focus on some of the key issues which any design needs to confront. For example, in the 1980s state-level powers of borrowing severely aggravated macroeconomic mismanagement. The accumulation of debts, state by state, poses a problem known as the 'tragedy of the commons': actions of each state individually are liable to undermine the national interest. The resolution of this problem requires some limitation on the rights of states to borrow. Ekpo and Englama chronicle the contentious history of revenue sharing, and outline the practical issues confronting Nigeria's federalism, such as the imbalances between assigned responsibilities and tax powers at different levels of government. Since the states have responsibility for many of the key components of spending that affect the lives of ordinary people, a well-functioning budgetary system at the state level is an important priority. Odoko and Nnanna (see www.csae.ox.ac.uk/books) marshal the evidence on how the budget is apportioned between the federation and each state, how state allocations relate to state needs, and how the money that states have received has been used to address those needs. The picture is one in which states have become increasingly important in their command over resources, but in which there is enormous variation in how those resources have been used. As assigned in the constitution, states and local governments play the most significant role in the delivery of basic services such as education, health, housing and water. Paradoxically, states in the zones that benefit from mineral derivation tend to perform relatively worse on basic indicators of access to services despite getting more money. Odoko and Nnanna suggest some options for rethinking fiscal federalism so that the system could efficiently and equitably deliver quality services to its citizens.

Section III covers policies for private sector development. Modern economies are integrated into global activity. The chapters discuss the policies that determine how well Nigeria harnesses the opportunities for private sector development with a particular focus on trade. For Nigeria the global economy is especially important because its large oil revenues provide it with the ability to purchase large imports but also potentially generate Dutch disease that makes other exports uncompetitive. The chapter by Malik and Teal covers manufacturing. Using evidence from surveys that track the performance and problems of 200 manufacturing firms it shows that the policy climate is markedly more difficult in Nigeria than elsewhere in West Africa. The most severe problems arise from failures in supply of electric power, but also in the lack of credit, the volatility of the economy, and difficulties in the supply of imported inputs. As a result of these problems productivity has been stagnant, investment has been very low, and there has been no overall growth. This constitutes a major missed opportunity since Lagos might have the potential to be an important global manufacturing centre, creating thousands of jobs for ordinary Nigerians.

With power by far the most important constraint on Nigerian manufacturing it is appropriate next to turn to why an oil-abundant country should have so mismanaged its power sector as to face severe shortages. The chapter by Tallapragada and Adebusuyi explains what went wrong and the options for reform. The problems are deeper than a shortage of installed capacity. An astonishingly high proportion of the power that is generated is lost in distribution, and of that distributed a further high proportion has been stolen – taken without payment. Even large increases in generation without improvements in distribution and payment would rapidly lead back to the nightmare of shortages. Tallapragada and Adebusuyi describe some of the reforms in the sector since 1999 to increase generation capacity, including through promotion of independent power plants. High on the agenda also is the introduction of commercial practices, and unbundling of the power authority as a step toward eventual private management. But the challenges in upgrading transmission and distribution and increasing access to power, particularly in the rural areas, still remain.

The next major bottleneck to be addressed is the ports. Although oil gives Nigeria the ability to pay for large imports, problems in the ports have dissipated this advantage. Oji and Agu use survey evidence to compare the operation of Nigeria's ports with those elsewhere in West Africa. They show that on a range of measures costs and delays are radically higher and that this is accounted for predominantly by human factors rather than by physical infrastructure. Globally, the efficiency of ports has been rising over time, and so standing still constitutes a growing competitive disadvantage. They draw an analogy between Lagos and the fate of the port of New York, which failed to keep up with technological innovation. As a result, not only did activity in the port of New York dwindle, but more importantly manufacturing relocated out of New York to be close to better-run ports. They then use the example of Buenos Aires to show how it is possible rapidly to turn a port round from being the worst in a region to being the best.

The chapter by Daramola, Ehui, Ukeje and McIntire (see www.csae.ox.ac.uk/books) focuses on export agriculture. Since the early 1970s Nigeria's agricultural exports have collapsed. This was not an inevitable consequence of oil: Indonesia, another oil exporter with a large agricultural sector, created a wide range of agricultural export activities including the very same crops that collapsed in Nigeria. The collapse of agricultural exports, with the consequent decline in the incomes of households engaged in the activity, occurred because the adverse effects of Dutch disease were intensified by mistakes in exchange rate and trade policy, rather than being mitigated by pro-agriculture spending policies. Both overvaluation of the exchange rate and import restrictions inadvertently were equivalent to the imposition of heavy taxes on agricultural exports. It was this taxation that was the predominant reason for the decline of export agriculture. In addition, the government gave a low priority to spending that would have helped exports, such as improving the rural road network, extension services, improved varieties, and marketing channels. The money spent subsidizing fertilizer was easily captured by the middle men in charge of distribution, rather than reaching the farmers. Daramola *et al.* argue that Nigeria now has the potential to earn much more from both traditional and non-traditional agricultural exports and that policies to improve competitiveness of small farmers in domestic and regional markets are the place to start.

Finally, Section IV focuses on households. Appleton, McKay and Alayande analyse the 2004 national household budget survey. This is by far the largest set of data on living conditions ever gathered in Nigeria and so is probably more reliable than any previous data. Appleton, McKay and Alayande show that other recent analyses of these data have made important methodological and conceptual errors that have produced misleading results. They find that poverty is deep and pervasive, and far higher than indicated in the studies from previous decades. By contrast, inequality seems to be little changed from twenty years ago. Hence, the widespread perceptions that poverty is coming down but inequality is rising do not find support in the national household data. While education has strong effects on the earnings of wage earners, since this is a relatively small proportion of the population, education does not have major effects on lowering overall poverty. People living in large families, and the self-employed, tend to be poorer.

While Appleton *et al.* focus on household consumption, Osili evaluates the impact on women of a major social policy initiative, the Universal Primary Education programme launched in 1976 and discontinued in 1981. The programme eliminated school fees at the primary level. Osili shows that this was very successful in decisively increasing enrolments and schooling years completed for women. Further, she shows that, although primary education has not directly increased incomes, it has generated important social returns. These originate with the lower fertility of women involved in the programme, and the lower mortality rates of their children. This calls into question the wisdom of the 1981 decision to discontinue free primary education at a time when huge expenditures continued to be incurred on projects which have yielded little. The abandonment of the programme without a proper evaluation of its effects is an example of what can happen in the absence of evidence-based policy-making.

The third chapter in this section, by Aromolaran, follows the theme of how education for women can improve the well-being of households through both labour market and social channels. Aromolaran finds that higher levels of female schooling are associated with greater participation in the labour market. The strongest effect of primary education is that more women work in self-employment, while post-secondary education has the largest impact on women becoming wage-earners. Osili showed the impact of education for women on household well-being, through smaller families and healthier children. Here we see one way this came about – by providing the opportunity for more women to join the labour market. Aromolaran also estimates that implementation of Universal Basic Education (UBE) could result on close to a doubling of the labour market participation rates of women, which the other chapters in this section would suggest could have large social returns.

To conclude, Nigerians confront the paradox that, despite three decades of oil revenues, the services normally provided by government are unusually bad and the scope for ordinary people to earn a decent living is unusually limited. These outcomes are the legacy of poor public choices over a long period. This book has documented some of these mistakes, such as the mismanagement of the ports and electricity provision, and the abandonment of free primary education. The current high level of oil prices offers Nigerians a second chance. The chapters in this book and on the associated website are a step along the road to evidence-based policy choices sustained by an informed society.

Section I

Oil and the Macroeconomy

1
Binding Constraints to Growth in Nigeria

Victoria Kwakwa, Adeola Adenikinju, Peter Mousley and Mavis Owusu-Gyamfi[1]

1.1 Introduction

In the 1970s, Nigeria appeared to have successfully leveraged two oil booms for economic progress. Growth was rapid in both industry and services, the economy grew 7.4 per cent on average annually and as high as 27 per cent in 1970. Per capita GDP increased 4 per cent annually. This growth episode was, however, short-lived and by the late 1970s had begun to slow. When oil prices crashed in the 1980s, the economy went through several years of contraction. Stagnation continued in the 1990s. Per capita GDP in Purchasing Power Parity (PPP) terms fell 40 per cent, from $1215 in 1980 to $706 in 2000 (CSAE, 2003). Income poverty level rose from 28.1 per cent to 65.6 per cent, and other indicators of welfare – notably access to education and health – also declined. The economy became more dependent on oil while productivity and competitiveness of the non-oil sector declined.

Nigeria is currently presented with a rare opportunity for growth. Oil prices are at unprecedented levels and projected to remain relatively high for the foreseeable future given significant upward structural shifts in global demand for oil. The government is putting in place new mechanisms to better manage oil revenues and reduce the inefficiency associated with past boom–bust cycles. Fundamental changes in economic direction are tackling distortions that have reduced incentives for investment and productive activity. Strengthening of democratic governance is building demand for accountability from political leaders and policymakers. These developments are helping to create the conditions for growth and strengthening confidence of investors in the economy.

The economy is experiencing the fastest growth in over two decades. Growth averaged 5.7 per cent annually between 2000 and 2005, picking up across a broad range of sectors (see Table A1.1 in the Appendix, www.csae.ox.ac.uk/books). The non-oil sector, which provides livelihoods for the majority of Nigerians, has grown at 5.9 per cent annually accelerating to 7.4 per cent in 2004 and 8.2 per cent in 2005. Data for the first half of 2006 suggest non-oil growth will reach about 8.9 per cent for the year. GDP per capita in current US dollars has more than doubled, from $358 in 2000 to $752 in 2005.

1.2 The challenge of sustaining recent growth

Five years of 5.7 per cent annual average growth – while laudable – is not enough to make a discernible impact on poverty in Nigeria. Estimates suggest that the economy will need to grow at least 8 per cent annually over decades to achieve major reduction in income poverty. In addition, growth needs to create more jobs and at higher wages than has been the case over the last few years. Only an estimated 5–10 per cent of the 6 million new entrants into the labour market find jobs.[2] Open unemployment of youth aged between 15 and 29 years is estimated at about 60 per cent.[3] The prospects for sustaining growth are stronger now than during past oil booms. First, this oil boom has been accompanied by fundamental improvements in policy direction. This was not the case in the past. In particular, the public-sector-driven import substitution approach that led to a highly distorted economy is being replaced with more focus on private sector leading of growth and more openness to external trade. The oil revenue cycle is being managed better with the introduction of the oil-price based fiscal rule. A second reason for optimism is that the non-oil sector has grown just as strongly as, and in the last two years more strongly than, the oil sector. In past oil booms, the oil sector grew much faster and agriculture in particular regressed. Previous oil booms led to massive debt accumulation as surpluses were quickly exhausted. In contrast, today, Nigeria's debt overhang has been addressed with the recent Paris Club debt deal and the government is implementing a more prudent external debt policy built around borrowing only on concessional terms. External debt has been reduced from $35.9 billion in 2004 to around $3.5 billion and about 3 per cent of GDP in 2006. Sizeable overall external surplus has allowed increases in gross international reserves to about $40 billion and about 13 months of imports.

All of these factors put Nigeria in a stronger position to preserve recent growth beyond a short-lived spurt. Nevertheless the challenge of sustaining growth cannot be taken for granted. Global evidence shows that, while most oil-dependent economies do well during oil booms, there is typically a sharp reversal of performance within a few years of the end of the boom. Moreover, despite recent progress the Nigerian economy continues to face significant competitiveness challenges. Total factor productivity growth[4] appears to have fallen consistently between 1970 and 2000 and increases in capital per worker have been negligible (Figure 1.1). By several measures it is still one of the least competitive, globally and even in Africa. On several of the 'Doing Business Indicators' Nigeria does poorly compared to most other economies including low income economies in Africa. The World Economic Forum (WEF) 2006 report ranks Nigeria 88 out of 117 countries on its Global Competitiveness Indicators (GCI) (Table 1.1). Despite the large domestic market, only a small proportion of producers have been able to develop into sizeable businesses able to compete internationally.

In agriculture, the largest non-oil sector, yields have been falling. Productivity has declined for both commercial and food crops over the last 20 years. For commercial crops, production levels have fallen as well. In contrast, production

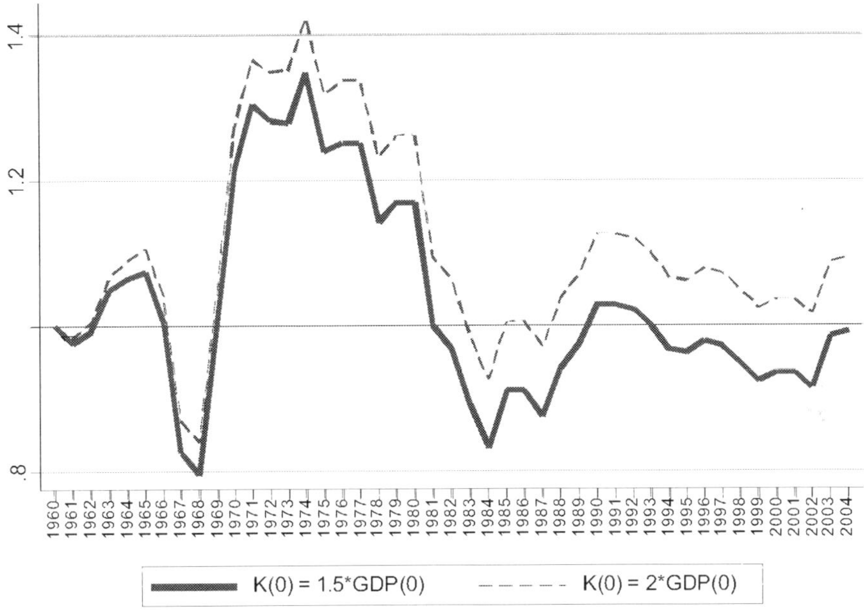

Figure 1.1 Cumulative TFP for alternative initial capital–output ratios.
Source: World Bank staff based on WDI data.

levels of food crops have increased substantially and Nigeria has overcome its extreme import dependence. However, this growth has been driven by steady and substantial increase in the area cultivated and harvested[5] and crop land expansion is increasingly taking place on marginal land where yields are lower (Table 1.2). Productivity as measured by yields per hectare has therefore declined whilst internationally yields have been rising. In the case of roots and tubers, for example, a fourfold increase in area planted since the mid-1980s has been accompanied by a decline in yields in excess of 40 per cent. Similar but less dramatic outcomes are observed for cereals, beans and groundnuts.[6]

The severe reduction in agricultural exports is further indication of the weak competitiveness of Nigerian agriculture. Agricultural exports fell from 2.5 per cent to 0.2 per cent of total exports between 1980 and 2005. Nigeria has lost market share for exports such as cocoa, palm oil and rubber. Non-traditional agricultural exports are limited. While agricultural exports have strengthened since 2000, performance is still far below the economy's potential. The share of manufacturing in GDP has declined, from 8.4 per cent in 1980 to 5.5 per cent in 1999 and 4.6 per cent in 2005. This compares poorly with other oil economies and even with some African countries (Table 1.3). Capacity utilization is about 50 per cent and value added per capita has stagnated at around $17 over the last decade and a half. This contrasts with increases from $133 to $273 for Indonesia and $600 to $1066

Table 1.1 Comparative indicators of competitiveness

Country	GCI 2005 Rank	GCI 2005 Score	GCI 2004 Rank
South Africa	42	4.31	41
India	50	4.04	55
Ghana	59	3.82	68
Brazil	65	3.69	57
Indonesia	74	3.53	69
Nigeria	88	3.23	93
Kenya	92	3.19	78

Source: World Economic Forum, 2006.

Table 1.2 Nigeria: main crops, area harvested, production and yield, 1999, 2003 and 2004

	Area harvested			Production			Yield		
	1999	**2003**	**2004**	**1999**	**2003**	**2004**	**1999**	**2003**	**2004**
Main cereals	18,437	24,133	25,515	22,478	29,186	31,477	1.22	1.21	1.23
Roots and tubers	6,849	9,300	10,344	66,076	78,830	84,465	9.65	8.48	8.17
Pulses	10,340	13,961	14,107	4,603	5,952	6,140	0.45	0.43	0.44
Others	5,294	7,180	6,787	6,586	7,776	8,230	1.24	1.08	1.21

Source: NBS, 2000, 2003, 2005a,b.

Table 1.3 Manufacturing value added, 1980–2005 (% of GDP)

	1980	**1990**	**2000**	**2005**
Nigeria	8.4	5.5	4.5	4.6
Mexico	22.3	20.8	20.3	17.7
Indonesia	13.0	20.7	27.7	28.1
Brazil	33.5	n.a.	17.1	n.a.
Ghana	7.8	9.8	9.0	8.6
South Africa	21.6	23.6	19.0	19.1

n.a., not available.
Source: World Bank database.

for Mexico over the same period. Recent evidence from Lagos State, which has the largest concentration of manufacturing firms, suggests that Nigerian firms are forgoing scale economics. As indicated above, many sectors have low levels of market competition, with small numbers of larger enterprises and a competitive fringe of smaller or tiny ones. However, even the largest firms are very small by international standards.

1.3 The binding constraints to growth in Nigeria

There are several factors in the still low productivity and efficiency of the Nigerian economy. Several of the ongoing reforms are trying to redress these factors but they cannot, and fortunately need not, all be addressed at the same time. Prioritizing and sequencing action is important to ensure that Nigeria's reform effort is focused and uses limited government capacity and political capital judiciously to achieve the biggest impact on growth. This requires a growth diagnostics analysis. The rest of this chapter identifies the binding constraints to growth or the factors that need the most immediate attention of policy-makers in order to begin to transform Nigeria's recent growth into a sustained long-term growth take-off.

The analysis follows the Hausmann–Rodrik–Velasco (HRV) approach (Hausmann *et al.*, 2005) to determining the binding constraints to growth. Starting from traditional growth theory which emphasizes the importance of savings and capital accumulation, the approach posits that low levels of private investment and growth are due to either low returns or low savings and associated high cost of finance. A decision tree methodology is used to drill down further to determine the binding constraint around which reform action could have the largest growth impact.

1.3.1 Are savings and accumulation in Nigeria low?

The accumulation of physical capital in Nigeria has been lower than in more successful and rapidly growing developing economies (Figure 1.2). Between 1980 and 2005, domestic investment to GDP averaged 19.5 per cent. Private investment has dominated public investment, averaging about 14.4 per cent of GDP between 1990 and 2005, but this has also been much lower than in comparator countries. In addition, the larger share of private investment has gone into the oil sector. Two other features of investment performance are striking: first its extreme

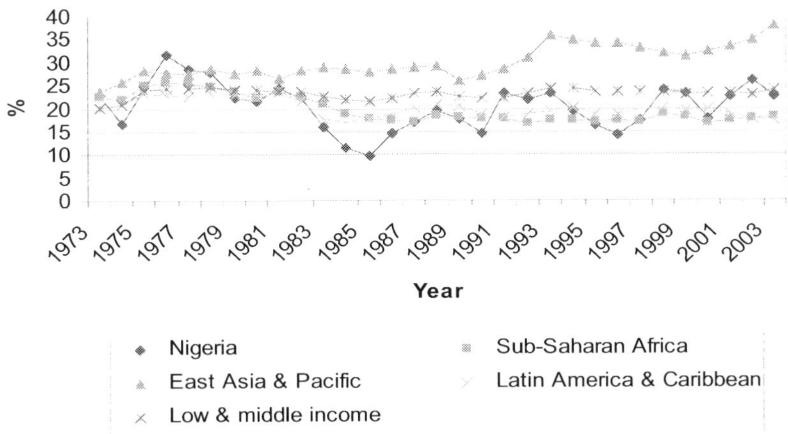

Figure 1.2 Gross fixed capital formation (% of GDP).
Source: World Bank, 2005a,b.

pro-cyclicality which is explained largely by the influence of the oil cycle and its low efficiency. Public investment in particular has been marked by low efficiency due to poor investment planning and corruption, and incremental capital output ratios (ICORs) have therefore been high averaging about 12.7 between 1974 and 2004.

Savings performance has lagged behind performance in comparator countries, averaging 18 per cent between 1980 and 2005 (Figure 1.3). In the last few years domestic saving has risen significantly mainly because of the oil boom.[7] Between 2000 and 2004, gross national savings averaged 25 per cent of GDP annually. A large share of this (17 per cent of GDP) is public saving, reflecting improved fiscal prudence through implementation of the oil-price based fiscal rule. Another feature of savings in Nigeria is the divergence between gross national and gross domestic savings. Gross domestic savings have consistently been higher than gross national savings, confirming net outflow of savings from Nigeria. The gap was much higher in the 1980s and early 1990s – as high as 10 percentage points in some years – but has narrowed down in more recent years.

1.3.2 Is return on capital in Nigeria low?

The low productivity of the economy suggests that overall return on capital in Nigeria is low. The available data supports a more nuanced conclusion: in a few select sectors returns to capital are very high, but returns appear to be low in most other sectors and particularly in the agriculture sector. High return sectors include oil, banking and finance and some parts of the food and beverage industry (Table 1.4. In the oil sector, high return is explained by the special nature of oil, and the fact that the industry operates at international standards using global

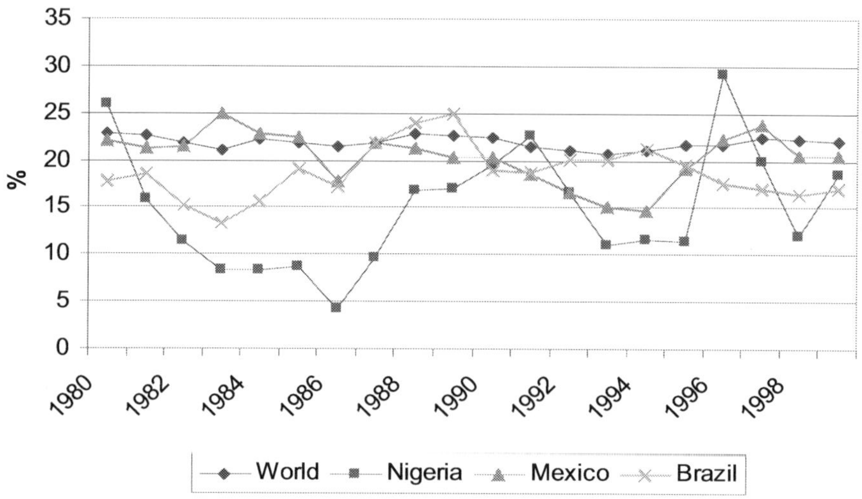

Figure 1.3 Gross national savings, including NCTR (% of GDP).
Source: World Bank, 2005a,b.

Table 1.4 Return on assets (%) in selected Nigeria formal manufacturing sectors

	2002	2003	2004	2005
Conglomerates	10.4	18.8	15.7	11.6
Building materials	8.8	9.2	16.4	22.9
Health care	16.2	12.5	18.7	17.3
Food and beverages	17.4	14.6	11.8	9.8
Breweries	13.9	12.7	11.2	10.6

technology. Thus even with considerable unrest in the Niger Delta and increased operating costs, including for security, returns are attractive enough to keep oil majors engaged and continuing to invest and expand their operations.

In the banking sector, before the recent bank consolidation reform, the more profitable banks averaged about 35–40 per cent on equity. What explains this? Compared with other developing countries, branch density is low in Nigeria, suggesting that Nigeria is under-banked. The high rate of return on equity therefore reflects high returns on marginal investment opportunity. As the banking sector is becoming more competitive after consolidation, there will be more competition for these investment opportunities and return on equity is likely to decline. However the high returns before consolidation also reflect distortions in the functioning of the sector. Large banks made their profits primarily from foreign exchange transactions and investment in government securities and not from lending. Moreover, some banks were more privileged than others in their access to foreign exchange and this could explain the lower return on equity for non-top-tier banks prior to consolidation. Thus the high return was not a reflection of a well functioning system. Instead the system was fragmented and delivered little credit to viable potential borrowers. A privileged tier of banks had superior access to foreign exchange which allowed them to make high returns.

Table 1.5 Productivity of investment – returns

Decade	AFR	EAP	ECA	LAC	MNA	SAR
1960–69	0.326	0.301	0.263	0.259	0.540	0.314
1970–79	0.243	0.316	0.215	0.274	0.239	0.225
1980–89	0.151	0.146	0.109	0.085	0.106	0.235
1990–99	0.074	0.191	–0.229	0.143	0.214	0.220
2000–2002	0.109	0.237	0.258	0.048	–0.022	0.175

AFR, Africa; EAP, East Asia and Pacific; ECA, Eastern and Central Asia; LAC, Latin America and the Caribbean; MNA, Middle East and North Africa; SAR, South Asian Region.
Source: World Bank, 2006.

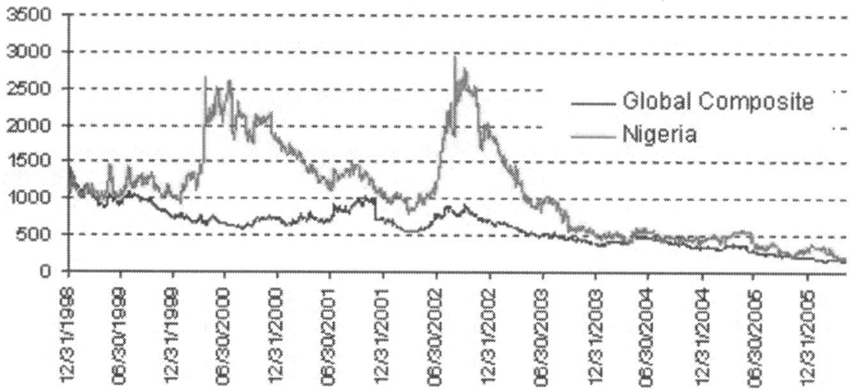

Figure 1.4 EMBI global stripped spreads (bps) of Nigeria's external debt.

In the food and beverage sector, the shrimp industry, for example, appears to be enjoying high returns because it has met international standards of quality and health safety and successfully cultivated and captured a segment of the international market. It is estimated that profits in the industry represent around 18 per cent of value added. Other businesses in the food and beverage sector – mainly multinationals such as Nestlé, Cadbury, Heineken – appear to achieve good returns and are expanding their investments while the bulk of firms are less successful. Another indication of high returns in some segments of the economy is the high market average price-to-earning ratio of 22.34 per cent for firms quoted on the Nigerian stock exchange. However, only 203 firms are registered on the stock exchange and the market capitalization is less than half of GDP, indicating again that this result is not necessarily widespread across the economy.

For the rest of the non-oil sector, particularly agriculture and the large informal economy, returns are low, evidenced in low levels of productivity and high levels of unused capacity in manufacturing. Therefore returns in Nigeria can be argued to be low. A low return in Nigeria is also consistent with low investment returns in Africa relative to other regions.

1.3.3 Is low investment due to low savings or due to low returns to investment?

If domestic savings were scarce and the binding constraint on investment, high foreign debt or a large current account deficit would signal that Nigeria is making extensive use of foreign savings. This was the case during the 1980s and 1990.[8] The external current account recorded persistent and significant deficits. External debt rose to 120 per cent of GDP by 1987. Repeated rescheduling and continuing external debt arrears effectively shut Nigeria out from international capital markets for most of the period. Evidence of this lack of market access is the prohibitive mark-ups that Nigeria would have had to pay on primary issues that can be derived from secondary market information.

This is not the case now. External debt following the recent Paris Club debt deal and the buy-back of part of the London Club debt is only 3 per cent of GDP, and the external current account has been in surplus averaging 4.8 per cent of GDP over the last three years. Nigeria's recent sovereign credit rating (BB–) has also improved access to foreign savings and finance. Markups that Nigeria would have had to pay on international markets have fallen to manageable levels. Export credit agencies are showing willingness to resume the full range of services to Nigeria after a long period of interruption. Remittances from Nigerians abroad are also an increasingly important element of private flows, reaching $3.5 billion (net) and about 3.5 per cent of GDP in 2005. Domestic commercial banks have traditionally been and continue to be highly liquid. In addition, while the private sector complains about the high cost of finance, real interest rates are comparable to or lower than in similar countries including Indonesia.

The high variability of interest rates and poor access to finance, especially long-term finance, are perhaps the more pressing challenges. Both are related to the poor development of the Nigerian financial system and its weak intermediation capacity. Private credit as a share of GDP has historically been lower in Nigeria than in other large oil economies and even countries in sub-Saharan Africa (SSA) (Table 1.6) although levels have been rising in the last few years. Bank credit remains the main source of funding of investment by Nigerian quoted firms. Relative to other emerging markets, the Nigerian stock market is also quite small. Although the number of listed securities is increasing, trading activity is still very thin because institutional and individual investors are reluctant to trade in the secondary market. But the recent bank consolidation has boosted trading in the market. Small businesses have little access to credit, unless they are willing to pay rapid turnover moneylender rates of up to 100 per cent annually. Sustainable micro-credit institutions, while now starting to enter the market since the December 2005 launch of the new Central Bank Microfinance Policy Framework, currently remain limited in reach and coverage. The equity market has only a small number of instruments and is accessed only by the largest firms, and the corporate bond market is virtually non-existent.

Term financing in particular is scarce and constrains productive investment. Less than 16 per cent of the 2002 RPED[9] private sector survey sample reported having loans longer than one year in duration. Existing loan maturities do not meet the long-term financing needs of enterprises and infrastructure projects. In a financial market characterized by volatile interest rates and short-term funding, banks have historically been willing to take maturity risk only on borrowers with outstanding credit quality. For blue chip clients, some banks are prepared to take refinancing risk and provide medium-term loans by rolling over short-term funds up to a maturity of 7–9 years. With the exception of the telecom sector, loan maturities fall short of the long-term financing horizon of 10–20 years required for investments in infrastructure and project finance.

The main cause of low investment and growth in Nigeria then appears to be not low savings but rather low returns to investment. This could in turn be the

Table 1.6A Banking sector liquidity

Nigeria	1998	1999	2000	2001	2002	2003	2004
Liquid assets/total deposits and short-term borrowing (%)	82	91	86	86	94	87	88
Liquid assets/total assets (%)	52	61	62	59	62	59	59
Banking liquidity index	10	10	10	9	10	10	10

Source: World Bank Financial Sector Development Indicators.

Table 1.6B Banking sector liquidity: cross-country comparison

	Liquid assets/total deposits and short-term borrowing (%)	Liquid assets/ total assets	Banking liquidity index
Nigeria	88	59	10
Kenya	14	30	5
Ghana	55	53	8
South Africa	24	13	4
Tanzania	48	54	10
Sub-Saharan Africa	44	40	6
Middle income	36	35	5
Low income	45	42	6

Source: World Bank Financial Sector Development Indicators, 2004.

result of low social returns and/or low ability of private sector to appropriate returns even where they exist or may be potentially high.

1.3.4 Is the problem low social returns or low private appropriability of returns?

Are low returns in Nigeria a problem of low social returns or is it that while social returns are high other factors constrain the ability of the private sector to access or appropriate these returns? The evidence suggests a combination of the two factors. Social return is determined by the underlying productivity of the particular economic activity. The low productivity of the Nigerian economy indicates that overall social return on capital in Nigeria would be low. But there is also evidence of high transaction costs that prevent economic agents from fully realizing potential returns. The relative importance of these two factors is also likely to be different across the different segments of the economy. In agriculture, for example, it is likely that low social returns, evidenced in low and declining yields, would be the more important of the two factors.

Table 1.7 Indicators of financial intermediation across countries (data for 2004–5)

	Liquid liabilities/ GDP (%)	Private credit/ GDP (%)	Overheads/total assets (%)	Net interest margin (%)	Stock market capitalization/GDP (%)	Life insurance premium volume/GDP (%)	Non-life insurance premium volume/GDP (%)
Nigeria	20.39	14.24	5.21	6.39	17.15	0.10	0.50
Ghana	30.3	12.0	8.77	9.54	19.02	–	–
Kenya	39.8	25.3	6.83	7.40	28.63	0.85	1.94
Tanzania	22.1	7.8	6.60	5.91		–	–
South Africa	61.51	106.89	5.29	6.89	213.51	10.80	3.02
Sub-Saharan Africa	32.33	20.90	5.88	7.36	47.76	4.02	1.92
Low income	31.15	17.99	5.00	6.28	30.35	0.86	0.71

Source: Thorsten *et al.*, 2000.

Low social returns

The HRV approach identifies three possible reasons for low productivity of an investment: (i) low human capital; (ii) bad infrastructure; (iii) poor geography.[10]

Low human capital. Recent growth literature gives much greater prominence to human capital as a factor in productivity and growth. Nigeria's population of 132 million is estimated to be growing at about 2.5 per cent annually. About 45 per cent of the population is under 15 years old. The dependency ratio of 0.9, though high, has been declining in recent years. Relative to Asian and several other large oil economies, this large human resource is poorly developed and lacks the skills needed to allow Nigeria to move onto a path of industrialization and integration into the global economy (Table 1.8).

Gross primary school enrolment is about 100 per cent but enrolment at secondary and tertiary levels is only 35 per cent and 10 per cent respectively, compared to 62 per cent and 16 per cent in Indonesia. Net enrolment at primary and secondary levels is lower at 88 per cent and 28 per cent respectively. At the tertiary level, there is also growing preference for non-science and non-technology related disciplines. Between 1991/92 and 2001/2002, the share of enrolment for science and engineering disciplines dropped from 27 per cent to 23.4 per cent because of lower returns on education in these fields from lower opportunities for employment. The quality of education has fallen at all levels over the last two decades. This is evidenced in worsening test scores, rising student–teacher ratios and other indictors of educational quality. Firms are also compelled to spend huge sums of money retraining new recruits or resort to the use of expatriates. Some firms now go overseas to recruit Nigerian graduates trained abroad[11] to ensure quality.

Nigerian manufacturing firms are preponderantly in sectors that require low skills. Most are found in labour- and resource-intensive, low-tech, low wage and low TFP growth sectors. In spite of Nigeria's relatively well developed manufacturing

Table 1.8 Indicators of size and quality of human capital

	Literacy rate		**Life expectancy at birth**		**Mortality rate**		**Public expenditure on education (% GDP)**
	1970	**2003**	**1970**	**2003**	**1970**	**2003**	**2004**
Nigeria	20.1	66.8	43.5	44.9	140	98	1.02
Indonesia	56.1	87.8	49.2	66.9	104	31	1.3
South Korea	n.a.	n.a.	61.4	74.2	43.0	5.0	4.3
Mexico	73.5	90.0	62.6	73.6	79.0	23.0	5.2
South Africa	69.5	86.0	53.9	45.7	n/a	53.0	5.4

n.a., not available.
Source: World Bank, 2005; CBN Statistical Bulletin, 2005.

sector compared to other SSA countries, it has fewer of its manufacturing firms in high-tech and high wage sectors (Table 1.9). In contrast to African countries with the best TFP estimates in Africa, Nigeria belongs to the poorest performing set of countries in Africa, together with Ethiopia, Zambia and Mozambique (Gelb *et al.*, 2005). This structure of firms in the Nigerian manufacturing sector could be due to the poor skills base of Nigerian labour, suggesting that weak human development is a binding constraint on the economy's ability to move to higher productivity investments. However, an alternative explanation could be that causality runs in the opposite direction and that the skills base of Nigerian labour (supply of skills) is low because there is low demand for skills by firms.

Clearly low human capital development is a factor in low productivity and returns in Nigeria but it is less clear that this is the binding constraint on growth. If low human capital were the binding constraint, we would expect to see high returns to education. The limited research and empirical analysis on this issue in Nigeria highlight the following results: (i) mean monthly earnings of workers increase with more years of schooling; (ii) private returns to primary and secondary education in Nigeria are low, having fallen substantially from 1966 estimates of 30 per cent to between 2–4 per cent per year; (iii) private wage returns to post-secondary education have also fallen to between 10 and 15 per cent per year compared to an estimated 34 per cent 40 years ago. The current estimates are low compared to results for Africa, Latin America and Asia estimated over 20 years ago (Table 1.10).

The low returns could be a reflection of the poor quality of education in Nigeria, and need further research. However it cannot be argued on the basis of the available data on returns to education that low human capital is the binding constraint on Nigeria's growth. Nevertheless the discussion above shows that strong human capital will be critical to Nigeria's ability to shift the composition of production towards higher productivity activities and thereby create more jobs at higher wages. Since building human capital takes a long time, it will be important for policy-makers to strengthen their efforts now.

Bad infrastructure. There is strong empirical evidence on the positive links between good infrastructure and economic growth and development. Access and quality across all key infrastructure sectors in Nigeria are significantly below levels in more rapidly growing economies. Electricity generation, for example, is below 4000 MW compared to about 39,000 MW in South Africa, with a population less than one third of Nigeria's. Per capita consumption of power is just a fraction of consumption in countries such as Malaysia, India, Indonesia, the Philippines and South Africa. Poor quality is evidenced in random and frequent power brownouts and blackouts and high variation in voltage quality which disrupts productive activity. This forces firms to divert substantial resources from reinvestment in their productive business to self-generation. Available estimates indicate that costs of infrastructure investments (power, road, water, telecoms) constitute upwards of 20 per cent of the cost of new investment projects in Nigeria. Staff costs to run and maintain self-generation efforts are in some cases as high as 10–15 per cent

Table 1.9 Comparative structure of manufacturing in Nigeria and SSA 1992 and 2002

	Nigeria		**Sub-Saharan Africa**	
Categories	**1992**	**2002**	**1992**	**2002**
Factor intensity				
Labour and resource intensive manufactures	63.4	62.9	71.4	70.4
Low skill technology, capital and scale intensive	14.6	14.7	10	10
Medium skill technology, capital and scale intensive	20.4	20.6	10	10.1
High skill technology, capital and scale intensive	1.8	1.8	6.7	7
Level of technology				
Low	65.3	64.8	74	73.2
Medium	34.6	34.9	23.3	23.4
High	0.3	0.3	0.8	0.9
Orientation				
Resource intensive	41	40.4	51.1	51.1
Scale intensive	32.28	26.8	23.2	22.1
Labour intensive	26.6	32.4	22.3	23.0
Science based	0.72	0.72	2.9	3.0
Wage type				
Low	65.9	66.1	67.4	64.7
Medium	32.5	32.1	24.3	26.2
High	1.8	1.8	6.5	6.8
Rate of productivity growth				
Low TFP growth sectors	32.9	32.7	44.5	43.8
Medium TFP growth	23.9	23.5	18.9	20.4
High TFP growth sectors	42.9[a]	43.3	33.7	32.5

a The high figure of Nigeria here is because the underlying framework we used adds textiles and clothing to the high TFP growth sectors.
Source: computed from UNIDO data.

of total payroll. Poor access to reliable power has a direct impact on the risks faced by enterprises. Particularly for start-up firms lacking experience and market knowledge, the risk that enough market share and adequate returns may not materialize is substantial. This is likely to discourage entry. Given poor access to finance it is additionally difficult to mobilize the funds for such high investment requirements. Thus older firms, particularly those who may have fully or

Table 1.10 Returns to education

	Africa (%)	Asia (%)	Latin America (%)
Primary	45	31	32
Secondary	26	15	23
University	33	18	23

Source: Psacharopoulos (1985).

substantially amortized their infrastructure service investments, are at a significant cost advantage relative to new entrants. Interviews with private sector firms indicate that the need for start-up companies to invest in backup generators is frequently a requirement for obtaining a commercial bank loan. With diesel prices uncertain and rising, it raises the risk perceptions enough to pose a barrier to entry. Thus competition for existing businesses from new entrants in any given sector is reduced.

Despite its good coastal location Nigeria has not been able to develop an efficient port service. For many value chains, port and related trade facilitation constraints constitute cost key drivers that undermine competitiveness. Nigerian port services are amongst the most inefficient and expensive in the world as evidenced by:

1 *High waiting times.* Ships wait up to 20 days for berths at the Apapa container terminal, which handles a large part of Nigeria's international trade in terms of value, excluding oil. These long queues at Apapa are very poor in comparison to container ports in other countries where waiting times are negligible.
2 *Low handling speeds.* The largest operators in Apapa average only about 6–7 crane moves per hour, in contrast to the 25 crane moves per hour achieved at efficient ports. Handling speeds for bulk and conventional cargo are also very low.
3 *High container 'dwell times'* (the times the boxes spend in the port). These average about 25–30 days, which is five times higher than international best practice standards. This results in severe congestion on the quays and further falls in container handling speeds due to congestion. Apapa should be able to handle about 1.2 million twenty-foot equivalent units (TEU) at operational levels in line with international standards but it is only handling 350,000 TEU and with great difficulty, as evidenced by the long queues.

As a result of these inefficiencies, costs of shipping spiralled upwards. The shipping lines have imposed surcharges of around $700 per TEU to cover the time ships spend waiting, adding about a third to freight rates from Europe. Surcharges are unusual in other countries, and where they exist are usually far below those applied at Lagos. For example, the port of Tema in Ghana has a surcharge of $150 per TEU and Cotonou $215 per TEU. There is no surcharge in Abidjan.

The costs of moving a container through the port are also very high. The basic container handling charges are about $223 per TEU (consisting of $187 for ship–shore handling and $35 for delivery). But the lines incur other transaction costs, including the costs of deploying their own staff to 'assist' the NPA staff. The cost of container handling in well-run international ports is often in the range $100–$125 per TEU: about half of that in Lagos. The government has recently completed concessioning of the ports. Combined with customs administrative reforms also under way in Lagos, as discussed in more detail later in this report, improvements to port efficiency and overall trade facilitation are already being recorded. However, this progress will need to be maintained and more done in order to bring costs in line with international best practices.

Poor roads are estimated to exact a cost on the economy of about 3 per cent of GDP. Poor quality and access to transport infrastructure increases time to market and is responsible for as much as 15–20 per cent of agricultural produce never reaching market. Some businesses report losses of up to 20 per cent of their output due to poor infrastructure, especially power. Nigeria's considerable infrastructure costs reduce firm profitability and returns to below levels for comparable activity in similar countries and potential levels in Nigeria. At the same time the relatively high levels of returns to investment for some existing firms indicate limited competition. This could be attributed to barriers to entry for new firms resulting from infrastructure deficiencies. Given their sunk investments in propriety infrastructure, firms are protected against competition from new market entrants. Relieving severe infrastructure constraints is critical for raising investment returns. But significant improvements in the efficiency of public spending are required in parallel with increased public spending in this area to achieve the desired impact. Bad infrastructure rather than low human capital then seems to be the more binding constraint.

Low private appropriability

While the 'hard' infrastructure issues discussed above affect the underlying productivity of investment activity, there are 'soft' infrastructure challenges that constrain the ability of economic agents to realize potential returns. These challenges

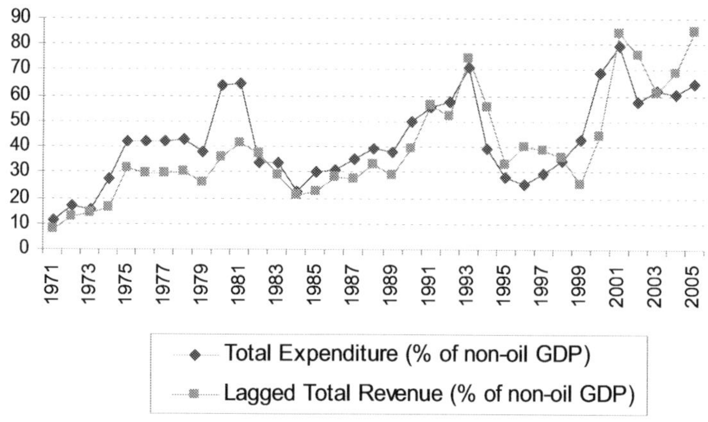

Figure 1.5 Revenues and expenditures, 1971–2005.
Source: Budina *et al.*, 2006.

manifest at both the macroeconomic and the microeconomic levels. Macroeconomic risks stem from historically weak macroeconomic management that has led to macroeconomic volatility and instability and other macro level distortions discussed in previous chapters. Micro level risks arise from the functioning of institutions, regulations and policies that are supposed to enable and promote investment. Both levels of risks reflect primarily massive failure of government: failure to manage the economy to avoid volatility from oil prices and the failure of government via the pervasive corruption created around state dominance of the lucrative oil sector. This has in turn weakened institutions' delivery of business enabling environment services to private sector entrepreneurs and unleashed predatory behaviour of public servants on private agents. Market failure evidenced in poor self discovery and poor public–private sector coordination are also factors.[12]

The high-risk business environment means that investors will require much higher levels of return to undertake investment activities. In addition, the investor class is confined to a smaller group that has high enough levels of risk aversion and/or has personal means at their disposal to mitigate against some of these risks. This means that capital is concentrated in relatively few hands and is not adequately dispersed. Both factors reduce investment levels and keep growth lower than potential.

Macroeconomic risks. A high degree of macroeconomic risk is evidenced in the high level of macroeconomic volatility which stems fundamentally from the historically poor management of the oil revenue cycle. Nigeria has tended to treat oil booms as permanent. Public expenditures have ratcheted out of control and beyond sustainable levels only to be followed by difficult and often inadequate adjustment to falling revenues when oil prices collapsed. This poor management of the oil revenue cycle has created excessive macroeconomic volatility. Recent analysis by Van Wijnbergen and Todorova (Budina *et al.*, 2006) also finds that Nigeria's economy has been more volatile than most, and more so than can be explained by oil price volatility alone. They show that fiscal policy has indeed exacerbated volatility and has not been used effectively to smooth the impact of volatile oil prices on the economy. Despite the government's attempts to save past oil windfalls, public expenditure remained highly correlated with oil fiscal revenue and fluctuated widely as a result of weak fiscal discipline and high oil price volatility. They conclude that volatility of spending, rather than its level, is therefore a strong explanatory factor for Nigeria's poor investment and growth performance. The macroeconomic instability and highly volatile real exchange rate from poor management of the oil revenue cycle have been a tax on investment.

Poor macroeconomic management also led to considerable exchange rate overvaluation. While flexible exchange rate policy could have been used to minimize the adverse macroeconomic impacts of massive oil revenue inflows, exchange rates were for a long time kept rigid with reliance on inflation and parallel markets to provide the needed real exchange rate adjustment. This only led to excessive real exchange rate appreciation and a shift in allocation of resources away from the non-oil tradable sectors, mainly agriculture. Real exchange rate overvaluation was evident in the rapid increases in the parallel market premium. In the last few years exchange rate management has improved significantly and the exchange rate premium has been virtually eliminated in 2006. Nevertheless, the continued appreciation of the real exchange rate reduces export competitiveness.

One implication of the volatility of the economy is the reluctance of banks to commit to long term financing to the business sector. Figure 1.6 shows the maturities of loans for Nigerian banks. There is a clear preference of deposit banks for loans of shorter maturities. The proportion of commercial banks' loans maturing over one year declined from 22 per cent of total loans in 1980 to 17 per cent in 1996 and in 2005 was only 14.2 per cent.

Policy instability and unpredictability has also been an important factor in the unstable macroeconomic environment. In particular, frequent changes in trade tariffs and in the use of import bans have been a major source of uncertainty for investors. Moreover, before the move to the ECOWAS Common External Tariff (CET) in October 2005, the Nigerian economy was one of the most protectionist.[13] In 2003, more than 42 import categories were banned, including most types of textiles and men's footwear. In 2005, the number stood at 44. This protectionist stance contributed to inefficiency, in part because firms were not compelled to seek competitiveness improvements. Nigeria's unweighted trade tariff has now declined to 12.1 per cent and the maximum tariff from 150 per cent to 50 per cent. There is, however, still considerable resort to ad hoc import bans.

Microeconomic risks. These also contribute to low private returns to investment in Nigeria. They stem fundamentally from weak institutions, poor public–private coordination, and corruption, which adversely impacts on the quality of services

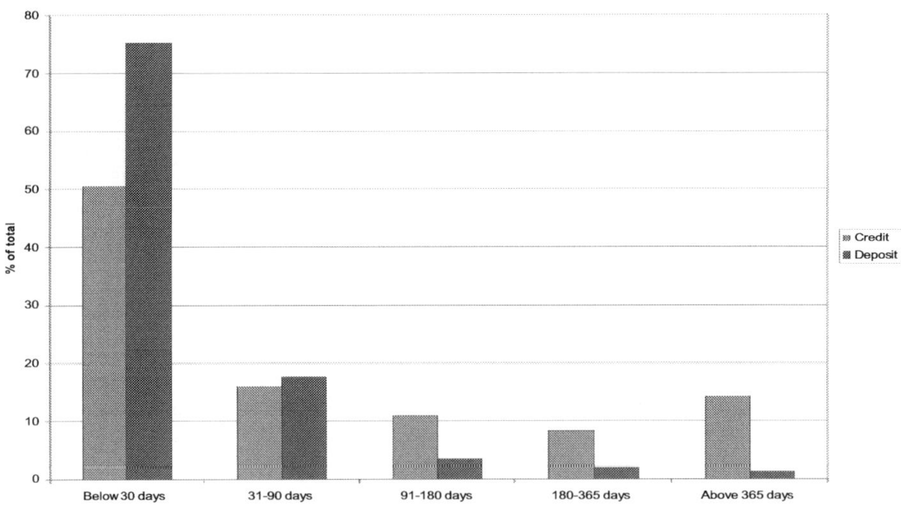

Figure 1.6 Deposit and credit structure of deposit banks in Nigeria (%), 2005.
Source: Soludo, 2006.

rendered by government agencies to private businesses and greatly increases transaction costs of doing business in Nigeria.

Problems of weak institutions, poor coordination and corruption are not uncommon in oil rich economies and Nigeria has suffered significantly from this. During decades of autocratic military rule both public and private institutions were systematically undermined and allowed to be run down. Power was concentrated in the executive. Other institutions of government, including the legislature, judiciary and civil service, had limited influence and capacity. In addition the larger society has had a limited voice in policy-making. Moreover, selected interest groups who have special access to those in authority are able to capture policy-making and exercise a considerably greater say. Policy decisions therefore often did not reflect broad economic interests. This has led to a shifting and unpredictable policy environment that has not been conducive to private investment. Since the return to democracy and constitutional rule, there has been a gradual shift in the balance of power. The National Assembly has begun to reassert itself, and some elements of the civil service linked to the reform programme have been reinvigorated. This being said, there was a substantial legacy of distrust between the public and private sector inherited by the administration in 1999 that will take a concerted effort over a period of time to fully overcome.

Corruption and rent-seeking thrived under weak institutions. Public sector dominance of the oil sector helped create a 'rentier' state whose principal concern was sharing resource rents through large-scale public spending, job creation in government and public enterprises, and protection of numerous sectors of the economy. In addition, patronage politics become pervasive. For long periods the lack of broader democratic legitimacy meant that in order to stay in power regimes have had to rely on dispensing patronage. In such conditions public resources were used wastefully and often for corrupt purposes. Because governments have not needed the private sector for revenue or job creation, they have failed to provide the public goods and conducive investment climate that are essential to enable the growth of a competitive private sector. The lack of diversification of the base of the economy led to a configuration of socio-economic interest groups, in which the most influential felt threatened in the short term by productivity- and competition-enhancing reforms.

Weak institutions and poor governance contributed substantially to Nigeria's public debt problems, as the majority of projects financed by public borrowing during the late 1970s and 1980s failed to generate an adequate rate of return needed to improve repayment capacity.[14] The resulting debt overhang constrained reduced incentives for investment. Corruption is also negatively and significantly associated with the accumulation of physical capital GDP growth (Mauro, 1995). Differences in institutional quality account for a major share of cross-country growth differences (Knack and Keefer, 1995). While Nigeria's corruption perception index[15] of 2.2 represents a significant improvement over the last few years the country still ranks 142 out of 163 countries ranked. Nigeria's score on the civil liberties scale was only surpassed by those of China and Vietnam. In addition, Nigeria had the worst score (–1.13) in the rule of law index. All of these indicators are hardly suggestive of an environment conducive to private sector growth (see Narula, 2004). Nigeria is also ranked poorly on other institutional and governance indexes (for example, Heritage Foundation). Weak institutions have increased the cost of doing business for Nigerian firms and lowered profits available to be made by businesses and firms. Different surveys have documented evidence that 'unofficial payments' by firms for access to even the most basic economic infrastructure is quite common. This is particularly in respect of public service connections, licensing and permit processing, government contracts and customs. Respondents also consistently rank the quality, integrity and efficiency of most public institutions as very poor. Firms report paying bribes to secure government contracts. The data show clearly that several of these indicators are improving which suggests some strengthening of institutions and declining corruption levels. Nevertheless, corruption and related weaknesses in institutions remain major contributors to high business transactions costs. This has created a business environment that is extremely hostile to competition, investment and growth because it severely limits private appropriability of returns.

The impact of weak institutions, poor public–private coordination mechanisms and corruption is amply evident in four critical aspects of the business environment where Nigeria performs most poorly and where improvements could have a significant short-term impact on enterprises: namely taxation, trade facilitation, business regulation and licensing and contract enforcement. Constraints in these areas of the business environment increase the micro level risks of doing business and also explain a large part of the informality in the Nigerian economy. Excessive regulations that place unnecessary burden on firms, coupled with what are viewed as unjust taxes and predatory behaviour by public agents, are a major determinant in a firm's decision not to operate in the formal sector.

With a marginal effective tax rate (METR) of 27.1 per cent, the tax burden on businesses in Nigeria is internationally competitive and compares well with countries such as India (43.2 per cent), Indonesia (38.8 per cent), Kenya (68.2 per cent) and South Africa (43.8 per cent). This competitiveness is, however, undermined by a burdensome tax administration process. It takes 1120 hours per year for a company to pay these taxes in Nigeria compared to 340 hours in Ghana and 350 hours in South Africa. This administrative burden represents one of the worst worldwide and is well beyond the best practice of 12 hours that prevails in the UAE. This administrative burden is compounded by the fact that taxes are administered by all three tiers of government. While each tier has a distinct role, there is insufficient coordination of these roles. The impact is a system of multiple taxes and a proliferation of taxes, some of which are illegal and not ratified by the appropriate legislature. In an attempt to improve revenue collection, many state governments have handed over their tax collection to private contractors, practising a system of tax farming that results in arbitrary assessments and the use of coercion (moral and physical) which all but destroys the integrity of the tax system in the eyes of individuals and businesses. Evasion is therefore widespread.

Despite the fact that Nigeria's tax burden relative to other countries is modest, enterprises invariably complain about the country's tax regime. This dissatisfaction derives from two factors. The first, which lies beyond the purview of the tax authorities, is the legitimate sense firms have that they do not get value for money for the taxes they pay – most specifically in terms of infrastructure services. The second key complaint is related to the administrative inefficiencies of the tax system managed across the three tiers of government. Firms, at least those that are able, have internalized the costs and constraints associated with their interface, finding ways to evade and avoid taxes and coping with the cost of compliance, and therefore tend to rank this constraint lower relative to other concerns (namely infrastructure and access to finance).

The true extent to which the tax regime constrains business is reflected in the results of recent surveys in Abia and Anambra States that sought to assess the problems experienced by businesses dealing with Nigeria's tax system (IFC and Skoup Consultants, 2003). Sixty-eight per cent of the firms surveyed rated tax regulations and high tax rates as a significant barrier to the growth and development of their business. This level of frustration encompasses issues such as the number and incidence of taxes, frequent changes in tax rates and procedures and the significant administrative burden associated with tax demands, including overlapping claims from the different levels of government. Table 1.11 outlines a list of complaints made by a cross-section of the businesses in eastern Nigeria. It includes both direct taxes and indirect costs. Direct taxes represent the multiple/duplicative taxes that businesses often find themselves paying. Indirect costs comprise the management resources that a firm must devote to deal with the inefficiency of the tax regime and the need to hire intermediaries to deal with overzealous tax officials. Almost 90 per cent of the firms interviewed employed full-time accountants and lawyers or outsourced their taxation/accounting requirements on an 'as needed' basis.

Federal government capacity to administer enterprise taxes is limited, particularly in relation to correctly assessing taxes. A recent study on tax policy reforms highlighted the fact that the number of tax administrators is limited and they are badly trained and equipped and poorly remunerated (Odusula, 2006). This administrative constraint is compounded by the lack of computerization and the multiple tax administrative activities emanating from the different tiers of government.[16] Specific transactions, such as tax refunds or duty drawbacks, are extremely difficult to obtain and can take extended periods to effect. Firms have limited access to up-to-date information on tax structure and the rates or levies applicable to different taxes.[17] There is therefore a lack of clarity as to what taxes should be paid, at what rates and to whom. Seeking redress through the court system is slow and expensive. The poor administration and multiple government layers represent a major disincentive to formalization of businesses and reduces the tax base as a result. The burden on management also detracts from other strategic responsibilities, driving down productivity and competitiveness.

The Doing Business Survey of 2006 rated Nigeria in the bottom 20 countries assessed globally on trade facilitation. It takes 53 days to clear goods from Lagos ports compared to 26 days in Senegal and 16 in Mauritius (Doing Business, 2006). The dire state of the Lagos ports contributes to the delays and increases the costs

Table 1.11 Common tax administrative complaints

Tax	Problem
Business Permit	Agents behave like touts in order to extort money Local Government does not provide any service
Capital Gains Tax	Since bills are estimated, overcharging occurs frequently
Company Income Tax	High and excessive Bills are estimated Assessment problem: arguments about what turnover actually is versus what the tax consultants want it to be Difficult to get a Tax Clearance
Excise Duty	Continuously on the increase
Property Tax	Corrupt officials Improper assessment leads to overestimation
Vehicle Emblem	Extortion and exploitation by local governments Regulations lacks clarity
Value Added Tax	Double taxation – e.g. VAT paid on raw materials and again on finished goods[a]

a FIRS make the point that VAT in Nigeria recognizes both input and output elements so that manufacturers are allowed to net-off input VAT charges. The problem reflected in this table is probably more to do with implementation rather than policy or legislation.

for firms who use them. Furthermore, the inefficiency provides incentives for informal trade. The very costly delays at the ports are further compounded by onerous administrative and customs procedures. Table 1.12 outlines the complex sequence of activities associated with import–export clearance for non-export processing zone (EPZ) firms. In response, Nigeria is embarking on significant trade facilitation reforms that complement the recently concluded port concessioning. First and foremost there is the new dynamic in place at the Apapa terminals in Lagos Port. New private sector operators concerned with the bottom line are working increasingly closely with customs to address time and cost concerns. This new commitment to coordination is key. And the customs service is responding with its own reform initiatives. This includes extended working hours and new procedures aimed at easing the process of clearing goods at ports. Nigeria has installed the ASYCUDA++ software and scanners to speed up the inspection of goods. In January 2006, as part of the government's move from pre-shipment inspection to a Destination Inspection regime, new scanning equipment was introduced by the inspection consultants. Additionally there is improved inter-agency collaboration resulting in a reduced number of inspections of cargo. The upshot, based on the most recent 2007 Doing Business Report, is a reduction in exporting time down to 25 days from 41, with importing time declining from 53 to 45 days.

Despite the recent progress, it needs to be borne in mind that Nigeria's competitor in Senegal is still able to import and export in half the time it will take at Apapa. And notwithstanding the reduced number of inspections, nevertheless a

Table 1.12 Import clearance sequence for non-EPZ firms

Rank	Activity	Time lapse	Cost
	Pre-shipment procedures		
1	Pro-forma invoice sent to clearing agent		
2	Clearing agent obtains and completes form M		
3	Clearing agent purchases cargo insurance and submits receipt to bank		
4	Bank approves Form M and sends to other agencies		
5	PSI agent assigns cargo an SEIC number and completes inspection and issues CRI		
	Post-shipment procedures		
6	Clearing agent obtains single goods declaration form and with documents provided calculates duties owed for company to pay at a bank		
7	Clearing agent takes all documents to CPS at port		
8	Deputy Comptroller reviews documents		
9	Desk Officer verifies documents		
10	Accounting Officer verifies documents and gives to Deputy Comptroller for final verification		
11	ASYCUDA assigns serial number		
12	Manifest department certifies Bill of Lading		
13	Customs examination shed officers check cargo against documents		
14	Valuation Unit inspects cargo and then releases it		
15	Clearing agent confirms payment and claims goods		

firm must go through 15 separate procedures to receive a cargo and 14 procedures to ship one. Studies demonstrate that these cross-border procedures increase import costs for firms in Nigeria by 45 per cent on average. Some enterprise managers noted that they must spend between 30 and 50 per cent of their time on procedures alone (World Bank, 2005a,b). This is considerably higher than the 14 per cent in Kenya, 13 per cent in India and 5 per cent in Indonesia (Yee *et al.*, 2005). The impact is a reduction of export volumes by 1 per cent in Nigeria. It is estimated that a reduction of 'factory-to-ship' time from 41 days to 27 could increase exports from Nigeria by almost 15 per cent (Djankov *et al.*, 2006).

As seen from Table 1.12 above, the sequence of activities associated with import–export clearance for non-EPZ firms is complex. Some 71 signatures on 13 different documents are required for imports into Nigeria. Clearing and forwarding agents note that importers typically avoid the principal import document (Form

M) and its financial obligations by dealing with port-based syndicates. For a fee of 1000–4500 naira these syndicates provide a Form M and forge bank signatures and stamps. Clearance procedures for an EPZ are significantly more streamlined but the EPZ still incurs many of these problems.

Over the past five years significant reforms have taken place in the process for business registration in Nigeria. The Corporate Affairs Council (CAC) has initiated a reform agenda which includes computerization, institutional renewal, staff reform and a programme of national outreach which resulted in the establishment of 25 state offices. In a recent survey taken in Abia and Anambra, 40 per cent of firms cited improvement in the last five years in the number of days it takes to register a business, and the average cost of business registration declined 46 per cent over the same period (Skoup, 2003). Figure 1.7 outlines the official steps for a new entrant firm in Nigeria and current estimates of the time required to complete each step. The outstanding challenge under the current reform programme is updating the current database to eliminate companies that are no longer operating and ensure that the annual reporting of registered companies is completed in a thorough and timely manner.

The process of licensing is still a significant challenge. Doing Business ranks Nigeria as the sixth worst performer on the speed of obtaining a licence. Although Nigeria and Ghana both have 16 procedures for obtaining a licence, it takes 121 days to complete the procedures in Ghana and 465 in Nigeria (Doing Business, 2006). A recent analysis of five major industries in Nigeria identified a list of annual and monthly licences that firms typically have to obtain to operate in a country. It identified 29 basic permits and inspections with which firms had to comply such as registration fee and expatriate entry and re-entry permits. In addition there are industry specific licences (for example, a shrimp company is required to secure 17 additional licences to operate (Consilium International, 2005)) which are often a duplication of the procedures the firm must go through at the federal

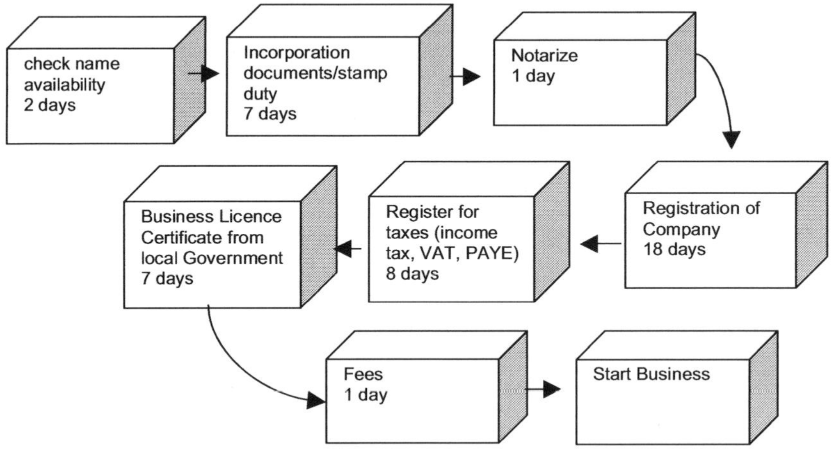

Figure 1.7 Entry procedures.

Table 1.13 Contract enforcement indicators

Country	No. of procedures	No. of days	Cost as % of debt claim
Angola	47	1,011	11.2
Cameroon	58	585	36.4
Ghana	23	200	14.4
Ivory Coast	25	525	47.6
Kenya	25	360	41.3
Nigeria	23	730	37.2
Sudan	67	915	30
United Arab Emirates	54	614	16
United Kingdom	14	288	17.2
United States of America	17	250	7.5

Source: World Bank, 2005a,b.

level. The plethora of licences at the federal level is compounded by state and local government licences which often duplicate federal-level processes. Box A1.1 in the Appendix (see www.csae.ox.ac.uk/books) further portrays this problem by detailing the licensing requirements for hotel operators.

The high cost of compliance associated with setting up a business and/or dealing with licences places an unnecessary burden on firms and can play a major role in their decisions to migrate to the formal economy. Registration processes can be streamlined further. However, reform of licensing is a more intractable challenge since it requires coordination across the three tiers of government and changes in the way public officials behave.

Nigeria ranks 119 out of 155 countries surveyed in Doing Business 2006 on contract enforcement. It takes 730 days and costs 37.2 per cent of the debt value for a business to settle a basic contractual dispute through the court system in Nigeria. This is 27 times the number of days it takes in Tunisia and almost four times the number of days in Ghana. This delay is a strong disincentive for a business to enter into contracts or risk funds beyond a trusted circle of family and business contacts, inhibiting investment, innovation and market exchange. At the same time, Nigeria is losing out on the economic benefits of an effective judicial system which include more bank credit to businesses, increased entry by new firms and hiring by established ones, and reduced demands on government budget.

The formal judicial system is currently faced with a huge backlog of cases. The costs and time delays involved in using the judicial system to settle a dispute vastly outweigh the potential benefits for the majority of plaintiffs. Therefore only large firms can afford to use the system. This problem is compounded by the fact that, in a number of critical areas, Nigerian legislation is outdated and inhibits modern business activity and practices. Much of this body of laws (dealing with issues like bankruptcy and insolvency) remains the same as at independence 45 years ago.

Experience has also shown that the Arbitration and Conciliation Act (ACA) has failed to achieve one of the underlying philosophies of the UNCITRAL Model Law, which is to minimize judicial intervention in the arbitral process. In Nigeria, arbitration is often perceived as the first step to litigation, and the arbitral process often becomes entangled in the extremely protracted and cumbersome process of Nigerian litigation.

Lack of 'self-discovery' and innovation. Productivity and innovation are critical for sustaining Nigeria's growth. Defining a product discovery as the growth of exports in a product category from less than $10,000 in each of three base years to more than $1 million in each of three target years (Klinger and Lederman, 2004), analysis conducted by Walkenhorst and Cattaneo (2006) at the SITC 4-digit level for export development between 1993–95 and 2002–2004 gives only one product discovery ('Liquefied natural gas'). If this criterion is modified by reducing the target year threshold from $1 million to $100,000, only two additional products are identified ('Waste and scrap of paper or paperboard' and 'Waste and scrap of cast iron'). None of these discoveries represents a productive non-oil output. In comparison, in a sample of 53 countries there was an average product discovery rate (at the HS 4-digit level) of more than six per country (Klinger and Lederman, 2004). In addition, measured by widely used indicators such as the Herfindahl index,[18] Nigeria has the most highly concentrated export structure in the world (UNCTAD, 2005). In 2003, the country had only 66 product groups with export values exceeding $100,000,[19] while five comparator countries had substantial exports in at least 175 product categories. On a per capita basis, only three countries in the world have lower non-oil merchandise exports, namely Burundi, Ethiopia and Rwanda (Nielsen, 2005). The dependence on fuels might even increase further in the medium term, as exports of natural gas, of which Nigeria has very substantial reserves, are projected to double within the next four to five years.

There are a few positive cases of cost discovery: for example the success of the light manufacturing clusters in Nnewi that have continued to survive and produce with very little external support, in the face of the most hostile business environment. Over the past 25 years, there have been significant cost discovery accomplishments realized in this cluster. Entrepreneurs have reached out to Taiwan in particular to obtain technology and know-how which have been introduced into their Nigeria operations.

Overall, however, there appears to be a deficit in Nigeria with respect to the uptake of new productive activities. The absence of these new ideas is a factor in low private returns to investment. Essentially this boils down to failure to identify considerable numbers of potentially profitable new non-traditional high-productivity investment opportunities. One way for government to help the discovery process and overcome possibly existing information and coordination deficiencies would be to reduce the anti-export bias in the trade regime and assist potential exporters in identifying new overseas opportunities by providing better developed and targeted market and industry information than is currently available to them. In other areas where there is clear additional export growth potential – such as leather and shrimps – specific strategies can be developed to foster improved performance and growth. In the case of leather, this could entail targeted market-driven performance-based initiatives to augment the quality of hides; for both activities, significant appropriability gains could be achieved with government streamlining of the licensing procedures that absorb significant management time and squeeze profit margins. Additionally the domestic catfish industry is a burgeoning market where better capture of information externalities – particularly in regard to access to and uptake of new technologies – together with improved coordination within the industry, could go a long way to providing the opportunity for better returns. These would be captured by those producers that can exploit quality improvement opportunities and convert these into successful cost discovery outcomes.

Recent econometric work (Iyigun and Rodrik, 2004) on entrepreneurship (measured in terms of cost or self-discovery, the policy and institutional environment in which it operates) and the role of reform in augmenting private-sector-led growth suggests that where there is poor cost discovery – arguably the current case in Nigeria – considerable entrepreneurial activity can be triggered by relatively modest, rather than major, structural and institutional reforms. This can certainly be seen to be the case for the value chains that are showing growth and resurgence (see Box A1.2 in the Appendix, www.csae.ox.ac.uk/books) – such as leather and shrimps. Entrepreneurship also thrived in Nnewi with the most modest of improvements. Some of the businesses in the cluster attributed this to their own ability to coordinate sufficiently to provide some basic defence to past highly predatory government behaviour that threatened private appropriability.

Private sector perceptions of the most severe constraints to their activities largely confirm some of the conclusions of the growth diagnostics. Various firm-level surveys have repeatedly identified infrastructure, access to and cost of finance, macroeconomic instability and business and regulatory impediments as the most severe constraint to economic activity. What is most striking about the survey analyses (see Box A1.3 in the Appendix, www.csae.ox.ac.uk/books) is the consistency in results across the surveys, each of which takes a different angle for analysis. Whether looking from a nationwide manufacturing enterprise perspective (RPED study), or focusing on specific States (cluster and Lagos surveys), or disaggregating according to firm size (Lagos study) or by industry (value chain analysis) we find infrastructure, access to finance and government policy and administration (whether measured in terms of uncertainties or the additional administrative management costs that end up being borne by the firm) revealed as the most severe impediments to improved investment levels and therefore to firm productivity improvements, growth and employment creation.

1.4 Conclusions

Nigeria's growth performance has strengthened since 2000. The economy needs to grow much faster and sustain such growth over a longer period of time to achieve appreciable impact on poverty. Sustaining recent growth will require focusing limited government capacity and political capital on addressing the most binding constraints to growth. The immediate threat to sustaining recent growth in Nigeria does not appear to be low savings but rather low productivity and efficiency of the economy which has led to low private returns. This is in turn a result of both low investment returns and limited capacity of the private sector to appropriate returns.

Reform and investments that will help raise investment returns, particularly reforms and investment to enhance access to and cost of physical infrastructure, seem the most urgent areas for action. The next area is reforms to raise the ability of economic agents to appropriate returns. This refers to actions to address macroeconomic instability, particularly from oil revenue volatility, and microeconomic risks, from corruption and related weaknesses of institutions, and regulations to guide investment behaviour. On the macroeconomic front, the most urgent issue for attention seems to be finding ways to institutionalize the oil-price based fiscal rule that has since 2004 been applied on the basis of political agreements between federal and state governments. Reducing micro-level risks by changing policies and procedures related to taxation, trade facilitation, business regulation and licensing is needed to help reduce predatory behaviour of public agents and limit opportunities for corruption. While the diagnostics suggest a higher priority to infrastructure, it is also clear that actions to strengthen the business environment would be generally easier to implement and could help deliver some quick wins. Targeting specific potential high value chains and selected growth poles, such as Lagos, could help demonstrate quick wins and also have the largest impact on the economy as a whole

Building human capital and skills does not come out unequivocally as a binding constraint to growth. Nevertheless, action is needed on this front since without stronger human capital and skills Nigeria cannot achieve the desired change in the competition of economic activity towards higher productivity activity. In addition Nigeria will not be able to benefit from full integration into global markets to sustain rapid growth over time. Action on this front needs to start immediately since results will take time to achieve. While savings are not the key factor in past low growth, enhancing access to capital, especially term finance, will be important for higher productivity including through promotion of longer-term investment.

Notes

1 The authors would also like to acknowledge the important contributions of others from the Infrastructure Team, including Justin Runji and Mohua Mukherjee, and from the Finance and Private Sector Team, including Shireen El Wahab, Uma Subramanian, Thomas Muller, Astrid Manroth and Michael Fuchs.

2 Federal Ministry of Labour and Productivity based on data from the Central Bank of Nigeria.

3 Federal Ministry of Labour and Productivity.

4 Other studies on productivity growth in Nigeria, including Adenikinju and Soludo (1997); Chete and Adenikinju (1996) and Adenikinju and Chete (1999), arrive at the same conclusion.
5 The statistics relate to area harvested and are likely to understate area cultivated since areas which yield no harvest are not included.
6 It should be noted that the table excludes the period 1972 to 1985, for which comparable information is not available, notably for area harvested and yields.
7 Using discount rate as a proxy.
8 During the mid to late 1980s, interest rate repression limited incentives to save and the economy relied strongly on foreign savings, evidenced in high levels of external debt and large current account deficits. But the low interest rate on deposits even after financial liberalization also suggests that, while important, savings might not have been a binding constraint to growth even during this period
9 Regional Program on Enterprise Development.
10 The issue of geography is not analysed in this chapter. Nigeria is neither landlocked nor resource poor. While being in the tropics imposes a higher burden of disease, other tropical countries such as India, Indonesia and Malaysia are doing well.
11 Some analysts are of the opinion that it is in the long-term interests of Nigerian firms and private sector at large to invest more in the Nigerian education sector.
12 For further elaboration of these concepts and their impact on growth and industry and sector development strategies, see Rodrik (2004).
13 Nigeria has formally adopted the ECOWAS CET with tariff bands of 0, 5, 10 and 20 per cent. However, a tariff band of 50 per cent will still be applicable in the interim for some selected import competing goods.
14 A study carried out by the Federal Ministry of Finance in 1996 of commercial external loans from bilateral and commercial creditors (amounting to about 70 per cent of external debt outstanding in 1996) has documented problems encountered by externally financed projects.
15 Measured by Transparency International.
16 Multiple taxation is clearly prohibited in the Constitution of the Federal Republic of Nigeria (paragraphs 8 and 10 of Part II of the Second Schedule). Businesses and stakeholders have been encouraged by the Joint Tax Board to stand up for their legal rights and challenge any tier of government that engages in multiple taxation, either individually or collectively through industry, trade or business associations.
17 Firms noted that this was particularly the case for customs duty laws where there is need for greater transparency regarding the base for calculation.
18 Calculated as the sum of the squares of product export-shares.
19 Although this was up from 37 in 2001.

Bibliography

Adenikinju, A. and C. Soludo, 1997, *Economic Policy and Total Factor Productivity in Nigeria's Manufacturing Sector*. Paris: OECD Development Centre.

Adenikinju, A.F. and L.N. Chete, 1999, 'Trade Liberalization, Market Structure and Productivity in Nigeria', *The Nigerian Journal of Economic and Social Studies*, 41, 385–403.

Aghion, P., P. Bacchetta and R. Ranciere, 2006, 'Exchange Rate Volatility and Productivity Growth: The Role of Financial Development', NBER Working Paper 12117.

Bhaumik, S., and S. Estrin, 2006, 'The Performance of Nigerian Firms in Lagos.' Report prepared for Lagos State Government as background to Lagos State Economic Development Strategy

Budina, N., G. Pang and S. van Wijnbergen, 2006, 'Nigeria's Growth Record: Dutch Disease or Debt Overhang?' Unpublished.

Central Bank of Nigeria, 2005, *Statistical Bulletin*. Abuja, Nigeria: CBN.

Centre for the Study of African Economies, 2003, 'Sources of Growth in Nigeria: An Initial Analysis', report prepared for DFID, Nigeria. Centre for the Study of African Economies, Department of Economics, University of Oxford, Oxford.

Chete, L. and A.F. Adenikinju, 1995, 'Productivity and Growth in Nigerian Manufacturing 1962–1985', *African Journal of Economic Policy*, 2, 77–88

Djankov, S., C. Freund, and C. Pham, 2006, 'Trading on Time.' Washington, DC: World Bank.

Eifert, B., A. Gelb, and V. Ramachandran, 2005, 'Business Environment and Comparative Advantage in Africa: Evidence from Investment Climate Data', presented at the World Bank Group Annual Conference on Development Economics held in Dakar, Senegal, in January 2005 (available at www.worldbank.org/afr/aftps).

Hausmann, R. and R. Rigobon, 2002, 'An Alternative Interpretation of the Resource Curse: Theory and Policy Implications', NBER Working Paper 9424.

Hausmann, R., and D. Rodrik, 2003, 'Economic Development as Self-Discovery', *Journal of Development Economics*, 72, 603–633.

Hausmann, R., D. Rodrik and A. Velasco, 2005, 'Growth Diagnostics', J. F. Kennedy School, Harvard University (available at http://ksghome.harvard.edu).

IMF, 2005, 'Nigeria: 2005 Article IV Consultation – Staff report; Staff Supplement; and Public Information Notice on the Executive Board Discussion', IMF country report no. 05/302.

Iyigun, M. and D. Rodrik, 2004, 'On Efficacy of Reforms: Policy Tinkering, Institutional Change and Entrepreneurship', NBER Working Paper 10455.

Klinger, B. and D. Lederman, 2004, 'Discovery and Development: An Empirical Exploration of "New" Products', World Bank Policy Research Working Paper no. 3450, World Bank, Washington, DC.

Knack, S. and P. Keefer, 1995, 'Institutions and Economic Performance: Cross-Country Tests Using Alternative Institutional Measures', *Economics and Politics*, 7, 207–227.

Marchat, J.M., J. Nasir, V. Ramachandran, *et al.*, 2002, 'Structure and Performance of Manufacturing Enterprises in Nigeria: Results of the RPED 2001 Nigeria Firm Survey', RPED Paper No. 118.

Mauro, P., 1995, 'Corruption and Growth', *Quarterly Journal of Economics*, 110.

Narula, R., 2004, 'Understanding Absorptive Capacities in an "Innovation System" Context: Consequences for Economic Growth.' Paper prepared for DRUID seminar conference, Elsinore, Denmark, 14–16 June 2004.

Nielsen, T., 2005, 'Nigerian Trade Policy.' In *International Monetary Fund, Nigeria: Selected Issues and Statistical Appendix*. Country Report No. 05/303, Washington, DC.

'Nigeria makes it easy for small businesses to register', USAID/Nigeria Program and Policy Development Office, Development Policy Series, No. 3, Abuja.

Nigeria National Bureau of Statistics, Federal Republic of Nigeria, 2000, *Annual Abstract of Statistics*, Lagos: Federal Government Publisher.

Nigeria National Bureau of Statistics, Federal Republic of Nigeria, 2003, *Annual Abstract of Statistics*, Lagos: Federal Government Publisher.

Nigeria National Bureau of Statistics, Federal Republic of Nigeria, 2005a, *The Nigerian Statistical Fact Sheets on Economic Development*, Lagos: Federal Government Publisher.

Nigeria National Bureau of Statistics, Federal Republic of Nigeria, 2005b, *Annual Abstract of Statistics*, Lagos: Federal Government Publisher.

Odusula, A., 2006, 'Tax Policy Reforms in Nigeria', research paper, UNU–WIDER.

Psacharopoulos, G., 1985, 'Returns to Education: A Further International Update and Implications.' *Journal of Human Resources* 20, 583–604.

Rankin N., M. Söderbom and F. Teal, 2004. 'Exporting from Manufacturing Firms in Sub-Saharan Africa: Micro Evidence for Macro Outcomes.' Working Paper. Centre for the Study of African Economies, Department of Economics, University of Oxford, Oxford.

Rodrik, D., 2004, 'Industrial Policy for the Twenty-First Century.' Unpublished.

Skoup and Company Ltd, 2003, 'Cluster Development Program in Eastern Nigeria: Administrative and Infrastructure Costs Survey of the Manufacturing Sector (Abia and Anambra States).' Report prepared for the IFC and World Bank.

Soludo, C.C., 2006, 'Nigeria: Economic Growth Drivers and Financing Challenges', presentation by the Governor of the Central Bank of Nigeria, 25 January 2006 (see Central Bank of Nigeria website: www.cenbank.org/publications).

Thorsten, B., A. Demirguc-Kunt and Ross E., 2000, 'A New Database on Financial Development and Structure', *World Bank Economic Review* 14, 597–605.

United Nations Conference on Trade and Development (UNCTAD), 2005, *UNCTAD Handbook of Statistics*, Geneva: UNCTAD.

Utomi P., A. Duncan and G. Williams, 2006, *Strengthening Incentives for Economic Growth: The Political Economy of Reform*.

Walkenhorst, P. and O. Cattaneo, 2006, 'Trade, Diversification and Growth in Nigeria'. Background Document for World Bank (2007) *Nigeria: Growth and Competitiveness*, Washington, DC: World Bank.

Willoughby, C,. 2006, *Infrastructure and Economic Growth in Nigeria*.

World Bank, 2005a, *World Development Indicators*, Washington, DC: World Bank.

World Bank, 2005b, *Doing Business in 2006: Creating Jobs*, Washington, DC: World Bank.

World Bank, 2006, *Challenges of African Growth*, Washington, DC: World Bank.

World Bank Financial Sector Development Indicators, various years, *Financial Sector Operations and Policy*, Washington, DC: World Bank.

World Economic Forum, 2006, *Global Competitiveness Report 2005–2006. Policies Underpinning Prosperity*, London: Palgrave MacMillan.

Yee P. and M. Paludetto, Consilium International Inc., 2005, 'Nigeria: Value and Supply Chain Study.' Report prepared for the World Bank.

2

Oil, Growth and Governance in Nigeria

Paul Collier

2.1 Introduction

Oil revenues are the single most important feature of the Nigerian economy. They constitute an enormous opportunity for growth. As is evident, over the entire period since they commenced, this opportunity has not been realized. At times of high oil prices the revenue has enabled both ordinary citizens and the state to achieve higher levels of consumption, but these levels have not proved sustainable: windfalls have not been converted into permanently higher levels of income. The disastrous failure of the previous oil boom of 1974–86 is often misunderstood in Nigeria. During the boom, consumption, both public and private, was high, and so living standards were temporarily high. The catastrophic failure of public policy was that the windfall was not transformed into a higher level of *sustainable* consumption. Indeed, on the contrary, policy during the windfall ensured that future consumption would be lower. This was because during the boom, instead of investing in productive assets, the government borrowed very heavily to finance consumption.

When the boom came to an end this borrowing stopped because the country was no longer credit-worthy and a start had to be made to repaying the accumulated debt. As a result, in 1986 Nigerian society faced a double shock: the world oil price crashed from $30 to $18, and there was a swing from borrowing to repaying. The debt shock was as large as the oil shock. Between them these two shocks roughly halved per capita real expenditure. Inevitably, the living standards of ordinary people crashed: on average they more or less halved. Had the boom been well managed, there need have been no shock to living standards at all: both government and private spending could have been protected from the decline in the oil price by a smoothing rule. As it was, poverty inevitably exploded. In one of the greatest public relations follies of all time, the World Bank chose this moment to trumpet a set of coping policies labelled the Structural Adjustment Programme (SAP). Unsurprisingly, Nigerians blamed SAP for the appalling increase in poverty. As a result, economic reform came to have a bad name and this legacy of misunderstanding has handicapped the society ever since. The SAP was, in fact, a straightforward set of coping policies centred around devaluation:

they were policies that the Indonesian government, faced with the same decline in oil prices, had carried out as a matter of course. Indeed, they were remarkably successful. Nigerian GDP – production – grew more rapidly during SAP than it had during the boom. Unfortunately, production is not the same as expenditure. More production produced less income because the crucial oil was worth so much less, and the income supported less expenditure because it was offset by debt repayment instead of being supplemented by borrowing. No authority with credibility with Nigerian citizens bothered to explain this to them and so the myth of SAP has persisted.

However, this chapter is about Nigeria's future rather than its past. The challenge is to make sure that the future is not a repeat of that past. In Section 2.2 I review the new global statistical evidence on how natural resource revenues affect growth. There are two key findings. First, high prices for commodity exports in general, and oil in particular, have radically different consequences in the short term from those in the long term. Secondly, the political economy of resource revenues is highly distinctive. Democracy seems to have very different effects on growth in the presence of large resource revenues such as prevail in Nigeria. In particular, electoral competition cannot be relied upon to discipline governments into a satisfactory transformation of oil into sustainable income.

Since something evidently typically goes seriously wrong in resource-rich countries, it is helpful to benchmark actual performance against the critical decisions that such an economy needs to get right. In Section 2.3 I therefore set out the principles of natural resource depletion, highlighting these critical decisions, and apply them to Nigeria. The first is the *savings decision*. As oil is depleted the revenue should be transformed into assets. These assets generate sustainable income and it is this income which can therefore safely be consumed, not the oil revenue itself. The second is the *asset composition decision*. The transformation of oil revenues into assets involves a key choice about the type of asset. Potentially, the revenue can be transformed into financial assets or real investment. If this choice is investment then a third decision is required on *which type of investment: structures or equipment?* The answer to these choices is likely to change over time, and depends upon the magnitude of the revenue. Hence, there is not a single right answer, but rather the need for a policy rule that makes choices contingent upon circumstances.

The range of options for how Nigerian society might handle these three decisions should be both politically realistic and technically sound. In the absence of systems that prevent them, both political mischief and technical errors are highly likely to frustrate the transformation of oil into sustained prosperity.

2.2 The evidence on resource riches and growth

Since the discovery of oil Nigeria has received revenues of around $300 billion but per capita income is little changed from before the discovery. Over the same period some other oil economies that are at least superficially similar, such as

Indonesia, have tripled per capita income. While something has evidently gone awry in Nigeria, the Nigerian experience is not exceptional: most oil-rich economies are not very successful in harnessing oil for growth.

There is a large literature on the 'resource curse' which brings out three distinct reasons why oil might have adverse effects: Dutch disease, volatility, and an erosion of governance (Gelb, 1989; Collier and Gunning, 1999). However, in apparent contradiction of the resource curse, since 2000, when the oil price has risen massively, Nigerian economic growth has accelerated. Is the oil curse a thing of the past?

Unfortunately, it is possible that an increase in the price of oil exports has short-run effects that are favourable even though its long-run effects are adverse. Collier and Goderis (2006) investigate the effect of the price of oil on the growth of oil exporting countries globally over a period of over forty years. A simple way of presenting their results is to consider the consequences of a doubling in the distribution of global oil prices which is then permanent. They find that, in the first four years following such an increase, growth is significantly higher. By the fifth year the effects on the growth rate have faded away, but by this time the faster growth in the four previous years has cumulated to a higher level on income of around 7 per cent. This is the short-run effect of a sustained increase in the oil price. Unfortunately, there is also a long-run effect that is significantly negative. After 17 years the permanently higher distribution of oil prices *lowers* the level of income by 10 per cent. So, the initial gain of 7 per cent is gradually eroded as the economy passes from a short phase of higher growth to a prolonged phase of lower growth. Evidently, the long-term effect cumulates to outweigh the favourable short-term effect: the economy ends up with a lower GDP than it would have had without the increase in the price of its oil exports.

This unpleasant result which describes the typical experience of resource exporters broadly conforms to Nigeria's own experience. Not only has Nigeria grown more slowly than a few other oil economies like Indonesia, but it has grown far more slowly than the typical economy that did not have oil or other natural resources. Oil has, in all probability, made Nigeria worse off.

Recall that the three routes by which oil has been postulated to undermine the economy are Dutch disease, volatility and the erosion of governance. Collier and Goderis try to assign the overall adverse effect of oil export revenue between these routes. Their results are not specific to Nigeria but represent the pattern in the typical oil-exporting developing country. They find some evidence for all three routes: problems generated by Dutch disease – that is the level of the real exchange rate; problems generated by high macroeconomic volatility; and problems generated by poor governance.

Each of these three routes reflects political choices: adverse consequences are not inevitable. Dutch disease is the least political of the routes. The appreciation of the real exchange rate consequent upon oil exports makes non-oil exports uncompetitive. However, whether Dutch disease is weak or powerful depends upon public spending priorities and trade policy. The more of the oil revenue that is spent by the government on non-tradable goods and services such as civil service salaries, the stronger will be Dutch disease. The less that is spent on reducing the costs faced by non-oil exporters, such as more efficient ports, the stronger will be Dutch disease. The more restrictive are the trade barriers that the government imposes the stronger will be Dutch disease. Nigerian policy choices created particularly strong Dutch disease effects and non-oil exports were virtually wiped out. This was avoidable. For example, over the same period that Nigerian cocoa exports collapsed, Indonesia, which also had large oil exports, created a cocoa industry which grew to be much larger than even peak Nigerian production.

Oil revenues are highly volatile. If this volatility is badly managed the results can be very costly. For example, public expenditure rises too rapidly during booms and in this atmosphere of expansion some very low-priority spending is started which then proves politically impossible to reverse. As a result, during the crash really important expenditures have to be reduced. However, as discussed below, if revenue volatility is well managed through expenditure smoothing, it need have no adverse consequences whatsoever. Hence, volatility places a premium on particularly good economic management. Good management is difficult because it requires technical expertise to know what to do and political choices that actually use this expertise. In practice, it is far easier to make good political choices if the principles coming from the technical analysis are embodied into some 'rules', although the force of these rules may range from being simply 'rules of thumb' to constitutional requirements. The key choices are obviously made during the booms. If the wrong choices are made during the booms, the periods of low oil prices are inevitably difficult. During the oil boom of 1974–86 Nigerian economic policy choices were very costly. During the boom that started around 2000, macroeconomic management was initially again questionable, but improved enormously during 2004.

Sometimes the blame for the mismanagement of Nigeria's oil resources is laid at the door of Nigeria's military governments. Certainly, these governments had some severe failings. However, by chance, both of the oil windfalls have accrued to governments that were democratically elected. In Nigeria, democracy alone has certainly not been sufficient to ensure that the oil revenues have been well used, and this turns out to reflect a general pattern. Globally, in the absence of resource riches, democracies tend to grow significantly faster than dictatorships. However, in the presence of sufficiently large natural resource revenues this is reversed: dictatorships outperform democracies (Collier and Hoeffler, 2006). The critical level of resource revenues at which performance switches is when the value of the resources accruing to government is around 20 per cent of GDP, and Nigeria is far above this figure. Fortunately, this does not imply that in economic terms Nigeria would be better off with dictatorship. It would not. The effect of dictatorship on growth depends not just upon the extent of natural resource revenues, but also upon the composition of the society: ethnically diverse societies are ill-suited to dictatorship (Collier, 2000, 2001). There is a simple reason for this. If the society is ethnically diverse, a dictatorship will usually imply that one ethnic group, namely that of the dictator, is in control. Further, in a diverse society, the ethnic group in power is unlikely to constitute a majority of the population. The group in power then has a strong incentive to advance its economic position by redistribution from other groups at the expense of overall national growth. This was indeed Nigeria's experience, and it has been common in many ethnically diverse societies. Nigeria needs democracy in order to avoid the economic costs of ethnically skewed concentrations of power.

Nevertheless, in the context of resource riches, democracy is not enough. Being ethnically diverse, as is Nigeria, does not make democracy work any better; it simply makes dictatorship work much worse. The question thus remains of how Nigeria might avoid the fate of the typical resource-rich democracy. In fact, democracies differ considerably and these differences prove to be critical for the management of resource wealth. A mature democracy combines two distinct features: electoral competition and multiple checks and balances. Electoral competition determines how a government *acquires* power, while checks and balances determine how it *uses* power. While a mature democracy has both, newer democracies tend to have plenty of electoral competition but few checks and balances. The reason for this is that it is a great deal easier to establish electoral competition than checks and balances. Electoral competition is easy because those who want power have an incentive to contest elections. Thus, even in the extremely difficult environments of Afghanistan and Iraq it has proved possible to hold hotly contested elections. By contrast, checks and balances are public goods that are in nobody's particular interest to provide, and indeed very much not in the interests of those with power to provide: checks and balances will limit how they can use power.

2.3 The economics of transforming oil into growth

Economics provides a helpful and straightforward framework for thinking through the three critical public decisions which are fundamental to whether oil is transformed into a sustained increase in living standards. I take them in turn.

2.3.1 Saving a depleting resource

Principles

Oil in the ground is a valuable asset. As it is brought out of the ground, how much of the resulting revenue should be consumed and how much saved? The appropriate rate of savings out of oil revenue depends upon two distinct assessments about global oil prices: their long-term trend, and whether they are currently above or below that trend.

Because oil is a depleting resource there is some expectation that over the long run it will gradually get more expensive. In the simplest framework, over the long term the world price should rise by around the world rate of interest. More sophisticated analyses must take into account extraction costs and tax incentives for oil companies. While these complicate the picture, what remains is a reasonable expectation that the world oil price will tend to rise in real terms albeit along a very volatile path. To see why this matters, suppose that on average it rises at the modest rate of 1 per cent per year. This implies that even the oil in the ground is an asset that is yielding an income and this can finance consumption on a sustainable basis.

The share of the revenue from oil extraction that can be consumed on a sustainable basis depends upon the extraction rate. Specifically, it is the expected rate of increase in the world oil price, divided by the extraction rate. If, for purposes of illustration, the expected increase in the oil price is 1 per cent, and the extraction rate is 3 per cent, implying that there is sufficient oil to sustain around 33 years of extraction at the present rate, then one third of the revenue from oil extraction can be consumed. This can be thought of as *the long-run savings rule*. If the remaining two thirds are saved in assets that yield more than the 1 per cent that would have accrued had the oil been left in the ground, then, as these savings build up, consumption can increase further.

The world oil price is extremely volatile. At any one time it is therefore likely to be either well above or well below the level implied by its long-run path. Just as some judgment has to be made on the rate at which oil prices can be expected to rise in the long term, so the savings decision has to be influenced by a judgment on the current deviation in the price from the long-run path. Income generated by a price judged to be above the long-run path needs to be saved. This can be thought of as *the medium-run oil price smoothing rule*. Thus, if the current world price is $60 but the normal price is judged to be $35, then the above-normal $25 per barrel should be saved. Unlike the savings generated by the long-run savings rule, these savings are intended to finance subsequent consumption during periods when the oil price is below its long-run path. There is thus a strong case for holding these assets in liquid form, which implies the acquisition of financial assets abroad.

An important consequence of holding these temporary savings abroad and then bringing them back at times of low prices is that this will dampen the volatility of the real exchange rate. Thus, the strategy has both a fiscal aspect and a foreign exchange market aspect – when times are good the government runs a fiscal surplus and the central bank accumulates foreign exchange reserves. The reduction in exchange rate volatility is directly beneficial to the private sector, from large businesses to small farmers. Hence, not only does it enable the government to smooth its own expenditures, with a payoff in terms of a higher quality of government spending, it also makes the environment for private activity less risky. The smoothing of government spending and the smoothing of the exchange rate are two sides of the same coin. It is not possible for the central bank to smooth the exchange rate unless the government is also smoothing its spending. Conversely, if the government tries to smooth its spending but the central bank fails to smooth the exchange rate the result will be to inflict massive volatility onto firms and households. As the chapter by Addison in this book shows, the Nigerian economy has in the past been among the most volatile in the world. The severe adverse consequences both for the quality of government spending and for the risks facing firms and households could be avoided in the future by adopting an *oil price smoothing rule*.

The oil price smoothing rule can only be introduced when the prevailing world price is above its expected path. This enables savings to build up which can then subsequently finance a period of dis-saving. If the rule were introduced at a time when the world price was judged to be below the expected world price there would be an initial period of borrowing, and such behaviour would be indistinguishable from straightforward fiscal irresponsibility. For credibility, a fiscal rule has to start with the politically more challenging decision of saving.

Let's now bring together *the long-run savings rule* and *the medium-run oil price smoothing rule*. I will continue to use the same numbers for illustration: the normal price is judged to be $35, the oil price is judged to be rising at 1 per cent per year, and the depletion rate is judged to be 3 per cent. With these judgments, one third of the $35 per barrel, namely $11.67, can safely be used to finance government consumption. The other two thirds, namely $23.33, should be used for long-term asset accumulation, to sustain consumption once oil revenues decline. But with the current price at $60, the remaining $25 per barrel should be put into more liquid assets, namely financial assets abroad, so that they can be spent on sustaining both consumption and investment when the oil price is below trend. Thus, around 19 per cent ($11.67/$60) of current oil revenues would be used to finance government consumption, around 33 per cent ($23.33/$60) would be used for long-term savings and investment, and around 42 per cent ($25/$60) would be saved in liquid form. Note that this illustration is simplified to abstract from any production costs of the oil. In reality, of course, when the oil price is $35, the Nigerian government does not get $35 of revenue per barrel, since costs of production, including reasonable profits of oil producing companies, must be deducted. However, the core ideas remain unchanged by this additional complication: some of the oil revenue can be consumed, some should be invested, and some should be saved temporarily and therefore kept liquid. The division between these three components reflects judgments about oil prices and depletion.

These judgments are almost certainly going to be wrong. There is thus a need both to allow for the likelihood of error and to enable revision of judgments as information builds up. The consequences of errors are not symmetrical between excessive optimism and excessive pessimism. If the judgement of the path of the long-term oil price is over-optimistic then the entire consumption strategy becomes unsustainable: the government runs out of money in circumstances of crisis. If the judgment is too pessimistic then all that happens is that assets accumulate more rapidly than would otherwise be the case. Hence, given the inevitability of error, it is wise to err on the side of caution, assuming a 'normal' path for the oil price that is probably lower than that which is likely. As assets accumulate faster than 'expected', the decision rules can gradually become a little less cautious.

Applying the principles to Nigeria

Historically, the Nigerian government has sometimes managed to save the peak of the oil windfalls, but these savings have been followed by very low levels of public saving at other times. The key issue is political: savings strategies have to be implemented day by day, year after year. A savings strategy is only as strong as the weakest link in the future political chain: one bad future politician could undo a decade of savings effort. How can society guard against such an eventuality?

There are two complementary approaches. One is to institutionalize the rules in a 'fiscal constitution'. Constitutional rules are indeed appropriate for decisions that need to be maintained over a long period and where there is a danger of short-term opportunism. This danger is particularly acute in the context of savings from oil revenues. As savings accumulate, the payoff to the opportunistic political strategy of raiding the assets to finance an unsustainable consumption boom becomes greater and greater. Hence, it is important to restrain the temptation for such a strategy by constitutional rules. The Fiscal Responsibility Bill is an enormously important step in this process of anchoring long-term economic decisions in a fiscal constitution. As with all constitutions, any act can be changed, but such constitutional change is something only to be done after serious consideration and debate across society. It thereby elevates the decision about savings out of oil revenue, from being merely part of the annual political haggle over the budget, to something based on long-term principles.

The second, complementary defence against opportunistic political decisions is to build an informed electorate. Here the Central Bank of Nigeria plays a critical role. Like many of the low-income democracies, Nigeria does not yet have a well developed coverage of economic issues in the popular media. As a result, the electorate is not adequately informed about vital economic decisions. The core role of a central bank in such an environment extends beyond the narrowly technocratic. It is to inform the electorate in an authoritative, simple and dispassionate manner about vital economic issues. The Central Bank should aim to be the natural source of objective information for citizens on such issues. That is one important reason why it has to be visibly independent of government: citizens must be able to distinguish between government information, which will inevitably be somewhat discounted as being partisan, and Central Bank information, which should come to be seen as politically unmotivated.

Only once a fiscal constitution is anchored through the support of an informed electorate is it properly defended against opportunism. An example is Indonesia. In the 1960s the Indonesian government so mismanaged the economy that it collapsed into hyperinflation, far worse than anything ever experienced anywhere in Africa. However, as a result of this a 'balanced budget' rule was enshrined into the Indonesian constitution. Further, the searing experience of hyperinflation immunized the population against macroeconomic opportunism. The resulting combination of a fiscal constitution grounded in popular support was a core component of the spectacular economic growth of the following thirty years: the sort of achievement that Nigeria needs over the next three decades.

2.3.2 Saving domestically versus accumulating reserves

Principles

I now focus on the second decision, where saving should be placed. This decision only applies to that part of the oil revenues that need to be saved in the long term.

In the illustration above this is 38 per cent of the oil revenues. The rest of the oil revenues are either consumed or saved in liquid form because they are only being saved temporarily.

The 38 per cent that is going to be saved in the long term could be invested either in the acquisition of foreign assets or in domestic capital formation. Note that if the money is used to acquire domestic financial assets the question must be pushed one stage further: what lies behind these financial assets? If the money that is put into domestic financial assets is used for consumption then it is not ultimately being saved. If it is put into foreign assets then that is its ultimate use, and if it is put into domestic capital formation then that is its ultimate use.

The decision between foreign assets and domestic investment should hinge upon the rate of return. Since the rate of return on foreign assets is known and stable, the key issue is the rate of return on domestic investment. This depends upon four factors: the initial stock of capital; the investment climate for the economy; the magnitude of savings from oil revenues; and the decision procedures of the government.

In a capital-short economy, the rate of return on capital should in principle be much higher than the world return. Thus, domestic investment should generate a higher sustainable income than the acquisition of foreign assets. However, one reason why the economy is short of capital might be that the investment climate is so poor that returns are very low. Even if the investment climate is satisfactory, if too much extra investment is attempted in a short period then the rate of return on domestic investment will be driven down. One reason for this is that during periods of boom the cost of those capital goods that can only be produced domestically gets driven up. This manifests itself as a construction boom, during which construction costs are unusually high. It therefore makes sense to defer some of investment expenditures until the construction boom has abated. By deferring these domestic investments the construction cycle is smoothed and public investment gets better value for money. Thus, at times when the overall savings from oil revenue are atypically high, a greater percentage of them should be temporarily saved abroad until construction costs have eased. These financial savings abroad can be thought of as *the short-run construction price smoothing rule*. In effect, the expansion of the construction sector needs to be planned so that it is reasonably orderly, rather than boom–bust. The government of Botswana, which managed its resource revenues brilliantly, actually had a plan-within-a-plan specifically for the construction sector, ensuring that demand and supply were broadly matched. Public investment projects were deferred if there were signs of congestion, and the emerging bottlenecks in the construction sector such as skill shortages were identified, by consulting the industry, and tackled.

Although both the *construction price smoothing rule* and the *oil price smoothing rule* involve temporarily saving abroad in financial assets, the uses to which these savings are then put when they are run down are distinct. The savings accumulated under the *construction price smoothing rule* are used to finance domestic investment involving construction when conditions in the construction sector are calmer. The savings accumulated under the *oil price smoothing rule* are used to finance both investment and consumption to prevent them from being reduced when the oil price is below trend.

Application to Nigeria

Nigeria is indeed very short of capital: it has a very low capital stock per member of the labour force. However, there is also strong evidence that the investment climate is a problem. As of 2006, the *Doing Business* survey which ranks countries globally by how investors perceive the business climate, ranked Nigeria 108th out of 175 countries. Nigerians themselves appear to regard other investment environments as more promising. Over the years there has been an enormous amount of capital flight: by 1998, according to the data from Coller *et al.* (2004), it had cumulated to around $107 billion.

The magnitude of savings from oil revenues will fluctuate with the current oil price and changes in the rate of extraction. Generally, limits to absorptive capacity for investment imply that there are diminishing returns. Hence, when savings are particularly high, the proportion of savings that are invested abroad rather than domestically should increase, at least temporarily. In Nigeria the capacity to absorb domestic investment is limited in the short and medium run because for around fifteen years domestic investment in structures was extremely low, so that the construction sector was tiny. The sector takes time to expand efficiently: for example, workers need to acquire skills. Hence, there is a strong case for spreading the desired investment in structures over a longer period through a phase of saving some of the oil revenues in financial assets.

The decision procedures of the government concerning investment are critical in determining the return that it will generate. In Nigeria during the oil windfall of 1974–86 the decision procedures for public investment were extremely poor, leading to astonishingly high levels of waste. Even the best decision rules cannot conjure up opportunities for productive investment beyond the limits set by absorptive capacity, but bad rules cause the society to miss such opportunities as are available. The worse is the investment climate and the decision rules the higher should be the share of the savings that is placed abroad. The savings abroad are generally in the form of foreign exchange reserves although a few governments have created investment funds that enable the purchase of equities. Over the longer term, equities have higher yields than the fixed interest government securities that constitute foreign exchange reserves. However, there is far more scope to raise the return on assets invested in Nigeria than to raise the return on foreign assets, and this should surely be the proper attention of government policy. Even with a very good investment climate and decision rules, the sheer volatility of oil revenues creates a need for medium-term smoothing of the rate of domestic investment by means of the temporary accumulation of foreign assets. But, since these assets are acquired only until the conditions are right for switching them into domestic investment, safe fixed-interest assets are appropriate.

A useful institutional practice is to subject all proposed public investment projects to a double-hurdle decision process: one hurdle for honesty, the other for efficiency. The objective of honesty in public investment is evidently enormously important: dishonesty can generate massive waste and rewards the wrong political actors. Honesty is not automatically ensured by democracy. For example, in 1978 during the previous Nigerian oil windfall, once the civilian government was installed one of its first decisions was to recall a contract for a dam which had been awarded at the price of $120 million and re-award it at the astonishingly inflated cost of $600 million (Bevan *et al.*, 1999). When the Nigerian government reintroduced the elementary requirement of competitive tendering for public investment projects in 2004, it recalled some contracts that had just been issued without it: as a result of competitive tendering, the average cost of these projects fell by 40 per cent. Honesty is thus vital and competitive tendering is a key process in achieving it. This was understandably the first priority for the reform of public investment and it has evidently been an important achievement.

However, honesty alone is not enough. An investment can be entirely honest and yet completely disastrous: investment projects must make economic sense. This is where the second hurdle is important. All proposed projects need to be subject to independent technical estimation of their likely rate of return. Projects whose likely rate of return falls below a critical threshold are then rejected. The political protection of the process of technical evaluation is critical: otherwise, estimates of returns can be manipulated to fit a political agenda. Thus, the technocrats doing these estimates need to be insulated, at least to a degree, from political power.

The combination of an honesty hurdle and an efficiency hurdle limits the number of public investment projects that should be undertaken at any one time. The difference between available savings and productive investment opportunities should then be saved abroad with the central bank accumulating foreign exchange reserves. Hence, the amount saved abroad is a residual that changes year by year, between savings and productive investment.

2.3.3 Public investment versus private investment

Principles

The final decision concerns the balance within domestic investment between public investment and private investment. A core distinction in investment is between 'structures' and 'equipment'. The two are complements: roads are an example of structures, and trucks are an example of equipment. Roads only have a good rate of return if there are trucks to drive on them; trucks only have a good rate of return if there are roads to drive on. Very obviously, the decisions to invest in roads and trucks are taken by different economic actors: investment in roads is undertaken by government, investment in trucks is undertaken by private firms. The oil revenue directly accrues to the government, but it only controls investment in roads, or more generally, in 'structures'. To make investment in structures productive requires that private firms also choose to invest. This does not happen automatically. How can the government increase the prospects that, during the current windfall, private actors will match the government investment boom in structures with their own complementary investment boom in equipment? The government does not directly control private investment and so it can only work indirectly. The government does, however, control to an extent the assets that the private sector holds. In particular, currently the private sector holds substantial claims on the government in the form of public domestic debt. If, through the Central Bank, the government uses oil revenues to repurchase this domestic debt, then the private sector has to switch into other assets (Collier and Gunning, 2005). In aggregate, if public domestic debt is reduced, the only choices open to the private sector are to increase domestic investment and to increase savings abroad. Since the private sector can be relied upon to do whichever of these choices is likely to be most profitable, it will indeed increase investment in the economy as long as the domestic investment climate is sufficiently good. Hence, a comprehensive investment policy out of oil revenue would be for the government to devote part of the savings to increased public investment, and part to the repurchase of its domestic debt, while simultaneously working to improve the investment climate. Potentially, beyond running down public debt, the government could also accumulate claims on the banking system, becoming a net depositor. The banking system can then on-lend this money to the private sector. In turn, this depends upon the capabilities of the financial sector to allocate capital efficiently,

Application to Nigeria

Nigeria is particularly short of private investment. This in part reflects the behaviour of private investment during the last Nigerian oil boom of 1974–86. The boom in oil revenues produced a boom in public investment as the government decided to save and invest the windfall, but by the middle of the boom the private sector started to *reduce* its own investment: private actors chose to send their savings abroad through capital flight. Hence, there is a case for inducing the private sector to invest in real assets by reducing the availability of financial claims on the government. Since this in turn depends upon the efficiency of the banking sector in making loans to the private sector, the reform and consolidation of the Nigerian banking system undertaken in 2005 was particularly important.

2.4 The political economy of public decisions on savings and asset choices

Recall from the global statistical evidence that Nigeria faces two acute problems in political design. First, typically in resource-rich democracies the political decision process is undermined by the combination of intense electoral competition and a lack of checks and balances. Second, typically in ethnically diverse societies collective action, which is necessary for the management of public resources, is much more difficult. Both of these features clearly describe Nigeria. As to the first, the experience of democracy produced poor public resource allocation both during the previous democratic episode under President Shagari and during the first term of President Obasanjo when inevitably there were no inherited checks and balances. As to the second, ethnic identity has repeatedly loomed large in Nigerian politics.

2.4.1 The need for checks and balances

Electoral competition without checks and balances is particularly dysfunctional in resource-rich societies. The absence of checks and balances *enables* politicians to divert public funds into patronage politics and the intensity of electoral competition *drives* them into doing so. In Nigeria electoral competition is intense; for example, between the first and second terms of President Obasanjo around 80 per cent of senators lost their seats. The average expenditure to get elected was around $500,000 – which had to be found somewhere. Such patronage politics is deadly for the wise use of oil revenues: politicians know that they may only have a brief tenure of office and so have an overwhelming interest in spending public money now rather than saving it wisely. To defend against this requires not only the specific practices discussed above, but a larger agenda in which politicians are freed from the burden of the pressure for patronage and so can pursue the larger public interest. The defences that honest politicians require are a wide range of checks and balances. One useful approach, followed for example in Britain, is to place severe limits on campaign expenditure combined with the provision of public funds for campaigns. This reduces both the scope for politicians to 'buy' votes through patronage, and the need for them to raise money for campaigning by selling favours. Obviously, such rules are only as effective as the scrutiny procedures that enforce them. A complementary approach is to introduce intense scrutiny of public spending so that it cannot so readily be diverted from legitimate uses. Since so much of Nigeria's public spending occurs at the state level rather than the federal, the publication of federal revenue releases to the states on a routine basis, as introduced in 2004, is a critical first step in such scrutiny. However, spending can usefully be scrutinized all the way along the money trail. Surveys which have tracked public spending elsewhere in Africa from its release by the Ministry of Finance to its eventual spending by its intended recipients such as schools and clinics have typically found very high rates of leakage. These leakages have been rectified once local scrutiny was introduced. A more conventional form of scrutiny to check on honesty is professional *audits*. As Stevens shows in a later chapter in this book, in Nigeria audits have typically been completed so late that their scope for accountability has been undermined. However, while such scrutiny can detect dishonesty, it cannot detect inefficiency. For this there is a need for professional *evaluation*. Evaluation can reveal whether public money has been usefully spent as distinct from whether it has been honestly spent. Evaluation needs some effort and skill: it requires data on both spending and its intended outcomes, and analysis of how the outcomes have actually been affected by the spending. However, it is now routine in all well run public sectors.

The most potent check and balance is an effective media. In Nigeria there is an enormous appetite for information that will enable citizens to hold government to account. Newspaper circulation spiked upwards on the day that the monthly releases from the Ministry of Finance to the state governors were published for the first time. In Peru a highly corrupt president was toppled by the effective reporting of a single small television station. Effectiveness depends upon the media having access to the audits and the evaluations, having the competence to understand their implications, and having the incentives to report them honestly. Just as politicians need checks and balances so do the media. Without them citizens may have no more reason to believe the media than they would casual rumour. Hence, defending the reputation of the media there needs to be an impartial judiciary able to enforce libel laws.

2.4.2 Coping with diversity

The problems inherent in all resource-rich societies are intensified in Nigeria because it is ethnically diverse. Globally, societies that are ethnically diverse find collective action more difficult because typically there are lower levels of trust between them than are found in a homogeneous society.

One appropriate way of coping with the greater difficulties of collective action implied by diversity is for the domain of the state to be more limited. Thus, at the margin, where activities can either be in the public sector or in the private sector, a diverse society tends to work better if they are in the private sector. In effect, Nigeria may be better to model the domain of the state on America, another diverse society, than on, say, France, a more homogenous society. As well as improving the performance of the activities that are assigned to the private sector, this enables the state to focus on the things that it really must do. Since in Nigeria the state will inevitably be large because of the scale of oil revenues, it may be better not to extend it beyond the many activities that cannot be shifted.

A second strategy that can be helpful in coping with ethnic diversity is decentralization. Nigeria is obviously much less ethnically diverse at the state level than at the federal level. Hence, the approach taken in the Nigerian constitution has a sound rationale in making collective action easier. However, a difficulty with decentralization is that administrative and managerial capacity in the public sector is limited, and so decisions are shifted to a level at which capacity is often scarce. In turn, this suggests that there is a massive need for capacity-building at the state level.

A third strategy for coping with ethnic diversity is the formal recognition of ethnic quotas in federal resource allocation. This is again something that is part of constitutional practice. Even highly developed diverse societies, such as Switzerland, operate a quota system for appointments in the civil service. Quotas are a sensible recognition that the reality of ethnic loyalties makes it difficult to have *credibly* neutral decisions from among an ethnically mixed field of candidates.

2.5 Conclusion

Nigerian society did not harness the opportunity of the previous oil boom of 1974–86. Consumption was high during the boom but policy mistakes made the bonanza unsustainable. The boom spanned both military dictatorship and democracy, but neither type of regime managed the windfall resources successfully. The society has had to wait two decades for a second chance. There is no way of telling how long the present boom will last but, since the depletion of Nigeria's oil can only continue for a few more decades before it is exhausted, it is imperative that the present opportunity be better managed than that of the past. Societies indeed often learn from failure. The hyperinflations in Indonesia in the 1960s and in Germany in the 1920s have both immunized their societies from a repetition of macroeconomic mistakes. But learning is not inevitable: it requires more than assertions that this time will be different. Major society-wide errors occur because of systematic features that propel the behaviour of individuals. The society avoids repeating these errors only if it goes through the difficult process of changing the incentives and restraints that face individuals. In Indonesia a balanced budget rule was enacted. In Germany the central bank was made independent of government. Nigeria might also choose to consolidate an equivalent change in its fiscal constitution. But fiscal constitutions are only as robust as the understanding of ordinary citizens and so any change in the formal rules would need to be underpinned by a society that is better informed about economic issues. In this situation the Central Bank of Nigeria is indeed critical. It has a dual role: it is likely to be a key component of any fiscal constitution, and it is surely the key authority on economic issues that ordinary Nigerian citizens can trust.

References

Bevan, D.L., P. Collier and J.W. Gunning, 1999, *The Political Economy of Poverty, Equity and Growth in Nigeria and Indonesia*, New York: Oxford University Press.

Collier, P., 2001, 'Implications of Ethnic Diversity', *Economic Policy*, 32, 127–166.

Collier, P., 2000, 'Ethnicity, Politics and Economic Performance', *Economics and Politics*, 12, 225–245.

Collier, P. and B. Goderis, 2006, 'Reconciling a Conundrum: Export Prices and Growth', mimeo, CSAE.

Collier, P. and J.W. Gunning, 1999, *Trade Shocks in Developing Countries*, Oxford: Clarendon Press.

Collier, P. and J.W. Gunning, 2005, 'Asset Policies during an Oil Windfall', *The World Economy*, 28, 1401–1415.

Collier, P. and A. Hoeffler, 2006, 'Testing the Neocon Agenda: Democracy and Resource Rents', mimeo, CSAE.

Collier, P., A. Hoeffler and C. Pattillo, 2004, 'Africa's Exodus', *Journal of African Economies*, 13 (suppl. 2), 15–54.

Gelb, A., 1989, *Oil Windfalls, Blessing or Curse?*, New York: Oxford University Press.

3

Addressing the Natural Resource Curse: An Illustration from Nigeria[1]

Xavier Sala-i-Martin and Arvind Subramanian

3.1 Introduction

Nigeria has been a disastrous development experience. On just about every conceivable metric, Nigeria's performance since independence has been dismal. In PPP terms, Nigeria's per capita GDP was $1113 in 1970 and is estimated to have remained at $1084 in 2000. The latter figure places Nigeria amongst the 15 poorest nations in the world for which such data are available.

Nigeria, unfortunately, fares much worse on measures of poverty too. Between 1970 and 2000, the poverty rate, measured as the share of the population subsisting on less than $1 per day, increased from close to 36 per cent to just under 70 per cent (Figure 3.1). This translates into an increase in the number of poor from about $19 million in 1970 to a staggering $90 million in 2000 (Figure 3.2).[2]

Table 3.1 reports the growth rate of GDP and its volatility for Nigeria. In terms of growth since 1960, Nigeria fared worse than the average country but better than oil-producing countries. It is also noteworthy that Nigeria's economy was substantially more unstable – reflected in the standard deviation and coefficient of variation of growth rates – than other countries, including other oil-producing countries.[3]

These developments, of course, coincided with the discovery of oil in Nigeria. Figure 3.3 depicts the revenues that Nigeria has obtained from oil since 1965. Over a 35-year period Nigeria's cumulative revenues from oil (after deducting the payments to the foreign oil companies) have amounted to about $350 billion at 1995 prices. In 1965, when oil revenue per capita was about $33, per capita GDP was $245. In 2000, when oil revenues were $325 per capita, per capita GDP remained at the 1965 level. In other words, all the oil revenues – $350 billion in total – did not seem to add to the standard of living at all. Worse, however, could it actually have contributed to a decline in the standard of living?

This chapter has three objectives developed in three sections. First, in Section 3.2 we use cross-section empirical analysis to demonstrate that stunted institutional development – a catch-all for a range of related pathologies, including corruption, weak governance, rent-seeking and plunder – is a problem intrinsic to countries that own natural resources such as oil or minerals. The resulting drag on long-run growth from having resources can be substantial. Second, in Section

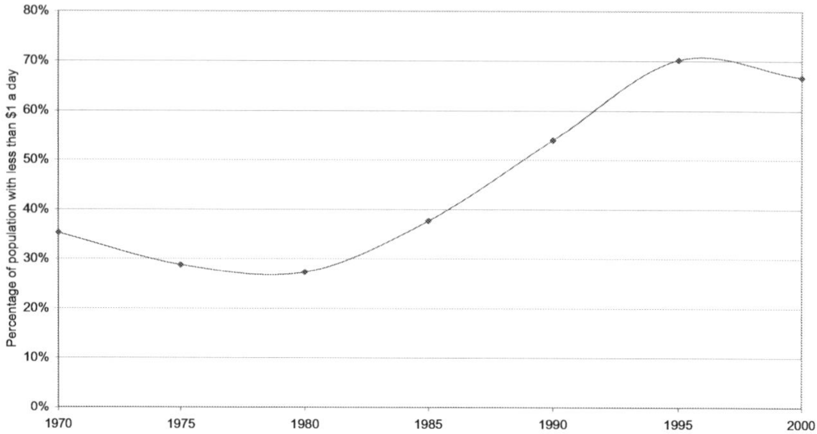

Figure 3.1 Poverty rates, 1970–2000.

3.3 we establish that Nigeria's poor economic performance stems largely from having wasted its resource income. Finally, in Section 3.4 we propose a solution for Nigeria to accelerate institutional change, which would involve distributing the bulk of the oil revenues directly to the people. In the absence of measures to improve the quality of institutions and avoid the problems created by oil rents, we remain deeply pessimistic about Nigeria's long-run prospects. The final section is the conclusion.

3.2 The natural resource curse: revisiting the empirical literature

Is the detrimental impact of oil on development unique to Nigeria or is it – the oft-cited 'natural resource curse' – a more general phenomenon? From a policy

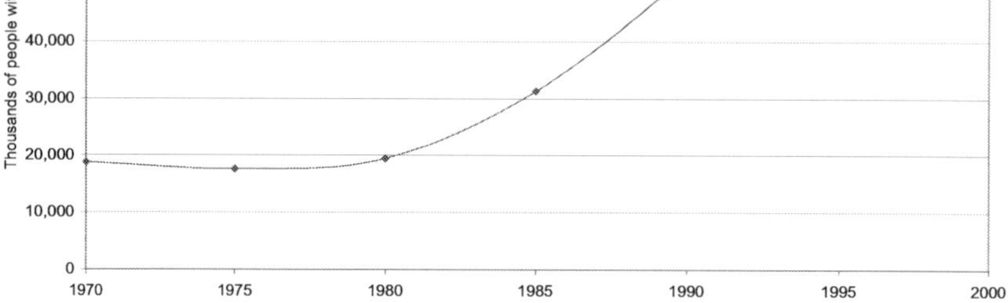

Figure 3.2 Poverty count, 1970–2000.
Source: Authors' calculations based on Sala-i-Martin (2003).

Table 3.1 Comparative indicators

	Nigeria	*Oil producing countries*	*Developing countries*	*All countries*
Per capita GDP, PPP, 1998	**955**	3579	2076	3029
Growth rate of per capita GDP, 1960-98	**1.336**	1.105	1.520	1.739
Standard deviation of growth of per capita GDP	**0.1465**	0.111	0.078	0.0703
Coefficient of variation	**0.110**	0.101	0.051	0.040

Source: World Bank's World Development Indicators.

perspective, while it is important to know if a curse exists, it is perhaps more important to know the mechanism by which it casts its spell. Identifying the mechanism allows a better stab to be made at prescription.

In the theoretical economics literature, three channels of causation from natural resource abundance to lower growth have been identified.[4] First, natural resources generate rents, which leads to rapacious rent-seeking (the voracity effect), whose adverse manifestation is felt through political economy effects as in Tornell and Lane (1999), and to increased corruption (Mauro, 1995; Leite and Weidmann, 1999), which adversely affects long-run growth. We shall refer to this effect more broadly as the institutional impact of natural resources.

Second, natural resource ownership exposes countries to volatility, particularly in commodity prices, which could have an adverse impact on growth through an increase in fertility. Finally, natural resource ownership makes countries susceptible to Dutch disease – the tendency for the real exchange rate to become overly

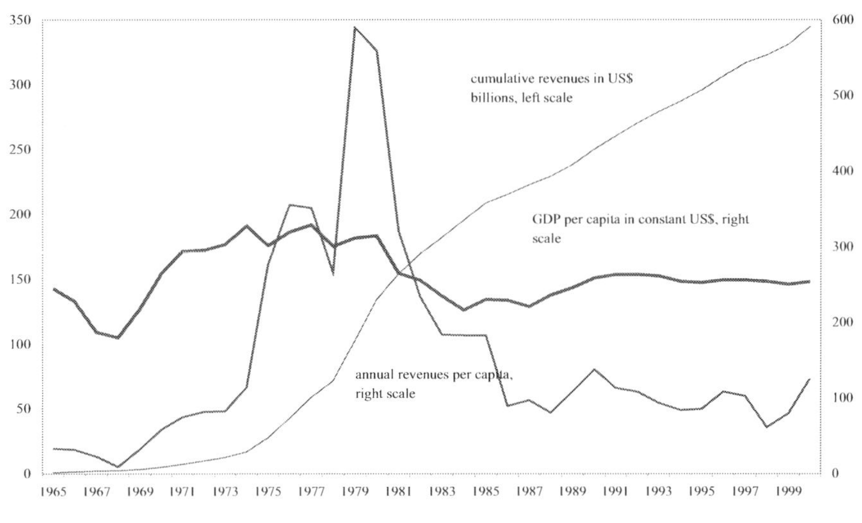

Figure 3.3 Cumulative revenues from oil, 1965–2000 (at 1995 prices).

appreciated in response to positive shocks – which leads to a contraction of the tradable sector. This outcome, combined with the (largely unproven) proposition that tradable (usually manufacturing) sectors are 'superior' because of learning-by-doing and other positive externalities, leads to the conclusion that natural resource ownership exerts a drag on long-run growth.

Hausman and Rigobon (2002) state our understanding of the impact of natural resources as follows:

> The concern that natural resource wealth may somehow be immiserating is a recurring theme in both policy discussions and in empirical analysis. The empirical regularity seems to be in the data but understanding its causes has been a much harder task.

This supposed empirical regularity derives originally from the work of Sachs and Warner (1995), who showed, based on standard cross-section growth regressions, that the curse of natural resource ownership is substantial, manifested in such countries growing slower, on average, by about 1 per cent per year during the period 1970–89. Variations of this basic result can be found in Leite and Weidmann (1999) and Bravo-Ortega and De Gregorio (2001).

In their empirical work, Sachs and Warner (1995) and Leite and Weidmann (1999) attempt to unravel the potential channel of causation, but without great success. Given the Nigerian experience, we are particularly interested in exploring the channel that operates through corruption and institutional quality. The recent work (Hall and Jones, 1999; Acemoglu *et al.*, 2001) on institutions provides another reason to revisit the natural resource literature. Our key results are in sharp contrast to the commonly held view about the impact of natural resources (especially Sachs and Warner, 1995), validating this revisiting of the empirical literature.

More recently, Collier and Hoeffler (2002) have shown that natural resources considerably increase the chances of civil conflict in a country. According to their estimates, the effect of natural resources on conflict is strong and non-linear. A country that has no natural resources faces a probability of civil conflict of 0.5 per cent, whereas a country with natural resources-to-GDP share of 26 per cent faces a probability of 23 per cent. Civil conflict, of course, is an extreme manifestation of institutional collapse and the work of Collier and Hoeffler (2002) is therefore suggestive of a role for natural resources in affecting institutional quality more generally.

A recent paper by Isham *et al.* (2003) tests the proposition that natural resources affect economic growth through their adverse effect on economic institutions. Although this chapter focuses on Nigeria, we do test a similar proposition in Section 3.3. Our Section 3.3 differs from the Isham *et al.* (2003) paper in some respects. First, we employ a different basis for measuring natural resources, which also allows us to test for nonlinear effects. Second, in order to deal with the usual problem of what additional explanatory variables to include, we use the robust variables identified by Sala-i-Martin *et al.* (2003). Third, and perhaps more importantly, our core results are subject to a greater degree of robustness checks than in the paper by Isham *et al.* (2003).

3.2.1 Econometric specification

As discussed earlier, three channels of influence from natural resources to growth have been identified in the literature: the impact through terms-of-trade volatility, overvaluation of the real exchange rate, and institutional quality. Our empirical specification is simple and general enough to capture these three effects:

$$\text{Growth}_{1970-98} = \mu + \beta\text{Conditioning variables}_i + \phi\text{Volatility of prices}_i + \delta\text{Overvaluation of exchange rate}_i + \gamma\text{Institutional Quality}_i + \lambda\text{Natural resources}_i + \varepsilon_i \quad (3.1)$$

where ε_i is the random error term. If all the channels of causation from natural resources to growth are captured in equation (3.1) and if all the variables are correctly measured, there should be no need for the natural resources term. In practice, however, neither of these can be ruled out, hence the inclusion of this term.

A number of specification issues arise. First, institutional quality will in general be endogenous and also subject to measurement error. Simple ordinary least squares estimation will therefore be incorrect. Accordingly, and in line with recent developments (Hall and Jones, 1999; Acemoglu *et al.*, 2001), we will adopt an instrumental variable (IV) estimation strategy, using the instruments recently identified in the literature. Two sets of instruments are available – mortality rates of colonial settlers (Acemoglu *et al.*, 2001) and fraction of the population speaking English and European languages (Hall and Jones, 1999). In much of this chapter we will rely on the latter set because they are available for a much larger group of countries, although we will also test whether our results are robust to the former set of instruments.

A second issue relates to the choice of conditioning variables and the problem of endogeneity related to them. In regard to the former, the strategy we deploy is to identify those variables that have been statistically proven to be the most robust determinants of growth. Sala-i-Martin *et al.* (2003) have shown that, out of a universe of about 70 variables that can plausibly affect growth, about 17 variables are statistically robust to deserve inclusion. In other words, for 17 of the 70 variables analysed the probability of inclusion increased after observing the data (so that the posterior was larger than the prior probability of inclusion). Sala-i-Martin *et al.* (2003) also show that the sign certainty probability for all these 'robust' variables is well over 95 per cent. We narrowed this further to five variables, which appear to be robust in the growth equations even after the inclusion of a measure for institutions (appropriately instrumented). Thus, we chose initial income (lnRGDP70), primary school enrolment (p60), the relative price of investment goods (iprice1), prevalence of malaria (MALFAL66), coastal population (within 100 km of coastline) over coastal area (DENS65C) as the set of covariates that feature in all the regressions. But to ensure that our choice is not selective or biased, we check the robustness of our results to inclusion of all of the other 12 covariates identified by Sala-i-Martin *et al.* (2003).

Clearly, many of these covariates – indicators of health and education – are endogenous in general. This is why we take the initial period values of these variables. Hence, the only variable we instrument for is institutions. This specification and estimation strategy yields implicitly a second equation that we estimate which will be very important for our analysis. This equation is the first-stage for the institution equation. Thus,

$$\text{Institutional quality}_i = \eta + \nu\text{Conditioning variables}_i + \theta\text{Volatility of prices}_i + \rho\text{Overvaluation of exchange rate}_i + \tau\text{Instruments for institutional quality}_i + \tau\text{Natural resources}_i + \upsilon_i \quad (3.2)$$

This equation will allow us to test whether natural resources have an indirect effect on growth (in addition to any possible direct effect captured in equation (3.1)) via their impact on institutional quality.[5] This equation represents one of the key innovations of this part of the chapter, allowing us to test for one of the channels of causation from natural resources to growth.

In this part of the chapter, we will therefore be interested in the sign, size and significance of the direct impacts of natural resources on growth and hence the coefficients β, ϕ, δ and γ in equation (3.1), and also of the indirect impacts via institutional quality and hence the coefficients θ, ρ and τ.

3.2.2 Data description and sources

The data and sources are described in detail in the appendix on pages 87–9. Here we highlight some key issues. Growth rates of per capita PPP GDP are from the World Bank's World Development Indicators. Following Rodrik *et al.* (2002) and Easterly and Levine (2002), the institutional quality measure we use is due to Kaufmann *et al.* (2002). This is a composite indicator of a number of elements that capture the protection afforded to property rights as well as the strength of the rule of law. We also check for robustness to the other measures of institution quality compiled by Kaufmann *et al.* (2002).

We measure natural resource endowments in different ways to ensure that our results are robust. Sachs and Warner's (1995) preferred measure was the share of exports of natural resources in GDP in 1970. We enlarge this to include (i) the share of the exports of four types of natural resources – fuel, ores and metals, agricultural raw materials, and food – in GDP and total exports; (ii) the share of the exports of all natural resources in total exports; and (iii) a dummy for oil producing countries. The question arises whether some of these variables could be endogenous – after all countries could have high share of natural resources in economic activity because of slow growth. To address this concern, we use initial period values of the natural resource variables for the estimations, with 1970 and 1980 serving as alternative initial periods.

3.2.3 Results

The results for the growth and institution equations are presented in Tables 3.2–3.8. All the tables, except except Table 3.7 and Table A3.1 in the Appendix (www.csae.ox.ac.uk/books), contain two panels – Panel A presents the estimation results for the second-stage equation for growth, and Panel B the corresponding first-stage regressions for institutional quality.

Table 3.2 presents the basic specification with natural resources treated as an aggregate and expressed in terms of their share in GDP (SHARENATRSGDP) or in total exports (SHARENATREEXP) for the two periods 1970 and 1980. All the equations include the five basic conditioning variables, all of which, in the growth equation, are significant and correctly signed with coefficient estimates that are close to that found in previous studies. In particular, it is worth noting that the convergence coefficient is between –1.6 per cent and –1.9 per cent, which is consistent with the magnitude obtained in growth regressions (Barro and Sala-i-Martin, 1995). The significance of the institutional quality terms is also consistent with the recent work of Acemoglu *et al.* (2002). The coefficient on the instability term (measured as the standard deviation of the terms of trade between 1970 and 1998 multiplied by the share of resource exports in GDP) is significant, although not consistently, and the overvaluation term is never significant and is hence dropped from all the equations.[6]

Table 3.2 Growth, institutions and natural resources in aggregate

	Panel A. Second stage: dependent variable is real per capita GDP growth, 1970-98					*Panel B. First stage: Dependent variable is rule of law*				
	(1)	*(2)*	*(3)*	*(4)*	*(5)*	*(1)*	*(2)*	*(3)*	*(4)*	*(5)*
Rule of Law	1.483	1.228	1.156	1.43	1.157					
	[0.666]	[0.785]	[0.514]	[0.789]	[0.550]					
lnRGDP70	-1.918	-1.678	-1.609	-1.738	-1.626	0.69	0.498	0.646	0.582	0.619
	[0.659]	[0.627]	[0.537]	[0.664]	[0.556]	[0.141]	[0.162]	[0.131]	[0.152]	[0.148]
P60	2.737	2.635	2.545	2.806	2.576	0.254	0.303	0.41	0.037	0.568
	[0.873]	[0.832]	[0.808]	[0.925]	[0.828]	[0.428]	[0.414]	[0.406]	[0.415]	[0.446]
IPRICE1	-0.009	-0.01	-0.009	-0.009	-0.009	-0.002	-0.002	-0.003	-0.002	-0.003
	[0.002]	[0.003]	[0.003]	[0.002]	[0.003]	[0.002]	[0.002]	[0.002]	[0.002]	[0.002]
MALFAL66	-1.048	-1.033	-1.079	-1.059	-1.141	-0.111	-0.108	-0.077	-0.062	-0.071
	[0.580]	[0.545]	[0.495]	[0.530]	[0.523]	[0.291]	[0.287]	[0.249]	[0.281]	[0.256]
DENS65C	0.001	0.001	0.001	0.001	0.001	0	0	0	0	0
	[0.000]	[0.000]	[0.000]	[0.000]	[0.000]	[0.000]	[0.000]	[0.000]	[0.000]	[0.000]
TOTvolatility7098	-0.014	-0.049	-0.073	-0.054	-0.065	-0.018	-0.008	0.003	-0.01	-0.006
	[0.053]	[0.029]	[0.020]	[0.027]	[0.025]	[0.021]	[0.013]	[0.008]	[0.011]	[0.011]
Overvaluation7098					-0.002					0.004
					[0.005]					[0.003]
EURFRAC						-0.569	-0.394	-0.661	-0.415	-0.622
						[0.241]	[0.220]	[0.232]	[0.217]	[0.228]
ENGFRAC						0.476	0.507	0.643	0.496	0.647
						[0.340]	[0.351]	[0.319]	[0.342]	[0.321]
naturalresourcesharegdp70	-2.427					-0.151				
	[3.025]					[0.973]				
naturalresourceshareexp70		0.001					-0.009			
		[0.010]					[0.004]			
naturalresourcesharegdp80			2.238		2.418			-2.29		-2.415
			[1.546]		[1.681]			[0.524]		[0.595]
naturalresourceshareexp80				0.009					-0.009	
				[0.010]					[0.004]	
Observations	71	71	71	71	69	71	71	71	71	69
Adjusted R-squared	0.57	0.6	0.63	0.59	0.62	0.64	0.68	0.69	0.68	0.69

Robust standard errors in brackets

As Panel A of the table shows, the different measures of natural resources are insignificant and change signs between 1970 and 1980, suggesting the lack of any direct impact from natural resources to growth. This is in contrast with the findings of Sachs and Warner (1995) who found a significant negative impact.

The institution regressions, in Panel B, however, present a different story. In four of the four cases, natural resources are significant (at the 5 and 1 per cent levels) and negatively signed, implying that natural resources are detrimental to institutional quality. The overall picture that appears to emerge is that natural resources have a negative impact on growth via their effect on institutions and that once institutions are controlled for they have no further impact on growth.

To gauge the quantitative significance of this indirect effect, consider the equations with natural resources expressed as a share of total exports. Note that the standard deviation for the share of natural resources in total exports is about 29 percentage points (mean of 66 per cent) in 1980 and the standard deviation for institutional quality is about 1.03. A unit standard deviation increase in the share of natural resources in total exports will lead to a deterioration in institutional quality of 0.259 (28.8*.009, where the latter is the coefficient of natural resources in the institution equation). This represents a 0.259 standard deviation change in institutional quality, which in turn results in a 0.36 per cent decline (0.259*1.43, where the latter is the coefficient on institutional quality in the growth equation) in the annual average rate of growth. Thus, a one standard deviation increase in the share of natural resources in exports is associated with a reduction in annual per capita GDP growth of about 0.36 per cent.[7]

Table 3.3 analyses whether it is appropriate to treat all natural resources alike. Theoretical models would suggest that, while they should exert similar effects in terms of their instability and overvaluation effects, the impact of different natural resources on institutional quality could be very different. In particular, oil and minerals give rise to massive rents in a way that food or agricultural resources do not. Isham *et al.* (2003) refer to them as 'point-source' natural resources. It is the lobbying for and allocation of the rents associated with such resources that is detrimental to economic and political institutions (as in Tornell and Lane, 1999). In Table 3.3, the four natural resources are combined into two – one for fuel and ores (fuelandmineralshare) and one for food and agricultural raw materials (foodandagrishare)[8] (measured in terms of their share in total GDP and exports) – and entered instead of the aggregate share.

The aggregate results in Table 3.2 appear to be an average of diverging effects at the level of individual resources. The coefficients on growth of the two natural resource terms are insignificant. But in the institution regressions, the coefficients of the fuel and mineral variable are consistently negative and significant, usually at the 1 per cent level, while the other natural resource term switches signs and is generally not insignificant, a pattern that will be evident in virtually all of the regressions. This strongly confirms our prior assumptions that fuel and minerals have different impacts on institutional quality compared with other natural resources, a finding confirmed by Isham *et al.* (2003).

Table 3.3 Growth, institutions and individual natural resources

	Panel A. Second stage: Dependent variable is real per capita GDP growth, 1970–98						*Panel B. First-stage: Dependent variable is rule of law*					
	(1)	*(2)*	*(3)*	*(4)*	*(5)*	*(6)*	*(1)*	*(2)*	*(3)*	*(4)*	*(5)*	*(6)*
Rule of Law	1.237	1.295	1.53	1.218	1.05	1.274						
	[0.745]	[0.568]	[0.682]	[0.495]	[0.478]	[0.578]						
lnRGDP70	-1.69	-1.728	-1.989	-1.743	-1.651	-1.754	0.528	0.66	0.746	0.726	0.705	0.7
	[0.624]	[0.551]	[0.692]	[0.541]	[0.494]	[0.576]	[0.150]	[0.136]	[0.133]	[0.126]	[0.133]	[0.127]
P60	2.651	2.911	2.89	2.864	2.324	2.608	0.257	0.026	0.039	0.172	0.271	0.289
	[0.864]	[0.925]	[1.002]	[0.837]	[0.703]	[0.764]	[0.439]	[0.396]	[0.512]	[0.427]	[0.474]	[0.398]
IPRICE1	-0.01	-0.01	-0.009	-0.01	-0.01	-0.01	-0.001	-0.001	-0.002	-0.002	-0.002	-0.002
	[0.003]	[0.002]	[0.002]	[0.002]	[0.002]	[0.002]	[0.001]	[0.002]	[0.001]	[0.002]	[0.002]	[0.002]
MALFAL66	-0.991	-0.739	-0.92	-0.928	-1.407	-1.101	-0.261	-0.329	-0.282	-0.188	-0.158	-0.069
	[0.630]	[0.539]	[0.695]	[0.481]	[0.389]	[0.473]	[0.316]	[0.288]	[0.358]	[0.260]	[0.274]	[0.237]
DENS65C	0.001	0.001	0	0.001	0.001	0.001	0	0	0	0	0	0
	[0.000]	[0.000]	[0.000]	[0.000]	[0.000]	[0.000]	[0.000]	[0.000]	[0.000]	[0.000]	[0.000]	[0.000]
totshkwtd7098	-0.053	-0.079	-0.029	-0.083	-0.011	-0.069	0.006	0.007	0.003	0.011	0.006	-0.007
	[0.035]	[0.025]	[0.062]	[0.021]	[0.015]	[0.013]	[0.015]	[0.009]	[0.029]	[0.008]	[0.010]	[0.007]
EURFRAC							-0.426	-0.588	-0.562	-0.679	-0.643	-0.579
							[0.234]	[0.226]	[0.240]	[0.232]	[0.233]	[0.213]
ENGFRAC							0.528	0.505	0.432	0.568	0.571	0.557
							[0.331]	[0.297]	[0.316]	[0.295]	[0.303]	[0.298]
fuelandmineralsgareexp70	0.002						0.012					
	[0.012]						[0.005]					
foodandagrishareexp70	0						-0.007					
	[0.009]						[0.004]					
fuelandmineralsgareexp80		0.011						-0.011				
		[0.009]						[0.003]				
foodandagrishareexp80		-0.001						-0.001				
		[0.008]						[0.004]				
fuelandmineralsgaregdp70			-1.474						-1.457			
			[3.544]						[1.554]			
foodandagrisharegdp70			-3.519						1.365			
			[3.865]						[1.311]			
fuelandmineralsgaregdp80				2.787						-2.587		
				[1.691]						[0.484]		
fuelandmineralsgaregdp80				-1.434						0.542		
				[3.170]						[1.195]		
fuelsharegdp80					2.549						-2.798	
					[1.537]						[0.530]	
mineralsharegdp80					-7.148						-1.497	
					[2.074]						[1.197]	
foodsharegdp80					-4.826						-0.354	
					[3.637]						[1.530]	
agrisharegdp80					7.446						3.095	
					[6.906]						[1.904]	
OIL dummy						1.559						-0.932
						[0.613]						[0.175]
Observations	71	71	71	71	71	71	71	71	71	71	71	71
Adjusted R-squared	0.59	0.63	0.56	0.64	0.73	0.67	0.68	0.71	0.65	0.71	0.71	0.71

Robust standard errors in brackets

The quantitative impact of the individual resources is broadly similar and potentially large. Taking column 4 as the core specification yields the result that one standard deviation in the endowment of minerals and ores is associated with *slower growth* of about 0.37 per cent per annum. Finally, column 6 in Table 3.3 introduces an oil dummy, which yields the interesting result that oil creates a beneficial effect on growth, once institutions are controlled for. But the impact on institutions of oil is significantly negative.[9]

Table A3.1 in the Appendix (www.csae.ox.ac.uk/books) explores whether the effect of natural resources depends upon the extent of dependence on natural resources. This is done by successively introducing dummies for shares in total exports exceeding 20, 30, 40, 50 60, 70 and 80 per cent, respectively. The interesting results relate to the institution equation (and hence the growth equations are not reported). The noteworthy regularity is the monotonic increase in the (absolute value of the) size of the coefficient and the precision of the estimates. For example, the coefficient on the dummy for fuel and mineral shares exceeding 80 per cent is –0.97, nearly three times that of the dummy for fuel share exceeding 20 per cent. Formally, these results suggest that the impact of natural resources is non-linear; that is, the marginal (negative) impact of natural resources on institutions depends positively on the level of natural resources itself. Evidently, oil corrupts and excess oil corrupts more than excessively.

Table 3.4 checks whether the results are sensitive to the list of the conditioning variables. As discussed earlier, Sala-i-Martin *et al.* (2003) identified 17 variables that are potentially worthy of inclusion. Our core specification contains five of these. We successively introduced in this core each of the other 12 variables, and Table 3.4 reports the results of introducing five of them – proportion of land area within tropics (TROPICAR), life expectancy at birth in 1960 (LIFE060), the number of years a country is open (YRSOPEN), ethnolinguistic fractionalization (AVELF) and a variable measuring the fraction of population that is Confucian (CONFU). The core result relating to the detrimental impact of fuel and minerals on institutions remains robust – even the magnitude of the coefficients is stable.[10]

In the last column of Table 3.4, we undertake a slightly different kind of robustness check relating to the institution equation. The finding that resources

Table 3.4 Growth, institutions and natural resources: robustness to covariates

	Panel A. Second stage: Dependent variable is real per capita GDP growth, 1970-98					*Panel B. First stage: Dependent variable is rule of law*					
	(1)	*(2)*	*(3)*	*(4)*	*(5)*	*(1)*	*(2)*	*(3)*	*(4)*	*(5)*	*(6)*
Rule of Law	0.035	1.154	1.072	1.408	0.992						
	[0.971]	[0.586]	[0.557]	[0.497]	[0.440]						
lnRGDP70 1/	-1.239	-2.023	-1.716	-1.91	-1.41	0.521	0.385	0.638	0.719	0.73	0.664
	[0.664]	[0.476]	[0.532]	[0.527]	[0.459]	[0.120]	[0.221]	[0.132]	[0.129]	[0.138]	[0.128]
P60	2.956	2.437	2.753	2.66	2.42	0.131	-0.334	0.066	0.116	0.159	0.578
	[0.775]	[1.147]	[0.843]	[0.850]	[0.762]	[0.357]	[0.434]	[0.437]	[0.400]	[0.459]	[0.375]
IPRICE1	-0.013	-0.01	-0.01	-0.01	-0.01	-0.002	-0.002	-0.001	-0.002	-0.002	-0.002
	[0.004]	[0.003]	[0.003]	[0.002]	[0.003]	[0.001]	[0.002]	[0.002]	[0.002]	[0.002]	[0.002]
MALFAL66	-0.112	-0.996	-0.914	-0.557	-0.859	0.29	-0.248	-0.149	-0.084	-0.185	-0.279
	[0.654]	[0.496]	[0.490]	[0.501]	[0.483]	[0.261]	[0.258]	[0.272]	[0.260]	[0.266]	[0.265]
DENS65C	0.002	0.001	0.001	0.001	0.001	0.001	0	0	0	0	0
	[0.001]	[0.000]	[0.000]	[0.000]	[0.000]	[0.000]	[0.000]	[0.000]	[0.000]	[0.000]	[0.000]
totshkwtd7098	-0.085	-0.083	-0.079	-0.088	-0.082	0.005	0.011	0.014	0.01	0.011	0.007
	[0.016]	[0.021]	[0.020]	[0.020]	[0.021]	[0.010]	[0.008]	[0.008]	[0.009]	[0.008]	[0.010]
EURFRAC						-0.239	-0.603	-0.6	-0.719	-0.675	-0.764
						[0.210]	[0.218]	[0.231]	[0.237]	[0.241]	[0.230]
ENGFRAC						0.487	0.434	0.576	0.588	0.565	0.568
						[0.221]	[0.288]	[0.297]	[0.307]	[0.302]	[0.304]
fuelmineralsharegdp80	2.556	3.127	2.539	3.674	2.59	-1.347	-2.004	-2.494	-2.461	-2.577	-2.53
	[1.468]	[1.644]	[1.631]	[1.708]	[1.665]	[0.577]	[0.478]	[0.510]	[0.544]	[0.501]	[0.537]
foodagrisharegdp80	3.434	-1.364	-1.476	-1.202	-0.162	2.195	0.667	0.344	0.66	0.573	-0.038
	[4.274]	[3.220]	[2.905]	[3.187]	[2.809]	[0.945]	[1.136]	[1.237]	[1.206]	[1.267]	[1.193]
TROPICAR	-1.998					-0.901					
	[1.065]					[0.270]					
LIFE060		0.036					0.039				
		[0.048]					[0.018]				
YRSOPEN			0.538					0.51			
			[0.648]					[0.256]			
AVELF				-1.009					-0.313		
				[0.509]					[0.325]		
CONFUC					4.547					0.127	
					[0.681]					[0.398]	
Observations	71	71	71	71	71	71	71	71	71	71	71
Adjusted R-squared	0.67	0.64	0.64	0.63	0.68	0.76	0.73	0.72	0.71	0.71	0.74

Robust standard errors in brackets

1/ In column 6, the intitial level of income refers to the year 1960 instead of 1970

have a negative effect on institutional quality controlling for the level of real income may not be terribly interesting or surprising. If natural resource income is indeed manna from heaven with no effect at all on institutions, then we would expect a negative correlation between natural resources and institutions conditional on total (resource and non-resource) income.[11] Hence, a test for whether natural resources have a negative effect on institutions should be conditioned not on total income but on non-resource income. To do this, we replaced the 1970 level of GDP in the institutions equation with that in 1960. Since many of the oil discoveries were made after 1960, one can expect that the 1960 level of income is relatively, albeit incompletely, uncontaminated by income from natural resources. The results, presented in column 6, suggest that the core result relating to the negative impact of natural resources remains robust.

Table 3.5 checks whether the results are robust to alternative measures of institutional quality. We replaced the rule of law variable successively by four other measures of institutional quality (from Kaufmann *et al.*, 2002) that capture respectively voice and accountability (VOICE), the effectiveness of government (GOVEFF), the control over corruption (CONCORR) and political stability (POLSTAB). The impact of natural resources on each of these measures is strong and statistically significant.

Table 3.6 undertakes other robustness checks.[12] In column 1, we use the Belsey–Kuh–Welsch (1980) test to check whether individual observations exert unusual leverage on the coefficient estimates, discarding those which do so. Two observations – Egypt and Malaysia – are influential. Even with these observations

Table 3.5 Growth, institutions and natural resources: robustness to alternative measures of institutions

	Panel A. Dependent variable is rate of growth of per capita GDP, 1970-98				*Panel B. Dependent variable is instituional quality*			
Institutional variable	*Voice and accountability*	*Government effectiveness*	*Control of corruption*	*Political Stability*	*Voice and accountability*	*Government effectiveness*	*Control of corruption*	*Political Stability*
Institutions	1.424	1.546	1.416	3.424				
	[1.440]	[0.694]	[0.648]	[3.666]				
lnRGDP70	-1.687	-1.946	-2.007	-2.557	0.554	0.706	0.817	0.495
	[1.039]	[0.664]	[0.724]	[1.983]	[0.100]	[0.121]	[0.126]	[0.118]
P60	2.263	2.841	2.708	1.544	0.426	0.083	0.237	0.411
	[1.017]	[0.883]	[0.920]	[1.606]	[0.418]	[0.357]	[0.379]	[0.423]
IPRICE1	-0.008	-0.012	-0.012	-0.004	-0.003	-0.001	0	-0.002
	[0.005]	[0.003]	[0.003]	[0.010]	[0.001]	[0.001]	[0.001]	[0.002]
MALFAL66	-1.274	-0.808	-0.856	-0.298	0.11	-0.168	-0.18	-0.223
	[0.721]	[0.483]	[0.571]	[1.116]	[0.194]	[0.229]	[0.222]	[0.242]
DENS65C	0.002	0	0.001	0	0	0	0	0
	[0.000]	[0.000]	[0.000]	[0.001]	[0.000]	[0.000]	[0.000]	[0.000]
totshkwtd7098	-0.079	-0.073	-0.073	-0.109	0.005	0.002	0.002	0.011
	[0.031]	[0.023]	[0.022]	[0.059]	[0.011]	[0.009]	[0.008]	[0.010]
fuelmingdp80	3.766	3.354	2.041	8.248	-2.793	-2.496	-1.77	-2.553
	[4.106]	[2.003]	[1.632]	[9.585]	[0.592]	[0.550]	[0.583]	[0.489]
foodaggdp80	-1.209	-1.793	-2.917	-6.711	0.212	0.669	1.647	1.728
	[4.350]	[2.931]	[4.070]	[9.114]	[1.160]	[1.185]	[1.197]	[1.014]
					-0.261	-0.493	-0.598	-0.208
					[0.188]	[0.200]	[0.231]	[0.249]
					0.47	0.491	0.487	0.227
					[0.191]	[0.286]	[0.268]	[0.202]
Observations	71	70	69	70	71	70	69	70
Adjusted R-squared	0.3	0.63	0.51	..	0.67	0.73	0.74	0.66

Robust standard errors in brackets

Table 3.6 Growth, institutions and natural resources: robustness to influential observations, regional dummies, sample and instrument for institutions

	Panel A. Second stage: Dependent variable is real per capita GDP growth, 1970-98				*Panel B. First stage: Dependent variable is rule of of law*			
	(1)	*(2)*	*(3)*	*(4)*	*(1)*	*(2)*	*(3)*	*(4)*
Rule of Law	1.027	1.128	1.564	3.408				
	[0.479]	[0.420]	[0.974]	[1.135]				
lnRGDP70	-1.533	-1.419	-1.645	-2.913	0.759	0.709	0.346	0.482
	[0.557]	[0.420]	[0.483]	[0.848]	[0.129]	[0.140]	[0.169]	[0.185]
P60	2.596	1.286	2.524	3.258	0.128	0.266	0.465	-0.151
	[0.847]	[0.728]	[0.928]	[1.332]	[0.424]	[0.561]	[0.428]	[0.483]
IPRICE1	-0.012	-0.008	-0.01	-0.008	-0.003	-0.002	-0.002	-0.001
	[0.002]	[0.002]	[0.003]	[0.004]	[0.001]	[0.002]	[0.002]	[0.002]
MALFAL66	-0.771	-0.044	-0.685		-0.044	-0.211	-0.38	
	[0.452]	[0.399]	[0.647]		[0.275]	[0.321]	[0.250]	
DENS65C	0.001	0.001	0.001		0	0	0	
	[0.000]	[0.000]	[0.001]		[0.000]	[0.000]	[0.000]	
totshkwtd7098	-0.079	-0.07	-0.087		0.009	0.01	0.011	
	[0.023]	[0.021]	[0.026]		[0.007]	[0.008]	[0.008]	
EURFRAC					-0.652	-0.699	-0.665	
					[0.234]	[0.266]	[0.288]	
ENGFRAC					0.572	0.573	0.387	
					[0.290]	[0.307]	[0.540]	
fuelmineralsharegdp80	1.591	2.367	3.164	5.561	-2.639	-2.571	-1.92	-1.599
	[1.582]	[1.555]	[2.186]	[2.685]	[0.507]	[0.480]	[0.487]	[0.529]
foodagrisharegdp80	-3.836	-0.762	-1.504	-3.586	0.337	0.534	0.671	0.796
	[2.821]	[2.165]	[4.056]	[3.498]	[1.338]	[1.245]	[1.390]	[1.427]
East Asia dummy		1.005				-0.103		
		[0.663]				[0.228]		
Sub-saharan Africa dummy		-1.498				0.042		
		[0.368]				[0.392]		
Log settler mortality								-0.217
								[0.109]
Observations	69 (influential observations: Egypt and Malaysia)	71	51 (sample = developing counries)	53	69	71	51	53
Adjusted R-squared	0.68	0.71	0.56	-0.04	0.72	0.7	0.42	0.52

Robust standard errors in brackets

dropped, the coefficient estimates in the growth and institution regressions remain statistically unaffected. In column 2, regional dummies are introduced. While the dummies for East Asia and sub-Saharan Africa are themselves significant in the growth regression, the results on the natural resource variables remain broadly unaffected.[13] Fuel and minerals continue to exert a strong negative impact on growth (significant again at the 1 per cent level) via their adverse effect on institutional quality. That the results on the fuel and minerals variable survive with the inclusion of the regional dummies is remarkable.

In column 3, we narrow the sample to developing countries. The results on fuel and minerals remain broadly unchanged. The coefficient on the fuel and minerals variable in the institution equation drops to –1.9, but the overall impact remains broadly unchanged because the coefficient of the institution variable in the growth equation goes up from 1.2 to 1.57. In column 3, we replace the Hall and Jones (1999) instrument for institutions with the Acemoglu *et al.* (2001) settler mortality. The negative effect of fuel and minerals on institutions remains robust and significant at the 1 per cent level. Interestingly, the settler mortality instrument sharply increases the convergence coefficient from less than –2 per cent to –2.9 per cent, which is on the high side, suggesting that this specification might be more fragile.

In the preceding tables, we held the sample size constant to facilitate comparison across specifications. In Table 3.7, we re-estimate the preferred specifications for larger samples. In view of the facts that the binding constraint on sample size is the growth variable and that we are particularly interested in the impact of natural resources on institutional quality, we report only the first-stage equations for institutions. In column 1, the basic specification using the individual natural resources is estimated with a sample size of 84 rather than 71 (see Table 3.3). In column 2, the sample is restricted to developing countries. In both cases, the negative impact of fuels on institutions and the insignificant impact of the other natural resources holds robustly. In columns 3 and 4 the same exercise is repeated replacing the natural resource variables with the oil dummy, and the results remain unchanged.

Table 3.7 Growth, institutions and natural resources: maximizing sample size

	First stage: Dependent variable is rule of law			
	(1)	*(2)*	*(3)*	*(4)*
lnRGDP70	0.683	0.242	0.77	0.365
	[0.131]	[0.156]	[0.111]	[0.123]
P60	0.396	0.601	0.089	0.282
	[0.397]	[0.356]	[0.349]	[0.327]
IPRICE1	-0.001	-0.002	-0.001	-0.001
	[0.002]	[0.002]	[0.002]	[0.002]
MALFAL66	-0.15	-0.359	-0.042	-0.259
	[0.238]	[0.232]	[0.229]	[0.227]
DENS65C	0	0	0	0
	[0.000]	[0.000]	[0.000]	[0.000]
totshkwtd7098	0.007	0.009	-0.004	0.001
	[0.011]	[0.009]	[0.008]	[0.008]
EURFRAC	-0.645	-0.546	-0.566	-0.53
	[0.212]	[0.257]	[0.196]	[0.241]
ENGFRAC	0.652	0.393	0.591	0.378
	[0.287]	[0.506]	[0.276]	[0.496]
fuelmineralsharegdp80	-2.388	-1.644		
	[0.478]	[0.494]		
foodagrisharegdp80	-0.335	-0.547		
	[1.060]	[1.247]		
OIL			-0.965	-0.659
			[0.175]	[0.136]
Observations	82	62 (sample = developing countries)	87	67 (sample = developing countries)
Adjusted R-squared	0.68	0.42	0.67	0.39

Robust standard errors in brackets

The results can be summarized as follows:

- First, in aggregate, the natural resources appear to have a strong, robust and negative effect on growth by impairing institutional quality. Once institutions are controlled for, there is either very little effect of natural resources on growth or even a positive effect. In other words, owning natural resources may still be a blessing on balance rather than a curse in contrast to the findings of Sachs and Warner (1995) and Isham *et al.* (2003). But there is a channel through which the curse operates, addressing which could make natural resources more of a blessing or less of a curse.
- Second, this aggregate picture, however, obscures diverging patterns between the different natural resources in one important respect. In particular, it is fuel and minerals – which typically generate rents that are easily appropriable ('point-source' natural resources) – that have a systematic and robust negative impact on growth via their detrimental effect on institutional quality. This effect is quantitatively significant, amounting to lower growth of about 0.36 per cent per year. Other resources do not seem to adversely affect institutional quality. This differential impact is significant in itself but is also consistent with the different attributes of natural resources.
- Third, the impact of natural resources is nonlinear. In particular, the negative marginal impact of resources on institutional quality depends on and increases with their level.

3.3 The Nigerian experience

Two broad themes pervade any macroeconomic account of Nigeria's post-independence development experience: waste and Dutch disease. We provide evidence that suggests that Dutch disease is an inadequate explanation for Nigeria's growth performance. The waste explanation, on the other hand, appears to be overwhelming, with oil a key factor causing a whole series of pathologies that have led to the waste.

3.3.1 The evidence on waste

Figure 3.4 provides a growth decomposition of Nigeria's performance since 1965. The two notable features are the rapid accumulation of physical capital, averaging 6.7 per cent per year; and *negative* TFP growth, averaging 1.2 per cent per year. That oil was responsible for the physical capital accumulation is suggested by the timing of the surge in investment: between 1973 and 1980, the years of the two major oil price shocks, the capital stock grew at an average rate of 14 per cent per year, which represented a threefold increase in the country's capital stock in eight years. A substantial part of the increase was accounted for by public capital spending financed by the surging oil revenues. Public investment as a share of GDP rose by over 7 percentage points during the period of the oil shocks. Between the 1960s and the end of the second oil shock the share of the public sector in capital formation increased from 20 per cent to 55 per cent.

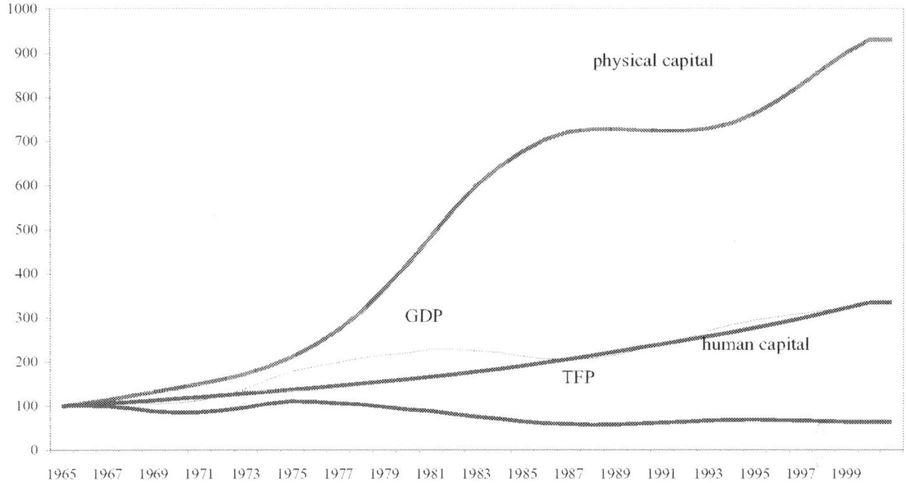

Figure 3.4 GDP, capital and TFP, 1965–2000 (index, 1965 = 100).
Source: Authors' calculations.

Another telling piece of evidence about the quality of investment comes from capacity utilization in manufacturing, a substantial portion of which is government-owned. Capacity utilization, which averaged about 77 per cent in 1975, started declining very quickly, to about 50 per cent in 1983 (see Figure A3.1 in the Appendix, www.csae.ox.ac.uk/books). Since the mid-1980s, capacity utilization has never exceeded 40 per cent, and has languished at around 35 per cent. In other words, two thirds of the investment in manufacturing by the government is consistently wasted.

The overall picture that emerges is that Nigeria has over-invested in physical capital and has suffered from poor productivity. Quality has suffered at the expense of quantity. Bevan *et al.* (1999) describe this accurately:

> This conjunction of a powerful political impetus to public investment and a lack of civil service skill is what makes Nigeria's economic history in this period so spectacular: almost the entire windfall was invested, and yet . . . there was nothing to show for it.
>
> (p. 67)

But how did oil make its impact felt in a way that affected Nigeria's economic fortunes and contributed to such spectacular inefficiency reflected in negative rates of TFP growth and substantial waste of the capital stock that had been built up based on oil revenues? Anecdotal evidence for this is abundant.

In fundamental ways, the politics of Nigeria has been shaped by getting access to the revenues from oil. The Biafran war of the late 1960s was in part an attempt by the eastern, predominantly Ibo, region to gain control over oil reserves. Successive military dictatorships have plundered oil wealth, the most notable being

General Abacha, and stories of transfers of large amounts of undisclosed wealth abroad are legion in Nigeria. The rise in government, following the surge in oil revenues, reflected an attempt by the North to appropriate oil revenues, and was manifested in the large share of the civil service being accounted for by Northerners. Oil revenues financed the building of the famous Ajakouta steel complex in the 1970s, which until today has not produced a commercial ton of steel. Moreover, as Bevan *et al.* (1999) note, the oil windfall enabled the government to increase its expenditures and thus provide increased opportunity for kickbacks.

Thus, it would seem plausible that not only has oil wealth been squandered but it has fundamentally altered politics and governance in Nigeria. More formal evidence for this is provided in Table 3.8, which examines whether Nigeria is an unusual performer in terms either of growth or of institutional development. This is done by introducing a Nigeria dummy in the core specifications. In column 1, the Nigeria dummy is significant: evidently, Nigeria fared significantly worse in terms of institutions but apparently significantly better in terms of growth. But when the natural resource variables are included (column 2), Nigeria continues to be a positive outlier in the growth equation, although it is no longer an outlier in the institution equation. In other words, Nigeria, like other oil and mineral producing countries, has suffered from poor institutional quality stemming from these resources. Based on the estimates in column 1, poor institutional quality in Nigeria has contributed to lower long-run growth of 0.5 per cent per year. This, in many ways, is the real legacy of oil in Nigeria.

3.3.2 Relative prices and the role of Dutch disease

In most accounts of Nigerian economic history, the impact of the oil windfall on the economy via its effect in raising the relative prices of nontradables to tradables occupies a central role in explaining poor economic performance. In this section, we explore this in further detail. We consider in turn what happened to relative prices and then to relative quantities.

In Figure 3.5A and B, we plot four indicators for the relative price of tradables to non-tradables; the first two might be called the external relative price and the latter two the internal relative price:

- the real effective exchange rate using the official rate;
- the real effective exchange rate using the parallel rate;[14]
- the relative prices of tradable to non-tradables in the GDP deflator;
- the relative prices of tradables to non-tradables in the CPI.

Since the early 1980s, all four indicators have moved in broadly the same direction: a substantial favouring of tradables in the 1980s and the first half of the 1990s which has been reversed since. For the 1970s, however, the indicators diverge. Specifically, the two internal price indicators suggest that, in fact, relative prices started moving in favour of tradables from 1970 onwards. The real effective exchange rate indicators, on the other hand, point to unfavourable tradable price movements for all of the 1970s, with the unfavourable trend being more pronounced for the official exchange rate indicator. A major reason for the diverging trends in these indicators is the behaviour of food prices in the aftermath of the first oil price shock. As Bevan *et al.* (1999) explain, the expansion in the size of

Table 3.8 Growth, institutions and natural resources: is Nigeria unusual?

	Panel A. Second stage: Dependent variable is real per capita GDP growth, 1970-98		*First stage: Dependent variable is rule of law*	
	(1)	*(2)*	*(1)*	*(2)*
Rule of Law	1.431	1.23		
	[0.661]	[0.502]		
lnRGDP70	-1.857	-1.758	0.698	0.726
	[0.652]	[0.548]	[0.139]	[0.127]
P60	2.722	2.877	0.236	0.172
	[0.874]	[0.842]	[0.428]	[0.431]
IPRICE1	-0.009	-0.01	-0.002	-0.002
	[0.002]	[0.002]	[0.002]	[0.002]
MALFAL66	-1.109	-1.006	-0.092	-0.189
	[0.563]	[0.486]	[0.292]	[0.266]
DENS65C	0.001	0.001	0	0
	[0.000]	[0.000]	[0.000]	[0.000]
totshkwtd7098	-0.051	-0.085	-0.018	0.011
	[0.030]	[0.019]	[0.016]	[0.008]
EURFRAC			-0.567	-0.679
			[0.238]	[0.234]
ENGFRAC			0.472	0.568
			[0.337]	[0.297]
naturalresourcesharegdp80				
fuelmineralsharegdp80		2.643		-2.59
		[1.722]		[0.494]
foodagrisharegdp80		-1.101		0.546
		[3.208]		[1.224]
Nigeria dummy	1.784	1.308	-0.349	0.017
	[0.355]	[0.317]	[0.174]	[0.143]
Observations	71	71	71	71
Adjusted R-squared	0.59	0.64	0.64	0.71

Robust standard errors in brackets

government led to a large influx of labour away from the rural toward the urban areas where job opportunities were growing. The resulting reduction in the size of the rural labour force led to a sharp decline in agricultural production and a rise in food prices.

Regardless of how the relative prices are measured, it seems that oil prices cannot account for their movements. For example, the correlation between oil prices and the two real exchange rate indices between 1968 and 2000 is –0.05 and –0.11, respectively; correctly signed but very weakly related (indeed statistically insignificant). The correlation between oil prices and the two internal price indicators is 0.39 and 0.26, respectively; statistically significant but incorrectly signed!

3.3.3 Relative quantity movements

The prime exhibits for the Dutch disease explanation of Nigerian economic decline is Figure 3.6 (see also Figure A3.2 in the Appendix, www.csae.ox.ac.uk/books), which show a decline in the share of agriculture in GDP from 68 per cent in 1965 to 35 per cent in 1981. The decline was especially pronounced for the cash crops

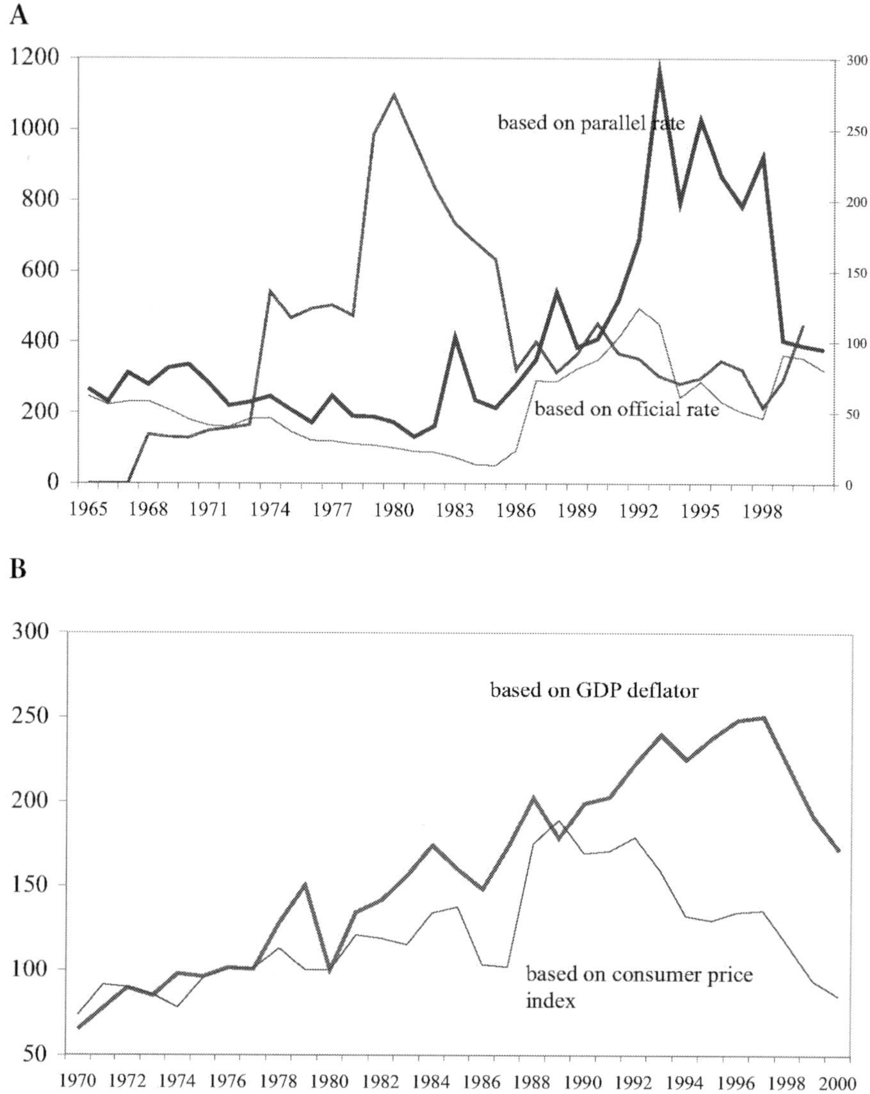

Figure 3.5 A. Nigeria: REER – official and parallel, 1965–2000. B. Nigeria: ratio of tradable to non-tradable prices, 1970–2000.
Source: Authors' calculations.

– cocoa, palm oil and rubber, which saw a decline in output of about 75 per cent between 1970 and 1981. Many commentators have argued that the big difference between the Indonesian and Nigerian response to oil windfalls was the ability of the Indonesian government to keep the exchange rate competitive and ensure the health of the agricultural sector through investments in technology, access to inputs and provision of extension services (see Gelb *et al.*, 1988).

The counterpart of the decline in agricultural sector was the rapid growth in the size of services (especially government services) and manufacturing, in which the government decided to invest heavily. The share of services and manufacturing over this same period grew by 16 and 8 percentage points respectively. This suggests that the real problem may well have been not that the agriculture sector declined but that the size of *government* in economic activity increased, with seriously detrimental effects in the long run.

Furthermore, it should be noted that this reallocation of resources had probably very little to do with relative price movements: they were simply the result of the government's decision on how to utilize the oil windfalls. In fact, if resources had moved in response to relative prices, manufacturing should not have seen the expansion that it did because if anything relative prices were moving against it. In the period of the windfalls, public absorption increased sharply while private absorption declined: changes in the share of agriculture (private sector) and services and manufacturing (public sector) thus were the counterparts in the production side of the national income accounts of the changes in absorption.

A final problem with the Dutch disease explanation for Nigeria is that, even if its detrimental effects in the 1970s were real, it is hard to explain why a reversal of the Dutch disease, indeed a sustained and prolonged depreciation for nearly 15 years, failed to offset or mitigate the previous problem. Looking at Figure 3.6 (see also Figure A3.2 in the Appendix, www.csae.ox.ac.uk/books), it is remarkable how constant the shares of the various sectors in GDP have been since 1980 despite some pronounced changes in relative prices. Agriculture witnessed a brief boom in the mid-1980s, but manufacturing has been in secular decline since the 1980s despite favourable relative price movements.

To summarize, the Dutch disease explanation for Nigerian economic performance is not entirely satisfactory because:

- It is not clear that relative price movements did in fact consistently disfavour the tradable sector even in the immediate aftermath of the oil windfalls.
- Relative price movements were not correlated with oil prices so that how oil windfalls were used rather than oil prices per se were more important in determining relative prices; in fact, decisions to keep the official exchange rate appreciated, were to a great extent related to the need to create rents (via the black market premium) at a time when oil revenues were in decline.[15] Thus exchange rate policy – clearly endogenous – was driven by rent and fiscal imperatives and the relative price consequences were almost a by-product (see Gelb *et al.*, 1988).
- The sustained movement of relative prices in favour of tradables in the 1980s and early 1990s did not reverse Nigeria's economic prospects.
- Although the role of the agricultural sector declined, it was offset by an increase in the size of the government sector in economic activity, and the poor performance of the latter may well be the more important for Nigeria's long-term economic decline.

If the investments in services and manufacturing that Nigeria made in the aftermath of the oil windfalls had been efficient, yielding the returns that they

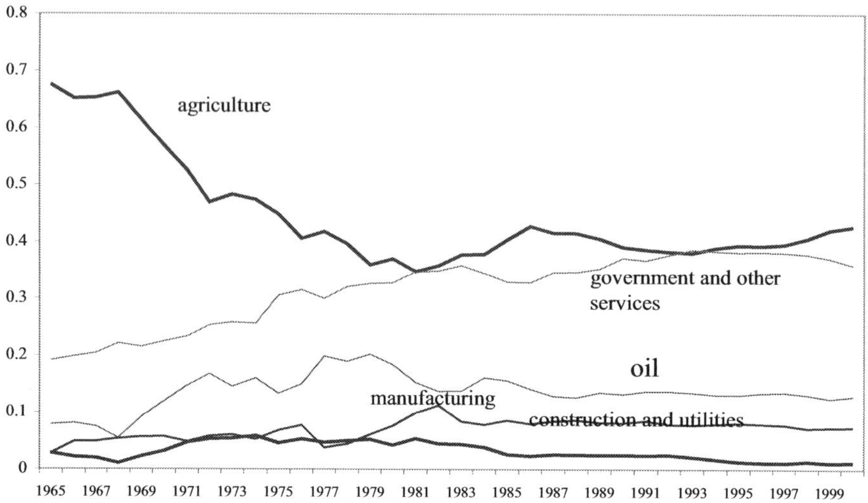

Figure 3.6 Nigeria: shares of sectors in real GDP.
Source: Authors' calculations.

did in, say, East Asia, we would now be celebrating successful diversification *away* from agriculture by the Tiger on the Niger rather than bemoaning the victimhood of agriculture.

3.4 Nigeria: from analysis to policy options

If natural resources do indeed lead and are intrinsic to a decline in institutional quality, what can be done to mitigate or offset this impact? Natural resources are an endowment, an unalterable geographical feature of the economic landscape. It would seem, therefore, that countries that have them are stuck, destined to institutional decline and poor growth.

But can there be a way out? One, somewhat glib, answer would be to say: increase transparency and accountability in the management of oil revenues. But who will exercise these functions? In the past, this proved impossible. With the ongoing consolidation of democracy in Nigeria, a positive response to this question is conceivable. But even the most optimistic observer would acknowledge that, given the inheritance of extremely weak public institutions bequeathed by four decades of military dictatorships, the transition from holding periodic democratic elections to having a fully functioning democracy is bound to be long. After all, institutions are known to exhibit stubborn persistence. In the case of Nigeria, this scepticism is warranted precisely because of oil revenues. While Nigeria is now a democracy, the balance of power between citizens and public officials, including those at state and local government levels, is inordinately skewed in favour of officials by virtue of their easy access to oil revenues. This perpetuates politics, even democratic politics, as patronage.

In the previous sections we showed that the main problem affecting the Nigerian economy is the fact that the oil revenues that the government gets are regarded as manna from heaven which tends to corrupt institutions and lower the long-term growth prospects. Starting from this premise, the logical conclusion is that the best way to deal with the problem is to transform Nigeria into a 'non-oil' economy. One way to do this is to prevent government officials from appropriating the oil resources directly. These resources should be distributed directly to the Nigerian citizens, ultimately their true and legitimate owners. This would replicate or simulate a situation in which the government has no easy access to natural resource revenue, just like governments in countries without natural resources. If this 'easy revenue' (and the incentives for corruption that it generates) were eliminated, much of the problem would disappear. One of the direct benefits of this would be that Nigerians would have an initial endowment superior to that of other nations.

Of course one implication of our proposal would be that the government would lose revenue. In fact, if our proposal were to be implemented, the government would lose all the revenue that it now collects directly from the sales of oil. Although this would seem tragic to some, this is indeed what happens to most governments in the world. And, like most of those governments, if the Nigerian authorities want to raise resources for necessary public expenditures, they would have to raise them by taxing the Nigerian citizens and companies. Our reading of the evidence is that it would be much more difficult to mismanage the resources that come from taxes than those that fall from the sky like manna. This would therefore create the right incentives for governance, incentives that are now sorely missing, and would contribute to reducing corruption and the rest of the problems that affect the Nigerian institutions today. The contrasting historical experiences of the US and Latin America suggest that institutional development is hindered where governments do not tax their citizenry (representation does seem to be difficult without taxation; Engerman and Sokoloff, 1994).

For reasons explained below, it would be desirable to embed our proposal in the constitution as an inalienable right of each Nigerian to have access to an equal share of oil proceeds. This would take the rents out of public officials' hands, thereby undermining the corroding process engendered by the rents, which have detrimental economic consequences. Of course, this is a radical proposal, and a number of issues arise in relation to it. We analyse each of them, but we would underscore that converting this idea into a concrete plan for implementation should be the task of Nigerians. Accordingly, we would suggest that a national conference, comprising a broad cross-section of Nigerian society, be convened at the earliest possible date to debate and give effect to this proposal.

This solution is rendered more urgent by the prospects of the future exploitation of Nigeria's vast reserves of natural gas. Nigerians celebrate the discovery of these reserves. However, it may be that natural gas may only aggravate and prolong the 'curse'.

Our estimates are that the likely magnitude of payments to individual households under our proposal would be large. We estimate them under two different scenarios: under current and future production levels each household would get about \$140, which would amount to \$425 in per capita PPP terms (roughly

$760 per adult), representing about 43 per cent of current per capita PPP GDP and well above the $1 per day poverty line. With full exploitation of gas, these amounts could increase to upwards of $750 per capita ($1330 per adult) in PPP terms.[16] Clearly these sums are non-negligible from the point of view of individual households.

3.4.1 Creating a Fund or distributing current revenues

One possible response to managing revenue volatility is to create a Fund.[17] The best-known examples are Norway and Kuwait, although there are many others (see Davis *et al.*, 2001). Based on an analysis of a number of countries, Davis *et al.* (2001) conclude that, funds 'are, however, not an easy – nor necessarily an appropriate – solution to the fiscal policy problems faced by these countries.' The underlying reasoning is that the conditions that generally thwart sound fiscal policy are likely to undermine the effectiveness of funds. Particularly, where institutional capacity – to monitor and exercise accountability – is weak, there is a very serious risk that Funds will be 'raided'. This temptation is likely to be greater the larger the size of the Fund. If the problem with oil is, as demonstrated above, weak institutions and corruption, a Fund is more likely to exacerbate the problem than address it. Hence, calling for the creation of a Fund in Nigeria with stringent mechanisms to 'ensure accountability and prevent the misuse of resources' raises the question of how these mechanisms can be created given the presence of oil. In this context, it is particularly inappropriate to invoke Norway as a model for Nigeria because Norway's oil discovery was made when its institutions were already highly developed.

For these reasons, the creation of a Fund in the spirit of the Alaska Fund, whereby what is distributed to the public is not the oil revenue directly but the income from the Fund, is not something that we would recommend. Moreover, if savings were an important issue, that could be addressed at the level of deciding how much oil to extract rather than 'over-extracting' and saving the proceeds, which has the pitfall noted earlier. Leaving oil in the ground, unextracted, is a form of saving.

3.4.2 Who should receive the revenues?

An important question is who should receive the oil revenues. Of course the natural answer would be: *all* Nigerian citizens! But when one thinks about this, some issues arise. For example, if all citizens, young and adult, are entitled to a lump-sum transfer, incentives to increase fertility (and therefore population growth) are introduced into the system. We do not think that distorting family incentives and introducing fiscally induced fertility is something that Nigeria needs today. If only adults should be entitled to the lump-sum transfer, the incentive to have more children would be lessened since the revenue associated with extra children would be postponed for 18 years.

It could also be argued that revenues should be distributed among women only. A number of studies have shown that development outcomes are strongly correlated with the degree of empowerment of women within a household (Sen, 1999). Whether this would be acceptable in Nigeria remains to be seen.

3.4.3 Fiscal issues

Another question is whether all the revenues should be distributed or a certain share should be retained because the government has to provide certain essential services (public goods). As mentioned earlier, our proposal is based on the conceptual principle of trying to convert an economy into one that notionally did not have oil. One way to achieve or simulate this would be to distribute *all* the revenues to the people and require the government to rely on normal fiscal principles to determine appropriate levels of taxation and expenditure.

This would create the right incentives for governance, incentives which are currently sorely missing. Currently, oil accounts for a substantial share of total government revenues. As such, the government has little incentive to provide services efficiently because the discipline exerted by the need to tax the public is largely absent: oil revenues are manna from heaven and keep flowing regardless of what the public sector delivers. Thus, even though some would argue that the point of distributing the money and getting it back would essentially constitute an administrative waste, we believe that this waste would be justified by the radically altered incentives for governance.

Of course, given that government cannot be starved of the revenue to provide essential services, there could be a transition period during which the share of overall revenues that is paid out progressively increases, culminating in a 100 per cent distribution, say at the end of a finite period.

The notion that fiscal issues, including those relating to fiscal federalism, should be addressed 'as if' Nigeria were a normal non-oil economy would argue in favour of making households or individuals rather than states the beneficiary of the revenues. One natural question that arises is whether regions or households in regions that are the victims of the environmental degradation caused by oil should be compensated in the form of greater revenues to reflect the marginal environmental cost. After all, the derivation principle in Nigeria, whereby oil-producing regions receive a higher share of revenues, is in part a response to these environmental costs. While this might be seen as politically desirable, we would argue that issues related to environmental compensation and other political considerations should be dealt with through normal tax/expenditure principles. The distribution of revenues is purely related to the initial allocation of endowments following which normal fiscal principles would take over. The endowment instrument should not be burdened with having to address other objectives. Moreover, given that not all the oil causes environmental degradation (a point that will become even more important as natural gas exploitation starts acquiring importance), it would seem more practicable and simple to treat all sources of revenues similarly. Indeed, Ahmad and Singh (2003) argue for oil production excises to address externalities.

Our proposal would have a radical impact on fiscal federalism discussions. Above all, it would create strong pressures for decentralization because the tax base would shift down toward the states and local governments, allowing social service expenditures, which are and should be delivered at the regional levels, to come closer to the unit of taxation.[18] Thus, expenditure and tax decision-making would be aligned more closely, improving fiscal management. Currently, there are significant vertical imbalances in Nigeria with revenues of sub-federal entities financing between 20 and 40 per cent of their current expenditures, with the rest made up of transfers of oil revenues from the federal level. Ahmad and Singh (2003) argue that the current revenue-sharing system is a key factor in predisposing the Nigerian intergovernmental arrangement to instability and inefficiency. In their view, a separation of revenues bases, with more stable revenue sources for the regions, would be desirable for countries such as Nigeria and Indonesia. They envisage the central government taking on the stabilization function. Our proposal would be in line with their proposals for a larger and more stable base for sub-federal levels, while at the same time obviating the need for the federal government to provide the stabilization function. As we argue below, this stabilization function is better provided by the private sector than by the government.

While there would still be a need to determine what goods should be provided at the federal levels, how they should be financed, and so on, there would be an improvement over the status quo, which is focused on sharing the 'manna from heaven' rather than on conducting discussions within the context of a normal fiscal framework. Our proposal would also create pressures to improve tax administration and collection, pressures for which are largely absent now.

3.4.4 Implementation issues

Implementing a system of transfer would no doubt raise huge administrative problems. The problems are very real and would have to be addressed. We would suggest that the transfers be made on a six-monthly or annual basis to minimize the administrative costs. Preferably, the payments should be made based on actual data made public by the government and the oil companies about how much revenue was paid by the companies to the government.

Citizenship or residence could be a condition for receiving these payments. Nigeria could take advantage of the fact that it has just implemented a voter ID system and issued cards to all eligible voters. It would therefore seem practical to link payments to voter identification and hence make payments to adults or adult women. Given Nigeria's short four-year election cycle, the voter ID would be periodically updated, facilitating the making of the oil payments. An unintended consequence of our scheme, and one that would facilitate participation in elections, would be the incentive to obtain voter registration.

Implementation would be facilitated if all eligible Nigerians had a bank account so that revenues could simply be transferred from government accounts to individual ones. Indeed, requiring a bank account as a precondition for receiving revenues could encourage financial intermediation. Alternatively, and as an interim arrangement, the government could post cheques to individual households as is done in the United States for tax refunds.

We are under no illusion about the likely corruption and leakage in the distribution process. Creative arrangements to minimize these should be devised. But we would argue that there is an important *ex post* check on the abuse that can result. Corruption and abuse will inevitably mean that some eligible households will not receive their rightful share of the oil proceeds. They would then have the constitutional right to seek redress through the judicial system, which, warts and all, appears to be one of the few institutions that function and that provide some scope for citizens to ensure accountability. In essence, the defaults between the current system and the one we are proposing would change: under the former, citizens rely on public officials and institutions for receiving the oil money indirectly through public services; under our proposal they would have an automatic – *and justiciable* – right to receive the proceeds directly.

3.4.5 Need for cooperation by foreign oil companies

Implementing our proposal and minimizing the corruption and waste would require the cooperation of the foreign oil companies in a number of important respects. To prevent the government from understating the revenues it has available for distribution, oil companies should independently report the exact amounts they have paid to the government, which could be verified by independent audit.[19] Information on their levels of production and the prices received would help in corroborating government figures.

3.4.6 Political economy

Our proposal is open to one fundamental criticism. If vested interests have been responsible for the squandering of oil revenues in the past, why would they allow our proposal, which would denude them of all money and power, and acquiesce to it?

Our response is that in some ways radical change of the sort we are proposing might be easier to accomplish than incremental change. Waste and corruption are issues that resonate deeply with every Nigerian: one could even hazard that the average Nigerian considers this to be the fundamental problem in Nigeria. Thus, it might be easier to rally popular opinion in favour of such a proposal in a way that the vested interests might find difficult to resist. And especially if the push for change can be codified as a constitutional right for every citizen, the consequences could be enormous. As argued above, this constitutional right can provide some scope for redress against inevitable abuse.

3.4.7 Macroeconomic consequences

How would the distribution of oil revenues directly to the people affect the ability of the economy to weather shocks, particularly those relating to oil prices? In terms of macro consequences, the proposal would essentially convert public windfall gains and losses from price volatility to private gains and losses. And this could have potential macroeconomic consequences.

Collier and Gunning (1996) provide an excellent analysis of the management of public and private windfalls, arguing that 'usually governments have proved themselves to be rather bad at coping with the revenue volatility that such a policy (custodial fiscal policy) entailed. By contrast, private agents respond much more appropriately than the argument for a custodial role presumed.'

The case for public management of shocks relies on government's being more able to distinguish temporary from permanent shocks and being more far-sighted in responding to them. Ideally, intertemporal consumption smoothing would require that a large portion of windfall gains be saved and that these savings be efficiently used. On the first, the evidence is that the private sector does no worse: Collier and Gunning (1996) report that savings from windfall gains were about the same whether the recipient agent was public or private.

As importantly, savings are much more efficiently used by the private than the public sector. This is an implication of our cross-section work, which shows that resources like oil, typically owned by the public sector, corrode institutions because of the lobbying for rents. And there can be no stronger support for this than Nigeria, where, as our analysis showed, the returns on investment have been abysmally low. Collier and Gunning (1996) also provide evidence that the quality of investment deteriorates during windfalls. Tanzania reintroduced its 'basic industries' investment programme during the coffee boom having previously abandoned it. Nigeria embarked on the famous or infamous Ajakouta steel complex during the oil price boom. More starkly, while there might be a legitimate custodial role for the state in managing windfalls, the question in this context is whether a weak state (with a demonstrably weak record) such as exists in Nigeria will be better at discharging this custodial role than the private sector.

In fact, Collier and Gunning (1996) discuss whether public windfalls should be transferred to the private sector through taxation or through the banking system, but they stop short, more on grounds of feasibility than of principle. Our proposal would just be a logical culmination of their analysis, albeit with other important justifications.

A related argument for custodial fiscal policy is the fear of a real appreciation and consequent Dutch disease when there is an unexpected positive shock. But if the private sector responds no worse or better than the public sector in terms of their savings behaviour, there should be no difference in terms of the impact on currency movements.

3.5 Concluding remarks

Natural resources such as oil and minerals may or may not be a curse on balance. But our work shows that they certainly have a seriously detrimental impact on the quality of domestic institutions and through this channel on long-run growth. Evidence from a cross-section of countries shows that this impact is very robust. We also find that the relation is nonlinear.

The Nigerian experience provides telling confirmation of this aspect of natural resources. Waste and corruption from oil rather than Dutch disease has been responsible for its poor long-run economic performance.

Exhortations to the new leadership to provide visionary leadership and implement the familiar litany of reforms – prudent macroeconomic policy, privatization, trade liberalization, strengthening the financial sector – would in our view be neither effective nor credible. Why should the new leadership be able to deliver where previous ones – dictators and democrats alike – have failed?

Our proposal to the new leadership would be to focus on one key issue: managing the revenues from oil. Actually, we would propose that the government stop managing these revenues and turn them over directly to the people. In particular, we propose that all Nigerians should have a constitutional right to an equal share of the proceeds.

We are under no illusion about the practical difficulties of implementing the proposal. Even with all the difficulties of corruption and inefficiency that will no doubt plague its actual implementation, in our view our proposal will, at the least, be much superior to the status quo. After all, the terrible current situation is the result of staggering corruption and waste over the last 40 years. At best, however, our proposal could fundamentally improve the quality of public institutions and, as a result, transform economics and politics in Nigeria for decades to come.

Further, we would argue that we may have understated the likelihood of our proposal being superior to the status quo. Our analysis was predominantly focused on average performance (economic growth), where Nigerian performance has been 'merely' bad. If proper account is taken of Nigerian performance on poverty and income distribution, which has been extremely bad and which is intimately related to oil and corruption, it would be difficult to imagine that the status quo cannot be improved upon.

Finally, the proposal presented in this chapter for Nigeria would apply to all countries that have a deep dependence on natural resources and that have suffered from the deteriorating institutions as a consequence. In some ways, countries such as Venezuela and Iraq may be even better candidates because the costs of administering our scheme may be lower. Ours is a proposal for Nigeria but it is applicable more broadly to all countries that are afflicted by the natural resource curse.

Appendix: data and sources

ABSLAT Distance from Equator of capital city measured as abs(Latitude)/90. Source: Rodrik *et al.* (2002).

AGRIshareEXP Share of exports of agricultural raw materials in total merchandise exports. Source: World Bank's World Development Indicators.

AGRIshareGDP Share of exports of agricultural raw materials in GDP. Source: World Bank's World Development Indicators.

AVELF Average of five different indices of ethnolinguistic fractionalization which is the probability of two random people in a country not speaking the same language. Source: Sala-i-Martin *et al.* (2003).

CONCORR Index of control over corruption. Source: Kaufmann *et al.* (2002).

CONFUC Fraction of population Confucian. Source: Sala-i-Martin *et al.* (2003).
DENS65C Coastal (within 100 km of coastline) population per coastal area in 1965. Source: Sala-i-Martin *et al.* (2003).
East Dummy variable taking value 1 if a country belongs to Asia, 0 otherwise.
ENGFRAC Fraction of the population speaking English. Source: Hall and Jones (1999).
EURFRAC Fraction of the population speaking one of the following major languages of Western Europe: English, French, German, Portuguese or Spanish. Source: Hall and Jones (1999).
FoodandagrishareEXP Share of exports of food and agricultural raw materials in total merchandise exports. Source: World Bank's World Development Indicators.
FoodandagrishareGDP Share of exports of food and agricultural raw materials in total GDP Source: World Bank's World Development Indicators.
FoodshareEXP Share of food exports in total merchandise exports. Source: World Bank's World Development Indicators.
FoodshareGDP Share of food exports in GDP. Source: World Bank's World Development Indicators.
FuelandmineralshareEXP Share of exports fuel and natural gas and ores and minerals in total merchandise exports. Source: World Bank's World Development Indicators.
FuelandmineralshareGDP Share of exports fuel and natural gas and ores and minerals in total GDP. Source: World Bank's World Development Indicators.
FuelshareEXP Share of fuel and natural gas exports in total merchandise exports. Source: World Bank's World Development Indicators.
FuelshareGDP Share of fuel and natural gas exports in GDP. Source: World Bank's World Development Indicators.
GOVEFF Index of effectiveness of government. Source: Kaufmann *et al.* (2002).
IPRICE1 Average investment price level between 1960 and 1964 on purchasing power parity basis. Source: Sala-i-Martin *et al.* (2003).
LAAM Dummy variable taking value 1 if a country belongs to Latin America or the Caribbean, 0 otherwise.
LCOPEN Natural logarithm of openness. Openness is given by the ratio of (nominal) imports plus exports to GDP (in nominal US dollars). Source: Rodrik *et al.* (2002).
LIFE060 Life expectancy in 1960. Source: Sala-i-Martin *et al.* (2003).
LNRDGP70 Natural logarithm of per capita PPP GDP in 1970. Source: Sala-i-Martin *et al.* (2003).
LOGEM4 Natural logarithm of estimated European settlers' mortality rate. Source: Acemoglu *et al.* (2001)
LOGFRANKROM Natural logarithm of predicted trade shares computed following Frankel and Romer (1999) from a bilateral trade equation with 'pure geography' variables. Source: Rodrik *et al.* (2002).
LSO Dummy variable taking a value of 1 if a country has a socialist legal system.
MALFAL66 Index of malaria prevalence in 1996. Source: Gallup and Sachs (1998).

MEANTEMP Average temperature (Celsius). Source: Sala-i-Martin *et al.* (2003).
MineralshareEXP Share of exports of ores and minerals in total merchandise exports. Source: World Bank's World Development Indicators.
MineralshareGDP Share of exports of ores and minerals in GDP. Source: World Bank's World Development Indicators.
NaturalresourceshareEXP Share of natural resources in total exports (calculated as the sum of the shares of individual resources). Source: World Bank's World Development Indicators.
NaturalresourceshareGDP Share of natural resources in GDP. Source: Sachs and Warner (1995).
NGA Dummy variable taking value 1 for Nigeria, 0 otherwise.
OIL Dummy variable taking value 1 for a country being major oil exporter, 0 otherwise.
OVERvaluation7098 measure of exchange rate overvaluation. Source: Easterly and Levine (2002).
P60 Enrolment rate in primary education in 1960. Source: Sala-i-Martin *et al.* (2003).
POLSTAB Index of political stability. Source: Kaufmann *et al.* (2002).
RULE Rule of Law index. Refers to 2001 and approximates for 1990's institutions. Source: Kaufmann *et al.* (2002).
SAFRICA Dummy variable taking value 1 if a country belongs to sub-Saharan Africa, 0 otherwise.
TOTshkwtd7098 Volatility in the terms of trade between 1970 and 1998 weighted by share of natural resource exports in GDP in 1970. Source: World Bank's World Development Indicators.
TROPICAR Percentage of tropical land area. Source: Sala-i-Martin *et al.* (2003).
VOICE Index of voice and accountability. Source: Kaufmann *et al.* (2002).
YRSOPEN Number of years economy has been open between 1950 and 1994. Source: Sala-i-Martin *et al.* (2003).

Notes

1 We are grateful to Francesco Trebbi for valuable research assistance. Thanks are due to Doug Addison, Peter Clark, James Daniel, José Fajgenbaum, Chris Lane and Dani Rodrik for helpful comments. Errors remain our own.
2 These calculations are based on Sala-i-Martin (2003). We use the original definition of poverty line of the World Bank, which is $1 per day in 1985 prices.
3 It turns out that the greater instability – relative to other oil producers – is not a consequence of oil's greater weight in GDP: in the sample, the share of oil in GDP for oil-producing countries was 9.5 per cent compared with 8.1 per cent for Nigeria.
4 Isham *et al.* (2003) provide an excellent summary of the mechanisms of causation identified in the economics as well as in the political science literature. In the latter, emphasis is placed on the 'rentier' effects, whereby large revenues from natural resources allow governments to mollify dissent and avoid accountability, insulating governments from pressures for institutional reform; and 'anti-modernization' effects, whereby governments successfully thwart pressures for modernization and institutional reform because

their 'budgetary revenues are derived from a small workforce that deploys sophisticated technical skills that can only be acquired abroad'.

5 The implied exclusion restriction is that the instrument INSTRi does not appear in equation (3.1).

6 The overvaluation term was insignificant in nearly all specifications when included on its own and also when interacted with the various natural resource variables.

7 Note that the equation with the share of natural resources in GDP in 1980 yields the same quantitative impact (standard deviation of SHARENATRSGDP80 in the sample is 0.115 and the coefficient is –2.29, yielding a growth impact of 0.37 per cent).

8 Respectively fuels, ores and metals, agricultural raw materials, and food.

9 In column 3 of Table 3.2, we enter the four different natural resource variables individually. In the institution equation, the fuel and minerals variables behave quite similarly, although they do appear to have different direct effects on growth.

10 The results when the other covariates are introduced are exactly the same and are not reported for efficiency. The only variable that changes the results is the Latin American dummy (see below).

11 We are grateful to Dani Rodrik for this point.

12 In the rest of the equations, column 4 in Table 3.3 is treated as the core specification. But virtually all the results obtain whether the individual natural resource variables are expressed in terms of export shares in 1970 or 1980, or for the period 1960–2000, or as a share of GDP in 1970, or the fuel variable is replaced by an oil dummy.

13 The dummy for Latin America is insignificant and its introduction renders the regression estimate very imprecise, yielding implausible coefficient values, and hence is dropped from the analysis.

14 Evidence in favour of Nigerian Dutch disease involves real effective exchange rate calculations using the official rate (see Pinto, 1987). It is not at all obvious why this is appropriate. As Reinhart and Rogoff (2002) remind us in their revision of post-World War II exchange rate history, parallel rates are the mechanism by which fixed exchange rate regimes become de facto floating ones. The more liberal the parallel market and the more the transactions carried out in it, the more appropriate it is to measure relative price movements based on the parallel rate.

15 In fact, the weak correlation between oil prices and the real exchange rate reported earlier may have stemmed precisely from the tendency of the government to keep the exchange rate appreciated during periods of low oil prices.

16 Considerable uncertainty surrounds the estimates of the future revenue flows from natural gas relating to the arrangements for their marketing and the terms offered to companies for its exploitation. But what is indisputable is the vast amount of reserves and its potential for exploitation.

17 Theoretically, a Fund could be created for two reasons: to manage volatility (stabilization funds) or to save for future generations (savings funds).

18 Of course, it is possible that consumers would rather not have the government provide some services; our proposal would allow consumers to decide on the scope of government itself, which might well lead to a reduction in government size.

19 Steps in this direction (including audits) have been taken under the Nigeria Extractive Industries Transparency Initiative (N-EITI) aimed at following due process and achieving transparency in payments by extractive industries companies to government, and in the revenues received and reported by government.

References

Acemoglu, Daron, Simon Johnson and James A. Robinson, 2001, 'The Colonial Origins of Comparative Development: An Empirical Investigation', *American Economic Review*, 91 (5), 1369–1401.

Acemoglu, Daron, S. Johnson, J. Robinson and Y. Thaicaroen, 2002, 'Institutional Causes, Macroeconomic Symptoms: Volatility, Crises and Growth', *Journal of Monetary Economics* (forthcoming), Carnegie–Rochester Conference Series.

Ahmad, E. and R. Singh, 2003, 'Political Economy of Oil-Revenue Sharing in a Developing Country: Illustrations from Nigeria', International Monetary Fund Working Paper WP/03/16, Washington, DC.

Barro, R. and X. Sala-i-Martin, 1995, *Economic Growth*, New York: MIT Press.

Belsey, D.A., E. Kuh and R.E. Welsch, 1980, *Regression Diagnostics*, New York: John Wiley and Sons.

Bevan, D., P. Collier and J.W. Gunning, 1999, *The Political Economy of Poverty, Equity, and Growth: Nigeria and Indonesia*, New York: Oxford University Press.

Bravo-Ortega, C. and J. De Gregorio, 2001, 'The Relative Richness of the Poor? Natural Resources, Human Capital, and Economic Growth', mimeo, University of California, Berkeley.

Collier, P. and J. Gunning, 1996, 'Policy Towards Commodity Shocks in Developing Countries', IMF Working paper WP/96/84, Washington, DC.

Collier, P. and A. Hoeffler, 2002, 'Greed and Grievance in African Civil Wars', *Quarterly Journal of Economics* (forthcoming).

Davis, J., R. Ossowski, J. Daniel and S. Barnett, 2001, 'Stabilization and Savings Funds for Nonrenewable Resources', International Monetary Fund Occasional Paper No. 205, Washington, DC.

Easterly, W. and R. Levine, 2002, 'Tropics, Germs, and Crops: How Endowments Influence Economic Development', mimeo, Center for Global Development and Institute for International Economics.

Engerman, Stanley L. and Kenneth L. Sokoloff, 1994, 'Factor Endowments, Institutions, and Differential Paths of Growth Among New World Economies: A View from Economic Historians of the United States', National Bureau of Economic Research Working Paper No. H0066.

Frankel, Jeffrey and David Romer, 1999, 'Does Trade Cause Growth?', *American Economic Review*, 89 (3), 379–399.

Gallup, J.L. and J.D. Sachs, 2001, 'The Economic Burden of Malaria', *American Journal of Tropical Medicine and Hygiene*, 64 (suppl. 1), 85–96.

Gelb, A. and Associates, 1988, *Oil Windfalls: Blessing or Curse?*, A World Bank Research Publication, New York: Oxford University Press.

Hall, Robert and Chad I. Jones, 1999, 'Why Do Some Countries Produce So Much More Output per Worker than Others?', *Quarterly Journal of Economics*, 114 (1), 83–116.

Hausman, R. and R. Rigobon, 2002, 'An Alternative Interpretation of the Resource Curse: Theory and Implications for Stabilization, Saving, and Beyond', paper prepared for the Conference on Fiscal Policy Formulation and Implementation in Oil Producing Countries, International Monetary Fund, Washington, DC.

Isham, J., L. Pritchett, M. Woolcock and G. Busby, 2003, 'The Varieties of the Resource Experience: How Natural Resource Export Structures Affect the Political Economy of Economic Growth', mimeo, World Bank, Washington, DC.

Kaufmann, D., A. Kraay and P. Zoido-Lobatón, 2002, 'Governance Matters II – Updated Indicators for 2000/01', World Bank Policy Research Department Working Paper No. 2772, Washington, DC.

Leite, C. and M. Weidmann, 1999, 'Does Mother Nature Corrupt? Natural Resources, Corruption and Economic Growth', IMF Working paper WP/99/85, Washington, DC.

Mauro, P., 1995, 'Corruption and Growth', *Quarterly Journal of Economics*, 90, 681–712.

Pinto, B., 1987, 'Nigeria During and After the Oil Boom: A Policy Comparison with Indonesia', *The World Bank Economic Review*, 1 (3), 419–445.

Reinhart, C.M. and K. Rogoff, 2002, 'The Modern History of Exchange Rate Arrangements: A Reinterpretation,' National Bureau of Economic Research Working Paper No. 8963.

Rodrik, D., A. Subramanian and F. Trebbi, 2002, 'Institutions Rule: The Primacy of Institutions Over Integration and Geography in Development', National Bureau of Economic Research Working Paper No. 9305.

Sachs, J. and A. Warner, 1995, 'Natural Resource Abundance and Economic Growth', in G. Meier and J. Rauch (eds), *Leading Issues in Economic Development*, New York: Oxford University Press.

Sala-i-Martin, Xavier, 2003, 'Estimating Poverty from the World Distribution of Consumption', mimeo, Columbia University.

Sala-i-Martin, Xavier, Gernot Doppelhofer and Ronald Miller, 2003, 'Determinants of Long-Term Growth: A Bayesian Averaging of Classical Estimates (BACE) Approach', *American Economic Review* (forthcoming).

Sen, A., 1999, *Development as Freedom*, New York: Norton.

Tornell, A. and P. Lane, 1999, 'Voracity and Growth', *American Economic Review*, 89, 22–46.

4

Modelling Policy Options for Nigeria: Fiscal Responsibility, Monetary Credibility, and Regional Integration[1]

Xavier Debrun, Paul Masson and Catherine Pattillo

4.1 Introduction

As in many other developing economies, establishing a low inflation environment has been a challenge in Nigeria; and ways to improve the formulation and implementation of monetary policy have been at the forefront of the policy debate. An array of institutional reforms expected to foster the credibility of a commitment to price stability could potentially be envisaged. In this chapter, we focus on two alternative reform paths currently under discussion, namely the formation of a monetary union with neighbouring countries, and strengthening the independence of the Central Bank while keeping a national currency. In contrast to most of the existing literature, our analysis is based on a model that incorporates two types of distortions leading to excessive inflation: the desire to stimulate output and the need to finance government spending. The model clarifies how the two specific policy frameworks considered here might remedy those problems. While both options can potentially yield significant credibility gains, the analysis points to the importance of capitalizing on the recent record of improved fiscal discipline. Specifically, structural fiscal reforms that would improve expenditure efficiency, and preclude interference between the conduct of monetary policy and public finances, appear to deliver significant credibility gains.

An objective of Nigerian policy has been to promote monetary cooperation with neighbouring countries, and the Obasanjo administration has been instrumental in pushing forward plans to create a common currency among the members of ECOWAS that are not presently part of the West African Economic and Monetary Union, or WAEMU. Countries in the WAEMU[2] share a common currency, the CFA franc, which is pegged to the euro through a financial arrangement with the French treasury. The non-WAEMU countries,[3] in particular Nigeria, Ghana, the Gambia, Guinea and Sierra Leone, aim to adopt a common currency by 2009. That project however has already been subject to several delays, since it was originally planned for 2003. The intention is to create a common currency area (the West African Monetary Zone, or WAMZ) among the above five countries, and eventually to merge it with the WAEMU to form a single-currency area for the whole of ECOWAS. At the same time, there is increasing interest in domestic monetary reform that would make the Central Bank more independent and clarify its mandate to target low inflation, thus making it more accountable.

The starting point for this chapter's formal analysis is the standard inflationary bias of national policy-makers who are unable to credibly commit to optimal monetary and fiscal policies. A key dimension of the model is that monetary authorities internalize public finance motives to generate inflation. To the extent that the socially optimal inflation tax is likely to be positive but low, there is a priori no reason for a central banker to completely ignore public finances. One problem, however, is that, if the monetary authorities are subject to political interference, they can be forced to raise the inflation tax in order to finance socially unproductive spending, resulting in a 'political' inflation bias. This chapter's model suggests that the effect of joining a regional monetary union is to dilute political interference: even if a regional central bank is still subject to the financing pressures from its members, the impact of any single government on monetary decisions is arguably less than if the latter were made by purely national central bankers. Moreover, conflicting demands by different member states may cancel out to the benefit of all.

The other option this chapter considers for fostering the credibility of a central bank's commitment to low (optimal) inflation is to make it more independent – that is formally insulated from political pressures. An independent central bank should in principle be more able to remain focused on the overarching objective of price stability. This requires institutional changes – legal, perhaps constitutional – that introduce (i) guarantees against political interference in regular monetary policy decisions, (ii) a mandate clarifying the objective(s) assigned to monetary policy and (iii) mechanisms by which the central bankers are held accountable for their actions.

This chapter provides a model-based assessment of the costs and benefits for Nigeria of the proposed regional monetary union, using a simple theoretical framework that includes the monetary policy commitment problems, traditional Optimum Currency Area (OCA) arguments, as well as new features particularly relevant for West Africa and Nigeria. The framework allows us to discuss the relationship between the two different and potentially complementary 'agencies of restraint': regional monetary union and an independent central bank with an inflation target. The model assumes the existence of a wedge between, on the one hand, public spending on socially beneficial items and, on the other hand, government resources stemming from distorting taxes, seigniorage, and other revenues, such as rents extracted from natural resources. That wedge reflects the possibility that some policy-makers or bureaucrats channel public funds toward projects that end up being socially useless, or that part of the revenues levied through distorting tax instruments is wasted in inefficient tax collection mechanisms.[4] As a result, the financing needs corresponding to a given level of productive public expenditure are artificially inflated. Politically dependent central banks could therefore be forced to accommodate higher financing needs by extracting suboptimally high seigniorage revenues. The analysis illustrates the point that differences in fiscal distortions affect incentives for Nigeria and the other countries to join a monetary union (WAMZ, or an ECOWAS-wide union), and the willingness of members in an existing monetary union (WAEMU) to accept new entrants.

It is important to keep in mind that the policy options investigated within the context of the model – regional monetary union and greater central bank independence – are only two among an array of possibilities. Also, our theoretical model emphasizes credibility issues. Institutional reforms affecting policy-makers' motivations therefore tend to be highly valued. Even though the model incorporates the costs of monetary unification as spelled out in the traditional OCA literature (through the asymmetry of terms-of-trade shocks), the relative weight of these costs in the welfare assessment is inevitably lower than in a standard OCA model. This is especially the case here as our model is calibrated for countries with at best a short record of macroeconomic stability. Also, the outcomes depend on estimates of unobservable variables, including in this case the extent of fiscal 'distortions'. Hence, the chapter should be viewed as an attempt to clarify first-order trade-offs between two specific policy options under discussion, and *not* as a normative exercise supporting either one of them. This chapter does not make policy recommendations.

4.2 Outline of the argument

Before proceeding to present in detail the model and results, it is useful to summarize some of our premises on the environment for monetary policy in Nigeria, assumptions and questions raised in the chapter.

As argued below, until recently monetary policy in Nigeria was severely constrained by fiscal dominance and volatility, the assignment of multiple objectives to the Central Bank, and limited Central Bank independence, as well as by other institutional and technical factors. Volatility of oil and fiscal revenues contributes to large liquidity shocks. Management of these liquidity surprises in an environment where the government could finance large budget deficits by automatic borrowing from the Central Bank at below market-clearing interest rates made the conduct of monetary policy very difficult, contributing to a history of high and volatile inflation (Batini, 2004).

The environment has now changed. The government's success in implementing the NEEDS reform programme, the adherence to an oil-based fiscal rule at all three levels of government, other fiscal reforms (discussed in other chapters in the current volume) and the recent banking sector consolidation have dramatically improved macroeconomic policy management, and have created the potential for more effective monetary policy.

Given this background, the chapter undertakes a theoretical analysis of two institutional changes that could potentially help Nigeria credibly strengthen its commitment to price stability. One alternative is that Nigeria could adopt a strategy geared at reforming monetary institutions: increasing legal, operational and instrumental independence of the Central Bank, continued strengthening of the conditions and conduct of monetary policy, and gradually moving toward an inflation-targeting regime. How can this option be compared with another proposal that has been officially supported (although the degree of high-level commitment is not clear), namely the planned WAMZ project?

This chapter addresses these issues by setting up and simulating a model to shed light on the following questions: could a regional monetary union have net benefits for Nigeria, and strengthen the commitment to price stability? If so, is the monetary union (either with other WAMZ members or with the whole of ECOWAS) feasible in the sense that other countries could also benefit and so would 'vote' to join? We discuss below the model's highlighting of fiscal distortions, so that members do not exert pressures for an overly expansionary monetary stance of the regional common central bank. If the monetary union is not currently feasible, what scale of further fiscal reforms would increase Nigeria's attractiveness as the natural anchor for a sustainable regional monetary union? As discussed below, fiscal reform in the context of this model means lasting improvements to public financial management, the composition and efficiency of expenditure and tax administration associated with strengthened fiscal institutions, all of which support a durable commitment to fiscal discipline. Turning to the option of reforming domestic monetary institutions, what degree of improvement in the Central Bank independence is needed to gain a similar benefit to that conferred by the discipline of a monetary union?

In the model discussed below, monetary unification brings about benefits which are similar in nature (though not necessarily in size) to those arising from reforming monetary institutions. This is so because monetary policy is credibly delegated to a regional central bank that is by its very design less dependent on domestic politics in any one country than a purely national institution. Hence, our analysis suggests that the monetary union and inflation-targeting independent central bank options can be considered as substitutes because each of them potentially leads to lower inflation and higher welfare. It can be argued, however, that they may also be complements. Stronger monetary institutions in Nigeria could make the monetary union project more attractive to the other countries in the region, if that credibility and independence from government interference also applied to Nigeria's representatives at the regional central bank. We do not treat issues that may also be relevant to a new regional institution, namely, the need for it to acquire credibility on its own (posing serious challenges),[5] and the real possibility that the regional institution would not command the same public respect as do national ones. In any case, in the context of the model, reforming monetary institutions therefore appears to be a win–win strategy: beneficial if in the longer run Nigeria moves to an inflation-targeting regime, or if the WAMZ project does in fact proceed. To date, the WAMZ countries have not demonstrated significant political will to move forward with the project, and the countries – including Nigeria – are generally silent in their national economic programmes on the implications of their policies for the agreed convergence process and other commitments to the transition programme. There is, however, some possibility that the WAMZ may be created, prompting this chapter's analysis.

The model that we use to analyse the potential monetary union captures familiar arguments in the optimum currency area literature, but identifies another important asymmetry: political distortions affecting fiscal policy decisions. The regional central bank is assumed not to be fully independent, but to set monetary policy to reflect *average* conditions (including financing needs inclusive of fiscal distortions) in the region. As a result, countries that are very different with respect to fiscal distortions would be unattractive partners for a monetary union, because the central bank would produce undesirable outcomes for some, or all, of them. A key linkage in the model is the effect of higher financing needs (including those motivated by wasteful spending) on inflation and taxes. The model recognizes that the government also has access to non-distorting revenues: more specifically in Nigeria's case, the rents extracted from natural resource endowments.

4.3 Institutional background

4.3.1 The WAMZ project

As outlined above, five ECOWAS countries, including Nigeria, have declared their intention to proceed to a monetary union, the WAMZ, as a first step toward a wider ECOWAS monetary union that would merge the WAMZ with the CFA franc zone countries in the WAEMU. The launch date for the WAMZ's common currency, initially set for 2003, was postponed to July 2005, and has been subsequently postponed until December 2009 because the WAMZ member states failed to achieve the convergence criteria.

A study by the West African Monetary Institute (WAMI), an institution set up to oversee the transition process to a monetary union and serve as a precursor to a common central bank, found that three main factors contributed to limited progress toward the monetary union objective during 2000–2004. These include constraints on macroeconomic convergence – largely because of fiscal dominance problems in a number of countries, but also relating to other fragilities of the economies, and the lingering effect of conflicts; the slow pace of economic policy harmonization; and the inability of countries to meet their financial obligations to the monetary union programme. These constraints reflect problems in macroeconomic policy management, and a lack of political will to push forward with the project. For example, although a Forum of Finance Ministers to coordinate fiscal policies met numerous times during the period, participation of finance ministers was poor, and there were no effective follow-ups to implement the recommendations of the forum.

The zone has set four primary convergence criteria that are prerequisites for entry into the monetary union: single-digit inflation; a fiscal deficit to GDP ratio (excluding grants) of 4 per cent or less; central bank financing of the fiscal deficit as a percentage of the previous year's tax revenue of 10 per cent or less; and gross international reserves equal to three months of imports or more. Progress on the primary convergence criteria has been mixed, based on end-2005 data.[6] Six secondary criteria are designed to facilitate achievement of the primary criteria and do not have to be met for the launch to take place. These include a positive real interest rate, a stable real exchange rate, the settlement of all public domestic arrears, targets for public investment and tax collection, and a ceiling on public wage expenditure.

4.3.2 Monetary policy and exchange rate regimes in Nigeria

Whereas the stated goals of monetary policy in Nigeria are output growth and low inflation, in the pre-NEEDS reform period, monetary policy was severely complicated by the legal, institutional and policy environment. The root of the problem was clearly the fiscal dominance and volatility associated with a highly expansionary fiscal stance. But the effectiveness of monetary policy was also hampered by the lack of central bank independence; the pursuit of multiple and often conflicting goals in addition to stated aims, such as interest rate stability, exchange rate stabilization, private sector credit growth, and strengthening the banking system; underdeveloped financial markets and instruments; banking sector unsoundness; and exchange rate inflexibility that made it more difficult to respond to shocks (IMF, 2003). In addition, the government's heavy reliance on Central Bank credit compromised the Central Bank's control of reserve money.

Operational and technical difficulties also impeded the effectiveness of monetary policy. The Central Bank could not meet one of its primary challenges of managing large liquidity injections originating from expansionary fiscal operations, given its involvement in the treasury bill market in a manner that limited interest rate movements, and a weak liquidity forecasting system.

The NEEDS reform package, including the fiscal reforms, and the more recent banking sector consolidation have dramatically changed the environment for monetary policy. Other specific reforms have helped improve monetary policy effectiveness, such as the movement to daily open market operations, and the gradual shift to market clearing interest rates in the government securities market.

But the management of liquidity in the recent period of booming oil revenues remains challenging. Substantial liquidity expansion resulted in a surge in inflation to the 20–30 per cent range in mid-2005, following which the Central Bank successfully tightened and brought down inflation through issuance of Central Bank and treasury bills, and special foreign exchange sales. In addition, steps have been taken to improve liquidity management capacities, such as the establishment of a monetary policy department, and a monetary policy implementation committee within the Central Bank. These steps are leading to tangible improvements in the effectiveness of monetary policy. The IMF has also encouraged the Central Bank to consider more far-reaching reforms such as phasing out the government's overdraft facility, and adoption of a proactive and forward-looking framework (IMF, 2005). These reforms could support the aim of moving, once conditions are judged right, toward an inflation-targeting regime.

Nigeria has had a long history of attempted exchange rate reforms aimed at a more flexible official nominal rate, reducing market segmentation and lowering the significant administrative and documentation requirements. Up until recently, these reforms have been largely unsuccessful because of a host of factors, including inconsistent monetary and exchange rate policies – alongside fiscal dominance, a weak banking system, the desire for a strong and stable nominal exchange rate, and the difficulties of selling the government's oil revenues to the market. Since 1986 there have been numerous regime changes: shifting between various types of dual markets (auctions, interbank markets, official rates, with restrictions on the types of transactions in each market) and administered rates, with continued existence of separate bureaux de change and parallel markets. At end-2005, the system included a retail, multiple-price Dutch Auction System (DAS) and an interbank market, together with the bureau de change and parallel market.

Following the major banking consolidation, the environment has become significantly more conducive for effective exchange market reform in 2006. In February 2006 a new wholesale DAS with free exchange of foreign exchange to the interbank market was established. Whereas the spread between the parallel market and the DAS/interbank rates had widened at the end of 2005, since mid-2006 the rates have been converging, following measures to increase foreign currency supply and extend official market access to the bureau de change.

4.4 Modelling institutional reform and regional integration

To assess the effects of alternative institutional frameworks on policy outcomes, we use a simple model that allows for an explicit characterization of time-consistent (that is, credible) monetary and fiscal policies under these different regimes. The model is a variant of the one proposed in Debrun *et al.* (2005) – hereafter DMP. In line with the early literature on the European Monetary Union, DMP emphasize the contribution of macroeconomic institutions to the credibility of a commitment to low inflation (see Martin, 1995; Beetsma and Bovenberg, 1998, 1999).[7] Conceptually, the solution to commitment problems is indeed central in characterizing desirable macroeconomic frameworks, whereas in practice the considerable progress achieved worldwide in controlling inflation can be partly attributed to successful institutional reforms.[8] As suggested above, that approach seems particularly relevant in the African context, where the risks to macroeconomic stability and the need for further institutional reforms are generally deemed higher than elsewhere.

4.4.1 The model

The DMP model considers a static, *n*-good, *n*-country economic area assumed to be small vis-à-vis the rest of the world so that policy-makers need not worry about the extra-regional consequences of their choices. The basic equations are spelled out in Table 4.1.[9] Additional details can also be found in DMP.

Countries differ only by the size of output (y_i), the propensity of their governments to spend public resources on socially wasteful projects (δ_i), the rent

Table 4.1 The DMP model in a nutshell (benchmark case of dependent central banks)

Basic equations (national policy-making)		
Supply function (Phillips curve)	$y_i = y_N + c\left(\pi_i - \pi_i^e - \tau_i\right) - \sum_{k \neq i, k=1}^{n} \theta_{i,k} c\left(\pi_k - \pi_k^e\right) + \varepsilon_i$, i=1,..., n	(4.1)
One-period budget constraint	$g_i = \bar{\rho}_i + \mu\pi_i + \tau_i - \delta_i$	(4.2)
Government's utility function	$U_i^G = \frac{1}{2}\left\{ -a\left(\pi_i - \pi\left(\varepsilon_i\right)\right)^2 - b\tau_i^2 - \gamma\left(g_i - g_i\right)^2 \right\} + y_i$	(4.3)
Trade-off between output and inflation variability	$\pi(\varepsilon_i) = -\eta\varepsilon_i$, so that $\pi(0) = 0$ and $\pi'_{\varepsilon_i} < 0$	(4.4)
Equation relevant in a monetary union M		
Phillips curve faced by the common central bank for each member of M	$y_i = y_N + c\left(1 - \theta_i^M\right)\left(\pi_M - \pi_M^e\right) - c\tau_i - \sum_{k \notin M} \theta_{i,k} c\left(\pi_k - \pi_k^e\right) + \varepsilon_i$, $\forall i \in M$, with $\theta_i^M = \sum_{k \in M} \theta_{i,k}$	(4.1′)

Key variables and parameters

π_i	Inflation rate in country *i*. A superscript 'e' designates a rationally expected value
y_i	Logarithm of output
y_N	Logarithm of the natural level of output at zero taxation. Without loss of generality, we assume $y_N = 0$
τ_i	Ad valorem corporate income tax rate (also tax revenues in per cent of output)
$\theta_{i,k}$	Marginal effect of monetary policy in country *k* on output in country *i*
ε_i	Terms-of-trade shock (zero-mean, transitory, and with finite variance)
g_i	Socially beneficial government expenditure in percentage of output
μ	Inflation tax base in percentage of output
$\bar{\rho}_i$	Permanent non-tax revenue from natural resource endowment in percentage of output
δ_i	Funds diverted from socially beneficial government expenditure in percentage of output
η	Relative preference for output stability against inflation stability
U_i^C	Utility function of a 'committed' agent (i.e. indifferent to the level of output y_i)

extracted (in a non-distorting way) from natural resource endowments ($\bar{\rho}_i$) and the random shocks (ε_i) affecting output. Output responds to monetary impulses (unexpected inflation stimulates activity, for instance, because nominal wages are set by contract before policies are decided) and to changes in tax rates (a higher rate τ_i reduces output). National monetary policies affect economic activity in other countries of the region, and that externality is negative: a monetary expansion (or devaluation) by one country reduces output in the other countries of the region. DMP discuss possible rationales for negative monetary policy externalities as modelled here, and they show that the magnitude of bilateral spillovers is proportional to the intensity of trade relations between two countries ($\theta_{i,k}$).

On the fiscal side, no accumulation of public debt is allowed, forcing revenues to match expenditure (Alesina and Tabellini, 1987). Introducing public debt would only complicate the formal analysis without qualitatively affecting our conclusions. In contrast to monetary decisions, fiscal policy changes have no direct spillover effects.

In the benchmark case of politically dependent central banks, governments are assumed to choose both monetary and fiscal policies that minimize deviations of the effective tax rate, public expenditure and inflation from specific objectives (respectively 0, g and $\pi(\varepsilon)$, see equation (4.3) in Table 4.1). Those objectives are non-negative constants except for inflation, which fluctuates to partly accommodate supply shocks. In other words, the authorities tolerate higher inflation in the face of an adverse shock, and aim at lower inflation in case of a positive shock. This captures the authorities' preferred trade-off between the *variability* of inflation and that of output. Finally, governments also care about the *level* of output, welcoming expansions and disliking contractions – technically the marginal utility of an increase in output is constant (and equal to 1, for simplicity).

The fact that monetary policy is also determined by fiscal objectives raises the issue of how one should formally characterize 'fiscal dominance' in the context of this model. As shown below, the Alesina–Tabellini (1987) framework treats inflation as any other source of distortive taxation. As a result, the existence of a link between public expenditure objectives and inflation is a feature of the socially optimal policy mix that even a perfectly independent central bank should take into account. By contrast, the fact that the government's financing need is distorted by δ_i (a pure dead weight loss) should not affect the decisions of an independent central bank. We therefore define fiscal dominance as the possibility for the government to force the central bank to take into account the financing of δ_i when setting inflation.

4.4.2 Equilibrium policies: discretion vs commitment

Our specification of policy-makers' objectives implies that they find the 'natural' level of output y_N too low. The first reason is that $y_N = 0$ whereas policy-makers welcome $y_N>0$ (Barro and Gordon, 1983), and the second that productive public expenditure has to be financed with taxes that bring the natural output level below y_N (Alesina and Tabellini, 1987).[10] The consequence is a systematic incentive to stimulate economic activity through expansionary monetary policies. As rational private agents understand that, they expect the authorities to deliver the inflation rate beyond which the marginal utility gain of a monetary expansion (increase in output) would be lower than the marginal cost of extra inflation. To prevent actual output from falling below its natural level, the best response of the monetary authorities is to deliver inflation in line with agents' expectations. In that case, equilibrium inflation is excessive, and any *ex ante* promise to keep it lower lacks credibility. The high-inflation equilibrium is typical of *discretionary* policy-making whereby policy-makers cannot credibly *commit ex ante* to deliver the socially optimal (low) inflation rate.

How does the inflationary bias impact discretionary fiscal policy? In comparison to the commitment solution, higher inflation boosts seigniorage revenues, which in turn allows the government to spend more on socially beneficial programmes and to tax less. The natural output level thus receives an indirect stimulus from lax monetary policy. However, the fiscal gains from higher inflation are of second order, and they cannot offset the first-order impact of excessive inflation on welfare.

In addition to the distortions arising from the lack of commitment, we introduce a political/institutional distortion δ_i that captures the propensity of policy-makers or government officials to allocate resources to socially wasteful projects – for instance, the white elephants – or to siphon off public funds to pursue private ends. Hence for a given level of productive public spending, g_i, financing needs increase, with inevitable repercussions on monetary, tax and expenditure decisions.

In equilibrium and all other things equal, more severe political distortions lead to higher inflation and tax rates, and lower productive expenditure. A key determinant of equilibrium policies is indeed the amount of resources (in terms of tax and seigniorage revenues) required to deliver the socially optimal level of productive expenditure. Specifically, in order to deliver desirable public goods and services equivalent to g_i, a government must actually find $g_i + \delta_i - \bar{\rho}_i$ in financing. We term this aggregate the 'unconstrained financing needs' or UFN. The latter includes the political dead weight loss δ_i but it excludes $\bar{\rho}_i$, a permanent, non-distorting source of revenue such as the rent extracted from natural resources.

Clearly, only structural fiscal reforms – aimed at increasing the accountability of decision-makers, fighting corruption and improving the efficiency of public administrations – can effectively address these political distortions.

4.4.3 Monetary reforms to improve the policy mix

How can we reduce equilibrium inflation in the absence of an intrinsic capacity to commit to the socially optimal policy? A vast literature has mushroomed around that question, suggesting that the inflationary bias can be reduced if monetary policy is *delegated* to an agency that is not subject to the same motivations as policy-makers themselves (Rogoff, 1985).[11] Concretely, that agency is an independent central bank whose objective function reflects a specific mandate assigned by the government.

Inflation targeting (IT) has now become the most common type of monetary policy framework whereby independent central banks that receive operational independence to exert full discretion on monetary policy are held directly accountable for delivering improved outcomes in terms of price stability. The inflation target (or range), often specified by the government, is then the benchmark against which the central banker's performance can be assessed. In the present model, inflation targeting would amount to assuming the appointment of a central banker who would be specifically instructed to deliver lower inflation. Since an independent central bank has no more intrinsic commitment capacity than elected policy-makers themselves, the successful appointee should be either one with more conservative views on inflation than the elected policy-maker, or at a bare minimum one that would respond to specific incentives to hold such views.[12]

The simplest way to model the central banker's aversion to inflation in a context of IT is to assume that the appointee has a lower inflation objective than society's at large (see Svensson, 1997): $\pi_{CB} = \bar{\pi}_i - \eta\varepsilon_i$. As can be seen from Table 4.2, appropriately setting $\bar{\pi}_i < 0$ ensures that the central bank will credibly deliver lower inflation on average while preserving the optimal trade-off between inflation variability and output variability (η is the same for the central banker as for an elected policy-maker). All that is needed is an incentive structure encouraging the central banker to prefer lower inflation more than elected policy-makers (or alternatively, an incentive structure that does not discourage such preference if it corresponds to a natural inclination of the appointee).

That said, if it is not exceedingly costly for a government to ignore or to interpret liberally the legal guarantees on political independence, IT may not deliver the expected reduction in inflation (McCallum, 1995). Here there is, in our view, a need to distinguish between the standard Barro–Gordon bias and our political inflation bias reflecting the dead weight loss δ_i on public expenditure. As regards the former, it is now widely accepted in policy circles worldwide that short-term monetary stimuli of economic activity are counterproductive in the longer run. This is even more likely to be the case in the African context, where the transmission channel of monetary policy to activity is arguably weaker and less certain than elsewhere. Hence, political pressures are less likely to be motivated by the desire to stimulate the economy than by the willingness to cover the government's financing needs.

Concretely, a weak enforcement of the institutional guarantees on independence, or biased appointment procedures whereby only government cronies would have a chance to be selected as central banker, may well allow a political inflation bias to survive. We illustrate this in Table 4.2, assuming that some features of fiscal dominance may survive the IT regime, preventing it from delivering the socially optimal inflation rate. Hence, a central bank that remains under influence of the government (λ_i is close to 0) could not reduce the political component of the inflationary bias (see Table 4.2).

Importantly, our model shows that IT with a fully independent central bank does not imply the appointment of an absolute inflation hawk. Indeed, aside from inflation, our central banker shares all the objectives of society and is consequently willing to operate socially optimal trade-offs among competing objectives. However, the mandate should ensure that he or she will face appropriate incentives to keep average inflation in line with the social optimum. This not only implies that he or she should be rewarded for holding more conservative views than society on what the appropriate level of inflation should be, but that he or she should also be protected by strict guarantees against fiscal dominance.

As indicated above, the main drawback of the central bank independence argument is that monetary delegation alone does not change the underlying motivations of governments. Independence itself could thus be threatened if the temptation to engineer a monetary expansion remains larger than the cost of reverting to pure discretion (McCallum, 1995). In other words, central bank independence can help alleviate the inflationary bias only if the costs of removing such independence (or of breaking the law) are large enough. In particular, countries with a long history of instability and failed institutional reforms may find it harder to reduce their inflationary bias because the new monetary regime is more likely to lack credibility.

If national reform is impossible or insufficiently credible, one alternative is to seek a credible nominal anchor outside national borders through the unilateral adoption of a foreign currency as the only legal tender (official dollarization), or the formation of a regional monetary union. We focus on the latter since that option is currently being given serious consideration.

A central feature of the DMP model is that monetary unification brings about some benefits akin to the credible delegation of monetary policy to an independent central bank, though not necessarily to the same extent. In comparison to purely national monetary policies, a regional policy is indeed less effective to stimulate output in individual countries because there are no gains to expect from a depreciation of the national currency vis-à-vis trading partners in the region. The term θ_A^M in equation (4.9) of Table 4.2 captures the extent of the monetary policy externalities internalized through participation in a hypothetical monetary union *M*. It is immediately evident that a higher θ_A^M (reflecting extended membership or more intense trade linkages among member states) will ensure that average equilibrium inflation in the monetary union will be lower. Specifically, the impact of θ_A^M on equilibrium inflation is akin to setting a negative value for $\bar{\pi}_i$ under an IT regime.

The credibility gains arising from regional monetary integration increase with the initial seriousness of the inflationary bias (which depends upon *c*, the effectiveness of monetary policy, *b*, the relative reluctance to tax, and γ, the preference for public spending), and with the determinants of θ_A^M, namely the size of the union and the intensity of intra-regional trade linkages. Hence, all other things being equal, the model implies that a large group of high-inflation countries with strong regional trade linkages would expect to gain more from monetary unification than a small group of low-inflation countries with limited regional trade. Again, the implicit assumption underlying that argument is that a regional monetary union is less easily reversible than a national reform that reduced π_{CB} and λ_i.

Table 4.2 Inflation rates under alternative monetary regimes

Monetary regime	**Equilibrium inflation**	
Autonomy (country *i*)		
Social optimum (without political distortion and in the absence of commitment problems, best)	$\pi_i^{***} = \frac{\gamma\mu b}{\Lambda}\left[g_i - \bar{\rho}_i\right] + \frac{\gamma\mu}{\Lambda}c - \frac{a\left(b+\gamma\right)\eta}{\Lambda}\varepsilon_i$, with $\Lambda = a\left(b+\gamma\right) + \gamma\mu^2 b > 0$	(4.5)
Commitment solution (with political distortion, second-best)	$\pi_i^{**} = \pi_i^{***} + \frac{\gamma\mu b}{\Lambda}\delta_i$	(4.6)
Equilibrium (time-consistent) inflation without IT	$\pi_i^{*} = \pi_i^{**} + \frac{\left(b+\gamma\right)}{\Lambda}c$	(4.7)

IT solution (equilibrium time-consistent inflation with possibility of residual fiscal dominance)	$\pi_i^{IT} = \pi_i^{**} + \frac{(b+\gamma)}{\Lambda} c + \frac{a(b+\gamma)}{\Lambda} \bar{\bar{\pi}}_i$	(4.8)
	$\bar{\bar{\pi}}_i^* = -\left[\frac{c}{a} + \frac{\lambda_i \gamma \mu b}{a\ (b+\gamma)} \delta_i \right] \Rightarrow \pi_i^{IT} = \pi_i^{***} + (1-\lambda_i) \frac{\gamma \mu b}{\Lambda} \delta_i$, with	
	$0 \leq \lambda_i \leq 1$, the strength of guarantees against fiscal dominance	
Monetary Union M without IT or precommitment	$\pi_i^{M*} = \frac{\gamma \mu b}{\Lambda} (UFN_A^M) + \frac{(1-\theta_A^M)\ (b+\gamma) + \gamma\mu}{\Lambda} c - \frac{a(b+\gamma)\eta}{\Lambda} \varepsilon_A^M$,	
	for all $i \in M$, with $x_A^M = \sum_{i \in M} \omega_i^M x_i$, for $x \in \{\ UFN, \theta, \varepsilon\ \}$	(4.9)
	(cross-country, output-weighted averages within M) so that $\pi_A^{M*} = \pi_A^* - \frac{\theta_A^M (b+\gamma)}{\Lambda} c$	

In particular, a regional central bank could pursue a specific mandate with greater independence because a joint decision by many different countries would be required to change that mandate. Of course, it leaves out any considerations related to the serious challenges that a new institution without a track record might face in acquiring credibility and generating public support for low inflation across the region.

The obvious drawback of the monetary integration strategy is that it also brings about costs that may exceed the credibility gains unless certain conditions are met. Clearly, the case where all countries jointly maximize the benefits from joining is one of countries with identical UFNs subject to the same terms-of-trade shocks ($\varepsilon_i = \varepsilon_j = \varepsilon_A^M$ for all $i \neq j$ in *M*). In such a configuration, the loss of monetary autonomy does not entail any cost because the common monetary policy fits everyone's needs, in terms both of optimal seigniorage and of macroeconomic stabilization. But monetary unification entails costs when potential members have different terms-of-trade shocks and UFNs – emphasized more in this chapter. DMP (2005) also highlight the welfare cost to monetary unification given asymmetry of terms-of-trade shocks; particularly since as an oil producer Nigeria's terms of trade differ from those of its neighbours.

Does this mean that no monetary union could ever emerge in a group of countries that widely differ in terms-of-trade disturbances, political distortions, resource endowments or social spending targets? In contrast to the standard literature, the DMP model provides a nuanced answer because structural cross-country differences (that is, all except supply disturbances)[13] do not necessarily reduce the net gains from monetary unification for all member states. On the one hand, differences in UFNs are a source of cost because the union-wide inflation rate will only by chance coincide with a country's desired trade-off between seigniorage and tax revenues. On the other hand, differences in UFNs may also be a source of gains depending on the country's position in the distribution of UFNs. More specifically, a government with a relatively high UFN may get additional gains from participating in a monetary union with low-UFN neighbours (that is countries with low spending targets, low political distortions and/or high resource endowments) because the latter, especially if they are large, exert a restraining influence on the regional central bank. From the point of view of high-UFN members, that 'imported' monetary restraint further reduces the inflationary bias under autonomy.

The mirror image of the above is that low-UFN members will incur additional losses stemming from the excessive demands of the others for monetary financing, pushing them away from their hypothetical commitment solution. Since the pressure exerted by a country on the regional central bank is assumed to be proportional to its size, the joint cross-country distribution of sizes and UFNs is critical to determine the equilibrium configuration of monetary union(s) in the region. That consideration emerges very clearly from the calibration exercises discussed below.

Overall, the message from the DMP approach for the desirability of West African monetary unions is potentially less negative than analyses based solely on OCA criteria (such as Bayoumi and Ostry, 1997). The reason is that credibility issues arguably remain important in comparison to the stabilization function of monetary policy. Our approach also points to interesting complementarities between national reforms and the creation of a regional currency. For instance, the model implies that limits on the credible institutional reforms achievable at the national level (formally, one could think of limits on λ_i and $\bar{\pi}_i$) could make regional monetary integration more attractive, other things being equal. In particular, the participation of large countries that have successfully implemented stability-oriented macroeconomic framework (low UFN and low λ_i) could boost the gains of smaller member states facing greater difficulties to achieve such reforms on their own (for example, because of capacity constraints).[14] The next section discusses the calibration of the model under alternative monetary regimes for WAMZ and ECOWAS countries.

4.5 Estimating fiscal distortions

The DMP model emphasizes the effect of political/institutional distortions on the conduct of fiscal policy, including inefficiencies in tax collection, the appropriation of tax revenues by corrupt officials, and the allocation of government resources to socially wasteful projects. In equation (4.2), these are summarized by a wedge (δ_i) between actual government revenues (from taxes and seigniorage) and socially beneficial (or productive) government spending (g_i). Hence, for any given level of g_i, the corresponding financing need is δ_i per cent of GDP higher than it would be in the absence of such distortions and, in equilibrium, the budget constraint requires higher inflation and taxes.

The key fiscal aggregate in equilibrium is the UFN ($g_i + \delta_i - \bar{\rho}_i$) which also accounts for the fact that natural resource endowments may provide a steady stream of revenues that ease the pressure on conventional financing means (Table 4.2). In other words, the UFN captures the resources that the government must collect through taxes and seigniorage in order to finance the socially optimal level of productive spending g_i. Calibrating our model requires country-specific estimates of UFN, which proves challenging because neither g_i nor δ_i is directly observable. Our calibration exercises below therefore discuss the robustness of our results to alternative UFN estimates.

To have a sense of δ_i, we need to quantify the impact of institutions on socially beneficial spending. In line with our conjecture that δ_i is positive, the existing literature emphasizes a *diversion effect*. Specifically, poor institutions (including an inefficient and corrupt bureaucracy, weak law enforcement and the absence of democratic accountability) distort the composition of expenditure because policy-makers pay insufficient attention to productive public spending. Also, even if priorities are appropriate *ex ante*, capacity constraints undermine the execution of the often complex and skill-intensive programmes characterizing sectors such as health and education. Finally, although poor institutions may cause pure waste (due for instance to X-inefficiency in public administration) and thereby inflate actual expenditure without raising welfare, such inefficiencies further discourage the allocation of scarce resources to priority programmes. The empirical literature confirms that bad scores on various institutional dimensions are associated with *underspending* on these programmes (see for example Mauro, 1998, for education spending).

Turning to the data, a simple cross-country regression allows us to identify and eventually estimate the effect of institutional variables on socially beneficial public spending in Africa. We focus on the health sector,[15] and then extrapolate our results to total government expenditure. In a cross-section of 33 African countries (with 2003 data[16]), there is robust evidence that weak institutions are linked to significant underspending (Table 4.3), confirming the outcome of a similar exercise – but with older data – in DMP. Underspending seems to originate in poor scores for politico-institutional dimensions that are more likely to distort budget priorities (democratic accountability) and failures in budget execution (bureaucratic quality, and law and order).[17]

The empirical model allows an approximation of resource diversion in ECOWAS countries. The simplest and most transparent measure of diversion is to take the difference between the expenditure on health predicted by the model under the highest possible ranking of institutional quality, and actual outlays. By doing so, we implicitly assume that only 'perfect' institutions lead to zero diversion

Table 4.3 Public spending on health and institutional quality (33 African countries, dependent variable is public spending on health in percentage of GDP)

	2003		**Average 1998–2003**	
	Coefficient	**t-statistic**	**Coefficient**	**t-statistic (robust)**
Constant	–2.72	(–1.44)	0.76	(0.41)
Log of GDP per capita	0.29*	(1.90)	0.10	(0.49)
HIV prevalence above 10 per cent (dummy)	0.72**	(2.57)	1.15***	(3.84)
Infant mortality	0.01*	(1.79)	0.00	(–0.34)
Life expectancy	0.01	(0.60)	–0.01	(–0.26)
Corruption	**–0.22*****	**(–3.02)**	**–0.24*****	**(–2.79)**
Other institutions[a]	**0.50*****	**(5.38)**	**0.40*****	**(3.74)**
R^2	0.71		0.69	
DW statistic	1.46		2.20	
White Heteroskedasticity F-test	1.20		2.80**	

Superscripts *, ** and *** indicate that the null hypothesis that the corresponding coefficient is equal to zero is rejected at the 10, 5 and 1 per cent threshold, respectively.

a This is the simple average of ICRG scores for democratic accountability, bureaucratic quality, and law and order.

Sources: World Bank (World Development Indicators), The PRS Group (International Country Risk Guide), and authors' calculations.

Table 4.4 Expenditure on health: estimates of resource diversion and UFN (in percentage of GDP in 2003, unless indicated otherwise)

	Actual 2003	Diversion from health	Diversion in % of no diversion	Total government spending actual (1997-2003)	Total government spending UFN
Benin 1/	1.9	n.a.	n.a.	19.4	23.8
Burkina Faso	2.6	1.0	28.1	21.1	24.1
Cote d'Ivoire	1.0	2.4	70.5	19.9	26.9
Gambia, The	2.9	1.1	27.6	24.5	27.9
Ghana	1.4	1.8	55.3	27.8	35.5
Guinea	0.9	1.8	66.9	18.1	24.2
Guinea-Bissau	2.6	2.8	52.5	36.4	45.9
Mali	2.8	2.0	41.5	22.3	27.0
Niger	2.5	1.4	35.2	17.6	20.7
Nigeria 2/	1.3	1.5	53.9	27.6	35.0
Senegal	2.1	1.4	38.8	21.6	25.7
Sierra Leone	2.0	2.9	58.5	25.9	33.5
Togo	1.4	2.0	58.5	15.0	19.4
ECOWAS average	2.0	1.8	48.9	22.9	28.4
WAEMU average	2.0	1.7	45.4	19.6	23.9
WAMZ average	1.8	1.7	49.6	23.6	29.5

Sources: ICRG database (The PRS Group); World Development Indicators (World Bank); Regional Economic Outlooks (IMF).

Note: The cross-country regression is based on 2003 data and includes a constant, the log of GDP per capita, at PPP, an aggregate index of institutional quality (simple average of ICRG indices for democratic accountability, bureaucratic quality, and law and order, all rescaled on the 0-10 range), the ICRG index for corruption (rescaled as well), a dummy identifying countries with HIV/AIDS prevalence rate above 10 percent, life expectancy and infant mortality. The sample consists of 33 African countries and estimates were obtained by OLS.

1/ Institutional data are not available for Benin. The unconstrained financing need is calculated using WAEMU average diversion.

2/ To account for the role of oil and gas revenues, total expenditure was reduced by the lowest amount of oil revenues recorded over the period 1992-2005.

and maximal efficiency.[18] The second column of Table 4.4 shows the hypothetical increment that would be spent if indices for accountability, bureaucratic quality, corruption, and law and order were at their optimum. It appears that, in many countries, governments divert more than half of the resources they would 'ideally' be expected to spend on health (third column). There are also significant differences across countries.

Because social (and governments') objectives in terms of public spending (that is, g_i) are unobservable as well, actual public expenditure is used as a proxy of the desired level of socially beneficial spending. This amounts to assume that the population would ideally like government to allocate actual outlays fully to items it deems desirable, which seems both legitimate and plausible. We allow for a positive $\bar{\rho}_i$ in the case of Nigeria only because ample government revenues from oil and gas (between 11 and 37 per cent of GDP over the last decade) significantly reduce the pressure of government spending on taxation and inflation. Specifically, we subtract from actual spending 10.9 per cent of GDP, corresponding to the lowest oil revenues recorded during 1992–2005.[19]

The UFN is obtained by extrapolating the diversion effect observed for health. To account for the fact that governments are likely to face trade-offs among alternative priority programmes (for example resources could be reallocated from health to education, or infrastructure investment), we assume that the diversion affecting total expenditure is only half that for health. The UFN is thus obtained by increasing actual public spending (our proxy for g_i) by a factor:

$$\left(1+\frac{\delta_i^{Health}}{2\left(g_i^{Health}+\delta_i^{Health}\right)}\right)$$

4.6 Model-based evaluation of the proposed monetary unions for the WAMZ and ECOWAS vs greater Central Bank of Nigeria independence

In DMP (2005), we utilized the model to evaluate the welfare gains and losses from proceeding with a monetary union among the WAMZ countries, and also a wider ECOWAS monetary union. We redo that model calibration here, with a refined methodology and updated figures for the fiscal positions of potential member countries.[20] A key input is our estimates of UFN because they approximate the likely intensity of pressures exerted by fiscal authorities on monetary policy. For Nigeria, financing requirements are reduced in the model calibration because of oil revenues, but adjustment is made for the fact that oil revenues fluctuate greatly. We assume an estimate for sustainable oil revenue to be the minimum value, as a ratio to GDP, that prevailed over the 1992–2005 period. The resulting figure for UFN, 35 per cent of GDP for Nigeria, is considerably above the levels for other ECOWAS countries, except for Ghana, Guinea-Bissau and Sierra Leone.

The last two are small economies whose level of expenditure reflects the ravages of civil wars.

In this section, simulations for ECOWAS countries allow us to answer the following two questions. First, in the context of the model, could a monetary union with its neighbours be an improvement over the current situation for Nigeria, because it would credibly strengthen the commitment to maintain price stability? And second, would such a monetary union, either with other WAMZ countries or the whole of ECOWAS, be incentive-compatible for those countries?

Estimates of UFN come from Table 4.4 above, whereas the parameters of the model and the variances and covariances of terms-of-trade shocks (the standard optimum currency area measures of shock asymmetry) are borrowed from our earlier paper because they are unlikely to have changed much.

Table 4.5 gives the model's evaluation of the welfare consequences of forming a monetary union among the WAMZ countries. It also reports each country's share of the union's output (ω), correlations between each country's terms-of-trade shocks and the union's average, and the ratio of the union's average UFN to the country's value (ψ). It is important to bear in mind that this exercise rests on a comparison of hypothetical time-consistent monetary and fiscal policies under two alternative regimes, assumed to be sustainable: one of complete monetary discretion with a flexible exchange rate and the other a monetary union with a flexible exchange rate vis-à-vis outside countries. The welfare gains are computed as the log difference in GDP equivalents. Thus, the model simulates that a WAMZ monetary union would, according to those figures, imply a permanent welfare gain for Nigeria equivalent to 1.88 per cent of GDP (increase in the level, not its rate of growth), a modest but non-negligible amount that does not account for other potential benefits stemming from a common currency, such as a reduction in transaction costs. However, the simulations suggest that the WAMZ project might not be in the interest of the other countries, and could therefore experience further delays unless sufficient homogeneity in fiscal behaviours is credibly achieved. Specifically, while Ghana and Sierra Leone are estimated to have small gains – considerably less than Nigeria's – the Gambia and Guinea-Bissau would incur substantial losses because the lower UFN in these countries point to a greater potential to achieve low inflation on their own. Of course, the decision

Table 4.5 WAMZ monetary union: net benefits for participants[a]

Country	ω	Net gain[b]	Correlation	ψ
Gambia	0.0103	–0.0351	0.1298	1.2149
Ghana	0.1833	0.0075	–0.4325	0.9548
Guinea	0.1016	–0.0442	0.6109	1.4006
Nigeria	0.6870	0.0188	0.9912	0.9684
Sierra Leone	0.0178	0.0023	–0.3191	1.0118

a Parameter values: $a = 0.9657$; $b = 9.0759$; $\gamma = 1.7723$; $c = 1$; $\eta = 1$; $\mu = 0.50$; $\theta^\wedge = 0.0201$.
b Net gain relative to independent currencies.

to go ahead is likely to be as much the result of political forces as anticipation of economic gains, so that continued strong Nigerian advocacy of the project might well bring it to fruition.

Table 4.6 provides a similar model-based assessment of the wider ECOWAS monetary union. This project is more distant and how it would come about is unclear. Details of its implementation would have to be worked out because the monetary arrangements of the WAEMU and non-WAEMU countries are different. The WAEMU countries, in addition to sharing a common currency, also peg that currency to the euro and have strong ties both to France and to the other CFA franc zone, the CEMAC in central Africa. Merging WAEMU and WAMZ would mean re-examining the external peg and probably forgoing France's support, since that country and her EU partners are reluctant to see the extension of France's financial guarantees to a wider set of countries.

We assume that a potential ECOWAS monetary union would not be able to rely on that support, nor would it peg to the euro. We calculate the welfare from such a 'free-standing' monetary union compared to the current situation governing the currencies of ECOWAS countries, in particular membership in WAEMU on the one hand and independent currencies for the non-WAEMU members of ECOWAS. The model suggests that an ECOWAS monetary union could be beneficial for Nigeria and its fellow WAMZ members, but not for any of the WAEMU countries (Table 4.6). The reason is fundamentally Nigeria's higher UFN – representing distortions that inflate financing needs from a given level of productive public expenditure, and evaluated to take account of the fact that the currently

Table 4.6 ECOWAS monetary union: net benefits for participants[a]

Country	ω	Net gain[b]	Correlation	ψ
Benin	0.0340	–0.0163	0.2677	1.2756
Burkina Faso	0.0406	–0.0157	0.1979	1.2597
Côte d'Ivoire	0.1706	–0.0162	0.0508	1.1286
Mali	0.0407	–0.0152	0.1523	1.1244
Niger	0.0301	–0.0157	–0.2465	1.4666
Senegal	0.0749	–0.0154	0.3455	1.1813
Togo	0.0215	–0.0150	0.4255	1.5649
Gambia	0.0061	0.0179	0.2277	1.0881
Ghana	0.1078	0.0605	–0.2748	0.8552
Guinea	0.0597	0.0082	0.5914	1.2545
Nigeria	0.4037	0.0602	0.9429	0.8674
Sierra Leone	0.0104	0.0544	–0.1986	0.9062

a Parameter values as above except $\theta^A = 0.0591$.
b Net gain relative to WAEMU for WAEMU countries; net gain relative to independent currencies for remaining (WAMZ) countries.

high oil revenues in terms of GDP are unlikely to persist in the long-run. Nigeria's estimated UFN – about 35 per cent of GDP – is more than 10 percentage points above the average for WAEMU. Turning to the non-WAEMU countries, model simulations suggest that all of them could benefit from membership in an ECOWAS union, both because they have UFNs that are closer to Nigeria's and because they currently have independent currencies – so, unlike the WAEMU countries, they do not already benefit from the stability that a currency union provides. Even the Gambia and Guinea-Bissau, which would suffer a net welfare loss from membership in WAMZ, could derive net benefits from being part of a wider regional grouping like ECOWAS, where the asymmetries from Nigeria's membership would be partially diluted by the WAEMU countries.

While these results are broadly similar to the conclusions of the earlier analysis of DMP (2005), the present model simulations suggest slightly better prospects for welfare gains from creation of new monetary unions in West Africa. The progress that Nigeria has made in improving its institutions and reining in fiscal excesses lowers its UFN and, on that score, could make regional monetary unions more incentive compatible for ECOWAS countries.

In that context, then, we use the model to estimate the further reduction in the fiscal diversion estimate – which we assume would follow from continued structural fiscal reforms – that would be needed to make Nigeria an acceptable partner for all the countries in the monetary union. If each WAEMU country had a veto on admitting new members, this would be a precondition for the full ECOWAS monetary union to go ahead – in the absence of other quid pro quo, which of course might be available. Specifically, we calculate the reduction of the fiscal diversion estimate in Nigeria (keeping total expenditures constant) that would be needed to make the most unfavourably affected WAEMU country (Benin in Table 4.6) just indifferent between its current situation in WAEMU and sharing the common ECOWAS currency with Nigeria. The needed decline in fiscal distortions would involve a reduction in UFN from the current 35 per cent to 27.4 per cent. At that level, Côte d'Ivoire would be just indifferent between joining a full ECOWAS monetary union and the current WAEMU monetary union and all other WAEMU countries would gain slightly (Table 4.7).

A UFN figure of 27.4 per cent of GDP implies, at given actual spending (net of 'normal' resource revenues) equal to 27.6 per cent of GDP, a *negative* diversion estimate of –1.4 per cent. Given our assumption that the best a country can do is zero diversion, this would be impossible. However, our initial estimate of sustainable resource revenues may have been unduly conservative. Table 4.8 gives some possible alternatives. The top line does not adjust at all for oil revenues, and gives a very high UFN; this should be considered an upper bound. Below it is the estimate we used above, based on the minimum over the past decade and a half. Using instead *average* oil revenues gives quite a rosy picture. Even with no improvement of diversion, Nigeria would qualify as one of the countries with the lowest UFN, and therefore would not be an obstacle to creating the ECOWAS monetary union. But oil revenues are in fact very variable, so it seems preferable to use an estimate that is below the mean. Adjusting down by one standard deviation gives a figure

Table 4.7 ECOWAS monetary union: net benefits for participants[a] (when Nigeria's UFN = 27.4 per cent of GDP)

Country	ω	Net gain[b]	Correlation	ψ
Benin	0.0340	0.0003	0.2677	1.1466
Burkina Faso	0.0406	0.0009	0.1979	1.1324
Côte d'Ivoire	0.1706	0.0000	0.0508	1.0145
Mali	0.0407	0.0011	0.1523	1.0107
Niger	0.0301	0.0013	–0.2465	1.3184
Senegal	0.0749	0.0010	0.3455	1.0619
Togo	0.0215	0.0022	0.4255	1.4067
Gambia	0.0061	0.0340	0.2277	0.9781
Ghana	0.1078	0.0757	–0.2748	0.7687
Guinea	0.0597	0.0248	0.5914	1.1277
Nigeria	0.4037	0.0370	0.9429	0.9960
Sierra Leone	0.0104	0.0698	–0.1986	0.8146

a Parameter values as above and $\theta^{A} = 0.0591$.
b Net gain relative to WAEMU for WAEMU countries; net gain relative to independent currencies for remaining (WAMZ) countries.

for UFN that is only 2.5 percentage points above the maximum UFN that would make all other ECOWAS countries at least indifferent to Nigeria's membership. This figure would imply that Nigeria's diversion (as a proportion of no-diversion spending) would have to decline from the 53.9 per cent of Table 4.4 to 32.2 per cent to lower UFN to the threshold level of 27.4 per cent of GDP. That figure for diversion would put it below the WAEMU average (45.4 per cent) but above that of Burkina Faso (28.1 per cent) and the Gambia (27.6 per cent). This is a sizeable decrease, which could require considerable effort on Nigeria's part to achieve.

It must be stressed that, in our view, the reduction of the type of diversion modelled in this chapter embodies a whole set of potential fiscal reforms that might include better public expenditure management, fiscal accountability, improvements in tax administration and collection, and reduction of corruption.

Table 4.8 Nigeria: alternative calibrations of UFN (in percentage of GDP); diversion = 53.9 per cent

	Actual	UFN
Total expenditure	38.5	48.8
minus:		
minimum oil revenues (1992-2005)	27.6	35.0
average oil revenues (1992-2005)	14.1	18.0
average minus 1 SD (1992-2005)	23.6	29.9
average minus 2 SD (1992-2005)	33.0	41.9

Also, since it is the overall UFN that matters in our model for a country's attractiveness as a potential monetary union partner, one could hypothetically have assumed an equal percentage reduction in actual government spending. In Nigeria's case, our assumption is that reductions in the estimated fiscal distortions would not be associated with lower government spending, given that the current fiscal stance is judged as broadly appropriate and in line with the government's reform programme, and that the country faces pressing needs for improved infrastructure, health care and education (IMF, 2006). Rather, we assume an emphasis on improvements to the composition and effectiveness of that spending, as emphasized in the government reform programme.

We have modelled one alternative to the 'imported' monetary discipline emerging from a monetary union, namely for Nigeria to develop greater 'home-grown' discipline through the ability of an independent central bank to pre-commit monetary policy to less expansive policies. In the model given above, this involves decreasing λ through institutional reforms that reduce the temptation to stimulate output, and bolstering the independence of the central bank, removing the pressure to finance fiscal deficits. Such an analysis would suggest that, for the parameter constellation retained here, home-grown reforms would have a fairly significant impact on the equilibrium inflation rate. An equivalent gain would result from an increase in λ of 0.0591, the proportion of trade to GDP internalized in the monetary union.

4.7 Conclusion

We calibrated a model to assess the potential gains and losses from a WAMZ and an ECOWAS-wide monetary union. In the model, monetary integration reduces the inflationary bias from incentives to conduct overly expansive monetary policies. The model also includes a fiscal distortion that causes government to aim for financing that is higher than the socially optimal level. We utilize country-level approximations for these unobservable financing needs in the model calibration to characterize first-order trade-offs between two particular options for enhancing monetary credibility – regional monetary union and domestic monetary reforms that would bolster central bank independence.

Model simulations bear out how the incentives to form a monetary union are strongly influenced by the differences in fiscal distortions across countries. In the context of the model, while Nigeria may benefit somewhat from the WAMZ, most of the other countries would not. Since Nigeria's estimated fiscal distortion is relatively high, it could gain by becoming part of a union where other countries with lower estimated fiscal distortions exert a restraining influence on the regional central bank, reducing the inflationary bias of national policy-makers who cannot credibly pre-commit to low inflation. Simulation results suggest that the more distant ECOWAS-wide monetary union, although potentially beneficial for Nigeria and its fellow WAMZ countries, may not be incentive-compatible for any of the WAEMU members.

What does the model imply concerning the scale of reduction in Nigeria's fiscal distortion that would be necessary for all WAEMU members to 'vote' to admit the WAMZ countries to an expanded union? The answer depends quite a bit on an assessment of the sustainable level of oil revenues to GDP for the medium to long term, since these provide a non-distortionary financing source for government spending. Using the relatively conservative assumption that sustainable oil revenues are one standard deviation below the average for the past decade and a half, we find that the required adjustment is substantial. We interpret this as suggesting that further structural reforms to public financial management, to the composition and effectiveness of government spending, and to tax administration, for example, would be needed to make the monetary union project potentially feasible. In sum the model suggests that monetary unification may generate only modest gains, and raises questions about the credibility and stability of a potential regional monetary union to the extent that large asymmetries in financing needs (importantly influenced by fiscal distortions) and, to a lesser extent, terms-of-trade shock asymmetries persist.

The model can also afford an assessment of the other alternative considered for 'tying the policy-maker's hands' for Nigeria: institutional reforms that decrease the temptation to boost output on the part of the Central Bank and remove pressures to finance government spending, paving the way for an inflation-targeting regime. The simulations suggest that the inflation-reduction gains from reforming domestic monetary institutions are potentially quite sizeable, and of a larger order of magnitude than the disciplinary effect of monetary union. In the context of the model, the strategy of continued reform of domestic monetary institutions has both this direct benefit and the indirect benefit that it could make the monetary union project – if it does in fact move forward – more acceptable to the other countries in the region, and potentially sustainable. By highlighting the interaction of monetary and fiscal policy, the model suggests that the credibility of a potential inflation-targeting regime is likely to be enhanced to the extent that the types of structural fiscal reforms noted above support lower financing needs and thus the minimum inflation rate that can be credibly achieved. At the same time, the model points to the important role of Central Bank independence in reducing the temptation to dissipate those potential gains.

Notes

1 An earlier version of this chapter was presented at an October 2006 workshop hosted by the Central Bank of Nigeria. We would like to thank, without implication, workshop participants, IMF staff and academic colleagues for useful comments. This work was prepared in order to stimulate discussion of Nigerian policy issues and provide a framework for thinking about them, not to come to specific conclusions about policy measures. The views expressed in this chapter are those of the authors and should not be attributed to the International Monetary Fund, its Executive Board, or its management.

2 Benin, Burkina Faso, Côte d'Ivoire, Guinea-Bissau, Mali, Niger, Senegal and Togo. Guinea-Bissau joined WAEMU in 1997. Data availability for that country is poor, and hence we do not analyse its impact on proposed monetary unions.

3 Liberia has declined to participate, while the remaining member of ECOWAS, Cape Verde, is pegged to the euro.
4 The ultimate causes for such inefficiencies are multiple. They range from imperfect information on the *ex ante* return of public investment projects, to X-inefficiency and corruption.
5 Unlike the underlying assumption in most of the literature on central bank independence (on which we draw), institutional reforms are unlikely to be a free lunch (bringing credibility instantly and at no cost) because the public needs time to fully grasp the true motivations of the new institution on the basis of its actions.
6 More progress made on convergence could contribute to reducing fiscal distortions and differences between the countries in their potential financing needs.
7 Monetary union may have other objectives – increasing trade, political solidarity for example – that clearly the model will not take into account.
8 It is of course difficult to disentangle the impact of institutional reforms from the role of greater competition in international markets, and the related deflationary pressures.
9 Analytical solutions are available upon request.
10 Of course, if all taxes were lump-sum, the need to finance productive public spending would not affect the natural level of output.
11 Inflation can also be reduced if policy-makers value reputation and endure penalties for succumbing to their penchant for monetary expansions. That approach relies on the infinite repetition of the interaction between policy-makers and the public, and is characterized by a multiplicity of equilibria. We prefer the analytically simpler route of a 'one-shot' interaction in alternative institutional set-ups.
12 As noted by Rogoff (1985), this may be why central bankers are more likely to be picked among groups with a stronger natural distaste for inflation such as financial market participants.
13 It is worth noting that the DMP model captures the essence of the OCA theory, assuming that the union-wide inflation target of the regional monetary authorities will only accommodate the common component of supply disturbances. This makes country-specific shocks costly and underscores the role of the joint distribution of supply disturbances as one of the determinants of the equilibrium configuration of monetary unions in the region.
14 In the presence of such constraints (like scarcity of skilled staff), good institutions have a public good dimension in the region.
15 We performed a similar exercise for public spending on education. However, data availability is more limited, and our estimates – although qualitatively similar to those obtained for government spending on health – were insufficiently precise to be used for calibration.
16 Interestingly, our simple empirical model shows that, all other things being equal (that is, once we account for the impact of other institutions), countries with less corruption manage to spend less, pointing to the empirical relevance of efficiency losses. In practice, of course, all things are not equal.
17 Perfect institutions and the absence of political distortions are not of this world so that, in line with our theoretical model, all countries in the world would be expected to exhibit a UFN that exceeds the government's spending target.
18 Our results also hold using averages over the period 1998–2003.
19 This amount lies within the two-standard deviation bounds from the mean of 24.3 per cent of GDP, and constitutes a conservative estimate of the permanent stream of revenues arising from abundant natural resources.
20 Sensitivity to parameter values is always a concern for calibrated models; sensitivity analysis undertaken in DMP (2005) indicated robustness to changes in some key parameters.

References

Alesina, A. and G. Tabellini, 1987, 'Rules and Discretion with Noncoordinated Monetary and Fiscal Policies', *Economic Inquiry*, 25, 619–30.

Barro, R. and D. Gordon, 1983, 'A Positive Theory of Monetary Policy in a Natural Rate Model', *Journal of Political Economy*, 91, 589–610.

Batini, N., 2004, 'Achieving and Maintaining Price Stability in Nigeria', IMF Working Paper 04/97, International Monetary Fund, Washington, DC.

Bayoumi, T. and J. Ostry, 1997, 'Macroeconomic Shocks and Trade Flows within Sub-Saharan Africa: Implications for Optimum Currency Arrangements', *Journal of African Economies*, 6, 412–44.

Beetsma, R.M.W.J. and A.L. Bovenberg, 1998, 'Monetary Union without Fiscal Coordination May Discipline Policymakers', *Journal of International Economics*, 45, 239–58.

Beetsma, R.M.W.J. and A.L. Bovenberg, 1999, 'Does Monetary Unification Lead to Excessive Debt Accumulation?', *Journal of Public Economics*, 74, 299–325.

Debrun, X., P. Masson and C. Pattillo, 2005, 'Monetary Unions in West Africa: Who Might Gain, Who Might Lose and Why?', *Canadian Journal of Economics*, 38, 454–81.

International Monetary Fund, 2003, 'Nigeria: Selected Issues and Statistical Appendix', IMF Country Report no. 03/60, International Monetary Fund, Washington, DC.

International Monetary Fund, 2005, 'Nigeria: 2005 Article IV Consultation – Staff Report; Staff Supplement; and Public Information Notice on the Executive Board Discussion', IMF Country Report 05/302, International Monetary Fund, Washington, DC.

International Monetary Fund, 2006, 'Nigeria: First Review Under the Policy Support Instrument – Staff Report; Press Release on the Executive Board Discussion; and Statement by the Executive Director for Nigeria', IMF Country Report 06/180, International Monetary Fund, Washington, DC.

McCallum, B., 1995, 'Two Fallacies Concerning Central-Bank Independence', *American Economic Review*, 85, 207–11.

Martin, P., 1995, 'Free-riding, Convergence and Two-speed Monetary Unification in Europe', *European Economic Review*, 39, 1345–64.

Mauro, P., 1998, 'Corruption and the Composition of Government Expenditure', *Journal of Public Economics*, 69 (2), 263–79.

Rogoff, K., 1985, 'The Optimal Degree of Commitment to an Intermediate Monetary Target', *Quarterly Journal of Economics*, 100, 1169–90.

Svensson, L.E.O., 1997, 'Optimal Inflation Targets, "Conservative" Central Banks, and Linear Inflation Contracts', *American Economic Review*, 87 (1), 98–114.

5

Monetary Policy and Oil Price Surges in Nigeria

Christopher Adam[1] *and Benedikt Goderis*

5.1 Introduction

The management of oil revenues is the past, present and future of macroeconomic policy in Nigeria. As Paul Collier describes (Chapter 2), the long history of fiscal mismanagement of oil booms in Nigeria saw the Central Bank of Nigeria's ability to pursue a coherent monetary policy severely circumscribed. Without the support of a disciplined and broadly predictable fiscal stance, the Central Bank was unable to make credible commitments to an inflation target or, indeed, to any other intermediate target such as the money supply or the exchange rate. Monetary policy could not reliably anchor inflation expectations. Since the turn of the century, however, the landscape has started to change. Harnessed to a stronger political commitment, the successful consolidation in the financial sector concluded at the end of 2005 and the de facto unification of the foreign exchange markets in early 2006, measures such as the Fiscal Responsibility Bill, currently working its way through the legislature, are laying the foundations for improved fiscal management of oil revenues. As a result, and for possibly the first time in its history, the prospects now exist for genuinely 'independent' Central Banking in Nigeria. It now makes sense to consider monetary policy playing a more central role in short-run macroeconomic management in Nigeria.

In this chapter, we are concerned with just one specific aspect of this management challenge. Specifically, we use a formal model that examines the properties of alternative monetary policy rules geared towards the efficient macroeconomic management of short-run volatility in oil revenues. In the model, we start from the premise that the Central Bank sees its core remit as pursuing low and stable inflation, even though it does not at present explicitly see itself as an 'inflation targeter'. However, we also assume that, quite reasonably, other concerns compete for the Central Bank's attention. First, there may be an anxiety about the level and volatility of the nominal and real exchange rates. Fears of adverse 'Dutch disease' effects accompanying oil surges may draw the authorities into attempts to prevent the temporary (or persistent) appreciation of the real exchange rate in order to forestall perceived losses in competitiveness. But concerns about exchange rate volatility may centre less on the question of competitiveness than on the political costs of temporary exchange rate appreciations which first confer big income gains on net consumers of imported goods before reversing them. The Central Bank may also be concerned about interest rate volatility. Attempts to address nominal (and real) exchange rate volatility through exchange rate intervention – a fear of floating – are often accompanied by a belief that some form of domestic liquidity sterilization is necessary to deliver on an inflation target. Sterilization, in turn, raises concerns over interest rate volatility, the effects on private investment, and the quasi-fiscal burden of increased domestic borrowing. Finally, the Central Bank may also seek to avoid excessive volatility in output, particularly in the non-tradable sector where prices are more likely to adjust sluggishly to demand shocks.

The challenge facing the Central Bank in dealing with oil price surges is to identify operational monetary rules that navigate these competing concerns without losing their anchor on inflation, or, more precisely, inflation expectations. This challenge can be distilled into three specific questions. First, to what extent does it make sense for the monetary authorities to seek to manage the path of the nominal exchange rate, if at all? Second, what is the role for using official foreign reserves as a buffer to smooth the spending and absorption of the oil windfall? Finally, how should windfall-related liquidity growth be sterilized, through bond sales or foreign exchange sales? This chapter, therefore, contributes to the making of monetary policy in Nigeria by examining the performance of a small set of alternative monetary policy rules in the face of volatile oil prices, holding other sources of volatility constant.

Two central messages emerge from our analysis. The first is that, when the fiscal response to oil surges significantly alters the path of domestic deficit financing needs, strategies involving significant foreign exchange intervention to offset the incipient nominal exchange rate appreciation deliver less volatile outcomes than those which allow the exchange rate to float freely. This intervention can be achieved by simple rules that match foreign exchange intervention directly to the saving out of the windfall (what we refer to as a *buffer-plus-float*) or through an explicit *exchange rate crawl* aimed at keeping the rate of nominal exchange rate depreciation close to the long-run inflation target. Both rules are much more effective at reducing short-run real and nominal volatility than a pure float. Second, judged solely against the narrow criteria of minimizing short-run price, exchange rate and output volatility, the crawl outperforms the buffer-plus-float. However, if, in addition to targeting macroeconomic volatility, the authorities are also concerned to develop the structural performance of domestic finance markets by promoting greater market-based exchange rate determination, the balance tips in favour of the buffer-plus-float.

The second main message is that, in the face of an oil price surge, the conventional case for domestic bond sterilization may be weaker than conventionally thought, even when the authorities' foreign exchange rate intervention leads to a growth in domestic liquidity. The reason is that the combination of income growth and a reduction in expected inflation arising from fiscal consolidation serves to increase the demand for domestic money thereby warranting the growth in liquidity arising from the authorities' accumulation of official net international reserves. Indeed, there may even be a case for 'reverse sterilization' where part of the oil windfall is used to buy back domestic debt. This may serve two purposes. First, a debt buy-back serves to crowd in private investment by temporarily lowering the real interest rate. At the same time, a debt buy-back at the beginning of an oil surge creates 'space' for the monetary authorities to more effectively manage the end of an oil price surge, especially in circumstances where the fiscal authorities cannot credibly commit to adjusting expenditure immediately as windfall revenue disappears.

Three important caveats apply to our model-based analysis, however. First, the strength of the case for foreign exchange intervention, and against bond sterilization, in the face of oil surges depends intimately on the assumed sensitivity of the private sector's demand for money to changes in expected inflation, and how heavily it discounts the future. Our simulations attempt to reflect the view that in contemporary Nigeria, especially as reforms in the financial sector begin to take root, portfolio effects appear to be relatively strong. However, these are only model-based assumptions: if in reality the inflation elasticity is low and horizons are short, portfolio effects on the demand for money will weaken, the distinction between alternative exchange rate rules will be less stark, and the case for a debt buy-back less powerful. Second, the analysis reported below is based on a model which de-emphasizes the role of the banking system in the transmission of monetary policy and hence the results do not do justice to the full range of policy instruments available to the Central Bank. Finally, and most importantly, we must reiterate a self-evident truth about monetary policy in Nigeria. With oil revenues constituting such a dominant share of total fiscal receipts, it will always be the case that monetary policy is conducted in the shadow of the *fiscal* management of oil revenues. Whilst it may be possible for the Central Bank to lean against weak fiscal management in the short run – for example by relying heavily on quantitative controls such as reserve requirements and Central Bank liabilities to mop up excess domestic liquidity – no long-run inflation target can succeed without a supportive fiscal policy. It follows, therefore, that, in the absence of a compatible fiscal policy, monetary policy options will remain heavily proscribed and strongly influenced by concerns about managing unsustainable liquidity growth. Other chapters in this volume address these broader issues of fiscal management directly; given the specific objectives of this chapter, we assume the existence of a broadly coherent fiscal stance.

The remainder of the chapter is structured as follows. Section 5.2 sets the scene by providing a brief sketch of the relevant monetary conditions in contemporary Nigeria. In Section 5.3 we motivate the formal simulation analysis by establishing the main lines of our argument, and in Section 5.4 we present and discuss the simulation results. Section 5.5 concludes with some brief comments on the question of fiscal credibility.

5.2 Monetary policy objectives and practice in contemporary Nigeria

In recent decades the declared objective of monetary policy in Nigeria has been to attain both price stability and exchange rate stability. The reality has, however, been rather different. Average inflation, which had stood at around 30 per cent per annum from most of the two decades since the 1974–1979 oil price boom, has fallen but has continued to be volatile (Figure 5.1).

Batini (2004) highlights two reasons for Nigeria's relatively poor historical record on inflation control. The first is a chronic 'fiscal dominance' problem which has frequently obliged the Central Bank to finance large and volatile fiscal deficits, and the second is the policy incoherence arising from attempts to satisfy the so-called 'impossible trinity' of monetary policy. This holds that, in countries with an open capital account, money supply and exchange rate targets cannot be pursued simultaneously so that, at some point in time, these two objectives will require mutually incompatible policy actions with the consequence that either or both targets will be jeopardized. These tensions between money supply and exchange rate objectives remain so that, while the authorities remain publicly committed to a programme in which broad money growth is the principal anchor, concerns about the path of the exchange rate are rarely far from the surface.[2]

Greater coherence has emerged in recent years, however, promoted in part by the National Economic Empowerment and Development Strategy (NEEDS) framework. A central pillar of NEEDS has been the development of an oil-price based fiscal rule, endorsed by the federal, state and local governments, under which the windfall oil revenues in excess of a budget reference price are saved. Under this rule, the fiscal stance has improved substantially in the last few years, despite the pressures to spend the large increase in oil revenue. The overall fiscal balance moved from a deficit of around 4 per cent of GDP in 2001 and 2002 to a surplus of roughly the same order of magnitude in 2004 and 2005, while the domestic debt ratio fell by around 5 percentage points of GDP over the same period. The focus

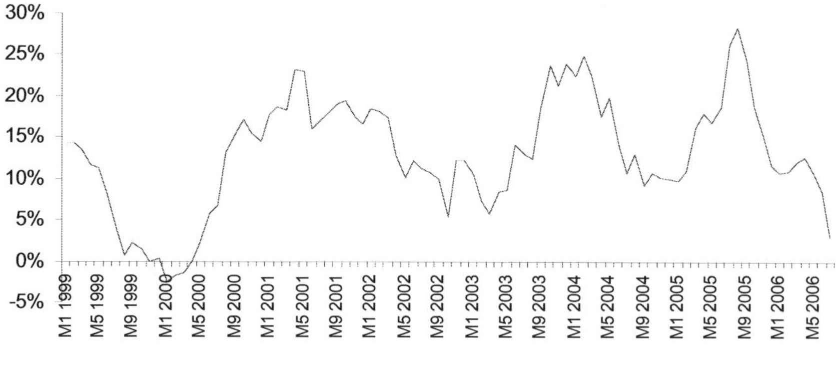

Figure 5.1 Inflation 1999–2006 (12-month percentage change in CPI).
Source: International Financial Statistics, IMF.

on improving fiscal discipline has also underpinned the Fiscal Responsibility Bill (FRB) – under review by the National Assembly at the time of writing – which seeks to establish better coordination of the fiscal policies of federal, state and local governments through formal fiscal rules and enhanced fiscal transparency and accountability, the lack of which has long been a problem in Nigeria (see Box 5.1).

Although the long-term success of the current initiatives remains to be seen, the first important and unprecedented steps have been made towards a sustainable fiscal policy framework. This improved fiscal outlook has immediate consequences for the conduct of monetary policy as well. In the presence of a certain degree of fiscal discipline and a credible money targeting regime, the question arises how the other objective of the Central Bank, exchange rate stability, should

Box 5.1 Allocation of oil resources and fiscal decentralization in Nigeria

The allocation of oil resources and fiscal decentralization in Nigeria has long been a topic of much controversy. The present system, embedded in the constitution, allocates a large share of revenues to the state and local governments. In particular, two categories of revenue are shared by the federal, state and local governments. The first consists of oil revenues net of expenditures, called 'First Charges', plus tax revenue collected by the federal government on behalf of the federation. This revenue is known as the Federation Account revenue and is allocated according to a rule that has changed over the years. In 2001, the rule allocated 48.5 per cent of the revenue to the federal government, 24 per cent to the state government, 20 per cent to the local government, and 3.5 per cent to special funds. The remaining 4 per cent was originally meant for other purposes but is now reallocated to the three government levels. The second category of revenue, the value added tax, is also collected at the federal level but is allocated to the three levels of government according to a different rule. In 2001, 50 per cent of the revenue was allocated to the local governments, whereas the state and federal governments received 35 per cent and 15 per cent, respectively.

While a large share of the revenues goes to the state and local governments, the responsibility for consolidated fiscal policy and macroeconomic stability lies at the level of the federal government. At the same time, the local and state governments are allowed to borrow domestically and hold no responsibility for fiscal prudence and macroeconomic stability. As a result, the current institutional structure makes it difficult for the federal government to exert control over the aggregated fiscal policy stance. It is this situation the Fiscal Responsibility Bill (2006) seeks to address by providing for formal fiscal rules aimed at improved coordination of the fiscal policies of federal, state and local governments.

be viewed, particularly in the face of volatile oil prices. It is to these issues that we now turn.

5.3 A simple framework for monetary policy analysis

5.3.1 The basic structure

Successful monetary management of volatile oil revenues turns on how this volatility translates into volatility in domestic deficit financing ('seigniorage'). As we show, this becomes a particularly important issue if fiscal policy is geared towards saving some of the oil windfall, either to reduce reliance on domestic deficit financing or to smooth the profile of government expenditure for a given fiscal stance (or some combination of the two). In such circumstances, simple monetary rules which stabilize the path of domestic financing through more or less exchange rate intervention turn out to have attractive properties. The reason for this is as follows: conventional wisdom concerning the choice of exchange rate regimes suggests that a floating exchange rate regime offers the economy the best protection against *real* shocks while a fixed (or crawling peg) regime provides better protection against *portfolio* shocks. The distinctive feature of oil price surges in Nigeria is that, while the originating shock is real, the authorities' fiscal choices, which alter the path of domestic deficit financing, convert the real shock into a mixed real and portfolio shock thus shifting the balance in favour of a degree of intervention aimed at managing the path of the exchange rate.

We examine the properties of two specific rules which achieve this objective, albeit in different ways. The first, which we refer to as a *buffer-plus-float*, directly stabilizes the path of seigniorage by synchronizing foreign exchange sales to the growth in liquidity generated by domestic spending out of the oil windfall. This entails initially accumulating oil proceeds as official foreign exchange reserves and then sterilizing the full domestic currency counterpart of non-import spending through foreign exchange sales as it occurs.[3]

The second rule, an exchange rate crawl, does not target liquidity growth directly but rather the authorities intervene in the foreign exchange market to keep the nominal exchange rate close to its long-run equilibrium rate of depreciation. In this case, foreign exchange intervention responds to the latent pressures coming through the private portfolio choices (between holding domestic and foreign denominated assets) which, in turn, reflect underlying changes in the supply of domestic liquidity arising from the fiscal intervention.

The simulation results presented later in this chapter are derived from a model based on O'Connell *et al.* (2006).[4] Although the model itself is quite detailed, its central insights can be derived directly from the basic accounting identities that frame the set of policy choices. The first is the consolidated budget constraint of the public sector which we define in naira terms as

$$(S_t - T_t^o) - E_t \Delta F_t = DF_t = \Delta H_t + \Delta B_t - \Delta NIR_t \tag{5.1}$$

where $S_t = (G_t + i_t^d B_{t-1} + E_t i_t^f F_{t-1} - T_t^{no})$ is the *non-oil* overall fiscal deficit before foreign financing, G is consolidated government expenditure, B and F represent domestic and external debt respectively (with domestic and foreign interest rates i^d and i^f), E is the nominal exchange rate, T^{no} is total non-oil revenue, and T^o windfall revenue from the oil sector. DF_i is therefore domestic financing of the consolidated public sector deficit. Equation (5.1) states that the fiscal deficit net of oil and any foreign financing is ultimately financed through some combination of the growth in the monetary base (ΔH), growth in public sector domestic debt (ΔB), and depletion of official net international reserves ($-\Delta NIR$).

The left hand side of (5.1) is the traditional province of fiscal policy. The fiscal spending decision determines the overall public sector domestic deficit net of oil proceeds period by period. In what follows we shall ignore the role of official foreign financing of the budget. For Nigeria this is of second-order importance to the overall budget: what really matters is the evolution of the fiscal deficit net of the oil windfall, $(S_t - T_t^o)$. The domain of monetary policy is then the *composition* of the right-hand side of (5.1), taking the left hand side as given. Choices over the exchange rate are implemented by the degree to which the monetary authorities target the evolution of official net international reserves. Net of choices over domestic debt issues (ΔB), seigniorage (ΔH) is the residual financing item which may, of course, be an intermediate policy target.[5]

It may also be the case that the fiscal authority explicitly chooses to run a foreign reserve buffer as part of a strategy to smooth its own expenditure. In this case we can re-define (5.1) as

$$(S_t - T_t^o) - E_t \Delta F_t + \Delta NIR_t^G = DF_t = \Delta H_t + \Delta B_t - \Delta NIR_t^C \qquad (5.1a)$$

where the superscripts G and C denote reserve accumulation decisions exercised by the fiscal and monetary authorities respectively.

These fiscal and monetary choices necessarily feed back onto the evolution of the external balance which can be defined as

$$-\Delta NFA - \Delta NIR = CAD^{no} - X^o \qquad (5.2)$$

where CAD^{no} is the non-oil current account deficit, X^o represents net oil proceeds and NFA private net foreign assets, and $NIR = NIR^G + NIR^C$. From (5.2), fiscal and monetary policy choices directly influence the contribution of official reserves to overall current account financing, which, in conjunction with the private sector's decision on net foreign asset accumulation, determines the extent to which the oil inflow is absorbed into the domestic economy. The private sector's portfolio choice, in other words their allocation of wealth between domestic bonds (B), foreign assets (NFA) and domestic assets (H), combined with the authorities' decisions over the supply of domestic liquidity simultaneously determine the real interest rate, inflation expectations and the private capital account response to the oil windfall. These two choices play a central role in shaping the short-run macroeconomic response of the economy to the oil price surge.

5.3.2 Formal model structure

The model is a stylized short-run open economy model with currency substitution. On the consumption side, households (characterized here by a representative agent) consume tradable and non-tradable goods, with the composition of expenditure being determined by the real exchange rate, given the parameters governing the elasticity of substitution. Their net financial wealth is held in terms of three assets: domestic government debt, money and foreign currency. Importantly, however, neither the representative household nor the government are fully integrated into world capital markets. Hence, while the private sector can accumulate foreign currency, it does not have direct, unrationed access to world capital markets. Similarly, world capital markets have no appetite for Nigerian government debt. Domestic public debt, on the other hand, is marketed but, given the lack of openness of the official capital account, it is, in effect, non-tradable. These assumptions may not be wholly realistic, but are made to allow for two important features that do characterize the Nigerian economy. The first is that domestic interest rates are not tied down by interest parity conditions but rather will move with supply and demand conditions in domestic markets – which are in turn influenced by fiscal and monetary policy choices – and the second is that the private sector capital account will constitute an important channel for adjustment to oil windfalls.

The private sector's naira money demand depends on its level of expenditure and the relative opportunity cost of holding domestic or foreign currency. The sensitivity of relative currency demand to these opportunity costs is an increasing function of the elasticity of currency substitution. Holding the nominal interest rate constant, an increase in expected exchange rate depreciation shifts desired portfolios in favour of foreign currency. The higher the elasticity of substitution between domestic and foreign money for any given change in relative returns, the stronger the desired portfolio reallocation and therefore the greater the pressure on the nominal exchange rate in response to shocks. We do not have any reliable empirical estimates of the size of this parameter for Nigeria, or indeed for other African countries, and so in this chapter we set this elasticity at around the mid-range values from the evidence on Latin American and other emerging markets. Given the calibration values used in the model, this implies an inflation elasticity of the demand for money of around 0.45.

Output consists of three forms: a non-tradable good, oil, and non-oil tradable output; although, for Nigeria, this third component represents a relatively small share of total production. Prices for tradable goods (on the production and consumption sides) are determined in world markets, while for non-tradables we allow for some price stickiness (Calvo, 1983).

The model is designed to consider issues of short-run volatility rather than longer-term response to *sustained* oil price surges. Hence, as we describe below, we examine the response of the economy to only the temporary component of oil price movements. The model does not concern itself with the medium-term evolution of the economy in response to sustained oil price increases.[6] Specifically, we do not consider the supply-side response to the oil windfall. Thus, the volume of tradable output is fixed, although the sticky-price assumption means non-tradable output is demand determined.

5.3.3 Oil shocks and policy responses

We use this model to examine the properties of alternative responses to oil price volatility holding constant all other sources of short-run macroeconomic volatility. In reality, the relevant volatility is in the value of oil proceeds which combine variations in production and exports with variations in the world price for Nigerian oil. In the interests of simplicity, however, we assume that the volume of oil output is constant and that all volatility arises from variations in the oil price. To focus attention on *short-run* volatility we represent the evolution of the oil price in terms of the following first-order autoregression:

$$(p^{oil} - \tilde{p}^{oil})_t = \gamma_0 + \gamma_1 (p^{oil} - \tilde{p}^{oil})_{t-1} + \varepsilon_t \tag{5.3}$$

where p_t^{oil} is the log of the world price for Nigerian Forcados crude oil in constant US dollars, and $\tilde{p}_t^{oil}$ represents a smoothed stochastic trend estimated using the Hodrick–Prescott filter. The key estimated parameters are $\hat{\varepsilon}_t$, the size of the oil shock relative to trend, and $\hat{\gamma}_1$, its persistence over time. Equation (5.3) is estimated on quarterly data from 1980(Q1) to 2005(Q4). The fitted trend and residual are shown in Figure 5.2. From the estimation we obtain a mean price shock of approximately 12.5 per cent and a persistence parameter of approximately 0.65. Given the share of oil in total government revenue, this translates into a revenue shock of just under 3.7 per cent of total revenue per quarter.

Other parameters calibrating the model to the key structural characteristics of the Nigerian economy are based on data for the period 2000–2004 so as to reflect the structure of the economy prior to the most recent oil price surge. Details of these parameters are provided in Appendix Table 5.A1 at the end of this chapter.

5.3.4 Fiscal and monetary rules

Our fiscal and monetary policy rules abstract from much of the detail of institutional structures in Nigeria but are sufficiently rich to reflect the principal macroeconomic choices confronting fiscal and monetary authorities. Given our concern with domestic financing we focus on the consolidated budget. On the revenue side we treat all non-oil sources of revenue as constant so that oil revenue is the only source of revenue volatility. Choices are more varied on the expenditure side. First, we assume the fiscal authorities can choose either to fully spend the oil revenue windfall or to save some portion of it. Specifically when oil revenues move above their long-run mean, a portion of the increase may be devoted to reducing the government's domestic financing needs; this we refer to as the

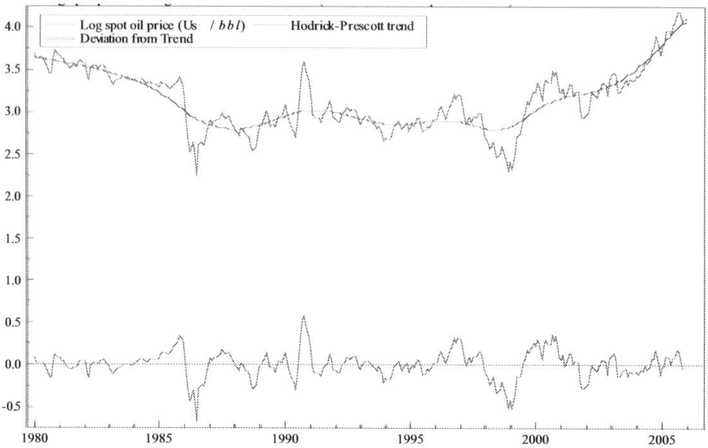

Figure 5.2 Log spot price for Nigerian Forcados crude oil (constant US$ per barrel) 1980–2005.

deficit-reducing (dr) component of the windfall. In the experiments reported below, we allow this saving to account for up to a quarter of the windfall.[7] Second, and in addition, the fiscal authorities may also run an explicit fiscal reserve programme aimed at smoothing the path of government expenditure relative to the path of the windfall. This may be for conventional consumption-smoothing reasons or to avoid short-run 'construction boom' effects. This expenditure smoothing is achieved through direct reserve accumulation on the part of the fiscal authorities through the operation of a 'reserve account'. In the face of an oil surge the government spends each period a constant fraction, μ, of the balance in the reserve account which consists of the opening balance in the account plus the windfall revenue accruing during the period:

$$g_t = \mu W_t = \mu[W_{t-1} + (1-dr)\tau^o{}_t] \tag{5.4}$$

where g_t is government expenditure, τ^o_t is the revenue value of the oil windfall, *dr* is the proportion of the windfall devoted to reducing the domestic deficit, and W_t is the reserve account. As $\mu \rightarrow 1$ the profile of expenditure matches that of the windfall. In the simulations reported below we fix μ=0.5. Given the estimated persistence of the oil price shock of 0.65, the half-life of the typical shock is just over one year, with 82 per cent of the windfall being received within four years. With μ=0.5, the half-life of spending is just over two years with only 68 per cent of the windfall being spent within four years. A value of μ=0.25 would increase the half-life of spending to almost four years. From a financing perspective, smoothing is different from deficit reduction since eventually the full value of the oil windfall is translated into spending. Smoothing alters the time-profile of spending and domestic deficit financing but not the present value; deficit reduction alters the present value. In terms of the simulations reported below, it is the latter that has the stronger impact on the path of domestic financing and hence the dynamics of inflation and the exchange rate.

The third dimension of expenditure choices concerns the composition of spending. We distinguish three alternatives. At one extreme – our reference simulations – we represent spending as consisting of a direct transfer to household by means of lump-sum transfers; this is, in effect, a version of the mechanism discussed by Sala-i-Martin and Subramanian (2003) with spending decisions out of the oil windfall fully aligned with the private sector's preferences, including their desire to smooth consumption inter-temporally. At the other extreme we assume simple allocation rules under which public spending at the margin is allocated on a current-income basis between tradable and non-tradable goods. Under this characterization we consider the propensity to spend out of the windfall (net of any deficit reduction) to be unity and spending to be allocated between tradable to non-tradable goods in the ratio of 0.15 to 0.85.

These three fiscal settings provide the background to the monetary policy rules. In its current form our model is relatively simple and, in particular, does not afford an explicit role for the banking system. This means, amongst other things, that the full range of monetary policy instruments, particularly the use of reserve requirements or statutory deposit instruments and other quantity-based instruments, cannot be investigated. Hence monetary policy choices centre on the Central Bank's transactions in foreign exchange and in government securities. Foreign exchange interventions can be summarized in the following reaction function:

$$\Delta z_{t-1} = -z_1 \cdot \dot{E}_t + z_2 .dr \cdot \tau_t^0 - z_3 \cdot (z_{t-1} - z_0). \tag{5.5}$$

where z_0 is the initial steady-state level of official reserves under the management of the Central Bank and $\dot{E}_t$ the rate of depreciation of the nominal exchange rate. The parameters z_1 and z_3 govern the degree of commitment to the steady-state rate of crawl, which is tied down by the long-run inflation rate, and the speed with which intervention is eventually unwound. As $z_1 \rightarrow \infty$ and $z_3 \rightarrow 0$, the regime approaches a predetermined crawl. Lower values of z_1 represent looser commitments to the reference rate of crawl. For $z_1 = 0$ the exchange rate floats: Central Bank intervention, if any, is independent of movements in the nominal exchange rate.[8] The term z_2 allows the Central Bank to tie foreign exchange sales directly to the time path of windfall-induced government spending. A policy of $z_2 = 1$ and $z_1 = 0$ corresponds to the buffer-plus-float strategy in which the Central Bank sells the oil revenue proceeds in the precise amount required to finance the domestic currency value of windfall-induced spending, while the *dr* component is then accumulated as reserves. Lower values of z_2 induce smaller foreign exchange sales and greater reserve accumulation, implying faster expansion of the monetary base, other things being equal.[9]

In addition, the Central Bank can engage in open market operations in the domestic bond markets. Bond operations are described by the following reaction function:

$$p_t \Delta b_t^P = b_1 \Delta j_t + b_2 dr.\tau_t^0 + b_3 p_t (\bar{b}^P - b_{t-1}^P) \tag{5.6}$$

where j denotes the sum of reserves under the management of the fiscal authorities (W) and the Central Bank itself (z). For $b_1 > 0$, bond operations are used to offset a portion of the impact of foreign exchange intervention on the monetary base, while for $b_2 > 0$ with $z_2 = 1$, intervention is used to sterilize the effect of the accumulation of reserves against the savings of government, whereas a strategy of $b_2 > 0$ with $z_2 = 1$ represents a reverse sterilization or debt buy-back operation.[10]

Both foreign exchange operations and bond operations are unwound over time, at rates determined by z_3 and b_3. These ensure that reserves eventually return to their original steady-state level, so that oil windfalls are ultimately fully absorbed regardless of the values of z_1, z_2 and dr, and leave interest payments and the fiscal deficit unchanged in the long run, as required by consistency with the long-run inflation target.

5.4 Results

5.4.1 Core results: impulse response functions

We begin by presenting a simple set of reference runs against which later analysis can be evaluated. Table 5.1 reports the impulse response functions for a one-time positive shock to the oil price under three alternative exchange rate rules. In doing so, we emphasize the effect of fiscal saving. In the first case, reported in panels A and B, we assume that the proceeds of the oil windfall are fully spent – but not 'overspent' – as and when they arrive. Government expenditure therefore follows, naira for naira, the rise and fall in oil revenues over the duration of the shock. In this base case, government spending is in the form of direct transfers to the representative private agent. In the second case, reported in panels C, D and E, we assume that the fiscal authorities use one quarter of the windfall revenue to reduce the demands on domestic deficit financing. In the context of equation (5.1) therefore, panels A and B correspond to the case where *DF* is unchanged, at least directly, while panels C, D and E correspond to the case where *DF* falls.

Two preliminary points should again be stressed. First, the model is stationary. The oil price shock is temporary and the economy reverts eventually to its initial equilibrium. Second, and related, the exchange rate regime is neutral in the long-run even though each has different short-run implications and different implications for the out-of-steady-state volatility of the economy. These are design choices allowing us to focus on short-run, day-to-day, monetary management issues. But they mean that we do not engage with issues of the medium-term response to persistent surges in the oil price, including questions of optimal oil extraction, investment behaviour, the long-run fiscal stance, and hence movements in the long-run equilibrium real exchange rate. All these features are subsumed in our 'steady state' equilibrium.

Table 5.1 Impulse responses to a 12.5 per cent positive shock to oil prices[a]

Period (quarters)	0	1	2	3	4	5	15
Oil revenue (% of total revenue)	3.70	2.41	1.57	1.02	0.66	0.43	0.00
Panel A: Clean float, oil windfall fully spent							
Inflation	–1.06	–0.96	–1.53	–1.64	–1.52	–1.31	–0.09
Nominal exchange rate[b]	–4.10	–0.94	–1.16	–1.20	–1.09	–0.93	–0.06
Real exchange rate[b]	–5.53	–5.49	–4.83	–4.03	–3.24	–2.59	–0.13
Real interest rate	–1.10	–1.20	–1.19	–1.06	–0.89	–0.73	–0.04
Non-tradable output	0.54	0.17	0.04	–0.02	–0.04	–0.05	–0.01
Current account	1.72	0.62	0.05	–0.22	–0.33	–0.34	–0.03
Private spending	4.05	3.53	2.96	2.39	1.89	1.46	0.07
Official reserves	0.00	0.00	0.00	0.00	0.00	0.00	0.00
Panel B: Crawl, oil windfall fully spent							
Inflation	2.26	0.08	–0.48	–0.68	–0.76	–0.78	–0.47
Nominal exchange rate[b]	–0.15	–0.17	–0.22	–0.31	–0.38	–0.45	–0.44
Real exchange rate[b]	–4.38	–4.84	–4.36	–3.67	–2.98	–2.38	0.23
Real interest rate	–1.08	–1.01	–0.99	–0.91	–0.78	–0.65	–0.05
Non-tradable output	0.79	0.20	0.06	0.01	0.00	–0.01	–0.01
Current account	1.95	0.81	0.18	–0.13	–0.27	–0.31	–0.07
Private spending	3.69	3.18	2.69	2.22	1.79	1.42	0.13
Official reserves	2.02	0.42	0.72	1.09	1.14	0.99	–0.36

Table 5.1 Continued

Period (quarters)	0	1	2	3	4	5	15
Panel C: Clean float, oil windfall partially spent							
Inflation	–12.94	–4.49	–3.73	–2.98	–2.32	–1.78	–0.08
Nominal exchange rate[b]	–17.41	–3.56	–3.01	–2.38	–1.82	–1.37	–0.06
Real exchange rate[b]	–8.14	–6.45	–5.22	–4.14	–3.22	–2.46	–0.12
Real interest rate	–1.10	–1.46	–1.32	–1.10	–0.89	–0.70	–0.04
Non-tradable output	–0.55	–0.19	–0.15	–0.14	–0.12	–0.09	–0.01
Current account	1.49	0.51	0.03	–0.19	–0.28	–0.29	–0.03
Private spending	4.15	3.63	2.93	2.31	1.78	1.36	0.06
Official reserves	0.00	0.00	0.00	0.00	0.00	0.00	0.00
Panel D: Crawl, oil windfall partially spent							
Inflation	1.15	–1.01	–1.66	–1.88	–1.96	–1.95	–1.10
Nominal exchange rate[b]	–0.89	–1.25	–1.46	–1.58	–1.65	–1.68	–1.07
Real exchange rate[b]	–3.73	–4.15	–3.78	–3.23	–2.69	–2.21	–0.36
Real interest rate	–0.97	–0.85	–0.82	–0.74	–0.64	–0.53	–0.05
Non-tradable output	0.73	0.19	0.06	0.01	–0.01	–0.02	–0.01
Current account	2.18	1.03	0.36	0.01	–0.17	–0.25	–0.10
Private spending	3.22	2.76	2.35	1.96	1.61	1.31	0.21
Official reserves	12.24	5.35	3.13	1.94	1.06	0.39	–1.03

Panel E: Buffer plus float, oil windfall partially spent							
Inflation	–5.44	–2.84	–2.31	–3.55	–2.69	–2.02	–0.08
Nominal exchange rate[b]	–7.49	–2.61	–1.98	–2.95	–2.18	–1.61	–0.06
Real exchange rate[b]	7.45	6.44	5.27	4.18	3.24	2.48	0.12
Real interest rate	–1.61	–1.49	–1.30	–1.09	–0.88	–0.69	–0.04
Non-tradable output	–0.08	–0.09	–0.10	–0.08	–0.16	–0.11	–0.07
Current account	1.45	0.52	0.04	–0.19	–0.27	–0.28	–0.03
Private spending	4.37	3.61	2.89	2.28	1.76	1.34	0.06
Official reserves	7.72	2.32	1.87	1.23	0.80	0.52	0.00

a Impulse responses are reported as percentage points for inflation, the nominal and real exchange rates and the interest rate. All other variables are measured as percentage point deviations from steady state values. See Appendix Table 5.A1.
b An increase in the nominal and real exchange rates indices denotes a depreciation.

With these ideas in place, we can turn to what our results do say. The first substantive point from Table 5.1 is that when the oil revenue is fully spent, and spent in line with optimal private sector consumption smoothing considerations (panels A and B), the real adjustment is relatively modest: the real exchange rate appreciates by between 4.3 and 5.5 per cent on impact while consumption rises by between 3.5 and 4 per cent on impact before adjusting smoothly to its original steady state level. The contrast is on the nominal side: under the float, the real exchange rate appreciation is achieved by a combination of a nominal exchange rate appreciation (of around 4 percentage points on impact) and an initial fall in inflation (of around 1 percentage point). Under the crawl, by contrast, given the stability of the nominal exchange rate relative to its steady state path, the appreciation requires a small transitory increase in inflation of around 2.3 per cent. In other respects there are no significant differences between the two adjustment paths: in both cases they describe an efficient adjustment to a temporary positive shock, with both consumption (*C*) and the current account balance (*ca*) rising and the real interest rate falling on impact and adjusting relatively smoothly back towards their equilibrium values.

Matters change when the fiscal authorities choose to use some of the proceeds of the windfall to reduce the domestic financing requirement of the budget deficit. This fiscal adjustment has two effects. The first is that the stronger savings response strengthens the real exchange rate appreciation. But, second, the change in the fiscal stance entails a sharp contraction in base money which, in turn, induces a drop in expected inflation and increases the demand for domestic money relative to foreign currency, depending of course on the strength of the inflation elasticity of the demand for money. Under a floating exchange rate, however, this shift in the private sector's portfolio – away from foreign currency and towards domestic – occurs against a background where the Central Bank does not intervene to alter relative supplies of domestic and foreign currency: the entire portfolio adjustment must therefore take place through the nominal exchange rate. As panel C indicates, the nominal exchange rate appreciation required to facilitate the desired portfolio adjustment is greater than the real appreciation required to absorb the windfall. As a result, both the nominal and real exchange rates overshoot which, with sticky prices, means that the non-traded goods sector experiences a sharp demand-switching recession.

The contrast with strategies that involve greater intervention is sharp. In terms of smoothing short-run volatility, of inflation, the exchange rate, output and interest rates, an aggressive crawl dramatically outperforms the clean float in this instance (panel D). In part this is because the intervention allows the desired portfolio adjustment to take place through quantity rather than price adjustment but, more importantly, because the intervention serves to limit the deviation of expected inflation from its long-run value and hence forestalls the short-run portfolio switching that so dominated outcomes under the float. How large this distinction is between a pure float and a crawl depends crucially on the underlying elasticity of demand for money with respect to expected inflation.

In practice, both the pure float and the aggressive crawl are polar extremes. In the final panel of Table 5.1 we consider a useful benchmark case which we refer to as a *buffer-plus-float*. In this instance, the monetary authorities accumulate reserves against that proportion of windfall allocated for deficit reduction but otherwise maintain a floating exchange rate regime. This strategy, which probably comes closer to actual practice than either of the other two rules, does not target the path of the exchange rate directly as in the crawl, and hence exhibits rather more inflation and exchange rate volatility, but nonetheless attacks the principal source of the volatility under the pure float, namely the sharp short-run contraction in base money growth brought about by the fiscal saving decision. Under this rule, however, intervention is significantly less aggressive than required to stabilize the path of the nominal exchange rate and inflation so that out-turns, for the parameters used here, lie somewhere closer to the float than the crawl.

Exactly where this outcome lies is less important than the implications, two of which are worth stressing. The first is that the outcome is consistent with well established views about efficient exchange rate responses to shocks which focus on the superiority of flexible exchange rates to current account (real) shocks and fixed or crawling rates to portfolio shocks. Although the originating shock in this case is a current account, terms-of-trade shock, macroeconomic volatility stems from a portfolio shock arising from the change in expected inflation and seigniorage requirements. To the extent that the intervention element of the buffer-plus-float goes some way to smoothing the impact of deficit reduction choices on the path for future seigniorage requirements, the otherwise disruptive portfolio adjustment is allowed to take place more smoothly.

The second point is that, while the buffer-plus-float may not be quite as effective as the aggressive crawl in terms of limiting short-run instability, it is nonetheless consistent with another objective of the Central Bank, namely to promote a more market-based integrated foreign exchange rate. The buffer-plus-float strategy commits the Central Bank to intervene with respect solely to that portion of the oil windfall that is saved but to observe a float with respect to all other sources of volatility and, more specifically, to sterilize the liquidity injections arising from the spending out of the windfall through foreign exchange sales (that is, a float).

5.4.2 Extending the analysis

The results in Table 5.1 provide a valuable background which allows us to focus on some key aspects of the problem. In what follows, however, we consider a slightly wider range of policy options but in the interests of clarity we report only the most salient results. In doing so we forgo the detailed examination of the impulse response functions presented in Table 5.1 and report instead the volatility of the variables of interest.[11]

We start by considering two particular variations of the fiscal response. First we assume that the spending patterns out of the windfall are heavily biased towards non-tradable goods. Second, and possibly in response to this, we assume that the fiscal authorities seek to smooth the profile of aggregate spending relative to the windfall. Since it may not be reasonable to assume that this occurs at all levels of government, the degree of smoothing that can be achieved is taken to be relatively moderate. In particular we assume that pressures to spend mean that smoothing falls some long way short of a rule which would tie consumption to the permanent income arising from the windfall.

Spending and smoothing

Table 5.2 summarizes the effects of altering these fiscal choices where in this case, rather than focusing on the profile of a single shock, we report the implied analytical standard deviations from the simulated model. Comparing panel B with panel A, two features stand out. The first is that the higher is the propensity to spend on non-tradables, the greater is the volatility in the real exchange rate, regardless of the nominal exchange rate regime. Although not reported in the table, the impact appreciation of the real exchange rate is almost twice as large as shown in Table 5.1. This differential behaviour is only partly related to the assumption that government has a stronger baseline preference for non-tradables per se. Rather it reflects the difference between 'rule-based' characterization of public expenditure and the extent to which this differs from the private sector's spending decisions which entail an efficient alteration of the composition of spending, both inter-sectorally and inter-temporally in response to a temporary income windfall. A similar pattern of response emerges even if we assume that the public sector's spending at the margin is biased towards the tradable sector. The message, therefore, is that rule-based 'myopic' public spending behaviour generates higher real exchange rate volatility than if the spending decision out of the windfall were handled by an optimizing private sector representative agent. The second feature of panel B is that the switch in demand at the margin towards non-tradables eases the up-front deflationary pressure that otherwise is present in Table 5.1 and hence reduces the inflation and nominal exchange rate volatility. Hence the benefits of intervention relative to the float are somewhat weakened although, as the evidence from the last three columns suggests, the pressures arising from the portfolio adjustment when the windfall is partly used for deficit reduction remain significant.

Aggregate expenditure smoothing on the part of the fiscal authorities also eases the pressure on monetary policy and narrows the gap between the exchange rate rules (Table 5.2, panel C). However, given the modest degree of smoothing considered in our experiments these effects are not dramatic and certainly not sufficient on their own to remove the instability caused by the effect of latent pressures for portfolio adjustment.

Bond sterilization and debt buy-backs

When exchange rate rules embody intervention it is common practice to consider issues of bond sterilization. The logic is simple: intervention implies a growth in net foreign assets relative to the counterfactual and hence, other things being equal, a growth in base money. This is certainly the case in debates on managing aid inflows (see, for example, IMF, 2005a) and would appear to be a perennial concern in Nigeria (IMF, 2005b). However, as Table 5.1 indicates, when an oil windfall is accompanied by a significant fiscal savings response, base money actually contracts in nominal terms relative to the counterfactual. The conventional rationale for bond sterilization does not seem quite so relevant here since non-sterilized intervention delivers a smooth path for base money as well as delivering a fair degree of stability in inflation and the exchange rate. Indeed, as the first two columns of Table 5.3, panel A, indicate, additional bond sterilization, in this case equivalent to 50 per cent of the intervention, delivers a marginal reduction in real exchange rate volatility but at the cost of somewhat higher price, exchange rate and interest rate volatility. Public debt management for the purpose of sterilization, therefore, does not appear to have substantial gains.

Looked at from the other side, however, this analysis suggests that there may be important gains to *reverse sterilization* in such circumstances. As the lower panel of Table 5.3 shows, our simple short-run model suggests that a debt buy-back may lead to a marginally stronger short-run real exchange rate appreciation but this is set off against a lower real interest rate trajectory over the lifetime of the shock. With no explicit modelling of the supply side of the economy, the real interest rate in this model serves solely as the relative price between present and future consumption. The lower path for the real interest rate therefore serves to 'tilt' consumption towards the present. However, in a medium model in which investment figures, the same profile represents an incentive to invest. The debt buy-back in this instance corresponds directly to the proposal advanced by Collier and Gunning (2005) and discussed in Chapter 2.

Using a temporary oil windfall to finance a debt buy-back may be attractive for other reasons. Buffie *et al.* (2006) consider the analogous case using (part of) an aid surge to finance a domestic debt buy-back in circumstances where government commitments to reduce public spending once the aid inflow has passed are less than fully credible. A fear of higher future domestic deficits reduces the private sector's willingness to increase its current demand for money and increases its incentives to resort to capital flight, thereby unwinding the benefits from the aid inflow. In these circumstances, a debt buy-back provides the government extra time to adjust expenditure as the boom passes since the Central Bank can resell the bonds in the future to control the temporary growth in domestic credit to government that will occur if the fiscal authorities struggle to realign expenditures with the new lower level of aid. The debt buy-back by the Central Bank in anticipation of a future surge in domestic deficit financing thus provides the mechanism to quell the private sector's pessimistic expectations concerning future financing. A directly analogous situation faces the Central Bank in Nigeria. Oil revenue is volatile and government commitments to fully align expenditure to future revenues are rarely fully credible (even in the presence of institutions such as the FRB). Monetary policy alone cannot solve the credibility problem but, with a suitable degree of fiscal discipline, can help to contain it.

Table 5.2 Standard deviations under alternative fiscal and monetary rules: responses to a 12.5 per cent shock to oil prices[a]

	Windfall fully spent		Windfall partially spent		
Period (quarters)	**Float**	**Crawl**	**Float**	**Crawl**	**Buffer plus float**
Panel A: Standard deviations from Table 5.1					
Inflation	3.76	3.54	14.93	6.87	9.22
Nominal exchange rate[b]	4.90	2.14	18.40	6.34	10.93
Real exchange rate[b]	11.24	9.94	13.28	8.86	10.91
Real interest rate	2.70	2.39	2.87	2.01	3.09
Non-tradable output	0.58	0.81	0.64	0.76	0.40
Current account	1.97	2.24	1.70	2.55	1.77
Private spending	7.20	6.66	7.18	5.93	7.27
Official reserves	0.00	3.31	0.00	14.50	8.43
Panel B: Expenditure biased towards non-tradables					
Inflation	4.89	5.93	10.58	7.23	8.03
Nominal exchange rate[b]	2.94	0.76	16.19	5.13	12.36
Real exchange rate[b]	19.87	19.57	19.87	15.95	17.49
Real interest rate	1.21	0.92	1.20	0.79	1.12
Non-tradable output	1.89	2.29	0.50	1.85	0.96
Current account	1.99	1.93	1.72	2.31	1.68
Private spending	3.29	3.18	4.09	3.34	3.85
Official reserves	0.00	8.63	0.00	16.65	8.43

Panel C: As Panel B with fiscal smoothing					
Inflation	2.24	3.82	12.57	6.36	7.68
Nominal exchange rate[b]	3.89	0.97	17.33	5.36	8.55
Real exchange rate[b]	18.42	17.97	18.46	14.86	9.07
Real interest rate	0.95	1.05	1.14	0.96	1.49
Non-tradable output	0.64	1.11	0.58	0.98	0.24
Current account	2.76	2.73	2.29	2.91	2.26
Private spending	2.96	2.92	3.84	3.16	3.91
Official reserves	0.00	7.98	0.00	17.27	8.43

a Standard deviations measured as percentage points.
b An increase in the nominal and real exchange rate indices denotes a depreciation.

Table 5.3 Standard deviations and impulse responses with bond sterilization: responses to a 12.5 per cent shock to oil prices[a]

	Windfall fully spent	Windfall partially spent	
Panel A: As Table 5.2, Panel A with bond sterilization			
	Crawl	**Crawl**	**Crawl with debt buy-back**
Inflation	3.27	9.04	5.80
Nominal exchange rate[b]	1.94	8.31	6.73
Real exchange rate[b]	9.91	9.07	8.08
Real interest rate	2.28	2.36	1.45
Non-tradable output	0.78	0.84	0.57
Current account	2.30	2.29	2.92
Private spending	6.60	6.24	5.78
Official reserves	5.93	7.78	33.22
Public debt	6.19	40.13	21.59

Panel B: Impulse response functions with reverse sterilization[c]

Period (quarters)	0	1	2	3	4	5	15
Oil revenue (% of total revenue)	3.70	2.41	1.57	1.02	0.66	0.43	0.00
Crawl, oil windfall partially saved, no sterilization (Table 5.1, Panel D)							
Inflation	1.15	–1.01	–1.66	–1.88	–1.96	–1.95	–1.10
Real exchange rate[b]	–3.73	–4.15	–3.78	–3.23	–2.69	–2.21	–0.36
Real interest rate	–0.97	–0.85	–0.82	–0.74	–0.64	–0.53	–0.05
Private spending	3.22	2.76	2.35	1.96	1.61	1.31	0.21
Crawl, oil windfall partially saved, reverse sterilization							
Inflation	–0.06	–1.67	–2.06	–2.09	–1.99	–1.83	–0.58
Real exchange rate[b]	–4.17	–4.24	–3.97	–3.44	–3.05	–2.61	–0.38
Real interest rate	–0.31	–0.38	–0.53	–0.57	–0.56	–0.51	–0.03
Private spending	3.76	3.22	2.75	2.06	1.78	1.51	0.33

a, b See Tables 5.1 and 5.2.
c Debt buy-back is equivalent to 50 per cent of the saving out of the oil windfall.

5.5 Conclusions

In the last few years, Nigeria has taken important steps to building solid foundations for effective macroeconomic management of oil revenues. While a coherent monetary policy will always require a compatible fiscal stance, demonstrable success in monetary management in current circumstances when a substantial measure of fiscal control does prevail can fuel its own virtuous circle, allowing the Central Bank's de facto independence to be enhanced and inflation expectations to be more firmly anchored in the future.

The credibility of monetary policy must be established across a range of issues and in the face of volatility from a variety of sources. In this chapter, we have focused on one particular aspect of the challenge facing the Central Bank, by examining the properties of a range of alternative strategies for exchange rate intervention and bond sterilization in the face of volatile oil revenues. Our analysis suggests that strategies that stabilize the path of domestic financing for a given fiscal response to the oil windfall have attractive properties relative to a range of conventional alternatives including those involving heavy reliance on bond sterilization and variants of a pure float. This is particularly the case if the fiscal authorities seek to save some portion of the windfall. Efficient alignment can be achieved by simple rules that match foreign exchange sterilization (that is, floating) directly to fiscal spending of the windfall while banking the unspent portion. However, an aggressive crawl aimed at keeping the rate of nominal exchange rate depreciation close to the long-run inflation target (a variant of a real exchange rate target) turns out to be rather more effective at reducing short-run real and nominal volatility. The attractive features of the crawl in this specific instance may, however, be over-sold if, in addition to targeting macroeconomic volatility, the authorities are also concerned to develop the structural performance of domestic finance markets by promoting greater market-based exchange rate determination.

The second main message is that the conventional case for domestic bond sterilization may need to be modified, particularly when a reasonable degree of fiscal discipline is in place. The combination of income growth and a reduction in expected inflation arising from fiscal consolidation serve to increase the demand for domestic money thereby warranting the growth in base money arising from growth in official net international reserves. By contrast, however, there may be a stronger case for reverse sterilization either as a means to stimulate private investment or as a way of providing some insurance against future deficit financing demands.

The research and policy agendas considered in this chapter are far from exhausted. Critically, the results and insights discussed here are model based and, as with all such exercises, are sensitive to underlying assumption. Although we are confident that the assumptions made throughout this chapter are sensible, good practice obviously demands that these be tested for robustness. Notwithstanding, the model used here can be extended in a number of directions as circumstances dictate. For example, it will be useful to examine the robustness of the simple policy rules as financial sector reforms take root and the private sector's asset demands evolve. Similarly for changes in fiscal structures and policies. The framework can also be readily extended to allow the authorities to be confronted by additional sources of volatility, for example climate-induced variability in agricultural output. Finally, the model could eventually be modified to reflect operating concerns as the authorities move closer to flexible inflation targeting.

Notes

1 This chapter draws heavily on joint work with Stephen O'Connell, Ed Buffie and Catherine Pattillo (see, for example, Adam *et al.*, 2006, Buffie *et al.*, 2006, and O'Connell *et al.*, 2006). We fully acknowledge our substantial debts to all three but stress that any remaining errors of commission and omission are our own responsibility. We thank participants at the Abuja conference for valuable comments on an earlier draft of this chapter. We also acknowledge the support of the UK Economic and Social Research Council (ESRC) under project RES-156-25-0001 *Managing Macroeconomic Risks in Developing Countries: Policies and Institutions.*

2 See for example IMF (2004, 2005b) and Central Bank of Nigeria (2006). It is clear from these reports that both the authorities and the IMF have been particularly exercised with the appropriate response to 'excess' spending out of oil windfalls and in particular how aggressively the authorities should seek to mop up excess liquidity through the domestic debt market.

3 Direct spending on imports is self-sterilizing and hence has no impact on the domestic deficit financing requirements of government.

4 A version of this model is also described in Adam *et al.* (2006).

5 We do not distinguish between bank and non-bank holdings of money which precludes a consideration of the role of reserve requirements as an instrument of monetary policy.

6 Nonetheless, these short-run shocks themselves are persistent.

7 Note that since we work with the consolidated budget this is an aggregate rate of fiscal saving and is consistent with differential rates of saving by state and federal levels of government.

Appendix Table 5.A1 Model calibration values

Parameter	Values
Non-tradable share (% private spending)	50.0
Private spending (% GDP)	77.0
Official reserves (% GDP)	12.0
Foreign currency (% GDP)	8.0
Domestic currency (% GDP)	17.0
Domestic debt (% GDP)	20.0
Real interest rate (% per annum)	5.0
Inflation (% per annum)	10.0
Implied values	
Nominal interest rate (% per annum)	15.5
Inflation elasticity of money demand	0.45

Source: IMF (2005b).

8 The intervention equation can also be defined in terms of the real exchange rate. Issues of real exchange rate targeting are important elements in the current discussion.
9 Until the oil revenue is spent the windfall has no impact on seigniorage, because net international reserves and net oil proceeds each change by the same amount. As the windfall revenue is spent (increasing the fiscal deficit), the import component of spending continues to leave domestic liquidity unchanged because net international reserves fall by the import component of the rise in the fiscal deficit (while, in the background, net domestic credit rises by the same amount). The liquidity injection associated with the oil windfall corresponds to the non-import component of windfall spending. A buffer-plus-float policy uses foreign exchange sales to sterilize this in full, leaving seigniorage unchanged.
10 An alternative, broadly equivalent, formulation of the sterilization rule would link sterilization directly to the growth rate of domestic liquidity rather than the level of intervention.
11 These volatilities (standard deviations) correspond to the analytical standard deviations of the model variables when the model is subjected to a *sequence* of oil shocks of the form analysed in Table 5.1. A complete set of results is available on request.

References

Adam, Christopher, Stephen O'Connell, Edward Buffie and Catherine Pattillo, 2006, 'Monetary Responses to Aid Surges in Africa', paper presented at WIDER conference on Aid Policies and Principles, Helsinki, June 2006.

Batini, Nicoletta, 2004, 'Achieving and Maintaining Price Stability in Nigeria', IMF Working Paper 04/97, Washington, DC.

Buffie, Edward, Christopher Adam, Stephen O'Connell and Catherine Pattillo, 2006, 'Fiscal Inertia, Donor Credibility and the Monetary Management of Aid Surges', mimeo, Department of Economics, Indiana University, Bloomington, IN.

Calvo, G., 1983, 'Staggered Prices in a Utility-Maximizing Framework', *Journal of Monetary Economics* 12 (3), 983–998.

Central Bank of Nigeria, 2006, *Economic Report for the First Half of 2006*, Abuja: Central Bank of Nigeria.

Collier, Paul and Jan Willem Gunning, 2005, 'Asset Policies During an Oil Windfall: Some Simple Analytics', *The World Economy* 28 (10), 1401–1415.

IMF, 2004, 'Nigeria: 2004 Article IV Consultation—Staff Report', IMF Country Report 04/239, IMF, Washington, DC.

IMF, 2005a, 'The Macroeconomics of Scaling up Aid: Lessons from Recent Experience', by Andrew Berg, Shekhar Aiyar, Mumtaz Hussain, Shaun Roache, Tokhir Mirzoev and Amber Mahone, IMF Occasional Papers 253, IMF, Washington, DC.

IMF, 2005b, 'Nigeria: 2005 Article IV Consultation—Staff Report', IMF Country Report 05/302, IMF, Washington, DC.

IMF, 2005c, 'Nigeria: Selected Issues and Statistical Appendix', IMF Country Report 05/303, IMF, Washington, DC.

O'Connell, Stephen, Christopher Adam, Edward Buffie and Catherine Pattillo, 2006, 'Managing External Volatility: Policy Options for Central Banks in Low Income Countries', in Nicoletta Batini (ed.), *Monetary Policy in Emerging Markets and Other Developing Countries*, New York: Nova Scientific Publishers.

Sala-i-Martin, Xavier and Arvind Subramanian, 2003, 'Addressing the Natural Resource Curse: An Illustration from Nigeria', IMF Working Paper 03/139, Washington, DC.

6

Trade Policy: Prospects and Challenges

Olumuyiwa Alaba, Adeola Adenikinju and Paul Collier

6.1 Introduction

As in many spheres of economic policy, Nigeria inherited from past military regimes a trade policy that was out of line with most other developing countries, and so an active process of reform was appropriate. Nigerian trade policy has been distinctive in imposing both quantitative bans on some imports, a practice now rarely used elsewhere, and high and variable tariffs on many other imports. Reform is thus likely to involve the abandonment of quantitative restrictions and the reduction and harmonization of tariffs.

The reform of Nigerian trade policy has always been controversial. Stiff opposition has arisen from interest groups including organized labour and local manufacturers. Some legislators and concerned groups are also worried about the impact of liberalization on the Nigerian economy. Among issues of concern are the fiscal implications and the effects on production, local costs of input and consumer goods, poverty and employment. This chapter analyses these concerns about liberalization.

The process of trade liberalization can potentially be undertaken following two different routes. One is for the Nigerian government to make the changes unilaterally; the other is for it to conform to the Economic Community of West African States (ECOWAS) rules of regional tariff harmonization on a structure of common external tariffs (CET). In 2005, the government announced a commitment to harmonize most tariffs with the CET, the exception being the retention of a much higher top band of 50 per cent, as against the CET top band of 20 per cent. There are advantages and disadvantages to each of these routes.

There are three significant advantages of the ECOWAS route. First, it provides a clear benchmark to which Nigerian tariffs can rapidly be lowered. Second, it provides a political lock-in mechanism that would restrain future increases in tariffs and so give greater credibility to any reform. Third, it would help to create a subregional market that would be significantly bigger than the Nigerian domestic market and so enable some scale economies to be reaped. There is, however, a significant disadvantage. Unlike most other ECOWAS members, Nigeria's exports are dominated by oil, and this makes the effects of any trade policy quite distinctive.

In turn, this makes it questionable whether the trade policy that is appropriate for Nigeria is the same as that for its non-oil-producing neighbours. As a result, the Nigerian government might find itself locked-in to a trade policy regime that is inappropriate for the country.

In Section 6.2, we set out the simple analytics of trade policy. Trade policy is one of the most counter-intuitive areas of economic policy: things are seldom what they seem. This section shows why. It shows, for example, why an oil economy is distinctive and the effects of a regional customs union. In Section 6.3, we describe the history of Nigerian trade policy. In Section 6.4, we analyse the impact of the 2005 tariff changes that harmonized with ECOWAS in more detail, using a simulation model to estimate some possible effects. In Section 6.5, we bring the analysis together with a brief conclusion.

6.2 The analytics of Nigerian trade policy

Unfortunately, the economic consequences of trade policies are not intuitively obvious. We set out some critical analytical building blocks that are pertinent for the particular features of the Nigerian economy.

6.2.1 The distinctive effects of oil

Trade policy in an oil-exporting economy is distinctive partly because it does not affect the overall volume of imports and partly because of the counter-intuitive implications for government revenue.

The effect on imports

Oil exports are evidently of value to Nigeria only because they pay for imports. Oil exports are determined by investment in the oil sector and by the world price of oil. Hence, the overall amount of Nigeria's imports is determined by these oil fundamentals, and not by trade policy. Trade restrictions, whether quantitative or tariff, merely change the composition of imports, shifting choices away from the more restricted items to the less restricted items. Hence, no matter how apparently 'protective' Nigerian trade policy is, it does not protect the Nigerian economy from imports, but merely protects some privileged sectors at the expense of increased imports in other sectors.

Some restrictions on imports are easy to justify: products such as hard drugs and guns should be curtailed, and preventing their import can be a good control mechanism. However, most restrictions of imports are not of this form but reflect competing domestic lobbies of producers striving to curtail competition from imports. As import restrictions on one commodity simply shift imports to other commodities, this is to an extent a 'zero-sum game', in which the gains for one set of producers are at the expense of other producers. However, it is more likely to be a 'negative-sum game', in which there are net losses, because Nigerian consumers end up worse off. This generates a tension between the private good and the public good. The private good is for individual producers to lobby for higher protection for their own products, while the public good is to avoid the resulting plethora of import restrictions. Indeed, the considerable resources devoted to lobbying government for protection constitute a further waste, which can best be avoided by the government pre-committing itself not to concede to such pressures. In most countries, this type of pre-commitment has been achieved through binding agreements under the auspices of the World Trade Organization (WTO): governments help each other credibly to resist lobbying by mutual commitments.

The effect on government revenue

While, from the viewpoint of efficient resource allocation, a regime of far fewer import restrictions seems appropriate, would this have adverse implications for government revenue? The second paradox of an oil-exporting economy is that, although tariffs appear to raise revenue for the government, in reality, they reduce its revenue. This is because, in an oil economy, the government gets its revenue not just from tariffs but also from oil. The direct effects of tariffs on revenue are more than undone by the indirect effects of tariffs on government oil revenues.

To see these effects, first consider a simple, stylized depiction of government revenue in the absence of any trade restrictions. The government gets a dollar income from oil and sells the dollars to citizens who use them to purchase imports. The value of the revenue in naira thus depends partly upon the dollar income, which we will treat as fixed, as well as partly upon the exchange rate, which is determined by the demand for imports. This is shown in Figure 6.1. This simply shows the demand curve for imports – demand is higher if the naira price of imports is lower – and the fixed total supply of imports, which is given by the fixed total value of oil exports. Government revenue is the shaded area – the naira price of imports multiplied by their quantity. The price of imports in this case is

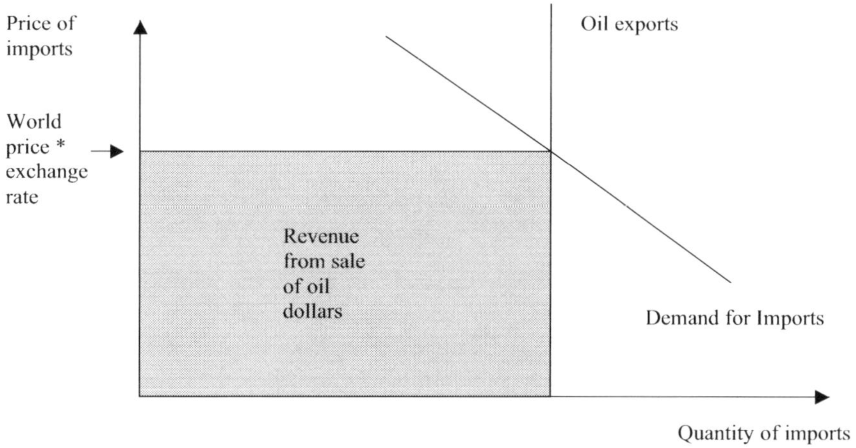

Figure 6.1 Government revenue from oil with no import restrictions.

simply the exchange rate: how much a dollar costs in terms of naira. Government revenue is determined by how much Nigerian importers are willing to pay for the amount of dollars that the Nigerian government is selling.

Now introduce import restrictions into the analysis, initially as a uniform tariff, say of 20 per cent. This does not change the price at which the demand for imports equals their supply. The only difference is that now the price that importers have to pay for imports has two components – the exchange rate at which they purchase dollars, and the tariff rate they pay when importing goods. Hence, as shown in Figure 6.2, the exchange rate appreciates to offset the tariff. The government gets the same total revenue as in the absence of tariffs, but now it raises it more laboriously, partly through the sale of dollars as before, but now also through a customs administration. Even if the customs administration is completely efficient and costless, it raises no net revenue. To the extent that it is corrupt or costly, it ends up reducing overall revenue.

Finally, introduce import restrictions that are not uniform. Instead of all imports paying 20 per cent, some pay more and some pay less. The effect of this is to shift the choice on imports to a pattern that importers would not otherwise have chosen, and so to a choice that they find less valuable. In terms of our figures, the whole demand curve for imports is shifted inwards – the same amount of dollars is now worth less in naira. The consequence is, as shown in Figure 6.3, that the overall value of government revenue is reduced relative to either a uniform tariff or unrestricted trade. Hence, the revenues reported to be generated by the customs service are an illusion: the present trade regime is costing the government money.

The effects of a customs union

We now review the simple analytics of a customs union such as membership of ECOWAS. The effects depend very much upon what the customs union is benchmarked against: continuing unilateral tariffs or unilateral tariff reduction. This

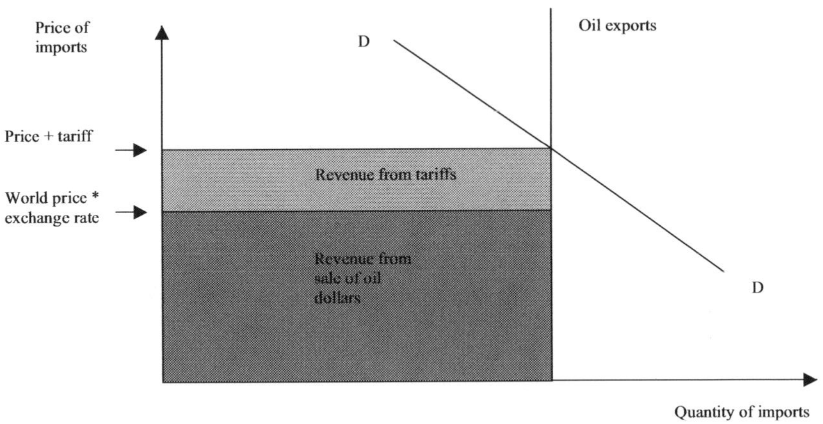

Figure 6.2 Government revenue from oil with a uniform import tariff.

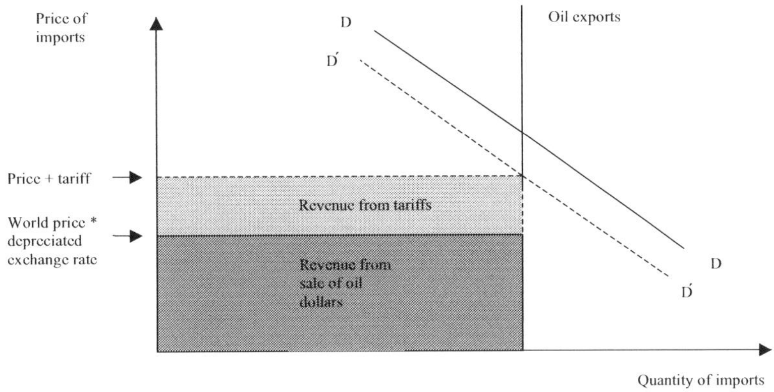

Figure 6.3 Government revenue from oil with multiple import tariffs.

broadly corresponds to the distinction between the short-run effects of ECOWAS, where the relevant comparison is with Nigeria's existing tariff policies, and the long-term effects of ECOWAS, where the relevant comparison is the best trade policy that Nigeria might otherwise adopt.

The short-run effect of joining a customs union such as ECOWAS is partly to lower the overall level of Nigerian tariff protection against non-ECOWAS countries and partly to create free trade with other ECOWAS members.

The tariff-lowering effect is likely to be beneficial overall, although it involves contraction of those activities that are currently most heavily protected and expansion of those that are less protected. The effect of free trade within ECOWAS is more complicated and ambiguous. As the Nigerian economy is roughly the same size as the rest of ECOWAS, the new market would be approximately double the size of the Nigerian market. This enables all firms to reap greater economies of scale, producing for the entire ECOWAS market rather than just for the Nigerian market. This scale effect generates overall net gains. However, a customs union also generates powerful transfers among its members, the magnitude of which depend upon the height of the common external tariff. ECOWAS proposes an external tariff on most final goods of 20 per cent, with the tariff on luxury goods set at 50 per cent, which are high rates by international standards, so the redistribution effect will be substantial. Nigeria might potentially gain at the expense of other ECOWAS members or lose to other members. Essentially, all products produced within ECOWAS that are also imported from the rest of the world will sell at around 20 per cent above their world price as a result of the tariff. The ECOWAS members that gain will be those that are net sellers of these protected products to other members.

The tariff-lowering effect concerns Nigeria's imports from outside ECOWAS, whereas the internal free trade effect concerns Nigeria's trade within ECOWAS. The size of these two trade flows is radically different. Overwhelmingly, most of Nigeria's trade is with Europe and North America. Very limited trading relationships exist with ECOWAS member states as evident from Figure 6.4.

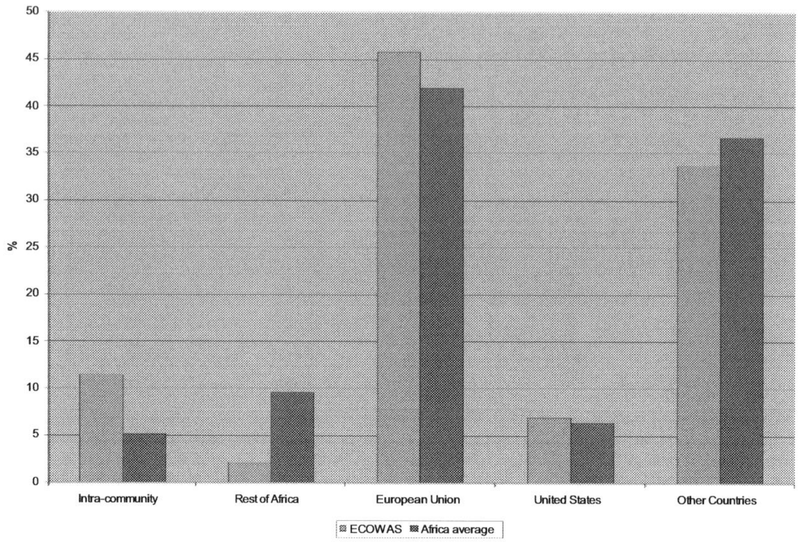

Figure 6.4 Sources of imports (%), 1994–2000.
Source: ECA (2004).

Within ECOWAS trade, whether Nigeria is a net seller or a net purchaser of manufactures will depend upon how competitive its manufacturing sector is relative to those of other members. At present, Nigeria is generally a high-cost production environment because of problems such as unreliable power and poorly functioning ports, as discussed elsewhere in this volume. For example, its ports are markedly less efficient than those elsewhere in West Africa, and this raises the costs of manufacturing production. Further, although Nigeria is a much larger economy than the other members of ECOWAS, its per capita income is much lower than some of them, such as Ghana and Senegal. The likely effect of a customs union among developing countries is to benefit the higher-income members at the expense of the lower-income members. This is because the common protection against the developed northern countries advantages those economies within ECOWAS that come closest to resembling those of the developed north. In effect, the poorer countries are forced to purchase their imports at higher prices from the richer ECOWAS members instead of at lower prices from the northern countries.

The long-run effects of adherence to the ECOWAS customs union depend upon what alternative policies they preclude. If the alternative is a reversion to a regime of high and volatile trade restrictions, then ECOWAS is likely to be beneficial through its imposition of a reasonably open and stable import regime. If the alternative is the best trade policy that Nigeria could have, then ECOWAS is likely to be costly, because it locks the government into higher tariffs than it would otherwise find efficient. In particular, as we discuss below, ECOWAS imposes 10 per cent tariffs on the inputs used in manufacturing processes. Tariffs on inputs are extremely important because modern manufacturing is no longer about complete processes of turning raw materials into finished products. Rather, firms find it more efficient to specialize in some particular stage of the manufacturing process, importing earlier stages and often exporting incomplete products for the next stage to be undertaken elsewhere: trade is now increasingly in tasks, not products. The countries that participate in this trade have very largely eliminated tariffs on inputs: high tariffs on inputs would render their firms uncompetitive. Hence, the ECOWAS tariffs on inputs will add to the cost of manufacturing inputs in Nigeria, making Nigeria uncompetitive in export markets beyond ECOWAS. As the ECOWAS market outside Nigeria is tiny relative to the world market, this may be important.

The long-term effects of ECOWAS thus depend upon the view taken about Nigeria's prospects in manufacturing. In the worst case, Nigerian manufacturing remains not only globally uncompetitive, but uncompetitive within the region. In this case, adoption of the ECOWAS common external tariff would lead to an income transfer to neighbours. Neighbouring countries will be net exporters of manufactures to Nigeria, and Nigerians will have to pay these firms prices 20 per cent above the world level on account of the tariff protection they enjoy.

In the most favourable case, Nigeria gradually exploits the magnificent location of Lagos, by reforming the power sector, the ports and other current impediments to world-class levels of production efficiency. If Lagos is thus turned into a location that has the potential to be globally competitive, the long-term effect of ECOWAS would be very costly, as the 10 per cent tariffs on manufacturing inputs would preclude it.

In between these two cases, Nigerian manufacturing might become sufficiently competitive to develop viable niches against ECOWAS competitors, but not sufficiently competitive to compete globally. In this case, Nigeria would benefit from ECOWAS, partly at the expense of other members. However, the composition of Nigerian manufacturing would inevitably change. The essence of manufacturing activity in a customs union is that each country tends to specialize in a few products, importing the rest from other members. As the Nigerian economy is around half of the total ECOWAS economy, in the 'neutral' circumstance in which Nigerian manufacturing was as competitive as the rest of the region, around half of present manufacturing activity would contract, and half would expand.

A long-term cost of taking the unilateral rather than the regional route is that Nigeria would face tariffs on its exports to its neighbours. Potentially, reciprocal regional liberalization on the model of the European Union (EU) is growth enhancing (Oyejide *et al.*, 2003). For example, Oyejide *et al.* (2003) find that belonging to the EU is growth enhancing through an efficiency gain effect, and Coe and Moghadam (1993) estimate that about 0.3 per cent of the growth experienced in France during the 1980s could be ascribed to its membership of the EU. The Cecchini Report (1988) estimates that between 2.5 per cent and 6.5 per cent of the increase in EU countries' income could be explained by the 1992 internal market arrangement. However, ECOWAS has two important differences from the EU. First, the common external tariff of the EU is much lower than that of ECOWAS and, second, intra-EU trade was already far larger than intra-ECOWAS trade. Both these effects suggest that ECOWAS will generate more income-reducing 'trade diversion' and less income-raising 'trade creation' than the EU. This is indeed consistent with the results of our simulation analysis in Section 6.4, which finds the eventual gains in terms of growth to be only around 0.1 per cent of GDP.

6.2.2 Nominal and 'effective' protection

Announced tariff rates give a misleading impression of the cost advantage they confer to protected activities. A useful concept is 'effective protection', which shows how much higher costs of production can be as a result of a tariff system. The concept is particularly important in a world of trade in 'tasks', as each firm adds only a small percentage to the value of the final product. The key point made by effective protection is that a tariff of say 20 per cent raises the price of the product by 20 per cent. Thus, if the firm only performs a task that contributes say 10 per cent to the true value of the product, the tariff allows the firm to have costs that are triple world levels. To see this, suppose that, in the absence of tariffs, the final product would sell for 100 naira. The firm imports inputs costing 90 naira and adds value by finishing the product, raising the value to 100 naira. With tariff protection, it is now able to sell the product at 120 naira, so that its costs of finishing the product can rise from 10 naira to 30 naira. In this example, although the nominal tariff rate is only 20 per cent, the rate of effective protection is a massive 200 per cent. Effective protection also takes into account tariffs on inputs, which tend to reduce the effective protective rate. Hence, the protection provided by a tariff system cannot be inferred directly from the announced rates, but must be calculated from the entire system. For example, the 50 per cent tariff on luxury imports that is part of the ECOWAS common external tariff structure generates extremely high effective protection for the domestic production of luxury goods. This induces firms to produce luxury goods even if virtually all the inputs are imported: because they attract much lower tariffs, the tiny amount of genuine value added is rewarded with very high returns, enabling production to be very inefficient and yet remain profitable.

6.2.3 'Parallel' trade

Trade restrictions drive a wedge between the domestic and the international prices of traded goods and, in so doing, provide incentives for illegal trade (Bhagwati and Hansen, 1973; Pitt, 1981). Illegal trade has three main impacts: it liberalizes the trade regime, shifts income from the private to the public sector and wastes resources (O'Connell, 1997). High tariff rates and non-tariff barriers adopted by Nigeria over the years have induced most of Nigeria's trade with ECOWAS members to take this parallel form: an estimated $2 billion annually. For instance, Benin and Cameroon act as 'warehouse states' for products that are either banned or highly taxed in Nigeria such as second-hand and retreaded tyres, second-hand clothes, textiles and garments, and used cars (Adenikinju and Alaba, 2004).

6.3 The practice of Nigerian trade policy

Successive Nigerian governments have made frequent changes to both tariff and non-tariff policies. Cumulatively, this has made the trade policy regime unpredictable, thereby increasing uncertainty and discouraging investment. It has also created a profusion of different restrictions, ostensibly imposed for widely different reasons. We consider the two forms of protection in turn.

6.3.1 Tariff policy

Tariffs were first introduced in the 1950s, with the motivation being revenue generation. Note that, as this pre-dated the arrival of oil, tariffs at this stage indeed generated net revenue to the government. Duties were placed on different categories of consumer goods imports from the latter part of the 1950s through to the very early 1960s. At that time, capital goods carried zero duty, and the duty on intermediate goods varied from 10 per cent to 15 per cent, while duties on consumer goods ranged from 25 per cent to 30 per cent.

However, tariff policy soon became used for the macroeconomic objective of balance of payments equilibrium. It is now recognized that trade policy is an inefficient way of attaining this objective, the exchange rate being the appropriate instrument. Tariffs increased between 1963 and 1965 with the introduction of the Approved User Scheme (AUS) and the Customs Tariff Act in 1964 and 1965, respectively, with differential rates sustained on various categories of goods. In addition to the balance of payments objective, there was some concern to develop the Nigerian manufacturing sector by means of protection from international competition. The AUS therefore gave large duty concessions to raw materials and other categories of intermediate imports. The review of rates continued as the economic situation of the country fluctuated. Thus, in 1966, there were drastic increases in rates on motor vehicles, intermediate and consumer goods imports, with the reviewed rates being as high as 150 per cent. In 1969, not only were tariffs increased further but duties on exports were introduced. The first oil boom of 1973 induced relaxation of the hitherto stringent trade policy practices. As oil revenues dipped in 1977, duties on items such as motor vehicles, garments and alcoholic drinks were increased to as high as between 100 and 150 per cent. The policy was intensified through to 1979 with minor exceptions. During the second oil boom, which started in 1980, tariffs were again reduced. The review came in the form of withdrawal of duties on vessels, while those on manufacturing raw materials were modified, with a number of them completely removed. Concessionary duties were also granted for importers and exporters far away from ports. For instance, duty on completely knocked down parts was 15 per cent in Enugu, but 20 per cent in Lagos. Import and export duties were also liberalized for a number of consumer items. Balance of payments and debt crises, which emerged in 1982 and 1983, motivated the authorities to adopt high tariffs and duties to discourage the importation of consumer goods, such as cigarettes and alcohol, while newly introduced tariff rates covered 49 new items. There were also drastic reductions with respect to import tariffs on items of 'public capital' such as electricity equipment. This continued until 1985, purposely to provide an enabling environment for production.

In 1986, with the use of the exchange rate for the balance of payments objective as part of the Structural Adjustment Programme (SAP), there was some liberalization of trade policy. However, post-SAP, tariff policy remains restrictive. The ostensible objectives are to protect existing domestic industries and to reduce the country's dependence on imports but, as noted in Section 6.2, this second objective is incoherent as imports are determined by the value of oil exports, not by trade policy. Despite massive global tariff reduction, Nigeria's tariff policy is still largely the same as that operated through the 1960s and the 1990s. The rates have escalated in respect of semi-processed and processed goods. High tariffs continued to apply to products that are available locally and those that the country has the potential to produce in the future (World Trade Organization, 1991, 1998, 2005a; Oyejide *et al.*, 2003).

6.3.2 Non-tariff policy

The history of non-tariff barriers started with the introduction of import licences in the early 1960s. The primary purpose of the policy was to address balance of payments problems, although there were also concerns expressed about 'dumping' and the need to safeguard the economy from the adverse consequences of international economic relations. The policy was initially directed at restricting textile products from Japan and Hong Kong. Non-tariff restrictions intensified in 1964 with specific embargoes on non-essential imports. By 1965, there was a blanket restriction on a number of products, including all products from Hong Kong and Japan, a measure that evidently inadvertently advantaged European suppliers. In the same year, there was also prohibition of direct repayments to overseas customers for imports, while certificates of import and multiple other documents had to be produced for all categories of imports. Trade restrictions were intensified until the oil boom.

With the onset of the oil windfall, relatively liberal policies became operational, reflecting the tendency of import restrictions to be used for balance of payments objectives. Reflecting this use of trade policy, during the dip in world oil prices between 1977 and 1979, import licences were reintroduced and a long list of items was banned outright. With the onset of the second oil boom in 1980, non-tariff barriers were again relaxed and, as oil revenues started to decline in 1982, they were retightened so that, by 1986, they were more severe than ever before. Through the mid-1980s and early 1990s, virtually all West African countries implemented unilateral trade liberalization programmes under various SAPs supported by the World Bank and the International Monetary Fund (IMF). However, despite these liberalizations, Nigerian trade policy remains unusually restrictive. Indeed, the import prohibition system is not compatible with the rules of the WTO. The Nigerian government has typically argued that import prohibitions are easier to monitor than price-based measures, as the presence of the products on local markets is in principle sufficient for enforcement, in contrast to tariffs, which may not be paid in practice (World Trade Organization, 1998). However, the larger point is that trade policy is not the appropriate instrument for balance of payments objectives as these are better achieved through adjusting the exchange rate.

6.3.3 The introduction of common external tariffs in West Africa

By the 1990s, Nigeria's trade policy was distinctive both in its overall restrictiveness and in its heavy reliance upon non-tariff measures. One approach to gradual trade liberalization has therefore been to move towards harmonization with neighbouring countries through the adoption of a common external tariff (CET) and free trade among members. This regional approach provides both a clear benchmark for tariff reduction and a subsequent enforcement mechanism once liberalization has been attained. Such an enforcement, or lock-in, mechanism is important in view of the history of Nigerian trade policy with trade restrictions going up and down so frequently as to introduce considerable unpredictability into policy.

By 2000, the UEMOA[1] group of West African countries had set up a customs union with a common external tariff that was much more liberal than Nigerian trade restrictions; the rates are shown in Table 6.1.

Nigeria and the other non-UEMOA countries in the ECOWAS community have long agreed to make moves to conform with these CET rates. However, this commitment has not been respected: only the UEMOA members have operated within the most favoured nation (MFN) applied and final bound tariff rates agreed by ECOWAS members. In other member-countries, the simple average tariff on all products ranged from 6.5 per cent in Guinea to 29.1 per cent in Nigeria in the period 2000–2004 (Table 6.2). The Economic Commission for Africa (ECA) has ranked government efforts to harmonize their trade policies within ECOWAS; the ranking is shown in Figure 6.5.

Countries' performances have varied in terms of their integration efforts. A recent publication by the ECA ranked all the countries in the sub-region by the intensity of efforts they have made in conforming with the goals of ECOWAS. The rankings are shown in Figure 6.2.

It is evident that Nigeria has been lagging behind. It has only meaningfully removed tariffs applying to unprocessed goods, but has maintained import prohibitions on some products, including those originating from ECOWAS member-states (Enterplan, 2005). A report further suggests that only 16 per cent of Nigeria's tariff lines are at or below the UEMOA target (see This Day,[2] 2005).

The level of tariff bindings across the sub-region gives a clearer picture of the constraints imposed by tariff policy on free flows of trade (specifically imports).

Table 6.1 The Common External Tariff structure

Classifications	Category of goods	Rates
Class 1	Essential social goods	0%
Class 2	Basic goods, raw material, capital goods	5%
Class 3	Semi-processed inputs and products	10%
Class 4	Customer goods and other products not mentioned above	20%

Table 6.2 MFN applied tariffs for West Africa (2000–2004)

	Simple average			Maximum		
Country	All	Agricultural	Non-agricultural	All	Agricultural	Non-agricultural
Benin	12.0	14.3	11.6	20	20	20
Burkina Faso	12.0	14.0	11.7	20	20	20
Côte d'Ivoire	12.0	14.3	11.6	20	20	20
Gambia	12.8	14.9	12.5	18	18	18
Ghana	13.1	17.3	12.5	233	20	233
Guinea	6.5	6.6	6.4	7	7	7
Guinea-Bissau	12.0	14.3	11.6	20	20	20
Mali	12.0	14.3	11.6	20	20	20
Niger	12.0	14.3	11.6	20	20	20
Nigeria	29.1	50.4	25.6	150	150	100
Senegal	12.0	14.3	11.6	20	20	20
Sierra Leone	13.7	16.4	13.3	30	30	30
Togo	12.0	14.3	11.6	20	20	20

Source: World Trade Organization (2005b).

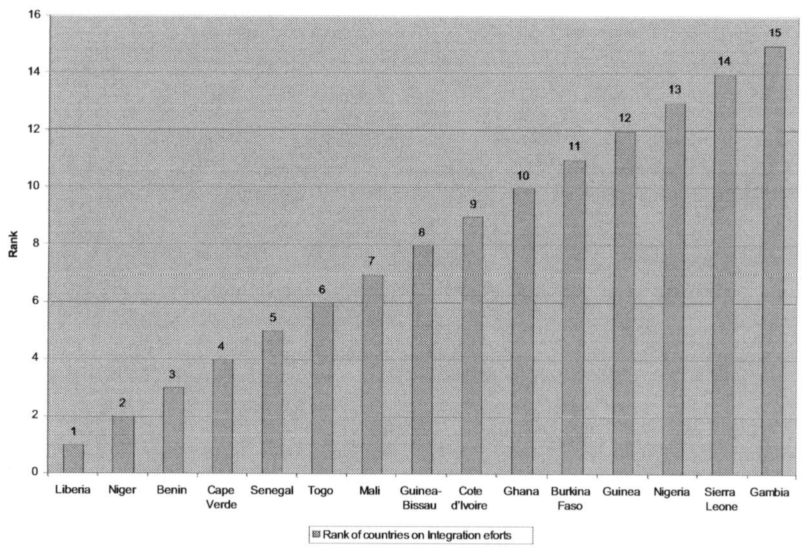

Figure 6.5 Ranking of countries within ECOWAS on integration efforts since 1994.
Note: Lower number indicates better performance.
Source: ECA (2004).

Intra-ECOWAS trade preferences are yet to be effective, and the MFN rates among the community's members are still very high (Table 6.3).

Both the average tariff rates and the level of binding are important. Binding, which reduces the uncertainty that otherwise surrounds trade policy, is limited in most West African countries, which do not wish to commit themselves in case they need to resort to higher tariffs for revenue purposes. Only Senegal, Sierra Leone, Niger and Guinea-Bissau have binding coverage approaching 100 per cent. Only 19 per cent of Nigeria's tariffs are bound.

In addition to tariff barriers, an important obstacle to inter-regional trade is the existence of 'checkpoints' at which officials can impede the transit of goods and extort unofficial payments. As shown in Table 6.4, Nigeria has more of these than any other ECOWAS country.

The analytics of a customs union suggest that, in a union among developing countries, the most developed will benefit more than the less developed. Most of the members of ECOWAS are 'least developed' with low income, small populations and little trade. Nigeria is the main outlier: its economy is particularly distinctive in view of the dominance of oil. Other than Nigeria, Côte d'Ivoire and Ghana are the only members that are not categorized as least developed. The population of ECOWAS is around 250 million with Nigeria alone accounting for half of this. Thus, ECOWAS is dramatically *less* important to Nigeria in terms of market expansion than to its other members.

Table 6.3 Final MFN bound tariffs (%), West African countries

	Binding coverage			**Maximum**		
Country	**All**	**Agricultural**	**Non-agricultural**	**All**	**Agricultural**	**Non-agricultural**
Benin	39.4	100	30.1	100	100	60
Burkina Faso	39.2	100	29.9	100	100	100
Côte d'Ivoire	33.1	100	22.9	64	64	25
Gambia	13.7	100	0.5	110	110	110
Ghana	14.3	100	1.2	99	99	99
Guinea	38.9	100	29.6	75	75	40
Guinea-Bissau	97.7	100	97.4	50	40	50
Mali	40.6	100	31.6	75	75	60
Niger	96.8	100	96.3	200	200	200
Nigeria	19.3	100	6.9	150	150	150
Senegal	100	100	100	30	30	30
Sierra Leone	100	100	100	80	80	80
Togo	14.0	100	0.9	80	80	80

Source: World Trade Organization (2005b).

Table 6.4 Official checkpoints on selected West African highways, December 2000

Highway	Distance (km)	No. of checkpoints	No. of checkpoints (per 100 km)
Lagos, Nigeria–Abidjan, Côte d'Ivoire	992	69	7
Lomé, Togo–Ouagadougou, Burkina Faso	989	34	4
Niamey, Niger–Ouagadougou, Burkina Faso	529	20	4
Abidjan, Côte d'Ivoire–Ouagadougou, Burkina Faso	1122	37	3
Cotonou, Benin–Niamey, Niger	1036	34	3
Accra, Ghana–Ouagadougou, Burkina Faso	972	15	2

Source: ECOWAS (2003).

The economic structure of ECOWAS members in shown in Table 6.5, which brings out how distinctive Nigeria is from other members. Despite being a large economy, Nigeria has an unusually small manufacturing sector.

Levels of gross domestic product (GDP) also vary massively. Gambia, Guinea-Bissau, Liberia and Cape Verde between them amount to only around $2 billion. Other than Nigeria, the three largest economies are Senegal, Ghana and Côte d'Ivoire, each in the range $8–16 billion. In contrast, Nigerian GDP is around $77 billion, half the entire GDP of ECOWAS. Only in respect of per capita GDP is Nigeria not an outlier. The range within ECOWAS is from $426 in Liberia to $5705 in Cape Verde, with Nigeria roughly in the middle at $2018.

6.4 A simulation of the impact of the ECOWAS common external tariff on Nigeria

In this section, we examine the impact of a 100 per cent adoption of the CET on the Nigerian economy using a dynamic computable general equilibrium (CGE) model. The structure of the model is described by Nwafor *et al.* (2006). The model results made a distinction between the initial impact of adoption of the policy on the economy (short run) and the final impact (long run). The qualitative and quantitative impacts of a policy in the short run are often not the same in the long run after several adjustments in capital and labour have worked themselves through the economy.

This is also consistent with the literature, which suggests that trade liberalization (tariff reduction) may have two potential impacts. One is the short-run impact on government revenue, production, consumption and income. The second is the long-run efficiency gain argument, which relates to a possible increase in output through economies of scale and long-run reduction in prices (Oyejide,

Table 6.5 Structure of ECOWAS economies in 2005 (as percentages of GDP)

Country	Agriculture	Industry (total)	Industry (manufacturing)	Services	Net duties and taxes on product
Benin	31.3	13.7	8.0	47.4	9.4
Burkina Faso	28.0	19.0	12.2	46.1	8.0
Cape Verde	9.92	13.9	4.7	69.0	10.1
Côte d'Ivoire	25.0	19.8	15.5	49.0	6.3
Gambia	25.9	8.1	3.1	57.1	9.8
Ghana	37.0	21.0	7.4	31.3	13.4
Guinea	21.6	30.9	3.4	41.9	5.9
Guinea-Bissau	52.0	12.1	7.3	33.4	2.5
Liberia	66.5	9.3	5.4	19.7	4.5
Mali	35.9	21.3	8.7	33.5	9.7
Niger	52.1	14.6	7.2	32.7	1.03
Nigeria	28.9	35.1	5.2	32.9	3.1
Senegal	14.4	21.7	13.9	52.2	12.7
Sierra Leone	43.0	27.2	1.6	24.6	5.8
Togo	39.5	16.4	7.8	36.8	9.0
ECOWAS average	29.1	28.2	7.5	37.0	5.7

Source: ECOWAS (2006).

1986; Kuji Ltd, 2002, Alaba, 2003; Nwafor *et al.*, 2006). There are several channels through which trade liberalization policies are transmitted into economic welfare: via the impact on production that comes through reduction in the cost of production and its consequent effects on demand and consumption; and through the impact of lower product prices on household income and welfare (Olofin *et al.*, 2001; Soludo *et al.*, 2003; Adenikinju and Alaba, 2004; Nwafor *et al.*, 2006).

In 2005, the highest tariffs recorded by the Nigerian customs were 150 per cent, and these were levied on two manufactured consumer goods – unsweetened water and tobacco. Most goods with tariffs above 100 per cent were consumer goods. The lowest tariffs were zero for some capital goods and medical equipment or inputs (chemicals and so on for medical activities) for example.

In implementing the ECOWAS tariffs, the Nigerian government adopted the following broad rates:

- 0 per cent for industrial machinery and necessities;
- 5 per cent for raw materials;
- 10 per cent for semi-finished goods;[3]
- 20 per cent for intermediate/finished goods;
- 50 per cent for luxury goods.

From this, we note that the government more or less chose to reduce tariffs on luxury consumer goods (and others) from their 150 per cent levels to 50 per cent rather than adopt the ECOWAS top rate of 20 per cent. On the basis of these new broad targets, a new tariff book for 2005/6 was published for imports at a ten-digit HS code level with a coverage of over 4000 tariff lines. This new tariff book formed the basis of the experiments considered in the study.

The adoption of the ECOWAS CET implies a major revision of the existing tariff structure of Nigeria. The revision will necessitate increases in tariff rates in some sectors and decreases in others. Agricultural food is not expected to be affected as the sector is not regarded as an importable sector. Average tariff rates will go up in the following sectors: oil and other mining and consumer goods manufacturing. Agricultural export, capital goods manufacturing and intermediate goods manufacturing will, however, experience a general reduction in existing import tariff rates. The changes in the average sectoral tariff rates for Nigeria consistent with the ECOWAS CET are shown in Table 6.6.

Analysis of the model results shows that there will be both economy-wide and sectoral impact of the tariff changes on the Nigerian economy. The short-run effects are also generally different from the long-run effects.[4] We discuss the two groups of effects here.

The adoption of the CET is expected to have a non-marginal impact on some macroeconomic aggregates including GDP. Table 6.7 summarizes these impacts for selected periods and the average for 2005–2020. The table shows that most macroeconomic variables are likely to decline after the adoption of the CET. In general, all prices including wages, consumer price index (CPI) and the prices of producer goods decline. This decline results essentially from increased competition in the economy due to expansion in supply and efficiency gains. The lower import tariffs will lower production costs, and competition from exports will enhance efficiency and lead to the exit of non-efficient firms.

The consumer price index falls by –1.57 per cent in the long run. The nominal wage rate also declines. However, while nominal consumption falls, the decline in CPI is faster, leading to some marginal increase in real consumption. The fall in nominal wages leads to a fall in nominal income for both urban and rural households. However, in real terms, urban households benefit from the tariff reductions as the fall in consumer prices is greater than the decline in nominal income. Rural households suffer from a decline in both real and nominal income.

Finally, although nominal GDP declines by a mean of –1.27 per cent over the period, real GDP rises marginally by 0.12 per cent. The marginal impact of the CET on real GDP is also consistent with an earlier study on the impact of trade liberalization in Nigeria (see Olofin *et al.*, 2001).

Effects at the sectoral level are also tiny. The output of agricultural food declines in both the short run and the long run because of increased competition from imports. However, the other sectors increase output due largely to a reduction in the cost of production. Oil and mining recorded the highest increase in output, 0.64 per cent over the base year output. Also, except for exports of oil and other mining, which declined in the short run, all other exportable sectors

Table 6.6 Direction of change in import tariffs due to the adoption of ECOWAS CET

Sector	2005 base tariffs (%)	% compliance with ECOWAS	% change in base tariffs
Agriculture – food	Not imported	Not imported	Not imported
Agriculture – export	20	13	–35
Oil and other mining	3	9	+200
Manufacturing – consumer goods	12	17	+42
Manufacturing – capital	9	8	–11
Manufacturing – intermediate	7	5	–29
Services	0 (approximation)	0 (approximation)	0

Source: Nwafor *et al.* (2006).

experienced an increase in exports after the adoption of the CET. The sectors' lower prices make their exports more attractive to the world market (Table 6.8).

The above discussion suggests that the CET will have only a very small impact on the Nigerian economy. This is consistent both with the structure of Nigeria's trade, which is overwhelmingly with countries outside ECOWAS, and also with the small size of the rest of ECOWAS. The main consequence of the CET is thus the tariff reduction effect, which brings Nigerian tariffs against non-ECOWAS members down to the CET rate.

Table 6.7 Impact of CET adoption (percentage increase over the base year)

	2006	2010	2015	2020	Mean
Wages	–2.14	–2.18	–2.24	–2.27	–2.21
Consumer prices	–1.51	–1.57	–1.60	–1.6	–1.57
Producer prices	–1.25	–1.39	–1.45	–1.46	–1.39
Capital goods prices	–1.15	–1.18	–1.16	–1.13	–1.16
Consumption	–1.49	–1.58	–1.65	–1.68	–1.56
Urban incomes (nominal)	–1.02	–1.10	–1.16	–1.18	–1.12
Rural incomes (nominal)	–2.18	–2.23	–2.29	–2.32	–2.26
Urban income (real)	0.49	0.47	0.45	0.44	0.46
Rural income (real)	–0.69	–0.67	–0.7	–0.73	–0.70
Government income	–1.16	–1.33	–1.38	–1.36	–1.32
Investment	–1.28	–1.54	–1.61	–1.58	–1.52
Nominal GDP	–1.18	–1.26	–1.31	–1.34	–1.27
Real GDP	0.07	0.13	0.14	0.13	0.12

Table 6.8 Changes in output after the adoption of ECOWAS tariffs (%)

	Gross output		Domestic output consumed domestically		Exports		Imports		Composite goods	
Sector	**SR**	**LR**	**SR**	**LR**	**SR**	**LR**	**SR**	**LR**	**SR**	**LR**
Agriculture – food	–0.33	–0.41	–0.33	–0.41			7.3	6.97	0.11	0.01
Agriculture – export	0.03	–0.07	0.03	–0.07	0.62	0.58			0.03	–0.07
Oil and other mining	0.03	0.64	0.56	0.26	–0.07	0.7	–9.52	–12	0.14	–0.07
Manufacturing – consumer goods	0.26	0.23	0.26	0.23	0.57	0.61	–4.35	–4.49	0.17	–0.23
Manufacturing – capital	0.31	0.42	–0.16	–0.2	0.47	0.62	0.54	–0.19	0.52	0.18
Manufacturing – intermediate	0.14	0.03	0.13	0.02	0.68	0.49	0.14	–0.03	0.1	0.01
Services	0.22	0.25	0.21	0.23	0.58	0.61	–0.38	–0.38	0.07	0.07

SR, short run; LR, long run.
Source: adapted from Nwafor *et al.* (2006).

Contrary to the usual resistance to CET by manufacturers' associations in Nigeria and related organizations, our result shows that CET is actually beneficial to the manufacturing sector, in terms of volume of trade and absorption of labour and ensuring consumers' welfare. The loss in terms of value of production, and probably profit, may be explained by challenges including inefficiency in production and, particularly, in responding to the export market opportunities in Nigeria. The above problems result from four major constraints in Nigeria, namely infrastructural constraints, access to credit, insufficient demand and policy uncertainty in Nigeria.

As discussed elsewhere in this book, infrastructure ranks as the greatest problem confronting manufacturing and production in general in Nigeria. Trade policy also matters but not because of insufficient protection. Rather, the malfunctioning of the customs service makes imported inputs unreliable and costly. In contrast, excessive imports appear not to be a severe problem.

6.5 Conclusion

Nigerian trade policy has been volatile and, on average, highly restrictive. It has predominantly been used to meet balance of payments objectives, a task better done by the exchange rate. Because Nigerian exports are dominated by oil, the revenue from which accrues to the government, the revenue consequences of trade taxes are not what they seem. Because of feedback effects, the net effect of Nigeria's tariffs is to reduce government revenue: oil revenue is reduced through exchange rate effects by more than the revenue collected by the customs service. Thus, Nigeria has a much stronger interest in trade liberalization than the rest of ECOWAS. It is therefore particularly paradoxical that, instead of having much lower trade restrictions than the rest of ECOWAS, which would be appropriate, Nigeria has had much more severe restrictions. As a result, the short-term effect of harmonizing with the ECOWAS common external tariff is favourable, largely because it thereby reduces Nigeria's tariff against non-ECOWAS members. However, in the long run, continued adherence to existing ECOWAS tariffs may be costly as it would lock Nigeria into tariffs that are still relatively high and would handicap an export manufacturing sector. Whether Nigerian manufacturing could ever be competitive on world markets depends not just upon the removal of tariffs on imported inputs, but on addressing a wide range of inefficiencies discussed elsewhere in this book. It is these that should be given priority attention rather than fostering additional distortions through import restrictions.

Notes

1 UEMOA countries are Benin, Burkina Faso, Chad, Côte d'Ivoire, Mali, Niger and Senegal.
2 www.thisday.com
3 Although we do not have the classification guidelines for distinguishing between raw materials/semi-finished goods/intermediate goods, it is clear the intention is to have

higher tariffs on more processed goods. The ambiguity posed by this broad classification is, however, removed in the tariff book where each product (as ten-digit HS codes) is assigned a tariff rate.

4 In observing the outcomes, we regard the effects in 2005 as short-run (SR) effects and those of 2020 as long-run (LR) effects.

References

Adenikinju, F.A. and O.B. Alaba, 2004, 'EU–ACP Economic Partnership Agreements: Implications for Trade and Development in West Africa', *Nigerian Journal of Economics and Social Studies*, 46 (2), 85–103.

Alaba, B.O., 2003, 'Balance of Payments Adjustment Mechanisms in Nigeria', unpublished PhD Thesis, Department of Economics, University of Ibadan, Nigeria.

Bhagwati, J. and B. Hansen, 1973, 'A Theoretical Analysis of Smuggling', *The Quarterly Journal of Economics*, 87 (2), 172–87.

Cecchini Report, 1988, *European Union 1992: The Overall Challenge*, EU Official Document no. SEC (88) 524 final.

Coe, D.T. and R. Moghadam, 1993, 'Capital and Trade as Engines of Growth in France', *IMF Staff Papers*, 40 (3), 542–66.

ECA, 2004, *Assessing Regional Integration in Africa*, ECA Policy Research Report, ECA, Addis Ababa.

ECOWAS, 2003, *ECOWAS Handbook of International Trade*, ECOWAS, Abuja.

ECOWAS, 2006, 'ECOWAS Social and Economic Indicators', mimeo, ECOWAS, Abuja.

Enterplan, 2005, *Impact Assessment Final Report. Government of Nigeria: Capacity Building in Support of Preparation of Economic Partnership Agreement*, Reading, UK: Enterplan.

Kuji Ltd, 2002, *Comprehensive Review of the Nigerian Customs and Excise Tariff 1995–2001: Implications for Nigeria of The ECOWAS Common External Tariff and Nigeria's Obligations/ Commitments under WTO, ECOWAS, AGOA AND ACP-EU*, A Report to the Federal Ministry of Finance, Abuja: Government of Nigeria.

Nwafor, M, O. Kanayo and A. Adenikinju, 2006, 'The Impact of Trade Liberalization in Nigeria: Dynamic Simulation in a Computable General Equilibrium Model', mimeo.

O'Connell, A.S., 1997, 'Macroeconomic Harmonization, Trade Reform and Regional Trade in Sub-Saharan Africa', in Oyejide, T.A., I. Elbadawi and P. Collier (eds), *Regional Integration and Trade Liberalization in Sub-Saharan Africa, Framework, Issues and Methodological Perspectives*, Vol. 1, London: Macmillan.

Olofin, S., A. Adenikinju and A. Iwayemi, 2001, 'A Computable General Equilibrium Model of Nigeria's Trade Competitiveness', Center for Econometric and Allied Research, Research Paper No. 2001/01, University of Ibadan, Ibadan.

Oyejide, T.A.,1986, *The Effects of Trade and Exchange Rate Policies on Agriculture in Nigeria*, International Food Policy Research Institute Research Report 55, Washington, DC: International Food Policy Research Institute.

Oyejide, T.A., E. Ogunkola, A. Adenikinju, A. Bankole and O. Alaba, 2003, 'Nigeria's Trade Policy Overview Assessment and Impediments to Integration into World Trade', A final report submitted to the World Bank, Washington, DC.

Pitt, M., 1981, 'Smuggling and Price Disparity', *Journal of International Economics*, 11, 447–58.

Soludo, C.C., O.G. Oji and C. Agu, 2003, 'Potential Impacts of Extension of UEMOA Tariffs to all ECOWAS Member States: A Case Study of Impacts on Revenue and Trade Balance in Nigeria', report prepared by the African Institute for Applied Economics, Enugu.

This Day, 2005, 'ACP–EU EPA, CET Economic Implications for Nigeria', ECOWAS, mimeo.

World Trade Organization, 1991, *Nigeria: Trade Policy Review*, Geneva: WTO.

World Trade Organization, 1998, *Nigeria: Trade Policy Review*, Geneva: WTO.

World Trade Organization, 2005a, *Nigeria: Trade Policy Review*, Geneva: WTO.

World Trade Organization, 2005b, *World Trade Report*, Geneva: WTO.

7

Economic Growth and Policy Choice in Nigeria: Lessons from the Asia Pacific

Obadiah Mailafia

7.1 Introduction

For more than three decades, the economic performance of the Asian economies, especially the so-called 'tigers' – Singapore, Hong Kong, South Korea and Taiwan – has been one of the remarkable features of international economic relations.[1] The literature on the 'Asian miracle' is vast and evolving. The key issue for scholars is seeking the explanatory variables and key determinants of economic success in the region (Acemoglu *et al.*, 2004). In Nigeria, as indeed in Africa and the rest of the developing world, there is renewed interest in emulating the economic policies that led to the rapid and sustained growth experienced in the Asia Pacific. Many countries in the developing world are seeking to understand the growth dynamics[2] sustained in the Asian countries and to find how best to replicate the East Asian experiences in their quest for economic growth and development.[3]

This chapter is premised on the proposition that there are indeed crucially important lessons that Nigeria and other African countries could learn from Asia. However, such emulation would have to be based on a proper understanding of the key ingredients that have spurred Asian economic development over the last decades and also a keen awareness of the fact that initial conditions and national specificities differ from country to country.

Several related questions have to be posed. First, what are the key characteristics in the Asian development model that are lacking in other developing countries? What were their sources of growth? What was the role of public policy in fostering that growth? Can policies that were successful in the Asian countries be replicated by other developing countries, such as Nigeria?

In this chapter, we examine economic development in the newly industrializing countries (NICs) of Asia and try to identify the key drivers of growth in the region, with the aim of critically ascertaining whether the Asian model is capable of adoption by the Nigerian economy. This issue becomes important in view of the efforts of the current administration to reform the economy and create a stable macroeconomic environment, diversify the economy and achieve non-inflationary gross domestic product (GDP) growth for poverty reduction.

The rest of the chapter is organized in four sections. Section 7.2 analyses macroeconomic developments in Nigeria and the current efforts at reforming the economy. Section 7.3 reviews developments in the emerging economies of Asia, particularly the high-performing economies (HPEs). Section 7.4 examines the issues and challenges facing Nigeria and the post-National Economic Empowerment and Development Strategy (NEEDS) agenda. Section 7.5 presents a summary and ideas about how Nigeria could adopt the Asian model to launch a path of sustained growth and development, through the pursuit of coordinated, wide-ranging economic policies and programmes.

7.2 Macroeconomic developments in Nigeria, 1980–2005

In this section, we analyse the developments in the Nigerian economy over the past two decades by examining the pattern of growth and sectoral contributions to GDP. The analysis is done using four time periods: 1980–86, which is described as the period of administrative controls; 1987–92, which was regarded as the period of the Structural Adjustment Programme (SAP); 1993–99, which represents the post-SAP period or period of 'guided deregulation'; and 2000–2005, which is the period of economic reform. The discussion focuses on the different policy regimes and how each regime impacted on economic development.

7.2.1 The structure and growth of the Nigerian economy, 1980–86

The period 1980–86 was characterized by administrative controls on the management of the Nigerian economy. Within this period, Nigeria operated a pegged exchange rate system that was characterized by a fixed official exchange rate and a parallel or black market, which operated side by side. In the same vein, strong barriers to entry, credit allocations as well as credit and interest rate ceilings characterized the banking sector. Furthermore, national development plans were used as the key strategy to promote economic development. In fact, the Fourth and Fifth National Development Plans were articulated and implemented within this period. The fourth plan emphasized, among other things, the balanced development of the

Table 7.1 Gross capital formation and gross savings as a ratio to GDP

Period	GDP at current market prices	Capital formation at current prices	National savings at current prices	Gross fixed domestic investment: GDP ratio (%)	Gross domestic savings:GDP ratio (%)
1980–86	59,660.70	8,632.30	4,252.40	15.30	7.90
1987–92	269,132.50	27,691.7	38,005.10	9.9	12.70
1993–99	2,217,758.60	146,689.30	200,055.80	7.40	8.20
2000–04	5,942,380.52	393,021.46	838,815.42	6.55	15.44

Source: Central Bank of Nigeria Statistical Division, 2006.

different sectors of the economy and the various geographical areas of the country. Consequently, about 924 million naira was allocated to the 11 River Basin Development Authorities, whose functions were, among other things, the construction of boreholes, dams, feeder roads and jetties. The period was also characterized by negative real GDP growth, except for the last two years, 1985 and 1986, which recorded positive growth.

The contribution of oil to GDP averaged 14 per cent during this period, while agriculture contributed more than 35 per cent in the same period. The manufactured goods share of GDP averaged 9 per cent. The sharp decline in the price of crude oil on the international market resulted in a decline in economic activities. However, the real effective exchange rate continued to appreciate, the agricultural sector remained weak, and the large-scale importation of goods and services continued unabated. It was also during this period, in 1982, that the first economic adjustment was introduced. The economic policy tagged 'austerity measures' was aimed at reducing private consumption and public spending. Although domestic investment averaged 15.3 per cent of GDP, indicating a fairly robust investment habit, the savings-to-income ratio averaged only 7.9 per cent of GDP. This reflected the low propensity to save following difficulties associated with austerity measures, which grossly reduced the disposable income of the working classes.

7.2.2 The period of the Structural Adjustment Programme (SAP), 1987–92

Nigeria introduced a Structural Adjustment Programme (SAP) in September 1986, which included, among other measures, liberalization of the foreign exchange market to include the Second Tier Foreign Exchange Market (SFEM) and shifts in trade regimes. The fixed official exchange rate was replaced by a floating, market-determined exchange rate system. As a result, the exchange rate of the naira depreciated from 1 naira/$1 at the beginning of 1986 to 63.2 naira/$1 by the end of the year. The policy of import and export licensing was abolished as most prices within the economy were deregulated. In addition, the government began a gradual process of abolishing sectoral allocation of credits as well as introducing and implementing privatization and commercialization policies to divest itself of its interests in some of the businesses that the government had previously been engaged in.

The immediate effects of these reforms were the restoration of incentives to export, a reduction in the incentive to import and an increase in the profitability of

Table 7.2 Sectoral contribution to GDP

Sector	1981	1985	1990	1995	2000	2004
Agriculture	28.3	32.7	31.5	34.2	35.8	34.8
Oil	35.7	40	37.6	33.3	32.6	32.7
Industry	7.8	6.4	5.7	5.2	4.5	4.9
Others	28.2	20.9	25.2	27.3	27.1	27.6

Source: Central Bank of Nigeria Statistical Division, 2006.

agriculture. While oil prices remained low during most of this period, the non-oil sector, especially the agricultural sector, recorded positive growth. With a shift in relative prices in favour of the rural sector, production of traditional food crops and cash crops increased, and agricultural outputs grew at an annual rate of 3.5 per cent during 1987–92,[4] with the real GDP growth rate averaging 5.3 per cent. The share of the GDP attributed to agriculture increased and averaged 37 per cent during this period, and that of domestic manufactures declined to about 5.6 per cent in the same period. The SAP failed to mobilize sufficient savings because of the unfriendly investment climate, as the ratio of domestic investment to GDP dropped from 15.3 per cent in 1983–86 to an average of 9.9 per cent during 1986–92. However, the savings-to-income ratio improved as the average increased from 7.9 per cent in the preceding period to 12.7 per cent.

7.2.3 The post-SAP or period of guided deregulation, 1993–99

In the post-SAP period of guided deregulation, many of the policies that contributed to growth were reversed. Consequently, the economy started to decline again. Real GDP growth rates fluctuated between 2.3 per cent in 1992, 0.2 per cent in 1994, 4.4 per cent in 1996 and 0.4 per cent in 1999. The share of the GDP attributed to agriculture declined to 35 per cent, and that of manufacturing also fell to 4.5 per cent. In 1994, the government introduced a new budget of 'guided deregulation' and began to reverse some of the previous policies that had contributed to stagnation, high inflation and reduction in income. As a result of the policy reversals, gross fixed capital investment as a percentage of GDP declined further to 7.4 per cent, while the savings-to-income ratio stood at 8.2 per cent. This reflects a decreased propensity to save as inflation rose much higher than the real interest rate.[5]

7.2.4 The Nigerian economy during the reform period, 2000–2005

The period 2000–2005 could be regarded as the period marking the beginning of genuine commitment to economic reform in Nigeria. This is because of the comprehensive reform agenda in both the real and the financial sectors of the economy. This exercise is being championed by a team of local experts called the Economic Team under the leadership of President Olusegun Obasanjo. The team produced a detailed economic reform blueprint called the National Economic Empowerment and Development Strategy (NEEDS). NEEDS is a strategy document. The main objectives of the programme are wealth creation, employment generation, poverty reduction and value reorientation. These objectives are to be attained through strategies anchored in empowering people, promoting private enterprises and changing the way in which government does business. Under this programme, governments have been able to privatize major companies including the national telecommunications carrier, NITEL, and to liberalize the downstream oil sub-sector. The national power agency, the National Electric Power Authority (NEPA), has also been unbundled in readiness for full privatization.

In the financial sector, reforms have focused on the recapitalization and consolidation of the banking and insurance industries. This exercise saw the emergence of 25 megabanks from the existing 89 banks. With this consolidation, the capital base of banks increased to 25 billion naira from 2 billion naira. The financial sector reforms, which started in July 2004, were predicated on the existence of small, fragile and uncompetitive banks that characterized the existing banking system in the country. For example, bank credit as a percentage of GDP in 2003 was only 24 per cent compared with over 100 per cent in South Africa. The system lacked the needed depositor confidence and could not support the economy. The reform seeks to establish Nigeria as Africa's financial centre, with the aim that, within ten years, Nigerian banks should be among the top 50–100 banks in the world. The key components of the reform are the recapitalization and consolidation of the banking sector through mergers and acquisition. The insurance industry is also being recapitalized to ensure an efficient and healthy financial system.

Although the reform exercise has not been under way for long, it has already recorded encouraging success. The banks have successfully recapitalized to 25 billion naira with minimal costs; about 350.2 billion naira of new investment (nearly $3 billion) was mobilized, while some $500 million of foreign capital inflows were registered in the sector.

This commitment to reform has resulted in enhanced macroeconomic performance in recent times. Real GDP grew at 5.4 per cent in 2000, 10.2 per cent in 2003 and 7.1 per cent in 2005. The manufacturing sector grew from 2.4 per cent in 1999 to 7.0 per cent in 2004. In the same vein, the non-oil sector grew from 4.9 per cent in 1999 to 7.3 per cent in 2004. The share of GDP attributable to agriculture ranged from 34.85 per cent in 2002 to 31.21 per cent in 2004, and that of manufacturing increased from 4.25 per cent in 2001 to 4.50 per cent in 2004. Gross fixed domestic investment as a percentage of GDP continued to decline. It averaged 6.55 per cent during the period, reflecting the harsh investment climate, while gross domestic savings as a percentage of GDP improved substantially to 15.44 per cent in the review period.

7.2.5 The potential for Nigeria to emerge as an economic power in Africa

Despite her lacklustre economic performance in the past, there is evidence that the Nigerian economy is at the threshold of renewed growth and recovery. Indeed, there is no doubt that the country possesses the potential to emerge as an economic power in Africa as well as the engine room that could drive the level of economic activities on the continent. Except for South Africa, Nigeria has the largest economy in sub-Saharan Africa and harbours the biggest local and foreign conglomerate and transnational operations in the West African sub-region, with an area of 924,000 square kilometres and an estimated population of 125 million in 2002 – nearly one-quarter of the population of sub-Saharan Africa.[6]

In addition, Nigeria accounts for more than 65 per cent of industrial infrastructure in the West African sub-region and contributes more than half of the sub-regional economic development. Nigeria's proven oil reserves are estimated to be 32 billion barrels. At the current rate of production, these reserves are sufficient to last for 37 years. Nigeria is a member of the Organization of Petroleum Exporting Countries (OPEC) and in 2003 its crude oil production averaged 2.2 million barrels per day.

Nigeria is currently the sixth largest producer of oil among the OPEC countries and the fifth largest source of US imported oil. A proven natural gas reserve is estimated at 174 trillion cubic feet, with an energy content slightly greater than the country's oil reserves. At the current level of production, these reserves will last 110 years.[7] Nigeria is also blessed with solid minerals such as coal, tin ore, kaolin, gypsum, columbite, gold, uranium, salt and so on.

Furthermore, Nigeria has the largest domestic market in sub-Saharan Africa, which could serve as a springboard for entering export markets worldwide. These and many other national assets could pave the way for seizing the development opportunities that come with cross-border cooperation and the globalization of industries, trade and investment. With skilful management, such opportunities could be converted into higher income per capita and enhancement of job creation.

7.3 Explaining the East Asian economic experience

The spectacular growth rate experienced by the many economies of East Asia, especially with respect to the most successful economies of Hong Kong, Korea, Singapore and Taiwan,[8] has puzzled many development economists. While many people have appreciated the growth achievements in these countries, there is no agreement on the single most important factor that has led to the tremendous growth rate experienced by these Asian countries.[9] However, there is no doubt that the implementation of sequential and coordinated government policies helped in jump-starting and sustaining economic growth in Asia. Yet, other scholars and policy analysts[10] are of the opinion that, despite the setbacks of the late 1990s, if the various governments in Asia continue to implement such innovative and effective policies, in another quarter of a century, they are likely to be on a par with the most advanced economies.

From 1960 to 1990, eight East Asian economies[11] achieved extraordinary economic success, with their economies recording tremendous growth in major macroeconomic aggregates. For example, per capita income grew more rapidly in South Korea, Singapore, Hong Kong, Taiwan and Japan than anywhere else in the world. The same was also true of Thailand, Malaysia and Indonesia. In South Korea, real per capita income increased from $900 to $6700, and economic growth was matched by improvements in life expectancy, gains in educational attainment and reductions in poverty.

East Asia's economic success affected not only the lives of the people in the region, it also helped in transforming the global economy. During this period, Japan's economy became the world's second largest, with its gross domestic product twice that of Germany and trailing only behind the United States. Because East Asian economies focused on manufacturing products for exports and in making substantial investments abroad, their international impact increased even more rapidly than their size. The success of the Asian economies has thus been attributed to a number of factors including:

- technological innovations;
- investments in agriculture;
- stabilizing population growth;
- investments in human capital development or education;

- infrastructure development;
- export promotion;
- increased savings and investment that led to a rapid increase in capital;
- promotion of productivity;
- shared growth.

The traditional growth account method recognizes that, for growth to occur, the three elements of land, labour and capital must be present. What is not certain is the contribution of each factor to the growth process. In essence, what is subject to debate is the contribution of the factors of production relative to that of technology. While some policy analysts believe that increased use of labour and capital explains growth, others have argued that the source of growth relies more on the use of efficient technology. This view suggests that technological progress is central to achieving significant and sustained rates of growth in output per person over a long period of time. Studies by both Solow (1956) and Lucas (1988) concluded that capital accumulation and increases in the labour participation rate have a relatively minor effect on growth, while technological progress accounts for most of the growth in per capita output. This has generally been referred to as the Solow residual in growth accounting. Based on this line of thought, experts conclude that East Asian economic growth was a result of their intense focus on technological catch-up in their economies. Growth in the sub-region occurred because these economies learned to use technology faster and more efficiently than their competitors.

The countries of the region also invested in agriculture and technological advancement, and that accounted for their relative success in feeding the population under severe land constraints. Governments' support for research launched the 'green revolution', the dramatic development and diffusion of modern rice and wheat varieties in tropical Asia starting in the 1960s. This innovative process involved the development of grains that were more responsive to fertilizers, agricultural research institutions that adapted modern grain varieties to local conditions, and new agricultural infrastructure, especially irrigation systems.

There were also developments in demographics that helped to spur growth in the region. After World War II, East Asian countries began to experience unprecedented growth in birth rates, which accelerated the growth in population. However, in the 1960s, the governments committed themselves to stabilizing population growth through national family planning programmes. Over the following decades, childbearing among Asian women declined (see Figure 7.1), partly in response to population programmes and partly to declining child mortality, urbanization, industrialization and higher educational attainment (especially for women). This rapid fertility decline produced important changes in age structure: decline in the relative number of children, a rise in the relative number of working age adults and, later, an increase in the relative number of the elderly. These changes are fundamental to understanding the link between population change and economic growth in the 'miracle' economies of Asia.

Even with the crisis of the 1990s, a study sponsored by the East–West Centre on six of these economies – Japan, South Korea, Taiwan, Singapore, Thailand and Indonesia – showed that population change played a fundamental role in East Asia's

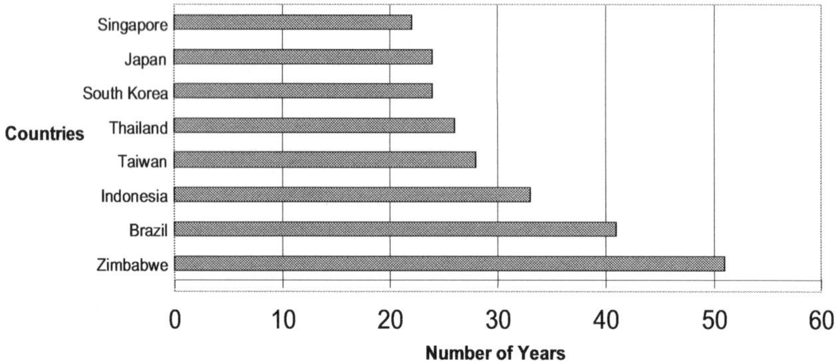

Figure 7.1 Years to complete transition from high to low birth and death rates.

economic success. The Asian experience shows that, for countries experiencing rapid population growth, family planning programmes can be an important tool to achieve higher standards of living. According to Mason (1997), 'rapid fertility decline and lower mortality rates created a window of opportunity, which when combined with effective economic policy, produced an era of remarkable economic progress'.

In nearly all the rapidly growing East Asian economies, the growth and transformation of the system of education and training during the past three decades has been dramatic. Education has been described as an 'engine of economic growth' in the region. The governments in the area instituted policies at primary and secondary levels that favoured economic growth. As early as 1965, most countries in the region achieved universal primary education, and enrolment in the region was higher than in many other developing countries. Even Indonesia, with its vast population, had an enrolment rate above 70 per cent. The achievement of high literacy and high cognitive skill levels substantially above that of other countries accelerated technology acquisition skills and made skill upgrading easier and quicker. Compared with other countries, including developed countries, by the end of 1993 the economies of East Asia ranked high in cognitive skill acquisition (Table 7.3).

The economies had more educational advantages than other developing countries and sustained them through explicit policies of investment in basic education. Public spending concentrated on primary and secondary education, as a large share of education spending was put into basic education. Declining fertility also meant more educational resource per child. Public funding of post-secondary education was used primarily for science and technology education.

The East Asian economies accumulated both physical and human capital much more rapidly and consistently than other developing economies. They encouraged investment by putting in place adequate infrastructure to complement private investment. Also, they created an investment-friendly climate through a combination of legal, tax and other measures that lowered the relative prices of capital goods by maintaining low tariffs on imported capital goods. While savings were increased by ensuring positive interest rates and deposits, lower lending rates subsidized investments and the production costs of corporations. In allocating accumulated human

Table 7.3 Percentage of children performing at or above level of mathematical scales by age 13 years

Country	Can add and subtract	Can solve simple problems	Can understand concepts	Can interpret data
Korea	100	95	40	5
Spain	99	91	14	1
UK	98	87	18	2
United States	97	78	9	1

Source: Birdsall and Sabot (1993) based on educational testing services.

and physical capital, these economies used a combination of market mechanisms and government intervention to guide decisions. They channelled their efforts into job creation, thus boosting the demand for labour. The rise in the demand for labour was followed by market-driven increases in real wages. Consequently, downward wage adjustments to macroeconomic shocks were minimal.

Another key factor accounting for the success of the East Asia economies was marrying imported technology and cheap labour to an export market. The view that investments and exports are engines of growth is based on both empirical and theoretical arguments. The empirical argument is that most East Asian countries that experienced phenomenal growth rates also enjoyed impressive rates of investment and are successful exporters. The theoretical argument as regards investment is that a high investment rate increases the capital stock (instruments of wealth creation) and that this can permanently increase the growth rate through economies of scale (for example bigger, more efficient factories and larger markets) and other beneficial side-effects. In the case of exports, the theoretical argument is that export orientation increases the openness of the economy and, by exposing it to foreign technology and foreign competition, provokes a rapid rate of technological progress. East Asian economies embarked on policies that were export intensive, thereby opening a window of opportunity and integrating the economies into the global economy.

Another argument often made is that growth in these regions was due to the high level of domestic savings, which allowed private enterprise and governments to fund investment without reliance on foreign finance. This reduced reliance avoided the debt-dependency spiral that afflicts many Third World countries, and also the profit repatriation that accompanies foreign investment in domestic businesses. It is certainly true that increased savings can assist already existing economic growth by providing cheap finance. However, it is not true that a greater pool of savings necessarily leads to greater economic growth. This depends on a multiplicity of factors, such as profitability, investment and access to markets. The critical combination in the NICs' case has been that between high domestic rates of profit (dependent most of all on low real wages), high demand abroad and conducive polices that promoted domestic investments. In the capital market, government intervened systematically both to control interest rates and to direct credit with strict performance criteria. However, the changing level of financial sector development and the increased openness of these economies to international capital flows decreased the availability of credit programmes.

Equally important, the coordinated investment in education helped to increase both the quality and the quantity of the labour force. These countries implemented the strategic actions of employing selective industrial policies and encouraging rapid export growth. They also engaged in technology acquisition through licences, capital goods imports and openness to direct foreign investments. They pursued a regime of policy liberalization, of both the exchange rate and trade, which promoted growth.

A particularly critical factor is that of commitment to shared growth. Countries such as Singapore inherited ethno-religious diversities that would have been a source of continuing conflict in other countries. However, as a result of the foresight of its leaders, Singapore was able to forge a sense of harmony and commitment to the common good of all its citizens (Ghesquiere, 2006). East Asian leaders supported the principle of shared growth, promising and delivering uniform growth to the populace. Policy reforms such as land reform, agricultural price policies, housing and wealth sharing, and incentives for small and medium-sized enterprises were adopted to ensure that the 'benefit of growth is equally distributed'.

7.4 Implications and challenges for the Nigerian economy

The current reform agenda being embarked upon by the Federal Government is trying to extend the privatization exercise and to diversify the economy away from the oil sector. The assessment of the economy under the NEEDS programme could be done by looking at Table 7.4. The growth rate of real GDP increased from 5.4 per cent in 2000 to 10.23 per cent in 2003 before declining to 6.2 per cent in 2005. This is an impressive performance if this figure is juxtaposed with the NEEDS target of 7 per cent at the end of 2007. In the same manner, the growth rate of the non-oil sector increased from 2.9 per cent in 2000 to 8.9 per cent in 2005. Growth in agriculture reached 7.0 per cent in 2003 before falling to 6.5 per cent in 2005. The manufacturing sector grew by 9.2 per cent in 2005. Export growth declined by –27.05 per cent in 2002. By 2004, exports grew by 38.85 per cent and, in 2005, the same sector recorded a growth rate of 64.96 per cent. On average, the current reform programme under NEEDS can be said to have fared well as most of the economic indicators have improved substantially.

In terms of growth, GDP growth rate has averaged 7.4 per cent since the reform exercise started (2003–2005). It is also important to note that the growth is being led by the non-oil sector. (The non-oil sector grew at 8.5 per cent per annum in 2005.) Furthermore, lending to the private sector rose by 40 per cent in 2005, higher than the programme target of 30 per cent.

In terms of price stability, although the goal of single-digit inflation has yet to be attained, the inflationary pressures in the economy have been managed in such a way that will ultimately achieve the target. For instance, despite food shortages in neighbouring countries that caused non-core inflation to peak at 38 per cent in August 2005, by November, headline inflation was brought down to an estimated 15.1 per

Table 7.4 Nigeria: selected macroeconomic indicators, 2000–2005

Item	2000	2001	2002	2003	2004	2005
Real GDP growth rate	5.40	4.60	3.50	10.23	6.09	6.20
Oil sector growth rate (%)	11.10	5.20	–5.70	23.90	3.30	2.80
Non-oil sector growth rate (%)	2.90	4.30	7.96	4.44	7.50	8.20
Agric sector growth rate (%)	2.90	3.90	4.30	7.00	6.50	6.50
Growth rate of manufacturing	3.44	6.99	10.07	5.66	10.00	9.20
Growth rate of export			–27.05	11.57	38.85	64.96
National disposable income growth rate (%)	4.30	4.60	3.90	4.40	6.37	6.82
Gross capital formation growth rate (%)	17.00	15.20	11.20	3.50	4.31	4.50
Savings (billion naira)	81.37	96.32	154.08	106.39	173.30	194.50
Gross fixed capital formation (billion naira)	41.53	32.42	39.00	58.53	84.03	97.21
Savings–investment gap (billion naira)	39.84	63.90	115.08	47.86	89.27	97.29
Inflation rate (%)	6.00	18.90	12.90	14.00	15.00	10.00
External reserve ($)	9.38	10.27	7.68	7.48	16.96	28.27

Source: National Bureau of Statistics, 2006.

cent while core inflation averaged 6.8 per cent. The exchange rate has also tended to remain stable, thanks to the reforms. Exchange rate stability was maintained around the predetermined band of ±3 per cent. In fact, the naira exchange rate appreciated by 3.1 per cent in 2004 and 3 per cent in 2005. This further reinforces the confidence of investors in the economy. Economic reform has also led to the successful negotiation of the country's debt with the Paris Club, resulting in a debt relief of $18 billion. The NEEDS document and commitment to its implementation formed the bedrock upon which the Paris Club group of creditors assessed Nigeria for debt relief. As of November 2006, the country's external reserve position has been beefed up to $41 billion, the highest in Africa.

7.4.1 Issues and challenges

Significant improvements have been recorded since the government embarked on the reform programmes. Despite these improvements, Nigeria still faces monumental developmental challenges. Some of these challenges centre on a number of issues that we shall dwell on briefly.

Among the most critical challenges is the question of poverty. In the last two decades, there has been little or no progress in alleviating poverty despite the massive efforts made and the many programmes established for that purpose. With a per capita income of $428 and a human development index of 0.453, Nigeria is a poor country, despite the abundance of human and material resources. According to the United Nations Human Development Report (UNDP, 2005), about 70.2 per cent of the Nigerian population live below the income poverty line of $1 per day, and about 90.8 per cent live below $2 per day. The majority of the poor, over 70 per cent, are located in the rural areas where most of the people and national resources are located. In the same report, Nigeria's human poverty index (HPI), at 44.2 per cent, ranks 87 out of the 103 developing countries for which the index was available. The HPI measures the extent of deprivation and the proportion of people in the community who are left out of progress. A survey on Nigeria carried out recently by the *Economist* (2005: 7) provides an alternative perspective on the poverty situation in Nigeria. According to the survey, Nigeria ranks 158 out of a total of 177 countries in its human development index (HDI). The HDI measures achievements in terms of life expectancy, education and real per capita income. Nigeria's average life expectancy is given as 50.1 years, infant mortality is 198 per 1000 live births, adult literacy rate is 59.5 per cent, and access to clean water is 50 per cent (Iyoha and Oriakhi, 2002). At this rate, it will take Nigeria about 40 years to achieve the Millennium Development Goals.

There is also the question of the infrastructure gap. Infrastructural facilities, according to Hirschman (1958), refer to those basic services without which primary, secondary and tertiary productive activities cannot function. In the wider sense, infrastructural facilities embrace all public services from law and order through education and public health to transportation, communication, ports and water supply. In other words, infrastructural facilities are key elements in the package of basic needs that a community would like to procure for a better life. The provision of rural infrastructure has for long been seen as a government concern, and the federal, state and local governments have tried in different ways to tackle the problems of rural infrastructure. One of the initial conditions for take-off in Asian economies was the availability of facilities such as telecommunications and transportation, power supply, railway systems and efficient ports.

One of the greatest challenges facing the Nigerian economy remains the provision of adequate infrastructural facilities to facilitate production. The synthesis of government activities reveals that, during the past few years, a series of constructive programmes and far-reaching actions was taken to combat rural infrastructural problems, which are far from being solved. Currently, there is a generally poor state of roads in the country and the railway system is almost moribund. Power supply has been fitful. In fact, most companies and organizations run their generating sets for almost 24 hours. The situation has resulted in high average costs of production with resultant cost-push inflation.

There is also the need to improve the investment climate. In general, Nigeria's investment climate, particularly the legal framework, is assessed as a weak foundation for supporting a competitive market economy (not yet competitive/anti-trust, weak protection of property rights and ineffectiveness of enforcement of legal requirements and commercial contracts). A friendly investment climate fosters domestic production for both domestic consumption and exports. For businesses in general, and for direct foreign investment in particular, the major concerns have been related to the policy discretions and uncertainty, the multiplication of rules and administrative procedures (red tape, complication, corruption). At present, Nigeria is judged to be a highly corrupt country. The corruption perception index, as assessed by Transparency International, places Nigeria as the third most corrupt country in the world, an improvement from the second position in 2003. The Asian economies of Hong Kong, Korea, Taiwan and China maintained effective and efficient legal systems, security of life and property, and they had to reform their attitudes before they could achieve substantial growth. It therefore behoves Nigeria to reform the judicial system, ensure security of life and property, and reform people's attitudes in order to attract much-needed investment – both domestic and foreign – into the economy.

In this connection, one must view favourably the current efforts at fighting corruption being championed by the Independent Corrupt Practices Commission (ICPC) and the Economic and Financial Crimes Commission (EFCC). However, it is crucial to bear in mind that corruption is not inherent or genetic in the Nigerian character; rather, it derives from the path dependence and collective mindset resulting from poor governance, lack of effective controls and the absence of a culture of democratic accountability, which have been the bane of the polity since independence. While the war against corruption must be waged on a vigorous and sustained basis, attention must also be given to the institutional environment of economic governance, in particular the regulatory regime for privatized utilities and a framework of anti-trust law to ensure healthy competition in the economy.

Another factor is the challenge of diversifying the economy away from dependence on oil. Nigeria's economic structure remains highly undiversified. Oil exports account for 95 per cent of total exports, while manufacturing accounts for less than 1 per cent. Since the 1970s, Nigeria has lost international market share even in her traditional (agricultural) exports. At independence in 1960, Nigeria was largely an agricultural country, producing food for her consumption and cash crops such as groundnuts, cocoa, rubber and palm oil for exports. Discovery of crude oil in commercial quantities came towards the end of the 1960s and began to bring about sizeable reductions in the agricultural share of GDP. Thus, from a GDP share of almost 64 per cent in 1960, agriculture accounted for only 28.3 per cent in 1981 and 34.8 per cent in 2004. The industrial share of output, which was 7.7 per cent in 1960, increased marginally to 7.8 per cent in 1981 and dropped drastically to 4.9 per cent in 2004. For the decade of the 1960s, the average share of services in output was a healthy 32.1 per cent but, by the end of 2004, this sector's share of GDP had dropped to 27.6 per cent.

The relative importance of crude oil to the economy has been enhanced by several factors including Nigeria's membership of OPEC and the ever-increasing price of oil, especially during periods of crisis, such as the Arab–Israeli war in 1973, the Gulf war of 1991 and the Middle East crises.

Lastly, there is the challenge of integrating the economy into the global marketplace in the context of our globalizing world economy. In the most basic terms, globalization of the world economy is the integration of economies throughout the world through trade, financial flows, the exchange of technology and information and the movement of people. The extent of the trend towards integration is clearly reflected in the rising importance of trade and capital flows. There has been phenomenal growth in cross-border financial flows, particularly in the form of private equity and portfolio investments, compared with the past. In addition, the evolution in communications and transportation technologies and the much improved availability of information have allowed individuals and firms to base their economic choices more and more on the quality of the economic environment in different countries.

It is clear that the trend towards more integrated world markets has opened up wide potentials for greater growth, and presents unparalleled opportunities for developing countries to raise their standards. At the same time, policy-makers try to focus attention on the downside of this trend, and concerns have been raised about the risk of marginalization of countries. What are the implications of globalization for the conduct of economic policy? What are its benefits and risks? What will Nigeria do to benefit from or to avoid the downside risks? While globalization rewards good policy, it also accentuates the cost of poor policy. Once lost, the credibility of economic policy becomes more difficult to regain. What is now critical is the perception of the markets that Nigerian economic policy formulation and implementation is consistent and predictable.

7.4.2 Towards a post-NEEDS agenda

Although the implementation of the current NEEDS document is on track and expected to continue even after 2007, there is a need to fine-tune the document to reflect, more appropriately, the changing needs of the people. The implementation of the current NEEDS has thrown up a number of issues that might need more diligence in policy formulations. For instance, observers point out (constructively) that, while the current reform agenda has resulted in higher growth (measured in real GDP), the employment content of this growth is not as impressive. The Nigerian Statistical Fact Sheets on Economic and Social Development gave the rate of unemployment in the country as 11.8 per cent in 2004, up from its level of 10.8 per cent in 2003. This is a major source of worry if we juxtapose this figure with the GDP growth rate of 7.1 per cent achieved in 2005. It is therefore appropriate to concentrate on employment as a driving force for sectoral growth in the post-NEEDS agenda.

Furthermore, despite progress recorded in the growth of real GDP in the past few years, the issue of poverty alleviation is critical and still remains unresolved. Ranking 158 out of 177 developing countries in the report, with a HDI of 0.453 and a HPI of 38.8 per cent, Nigeria remains one of the poorest nations in the world. Income distribution is highly skewed as the richest 20 per cent of the population controls 55.7 per cent of national income while the poorest 20 per cent of the population has a paltry share of 4.4 per cent (Human Development Report, 2005: 272). It is therefore pertinent that the issue of poverty alleviation, especially income distribution, is addressed with more vigour than hitherto. The agenda for post-NEEDS development should therefore focus on poverty and income distribution if a meaningful result is to be obtained.

It is also hoped that the post-NEEDS agenda will add more vigour to the issue of corruption and institutional reforms. This will certainly improve service delivery in the economy. While the current efforts in this direction by the present administration are commendable, it is worth mentioning here that much still needs to be done.

Attitudes and beliefs must change for Nigeria to make a quantum leap out of our present condition.

7.5 Summary and implications

We have tried to establish that the key success factors that led to the emergence of the highly industrialized economies of East Asia, particularly those of Thailand, Korea, Taiwan, Malaysia, Japan and, to some extent, Indonesia, were their exceptional use of technology and cheap labour to promote their exports market, the encouragement of private domestic investment and rapid growth in human capital, which precipitated the high level of economic growth and development witnessed in these economies in recent years. The high level of domestic financial savings sustained high investment levels, such that, although agriculture declined in relative importance, their economies experienced rapid growth and productivity improvements. The population growth rates in these economies also declined more rapidly than in most developing countries, and they also had a more educated labour force, a more effective system of public administration and clear performance criteria for selective intervention and performance monitoring. These factors combined to give East Asia the 'miracle' it has come to be associated with in recent times.

A critical look at these Asian economies suggests that their successes were closely linked to the appropriate combination of policies anchored on three macroeconomic objectives, namely achieving and preserving macroeconomic stability, promoting openness to trade and capital flows, and limiting government intervention to areas of genuine market failure and the provision of necessary social and economic infrastructure. Most importantly, no one set of policies was a sufficient condition for success. Indeed, the experience of the Asian economies has shown that poor policies in one area could obstruct progress in another, even if policies in those other areas were good. In East Asia, there was a well-coordinated and comprehensive set of macroeconomic programmes that were fully supported by committed governments willing to implement them.

We have also seen the potential of Nigeria, not only in sub-Saharan Africa, but also in the rest of the developing world, and asked the question, how can Nigeria use the lessons and experiences of East Asia to launch a path of economic growth and development? How do we emerge as an economic power within sub-Saharan Africa and the rest of the world? In the paragraphs that follow, I would like to share some of my thoughts on these questions with you.

The economies of East Asia succeeded in recording tremendous economic growth and development because they focused on technological progress, invested in human capital development, developed their infrastructure, had increased savings and promoted the export of goods and services, while discouraging the import of consumables. These Asian economies also implemented well-coordinated government policies aimed at improving their demographics, while keeping population numbers well under control. They promoted productivity growth while encouraging shared growth in key sectors of their economies.

Considering its vast natural resources and vigorous and energetic population, Nigeria has not just the potential but also the capability to grow its economy to heights equal to those of the best in East Asia. The achievements recorded recently through the current economic reform process are testimony that it can be done. With a committed and purposeful leadership that is focused within a well-defined and coordinated economic blueprint, Nigeria can indeed emerge as an economic power in Africa and the world at large.

The country faces another challenging democratic transition. A successful leadership would have to build on the foundations that have already been established. There is a need to focus on the quality of government and the efficiency and effectiveness of the bureaucracy in implementing economic policy (Mailafia, 1997). The focus on implementation, which has been the bane of governments throughout Africa, will be absolutely vital. The half-hearted reforms that have been undertaken in the public sector must be relaunched with vigour. The Singapore experience shows that the quality of government and the existence of a highly competent core of technocrats is critical in promoting rapid growth (Avellaneda, 2006). So also is the need to enhance the rule of law and to promote social harmony. Major work remains to be done in the area of institutional reforms in order to create a sound framework for public management and economic growth (Bardhan, 1996; Mabogunje, 2000).

Effective financing mechanisms have to be devised for the infrastructures sector, with a critical focus on the binding constraints for long-term growth. Human capital development must also be given top priority, from universal basic education to adult literacy, technical and skills development to higher education, technology and innovation. While agriculture holds the key to long-term poverty alleviation, increasing attention has to be given to industrialization, in particular enhancing the added value of agricultural products and building niche industries for exports that would boost employment and productivity. While markets are vital, the state must guide markets in a manner in keeping with social conscience that leads to the creation of a harmonious and inclusive social order.

To echo William Shakespeare, 'some [nations] are born great, some achieve greatness, and some have greatness thrust upon them'. Nigeria may be one of the few countries that were born great – or were born with all the attributes of national greatness already embedded in them. Sadly, the country has hitherto failed to fulfil its promise because of a combination of poor leadership and wrong-headed policy choices. Drawing from the Asian experience and from the impact of recent reforms in Nigeria, this chapter shows that it is possible – through resolute and purposeful leadership and the right mix of policies – to galvanize the country into the orbit of self-propelling growth.

Notes

1 For the purposes of this chapter, our focus is on the Asia Pacific countries, excluding China and India, whose recent resurgence would also be an interesting subject of study.

2 Cf. Sarel (1997).

3 The ultimate goal of economic development is to achieve the greatest material good for the greatest number of people.

4 Saji and Canagarajah (2002).
5 There was a negative real interest rate in the economy.
6 See the NEEDS document (2004).
7 See National Planning Commission (2004: 3).
8 The four countries are usually referred to as the Asian tigers, because of their powerful and intimidating economic performance. While many countries in Asia grew at the same rate as the rest of the world, averaging 2 per cent GPD growth annually, countries in the east enjoyed superior performance, achieving a growth rate of 3–5 per cent per capita. This impressive achievement is even lower compared with the phenomenal growth of the tigers, which recorded annual growth rates in excess of 6 per cent of GDP per capita.
9 The ensuing debate has provided a field-day for neoliberals and neo-Keynesians alike, in addition to the new institutionalists who emphasize the role of government in promoting Asian industrialization. Cf. Bhagwati (1996), Lall (1994) and Wade (1990).
10 See Manson (1997).
11 These are South Korea, Singapore, Hong Kong, Taiwan, Japan, Thailand, Malaysia and, to some extent, Indonesia.

References

Acemoglu, D., S. Johnson and J.A. Robinson, 2004, 'Institutions as the Fundamental Cause of Long Run Growth', in P. Aghion and S. Durlaug (eds), *Handbook of Economic Growth*, Amsterdam: North Holland.

Avellaneda, S.D., 2006, 'Good Governance, Institutions and Economic Development: Beyond the Conventional Wisdom', mimeo, paper presented at the Forum de Recerca, Departament de Ciencies Politiques i Socials, Universat Pompeu Fabra, Barcelona, 3 May.

Bardhan, P., 1996, 'The Nature of Institutional Impediments to Economic Development', mimeo, Centre for International and Development Economics Research, University of California, Berkeley, CA.

Bhagwati, J., 1996, 'The Miracle that Did Happen: Understanding East Asia in Comparative Perspective', mimeo, text of keynote speech at Cornell University on the occasion of the Conference on Government and Market: The Relevance of the Taiwanese Performance to Development Theory and Policy, May.

Birdsall, N. and R. Sabot, 1993, *Virtuous Cycles: Human Capital, Growth and Equity in East Asia*, Washington, DC: World Bank.

Central Bank of Nigeria Statistical Division, 2006.

The Economist, 2005, Economist Intelligence Unit Report.

Ghesquiere, H., 2006, *Singapore's Success: Engineering Economic Growth*, London: Thomson.

Hirschman, A.O., 1958, *The Strategy of Economic Development*, New Haven: Yale University Press.

Iyoha, M.A. and D. Oriakhi, 2002, *Explaining African Economic Growth Performance: The Case of Nigeria*, Benin, Nigeria: African Economic Research Consortium.

Lall, S., 1994, 'The East Asian Miracle: Does the Bell Toll for Industrial Strategy?', *World Development*, 22 (4), 645–54.

Lucas, R. E., 1988, 'On the Mechanics of Economic Development', *Journal of Modern Economics*, 22, 3–42.

Mabogunje, A.L., 2000, 'Institutional Radicalisation, the State and the Development Process, Inaugural Address', *Proceedings of the National Academy of Sciences of the United States*, 97 (25), 107–14.

Mailafia, O., 1997, *Europe and Economic Growth in Africa: Structural Adjustment and Economic Diplomacy*, London: Routledge.

Mason, A., 1997, 'Will Population Change Sustain the Asian Economic Miracle?', East–West Centre Working Paper No. 33. Honolulu: East–West Centre.

National Bureau of Statistics, 2006, *The Nigerian Statistical Facts Sheet on Economic and Social Development*, Abuja, Nigeria.

National Planning Commission, 2004, 'The National Economic Empowerment and Development Strategy', Abuja, Nigeria.

Saji, T. and S. Canagarajah, 2002, 'Poverty in a Wealthy Economy: The Case of Nigeria', IMF Working Paper No. WP/02/114, Washington, DC: The International Monetary Fund.

Sarel, M., 1997, *Growth in East Asia: What Can We and What Can We Not Infer?*, Washington, DC: The International Monetary Fund.

Solow, R., 1956, 'A Contribution to the Theory of Economic Growth', Quarterly Journal of. Economics, 70, 65–94.

UNDP, 2005, *Human Development Report*, New York and Oxford: UNDP/Oxford University Press.

Wade, R., 1990, *Governing the Market: Economic Theory and the Role of Government in East Asian Industrialisation*, Princeton, NJ: Princeton University Press.

Section II

Government: Fiscal Management within a Federal System

8

Issues in Fiscal Policy Management under the Economic Reforms (2003–7)

Bright Okogu and Philip Osafo-Kwaako

8.1 Introduction

Oil-dependent economies face two interrelated challenges in the management of oil resources: in the short run, there is the need to create a stable macroeconomic environment by delinking oil revenue earnings from public expenditures, while in the long run it is necessary to maintain a sustainable use of resources that ensures intergenerational equity. In most of the past three decades, Nigeria's management of oil resources was poor. The Nigerian economy has experienced significant macroeconomic volatility, driven largely by external terms-of-trade shocks, the country's large reliance on oil export earnings and poor policy choices in the management of oil revenues. By some measures, Nigeria ranked among the most volatile economies in the world for the period 1960–2000 (Chapter 3). Moreover, contrary to the received wisdom of increasing financial assets as a means of saving oil revenues, Nigeria had accrued significant domestic and foreign liabilities.

With the introduction of a reform programme under the second Obasanjo administration (2003–7), progress has been made in improving fiscal policy management in the country, particularly with the adoption of an oil-price based fiscal rule as well as the introduction of a medium-term expenditure framework and medium-term sector strategies to guide the planning of government budgets. These fiscal policy developments constitute a subset of a larger reform programme, the National Economic Empowerment and Development Strategy (NEEDS), adopted since 2003. The development of NEEDS at the federal level was also complemented by individual State Economic Empowerment and Development Strategies (SEEDS), which were prepared by all 36 Nigerian states and the Federal Capital Territory (FCT). The NEEDS programme emphasized the importance of private sector development to support wealth creation and poverty reduction in the country, and focused on four primary areas of reform, namely macroeconomic reform, structural reform, public sector reform and institutional and governance reform.

This chapter reviews recent policy measures introduced by the federal government to enable a more prudent management of oil revenue and also to improve the quality of the government's capital spending. The broad conclusion of this chapter is that, although recent fiscal policy measures have yielded significant positive results, these measures need to be sustained in order to maintain a stable macroeconomic environment, which is a precondition for sustained long-term growth. In addition, by consolidating recent improvements in budget planning, execution and monitoring, as well as in implementation of programmes based on the Millennium Development Goals (MDGs), the Nigerian government can make significant progress in improving service delivery to its citizens. Large capital investments projects which are currently being implemented by the government must also be closely monitored to ensure the quality and effectiveness of such expenditures.

The rest of this chapter is structured as follows. In Section 8.2 we discuss the theoretical literature on the challenges of revenue management in oil-dependent countries. In Section 8.3 we review Nigeria's history of oil revenue management, examining its effects on macroeconomic volatility as well as public savings. In Section 8.4 we discuss recent policy measures that have been introduced by the federal government as a means of improving the management of oil resources. Challenges in sustaining the fiscal reforms are discussed in Section 8.5, while conclusions are presented in Section 8.6.

8.2 Review of the literature on oil revenue management

The central policy challenge in oil-dependent economies arises from two observations: the volatility of oil prices and the exhaustible nature of oil resources. First, in the absence of appropriate domestic policies, the volatility of oil prices (and therefore of oil revenues) is transmitted into the economy, resulting in macroeconomic volatility, which hinders long-term fiscal planning. Second, the exhaustible character of the resource also implies that due care must be taken of intergenerational equity issues, in order to ensure that future generations also partly benefit from the oil wealth. This entails limiting current consumption in any period to the size of the permanent income flow from the stock of oil wealth. The volatility of oil prices therefore raises short-term challenges with ensuring macroeconomic stability, whereas the exhaustible nature of the oil resource raises a long-term issue of intergenerational equity. Below, we briefly examine each of these short-term and long-term challenges.

8.2.1 The volatility of oil prices

The historical behaviour of oil prices indicates that they tend to be susceptible to huge shocks. These shocks are often persistent, and mean reversion tends to be slow (IMF, 2005a,b; Okogu, forthcoming). Volatility of oil prices results in significant terms-of-trade volatility, particularly in countries with a large concentration of exports in the oil sector. If oil earnings constitute a significant share of total government revenue, external volatility results in substantial revenue volatility which may result in fluctuations in public expenditure. In principle, revenue fluctuations should not result in macroeconomic volatility if the government is able to smooth public expenditures either by saving or by borrowing. However, few oil-dependent countries have a successful oil savings programme, and these countries often have limited access to international financial markets during periods when they most need it: when the international oil market is weak.

Large fluctuations in public expenditure that move in tandem with oil revenue earnings result in macroeconomic instability, which is harmful for growth. A procyclical fiscal policy affects the short-run dynamics of macroeconomic variables: sudden increases in government expenditure tend to be inflationary; volatility in government spending may cause resources to be reallocated to accommodate changes in domestic demand and prices with significant adjustment costs. Volatile fiscal spending also tends to destabilize the real effective exchange rate; in particular, a fiscal expansion driven by oil revenues may result in an appreciation of the domestic currency, creating Dutch disease concerns, and reducing competitiveness of the non-oil economy (Barnett and Ossowski, 2002). An unstable macroeconomic environment is undesirable, as it lowers long-run economic growth, particularly in low-income countries with weak domestic institutions (Hnatkovska and Loayza, 2003). Volatility can lower growth via a number of channels, such as by reducing the productivity of the government's public spending or by reducing the level of private investments. For example, an unstable macroeconomic environment creates uncertainty, which hinders planning by the private sector and reduces long-term private investments (Aghion *et al.*, 2004; Aizenman and Marion, 1993).

8.2.2 Exhaustible nature of oil resources

Oil is an exhaustible resource, which should benefit all citizens of the country in the present generation as well as future generations. In the long run, it is important to achieve a sustainable use of resources that ensures intergenerational equity by spreading government wealth over time. In other words, it is important that oil income, or financial assets obtained from such income, is consumed over a long period, and adequately preserved for future generations.

In the standard framework, government wealth is viewed as the sum of oil wealth (present discounted value of future oil revenues), financial assets and physical assets. In each period, the model assumes that oil wealth is converted into assets; fiscal policy aims at distributing the total wealth equitably across generations by restricting government expenditure in each period to only the *implicit return* obtained on the total government wealth. This is not always easy to measure because, for example, the returns from physical infrastructure are not easily quantifiable, even though productive infrastructure is widely viewed as important for economic growth. However, the limitation of current consumption to the permanent income flow requires a calculation of the size of the total wealth. In reality, this cannot be done with any degree of certainty because the underlying variables, such as the size of recoverable reserves, future price of oil and cost of production, are uncertain. Assuming risk-averse behaviour, decision-making under conditions of uncertainty requires that the government adopts a conservative fiscal policy stance.

A more stringent variant of the above theoretical position is the so-called 'bird-in-hand' approach, which proposes that the projected income should be the income on the financial asset *already in hand* rather than the totality of all income that includes an estimate of oil still in the ground (Barnett and Ossowski, 2002). This model, though somewhat unrealistic because it totally ignores the value of the existing reserves, has the main advantage of protecting the financial planning process from the risk of obsolescence of oil (no matter how small the probability).[1] This realization has the potential to force the government to be more fiscally responsible. Overall, for countries that depend on an exhaustible resource, the objective of fiscal policy should be to accumulate as much stock of financial assets as possible, particularly when market conditions are favourable, such that the flow of income from the stock can finance the non-oil fiscal deficit after the exhaustion of oil.

An important consideration in determining the optimal level of current fiscal spending relates to the size of financial assets already saved. Some countries like Kuwait have built up dedicated funds for future generations (complemented by a stabilization fund for budget support purposes) whereas others have oil stabilization funds (such as Libya, Oman, Qatar, Azerbaijan). The purpose of these funds is to smooth financing of annual budgets, and strengthen the structure of the budget from both the revenue and expenditure sides.

In the conversion of oil wealth into assets, the government is also faced with a choice between *financial assets* and *physical assets*. It is often the case that, following the discovery of oil in commercial quantity, there is an immediate pressure for large capital expenditures based on the political economy of such developments. This may be justified if the existing stock of productive government capital (such as roads and bridges) is particularly low or if infrastructure is needed to improve development targets (for example in hospitals and schools). Yet the empirical reviews suggest that over-investment in infrastructure has sometimes been the cause of weak growth of oil-dependent countries, following resource discovery, partly because of poorly conceived projects as well as weak governance issues (Rodríguez and Sachs, 1999). Although public investments are important, it is critical that they are aimed at productive infrastructure which is likely to yield positive returns. Moreover, from an implementation viewpoint, a sudden upsurge in fiscal expenditure programmes may also suffer from poor quality in design and programme implementation. Rapid expenditure growth during commodity booms is often inflationary, quite apart from threatening the quality of projects.

A related viewpoint is that many oil-producing countries have not always been successful in managing their oil funds, either because there is usually a strong temptation to dip into the funds or, more disturbingly, because less prudent future leaders fritter away the savings of many prior years. In order to guard against these eventualities, some studies propose a radical alternative under which the funds are committed to worthy uses that would have a long-term benefit for the economy. For example, Sala-i-Martin and Subramanian (2003; also Chapter 4 in this volume) have argued that all revenue accruing from oil, after some transition period, should be distributed directly to adult women in Nigeria. Arguments of this nature have some merit – there is evidence that women tend to be more prudent custodians of household resources, and may probably be better channels for delivering some social services (see Duflo, 2000). However, distributing a nation's entire revenues to women for social programmes appears rather drastic, and is premised on the negative assumption that resource-based developing countries are not capable of improving institutional quality over the long term. It is a frustration-driven proposal – frustration with the failure of Nigerian menfolk as managers of the nation's resources, and frustration with existing institutions in Nigeria. Such a proposition risks trivializing a serious issue, and detracts from the central question of the need to improve public investments in productive infrastructure and to address institutional weaknesses. The subject of strengthening domestic institutions is revisited in Section 8.5.

8.3 History of oil revenue management in Nigeria

Prior to recent economic reforms, Nigeria's history of oil revenue management had generally been poor. Addison (Chapter 3 above) notes that Nigeria was one of the most volatile economies in the world over the period 1961–2000, as observed by the standard deviation of the growth rates in its real variables, domestic prices and money growth. According to these estimates, Nigeria ranked among the top 10 economies in terms of volatility of government revenues, terms-of-trade volatility, real exchange rate volatility and volatility of real GDP growth. Moreover, volatility in oil revenue earnings was often directly transferred into the domestic economy via fluctuations in public expenditures. Public expenditures closely followed oil revenue inflows as shown in Figure 8.1.

The costs of such macroeconomic volatility were significant for Nigeria.[2] First, expenditure volatility resulted in low quality of government public spending, often resulting in many abandoned government capital projects, and accrual of arrears to local contractors. Second, macroeconomic stability also hindered long-term planning by the private sector, resulting in low investment and low growth (see Table A8.1 in the Appendix, www.csae.ox.ac.uk/books). There was an increased concentration of economic activity in various short-term arbitrage opportunities (particularly in retail trade) rather than productive long-term investments. Overall, Addison (Chapter 3) estimates that, compared with other countries, macroeconomic volatility could have reduced growth in Nigeria by as much as 3.4 percentage points per annum.

Moreover, contrary to the conventional wisdom of increasing financial assets (as a means of saving oil revenues), the Nigerian government in the 1980s and 1990s had accrued significant financial liabilities particularly in the form of external debts to both the Paris Club and London Club creditors (see Table 8.1). By 2002, Nigeria's stock of debt amounted to about $40.5 billion (about 87.9 per cent of GDP), of which $31.0 billion was in external debt and the equivalent of $9.5 billion of domestic debt. High debt servicing costs placed a significant strain

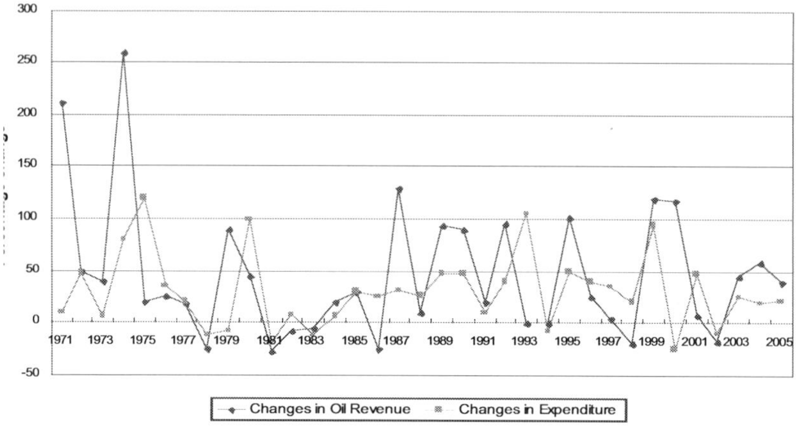

Figure 8.1 Pro-cyclical public expenditure pattern, 1992–2005.
Source: Federal Government of Nigeria estimates.

on government fiscal resources, and crowded out space for other necessary social expenditure and public investments.

In the late 1980s, attempts were made to smooth government revenues by saving incomes above a reference price for oil in a special stabilization fund. The operation of such funds was generally weak owing to a lack of transparency and fiscal discipline governing the use of such funds. As an example, in 1989, a total of 14.6 billion naira accrued into this fund, of which about 6 billion naira was withdrawn for use by the federal government despite rising oil prices (see World Bank, 2003).

8.4 Recent policy measures and results

Based on the above short- and long-term considerations, the literature on fiscal management recommends a number of prudent practices for oil-dependent economies such as Nigeria which are summarized below.

1. Institute appropriate rules to avoid pro-cyclical government spending patterns and to foster a stable macroeconomic environment, for example by using fiscal rules to insulate domestic fiscal programmes from external oil shocks.
2. Develop some form of a rules-based stabilization fund, thereby creating a form of precautionary savings. A stabilization fund or, alternatively, accumulation of government reserves serves as an insurance tool by providing resources for future fiscal activities in case of unforeseen adverse oil market developments. This follows from theory that income uncertainty results in reduced consumption decisions and higher savings (Deaton, 1992; IMF, 2005a).
3. Aim at ensuring long-term income (after natural resources are exhausted), by converting the natural resource into physical and financial assets, while also taking steps to reduce external debt as an integral part of prudent fiscal policy (World Bank, 2003; Barnett and Ossowski, 2002). A reduction in the overall

Table 8.1 Consolidated government operations

	1999	2000	2001	2002
Total revenue (% of GDP)	30.7	45.0	46.9	36.4
Total expenditure (% of GDP)	38.0	38.6	50.2	40.7
Fiscal balance (% of GDP)	–7.4	6.4	–3.3	–4.2
Total debt (% of GDP)	106.3	89.2	81.3	87.9
External debt (% of GDP)	81.8	69.1	62.2	67.2
Domestic debt (% of GDP)	24.5	20.1	19	20.7
Total debt ($ billions)	37.3	39.0	38.8	40.5
External debt	28.7	30.2	29.7	31.0
Domestic debt	8.6	8.8	9.1	9.5

Source: IMF (2001, 2003, 2005) and Federal Government of Nigeria (unpublished data).

stock of public debt reduces future debt service obligations, and thereby creates additional fiscal space for social expenditures.

4 For physical assets, it is important to invest in productive, public infrastructure and to minimize prestige 'white elephant' type projects. Projects must target productive public investments (in roads, bridges, power plants and so on) that reduce private sector 'transaction costs', and enhance productivity in the economy. In this context, an *ex ante* system of cost–benefit analysis framework is needed (incorporating costs, anticipated social benefits and the like) to guide government investments.

5 Finally, it is important to improve transparency in the oil sector as a means of strengthening governance of the sector, and reducing the likelihood of conflict (Collier *et al.*, 2003). This is an important recommendation as the lack of transparency in natural resource sectors, as well as competition over resource rents, could result in conflict particularly in ethnically fragmented societies such as Nigeria.

As part of the recent economic reforms by the Obasanjo administration, many components of these policies have been implemented. Progress has been made by introducing an oil-price based fiscal rule, by strengthening the budget planning process (via the use of the Medium-Term Expenditure Framework, MTEF, and the Medium-Term Sector Strategy, MTSS), by improving the efficiency of government spending, and by targeting expenditures for the MDG-based activities. In addition, a number of initiatives have been introduced to improve transparency in government public expenditures as well as in the oil and gas sector. Sections 8.4.1 to 8.4.6 below review some of the recent areas of reform.

8.4.1 Use of an oil price-based fiscal rule

The operation of fiscal policy in Nigeria under the reform programme has revolved around the adoption of an oil-price based fiscal rule and strict adherence to that rule in budget implementation. Any revenue earned above the benchmark price is saved in a common account ('the excess crude account') for all tiers of government. Benchmark prices of $25/barrel, $30/barrel and $35/barrel were used in 2004, 2005 and 2006 respectively, despite higher realized prices of $38.3 and $54.2 in 2004 and 2005 respectively and a projected average price of $68.0 for 2006. The 2007 budget, which was passed by the National Assembly in December 2006, was based on an oil price of $40 per barrel. Adoption of the fiscal rule has resulted in a significant fiscal surplus for the federal government, as well as for the federation on a consolidated basis: a consolidated fiscal surplus of about 9.9 per cent of GDP in 2004, increased slightly to about 10.7 per cent of GDP in 2005, and estimated to be about 11.9 per cent in 2006. Following the strong performance of the fiscal sector, international reserves grew steadily from about $7.5 billion at the end of 2003 to about $43.8 billion at the end of 2006 (Table 8.2). The increased level of reserves has partly underpinned the attainment of a stable exchange rate, with the elimination of a previous black market premium.

Fiscal management has been further strengthened by the management of government finances by a Cash Management Committee. For the period 2004–6, government did not utilize the Ways and Means window of the Central Bank, nor did it borrow from the banking sector.[3] The growth of excess liquidity was curtailed, thereby enabling the Central Bank of Nigeria (CBN) to meet its broad money targets in recent years. This has resulted in a significant reduction in inflation levels: end-year inflation (point-to-point) declined from 21.8 per cent in 2003 to 10.0 per cent in 2004. Inflation increased slightly to 11.6 per cent at the end of 2005 but declined to 8.5 per cent at the end of 2006 (CBN, 2006).[4]

However, an important result of the introduction of the oil-price based fiscal rule has been the increase in government public savings: a total of $5.9 billion was saved in the excess crude oil account in 2004 and a further $13.4 billion in 2005.[5] In a sense, the Nigerian excess crude account serves as both a savings and a stabilization fund. In keeping with prudent policy, savings in the fund have, in particular, been used for reducing Nigeria's financial liabilities (Table 8.3): primarily in financing Nigeria's payment of its debt obligations to the Paris Club[6] and, more recently, part of its London Club debt.

8.4.2 Strengthening the budget planning process

The actual budget preparation process has also been strengthened in order to increase the efficiency of government capital spending and also improve service delivery. As part of recent economic reforms, an annual fiscal strategy paper is prepared which outlines the government's anticipated expenditures and projected revenue earnings. Medium-term expenditure frameworks (MTEFs) and medium-term sector strategies (MTSSs) have been introduced to ensure that sectoral spending plans reflect existing government development priorities and are also in line with their projected resource envelopes. These three-year rolling budget frameworks have the advantage of ensuring that projects that span more than one year can be adequately budgeted for, with a clear plan for funding such projects over succeeding budget years, and thus avoiding the incidence of abandoned projects

Table 8.2 Selected economic indicators

	1992–8 (average)	1999–2001 (average)	2002	2003	2004	2005	2006
Real GDP (at 1990 factor cost) (% change)	1.84	3.48	1.42	10.90	6.10	7.20	5.67
Oil GDP (% change)	0.91	2.94	–11.63	26.50	3.50	4.20	–4.51
Non-oil GDP (% change)	2.37	3.84	7.96	4.40	7.40	8.60	8.93
Inflation rate (% change)	39.27	10.40	12.20	21.80	10.10	11.60	8.50
Money supply (M2) (% change)	...	35.03	21.55	24.11	14.02	16.03	28.40[a]
Exchange rate (IFEM/DAS) (naira/$, average)	...	102.3	121.30	129.50	133.5	131.8	126.50
External reserves ($ billion)	3.60	8.40	7.70	7.50	17.00	28.30	43.80
Total revenue (consolidated) (% of GDP)	...	40.90	36.40	37.10	43.00	43.50	45.40
Total expenditure (consolidated) (% of GDP)	...	42.30	39.00	37.10	35.30	34.20	33.50
Fiscal balance (% of GDP)	...	–1.40	–2.50	0.00	7.70	9.30	11.90

a estimated.
Source: Central Bank of Nigeria (2001, 2004, 2005, 2006), Federal Government of Nigeria (unpublished data), IMF (2001, 2003, 2005).

Table 8.3 Total public debt (1999–2006)

	1999	2000	2001	2002	2003	2004	2005	2006
Total debt ($ billion)	37.3	39.0	38.8	40.5	43.1	46.6	31.9	17.7
External debt ($ billion)	28.7	30.2	29.7	31.0	32.9	35.9	20.5	3.5
Domestic debt ($ billion)	8.6	8.8	9.1	9.5	10.2	10.7	11.4	14.2
Total debt (% GDP)	106.3	89.2	81.3	87.9	74.8	65.3	32.5	15.1
External debt (% GDP)	81.8	69.1	62.3	67.2	57.1	50.2	20.9	3.0
Domestic debt (% GDP)	24.5	20.1	19.0	20.7	17.7	15.1	11.6	12.1

Source: Federal Government of Nigeria (unpublished data) and IMF (2001, 2003, 2005).

that historically plagued the economy. The MTEF and MTSS process also forces government agencies to make hard choices between using available resources to start new projects and completing existing ones. Partly as a result of these recent measures, there has been a notable improvement in the implementation ratio of government capital budgets to about 90 per cent in 2004 and 2005 (albeit with some extension beyond the fiscal year; see Federal Ministry of Finance, 2005, 2006).

8.4.3 Improving the efficiency of government capital spending

Following an extensive review of public procurement systems in Nigeria, a Value for Money audit or Due Process mechanism was introduced in government procurement contracts. The Due Process mechanism has promoted an open tenders process with competitive bidding for government contracts. Any projects exceeding 50 million naira (or $400,000) in value require formal approval from the designated government agency (the Budget Monitoring and Price Intelligence Unit, BMPIU) and the award of a due process certificate. To ensure competitive costing of contracts, a database of international prices has also been developed to serve as a guide during the bidding process, while a public tenders journal is also regularly published by the government as a means of reducing patronage in the award of contracts. Finally, certification of completed government projects is also required before payments are made. With the introduction of the due process mechanism, there has been a notable improvement in the efficiency of capital spending. It is estimated that by the application of this policy the federal government has saved over 200 billion naira (approximately $1.5 billion) since 2001 in the form of reductions from otherwise inflated contract prices.[7] Moreover, in recent years, initial prices quoted by various government contractors have also declined significantly as a direct result of the vigilance of the Due Process mechanism.

8.4.4 Improving pro-poor, MDG-based, expenditures

In the process of strengthening fiscal policy management in the country, particular attention was also given to pro-poor expenditures within the budget which were needed to improve Nigeria's MDG indicators. The quantity and quality of social sector spending had declined significantly in Nigeria following years of military rule and poor economic management. In many cases, human development indicators in Nigeria at the end of the 1990s were comparable to those of other least developed countries. To address the deteriorating human development indicators in the country, annual savings from debt servicing (amounting to about $1 billion, with a federal government share of $0.75 billion) were channelled to various poverty reduction programmes. The utilization of debt relief savings is being monitored through a Virtual Poverty Fund Mechanism, named OPEN (Overview of Public Expenditure in NEEDS), which was designed to track utilization of these funds in the budget on pro-poor programmes. In the 2006 budget, OPEN was piloted by 10 government ministries, departments and agencies (MDAs): the Ministries of Health, Education, Water, Agriculture, Power, Works, Housing and

Development, Environment, Women Affairs and Youth. As an example, in the 2006 budget, the Delta State in the South South zone of Nigeria obtained financing for primary health care centres, for refurbishment of the local college for education, and for irrigation and rural water supply projects, as well as various rural electrification projects.

8.4.5 Improving transparency in public finances

In the past, poor public expenditure management in Nigeria greatly hampered the quality of government capital projects, resulting in poor service delivery to citizens. Oversight of public expenditures was further made difficult by fiscal decentralization in Nigeria, which allocates about half of total government revenues to states and local governments, with the remainder being allocated to the federal government. While increased resource allocation to states and local governments may potentially encourage more direct interventions in pro-poor programmes, capacity constraints and the lack of transparency at the sub-national level posed serious challenges. Therefore, to improve transparency at all levels of government, but particularly the sub-national level, a monthly publication of federal, state and local government shares of revenue from the country's federation account was introduced. Since January 2004, details of these revenue shares have been published: for the federal government, the 36 state governments and the Federal Capital Territory (FCT) as well as 774 local governments. The publication has increased transparency, particularly of sub-national finances, and opened up a dialogue on public revenues and expenditures at all tiers of government. Prior to this initiative, citizens had no way of challenging their governments on the size of funds received from the federal government. In the 1990s, it was quite common for teachers and other civil servants to go without pay for several months, and it was not unusual for state governments to blame such salary arrears on delays in receiving funds from the central government. In most cases this was correct, but there were other instances when it was simply used as a convenient excuse for poor management of public resources.

8.4.6 The oil and gas sector and the N-EITI initiative

The lack of transparency in the Nigerian oil and gas sector, particularly under past military administrations, also presented a major governance issue. The necessity for the establishment of the Nigerian Extractive Industries Transparency Initiative (N-EITI) became obvious after a government-commissioned study by the World Bank in 2000 revealed some disturbing findings.[8] Among other things, it found lapses in four broad areas: crude oil output and disposal; funds inflows; funds outflow; and institutional effectiveness. Clearly, such lapses created a fertile environment for corrupt practices to thrive. It became imperative for the administration to take decisive steps to institutionalize a system of regular independent audits of hydrocarbons reserves, financial flows and practices in the extractive industry. In this regard, Nigeria was the first country to sign on to the EITI in the fourth quarter of 2003, and the federal government inaugurated the National Stakeholders

Working Group (NSWG) in February 2004 to help improve governance of the sector.[9] Specifically, the NEITI commissioned an independent audit of the oil and gas sector for the period 1999–2004, comprising financial, physical and process audits.

The audit report presented a number of instructive findings. It pointed to a history of poor data-keeping, particularly in the financial and physical audits of the oil and gas sector. On the financial audit, only minor disparities were observed between revenues that oil companies reported as paid and the actual amounts reported as having been received by the Central Bank.[10] However, the coordination among government agencies was found to be weak, and government data-keeping was also poor, such that reported revenues fluctuated: in some years reported income exceeded what the Central Bank received, whereas in other years the reverse occurred. The physical audit pointed to the systematic loss of crude oil between the wellhead and export metering terminals. Poor metering infrastructure also hampered proper data collection on gross volumes. Finally, the process audit highlighted some concerns with the discretionary powers of the Petroleum Minister in oil block allocation, arising from the Petroleum Act of 1969. The findings of the study were subsequently disseminated to the general public, while remediation measures were initiated by the government.[11]

8.5 Challenges in sustaining the fiscal reforms

Given its history of poor oil revenue management, Nigeria has recently made significant progress in improving its fiscal policy management as part of current economic reforms. However, despite recent improvements in the management of oil resources and public expenditures in Nigeria, significant challenges remain. We focus here on two main challenges: first, the need to institutionalize recent reforms; and second, the challenge of extending reforms to the sub-national level.

8.5.1 Institutionalizing recent reforms

The strategy for sustaining and deepening the reforms lies in institutionalizing them through appropriate legislation to lock in the reforms – a strategy that has always been emphasized by the government. The role of institutions in economic development is now widely recognized, as most social scientists now agree that 'institutions matter' in the development process. The presence of strong institutions insulates the reform process to the extent that there is much less dependency on the personality of the leadership. With strong domestic institutions, private sector investors are less concerned about the risks of policy reversals by future administrations. Strong institutions prevent arbitrary reversals of policy and underscore the rule of law.

The centrality of institutions was well argued in the 1970s by Douglas North, who stressed that strong institutions were an important factor in explaining the rise of the Western economies in the eighteenth and nineteenth centuries. More recently, Acemoglu, Rodrik and others have also stressed the importance of institutions in explaining cross-country growth differences among developing countries (Acemoglu *et al.*, 2001; Rodrik, 2003). For example, Acemoglu discusses the case of Botswana, where strong economic performance was closely linked with the development of institutions to secure property rights, to ensure law and order, and also to improve governance of diamond resources (Acemoglu *et al.*, 2003). In the area of macroeconomic management, Satyanath and Subramanian (2004) have also observed the importance of democratic institutions in promoting disciplined monetary policy and supporting macroeconomic stability. As Fukuyama (2005) has noted:

> Recognition that 'institutions matter' and that good governance is a key part of any development strategy has become widely accepted within the development policy community in recent years. ... reforms need to be accompanied by positive acts of institutional reform and state-building.

From interactions with the Nigerian public, who have seen several false starts in economic policy, it is clear that sustainability of the reforms is the single most important issue to them.[12] Accordingly, the government has initiated several bills designed to institutionalize the recent reform measures. Several bills directly related to the economic reforms are currently under consideration by the National Assembly, including the Fiscal Responsibility Bill, the N-EITI Bill, the Public Procurement Bill, various Tax Reform Bills, the Central Bank of Nigeria/Bank and Other Financial Institutions Act Amendment Bill, the Anti-Trust Bill, the Ports Reform Bill and the Downstream Gas Bill. In particular, the passage of three of the above-mentioned bills would be crucial: the Fiscal Responsibility Bill, which sets limits on government borrowing; the Public Procurement Bill, which enshrines the Due Process mechanism in law; and the N-EITI Bill, which will institutionalize the Nigerian EITI. A number of bills have already been passed into law, including the Public/Private Partnerships Bill, the ICPC and EFCC Bills, the Pension Reform Bill, and the Power Sector Reform Bill. Passing appropriate legislation to institutionalize the reforms will help ensure the long-term sustenance of recent reform measures.

8.5.2 Extending reforms to the sub-national level

A second major challenge concerns the need to extend recent reforms to the sub-national level. The implementation of fiscal decentralization in Nigeria implies that about half of consolidated government spending is executed by states and local governments. Sub-national governments also possess significant independence regarding their expenditure decisions, which are intended to be primarily in delivering social services. However, weak capacity and the lack of fiscal transparency at the state and local government level often limit the quality of their public expenditures. Extending reforms to the sub-national level can assist in improving their fiscal policy management. Therefore a major challenge for the future would be to encourage states and local governments to adopt recent federal government reform measures, particularly in the areas of public procurement and expenditure management.

8.6 Conclusions and way forward

The reform of the fiscal sector has been at the heart of the ongoing economic reform programme and the success so far recorded. The introduction of an oil-price based fiscal rule enabled the government to reverse the trend of procyclical expenditure patterns, thereby strengthening the structure of the budget, controlling excess liquidity and generally engendering a stable macroeconomic environment. The policy has translated into substantial public sector savings, part of which was used to resolve the debt problem and introduce additional fiscal space in Nigeria's public finances. A related benefit has been the accumulation of significant international reserves. The strong fiscal performance was complemented by a sound monetary policy that has brought improvements to key variables such as inflation, interest rates and the stability of the exchange rate.

Nevertheless, several challenges remain, mostly relating to the need to institutionalize the reforms, to ring-fence public finances, and to build on the gains already made. A further area of critical importance is how to deepen the reforms to the sub-national levels in order to improve service delivery to ordinary Nigerians and help in tackling poverty. In this context, several bills, including the Fiscal Responsibility Bill, the Public Procurement Bill, the N-EITI Bill and some tax bills, are currently under consideration by the National Assembly and are at different stages of passage. Their swift passage into law would not only help to institutionalize the reforms, but also quicken the drive to transmit the benefits of reforms to Nigerians.

Notes

1 Obsolescence in this case does not necessarily mean that oil usage would be obsolete but that technological advancement might make alternative fuels more competitive in the energy markets so that it will no longer be competitive to invest in oil production.
2 For further discussion on the impact of volatility on growth, see Bleaney and Greenaway (2001), Fatas and Mihov (2003) and Servén (2003).
3 In 2005, the CBN granted total advances of 54.04 billion naira in a Ways and Means overdraft facility to the federal government. However, this facility was within accepted limits of the West African Monetary Zone (WAMZ), and was repaid by the end of December 2005, in line with statutory requirements.
4 The slight increase in inflation during 2005 was attributed to increases in food prices caused by a rise in food exports (particularly cassava and grains) to neighbouring countries, Chad and Niger, during their drought episode in 2005.
5 Of the amount saved in 2004, 50 per cent was shared among all tiers of government in 2005, leaving the balance on the account at $16.3 billion at the end of December 2005.
6 As part of a debt agreement with the Paris Club, Nigeria paid its outstanding arrears of $6.4 billion, received a debt write-off of $16 billion on the remaining debt stock (as under Naples terms), and purchased its outstanding debt under a buy-back agreement at 25 per cent discount for $6 billion. The entire debt relief package cost $12.4 billion

in payment of arrears and buy-back, in return for $18 billion or 60 per cent debt write-off.

7 Source: Government of Nigeria (Budget Monitoring and Price Intelligence Unit, BM-PIU).

8 The EITI scheme is a 'publish what you pay' scheme initiated by Tony Blair and George Soros, and aims at improving transparency in the oil and gas sector of the country. The Nigerian EITI (N-EITI) acts as the secretariat for the Initiative and carries out the day-to-day work of the agency.

9 The National Stakeholders Working Group (NSWG) is comprised of representatives from government, the national assembly, the oil industry, civil society, trade unions and the media.

10 The final audit report showed that only 0.01 per cent of aggregate revenue for the period was unaccounted for, mostly in the form of old invoices. The auditors have pointed out that this is within the conventional margin of error of 5 per cent for auditors.

11 Also available online at www.neiti.org.

12 See also, for example, Business Day newspaper of Tuesday 16 January 2007.

References

Acemoglu, Daron, Simon Johnson and James A. Robinson, 2001, 'The Colonial Origins of Comparative Development: An Empirical Investigation', *American Economic Review*, 91, 1369–1401.

Acemoglu, Daron, Simon Johnson and James Robinson, 2003, 'An African Success Story: Botswana', in Dani Rodrik (ed.), *In Search of Prosperity*, Princeton, NJ: Princeton University Press.

Aghion, Philippe, Angeletos George-Marios, Abhijit Banerjee and Kalina Manova, 2004, 'Volatility and Growth: Financial Development and the Cyclical Composition of Investment', MIT Working Paper, Cambridge, MA: MIT Press.

Aizenman, Joshua and Nancy P. Marion, 1993, 'Policy Uncertainty, Persistence, and Growth', *Review of International Economics*, 1 (June), 145–63.

Barnett, Steven and Rolando Ossowski, 2002, 'Operational Aspects of Fiscal Policy in Oil-Producing Countries', IMF Working Paper WP/02/177, Washington, DC.

Bleaney, M. and David Greenaway, 2001, 'The Impact of Terms of Trade and Real Exchange Rate Volatility on Investment and Growth in Sub-Saharan Africa', *Journal of Development Economics*, 65 (2), 491–500.

CBN, 2006, *Annual Report and Statement of Accounts for the Year Ended 31st December, 2005*, Abuja: Central Bank of Nigeria.

Collier, Paul, V.L. Elliott, Havard Hegre, Anke Hoeffler, Marta Reynal-Querol and Nicholas Sambanis, 2003, *Breaking the Conflict Trap: Civil War and Development Policy*, Washington, DC: World Bank and Oxford: Oxford University Press.

Deaton, Angus, 1992, *Understanding Consumption*, Oxford: Clarendon Press.

Duflo, Esther, 2000, 'Grandmothers and Granddaughters: Old-Age Pensions and Intrahousehold Allocation in South Africa', *World Bank Economic Review*, 17 (1), 1–25.

Fatas, Antonio and Ilian Mihov, 2003, 'The Case for Restricting Fiscal Policy Discretion', *Quarterly Journal of Economics*, 118 (November), 1419–47.

Federal Ministry of Finance, 2005, *Report on the Implementation of the 2004 Budget*, Abuja: Federal Ministry of Finance.

Federal Ministry of Finance, 2006, *Report on the Implementation of the 2005 Budget*, Abuja: Federal Ministry of Finance.

Fukuyama, Francis, 2005, *State Building: Governance and the World Order in the 21st Century*, Ithaca, NY: Cornell University Press.

Hnatkovska, V. and N. Loayza, 2003, 'Volatility and Growth', Working Paper WPS 3184, Washington, DC: The World Bank.

IMF, 2001, 'Nigeria: 2001 Article IV Consultation', IMF Country Report No. 01/131, Washington, DC: International Monetary Fund.

IMF, 2003, 'Nigeria: 2002 Article IV Consultation', IMF Country Report No. 03/3, Washington, DC: International Monetary Fund.

IMF, 2005a, *Nigeria: Selected Issues and Statistical Appendix*, Washington, DC: International Monetary Fund.

IMF, 2005b, *World Economic Outlook: Globalization and External Imbalances*, Washington, DC: International Monetary Fund.

Okogu, B.E., forthcoming, 'Characterizing the Oil Price Behavior: Unit Root Tests with and without Structural Breaks, and Fiscal Policy Implications', IMF Working Paper.

Rodríguez, Francisco and Jeffrey D. Sachs, 1999, 'Why Do Resource-Abundant Economies Grow More Slowly?', *Journal of Economic Growth*, 4 (September), 277–303.

Rodrik, Dani, 2003, 'Introduction: What do we Learn from Country Narratives', in Dani Rodrik (ed.), *In Search of Prosperity*, Princeton, NJ: Princeton University Press.

Sala-i-Martin, Xavier and Arvind Subramanian, 2003, 'Addressing the Natural Resource Curse: An Illustration from Nigeria', IMF Working Papers 03/139, Washington, DC.

Satyanath, Shanker and Arvind Subramanian, 2004, 'What Determines Long-Run Macroeconomic Stability? Democratic Institutions', IMF Working Paper 04/215, Washington, DC.

Servén, L., 2003, 'Real Exchange Rate Uncertainty and Private Investment in LDCs', *Review of Economics and Statistics*, 85 (1), 212–18.

World Bank, 2003, *Nigeria Policy Options for Growth and Stability*, Report No. 26215-NGA, Washington, DC: The World Bank.

9

Towards Securing Fiscal Policy Coordination in Nigeria

Olu Ajakaiye

9.1 Introduction

A federal state, or a federation, is one in which political power is shared among central or national authority and a number of sub-national authorities, generally under the terms of a constitution (Roberts, 1999). In a federation, definite powers are allotted to the central government, and the actions of the central government in exercising the powers conferred on it by the constitution may directly and/or indirectly affect the sub-national governments and vice versa.

Fiscal policy refers to that part of government policy concerning the raising of revenue through taxation and other means, and deciding on the level and pattern of expenditure for the purpose of influencing economic activities or attaining specified desired macroeconomic objectives (Anyanwu, 1997). Fiscal policy has at least three broad aspects, namely stabilization, distribution and allocation. *Stabilization* aspects relate to managing unemployment, inflation and economic development in general. *Distribution* aspects relate to changes in the distribution of income through spending and taxing policy. *Allocation* aspects deal with the provision of goods and services efficiently and effectively. In a federation, the stabilization and distribution aspects of fiscal policy normally belong to the central government, whereas the allocation function is performed by jurisdictions defined as benefit areas, which may be local, regional or national in scope (Musgrave and Musgrave, 1976: 625). In other words, while the stabilization and distribution aspects of fiscal policy are generally reserved for the federal government, the allocation aspects are within the purview of all levels of government.

Meanwhile, regardless of the purpose, in determining fiscal policy, a government has to decide various things, including how much to raise through taxes, how much to allocate to recurrent expenditure (personnel and overhead costs) and how much to allocate to capital expenditure on items such as schools, hospitals, housing construction, road construction and so on. Also, regardless of the level, a government may choose to spend more than it raises as revenue and so run a budget deficit. If the deficit is financed by printing money, then there is the risk of inflation. Needless to say, an important indicator of macroeconomic instability is rising inflation. Also, if interest rates are rising, this may adversely affect production activities, leading to unemployment. Clearly, rising unemployment is another key indicator of macroeconomic instability. An economy that is confronted with rising inflation and unemployment is unlikely to secure decent economic growth and transformation, both of which are required for economic development (NISER, 2000). This is precisely why the fiscal policy actions of a government in a federation can threaten macroeconomic stability, which is normally the primary preoccupation of the central government.

Therefore, fiscal policy coordination is imperative in a federal state if fiscal policy is to be able to secure macroeconomic stability. In this respect, fiscal policy coordination in a federation such as Nigeria will require adherence to fiscal discipline (observing the fiscal deficit rule similar to that currently in place in the Eurozone) by federal and state governments as well as adherence to the strategies for dealing with other externalities that cannot be addressed through fiscal discipline alone. See Pisani-Ferry (2002) for a discussion of fiscal policy discipline and policy coordination in the Eurozone. In the Nigerian context, the 1999 Constitution already grants full autonomy to state governments with respect to powers and the control of public funds (Federal Republic of Nigeria, 1999: Sections 120–9). In the absence of a fiscal policy rule to which all levels of government can adhere, that component of fiscal policy coordination is blunted. At the same time, there are no strategies for dealing with other externalities, such as unanticipated upsurge or decline in revenues whose rates and/or bases cannot be significantly influenced by the Nigerian authorities at the federal and/or state level. Moreover, as will be seen later, all levels of government depend excessively on oil for revenue. The major determinants of oil revenue, namely quantity and price of oil export, are really exogenously determined by the Organization of Petroleum Exporting Countries (OPEC), the oil-producing companies and oil importers. With a relatively small proportion of government revenue coming from internal sources, fiscal policy coordination can be secured mainly through expenditure management.

Meanwhile, the state governments, relishing constitutionally guaranteed autonomy, are unwilling to voluntarily surrender to the tenets of fiscal responsibility, namely adherence to a reasonable fiscal deficit rule and strategies for dealing with exogenous revenue shocks. This is particularly so as the Constitution also guarantees the rights of state governments to their portion of the Federation Account proceeds. The Federation Account receives all federally collected revenue with the exception of personal income tax from the personnel of the armed forces, the Nigeria Police, Foreign Affairs and the residents of the Federal Capital Territory. These revenues are retained by the federal government. Clearly, fiscal policy coordination in Nigeria can only occur accidentally. Fortuitous fiscal policy coordination in a federation does not augur well, for fiscal policy is unlikely to be an effective tool of stabilization, distribution and allocation, all of which are necessary ingredients for sustainable growth and development.

Against this background, it is necessary to examine strategies for securing fiscal policy coordination in the Nigerian Federation, especially since 1999 when the new constitution came into effect and democratic governance resumed. Accordingly, the rest of the chapter is structured as follows. In the next section, threats to fiscal policy coordination in a federal state are identified. This is followed by a review of experiences in dealing with some of these threats, drawing on the experiences of other federations. In the concluding section, options for fiscal policy coordination necessary for dealing with these threats in Nigeria are proposed.

9.2 Threats to fiscal policy coordination in a federal state

Drawing inspiration from the works of Mbanefoh (1992), Tanzi (1995), Shah (1998), Anyanwu (1997), Burki *et al.* (1999) and Kwakwa (2003a), at least nine threats to fiscal policy coordination in a federal state can be identified. First, if *a large proportion of the national government revenue derives from an exogenous source,* then fiscal policy coordination will be particularly difficult. This is especially the case in countries where a large proportion of national government revenue derives from the export proceeds of crude mineral resources such as crude oil and unprocessed solid minerals. Such economies are prone to severe external shocks likely to render the entire fiscal policy unimplementable, let alone coordinated. In essence, if the base and/or rate of a tax are completely exogenous to the economy, then fiscal policy programmes are very vulnerable to external shock, and this can render fiscal policy coordination unworkable.

Second, when the incidence of *business cycles is not uniformly distributed across space in the country,* the severely affected states will tend to run budget deficits, thereby complicating macroeconomic stability. For example, if one state in a federation depends heavily on agricultural export produce tax for its revenue and there is a major decline in the international price of the commodity arising from, say, a business cycle in the importing countries, such a state is unlikely to agree to a fiscal policy coordination that will compel it to pursue counter-cyclical fiscal policy.

Third, in a multi-party federal system, different states are likely to be governed by different political parties. If there are *philosophical differences among political parties,* this may be manifest in their preference for certain macroeconomic variables or development strategy. For example, it is possible for a state to prefer less inflation while another may prefer less unemployment. Another example is for some states to embrace privatization while others favour continuing and even enlarging government participation in directly productive activities through public enterprises. Under these circumstances, it will be difficult to secure a robust fiscal policy coordination.

Fourth, if the *budget does not derive from an underlying medium-term development plan,* there will be no anchor for fiscal policy coordination, and this will make it more difficult to convince sub-national governments that fiscal policy coordination is advantageous to them. Specifically, if the budget is anchored on an underlying harmonized medium-term development plan at all levels of government, it will be easier to secure fiscal policy coordination as other sub-national governments will put pressure on the particular erring government, be it the central or a sub-national government, in the realization that the actions of such a government can complicate macroeconomic stability and threaten the achievement of their agreed growth and development targets.

Fifth, if there is a *mismatch between spending responsibilities and resource allocation* among the different tiers of government, fiscal policy coordination will be difficult. For example, if sub-national governments are assigned high spending responsibilities while a disproportionately large share of national revenue is retained at the federal level, the sub-national governments will tend to incur budget deficits, which may be financed in several ways, including explicit borrowing from the banking system and incurring 'hidden' debts in the form of suppliers' credit and unpaid salary arrears and pension arrears.

Sixth, if the *assignment of spending responsibilities is vague,* there is a risk that both the central and the sub-national governments will be spending on the same item, and this may lead to wasteful duplication and inefficiency. In such a case, fiscal policy coordination will be difficult as the sub-national governments may perceive the initiative as an attempt by the central government to make them unpopular among the electorate.

Seventh, the *lack of incentive for sub-national governments not to borrow* can make fiscal policy coordination difficult. For example, if there are no constitutional limitations preventing sub-national governments from borrowing, if the banks are not discouraged from lending to sub-national governments, if the capital market is unable to impose discipline on the borrowing sub-national governments and/or if the central government is likely to intervene with a bailout, then there will be incentives to borrow, thus complicating macroeconomic stability.

Eighth, *weak public expenditure management* is another possible threat to fiscal policy coordination in a federal state. In such situations, the lack of information and capacity necessary for a well-articulated, medium-term development plan will make fiscal policy coordination a mirage.

Finally, and probably most importantly, is the problem of *endemic corruption.* Where corruption pervades the public and private sectors, the efficacy of fiscal policy coordination for macroeconomic stability will be blunted. This is because the injections will be far larger than the real goods and services provided, and this will certainly cause inflation immediately, and unemployment will eventually follow.

9.3 Strategies for dealing with threats to fiscal policy coordination

Beginning with the threat posed by *exogeneity of revenue sources,* a number of countries have developed strategies for dealing with the problems of uncertainty in revenue streams as well as the non-renewable nature of some of these resources. Instability of revenues makes fiscal policy coordination quite difficult basically because of the need to adjust to unanticipated positive and negative shocks. Several countries have responded to these challenges by setting up stabilization funds into which a specified proportion of the share of revenue from these sources is paid. In Kuwait, for example, a Reserve Fund for Future Generations (RFFG) was established in 1960 into which 10 per cent of the revenue from oil was paid. The main purpose of the fund is to protect public investment and social programmes from the impact of a fall in the world price of oil. The Kuwait Investment Authority decides the RFFG portfolio, which includes investment in domestic equity, equity and international financial assets.

In Chile, a Copper Stabilization Fund was set up in 1985, into which revenue in excess of projected revenues is paid. The purpose of the fund is to smooth the revenue profile by withdrawing from the fund whenever the actual revenue falls below the projected revenue.

It is significant to note that copper revenue projection is based on a reference price that is not too optimistic. In the state of Alaska, USA, an Alaska Permanent Fund (APF) was established into which 22 per cent of its oil revenue is paid. The fund is intended for the benefit of future generations, to smooth revenue streams from oil and also to fund economic diversification programmes. The APF has grown so large that Alaskan residents are currently paid an annual dividend from APF income.

In Venezuela, a Macroeconomic Stabilization Fund was established in 1998 to help to smooth expenditures. The government was required to make a mandatory payment into this fund. However, owing to political interference and budget indiscipline, the fund has performed poorly. The situation has deteriorated to the point at which the government was only able to make the mandatory payment into the account by borrowing domestically.

In Nigeria, a stabilization fund was established in 1993 into which 0.5 per cent of the federation accounts proceeds was paid. Experience with the management of the fund was not too encouraging largely because of fiscal indiscipline, particularly under military rule. The Supreme Court Ruling of 2003 on the Resource Control Suit has compelled the termination of payments into the fund.

The upshot of the foregoing is that the establishment of a fund to smooth expenditure is not enough to facilitate fiscal policy coordination. There must be resolute fiscal discipline and strict expenditure control, without which expenditure will tend to follow revenue during booms and excessive deficits during busts. In such a situation, fiscal policy coordination will remain difficult.

With respect to the uneven distribution of the *impact of business cycles on revenue across the regions of a large federal state such as Nigeria,* the prior existence of certain policy rules that require sub-national governments to balance their budgets is perhaps the best strategy. This is the so-called hard budget constraint scenario. Where the fiscal policy rule allows sub-national governments to run budget deficits, there should also be a clear rule forbidding bailouts. In essence, the fiscal policy rules and intergovernmental fiscal relations should be such as to discourage borrowing by sub-national governments. In order to manage the problem of excessive injection in the case of uneven distribution of the positive impact of business cycles on the revenue of sub-national government, the strategies for managing situations of exogenous revenue sources discussed above should be applicable. Again, for these strategies to be effective, there should be considerable fiscal discipline at all levels of government.

A strategy for dealing with the threat of *philosophical differences among parties in a federal state* is to establish and enforce a hard budget constraint regime.

Under such circumstances, the implication of the differences in preferences on macroeconomic stability will be manageable. In the absence of a hard budget constraint, there must be a fiscal policy rule that discourages excessive borrowing by sub-national governments and prevents bailouts.

The threats of *mismatch between spending responsibilities and resource allocation as well as vague assignment of spending responsibilities* can be addressed by making necessary adjustments in the assignment of responsibilities and/or resource allocation. However, in federations where spending responsibilities as well as resource allocation are constitutional matters, it can be quite difficult to make these adjustments. This calls for a very careful articulation of these aspects of the constitution.

It is perhaps easier to deal with the threat of *weak public expenditure management* provided there is an appreciation of the need to invest judiciously in capacity building and the statistical system. It turns out that, in Nigeria and many developing countries, investment in capacity building and statistical systems is seen as investment in luxury activities. Unfortunately, no matter how sound the rules are, if the capacity of the public servants to articulate, implement, monitor and assess the impact of policies and programmes is not built and sustained, the achievement of fiscal and, indeed, all other policies will remain largely a paper exercise. Therefore, statistical agencies, research, training and other capacity-building institutions should be well established and resourced in order to create the enabling environment for the effectiveness of otherwise well-formulated fiscal policy rules.

In order to deal with the *threat of weak or non-existent plan–budget links,* there must be full appreciation by the leadership at all levels of government of the relevance of planning, even in a market-oriented developing economy. The prevailing tendency on the part of the leadership in several developing countries to vacate planning on the pretext that it is incompatible with the market system is both theoretically flawed and creates room for arbitrariness, disorderliness and unpredictability in government actions, which adversely affect private sector operations.

It should be acknowledged that Professor Soludo, the current Governor of the Central Bank of Nigeria, while serving as Economic Adviser to the President and Chief Executive Officer of the National Planning Commission, successfully convinced the leadership of the executive and legislative arms of government at all levels to accept the inevitability of planning even in a market-oriented economy. Under his leadership, a medium-term plan called the National Economic Empowerment and Development Strategy (NEEDS), 2003–2007, was prepared. NEEDS was the federal government component of a nationally coordinated development plan, while the state governments were encouraged and supported to develop State Economic Empowerment and Development Strategies (SEEDS). An elaborate institutional framework for implementing the NEEDS and SEEDS was articulated. With the departure of the champion of the initiative, enthusiasm for implementing NEEDS and, by extension, SEEDS waned and, correspondingly, there has been no cause to embark on a review of the implementation and performance of these programmes against the well-stated objectives. Thus, the much anticipated commitment of the leadership in the executive and legislative arms of government at all levels to plan and budget with discipline failed to materialize. Also, the anticipated follow-up institutional framework for harmonized development planning in a federal state necessary to make planning inescapable could not be articulated, let alone enacted to law. The result is that commitment to planning continues to remain optional.

Turning to the *threat of lack of incentive to sub-national governments not to borrow*, the appropriate fiscal policy rule that imposes constitutional limitations on borrowing by all levels of government is an effective strategy adopted in several federations. The limitations on borrowing by sub-national governments are typically enshrined in a fiscal responsibility law, as has been done in Brazil for example. The limitation on borrowing by the central government should be part of the act establishing the central bank, and the act should guarantee full autonomy of the central bank. In fact, the central bank should be answerable only to the senate in a bicameral national assembly. This should be complemented with a well-regulated banking system and capital market in order to ensure that market discipline is imposed on all categories of borrowers, especially the governments. As noted earlier, the fiscal policy rule should oust bailouts under any guise.

Finally, the *threat of corruption* to fiscal policy coordination can be addressed by the establishment of a virile financial crime prevention scheme. In particular, the regular law enforcement agencies should be well structured, trained and equipped to prevent, detect and prosecute cases of financial crime. This should be complemented by the enactment and strict enforcement of special anti-corruption laws, the installation of an effective procurement procedure, ensuring full compliance with due process in contract awards and regular as well as timely auditing of government finances with swift implementation of redress procedures in cases of proven infractions of the rules and regulations.

9.4 Options for securing fiscal policy coordination in Nigeria

In attempting to propose options for securing fiscal policy coordination in Nigeria, it is perhaps pertinent to contextualize the problem. Perhaps the first feature of the Nigerian situation is the fact that the structure of public finance at all levels of government in Nigeria is inimical to effective fiscal policy coordination.

Table 9.1 shows that the revenue base of all the Nigerian governments is essentially exogenous. For this purpose, a revenue source is classified as fully exogenous if both the base and the rate cannot be directly and effectively influenced by the policy of the Nigerian government. If either the base or the rate cannot be directly and effectively influenced by the policy of the Nigerian government, then such a revenue is classified as partially exogenous. Finally, a revenue is classified as endogenous if both the rate and the base can be directly and effectively influenced by the policy of the Nigerian government.

On the basis of this classification, it is clear from Table 9.1 that, between 1999 and 2001, the portion of federation account revenue that could be directly and effectively influenced by the Nigerian authorities was below 15 per cent. In 2002, when the government succeeded in raising the domestic prices of petroleum products, the figure rose to 28 per cent. Being a once and for all increase, the figure declined sharply to 21.6 per cent in 2003 and further to 20.6 per cent in 2004. In such a situation, fiscal policy coordination at the level of revenue is essentially blunted.

Furthermore, a look at Tables 9.2, 9.3 and 9.4 will reveal that all levels of government depend chronically on exogenous revenues. For example, total revenue less the largely endogenous independent revenue of the federal government exceeded 90 per cent in 2004. The same situation is observable in the case of local governments. While the situation of state governments appeared to be slightly better, a closer look at Table 9.3 will show that the proportion of internally generated revenue declined from over 20 per cent in 1999 to about 12 per cent in 2004. Finally, it should be observed that, apart from state governments, recurrent expenditure of the other two levels of government accounted for well over half the total expenditure as of 2004, with personnel costs taking the lion's share.

Table 9.1 Structure of Federation Account Revenue, 1999–2004 (in percentages)

	1999	2000	2001	2002	2003	2004
Domestic crude oil sales	4.86	5.06	5.45	17.57	15.01	16.29
Companies' income tax	4.87	2.68	3.08	5.15	4.46	3.33
Independent revenue of the federal government	2.12	2.00	1.99	3.93	2.10	1.02
Education tax	0.00	0.39	0.73	0.59	0.00	0.00
Others	0.95	0.74	1.08	1.37	0.00	0.00
Tax on petroleum products	1.51	1.34	1.36	0.00	0.00	0.00
Total fully endogenous revenue	14.31	12.21	13.68	28.61	21.57	20.64
Custom and excise	9.26	5.33	7.64	10.47	7.59	5.56
Value added tax	4.97	3.07	4.11	6.27	5.2	4.09
Petroleum profit tax and royalties	17.31	27.55	28.65	22.65	26.54	30.34
Others	0.00	1.21	0.56	2.20	0.33	0.52
Total partially exogenous revenue	31.53	37.15	40.96	41.59	39.66	40.50
Crude oil exports	54.16	49.69	41.87	28.66	38.77	38.41
Total fully exogenous revenue	54.16	49.69	41.87	28.66	38.77	38.41
Privatization proceeds	0.00	0.95	3.49	1.14	0.00	0.00
Total transitory revenue	0.00	0.95	3.49	1.14	0.00	0.00
Grand total	100.00	100.00	100.00	100.00	100.00	100.00

Source: Underlying data obtained from CBN Annual Reports (various issues).

Table 9.2 Summary of federal government finances, 1999–2004 (in percentages)

	1999	2000	2001	2002	2003	2004
Total federal retained revenue	100.00	100.00	100.00	100.00	100.00	100.00
Share of federation account	33.03	84.10	66.58	70.10	86.90	92.98
Share of value added tax	1.07	1.38	1.68	1.65	1.95	1.93
Federal government independent revenue	1.74	6.37	5.57	7.26	5.30	3.23
Share of reserve	5.66	0.00	14.68	0.00	0.00	0.00
Education tax	0.55	0.00	0.00	0.00	5.21	0.00
Privatization and Global System of Mobile Phone proceeds	0.00	3.03	4.74	3.24	0.00	0.00
Custom levies	1.29	0.00	0.00	0.00	0.00	0.00
Petroleum Subsidy Trust Fund revenues	1.48	0.00	0.00	0.00	0.00	0.00
First charges	54.09	0.00	0.00	11.80	0.00	0.00
Others	1.08	5.12	6.74	5.61	0.64	1.86
Total expenditure	100.00	100.00	100.00	100.00	100.00	100.00
Recurrent expenditure	47.45	65.84	56.91	68.43	80.29	77.16
Personnel costs	30.00	39.75	28.01	36.26	30.42	32.14
Overhead costs	13.07	10.18	11.59	10.72	11.94	9.30
National Poverty Eradication Programme	0.00	0.00	0.12	0.00	0.00	0.00
Others	0.81	0.00	1.93	1.43	8.43	6.88
Federal government external obligations	1.90	0.66	0.00	0.00	0.00	0.00
Federal government extra-budgetary expenditure	15.69	0.00	0.00	0.00	0.00	0.00
Shortfall in exchange conversion	10.08	0.00	0.00	0.00	0.00	0.00
Interest payment	28.46	15.48	15.27	20.03	29.90	28.85
Foreign	10.76	0.00	0.00	3.27	15.80	14.06
Domestic	17.70	15.48	15.27	16.76	14.10	14.79
Capital expenditure	52.55	34.16	43.09	31.56	19.71	22.84

Source: Underlying data obtained from CBN Annual Reports (various issues).

Table 9.3 Summary of state government expenditure, 1999–2004 (in percentages)

	1999	2000	2001	2002	2003	2004
Current revenue	100.00	100.00	100.00	100.00	100.00	100.00
Federal Account	61.34	70.07	70.46	57.96	62.59	69.75
Value added tax	14.05	8.53	7.83	7.86	7.71	8.64
Internally generated revenue	20.18	10.52	10.36	13.38	13.89	12.05
Grants, etc.	3.88	9.27	10.12	19.37	15.69	9.38
Stabilization fund receipts	0.55	1.61	1.23	1.43	0.12	0.18
Recurrent expenditure	61.17	54.71	49.37	58.55	59.20	49.49
Current surplus	39.23	45.20	48.62	33.90	33.62	49.52
Capital expenditure	35.99	44.18	39.41	39.12	35.18	36.70
Extra-budgetary expenditure	2.84	1.11	11.22	2.33	5.62	13.81
Total expenditure	100.00	100.00	100.00	100.00	100.00	100.00

Source: Underlying data obtained from CBN Annual Reports (various issues).

Table 9.4 Summary of local government finances, 1999–2004 (in percentages)

	1999	2000	2001	2002	2003	2004
Current revenue	100.00	100.00	100.00	100.00	100.00	100.00
IGR	7.70	5.08	5.91	6.05	5.45	4.78
Tax revenue	1.99	1.26	2.17	1.90	0.94	1.04
Non-tax revenue	5.71	3.82	3.74	4.16	4.51	3.74
Federation Account	72.15	77.65	71.11	74.87	78.72	80.22
Value added tax	15.72	9.15	11.63	10.88	10.71	9.82
Stabilization fund and ecology	1.74	3.57	7.26	5.75	1.25	1.30
State allocation	0.69	1.30	0.77	0.97	0.57	0.77
Grants, etc.	1.99	3.26	3.31	1.47	3.30	3.10
Total expenditure	100.00	100.00	100.00	100.00	100.00	100.00
Recurrent	68.94	62.11	70.97	73.43	58.50	64.13
Personnel costs	54.72	44.39	50.42	41.43	63.40	62.92
Overhead costs	39.25	44.45	36.86	25.93	29.86	31.87
Consolidated Revenue Fund Charges, etc.	6.03	11.17	12.72	6.07	6.74	5.21
Capital	31.06	37.89	29.03	26.57	41.50	35.87

Source: Underlying data obtained from CBN Annual Reports (various issues).

The upshot of the foregoing is that all governments in Nigeria are extremely vulnerable to external shocks. They all have high recurrent expenditure dominated by personnel costs, implying that there is very little room for adjustment to external shocks without deleterious effects on stabilization in terms of either running high deficits, with adverse effects on inflation, or retrenchment, with adverse effects on unemployment and the poverty situation.

It is against the background of these features of the Nigerian fiscal operations that options for securing fiscal policy coordination are explored in the rest of this chapter. The first option is to seek ways of reducing government dependence on exogenous sources of revenue. This may be achieved by vigorous efforts to diversify the economic base away from crude oil towards more endogenous sources, especially corporate income tax and excise duties as well as value added tax (VAT) on locally produced goods and services. At the moment, over 80 per cent of VAT is on imports, making this source of revenue essentially exogenous. The thinking is that when larger proportions of revenue at all levels are fully endogenous, fiscal policy coordination will become less difficult and contentious. Therefore, serious efforts should be made to encourage domestic production and investment, especially in labour-intensive manufacturing. Towards this end, the constraints posed by weak infrastructure, especially electricity, water and transportation, should continue to receive attention at all levels of government.

With respect to the preponderance of personnel costs in total government expenditure at all levels, there is a need for cooperation on the part of the labour force to reduce pressure for nominal wage increases because this reduces the opportunity for adjustment to inevitable external shocks. On the part of government, there is need for caution in pursuing cost- and price-escalating policies. In particular, it should be helpful if serious efforts are made to resolve the problems that are militating against reliable domestic supply of petroleum products as opposed to exclusive reliance on intermittent tinkering with prices of these products as a strategy for managing demand. In the spirit of burden sharing, the manufacturers and other producers of goods and services may also assist by absorbing at least part of the inevitable price increases, instead of magnifying and passing on the cost implications to prices, thereby creating conditions for pressure for wage increases. The monetary authorities and banking sector operators could complement government efforts by progressively reducing MPR as appropriate while the banks respond by reducing bank lending rates.

In the meantime, options for addressing the stark reality of unstable revenue flow from exogenous sources, in other words oil, should be considered. In this regard one possibility is the passage of a well-articulated *National Reserve Fund Act* to law. Such an act could specify a minimum percentage of oil revenue to be paid into the Reserve Fund for the benefit of future generations. Another possibility is to require that any excess crude oil earnings at the end of a fiscal year should also be paid into the fund, thereby formalizing the current practice of sterilizing excess crude oil earnings. The fund may also be kept with the Central Bank of Nigeria for investment mainly in the Nigerian capital market as a strategy for supporting the growth and development of this market. The possibility of investing part of the fund in the international capital market subject to necessary safeguards against excessive risks and graft should be explored. For this purpose, the fund should be audited regularly, and the audit report should be widely publicized. During periods of severe depression in the international oil market similar to the one witnessed in 1985–86, part of the proceeds of investment (not the capital) may be used to supplement the federation account in order to avoid severe economic depression. Of course, the withdrawal from the account should be distributed among all levels of government according to the prevailing revenue allocation formula.

Second, the price of oil for the purposes of making revenue projections may be based on rules such as production cost plus a mark-up. The mark-up should not exceed the norm in the industry over time. In order to avoid pressure to distribute any receipts in excess of the projection at any time, a *National Revenue Act* may be enacted into law every year prior to the Appropriation Act. Any excess revenue may be retained in the Federation Account and be distributed within the year only with the passage of a *National Supplementary Revenue Act*.

Each state assembly may be encouraged to enact its own *State Revenue Act* as well, and the instrumentality of the *State Supplementary Revenue Act* may be used if there is a need to distribute all or part of the excess revenue. If found suitable, states may also establish State Reserve Funds managed along similar lines to those proposed for the National Reserve Fund.

Another complementary option is to create strong incentives for not borrowing by state and local governments. This can be achieved through the instrumentality of a *Fiscal Responsibility Law*. A draft Fiscal Responsibility Law was pending with the outgoing National Assembly. It may be useful if this draft law is considered and passed into law soon after the new National Assembly is inaugurated in 2007. The act may outlaw borrowing by state and local governments from the banking industry and federal government guarantees and bailouts, thereby imposing hard budget constraints on these levels of government. In this way, each state and local government will be constrained to borrowing only from the capital market, where market discipline should hold sway.

The Fiscal Responsibility Law may also require that the Appropriation Bill presented to the National Assembly by the Executive be accompanied by the underlying medium-term plan and Statement of Compatibility with the underlying plan. The Statement of Compatibility should include justifications for deviations from the plan for consideration by the National Assembly. In this way, the incidence of plan and budget indiscipline may be reduced considerably, thereby enhancing credibility of government polices and programmes.

In order to entrench and deepen the participatory and nationally coordinated planning approach used in the preparation of NEEDS and SEEDS as well as to promote effective implementation, the government may consider a new institutional arrangement for development planning. To this end, a *Federal Ministry of National Economy and Development (MNED)* should be created. The ministry may be responsible for coordinating all national development policy formulation, in which case it should function as a specialized professional body, whose professional staff may not suffer any disadvantage in terms of career progression and/or opportunity to reach the top of the civil service. Also, the ministry may be the Secretariat of the National Economic Council and the National Council of States. Finally, the ministry may ensure that all programmes and projects seeking external assistance should be conceived and implemented within the framework of the plan, and ensure that only commitments with the donors, including the Bretton Woods institutions, that are consistent with the goals and aspirations of the plan should be made. Each state may consider a similar institutional arrangement to enhance coordination and complementarity among all levels of government. In that case, it may be instrumental to revise and re-invigorate the Joint Planning Board and National Council on Development Planning to provide a platform for regular exchange of ideas among the leadership of planning agencies at the federal and state levels.

In order to impose a similarly hard budget constraint on the federal government without blunting the efficacy of fiscal policy as a tool for economic management, the *Central Bank Act may be amended to make it responsible only to the Senate.* The independence thus guaranteed will make it possible for the Central Bank to insist on full compliance with the provisions of the Central Bank Act with respect to government borrowing from the bank.

At the moment, there are no explicit and discernible philosophical differences among the political parties in Nigeria. Whenever this arises, the existence of a hard budget constraint implied by the Fiscal Responsibility Law and strict observance of the Central Bank Act duly amended as proposed may suffice.

In order to deal with the problem of weak public expenditure management, government at all levels should take the issue of training and retraining its work force very seriously. Also, *research and training institutions should be adequately funded to enable them to deliver pertinent policy advice and cutting edge capacity-building programmes, respectively.* With respect to information and analytical input into the public expenditure management processes, the new National Bureau of Statistics should be fully and effectively funded to carry out the necessary surveys and produce high-quality data on a timely basis and with appropriate frequency. A situation whereby there are no quarterly GDP estimates will make fiscal policy coordination more difficult as the impact of fiscal misalignment will become obvious only with a long time lag, and this will render remedial action ineffectual. Also, the National Bureau of Statistics should embark on producing state-level GDP by sectors. Needless to say, adequate data will provide a useful guide to policy-making only if they are promptly analysed and the results made available to requisite stakeholders. This calls for proper funding of policy research institutes such as the Nigerian Institute of Social and Economic Research (NISER) and the universities.

Finally, the scourge of corrupt practices in all sectors of Nigerian society should be vigorously addressed. In this regard, the Independent Corrupt Practice and Related Offences Commission (ICPC) and the Economic and Financial Crime Commission (EFCC) may be quite instrumental, just like the extant rules surrounding the award of contracts in the public sector.

In conclusion, without prejudice to the efficacy of laws and regulations, the ultimate determinant of success in securing fiscal policy coordination in a federation such as Nigeria is the level of personal discipline and integrity of the operators of the system. Also, their commitment to national development and a full realization of the need and readiness on their part to serve, rather than to be served, while in office are important. Unfortunately, none of these requirements can be legislated into law. They are really traits that are acquired through proper socialization.

Bibliography

Aboyade, O., 1983, *Integrated Economics: A Study of Developing Economies*, New York: Addison-Wesley Publishers.

Ajakaiye, O., 2001, 'Promoting Economic Growth Through Synchronized Fiscal and Monetary Policies in Year 2001', paper presented at the National Workshop on Monetary and Financial Policy Management Organized by the Chartered Institute of Bankers of Nigeria, Lagos.

Ajakaiye, O., 2003, 'Fiscal Policy Coordination For Macroeconomic Stability in a Federal State', paper presented at the one-day Seminar of the Nigerian Economic Society on Fiscal Policy Management in Nigeria, the Muson Centre, Onikan, Lagos, 22 May.

Ajakaiye, O. and S.A. Benjamin (eds), 1999, *Issues in the Review of the 1999 Constitution of the Federal Republic of Nigeria*, Ibadan: NISER.

Anyanwu, J.C., 1997, *Nigerian Public Finance*, Onitsha, Nigeria: Joanee Educational Publishers.

Aron, J., 1996 'The Institutional Foundations of Growth', in S. Ellis (ed.), *Africa Now, People, Policies and Institutions*, Hague: Ministry of Foreign Affairs.

Burki, S.J., G. Perry and W. Dillinger, 1999, 'Addressing the Macroeconomic Threats: The Quest for Hard Budget Constraints', in Burki, S.J., G. Perry and W. Dillinger (eds), *Beyond the Center: Decentralizing the State*, World Bank Latin American Studies, Washington, DC: World Bank.

Central Bank of Nigeria, various years, *Annual Report and Statement of Accounts*, Lagos: Central Bank of Nigeria.

Chowdhury, A. and C. Kirkpatrick, 1994, *Development Policy and Planning*, London: Routledge.

El Dersh, A., 2002, 'Planning in a Market Economy: What, Why and How', luncheon speech on Planning in a Market Driven Economy, Semiramis Inter-Continental, Cairo, Egypt, 16 October.

Federal Republic of Nigeria, various issues, *National Rolling Plan of Nigeria*, Lagos: National Planning Commission.

Federal Republic of Nigeria, 1962, *Nigerian National Development Plan, 1962–68*, Lagos: Federal Government Printers.

Federal Republic of Nigeria, 1970, *Second National Development Plan, 1970–74*, Lagos: Federal Government Printers.

Federal Republic of Nigeria, 1975, *Third National Development Plan, 1975–80*, Lagos: Federal Government Printers.

Federal Republic of Nigeria, 1981, *Fourth National Development Plan, 1981–85*, Lagos: Federal Government Printers.

Federal Republic of Nigeria, 1986, *The Structural Adjustment Programme for Nigeria, 1986–88*, Lagos: Federal Government Printers.

Federal Republic of Nigeria, 1999, *The 1999 Constitution of the Federal Republic of Nigeria*, Abuja: Government Press.

Federal Republic of Nigeria, 2004, *Nigeria: National Economic Empowerment and Development Strategy (NEEDS)*, Abuja: The NEEDS Secretariat, National Planning Commission, Federal Secretariat.

Government of Brazil, 1998, *Fiscal Responsibility Law*, Brasilia: Federal Ministry of Budget and Management.

Government of India, 2001, *Approach Paper to the Tenth Five Year Plan, 2002–2007*, New Delhi: Planning Commission.

Kaplan, E.J., 1972, *Japan: The Government–Business Relationship*, Washington, DC: US Department of Commerce.

Kwakwa, V., 2003a, *Mechanisms for Fiscal Policy Coordination and Cooperation Between The Three Tiers of Government in Nigeria*, Abuja: World Bank.

Kwakwa, V., 2003b, *Managing Oil Revenues: Lessons from Global Experience*, Abuja: World Bank.

Mbanefoh, G.F., 1992, 'Nigerian Fiscal Federalism: Assignment of Functions and Tax Powers', Paper presented at the National Seminar of the Revenue Mobilization, Allocation and Fiscal Commission, Enugu.

Musgrave, R.A. and P.B. Musgrave, 1976, *Public Finance in Theory and Practice*, New York: McGraw-Hill.

NISER, 2000, *NISER Review of Nigerian Development: The State in Nigerian Development*, Ibadan: NISER.

Obadan, M.I., 2002, 'Stabilization Funds in Nigeria as a Source of Cheap Funds for the Real Sector', paper presented at a two-day seminar on Obtaining and Managing Long-Term Low Interest Funds for Real Sector in Nigeria, organized by the Office of the Vice-President, Abuja, March.

Obasanjo, O.O., 1999, 'Economic Priorities: Statement on the Budget Review to the National Assembly', in Obe, Ad'Obe (ed.), *A New Dawn: Selected Speeches by Olusegun Obasanjo*, Abuja: Presidential Communications Unit, Office of the President.

Olomola, A.S., 1999, 'Institutional Implications of the 1999 Constitution', in Ajakaiye, O. and S.A. Benjamin (eds), *Issues in the Review of the 1999 Constitution of the Federal Republic of Nigeria*, Ibadan: NISER.

Omole, D.A., 1999, '1999 Constitution of the Federal Republic of Nigeria: Implications for Fiscal Federalism and Economic Management', in Ajakaiye, O. and S.A. Benjamin (eds), *Issues in the Review of the 1999 Constitution of the Federal Republic of Nigeria*, Ibadan: NISER.

Onimode, B., 1997, 'Resources Derivation, Allocation and Utilization', in *Constitutions and Federalism, Proceedings of the Conference on Constitutions and Federalism*, Lagos: Friedrich Ebert Foundation.

Onimode, B., 2000, 'Fiscal Federalism in Nigeria: Options for the 21st Century', a research report submitted to the Ford Foundation, New York.

Pisani-Ferry, J., 2002, 'Fiscal Discipline and Policy Coordinaton in Eurozone: Assessment and Proposals', paper prepared for the European Commission President's Group of Economic Analysis.

Roberts, F.O.N., 1999, 'The 1999 Constitution of the Federal Republic of Nigeria: Implications for Intergovernmental Relations', in Ajakaiye, O. and S.A. Benjamin (eds), *Issues in the Review of the 1999 Constitution of the Federal Republic of Nigeria*, Ibadan: NISER.

Sen, A.K., 2000, *Development As Freedom*, New Delhi: Oxford University Press.

Shah, A., 1998, 'Fiscal Federalism and Macroeconomic Governance: For Better or For Worse?', Policy Research Working Paper No. 2005, World Bank Operations Evaluation Department.

Tanzi, V., 1995, 'Fiscal Federalism and Decentralization: A Review of Some Efficiency and Macroeconomic Aspects', in *Proceedings of the Annual Conference on Development Economics*, World Bank.

Tendulkar, S.D., 1991, 'The Role of Policy Research in the Formulation and Implementation of Macroeconomic Strategies and Policies in India', in UNESCAFE Institutional Relations in Development, Development Papers, No. 8, UNESCAFE, 31–50.

Uddin, F., 2000, *Planning in Free Market Economy*, Internet Edition, Dawn, 8 May.

10

Fiscal Federalism in Nigeria: Issues, Challenges and Agenda for Reform

Akpan H. Ekpo[1] *and Abwaku Englama*[2]

10.1 Introduction

Resource allocation and management as well as fiscal federalism/decentralization have remained contentious issues in a federal state such as Nigeria. This is because the essence of government at all levels is to bring about rapid economic development through adequate provisions of social and economic infrastructures for the citizenry. The fiscal arrangement within the federation should, therefore, adequately cater for the federating units to enable them to discharge their constitutional responsibilities. Consequently, the struggle for control of power and equitable distribution of resources by the component units that make up the federation is driven by the need for balanced development, fiscal justice and fair play. Fiscal federalism has, therefore, become part of a worldwide 'reform' agenda supported by the Bretton Woods institutions such as the World Bank and the International Monetary Fund (IMF), and several international institutions such as the United States Agency for International Development (USAID) and Asian Development Bank. It has become an integral part of economic development and governance in developing and transitional economies (Bahl, 1999). Fiscal decentralization and the desire for local discretion and devolution of power is often seen by the World Bank as a vehicle to promote governance and development in developing countries such as Nigeria. James (2003) observed that the underlying basis for the renewed interest in fiscal federalism/decentralization as an aspect of any reform agenda includes the following: (i) central governments have discovered that it is impossible for them to meet all the competing needs of their various constituencies and are therefore attempting to build local capacity by delegating responsibilities downward to their regional governments, (ii) central governments expect regional and sub-regional governments to implement national economic development strategies and (iii) regional and local political leaders are demanding more autonomy and want the taxation powers that go along with their expenditures.

The situation in Nigeria is, however, different. The paradox of Nigeria's fiscal system is that it focuses more attention on 'sharing' than 'generating'. In other words, increased revenue generation has attracted less attention than revenue sharing. This is because oil remains the highest contributor to the distributable pool of the federation. In fact, the over-dependence on oil has become a propelling wind of regional agitations instead of energizing efforts towards diversification of the economic base for a virile and durable economy. For instance, the crisis in the Niger Delta has been traced to inequitable fiscal systems among others. The issues that need to be addressed therefore are: (i) Has the current fiscal system resulted in desired development by the citizenry? (ii) What are the consequences of the sustainability of the current fiscal system on the 'Nigeria Project'? (iii) What policy measures should be adopted to achieve balanced development among the component units of the federation? (iv) What are the challenges for promoting fiscal harmony in the Nigerian federation? The answers to these issues have become imperative against the backdrop that fiscal decentralization has become a global reform agenda for meeting the challenges of the Millennium Development Goals (MDGs). In the Nigerian federation, struggles between federal and state governments remain significant obstacles to the realization of the goals of the ongoing economic reform under the aegis of National Economic Empowerment and Development Strategy (NEEDS).

In analysing fiscal federalism in Nigeria, it is important to view the federal government of Nigeria as one, with both centralized and decentralized levels of decision-making in which choices made at each level concerning the provision of public services are determined mainly by the demands for those services by those residing in the respective jurisdiction.

Sub-national governments in Nigeria can be justified for three reasons. (i) The present democratic experiment seems to work best the closer the government is to its constituency. The assumption here is that a sub-national government such as a local government will be better at perceiving the desires and demands of its constituents for public services than a centralized government far away in Abuja. (ii) People living in the various states and local governments have the right to demand different types and quantities of public goods and services; states and local governments have been agitating that they are better placed to provide certain utilities that are currently being provided by the federal government. For example, the federal government seems to have failed in attempting to provide electricity. However, while states argue that they are in a better position to provide electricity, the federal government is still insisting on doing same by investing in independent power plants. (iii) Finally, to reduce ethnic tension. This is broadly at two levels – federal and state. At the federal level, there exists some understanding that power is being shared among the three major ethnic groups.

The creation of states, apart from decentralizing decision-making, also gave minority ethnic groups a sense of being part of the federation. This is not to suggest that there are no ethnic tensions within states. On the contrary, ethnic tension does exist but perhaps better than would have been the situation if states were not created. For example, in Akwa Ibom State in the south-eastern part of the country, the majority ethnic group (the Ibibios) are about 2.5 million in population. In the Nigerian context, the group is a minority one but in the state, it is a majority ethnic group co-existing with other smaller ethnic groups. Ethnic tension is, therefore, better managed at the lower levels of government. With over 250 ethnic groups in the country, the creation of sub-national governments partly guarantees the existence of the Nigerian nation.

Using the Musgravian framework, decision-making should take place at the lowest level of government, and this is consistent with the twin objectives of allocational efficiency and distributional equity. However, in the Nigerian federation, as presently constituted, sub-national governments such as states and local governments do not have the capacity to perform certain functions. It is, therefore, imperative that capacity be built at the lower levels of government. It is because of this lack of capacity at the lower levels that the federal government continues to perform the functions discussed in this chapter.

It is against this background that this chapter seeks to examine fiscal federalism in Nigeria with a view to bringing out the salient issues that have marred its performances over the years and proffering policy actions for improvement. Following the introduction, the next section discusses the theoretical framework of fiscal decentralization. In Section 10.3, an analysis of the history of revenue allocation in Nigeria is presented. The issues and challenges arising from the practice of fiscal federalism in Nigeria form the focus of Section 10.4, while Section 10.5 concludes the chapter.

10.2 The theoretical framework for fiscal decentralization

There are several economic and political arguments for the practice of fiscal federalism in a country. While the political arguments are largely based on the heterogeneous characteristics of the different regions making up the federation, the economic justification is usually based on the need to promote efficiency in the use of national resources (Alade *et al.*, 2003). Thus, in discussing issues of fiscal federalism and macroeconomic governance generally, the roles of the various levels of government and their partnership arrangements with society, in respect of the management of the economy, are usually the focus of attention.

Federalism has been defined as the amalgam of sub-units of a national sovereign government that operate independently within a constitutionally defined sphere of functional competence (Oates, 1972). The federating units in a federal system voluntarily give up sovereignty in several respects of their operations in order to achieve the benefits of national unity in some areas of government activities, while retaining a measure of autonomy in others. It can also be defined as a compromise solution in a multidimensional state, between two types of self-determination. In fact, the important aspects of intergovernmental fiscal relations (IGFR) can be located within the concept of federalism. Thus, federalism could be taken to mean a system of government in which revenue and expenditure functions are divided among the tiers/levels of government. This division is usually done to enhance the government's effective provision of public goods and services at different levels to the citizens. It has been generally opined that revenue generating and spending responsibilities, intergovernmental transfer and the administrative aspects of fiscal decentralization are, in fact, the real issues involved in intergovernmental fiscal relations, or fiscal federalism as it is usually known. Specifically, the Nigerian fiscal federalism structure involves the allocation of expenditure and tax-raising powers among the federal, state and local governments.

According to Alade *et al.* (2003) and Sanni (2003) the objectives of fiscal relations among units in a federation include among others (i) ensuring correspondence between sub-national expenditure responsibilities and their financial resources, (ii) increasing the autonomy of sub-national governments by incorporating incentives for them to mobilize revenues of their own, (iii) ensuring that the macroeconomic management policies of the government are not undermined or compromised and (iv) giving expenditure discretion to sub-national governments in appropriate areas in order to increase the efficiency of public spending and improve accountability of sub-national officers to their constituents.

Fiscal decentralization entails the process of reassigning expenditure functions and tax resources to the lower tiers of government with a view to decentralizing policy-making and implementation. James (2003) defined fiscal decentralization as the devolution by the central government to local governments of specific functions with the administrative authority and fiscal revenue to perform those functions. Thus, this arrangement ensures that each level of government is free to take decisions and allocate resources according to its own priorities in its area of jurisdiction.

The distribution of tax authority and expenditure responsibility in a federal state such as the United States of America, People's Republic of China or Nigeria is an extremely complex issue. Economists generally focus on issues of efficiency and equity, while public administration and political scientists tend to focus on distribution of powers, responsiveness and accountability, and tax competition and coordination. Musgrave's framework for analysing the roles or functions is widely accepted (Musgrave, 1964). Musgrave described the functions performed by the government as stabilization, distribution and allocation. The stabilization function involves the role of tax and spending policies and monetary policy in the overall level of economic activity. It is widely believed among scholars that this role should be assigned to the national government. This implies that the national government must have a broad-based tax suitable for this role (James, 2003).

The distribution function explains the role of government in changing the distribution of income, wealth or other indicators of economic well-being to make them more equitable than would otherwise be the case. The case for assigning this function to the national government rests on two assumptions: (i) that the national government's broad taxing powers can more easily redistribute income and (ii) that the ability of the taxpayers to move from one jurisdiction to another to take advantage of more attractive spending and taxation policies weakens local government's ability to mobilize resources for development. The allocation function is the government's role in deciding the mix of public and private goods that are provided by the economy or by the government. Each level of government may be more efficient in delivering certain governmental goods and services.

In other words, allocation functions are dictated by the rule that the national government should handle responsibilities whose spillover effects are national in character while the state and local authorities should perform those matters whose benefits are local. Thus, defence, foreign affairs, space exploration research and development are usually left to the central government.

The Musgrave framework has been helpful in deciding which taxes are levied at each level. The principle is that 'finance should follow function'. This implies that expenditure function should be matched by tax responsibilities. If tax collection falls short of expenditure responsibilities then that level of government must have additional taxing authority, or rely on intergovernmental transfers (such as grants and shared taxes) to support its expenditures (James, 2003).

The modern case for decentralized fiscals was articulated by Oates (1999). His arguments were based on two aspects: efficiency and governance values. The core of the efficiency value is the maximization of social welfare. It is argued that the public sector does not possess the same price signals as the private sector for it to regulate supply and demand and that within a political jurisdiction there is the likelihood that there will be divergence between the preferences of the individual community members. Thus, the tax and service package reflects the aggregate community preferences. Fiscal decentralization is, therefore, expected to cater for the divergent needs of the society.

Tanzi (1995) summarizes a number of situations or conditions, especially in developing countries, where decentralization may lead to less than an optimal result: taxpayers may have insufficient information or no political power to pressure local policy-makers to make resource-efficient decisions; local politicians may be more corrupt than national politicians or at least find themselves in more corrupting situations; the quality of national bureaucracies is also likely to be better than local bureaucracies; technological change and increased mobility may reduce the number of services that are truly 'local' in nature; and local governments often lack good public expenditure management systems to assist them in their tax and budget choices. Fiscal decentralization may, therefore, exacerbate a central government's ability to deal with structural fiscal imbalances.

Prud'homme (1995) argues that fiscal inequities may actually increase with decentralization. In addition, localities might engage in destructive competition to attract industry. He also argues that the rationale for decentralization of revenues is not the same as expenditure, and in many cases the issue is not whether a certain service should be provided by a central, regional or local government, but rather how to organize the joint production of the service by the various levels.

Shah (1998) concludes that, contrary to a common misconception, decentralized fiscal systems offer more potential for improved macroeconomic governance than do centralized fiscal systems, because they require greater clarity about the roles of various players and decision-makers and – to ensure fair play – greater transparency in rules governing interactions. In order to ensure that fiscal decentralization contributes meaningfully to growth and development, he advocated that monetary policy is best entrusted to an independent central bank with a mandate for price stability. Fiscal rules accompanied by 'gatekeeper' intergovernmental councils or committees provide a useful framework for fiscal discipline and coordination of fiscal policy. The integrity and independence of the financial sector contribute to fiscal prudence in the public sector. To ensure fiscal discipline, governments at all levels must be made to face the financial consequences of their decisions, and societal norms and consensus about the roles of various levels of government and limits to their authority are vital to the success of decentralized decision-making. He also states that tax decentralization is a prerequisite for sub-national access to credit markets, and higher-level institutional assistance may be needed to finance local capital projects in situations of insufficient fiscal resources; an internal common market is best preserved by constitutional guarantees.

Intergovernmental transfers in developing countries undermine fiscal discipline and accountability while building transfer dependencies that cause a slow economic strangulation of fiscally disadvantaged regions; periodic review of jurisdictional assignments is essential to realign responsibilities with changing economic and political realities. He concluded that decentralized fiscal systems offer more potential for improved macroeconomic governance than do centralized fiscal systems.

10.3 History of revenue allocation

The task of revenue sharing in Nigeria has been daunting, so the sharing formula has continuously changed to meet the exigencies of the country at every stage of her development. Revenue sharing in Nigeria began in 1946 when the Richards Constitution granted internal autonomy to regional governments. The arrangement for sharing of responsibilities between the national and regional governments made it necessary to make available to the regions revenues with which to undertake their new functions. The Philipson Commission of 1946 recommended only three principles of revenue allocation, which were derivation, even progress and population. But in the absence of statistical data only the population principle was applied. Regional revenues were divided into declared and undeclared revenues and shared on a horizontal basis, as there was no vertical sharing system then. A region was given a sum relative to its contribution to the central revenue while even progress as a factor was used to allocate more revenues to backward areas to enable them catch up with the rest of the country. This, indeed, justifies the notion that revenue allocation is more or less a political issue.

The Hicks–Philipson Commission report of 1951 on revenue sharing developed a scheme based on the 1951 McPherson Constitution, which introduced a quasi-federal structure of government. The Commission recommended four general principles of sharing, namely independent revenues, derivation, need and national interest. For instance, under the derivation principle, the Commission gave 50 per cent of the import and excise duty on tobacco and 100 per cent of the duties on motor fuel to the regions.

The Chicks Commission's report of 1953 recommended derivation as the only factor of revenue sharing and virtually ignored other principles. It recommended 50 per cent to regions on import duties on goods and excise taxes on tobacco in accordance with regional consumption, 50 per cent on import duties on goods other than tobacco, 50 per cent on hides and skin. All proceeds from import duty on motor spirit and mineral royalties were allocated in full to the regions. The Commission's underlying philosophy then was that the principle of derivation is followed to the fullest degree compatible with meeting the reasonable needs of the centre and each of the regions.

The Raisman Commission report of 1958 came as a result of disenchantment from the regions with the mode of sharing, especially the derivation principles. The Commission on its part recommended that all proceeds of both import and excise duties should be distributed in full among the regions. This was to avoid an allocation system that depended too much on derivation and also to take into account differing needs of the regions. The Commission created a Distributable Pool Account into which 30 per cent of the revenues from mining rents and royalties and 30 per cent of the revenues from other import duties would be paid. Revenues from mining rents and royalties were to be allocated between the regions in whose areas the mineral existed, the centre, and the Distributable Pool Account in the ratio of 50:20:30 respectively.

The Binns Commission's report of 1964 rejected sharing among the regions on the basis of derivation and recommended an increase from 30 per cent to 35 per cent of duties on general import and revenue from mining rents and royalties, payable to the Distributable Pool Account. The Dina Interim Revenue Allocation Review of 1968 recommended the renaming of the Distributable Pool Account as the State Joint Account and the creation of a Special Grants Account. It advocated a Permanent Planning and Fiscal Commission. Dina's report was rejected by the then military government, which promulgated Decree No. 13 of 1970, which reduced the state's shares of export duty revenue from 100 per cent to 60 per cent and of excise duty revenue from 100 per cent to 50 per cent. The federal government was to receive 5 per cent of mining rents and royalties taken out of the 50 per cent that went to the states by derivation.

Decree No. 9 of 1971 allowed the transfer of rents and royalties of offshore petroleum and mines from the states to the centre, while Decree No. 6 of 1975 ruled that all revenues to be shared by the states had to pass through the Distributive Pool Account except 20 per cent of onshore mining rents and royalties due to the states of origin on the principle of derivation.

The Aboyade Report of 1977 recommended five principles for revenue allocation: equality of access of development opportunities; national minimum standard for national integration; absorptive capacity; independent revenue and minimum tax effort; and fiscal efficiency. This report was, however, rejected because it was found to be too technical.

In 1979, the Okigbo Commission's report recommended principles such as minimum responsibilities of government, population, social development factors and internal revenue effort among others in the sharing of revenue. The report further argued on the principle of derivation that oil-producing states advanced the inclusion of derivation based on history, legal right and equity. The Report felt that appeal to history was not persuasive enough while that of ownership was judicial. Thus, while legislation vested the ownership of land to states, it vested the ownership of minerals in the federal government. The Okigbo Commission took the view that mining rents should be paid directly to the oil-producing states as right under existing laws and that the Federal Government had a duty to make some restitution to those states for the damage caused by the exploitation of the mineral wealth. Hence, a provision of 2 per cent of the Federation Account as a Special Fund was advocated to be applied exclusively to the rehabilitation of the mineral-producing areas and no distinction was made between offshore and onshore.

In 1984, an amendment to the Allocation of Revenue Act of 1982 was promulgated as Amendment Decree No. 34 of 1984, stipulating that 2 per cent should be paid to mineral-producing areas on the basis of derivation and 1.5 per cent of the Federation Account should be set aside for the development of mineral-producing areas.

It is instructive to note that, despite the need to have complex sharing formula by several commissions, the exercise has been made difficult by lack of adequate data. As part of the solution, the Okigbo Commission stressed the recommendation of the Dina Commission of 1968 of the need for the continuous development, refining and updating of the principles and data needed for operational and less subjective works in revenue allocation, through the creation of a permanent special commission charged with the responsibility for mobilization, monitoring and evaluating revenue allocation issues, on a continuous basis. The Political Bureau, set up by the Babangida administration, further endorsed the recommendation.

In September 1988, the then federal military government through Decree No. 49 of 1989 inaugurated the National Revenue Mobilization Allocation and Fiscal Commission under the Chairmanship of General T.Y. Danjuma (retired). The Commission's Report recommended that the following be taken into account in revenue sharing: equality of states; population; social development factor; landmass and terrain; and internal revenue effort. However, in 1990, under horizontal sharing, the Social Development Factor was made to include education, health and water, while the vertical formula was made 50 per cent in favour of the federal government. In 1992, the vertical share of the local government was increased to 20 per cent while that of the state was reduced to 25 per cent. In the same vein, in June 1992 the state share in the vertical formula was further reduced to 24 per cent and the share dedicated to ecology was increased to 2 per cent from 1 per cent and that for development of mineral-producing areas rose to 3 per cent. Derivation remained 1 per cent and this was allocated directly to the states based on production quantum (Ekpo, 1994).

Here, it is pertinent to note that since 1982, when the Shagari administration passed the Revenue Allocation Act, the system of revenue sharing has been shrouded by the whims and caprices of the succeeding military administrations.

The period of Babangida's administration of 1985 to 1993 was extraordinary. Even after the National Revenue Mobilization Allocation and Fiscal Commission were set up, their recommendation was subjected to a thorough review that eventually skewed the system of revenue allocation in favour of the centre. The system of revenue sharing then was more of a grant to subordinate tiers. A striking example was in 1992 when the nation's revenue formula was changed twice via budget and national broadcast.

It is disheartening to say that since 1992 to date, the nation's revenue sharing system has remained unchanged except for minor changes occasioned by the Supreme Court ruling of 5 April 2002, otherwise known as the Resource Control Suit.

10.3.1 Principles of revenue sharing in Nigeria

The history of revenue allocation as discussed in the preceding section has shown that revenue allocation among the federating units is contingent on several socio-economic factors but the ultimate goal is to ensure the overall development of the country with each unit having a fair share of the national resources. Revenue sharing is therefore guided by certain principles. Soyode (2004) and Agiobenebo (2003) identified some fundamental principles of fiscal federalism that have been evolved to guide intergovernmental fiscal relations in practice. These include:

- *The Principle of Diversity* One of the arguments for the federal system is its ability to accommodate a large variety of diversities. So the fiscal system must provide scope for variety and differences to accommodate adequately the supply of national, regional (state) and local public goods.
- *The Principle of Equivalence* The geographical incidence of the various public goods differs. Therefore, allocative efficiency requires the equalization of locational advantages arising from inter-jurisdictional differences with a combination of taxes and public goods and services.
- *The Principle of Centralized Stabilization* This principle requires the use of fiscal instruments for achieving macroeconomic policy objectives (such as stabilization and growth) at the national level.
- *Correction of Spillover Effects* Efficiency of fiscal federalism requires that inter-jurisdictional externalities be corrected for by the system. Spillover effects or inter-jurisdictional externalities refer to externalities (both benefits enjoyed and harm suffered) by residents of geopolitical units because benefits for regions for many public goods and services are open entities. This requirement is intended to control for what in the fiscal decentralization literature is referred to as the 'central city exploitation thesis'. In addition, it involves the exploitation of the economies of scale as well as the rationale for intergovernmental grants. Efficiency and equity require that the emitting entity should internalize the cost of the external diseconomy. In the alternative, if this external diseconomy is across states, then the national government and the state should intervene. The important requirement is that the fiscal system should internalize the cost to achieve allocative efficiency and even equity in the use of resources.

Table 10.1 Assignment of expenditure responsibilities in Nigeria

Level of government	Expenditure category
Federal only (exclusive list)	Aviation including airports Award of national titles of honour, decorations and other dignitaries Bankruptcy and insolvency, exchange and currency, coinage and legal tender Construction and maintenance of federal trunk roads Defence Deportation of non-citizens Diplomatic, consular and trade representation Drugs and poison Elections (excluding elections to local government councils) External affairs Fingerprints, identification and criminal records Immigration into and emigration from Nigeria Meteorology Military (Army, Navy and Air Force) Mining and minerals, including oil fields, oil mining, geological surveys and natural gas National Parks Nuclear energy Pension, gratuities and other benefits payable out of the Consolidated Revenue Fund of the Federation Police and other government security services established by law Posts, telegraphs and telephones Prisons Public services of the Federation Railways Price control of goods designated as essential by the National Assembly Traffic and federal trunk roads
Federal–state (concurrent list)	Antiquities and monuments Archives Electoral law Electric power Exhibition of cinematograph films Industrial, commercial or agricultural development Scientific and technological research Statistics Trigonometrical, cadastral and topographical surveys University, technological and post-primary education
State only (so-called Residual Powers)	Any matters not included in the Exclusive Legislative List

- *Minimum Provision of Essential Public Goods and Services* This principle requires that fiscal federalism should assure each citizen that, irrespective of where he or she resides, a minimum level of certain essential public goods and services will be provided.

Table 10.1 Continued

Level of government	Expenditure category
Local government	Participation with the state in economic planning and development Establishment and maintenance of cemeteries, burial grounds and homes for the destitute or infirm Establishment, maintenance and regulation of slaughter houses, markets, motor parks and public conveniences Construction and maintenance of roads, streets, street lightings, drains and other public highways, parks and gardens Provision and maintenance of public conveniences, sewage and refuse disposal Participation with state in the provision and maintenance of primary, adult and vocational education Participation with state in the development of agriculture and natural resources other than the exploitation of minerals Participation with state in the provision and maintenance of health services

For a comprehensive listing of the functions, see Section 4 and the Second Schedule and Section 7 and the Fourth Schedule of the 1999 Constitution.
Source: Federal Republic of Nigeria (1999).

- *The Fiscal Equalization Principle* The existence of sharp regional differences in resource endowment and concomitant differences in fiscal capacity and state and local governments would indicate that some degree of fiscal equalization among the various levels and units of governments is required in order to ensure minimum level of public goods and services available to citizens irrespective of where they reside.
- *The Efficiency Principle* This principle has two dimensions in a two-step sequence. At the first level, it requires that collectively the set criteria directing fiscal federalism should ensure efficiency criterion in the Pareto sense. The efficiency criterion in practice is implemented partially and loosely through the criterion of absorptive capacity, which is not adequate. At the second level, it requires that the collective principles of intergovernment fiscal relations should ensure that each level of government has maximized its internal revenue earnings at minimum tax efforts with optimal distortion.
- *The Principle of Derivation* It requires that the component units of a federation be able to control some of their preferences in their own way and with their own resources.
- *The Principle of Locational Neutrality* Inter-regional fiscal differences tend to influence locational choices of both individuals and firms. Given the natural differences in resource endowments, tax capacity and effort, some degree of locational interference appears to be an inevitable cost of fiscal federalism. The focus of policy, therefore, is to minimize the distortions arising from such interference. Consequently, it is recommended that differential taxes, which cause locational distortions, should be avoided as much as practicable.
- *The Principle of Centralized Redistribution* The redistribution function of fiscal policy through progressive taxation and expenditure programmes should be

centralized at the federal level. This principle is mutually consistent with that of the principle of locational neutrality. In other words, if the redistribution function is decentralized, it could lead to distortions in the location decisions.

10.3.2 The practice of fiscal federalism in Nigeria

The experience of fiscal federalism in Nigeria raises important issues.

Imbalance between assigned responsibilities and tax powers

In a federal structure, each level of government is given adequate resources to enable it carry out its responsibilities. However, in practice, it is often difficult. The result is that one level of government may end up with more financial power than it actually needs while another may have less than it needs. The fiscal arrangement in Nigeria heavily concentrates on fiscal powers in the federal government. Consequently, there is a lack of correspondence between the spending responsibilities and the tax powers/revenue resources assigned to the different levels of government. The federal government becomes the 'surplus unit' while state and local governments are 'deficit units'. The allocation of tax powers is influenced by administrative efficiency and fiscal independence. In Nigeria, the weighting has always been in favour of the efficiency criterion which allows for concentration of taxing powers at the federal government. This has resulted in the over-dependence of state and local governments on federal sources of funding, often confused with dependence on the centre.

The federal government is assigned to administer the most lucrative sources of revenue because it is in a better position to administer those taxes efficiently. Therefore, the federal government is administering those taxes on behalf of all the governments of the federation. Thus, the federal government has no more right over the moneys collected by it than the state and local governments. 'It follows that in sharing the revenues collected by the Federal Government on behalf of itself and the other tiers of government, it is not correct to assert that the lower levels of government depend on the centre. In fact, the Federal Government is not constitutionally assigned to collect such revenues' (Mbanefoh, 1992).

The present fiscal arrangement is characterized by weak fiscal capacity of the state and local governments. An assessment of the current expenditure assignment, tax assignment and revenue-sharing formula points to the need for policy reforms. For example, solid mineral development, ports, defence and security, and aviation are assigned to the federal government while the responsibilities for primary education, town planning, and urban and rural water lie with the state governments. For each tier to execute the responsibilities assigned to it, it accesses funds through assigned tax bases. However, internally generated revenue of state and local governments compared with their shared revenue is very low. For instance, between 1991 and 2002, internally generated revenue of state governments averaged 6.8 per cent. The low internal revenue base resulted from the types of taxes assigned, which have low yields, and high cost of administration. Such taxes include property and personal income taxes.

Table 10.2 Disposition of major tax powers among the three tiers of government

Serial number	Federal government of Nigeria	State government	Local government
1.	Import duties	Personal income tax (administration and collection)	Property taxes and ratings (tenement rate)
2.	Companies income tax	Withholding tax (on individuals)	Market and trading licences and fees
3.	Withholding tax on companies	Capital gains tax (administration and on individuals)	Motor park dues
4.	Petroleum profit tax	Stamp duties on individuals	Radio and television licences (other than radio and television transmitters)
5.	Capital gains tax (legal basis)	Entertainment tax	Marriage, birth and death registration fees
6.	Mining rents and royalties	Road taxes (motor vehicle and drivers' licences)	Bicycles, trunk, canoe and wheelbarrow fees
7.	Stamp duties on corporate bodies	Pools betting and lotteries and gaming taxes	Public convenience, sewage and refuse disposal fees
8.	Value added tax (VAT)	Land registration and survey fees	Signboard and advertisement permit fees
9.	Education tax	Development levy	
10.	Personal income tax (except in respect of members of the Armed Forces of the Federation, members of the Nigerian Police Force, residents of the Federal Capital Territory, Abuja, and staff of the Ministry of Foreign Affairs and non-resident individuals)	Property taxes	

Source: Nigerian Constitutions, fiscal commissions, Revenue Mobilization and Fiscal Commission and Value Added Tax (VAT) Decree of 1993 and subsequent amendment of 1996.

In the Nigerian context, therefore, it would seem that the most viable option for addressing the problem of imbalance between the functions and the tax powers assigned to the different levels of government is adjustments in the revenue-sharing formula.

The Federation Account

Section 162(1) of the 1999 Constitution states that the Federation shall maintain a special account to be called 'The Federation Account into which shall be paid all revenues collected by the Federal Government'. Section 162(2) of the same constitution makes provisions for sharing the Federation Account among the three levels of government.

Before the Resources Control suit, the areas of contention with respect to the Federation Account centred on the non-payment of some revenues collected by the federal government into the Account and some deductions from the Account before sharing among the three tiers of government. The Supreme Court decision declared both actions of the federal government illegal. However, the amount within the Federation Account set aside as 'Special Fund' is still controversial.

The present debate on the Special Fund tends to confuse the need for funding some activities with who foots the bill. For example, no one can fault the case of developing the Federal Capital Territory (FCT). However, there is also the need to develop the 36 state capitals, particularly those of the newer states. Some of these state capitals still have features of rural settings and need to be developed. This would decongest Lagos and Abuja. If we accept the case for the development of state capitals to be funded by state governments, then there is no reason why the federal government cannot fund the development of the FCT out of its resources particularly when we examine the proportion of the Federation Account that goes to the federal government.

It should be noted that, though the Supreme Court's decision of April 2002 voided the distribution of the Federation Account to the special funds, a presidential order simply transferred the Special Funds to the federal government's share thus increasing it from 48.5 per cent to 56 per cent. The states were unsuccessful in challenging the presidential order in the Supreme Court in January, 2003.

Vertical revenue allocation

Another issue in Nigeria's fiscal federalism is how to devise a rational and equitable allocation of the country's resources among the different tiers of government that would minimize inter-government and inter-group tension to promote national unity and development. Can the federal government's retention of the lion's share of the Federal Account be justified on the basis of the relative *weight* of functions assigned to it or is this just a legacy of a past attitude that assigned a major role to the federal government in the field of economic development in the absence of a viable private sector. The federal government may need to limit its role with respect to the regulatory aspects of such functions and in productive activities. For example, with the increase in private courier services and Global

Systems for Mobile Telecommunications operators, how important are the port office and Nigerian Telecommunications Company Limited?

The current policy of privatization suggests the need to shed a lot of expenditure responsibilities on the part of the federal government by way of reduced funding of public monopolies. It may be necessary to re-examine the weight of federal functions, and by implication, the share of the federal government in the Federation Account.

Horizontal revenue allocation

Another reason for intergovernmental transfer is to correct horizontal imbalances. The imbalances may be due to the fact that some jurisdictions have higher tax bases than others or have higher expenditure needs or greater extraordinary expenditure. The aim of the fiscal transfer is to attempt to close the gap between fiscal capacities and fiscal needs of the sub-units. The horizontal revenue allocation in Nigeria is, thus, a kind of unconditional block grant to states and local governments to correct horizontal fiscal imbalances among them. The question to address is whether the existing formulas or principles used for horizontal revenue allocation can solve the problem of horizontal fiscal imbalances. In addition, what is the extent of the horizontal fiscal imbalances among the states and local governments? In order to properly examine this matter, it is necessary to ascertain the fiscal capacities and fiscal needs of the lower levels of government.

However, in examining the principles applied in horizontal revenue sharing, the following variables need to be considered:

- population;
- internal revenue effort;
- land mass;
- derivation.

Each of these variables remains contentious in Nigeria's fiscal federalism (Ekpo and Ubok-Udom, 2003).

Oil-producing areas and resource control

That crude oil production has been the most important economic activity in the Nigerian economy since the early 1970s is not subject to debate. Its impact is not limited to its contributing almost 90 per cent of Nigeria's total foreign exchange earnings; in addition, national budgets are predicated on the expected annual production and price of crude oil. Therefore, crude oil is the primary engine for national economic growth and development. It is, thus, quite reasonable to expect that the areas producing the nation's crude oil would be very highly developed as compensation for what is taken away as well as for the devastation on the land engendered by the exploration process.

The Niger Delta area suffers from near total neglect by both the federal government, which claims ownership of the oil, and the multinational companies, which actually exploit the oil reserves. Theirs is a picture of wanton environmental degradation of all types – land (despoliation of farmlands), water (destruction

Table 10.3 Nigeria: State Governments' Finances, 2001–2005 (as percentage of totals)

Fiscal indicator	2001	2002	2003	2004	2005	Average (2001–2005)
Federation Account revenue as percentage of total revenue	78.29	65.83	70.30	78.41	71.03	72.77
Internally generated revenue (IGR) as percentage of total revenue	10.36	13.38	13.89	12.05	8.65	11.66
Other revenues as percentage of total revenue	11.35	20.79	15.81	9.55	20.32	15.57
Recurrent expenditure as percentage of total expenditure	55.61	59.94	62.73	57.42	39.48	40.76
Capital expenditure as percentage of total expenditure	44.39	40.06	37.27	42.58	39.48	40.76
Overall deficit as percentage of total revenue	4.08	8.17	7.74	1.00	4.15	5.03

Source: Eboh *et al.* (2006).

of fishing areas and sources of drinking water) and air (release of many pollutants causing diseases in humans, animals and plants). The wanton devastation and degradation suffered by the oil-producing areas are indications of extraordinary expenditure needs of those areas which ought to be addressed by intergovernmental transfer. While the intervention of the federal government through the Niger Delta Development Commission (NDDC) is a welcome development, we still believe that enough weight ought to be given to derivation to enable the state and local governments of the oil-producing areas to handle their developmental problems according to their own felt needs and priorities. The minimization of the derivation factor over the years – from the earlier 50 per cent to 1 per cent and now 13 per cent only – particularly as it affects oil exploration and production, seems unjust and unfair.

Channelling allocation to local governments

Section 162(5)–(6) of the 1999 Constitution makes for the channelling of local government share of the Federation Account to local government councils as follows:

- The amount standing to the credit of local government councils in the Federation Account shall be allocated to the states for the benefit of their local government councils on such terms and in such manner as may be prescribed by the National Assembly.
- Each state shall maintain a special account to be called 'State Joint Local Government Account' into which shall be paid all allocations to the local government councils of the state from the Federation Account and from the Government of the State.

Table 10.4 Nigeria: Local governments' finances, 2001–2005 (as percentage of totals)

Fiscal indicator	**2001**	**2002**	**2003**	**2004**	**2005**	**Average (2001–2005)**
Federation Account as percentage of gross revenue	86.64	85.75	89.43	90.04	91.10	88.59
IGR as percentage of gross revenue	3.51	6.05	5.45	4.78	4.00	4.76
Other revenues as percentage of gross revenue	9.85	8.19	5.12	5.18	4.91	6.65
Recurrent expenditure share of total expenditure	71.61	73.43	58.50	64.13	66.31	66.79
Capital expenditure share of total expenditure	28.39	26.57	41.50	35.87	33.69	33.21
Overall deficit share of gross revenue	0.09	1.35	2.27	1.55	0.45	1.14

Source: see Table 10.3.

On payment into the State Joint Local Government Account from the Government of the State, Section 162(7) of the constitution provides that each state shall pay to the local government councils in its area of jurisdiction such proportion of its total revenue on such terms and in such manner as may be prescribed by the National Assembly. A number of issues still remain unresolved in respect of channelling to local government councils amounts standing to their credit from the Federation Account and from the government of the state. The local government councils complain that not all the amounts due to them from the Federation Account are paid into the State Joint Local Government Account. They complain that state governments find all sorts of reasons to make deductions at source before payment of Federation Account proceeds into the Joint Account; and that hardly any state government has paid the stipulated percentage of its internally generated revenue into the Joint Account, contrary to Section 162(7) of the Constitution.

It is evident from the above analysis that it is important to fine-tune the revenue-sharing formula as well as re-examine the fiscal performances of sub-national governments in Nigeria. From Table 10.3 above, between 2001 and 2005, state governments depended on the federal government for about 73 per cent of their revenues on average while local governments relied on the federal government for about 89 per cent of their revenues. The data clearly indicate heavy dependence on the centre by both state and local governments for revenues needed to run their economies.

Internally generated revenue (IGR) averaged 11.6 per cent for state governments and 4.8 per cent for local governments during the period 2000–2005. The low level of internal revenue generation is not surprising given the dependence on the centre. If the lower levels of government were to reduce dependence on the centre then efforts would be made to boost internal revenue. As was argued above, the weight placed on efforts to generate revenue internally remains controversial.

It is also interesting to note, particularly at the local government level, that the bulk of expenditure is on recurrent matters, showing the nature and extent of the fiscal burden evidenced by the size of government. Recurrent expenditure share in total expenditure averaged about 67 per cent during the period 2001–2005 (see Table 10.4 above). For the state governments note that, from 2001 to 2005, average share of social services in recurrent and capital expenditures of the 36 states (pooled) totalled about 42 per cent and 35 per cent respectively (Eboh *et al.*, 2006). Economic services received the highest simple average yearly share of capital spending by all the states.

Macroeconomic management

The Nigerian economy has experienced persistent budget deficits over the years; budget deficits at the lower levels of government also create problems for the wider economy. Fiscal coordination at all levels appears difficult and remains an issue in Nigeria fiscal federalism. In order to improve the management of the economy at all levels of government, a Fiscal Responsibility Bill (FRB) is before the House of Assembly. The Bill aims at committing all tiers of government to effective, disciplined and coordinated budgetary planning, implementation and reporting.

The major features of the Act include, among others, institutionalizing a stabilization strategy of saving windfall oil revenues to smoothen consumption during periods of decline in oil revenues, as well as purposeful investment of the windfall; reduction in fiscal deficits by providing guidelines against over-borrowing and incurring unjustified debts; providing a standard format for reporting and evaluation of budgetary goals and performance; providing guidelines to stem the culture of indiscipline, waste and corruption in Nigeria public finance in order to improve transparency and accountability; and establishing high standards of financial disclosure and public access to information on government finances. The Fiscal Responsibility Bill has gone through the various stages in the Houses of Parliament and will soon become law.

Fiscal federalism, democracy and good governance

Another important matter is the dynamics of fiscal federalism within Nigeria's new democracy and the need for good governance. It follows that proper devolution of powers has inherent democratic values. At all levels of government, transparency, accountability and probity are necessary ingredients for sustaining democracy. It is, thus, instructive how the recent fight against corruption in all its ramifications (abuse of office, money laundering) has been generally received by the populace. For example, corruption at the local government levels denies the people the needed resources for economic development.

10.4 Challenges facing Nigerian fiscal federalism

The challenges confronting Nigeria's fiscal federalism include the following:

- The lopsidedness of Nigeria's fiscal system since independence has continued to undermine the efficacy of fiscal and monetary policies. Hence, the challenge is how to make the fiscal system conform to international best practices to enable it to contribute to growth and development. There is need for a critical review of the divisions of functions among the various tiers of government as well as the revenue-sharing arrangements in order to substantially improve the delivery of public goods and services. This lopsidedness, besides increasing the desperation of the different levels of government for more funds, has also resulted in non-performance and high level of corruption and bloated government apparatus in each of the levels of government leading to waste and unnecessary expenditure. The overall impact is that fiscal federalism in Nigeria has not been able to contribute optimally to social and economic development despite the considerable increase in the number of administrative units. Real economic growth and development in Nigeria has been dwindling since the suspension of regionalism in 1966 and the levels of per capita income have continued to decline, indicating that the creation of more states and local governments has not translated into substantial improvement in the delivery of public goods and services or the promotion of real economic growth (Soyode, 2004).

- Given the dependence of all tiers of government on centrally collected revenue, especially from oil and gas production, the competing demand by each tier for a bigger share of revenue remains a major challenge. Historically, the federal government under successive military regimes has had the lion's share of federally collected revenue. However, with the return of civil democratic rule in 1999, there has been strong agitation by the states, particularly those in the resources-rich Niger Delta region, for a greater share of national revenue. A case in point is the resource control struggle by states in the Niger Delta region. The 1999 Constitution provides for a periodic review of the sharing rules to reflect changing economic and social realities. However, because there has been no such review since the operation of the 1999 Constitution, agitations for a greater share of the so-called 'national cake' have continued unabated. Therefore, while the constitutional provision is for derivation to be given a weight of not less than 13 per cent in the sharing formula, advocates of 'resource control' in the Niger Delta have continued to insist on a higher percentage, say between 25 and 50 per cent.
- Another challenge, perhaps, is the controversy surrounding the way and manner in which the federal government operates the Federation Account. The issue of illegal and unconstitutional deductions from this account has been settled by the Supreme Court in its ruling of April 2002. However, the federal government continues to operate this account with total disregard for the Constitution and the Supreme Court ruling. For example, the federal government continues to divert revenues meant for the Federation Account into so-called dedicated accounts such as the Nigerian National Petroleum Corporation (NNPC) expenditure account and the excess crude oil revenue account.
- There is the challenge of the custodian of the Federation Account. The federal government has conducted itself as the custodian and owner of the Federation Account. This claim was, however, not sustained in the judgment of the Supreme Court in the case of *Lagos State* vs. *the Federal Government* when the court ruled that the federal government or President has not been conferred the powers of custodian and trustee to this account and, hence, cannot proceed to operate it in any manner it deems fit.
- The issue of distributive justice in the provision of public goods and services remains a serious challenge. That is to say, the adjustment of income and wealth to ensure conformity with what the society considers a just and fair distribution. As expected, distribution issues are frequently the major controversy in the determination of public policy. They play a key role in determining tax and transfer policies. Musgrave and Musgrave (1984) suggest that answers to questions of distributive justice involve consideration of social philosophy and value judgment. Thus, distribution is both a market problem and a social policy problem.

- Lack of coordination between fiscal and monetary policies remains a threat to macroeconomic stability. The economy is still characterized by excessive government spending which has continued to exacerbate the liquidity surfeit in the system. More importantly, unguided expenditure by the state and local government despite the activities of the Economic and Financial Crimes Commission (EFCC) has heightened the level of corrupt practices at these levels. The due process principle appears not to have been imbibed by other levels of government. Therefore, the issue of domesticating the due process principle by states and local governments is essential for controlling their fiscal operations.
- Another challenge is the passage of the Fiscal Responsibility Bill by the National Assembly. Its passage will strengthen the effective adoption of the fiscal rule. Fiscal rule is needed for an oil-dependent economy such as Nigeria to insulate the fiscal policy from oil price and revenue volatility. The passage of the Bill, which represents a bold attempt to legalize fiscal coordination, will pose an implementation challenge.

10.5 Conclusion

We have examined issues and challenges confronting Nigeria's fiscal federalism. It is clear that fiscal federalism in Nigeria has generated several contending issues, particularly factors that would ensure an equitable and stable revenue allocation among the three levels of government. These factors include: (i) adopting a uniform derivation principle; (ii) giving adequate weight to the equality of states; (iii) paying attention to the development of the natural resources-producing areas; and (iv) the sharing of revenue based on the responsibilities of each tier of government.

Any meaningful reform that will optimize the principles and practice of fiscal federalism in Nigeria ought to address the following:

- The adoption of fiscal rules must be accompanied by setting up an independent intergovernmental committee to promote a useful framework for fiscal discipline and fiscal policy coordination. Transparency of the budgetary processes and institutions, accountability to the electorate and general availability of comparative data on fiscal positions at all levels of government will further strengthen fiscal discipline.
- It may be necessary to decentralize tax administration in the country. The decentralization should be done to enhance the fiscal capacity of the federating units to enable them to carry out their constitutional responsibilities. Tax decentralization will restore private sector confidence in lending to local governments, thus sharing the risks and rewards of such lending.
- A general review or an amendment of the 1999 constitution is imminent. The review should examine the issue of the devolution of more power by the central government to the lower levels of government. The role and functions

of each level should be clearly expressed and more tax responsibility should be assigned to states and local governments.

- The agitations for increased derivation by the Niger Delta region should be addressed. There is need for deliberate government intervention (more than the present NDDC) in the region to reverse its continued underdevelopment. The development of the region will be in the overall interest of the polity.

The issues and challenges discussed in this chapter represent a template for reforms in Nigeria's fiscal federalism. The attempt to practise true federalism will sustain the country's democracy and the associated economic reform agenda.

Notes

1 Akpan H. Ekpo is a Professor of Economics and former Vice-Chancellor, Federal University of Uyo. He is currently the Pioneer Vice-Chancellor, Akwa Ibom State University of Technology, Uyo, Nigeria.

2 Abwaku Englama is with the Research Department, Central Bank of Nigeria, Abuja.

We thank the participants of the workshop on Economic Policy Options for a Prosperous Nigeria, Abuja, 23–24 October 2006, for their useful comments on an earlier draft of this chapter. The usual disclaimer applies.

Bibliography

Adedeji, A., 1969, *Nigerian Federal Finance*, London: Hutchinson Educational.

Alade, S.O., J.O. Ebajemita, S.C. Rapu and Moses Tule, 2003, 'Fiscal Federalism and Macroeconomic Governance', in *Contemporary Economic Issues in Nigeria*, Abuja: Central Bank of Nigeria.

Agiobenebo, T.T., 2003, 'Issues in Fiscal Management: Implications for Monetary Policy in Nigeria', paper presented at the Third Annual Central Bank of Nigeria Conference, Abuja, November.

Bahl, R.S., 1999, *Fiscal Decentralization as Developmental Policy*, Washington, DC: Public Budgeting and Finance.

Central Bank of Nigeria, 2005, *Annual Reports and Statement of Accounts*, Abuja: Central Bank of Nigeria.

Eboh, E., U.S. Amakoro and M. Uduh, 2006, *Budget and Public Expenditure across Nigerian States*, Enugu: AIAE.

Ekpo, Akpan H., 1994, 'Fiscal Federalism: Nigeria's Post-Independence Experience, 1960–90', *World Development*, 22 (8), 1129–1146.

Ekpo, Akpan H., 1999, 'Fiscal Federalism and Local Government Finances in Nigeria', in *Fiscal Federalism and Nigeria's Economic Development*, Ibadan: Nigerian Economy Society.

Ekpo, Akpan H., 2005, *Fiscal Theory and Policy: Selected Essays*, Lagos: Somaprint.

Ekpo, Akpan H. and Enamidem Ubok-Udom (eds), 2003, *Issues in Fiscal Federalism and Revenue Allocation in Nigeria*, Ibadan: Future Publishing.

Ekpo, Udeme, 2004, *The Niger Delta and Oil Politics*, Lagos: International Energy Communications.

Emenuga, Chidozie, 1993, 'Nigeria: In Search of Acceptance Revenue Allocation Formula', in *The National Question and Economic Development in Nigeria*, Ibadan: Nigerian Economic Society.

Federal Republic of Nigeria, 1977, *Report of the Presidential Commission on Revenue Allocation, Vol. 1*, Main Report, Apapa: Government Press.

Federal Republic of Nigeria, 1999, *Constitution of the Federal Republic of Nigeria 1999*, Apapa, Lagos: Federal Government Press.

James, E.K., 2003, 'Fiscal Decentralization: Theory and Reform', in *Contemporary Economic Issues*, Abuja: Central Bank of Nigeria.

Mbanefoh, G.F., 1986, 'Military Presence and the Future of Nigerian Fiscal Federalism', Faculty Lecture Series 1, Faculty of the Social Sciences, University of Ibadan, Ibadan.

Mbanefoh, G.F., 1992, 'Nigerian Fiscal Federalism: Assignment of Functions and Tax Powers', paper presented at the National Seminar on Revenue Mobilization, organized by the Revenue Mobilization, Allocation and Fiscal Commission, Enugu, 21–23 April.

Mbanefoh, G.F., 1993a, 'Unsettled Issues in Nigeria's Fiscal Federation and the National Question', in *The National Question and Economic Development in Nigeria*, Ibadan: Nigerian Economic Society.

Mbanefoh, G.F., 1993b, 'Federalism and Common Property', *The Guardian*, Saturday 20 February 1993, 13.

Mbanefoh, G.F. and Akpan H. Ekpo, 2005, *Review of Constitutional Provisions on Fiscal Federation in Nigeria Processed*, Abuja: World Bank.

Musgrave, R.A., 1964, *The Theory of Public Finance. A Study in Public Economy*, New York: Mcgraw-Hill Book Company.

Musgrave, R.A. and P.B. Musgrave, 1984, *Public Finance in Theory and Practice*, New York: Mcgraw-Hill Book Company.

Nwabueze, B.O., 2002, *Federalism in Nigeria under the Presidential Constitution*, Lagos: Lagos State Ministry of Justice.

Nyong, M.O., 2003, 'Fiscal Federalism, Revenue Allocation Formula and Economic Development in Nigeria', in Akpan H. Ekpo and Enamidem Ubok-Udom (eds), *Issues in Fiscal Federalism and Revenue Allocation in Nigeria*, Ibadan: Future Publishing.

Oates, Wallace, 1972, *Fiscal Federalism*, New York: Harcourt Brace.

Oates, Wallace E., 1999, 'An Essay on Fiscal Federalism', *Journal of Economic Literature*, 37, 1120–49.

Okigbo, P.N.C., 1965, *Nigerian Public Finance*, London: Longmans.

Osayinwese, Izevbuwa and Sunday Iyare, 1991, 'The Economics of Nigerian Federalism: Selected Issues in Economic Management', *Publius*: *The Journal of Federalism*, 21, Fall, 89–101.

Phillips, Adedotun O., 1991, 'Four Decades of Fiscal Federalism in Nigeria', *Publius*: *The Journal of Federalism*, 21, Fall, 103–111.

Prud'homme, R., 1995, 'On the Dangers of Decentralization', *World Research Observer*, 10 (2), 202–20.

Sanni, G.K., 2003, 'Emerging Issues in Nigeria's Fiscal Federalism', *Central Bank of Nigeria Bullion*, 27 (3), July/September, 10–21.

Shah, A., 1998, 'Fiscal Decentralization: An Elusive Goal? A Case Study of Indonesia and Pakistan Experience', paper presented at the International Conference on Fiscal Decentralization on Developing Countries, Washington, DC.

Soyode, A., 2004, Fiscal Federalism in an Emerging Democracy: Nigeria as a Case Study, Ibadan: Nigeria Economic Society.

Tanzi, V., 1995, 'Fiscal Federalism and Decentralization: A Review of Some Efficiency and Macro-economic Aspects', paper presented at the Annual World Bank Conference on Development Economics, World Bank, Washington, DC.

Tukur, H.A., 2005, *Revenue Mobilization and Allocation in Nigeria: Performance and Prospects*, Abuja: NRMAC.

Section III

Firms and Farms: The Policy Climate for Private Activity

11

Towards a More Competitive Manufacturing Sector[1]

Adeel Malik and Francis Teal

11.1 Introduction

If oil lies at the core of Nigeria's economic and political problems, a vibrant manufacturing sector is part of the solution. In analysing Nigeria's economic challenges, the buck often stops at the manufacturing sector, since its role remains central to any attempt at reducing oil dependence and promoting economic diversification. Previous chapters have posed a broad range of questions: How to avoid the adverse effects of oil dependence on institutions? How to cope with the extreme volatility induced by fluctuations in the terms of trade? How to create a competitive tradable sector? How to generate pro-poor growth? It is these questions that inform the focus on the manufacturing sector and underscore the need for reform. Reviving manufacturing activity in Nigeria is the *sine qua non* of any serious policy effort for economic reform.

Nigeria's manufacturing sector is weak, uncompetitive and suffers from low capacity utilization. Its contribution to the national economy is both low and declining. The share of manufacturing in GDP has nearly halved, from 8.4 per cent in 1980 to 4.6 per cent in 2005. The aim of this chapter is to underline the key challenges facing Nigeria's manufacturing sector. We approach these issues by drawing on micro-data from Nigerian firms. Since the private sector is the principal stakeholder of any reform effort, we analyse these challenges through their prism, using a wealth of information that is now available from a decade of firm level surveys and interviews in Nigeria.

These firm-level surveys – covering broad sectors, geographical regions and firms of various sizes – have generated a wealth of information on Nigeria's manufacturing sector. Some of the more notable attempts in this regard include surveys conducted by the World Bank: the Regional Programme on Enterprise and Development (RPED) survey, the Investment Climate Survey (ICS) and the World Business Environment Survey (WBES). In a collaborative effort, UNIDO, DfID and the Centre for the Study of African Economies (CSAE) have carried out two waves of Nigerian Manufacturing Enterprise Survey (NMES) in 2001 and 2005. Since the latter survey provides the most up-to-date information on firm perceptions, this chapter will rely quite heavily on its findings; see CSAE (2005).[2]

Before proceeding further, a few clarifications are in order. First, the findings based on firm perceptions are subject to the usual caveat that different respondents may not use the same benchmark in giving their responses (Lall, 2001). Second, Nigeria has recently undertaken a series of economic reforms in the financial sector. Recent firm surveys were carried out either before or during these reforms. This chapter will, therefore, not have much to say about the impact of these reforms. Third, one of the limitations of existing surveys is insufficient coverage of the export-oriented firms, which is partly a manifestation of the conspicuous absence of Nigeria from the global export market. Our analysis in this regard will inevitably be more general.

Before presenting the detailed findings of firm surveys, it is instructive to identify some common threads uniting various sections in this chapter. We can delineate at least four broad patterns. First, regardless of the types of performance indicators, Nigeria suffers from an extremely poor investment climate. Second, the investment climate in Nigeria is worse than even some of its African counterparts, not to mention the competitors from Asia and Latin America. Third, it is rare to find signs of improvement. Temporal patterns – in indicators of both investment climate and firm performance – reveal more persistence than change. Fourth, the evidence points towards the presence of asymmetric effects, with firm performance varying markedly across firms of various sizes. Importantly, size differences appear more critical than differences across sectors or geographical regions.

This chapter is divided into four interconnected sections. Section 11.2 will describe firm perceptions regarding their business environment. Section 11.3 provides concrete evidence on various dimensions of firm performance, such as firm profitability, labour productivity, investment patterns, recent trends in output and propensity to export. Section 11.4 considers issues of earnings, skills and education in Nigerian manufacturing, especially in relation to their potential for poverty reduction. The final section will offer concluding remarks and suggest policy implications.

11.2 A poor investment climate

There is a wide consensus that a vibrant private sector cannot exist without a sound investment climate. Investment activity does not take place in a vacuum – it requires effective public inputs such as well functioning roads, reliable electricity and speedy ports. A prosperous private sector is often built on the back of well defined property rights, a well developed financial sector and a stable and sound policy environment. These attributes of the investment climate are important because they create the enabling environment for investment and determine the 'opportunities and incentives for firms to invest productively, create jobs and expand'. In their absence, the returns to investment are low, which lowers investment levels and prevents firms from exploiting growth opportunities.

Micro-data from firm surveys furnish rich evidence on various dimensions of the prevailing business environment. The overall evidence paints a bleak picture. The vast majority of Nigerian manufacturers face an adverse investment climate, characterized by poor provision of public services, an inaccessible and costly financial system and high levels of policy uncertainty. This adverse climate compounds the cost of doing business, prevents firms from growing and making new investments, and damages their competitive edge in the face of rising competition from global trade.

What is going wrong with the investment climate in Nigeria? Firm surveys begin by seeking firms' opinions about major constraints to their performance. Firm respondents are generally asked to indicate their three biggest problems from a large menu of options, which include different factors affecting their investment climate. Findings from various surveys point to the perceived importance of at least four factors in varying degrees of importance: physical infrastructure, access to credit, uncertainty of government policies, and demand conditions.

These concerns recur with surprising consistency across various firm surveys. Respondents in the RPED survey, for instance, ranked lack of infrastructure, access to finance, and uncertainty due to fluctuations in government policies as their three biggest concerns. A more recent survey by UNIDO flagged infrastructural constraints, access to credit and the broader macroeconomic conditions affecting the demand for goods produced by the manufacturing sector as the three principal constraints affecting their performance (CSAE, 2005).

Figure 11.1 shows the nine most frequently cited problems, which were identified by respondents as one of their three principal constraints in 2004.[3] Physical infrastructure tops the list of concerns: about 55 per cent of the firms regarded ineffective provision of physical infrastructure as one of their three biggest problems. This is consistent with findings from a firm survey in Lagos that regarded the ineffective provision of electric supply as the most serious problem faced by Nigerian firms (World Bank, 2006). A second most important constraint perceived by firms in the sample was inadequate access to credit: 47 per cent of the firms placed access to credit among their top three problems. The third most frequently cited concern of the firms was the problem of insufficient demand (31 per cent).

Clearly, these concerns appear to be more pronounced for small and medium-sized firms. For instance, access to credit is more often cited as the core problem by micro and small firms than by medium and large firms. One third of the micro firms, and 18 per cent of the small firms, rate lack of access to credit as their main problem, while only 11 per cent of firms in the two largest categories rate credit access as their biggest problem.

Having introduced these leading constraints, it is useful to dig a bit deeper into the problems of physical and financial infrastructure which have such a profound impact on Nigerian manufacturing.

11.2.1 Ineffective provision of physical infrastructure

Ineffective provision of infrastructure is a recurring concern of the Nigerian manufacturers. In the World Bank's investment climate survey infrastructure problems were rated as nearly two-and-a-half times worse than the next biggest problem, 'access to finance' (World Bank, 2002).

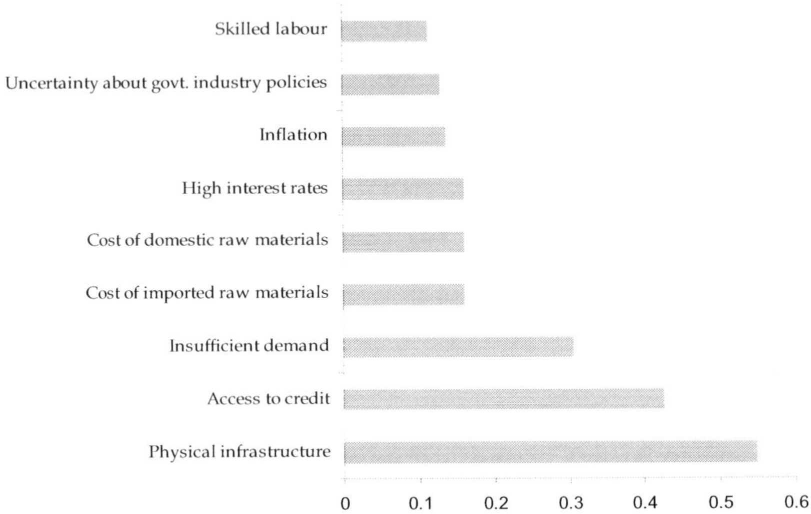

Figure 11.1 Perceived main problems.
The chart shows the percentage of firms considering a particular category as one of its three principal constraints [$n=124$].

By far, the most pressing infrastructure constraint relates to the provision of electricity. Evidence from the RPED survey shows that about 94 per cent of the firms believed that the biggest infrastructure problem relates to electricity (World Bank, 2002). Publicly provided electricity is often unreliable, irregular and insufficient to meet the growing needs of manufacturers. The unpredictability of power failures makes matters worse and precludes an efficient reorganization of manufacturing activities. A recent survey of Lagos firms discovered that only 2 per cent of large manufacturing firms obtained a prior notice of power failures (World Bank, 2006). Power outages are a common occurrence and are often blamed for damage to machinery and equipment. According to the RPED survey, such damage reportedly accounts for 3.3 per cent of the total value of equipment and machinery.

Few public services are viewed with such disdain as the provision of electricity. Firms participating in the UNIDO survey generally had mains electricity for less than three days per week. A majority of firms interviewed in recent surveys expressed a growing dissatisfaction with the services provided by the National Electric Power Authority (NEPA). Behind the poor service provided by NEPA lie a multitude of problems, which include among others inaccurate billing, a high degree of default, widespread corruption and mismanagement, and price distortion due to government subsidies. These inefficiencies are best manifested in the excessively high cost of electricity generation: for NEPA each KwH of electricity costs nearly twice as much as the global average (World Bank, 2002: 57).

When electric supply is unreliable and unaffordable, manufacturers are forced to depend on more costly alternatives, such as the private provision of electricity. A common practice among manufacturers is to rely on personal generators, voltage stabilizers and motors to avoid production stoppages. As the RPED survey shows, most firms are privately providing electricity 67 per cent of the time on average. As Table 11.1 indicates, reliance on privately provided electricity is considerably high for most firms regardless of location and size. However, firms in the East and in the South depend more on private provision compared to those in the North, although the difference is far from significant.

Privately generated electricity can be a poor substitute for publicly provided power supply. First, self-supply of electricity can be considerably more expensive – about three times more expensive than NEPA. Second, reliance on private generators imposes additional costs through capital and maintenance expenses. A World Bank survey in 2002 revealed that generators and accessories accounted for about 22 per cent of the total value of equipment and machinery (World Bank, 2002). This has non-trivial implications for firm performance. To start with, as evidence from a 2004 survey suggests, real electricity costs have escalated substantially since 2001 (CSAE, 2005). It is safe to assume that a large part of this rising cost is attributable to reliance on private generators that run on expensive fuel.

How does this all add up for private firms, especially for small firms that are relatively underprivileged? Electricity problems can lead to significant output losses which, as a recent survey assessment notes, can be as high as 30 per cent (World Bank, 2002). Small firms lost 24 per cent of their output to power outages, medium firms lost 14 per cent and large firms 17 per cent (World Bank, 2005: 132). Defective power supply can also affect the mix of products that firms produce. As the World Bank ICS observes, firms may switch to products that require a less intensive use of electricity.

Firm-level surveys have consistently shown that unreliable power supply is a more pressing concern for smaller enterprises. The micro and small firms have mains electricity an average of 2.58 days per week compared to the 3.39 days per week of mains electricity for an average large/macro firm. Small and medium enterprises are particularly badly affected by power breakdowns as well. A report

Table 11.1 Reliance on privately provided electricity

	Location			
	East	**North**	**South**	**All**
20–49	68.9	49.0	68.9	65.5
50–99	77.8	54.3	71.2	67.2
100–199	67.6	66.7	71.2	69.5
200–499	74.5	58.6	68.6	67.3
500–999	77.5	38.3	69.3	64.2
1000 and over	53.3	53.2	72.5	62.9
All	70.7	55.9	70.0	66.8

Percentage of privately provided electricity out of total firm demand.
Source: World Bank (2002).

on a recent survey in Lagos notes: 'while in no firm type do we find less than 60% of firms affected by a power breakdown every day, the figure is 75% for informal sector firms and 80% for SMEs' (World Bank, 2006). This is partly because of the greater dependence of smaller firms on publicly provided electricity: according to independent estimates 16 per cent of small firms relied only on NEPA service. Such dependence was rarely observed for medium and large firms.

While power supply is by far the biggest infrastructure problem, it is by no means the only infrastructure constraint faced by Nigerian manufacturers. Other elements of the enabling infrastructure – such as roads, water and telephone connections – are often missing or non-functional for many firms – see Table 11.2. Limited and unreliable water supply is one such concern. Firms had an adequate water supply for an average of two days per week only. Large firms are particularly badly affected with less than two days of adequate water supply a week. A survey report of Lagos firms corroborates this by noting that 'the issue that generates the largest number of major concerns for large manufacturing firms is actually the reliability of water supplies (62%)' (World Bank, 2006).

Just as in the case of power supply, firms with water shortages are compelled to look for private alternatives. Firms whose production relies quite heavily on water, such as the cosmetics and foam industries, have especially reduced their dependence on publicly provided water supply. However, this generally entails additional costs that could have been easily avoided. Telephone connections work better – on average, 4.66 days per week. Mobile telephones have increased the access and reduced the cost of communication. There is no waiting time for obtaining a connection and the service is more reliable.

Another key aspect of the physical infrastructure relates to the condition of roads. A good road infrastructure is essential for connecting markets, bringing together buyers and sellers. Roads in Nigeria are often run-down and poorly maintained, which forces many manufacturers to connect their factories to the main road themselves. The CSAE–UNIDO surveys have collected some objective information regarding the condition of roads directly outside the enterprise. As Figure 11.2 shows, most of the surveyed firms had a road directly outside the enterprise: only about 2.5 per cent of the firms lacked a road in the immediate

Table 11.2 Supply and reliability of utilities

	All	**Micro/ small**	**Medium**	**Large/ macro**
How many days per week do you have mains electricity?	2.98	2.58	2.98	3.39
How many days per week do the telephones work?	4.66	3.89	5.52	5.01
How many days per week do you have an adequate water supply?	2.00	2.06	1.92	1.97
Total number of firms	121	49	25	47

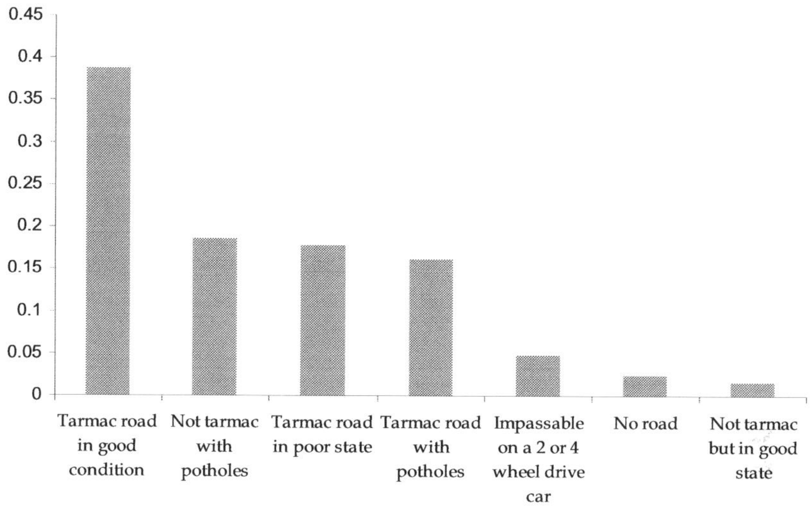

Figure 11.2 The state of roads directly outside the enterprise.
The graph shows proportions of firms in each category. The total number of firms in these calculations is 114.

vicinity. However, despite the existence of a road only 38 per cent of firms in the sample have a tarmac road 'in good condition'. The next largest category was 'not tarmac with potholes and bumps' – this was reported to be the case by 18.5 per cent of the firms. This was followed by tarmac road in poor state of repair (17.7 per cent) or with potholes (16 per cent).

Like other public services, the poor condition of road infrastructure particularly affects the smaller and medium-sized firms. Given that medium-sized firms make a more intensive use of the infrastructure, the absence of good roads is particularly costly for them. Medium and small firms were less likely to have a tarmac road in good condition: only 28 per cent of medium firms and 35 per cent of small firms had a tarmac road in a good condition, as opposed to the corresponding figure of 44 per cent for large firms (CSAE, 2005).

In many ways, problems of physical infrastructure are more acute in Nigeria than in many even of its African neighbours. Publicly provided power supply provides an interesting reference point for comparison. Even though the cost of publicly provided electricity is nearly as much in Ghana as in Nigeria, firms report a superior service in Ghana. As a result, the reliance on privately generated electricity remains significantly lower in Ghana: while Nigerian firms rely on private provision 67 per cent of the time, the corresponding figure in Ghana is only 10 per cent.

11.2.2 Bank finance – costly and inaccessible

Investment is a long-term decision – and therefore hinges on the availability of long-term finance. Nigerian entrepreneurs are rarely short of sound business ideas and profitable investment opportunities. What they often lack is access to long-term funds to tap these productive opportunities. No wonder that access to credit is consistently ranked as a leading investment constraint by Nigerian firms. According to a recent survey, 'access to credit' was regarded as the second most pressing constraint by the firms (CSAE, 2005, see Figure 11.1). According to the RPED survey in Nigeria, inadequate access to finance is ranked as the third most important constraint faced by the manufacturing sector (World Bank, 2002).

Judging by various macro indicators, the financial sector in Nigeria is chronically underdeveloped. This is borne out by a low M2 to GDP ratio (13 per cent). The level of credit extended to the private sector as a ratio of GDP also remains quite low at 9.5 per cent of GDP. Nigerian firms face high interest rates and have to cope with difficult collateral requirements, a near absence of long-term bank finance, and fewer alternatives to bank finance in the form of insurance companies, pension funds, capital markets or equity capital.

The reality for an average Nigerian firm is simple and crushing: bank finance is both costly and limited, hence a privilege of the few. The bulk of lending takes place through short-term loans or overdrafts. Firms that are small, less connected and lacking collateral are effectively abandoned by the banking system. By and large, Nigeria's financial system is poorly prepared to meet the financing needs of the private sector.

The costs of an inadequate financial infrastructure are demonstrably higher for small and medium-sized firms, because these firms are not well connected to lenders and often lack the necessary credit history and collateral required for accessing bank finance. Cross-country evidence from investment surveys suggests that smaller firms are 50 per cent more likely to view access to credit as a severe constraint (World Bank, 2005). Yet it is precisely these smaller and less privileged firms that are especially important for generating investment and job opportunities for the poor.

Nigeria's financial system does badly in reaching out to the smaller firms, especially when compared to other African countries. In a World Bank survey that was carried out for 53 countries, Nigeria fared poorly even with respect to other African countries for which comparable data were available (see Figure 11.3). In the Nigerian sample only 11.1 per cent of small firms had access to bank loans – which was the lowest percentage compared with other African countries in the project.

Liquidity shortages are prevalent – and a fact of life

Liquidity or cash flow problems are rife – scarcely any firm is safe from them. Irrespective of size and influence, most firms interviewed for the NMES survey acknowledged facing liquidity problems. When asked if they witnessed cash flow problems in 2003, a staggering 81 per cent of the interviewed firms acknowledged facing liquidity problems (see Figure 11.4). Clearly, these liquidity problems are even more serious for small and medium-sized firms: 96 per cent of the small firms admitted having cash flow problems whereas the corresponding ratio for large firms was 62 per cent.

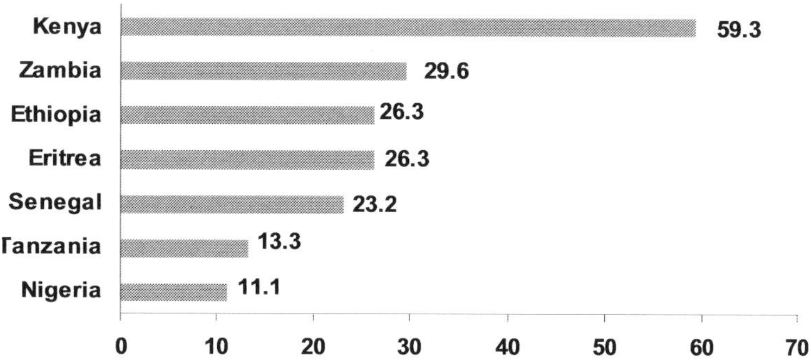

Figure 11.3 Proportion of firms with access to bank loans in 2003.
Source: World Bank (2005).

In the face of cash shortages, banks are seldom lenders of first resort

While cash flow problems are widespread, bank finance is hard to access. The banking system in Nigeria is rarely a lender of first resort. In countries with well developed financial systems, firms mitigate their credit problems by resorting to bank finance, whether through bank loans or overdrafts. This is rare in Nigeria. The NMES survey directly enquired how firms coped with liquidity problems. Figure 11.5 summarizes five major firm responses for overcoming liquidity problems.[4] Only about 35 per cent of the respondents regarded bank borrowing as their principal means of overcoming cash flow problems.

For firms that could afford it, drawing on personal cash reserves was an important alternative. Roughly 28 per cent of firms in the sample relied on personal

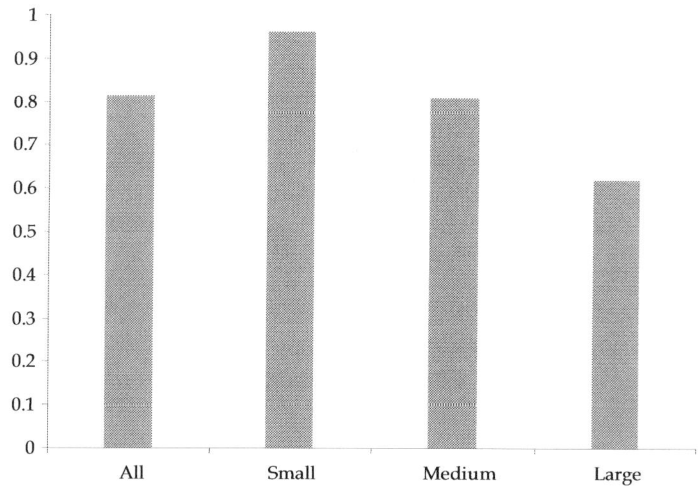

Figure 11.4 Proportion of firms facing liquidity problems in 2003.
The graph shows proportions of firms in each category. The total number of firms in these calculations is 124.

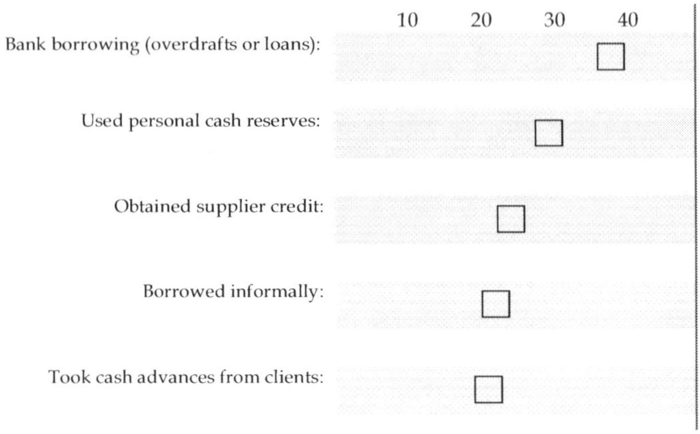

Figure 11.5 How do firms respond to liquidity problems?
Share of firms reporting a response to liquidity problems. The total number of firms in these calculations is 101.

cash reserves to deal with acute cash shortages. Other important responses included obtaining supplier credit (21 per cent), taking cash advances from clients (19 per cent) and borrowing from friends and relatives (20 per cent). In short, the majority of the sampled firms mitigated their liquidity problems by using means other than bank borrowing. A recent study of firms in the Lagos region confirms the limited reliance on bank borrowing and concludes that two thirds of investment finance was provided by retained earnings (World Bank, 2006).

Overall, there is now a powerful body of survey evidence that indicates an extremely limited reliance of firms on bank loans. According to the Investment Climate Survey (ICS) only 23 per cent of sampled firms reported having bank loans (World Bank, 2002). Long-term loans – that is, loans of more than one year in term – remain a rarity in the sample. In the ICS fewer than 16 per cent of firms reported having long-term loans and these were mainly medium-sized and large firms.

Most firms have little faith in the ability of the banking system to alleviate their credit constraints. High cost, limited access and complicated procedures for obtaining credit make bank finance not an option. Evidence from the ICS suggests that more than half the firms declared that they never applied for a loan. Similar trends were observed in the NMES sample: at most 27 per cent of the firms submitted a loan application (see Figure 11.6). Firms that do apply for loans are usually those with more promising chances of acceptance. Of those firms that submitted applications, between 75 and 86 per cent had their applications accepted.

Perhaps owing to their size and influence, large firms enjoy greater access to bank finance. No wonder that loan applications in the NMES sample primarily came from large firms: only about 18 per cent of the submitting firms were characterized as small. Firms that are subsidiaries of large groups and are capable of providing guarantees are also more likely to seek bank finance. In the RPED survey foreign-owned firms were twice as likely to have long-term loans as indigenous firms (World Bank, 2002: 48).

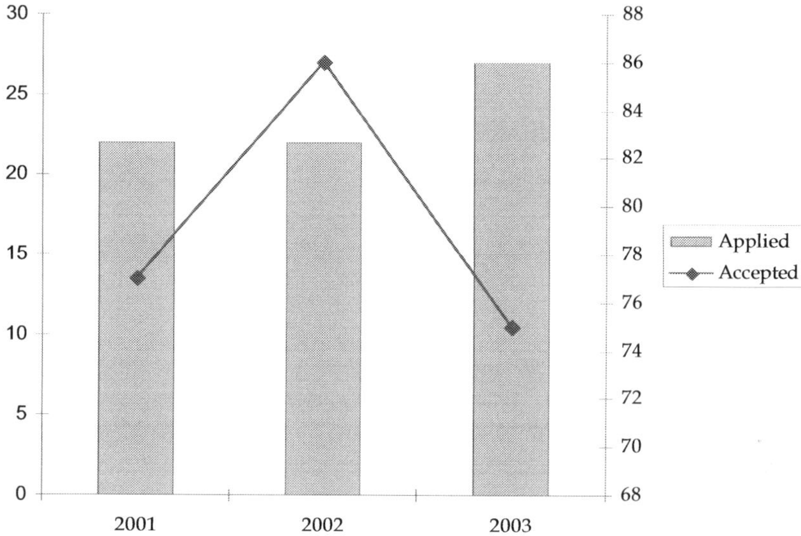

Figure 11.6 Reliance on bank loans remains limited.
Share of firms in each category.

By contrast, reliance on the banking sector is much more limited amongst smaller and informal sector firms. A recent study of Lagos firms has shown that small and medium enterprises receive no more than 4 per cent of their working capital from the banking sector. Only 7.5 per cent of firms in the informal sector received bank loans for starting a business. Very few of these firms actually have a bank account: barely 40 per cent of the informal sector firms have a bank account (World Bank, 2006).

Compared to bank loans, there is an extensive reliance on overdrafts, which are now the dominant mode of financing for private firms. Roughly 96 per cent of bank loans have a maturity of 12 months or less. Whereas a mere 18 per cent of firms obtained bank loans, about 42 per cent of the sampled firms availed themselves of some kind of overdraft facility. Overdrafts are essentially short-term loans that are normally returned or renewed on an annual basis. Like long-term loans, obtaining overdrafts entails substantial collateral requirements, and the annual interest rate charged on these overdrafts can range between 21 and 25 per cent. Although interest rates have come down from a high range of 30–35 per cent less than a decade ago, most firms still consider them high. This is because effective borrowing cost remains high as various hidden costs in the guise of bank charges and special conditions add to the overall cost.

By their very nature, overdraft facilities are merely helpful in mitigating urgent cash shortfalls and in maintaining the necessary cash flow. Small firms with big ideas stand to lose, as few good projects can deliver returns that could justify a one-year loan. Understandably then, large and established firms continue to be the prime beneficiaries of overdraft arrangements. According to the NMES survey 83 per cent of the large firms had taken overdrafts from banks during the period 2001–2003. By contrast, 46 per cent of the medium-sized firms and only 11 per cent of the smaller firms had any overdraft arrangement during the above period.

Why such limited reliance on bank finance?

How to explain such limited reliance on long-term bank finance? It appears that high interest rates, collateral requirements, lack of faith in the banking system and complicated loan processes are partly to blame. This was more systematically probed in the NMES survey that asked firms to identify possible reasons for not making a loan application during the period 2001–2003. Figure 11.7 summarizes these firm responses. High interest rates – cited by 31 per cent of firms – appear as a major deterrent against making loan applications. About 22 per cent of firms did not want to incur debt – and this is not because they do not require a loan but because they lack any hope of obtaining it. In fact, firms unanimously disagreed with the statement that their enterprise does not require a loan.

Significant collateral requirements also prevent firms from applying for loans. Most banks require collateral in the form of plant, property and other fixed company assets, and the average reported level of collateral could be as high as 151 per cent of the value of the loan (World Bank, 2002). Inadequate collateral was cited by 16 per cent of firms as another major reason for the absence of loan applications. This is especially relevant for small and medium enterprises that are more likely to lack collateralizable assets.

'Poor access to long-term funds' is symptomatic of the deeper problems of the financial sector. Nigeria's financial sector is afflicted by a certain degree of *short-termism* – in the sense that banks are generally hesitant to engage in long-term

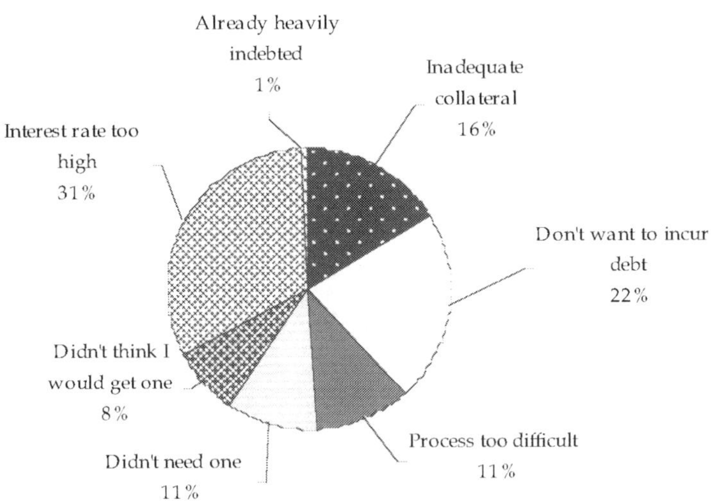

Figure 11.7 Reasons for not applying for a bank loan.
Share of firms reporting a particular reason. The total number of firms in these calculations is 101.

lending. In private interviews firm managers frequently complain about the banks' refusal to advance long-term loans. Many entrepreneurs hold the perception that banks are interested in making a quick return through short-term loans.

However, a closer inspection of the banking sector reveals a more complex story. Most Nigerian banks are undercapitalized and suffer from limited resource flexibility. During the last few decades, the banking system has been considerably stressed by pressures for government borrowing and lending to parastatals. The banking system faces a multitude of challenges, such as high deposit requirements, administrative inefficiency (manifested in high non-interest expense) and the shortage of professional banking skills. Absence of proper contract enforcement, judicial weaknesses and various informational imperfections compromise the financial sector's ability to scrutinize investment opportunities and to distinguish between good and bad borrowers. Instead, banks find it easier to control borrowers through short-term debt or overdrafts renewed on an annual basis. Much of this is changing with ongoing financial reforms, but it will take time before these reforms translate into easier access to credit for private firms.

An uncertain business environment – partly a consequence of macroeconomic and political uncertainty – also influences the lending behaviour of banks. Macroeconomic distortions, regular depreciation episodes and low credibility of public policies may have created an environment where banks are hesitant to commit financial resources for longer time periods. Uncertainty – by affecting the lending behaviour of financial institutions – is thus a double deprivation for countries such as Nigeria that have low levels of financial development.

11.2.3 Poor governance constitutes a non-trivial cost of doing business

As chapters by Collier and Sala-i-Martin and Subramanian have convincingly argued in this volume, Nigeria's oil riches remain an important source of rent-seeking and patronage politics. In this milieu, it is not surprising that Nigeria occupies a prominent place on international corruption rankings.[5] Corruption is deeply embedded in the Nigerian society and has eroded the very legitimacy of state institutions. This misgovernance is most vividly reflected in the failure of public institutions to deliver vital public services, which, as previous sections show, affects private firms in a very direct and tangible way.

Corruption is a daily reality for most firms and affects them in the provision of core public services, the design and enforcement of regulations, the administration and collection of taxes, clearance of imported goods from customs, obtaining duty exemptions and winning government contracts. This could raise the cost of production, create additional barriers to entry for potential investors, encourage tax evasion and hinder the efficient conduct of important business operations.

Absence of law and order

Corruption is by no means the only aspect of misgovernance. Other key elements of an enabling investment climate that are missing include law and order, a reliable judicial system and no administrative barriers to investment. An RPED survey conducted by the World Bank showed that 36.3 per cent of the firms reported crime as a major constraint. A survey of firms in Lagos revealed that one in every four large manufacturing firms in 2003 was affected by crime. Larger and more successful firms were generally found to face higher crime levels (World Bank, 2006).

Nigeria has a deficient legal framework. The judicial process is slow, cumbersome and significantly backlogged with cases. 'On average it takes three years for a claim to be heard at the court' (World Bank, 2002). As a result, businesses have a limited faith in the ability of courts to settle commercial disputes, secure property rights or enforce contracts.

Procedural barriers to investment

The World Bank's *Doing Business Project* furnishes objective information on the procedural barriers to investment. As Table 11.3 shows, the number of days and procedures required to start a business in Nigeria can compare favourably to those in sub-Saharan Africa and East Asia. However, contract enforcement and registration of property are significantly more difficult in Nigeria. Although there are fewer procedures to enforce a contract in Nigeria, it takes significantly longer: it takes 730 days to enforce a contract in Nigeria compared with the regional average of 434 days for sub-Saharan Africa. Similarly, on average it takes more than twice as many days and three times as many procedures to register a property in Nigeria than for those in sub-Saharan Africa.

Unofficial payments to access public services

Governance problems constitute an invisible yet *non-trivial* cost of doing business. For firms that are already encumbered by poor infrastructure, low demand and limited access to capital, corruption adds to the costs of doing business. Firms often need to bribe officials for accessing routine public services – such as getting connected to electricity, clearing goods through customs, obtaining business licenses, submitting tax returns. None of these interactions is costless in terms of

Table 11.3 The procedural barriers to investment

	Starting a business		**Enforcing a contract**		**Registering property**	
	Days	**Procedures**	**Days**	**Procedures**	**Days**	**Procedures**
Nigeria	44	10.0	730	23.0	274	21
Sub-Saharan Africa	63.2	11.2	434.2	35.2	114.2	6.9
East Asia and Pacific	72.9	9.9	373.8	31.0	59.4	5.2

Source: World Bank (2005).

time and money. Producers must factor these additional costs in their outlays and this could have clear implications for their productivity and efficiency.

Firms in Nigeria are routinely required to pay hidden charges for steady supply of services. For instance, secure supply of water and electricity remains a key challenge for Nigerian manufacturers. Firms have often complained in survey interviews about regular power failures and about the need to make hidden payments to NEPA officials to secure electricity connections. More systematic evidence indicates the high prevalence of unofficial payments in accessing various public services. Figure 11.8 illustrates the incidence of additional unofficial payments in five different situations.[6] Of the five situations referred to here, public service connection appears to be the one with the highest incidence of additional payments, 57 per cent, followed by government contracts (54 per cent), customs (51 per cent), licence/permit processing (44 per cent) and tax collection (38 per cent).

When asked to rate the overall quality, integrity and efficiency of public services, firm respondents judged the state of public services quite poorly. The worst average score is given to the electricity service, 3.26, confirming earlier results about the dilapidated state of infrastructure and the growing dissatisfaction on the services offered by NEPA. This was followed by the police at 2.60, water services, 2.58, and roads, 2.26.

Hidden payments for securing business contracts

For many firms aspiring to government contracts, unofficial payments for securing contracts are a routine practice. About 56 per cent of the firms admitted that firms in their industry pay some proportion of the contract value as a bribe,

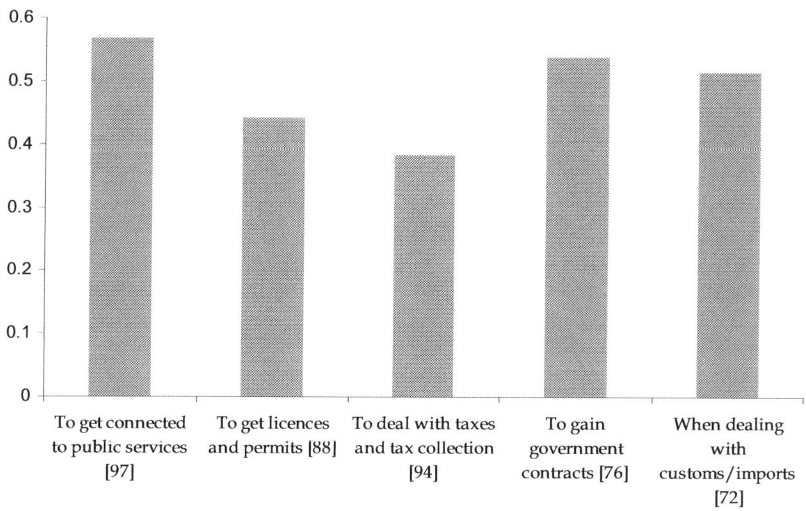

Figure 11.8 Unofficial payments in the provision of public services.
Proportions of firms that 'always', 'usually', or 'frequently' need to make unofficial payments. The question asked of the respondents refers to 'firms like yours'. Number in brackets denotes how many firms responded to the question.

ranging from less than 1 per cent to more than 25 per cent. Twenty-three per cent of the firms believed this unofficial payment to be 10–17 per cent of the original contract value; 15 per cent of the firms placed this in the range of 2–9 per cent of the contract value; and 14 per cent considered this bribe to be more than 18 per cent of the contract value. Presumably, the costs of bureaucratic corruption are potentially more serious for larger firms. In Lagos, large manufacturing firms reported that '81% of licensing officials with whom they deal expect a bribe, but the figure is only 34% for SMEs' (World Bank, 2006).

Delays at ports

Manufacturing firms frequently need to purchase imported machinery, spare parts and raw materials that are crucial to the production process. This requires customs clearance at ports, which many firms complain is excessively delayed to extort hidden payments from importers. As Figure 11.9 shows, customs delays appear to be more pronounced in Nigeria than in many African countries for which data are available. It takes on average 18 days to clear custom goods in Nigeria, compared with 13.5 in Ethiopia, 9.1 in Eritrea and 4.8 in Zambia.

In order to prevent these delays, most importers are now turning towards professional clearing agents that specialize in customs clearance – and this clearly adds to the overall cost of production. More than the financial costs, such delays can waste precious managerial time and interfere with crucial firm planning. Some firm managers reported that 50 per cent of their time was spent with government officials, negotiating contracts, dealing with tax authorities or solving anomalies on import duties.

11.3 Delineating trends in firm performance

Nigerian firms fare badly on various indicators of firm performance calculated from micro-data. Given the poor state of business environment illustrated earlier,

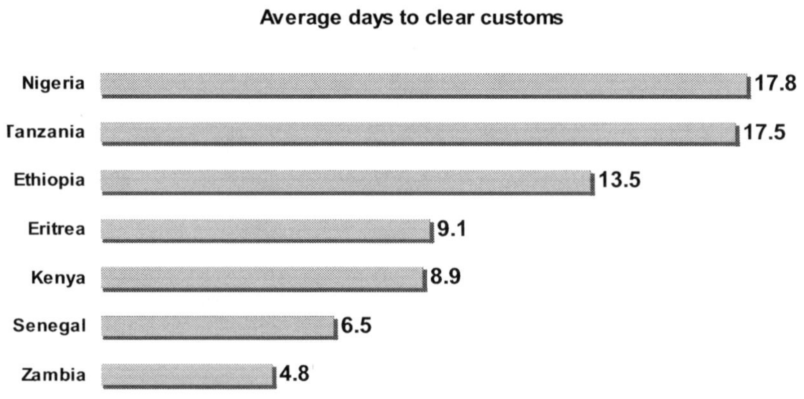

Figure 11.9 Customs delays.
Source: World Bank Investment Climate Surveys (http://www.enterprisesurveys.org/).

it comes as no surprise that Nigerian firms are failing to meet their potential. Existing evidence paints a bleak picture, characterized by output stagnation, absence of any meaningful improvement in productivity, low and sporadic investment, dwindling rates of capacity utilization, and limited participation in export markets. This section will provide a quick review of the salient trends in key performance indicators over the period for which firm data is readily available.[7]

11.3.1 There has been no marked increase in real output during 1998–2003

Firm growth – whether measured by employment or output – has been virtually zero in the NMES sample, and appears not to have varied either by the sector of the firm or by its size. As Figure 11.10 shows, irrespective of firm size there has been no meaningful change in real output over the 1998–2003 period – suggesting that firm growth in the sample has been negligible. It needs to be stressed that this is a result for our sample and that our sample is not representative of all firms in Nigeria's manufacturing sector. It is possible – indeed probable – that large numbers of firms have been both entering and leaving the sector. However, one may draw an important inference from Figure 11.10. Provided the NMES sample is representative of firms of particular sizes, we can argue that whatever firm growth has occurred would have been the result of net new entrants, and not due to expansion within existing firms.

11.3.2 There has been no discernable improvement in the efficiency of firms

There is no noticeable change in labour productivity over the sample period (see Figure 11.11). At a first glance, Figure 11.11 does suggest a slight downward trend of real output per employee for small and medium firms and a similar upward trend for large firms, but this simply reflects changes in the underlying sample.[8]

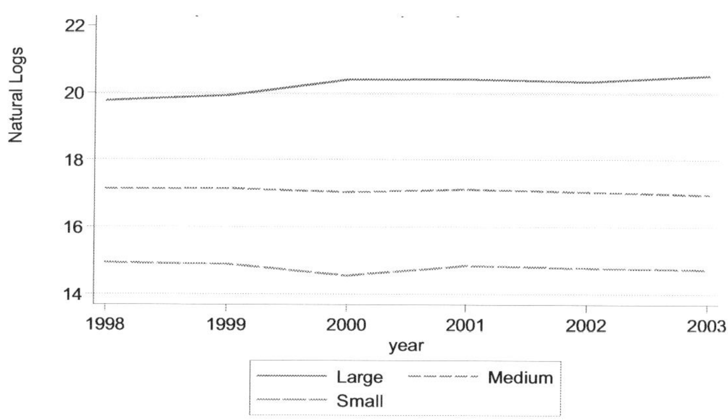

Figure 11.10 Real output by average firm size, 1998–2003.
A small firm is one employing fewer than 20 workers; medium is from 21 to 75; large is more than 75.

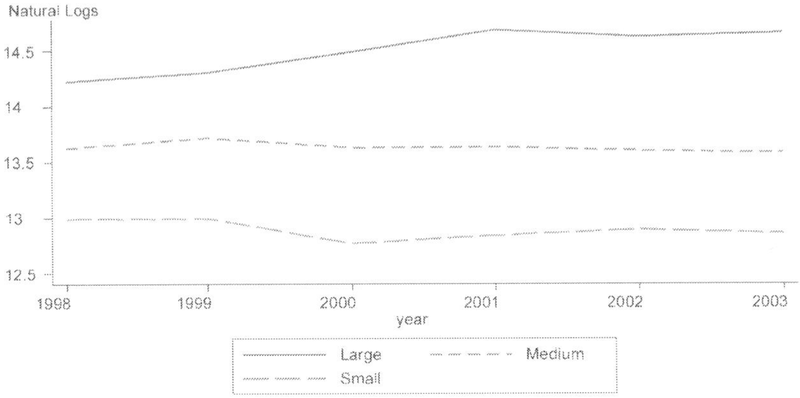

Figure 11.11 Real output per employee, 1998–2003.

How should this stagnation of labour productivity be interpreted? It appears that Nigerian firms did not get better at changing inputs into outputs during the 1998–2003 period – or that there has been no discernible improvement in the efficiency with which firms have operated.

Aggregating across sectors, labour productivity appears to increase monotonically with firm size (see Figure 11.12). The difference between the two largest size groups amounts to roughly 115 per cent. However, the difference between small and medium firms is even more pronounced, with medium-sized firms in this sample producing around 190 per cent more output per worker. The rather remarkable finding from the data is that, while there are small differences in productivity by sector, by far the most important difference is due to differences in firm size.

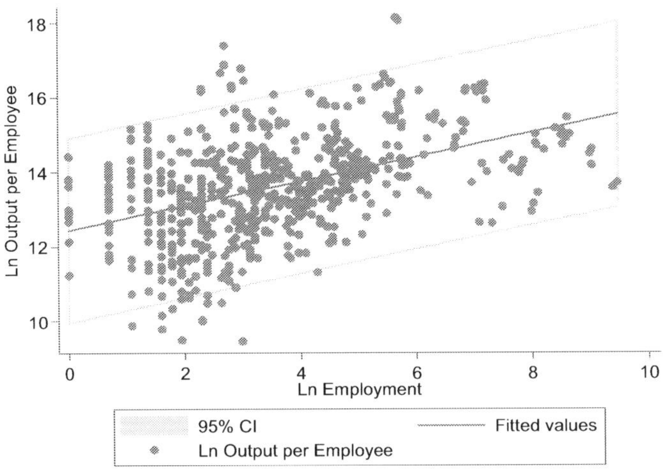

Figure 11.12 Output per employee and capital intensity by firm size.

It appears that much of the differences in labour productivity can be explained by differences in capital intensity, which measures the relative use of capital to other factors, such as labour, in the production process. Both labour productivity and capital intensity increase with firm size.

11.3.3 There is no evidence that larger firms are more efficient

It is important to ask if larger firms are more efficient in the sense that there is evidence in the data for increasing returns to scale. If larger firms are to be more efficient in the sense of benefiting from returns to scale it would be true that for any given percentage increase in inputs there was a larger percentage increase in output. There is very little evidence for any but the most modest returns to scale. In fact most of the evidence points to constant returns to scale. There is thus no evidence that larger firms are more efficient.

11.3.4 Profitability falls by firm size

What are the implications of the findings of the last two sections for the profitability of firms in Nigerian manufacturing? Figure 11.13 plots the log of the profit rate (defined as the ratio of profits to the value of capital) against the log of employment, a possible measure for firm size. The profit rate so defined is close to the return on capital to the firm. As is clear from the figure, the profit rate falls with firm size in the sense that larger firms have a lower profit rate. It does not necessarily imply that large firms are less profitable but that they face a lower cost of capital and thus require a lower return on capital to stay in business. In fact, the differing profitability of firms over the size range reflects differences in the use of capital per employee – clearly, larger firms use far more capital per employee than smaller firms.

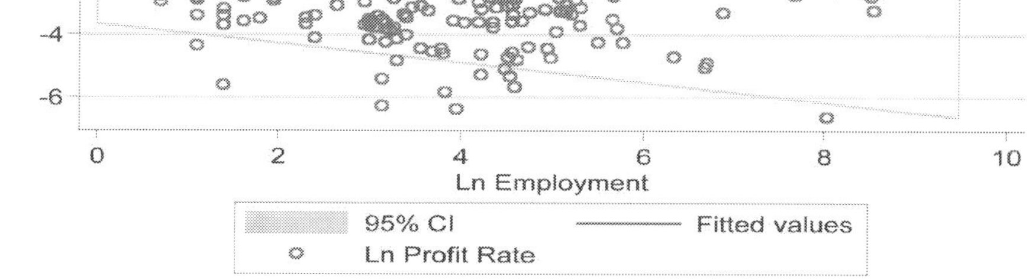

Figure 11.13 Firm profitability.
The profit rate is defined as profits (value added less wages) over the value of the capital stock.

11.3.5 More than half the firms report zero investment in a given year and the propensity to invest is markedly lower for smaller firms

Investment activity is rare among Nigerian firms. This is consistent with findings from firm-level surveys across Africa that discovered the high frequency of zero investment by manufacturing firms. One of the difficulties encountered in the analysis of firm-level investment is that investment is not a smooth process; the majority of firms do not invest in any given year. In the NMES sample, only 48 per cent of the firms reported non-zero investments in any given year. The average investment rate in the sample of firms that do invest is about 0.12, which is not atypical when compared with similar numbers from other African countries. This suggests that for more than half of the firms capital stock is actually declining as value lost through depreciation is not being replaced. Like other aspects of firm performance, firm size is a critical determinant of the propensity to invest. Only 28 per cent of small firms invest, compared with 44 per cent of medium firms and 80 per cent of large firms.

11.3.6 There is a discrete nature of investments: larger firms invest more often, but relatively smaller amounts

Although small firms may be less likely to invest, when they do, the amount invested is larger as a proportion of their capital stock than that of either medium or large firms. Once a small firm takes the decision to invest, it invests on average about 55 per cent of the existing capital stock. However, in aggregate the total amount invested by small firms would be less than that for the other size categories owing to their smaller capital stocks. Clearly, there is a discrete nature of investments suggesting that there are significant fixed costs or returns to scale to investment. Larger firms invest relatively smaller (but absolutely bigger) amounts more often, while smaller firms are characterised by periods of zero investment followed by substantial discrete jumps.

11.3.7 There are several possible explanations for low rates of investment

What accounts for relatively low levels of investment in Nigeria? Firm-level evidence for many African countries including Nigeria points to the role of high indirect costs in depressing investment rates. These high indirect costs take the guise of bureaucratic inefficiencies, corruption, infrastructural bottlenecks, especially the ineffective provision of power supply. For instance, analysis based on data for Lagos firms shows that poor infrastructure negatively affects investment (World Bank, 2006). Also older firms are considerably less likely to invest, underlining the need for policies to allow for greater entry and firm mobility.

Besides infrastructure, lack of access to finance and low level of demand are frequently flagged as important explanations for underinvestment. Like other African countries, domestic markets are quite small in Nigeria and the export potential remains largely unexplored. This puts African firms at a significant disadvantage compared to their East Asian counterparts (Eifert *et al.*, 2005). When demand constraints are alleviated – for example through government tenders or other industry-specific conditions – firms are generally more inclined to invest.

But perhaps one of the most pressing constraints on investment is uncertain business environment. Bigsten and Söderbom (2006) argue that uncertainty is a bigger constraint for investment in African countries than other factors such as inadequate access to credit. Investment is a forward-looking variable, requiring a longer planning horizon. It can involve significant fixed costs, which may be sunk and irreversible. Uncertainty – whether economic or political – thus tends to reduce investment. As Gunning and Mengistae (2001) correctly note, 'investments in African manufacturing have been held back by high risk rather than low return on investments'. Nigerian firms face a high level of risk, stemming in part from high levels of political and economic uncertainty. The market for second-hand capital goods is not well developed, with the result that investments in fixed capital often constitute sunk costs and are treated as irreversible.

11.3.8 Rates of capacity utilization are worryingly low

Findings from various surveys point towards limited capacity utilization in Nigerian firms. A survey of Lagos firms shows that 'more than half of large manufacturing firms report using only a single shift, and only a very small number are working flat out, using three shifts' (World Bank, 2006). The average capacity utilization rate was 44 per cent in the NMES sample. Medium-sized firms had a slightly better rate of capacity utilization – about 5 percentage points higher than the larger firms (see Figure A11.1 in the Appendix, www.csae.ox.ac.uk/books). Overall, capacity utilization rates remain low by international standards, suggesting ample excess capacity.

Firms cite electricity problems and lack of demand as major reasons for idle capacity. The large majority of firms – about 69 per cent – regarded ineffective provision of power supply as one of the major reasons for idle capacity; 62 per cent cited lack of demand for their products as a major reason for idle capacity. Other important reasons include lack of capital and raw materials – both domestic and imported (see Figure 11.14).

11.3.9 A tiny percentage of the sampled firms is engaged in exports

The problems of limited productivity growth and low levels of investment and output are ultimately tied to the wider problem of low export volumes. The poor performance of manufacturing firms in Nigeria is best manifested in limited exposure to export markets, denying them the benefits of exporting. The vast majority of Nigerian firms primarily serve the domestic market. Survey evidence suggests that Nigerian firms are highly unlikely to export, with only 10 per cent of firms involved in the export market. A recent survey of Lagos firms tends to confirm this low participation in foreign trade: a mere 18 per cent of the large manufacturing firms and 16 per cent of SMEs were involved in foreign trade activities, exports and imports combined (World Bank, 2006). Here Nigerian firms are particularly disadvantaged compared with their African neighbours. For given characteristics,

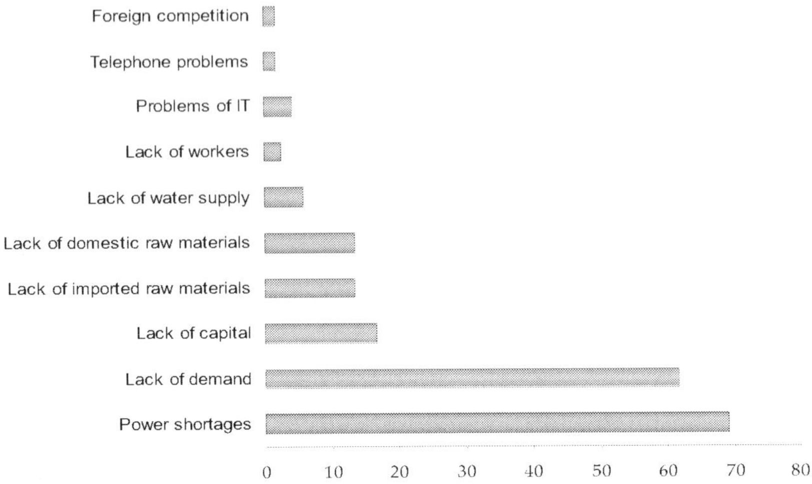

Figure 11.14 Reported reasons for idle capacity (%).
Each category on the *y*-axis represents one of the multiple reasons cited.

Nigerian firms are 15 percentage points less likely to enter the export market than firms in Ghana and Tanzania – see Figure 11.15 (CSAE, 2003).

What accounts for such low propensity to export? First of all, very limited data exists on exporting firms in Nigerian surveys. This precludes any serious analysis of determinants of exporting behaviour. However, to the extent that research on export-oriented firms in Africa is relevant to the Nigerian context, a number of observations could be made.

First, 'past export status' predicts propensity to export – indicating that there may be fixed costs to entering the export market (Bigsten *et al.* 2004). Once firms participate in exporting, they are likely to continue exporting. Second, firms that are relatively more efficient are generally perceived as self-selecting into export markets. This may also suggest that 'firms may have to be more efficient in order to overcome high transaction costs associated with the export market' (Söderbom and Teal 2002). Firms may also become more efficient through exporting. Third, weak financial infrastructure that restricts access to finance can add to the difficulties of firms wishing to enter the export market. In a recent study for Lagos firms, the World Bank (2006) describes access to finance as a 'binding constraint' for the ability to export. It also finds that firms that specialize at the higher end of the value chain are more likely to export.

11.4 Pathway out of poverty: skills and earnings in Nigerian manufacturing

The last section focused on sketching areas where the performance of firms in Nigeria's manufacturing sector is poor. This section focuses on another key policy objective that superior firm performance can help to achieve – the creation of

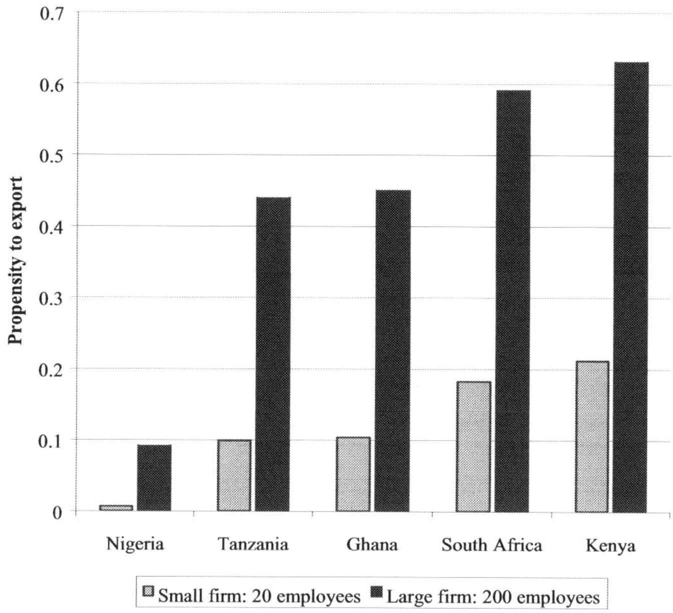

Figure 11.15 Propensity to export: Nigeria compared with Africa.
Source: CSAE (2003).

better-paid jobs. The poor could be lifted out of poverty if they get more and better-paid jobs. Evidence from firm surveys shows that in real terms skilled workers earn almost twice as much as unskilled workers.[9] Given this positive association between skills and earnings, skill acquisition may offer a pathway out of poverty.

However, any fresh thinking on this must confront two key facts. First, job creation in Nigeria during the last decade has primarily taken place in the self-employment sector, especially in urban areas. During the late 1990s total wage employment was no more than 12 per cent of the labour force in household samples (Aromolaran, 2004). The growth in self-employment rather than in wage jobs means that, with the expansion of education, the number of formal sector jobs is failing to keep pace with the growth of school leavers. And this brings us to the second fact. Returns to education – the extent to which earnings increase with the level of education – are greater for higher levels of education (Aromolaran, 2004).

Evidence from firm-level surveys corroborates this. There appears to be a non-linear relation between earnings and education. Real earnings only start to increase at the completion of secondary school. Secondary school graduates earn about 35 per cent more than primary graduates but those with post-secondary education earn almost twice as much as secondary school graduates. This means that there is little or no income gain from education until a certain critical level is reached, which is 10 years of education in the NMES sample. This finding is important for policy as it implies that an expansion of education at the primary and secondary level may not generate increases in income for those who stop education before the end of secondary school.

In this context, it is important to ask: Which firms have the greatest potential for job creation? Where is the labour demand highest for unskilled workers? What is happening to wages of unskilled workers in Nigeria? The availability of matched worker data from Nigerian firm surveys enables a systematic analysis of these issues that are so central to policy-making.

11.4.1 Small firms have a greater potential for job creation

Evidence suggests that, for a given level of investment, the micro and small firms have a greater potential for job creation. Figure 11.16 uses survey results to show how many jobs are created for $100,000, depending on the size of the firm. A micro firm, defined as one with fewer than six employees, creates more than 100 jobs for $100,000 of investment. This compares with about 10 for very large firms, defined as those with more than 200 employees. Thus, jobs in micro firms cost about $1000 in terms of investment while those in very large firms cost 10 times as much at $10,000. If 200 micro firms were founded they would generate the same number of jobs as the present typical very large firm but the amount of capital required for this task would be only $400,000, less than 5 per cent of the capital used in the very large firm.[10] In practice, firms have a limited ability to invest, and capital sums as large as $2000 are very high for most Nigerian entrepreneurs.

11.4.2 ... but small firms pay less than larger firms

Despite having a greater potential for job creation, smaller firms suffer from two important limitations. First, small firms typically have low propensity to invest.

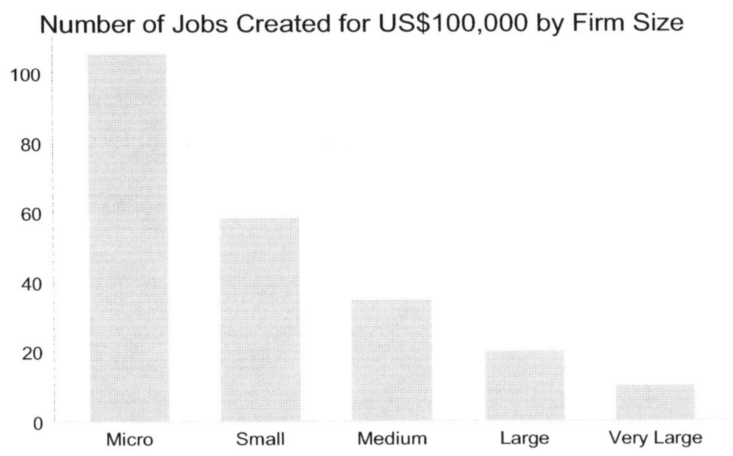

Figure 11.16 Where do jobs get created?
A micro firm is one employing fewer than six workers; small is from 6 to 20; medium is from 21 to 75; large is from 76 to 200; and very large is over 200.

While a lot of jobs are created per unit of investment, the amounts of investment may be very low. This is a mirror image of the point that micro firms use capital very economically – because it is scarce and expensive for them as the last section showed. Second, even if small firms were to invest, they tend to generate relatively low-paid jobs. In particular, unskilled workers tend to earn more in larger firms. Figure 11.17 documents the pattern of earnings which results across firm size after holding the skills and age of the worker constant. The wages for unskilled workers in micro firms were just over $20 per month. This rises to $30 for firms employing 50 workers and continues to rise, although less rapidly for firms with 100 or more workers. It is clear that while micro firms produce a lot of jobs per unit of investment they pay much less than larger firms.

11.5 Some implications for policy reform

An efficient infrastructure connects markets and expands investment opportunities. The absence of a well-functioning infrastructure – electricity, water, roads and telephones – acts as a severe handicap for Nigerian manufacturers. The stark reality for most Nigerian firms is that the most basic public inputs for production are either missing or of such poor quality that firms are forced to rely on costly alternatives. The weight of evidence from firm surveys over the past decade in Nigeria points towards an urgent need for reforming the country's infrastructure – both physical and financial.

Perhaps the single most important aspect of infrastructure that deserves immediate attention from Nigerian policy-makers lies in the domain of electricity provision. Defective power supply is a problem of crisis proportions in Nigeria.

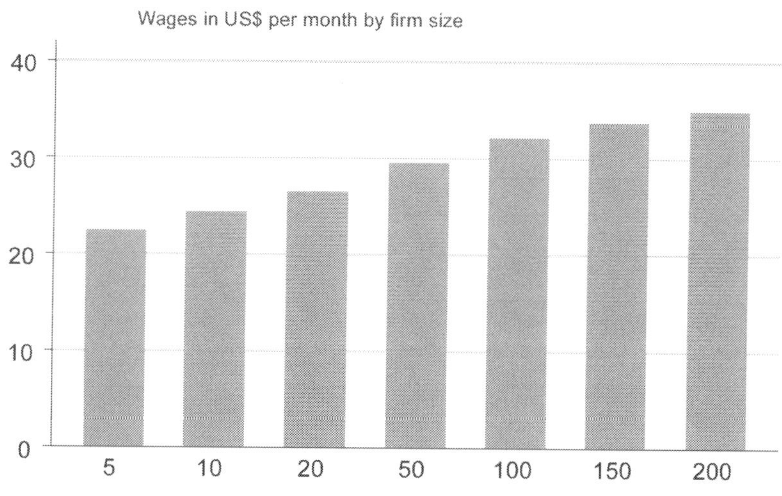

Figure 11.17 Where do better jobs get created?
The wages are calculated for an unskilled male worker over the period from 2000 to 2004, aged 20 with nine years of education and just starting out in the labour force.

This chapter has highlighted the enormous costs of ineffective provision of electricity – and the different ways in which it hampers firm performance: output losses, damage to machinery and equipment, altered mix of products and a significant escalation of indirect costs. The need for reforming NEPA is real and urgent, which is also a subject of Chapter 16 in this book.

Lack of access to finance is another pressing constraint. Nigeria's financial system is notoriously underdeveloped, characterized by poor access to long-term funds, significant collateral requirements and an over-reliance on overdrafts as the primary means of finance. Bank finance is a privilege of the few – to the extent that small and medium firms are virtually crowded out of the financial market. This situation must change to afford private firms greater opportunities for investment and growth. A weak financial sector can be a major hindrance to reviving Nigerian manufacturing, since it lowers competitiveness, impedes the growth of innovative firms, prevents efficient risk-taking by entrepreneurs and deters investment. Nigerian policy-makers are alert to the need for reform in this area. The recently introduced financial sector reforms are a welcome step forward.

In face of this adverse investment climate, it is hardly a surprise that Nigerian firms are failing to deliver on conventional measures of firm performance. Consider any measure of firm performance – whether growth of real output, labour productivity, investment rates, firm profitability or capacity utilization – and the pattern manifested in micro-data is one of stagnation rather than change. Firm growth is virtually zero. Investment levels are low and sporadic and there are no visible signs of improvement in the efficiency with which firms operate.

Such an abysmal record of firm performance should be alarming for policy-makers, since without a vibrant manufacturing sector job creation and poverty reduction will remain distant dreams. Firms must grow – and grow very rapidly – in order to create more jobs for the poor. Nigeria urgently requires a private sector that is both industrially competitive and labour-intensive. So how can more, better paying, jobs best be created? First, it is necessary that firm expansion be linked to employment creation. Second, the increase in labour demand needs to be concentrated among relatively unskilled workers. It is these workers who have low incomes and for whom more employment opportunities are urgently required. Third, more skills are required among the workforce but it has been argued that the value of these skills – both to those acquiring them and the economy – will depend on the ability of firms to grow rapidly.

It is not simply the number of jobs that is of policy concern. It is also the wages these jobs pay. Policy needs to focus on creating high wage jobs. If those making a marginal living in the self-employed sector could be absorbed into a higher paying wage sector this would provide a powerful mechanism by which incomes for the poorest could expand. It is a mechanism that is powerfully driving the growth of the Chinese economy at present and this mechanism is conspicuously absent both in Nigeria and in most African countries. Creating a high wage job creation machine needs to be a central objective of any policy.

What is the key to rapid firm expansion? It is here that we can discern a link between inadequacies of infrastructure and poor firm performance. Some 30 per cent of the firms cited a lack of demand for their products as one of their three principal problems. For firms in the manufacturing sector there are two possible sources of demand – demand driven by the domestic market and demand for exports. As discussed in this chapter, very few firms in Nigeria export their products to foreign markets – hence most are overwhelmingly reliant on the domestic market. So at present the growth of firms is tied to the growth of the economy, which has historically been uncertain, volatile and linked to oil price fluctuations.

It is very unlikely that domestic demand alone will be able to provide the necessary growth for the massive creation of jobs that is required to lift people out of poverty. Nigerian firms must break into global markets to reap the benefits of exporting. There is sufficient evidence now that firms become more efficient by exporting. However, there may be significant fixed costs to entering the export market. Once a firm enters the export market it continues to export. An important policy priority in Nigeria should thus be on reducing barriers to exporting and on creating a policy environment that is conducive to export-oriented industrialization.

Notes

1 This chapter is based on two rounds of the Nigerian Manufacturing Enterprise Survey (NMES) undertaken by UNIDO with the assistance of the Centre for the Study of African Economies (CSAE). The first round was carried out in the summer 2001 and the second in winter 2004. As recall questions were asked it has proved possible to construct a panel dataset covering six years. UNIDO representative in Nigeria, Dr David Tommy, offered excellent organizational and other support for the survey. Dr Thiam Hee Ng at the UNIDO office in Vienna provided the necessary official support and both Danjuma Mahmoud and Obi Okoye provided technical input into the questionnaire and survey implementation. Neil Rankin and Simon Baptist provided a very substantial input into creating the dataset which forms the basis of the analysis presented in this chapter.

2 Recently, the World Bank has sponsored a survey of the Lagos business sector. We will draw on some of their findings as well. For details, see World Bank (2006).

3 Multiple responses were permitted (percentages do not add up to 100).

4 Since each respondent was allowed to report multiple answers, figures in the chart do not add up to 100.

5 See, for example the international corruption rankings produced by Transparency International (TI) (http://www.transparency.org/policy_research/surveys_indices/global/cpi).

6 The data used for these calculations were based on a question asking respondents to indicate how often 'firms like yours' need to make extra, unofficial payments in various situations.

7 The findings of this section are mainly based on the two waves of NMES surveys. We have classified firms by their average size over the whole period into three classes: small firms, which are firms employing fewer than 20 workers; medium firms, which employ from 21 to 75 workers; and large ones, which are those employing more than 75 workers. This procedure can mask firm growth if, as measured by employment, firm growth had varied across firms of different sizes. We have investigated whether this is the case and can find no evidence that either size or any of the time-invariant characteristics of the firms influences long-run growth rates of the firms.

8 For a more technical analysis on productivity, see CSAE (2005).

9 The occupation in which the individual works may provide another indication of the skills of the worker, which in turn may affect earnings. A skilled worker is defined as

one belonging to one of the following occupations: managers; professionals (engineers, accountants, economists, technicians); skilled office workers; sales personnel; and supervisors. Unskilled labour includes unskilled office workers, service employees such as cleaners and guards, and production workers.

10 At present, the median micro firm employs four workers and has a capital stock of $2,000. In contrast, the median very large firm employs 800 people with a total capital stock of $9 million.

References

Aromolaran, Adebayo, 2004, 'Wage Returns to Schooling in Nigeria', *African Development Review*, 16 (3), 433–455.

Bigsten, Arne and Mans Söderbom, 2006, 'What Have We Learnt from a Decade of Manufacturing Enterprise Surveys in Africa?', *World Bank Research Observer*, 21 (2), 241–265.

Bigsten, Arne, Paul Collier, Stefan Dercon, Marcel Fafchamps, Bernard Gauthier, Jan Willem Gunning, Abena Oduro, Remco Oostendorp, Catherine Pattillo, Mans Söderbom, Francis Teal and Albert Zeufack, 2004, 'Do African Manufacturing Firms Learn from Exporting?', *Journal of Development Studies*, 40 (3), 115–171.

Centre for the Study of African Economies, 2003, 'Sources of Growth in Nigeria: An Initial Analysis', report prepared for DfID, mimeo, Oxford University.

Centre for the Study of African Economies, 2005, *Report on the Nigerian Manufacturing Enterprise Survey 2004*, Oxford: UNIDO and CSAE.

Eifer, Benn, Alan Gelb and Vijaya Ramachandran, 2005, 'Business Environment and Comparative Advantage in Africa: Evidence from the Investment Climate Data', (available at http://www1.worldbank.org/rped/documents/rped126.pdf).

Gunning, Jan Willem and Taye Mengistae, 2001, 'Determinants of African Manufacturing Investment: the Microeconomic Evidence', *Journal of African Economies*, 10, 48–80.

Lall, Sanjaya, 2001, 'Competitiveness Indices and Developing Countries: An Economic Evaluation of the Global Competitiveness Report', *World Development*, 29 (9), 1501–1525.

Söderbom, Mans and Francis Teal, 2002, *Report on the Nigerian Manufacturing Enterprise Survey 2001*, Oxford: UNIDO and CSAE.

World Bank, 2002, *An Assessment of the Private Sector in Nigeria*, Washington, DC: World Bank.

World Bank, 2005, *World Development Report 2005*, Washington, DC: World Bank.

World Bank, 2006, 'Lagos Strategy for Economic Development and Poverty Reduction', MEPB firm surveys 2005, 'The Performance of Nigerian Firms in Lagos, Nigeria', a report by Sumon Bhaumik and Saul Estrin, Washington, DC: World Bank.

12
How Competitive and Efficient are Nigerian Ports?

Okechukwu George Oji and Chukwuma Agu

12.1 Introduction: Why ports? Why Nigerian ports?

It was not really a spectacular sight: a refitted World War II tanker, Ideal-X, moving from New Jersey to Houston carrying 58 aluminium truck bodies. When it stopped, the trucks were unloaded, dropped onto trailer chassis, and hauled to their final destinations. The date was April 1956. It was not a spectacular event either, but it marked the beginning of a global revolution in sea transport, the beginning of containerization. It was not only to change global trade in significant ways; it was also to change the destiny of people and cities. Marc Levinson (2006) chronicles the impact of this small revolution in shipping on world trade. He noted that:

> the introduction of container shipping in the late 1950s and early 1960s ... represents a major technological advance with significant economic consequences. By dramatically lowering the cost of freight handling, the container reduced the need for factories to be near suppliers and markets and opened the way for manufacturing to move out of urban centers, first domestically and then abroad. This impact was particularly intense in New York City, where the container revolution began. Containerization had a devastating impact on New York City's economy and was a major contributor to the collapse of its industrial base between 1967 and 1975.

Nigeria potentially has the largest market and economy in West Africa. But over the years it has continued to lose market share in sea transport and cargo in Africa. The combination of poor management, high transaction costs, high tariffs and insecurity of cargo has made Nigerian ports very unattractive to users. Many Nigerian firms were faced with two options under this development. Some of the firms turned Cotonou in the Republic of Benin into their New Jersey and so relocated. Currently, a number of Nigerian firms keep their head offices in Cotonou to be able to have access to more efficient port services. The others that were not able to find their New Jersey in Cotonou generally died, leading to high industry mortality beginning in the mid-1980s. Anecdotal evidence points to the fact that imports into Cotonou seem to be far higher than the country's capacity. Much of the excess is destined for Nigeria and neighbouring countries. Government has had to increase security at the borders to check the onward transmission of those goods into the Nigerian market through land borders, officially tagging this 'smuggling'.

Unfortunately, while the country stalls or is prejudiced in its response to this challenge, the global target keeps moving. The Port Authority of New York and New Jersey recently declared that its first priority investment is the deepening of the port's channels to 45 ft by 2004, to accommodate larger, deeper draught vessels, and down to 50 ft by 2009. Ship sizes are growing fast; larger twenty-foot equivalent unit (TEU) container ships are now being considered immediate possibilities and some ports like Singapore are quickly preparing to receive these large ships. New techniques and measures are being experimented with and adopted regularly as countries work hard not to be left behind in the fast changing world of global shipping and trading.

With impending common external tariffs – and probably a common market – in West Africa, there is now a clamorous need to fix Nigerian ports. There are huge costs incurred in the course of maintaining the large public outlay in ports authority, customs and ministerial/civil service positions in the ports. But the heavier and more worrisome costs to the economy are in terms of the efficiency and job losses attendant upon a dysfunctional port system. A number of studies (among others Soludo *et al.*, 2003; Oji, 2005) have pointed to port reforms as one of the requisite complementary measures for reducing the chances of economic suicide for Nigeria in the event of the full implementation of the common market in West Africa.

The key task in this chapter is therefore to present facts on the state of Nigerian ports relative to global and regional demands. This is undertaken in two dimensions. First, using data on material and time costs for exports and imports, we place the competitiveness of Nigeria's ports and processes within the multilateral and regional context and outline the key areas for policy intervention. Second, we analyse the results of a survey of major stakeholders in ports services in Lagos (Nigeria) and Cotonou (Republic of Benin). The survey seeks to obtain stakeholders' views on relative costs of doing business in the ports as they relate to services, nature of roads/network, security, corruption, road charges/levies and pilferage, existence of – and extent of inhibitions by – other costs of doing business in the ports. Using estimates from a simple econometric model we establish the most important obstacles to efficiency in Nigerian ports.

12.2 The context

Africa continues to lag behind the world in institutional and infrastructure development, particularly in transport. This hinders its participation in international trade (Limao and Venables, 2001). In the 2005 and 2006 Global Competitiveness Reports (GCR), most African countries competed with one another at the bottom of the tables (Table 12.1). In almost every aspect – infrastructure, institutions, macroeconomy, social sector development innovation, market efficiency and technological readiness – the continent performed much worse than the rest of the world. In particular, transportation limitations in the continent are daunting. Even the railroad, virtually ubiquitous in other parts of the world, is yet to reach most of Africa. The number of highway miles is quite small relative to the size of the countries, and air transportation is scarce and costly. Roads, ports and railways have deteriorated in many countries over the past two decades. Possible causes fingered in debates include economic stagnation, strained government finances, inefficient state operation of the transportation system, and conflict. It has been estimated that Africa needs $18 billion per year in infrastructure investment in order to even marginally improve on its competitiveness (World Bank, 2001). But how far investments alone can go in redressing this backwardness particularly in

Table 12.1 Global competitiveness ranking, 2005 and 2006, shifts in position among African countries

Country	**2006 ranking**	**2006 score**	**2005 ranking**	**Change in position**
Nigeria	101	3.45	83	–18
Uganda	113	3.19	103	–10
Botswana	81	3.79	72	–9
Cameroon	108	3.30	99	–9
Zimbabwe	119	3.01	110	–9
Mozambique	121	2.94	112	–9
Chad	123	2.61	117	–6
South Africa	45	4.36	40	–5
Namibia	84	3.74	79	–5
Ethiopia	120	2.99	116	–4
Malawi	117	3.07	114	–3
Mali	118	3.02	115	–3
Madagascar	109	3.27	107	–2
Kenya	94	3.57	93	–1
Tanzania	104	3.39	105	1
Benin	105	3.37	106	1
Morocco	70	4.01	76	6
Algeria	76	3.90	82	6
Gambia	102	3.43	109	7
Lesotho	112	3.22	—	
Mauritania	114	3.17	—	
Zambia	115	3.16	—	
Burkina Faso	116	3.07	—	

the face of high corruption and entrenched interests as well as cost recovery and maintenance imperatives remains an empirical question.

Nigeria seems to have led the rest of the continent in low and falling competitiveness and capacity to provide basic infrastructure. The 2005 GCR ranked Nigeria 83rd out of 125 countries in overall competitiveness. Within just one year, in the 2006 report, the country went down 18 places to the 101st position. Despite its vast resources and potentials, the transportation system within Nigeria and between Nigeria and the rest of the world is best termed 'sick'. The roads are in a parlous state and road transportation is a continual risk. Air transport fares no better, while dredging of the two most important rivers (Niger and Benue) has been in the pipeline for over two decades, and the work remains undone. In effect, none of the rivers is currently serving effective internal transport purposes. The railway system fares even worse than the other modes of transportation. The country still subsists on 3557 km of rail lines consisting of the Lagos–Nguru and Port Harcourt–Maiduguri rail lines. The last railway line was laid in 1958 and the system has been largely neglected since. At present, 3505 km of the railways consist of narrow gauge. Presently, Nigeria does not have any rail link with any of its neighbours. Overall, transport infrastructure in Nigeria presents a case study for poor initial planning and long-term negligence. Lack (or mismanagement) of resources makes improvement and repair of roads, boat docks, airports and railways difficult.

But while the roads, inland waterways and railways are important to reduce domestic production and transaction costs, the seaports link the country with the external world. By default then, they largely determine the country's competitiveness relative to the rest of the world. The Lagos port is by far the most important of the ports in Nigeria, handling more than 75 per cent of the country's general cargo. Over the years, the country's ports, which have been under the management of the Nigerian Ports Authority, have fallen far behind international standards in terms of the quality of facilities and operational efficiency.

The challenges are growing, the environment changing and the expectations rising with new developments in the global economic arena. Globalization and 'regionalization' of trade are now stark realities. Within the context of a globalizing world, as the country tries to meet old benchmarks, new ones emerge. Thus the challenges for faster lowering of barriers to growth and trade are mounting. As shipbuilding technology advances, many ports around the world are being constructed to meet the challenges when they come. At the regional level, having signed on to the Economic Community of West African States (ECOWAS), the country has bound itself to the Common External Tariff (CET) of ECOWAS in March 2006. But several (commissioned) studies evaluating the implications of the CET show that it is potentially disastrous for the country to latch on to the CET without paying adequate attention to its cost of doing business and necessary reforms in the ports (see Soludo *et al.*, 2003; Rajhi and Marchat, 2003 among others).

In recognizing these challenges, the Obasanjo administration has taken some steps to improve transport infrastructure and reform port operations in Nigeria.

It has sought to privatize the Nigerian Railroad Corporation; plans are well under way to introduce private–public partnership in the construction and management of roads, while the Nigerian Ports Authority (NPA) is pursuing partial privatization of the ports by means of granting concessions to private port operators. But the challenges remain. Privatization is currently not politically acceptable to different stakeholders, especially the organized private sector. Labour groups and organizations perceive the reforms as reducing their bargaining powers. Individual customs officials hardly see the 'big picture' of national competitiveness loss arising from their commitment to ensure that full institutional set-ups are utilized in curbing the excesses of 'erring' importers. Infrastructure at the ports is obviously overstretched, corruption seems high, documentation requirements are excessive and many importers would rather import through neighbouring Cotonou than through Lagos, leading to increased imports into the country without resulting revenue for government.

12.3 Global port services and an emerging 'efficiency' paradigm

While sea transport as an instrument of international trade is as old as civilization, there have been very significant revolutions in recent years in its capacity to deliver responsive services. The predominant view of ports as instruments of state control prior to the second half of the twentieth century has largely given way to intense competition among ports in the twenty-first century. With huge reductions in ocean transport, a lot of attention has been turned of late to ports as a key measure for significantly increasing global trade (World Bank, 2001).

Thus, pressure will continue to mount on ports and ocean transport services to increase in efficiency. In particular, several other aspects of costs for ocean transport services seem to be lowering with technological improvements. Since the introduction of containerization, there have been continual increases in the number and average size of container ships. Presently, ships with 10,000 to 12,000 TEUs are increasingly becoming possibilities and some ports (Singapore, Shanghai and Rotterdam among others) are already setting the logistics for the berthing of such ships. Ships of much higher speeds and sizes are also being contemplated in the near future. In all, these reduce the costs and delays associated with ocean travel and put pressures on ports to increase their efficiency and ability to handle the increasing global business.

The World Bank Toolkit (2001), for example, identifies five factors that naturally shape the competitive landscape of ports: (i) the state of rivalry among existing competitors; (ii) the threat of new competitors; (iii) the potential for global substitutes; (iv) the bargaining power of port users; and (v) the bargaining power of port service providers.

Standard methodologies can help to measure the efficiency gains from reforming the organization of port infrastructure, how those measures can be used to promote competition between ports, and how competition can be built into an incentive-driven regulatory regime. But they do not seem to be adequate to measure the efficiency of factors in ports, particularly the efficiency of labour. For example, Tovar *et al.* (2003) conducted the efficiency analysis of port restructuring in Mexico in 1993 using the stochastic production frontier method. His results show that Mexico has achieved annual efficiency gains of 6–8 per cent in the use of port infrastructure since assigning its management to independent, decentralized operators. His assessment of changes in relative performance ratings identifies consistent sets of leaders and laggards, including some that would not have been identified by partial productivity indicators commonly used in the sector. In more general terms, some of the major determinants of port efficiency outlined in the literature include not only activities that depend on port infrastructure, like pilotage, towing and tug assistance, or cargo handling (among others), but also activities related to customs requirements. It is often claimed that 'the (in)efficiency, even timing, of many port operations is strongly influenced (if not dictated) by customs' (Clark *et al.*, 2004).

In addition, it is now increasingly the case that a number of port services are outsourced to specialized private sector service providers via a number of different methods. In any case, the amount of cargo to be handled has no regular pattern and therefore daily employment is always widely different from the muster-roll. Thus, output per worker will be a gross underestimation of productivity of port workers. The more valid concept of labour productivity in this context would be the output per man-hour. A more direct measure of labour productivity in ports is the cargo handled per man-hour. A major problem encountered using total factor productivity measure is that increases in total factor productivity are attributable to the contributions of all the productive forces whose individual measurement is not possible. When policy and social changes like liberalization, globalization, privatization, consumer tastes and preferences, cause a change in the total productivity in post-reform ports, it is even more difficult to capture the productivity of individual agents in the ports. In all, though, a long-standing method of capturing overall efficiency of a port is to see how fast ships are being cleared from the port, in other words the turnaround time of ships. Average turnaround time and berth occupancy have for long been considered surrogate methods to measure port productivity. The berthing and cargo handling facilities available, coordination and supervision within the port and labour efficiency influence the turnaround time.

12.4 Global efficiency imperatives – Nigeria's response

12.4.1 Evidence from secondary data

With approximately 13 per cent of the world's population, Africa's performance in shipping, port services and container terminal handling is well below its potential. By 2001, only 6 per cent of waterborne cargo traffic and 3 per cent (8 million TEU) of container traffic worldwide took place in Africa. Equally, while about 70 per cent (approximately 172 million TEU) of global container terminal handling capacity and port services is in the hands of the private sector, governments and the public sector in Africa still own 90 per cent.

Cargo traffic is not evenly distributed among countries in the continent. There are wide variations in both regional and country experiences and performance in port services and sea transport (Table 12.2). Of the 54 countries in the continent, 15 are landlocked, leaving 39 owning 90 seaports. North Africa came from behind with only 15 per cent of total cargo in 1980 to being the destination for nearly 35 per cent of total cargo in the continent by 2002. There was also some improvement in East Africa whose share as at 1980 was 8 per cent but has grown to about 15 per cent in 2002. The gains by these two regions were, however, at the expense of the west and south of Africa. South Africa, which handled 41 per cent of total cargo in 1980, currently handles less than 30 per cent and West Africa, which was the destination of about 36 per cent of total cargo in 1980, now makes do with only 23 per cent. Africa's larger economies (including South Africa, Egypt, Côte d'Ivoire, Morocco, Kenya and Nigeria) with access to the sea account for a disproportionately high proportion (71.3 per cent in 2002) of total cargo in the continent. Yet even among these, there are still differences in the share of the gains each country has been capable of appropriating, determined mainly by progresses made in reform on port services and overall economic growth.

As is always the case, Nigeria is the major factor behind West Africa's poor and dwindling performance in cargo handling and port services. With about 50 per cent of the regional population and GDP, the country's performance will always be critical to the positioning of the West African sub-region. Between 1980 and 2002, the country's share in total traffic of the six larger economies fell from 19 per cent to only 5.2 per cent (Table 12.3). At the same time, Egypt rose from only 9 per cent of traffic of the six large economies to controlling 34 per cent in 2002! Kenya and Morocco also gained. A few other countries, notably South Africa and Côte d'Ivoire, reduced their share of control from 53 per cent to 39 per cent and from 12 per cent to 9.3 per cent respectively. In the latter case, around 50 per cent of output is trans-shipment and was highly affected by instability in government in the late 1990s and early 2000s. But even at that, none of the losses by any of the countries was as dramatic as the reduction in size for Nigeria. 'Coincidentally', these losses also mirror overall economic growth performance over the period.

Table 12.2 TEU of shipment to Africa by regions

Region	1980	%	1992	%	2002	%
N. Africa	217,067	15	956,355	30	2,782,582	34.40
E. Africa	110,254	8	528,304	16	1,172,356	14.50
S. Africa	599,531	41	923,404	29	2,251,206	27.90
W. Africa	527,083	36	813,356	25	1,872,667	23.20
Total	**1,453,935**	**100**	**3,221,419**	**100**	**8,078,811**	**100.00**

Source: Cameron (2003).

Table 12.3 TEU of shipment handled by countries

Top countries	1980	%	1992	%	2002	%
South Africa	599,531	53	923,404	41	2,251,206	39.1
Egypt	104,111	9	682,937	30	1,969,642	34.2
Côte d'Ivoire	133,858	12	188,727	8	535,000	9.3
Morocco	60,270	5	147,684	7	392,000	6.8
Kenya	30,660	3	135,325	6	310,835	5.4
Nigeria	210,805	19	169,340	8	301,000	5.2
Total	**1,139,235**	**100**	**2,247,417**	**100**	**5,759,683**	**100**

Source: Cameron (2003).

Indications from both primary and secondary data seem to point to inefficiency in services as responsible for the dwindling fortunes of Nigerian ports. The 2006 Doing Business survey shows that Nigeria does not fare too well in two of the three indicators of border trade – the number of documents and the time statutorily required from importers and exporters to operate (Table 12.4; Figures 12.1 and 12.2). Nigeria's performance in overall ranking is somewhat better than the average performance of West African countries, but its performance in cross-border trade is comparatively poor. Nigeria is on top of the chart for documentation requirements for imports with an average of 13 documents required. This compares less favourably with an average of 12 for SSA, 12.5 in South Asia, 10.3 in the Middle East and North African region, 9.5 in Latin America, 9.3 in East Asia and 6 in the OECD. In other words, even by sub-Saharan African standards, Nigeria's documentation requirements for imports are excessive. The situation is not different in documentary requirements for exports despite ongoing government 'enhancements and promotions' programmes for non-oil exports, as can be seen from Figure 12.1.

Nigeria's low and falling traffic in total ports is not an accident. Poor investment, high-handed government control of the sector and lack of planning for development have all combined to give rise to gross inefficiency and loss of market share for Nigerian seaports. The combination of corruption, inefficiency, poor infrastructure and other factors have made Lagos port amongst the most expensive in the world. Estimates by private shippers suggest that 'associated port costs' at Lagos are roughly three times higher than any other West African port. Import clearance takes 10 to 25 days on average. The result is a business environment where barriers to entry are high, large firms are favoured, political connections are important for business success, and uncertainty constrains firms' willingness to invest (World Bank, 2002). The Bureau of Public Enterprises (BPE) summarized attributes of Nigerian ports as including corruption, intimidation, extortion, high levels of indiscipline and vice among the dock workers' labour leadership, and the existence of 'wharf rats' and their disruptive and destructive activities. Lagos, for example, has remained a 'must call' port for about three decades and very

Table 12.4 Documents, time and cost of imports and exports in Nigeria and selected regions

Region	Documents for export (no.)	Time for export (days)	Cost to export ($ per container)	Documents for import (no.)	Time for import (days)	Cost to import ($ per container)	Percentage difference between documents required for export and import	Percentage difference between time required for export and import
E. Asia and Pacific	6.9	23.9	884.8	9.3	25.9	1,037.10	34.8	8.4
Europe and Central Asia	7.4	29.2	1,450.20	10	37.1	1,589.30	35.1	27.1
Latin America and Caribbean	7.3	22.2	1,067.50	9.5	27.9	1,225.50	30.1	25.7
Middle East and N. Africa	7.1	27.1	923.9	10.3	35.4	1,182.80	45.1	30.6
OECD	4.8	10.5	811	5.9	12.2	882.6	22.9	16.2
S. Asia	8.1	34.4	1,236.00	12.5	41.5	1,494.90	54.3	20.6
Sub-Saharan Africa	8.2	40	1,561.10	12.2	51.5	1,946.90	48.8	28.8
Nigeria	11	25	798	13	45	1,460	18.2	80.0

Source: World Bank (2006).

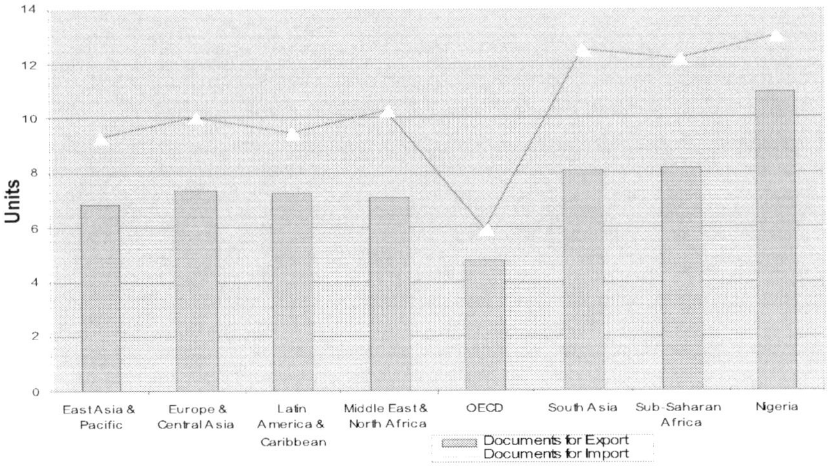

Figure 12.1 Number of documents required for exports and imports.

little has been done to increase the capacity of other ports around the country to reduce the traffic in Lagos. Vested interests and over-centralized control and the resultant inefficiency in administration ensured there were no investments in Lagos to match the increasing operational demands of a growing population and economy. In effect, while activities have grown considerably over time, the capacity of the port to bear them did not grow in tandem, leading to a crisis in port operations. The resultant expensive, lengthy and generally tortuous cargo inspection processes have meant an implicit high cost on the port user for the same port services. In 2001 and 2002, the climax of the congestion arising from these led to a diversion of cargo via other ports. Many shipping lines then applied

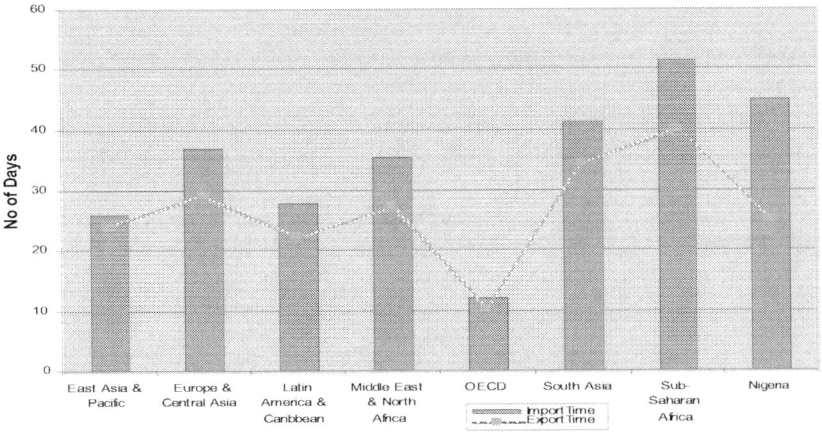

Figure 12.2 Time required for exports and imports (days).

a congestion surcharge on Lagos. Thus, relative to its Francophone neighbours (Dakar, Abidjan and Douala), stevedoring costs in Lagos rose sharply, standing at $200 per 20 ft container as against $60–$75 in these neighbouring ports. Total stevedoring and operating charges were $450 higher in Lagos for every TEU, or $80 million per year of port service, than in Thamesport and Teesport in the UK.

12.4.2 Port users' assessment of Nigerian ports

To supplement the foregoing analysis, a small survey was carried out in Lagos and Cotonou ports. One hundred and eighty-six stakeholders were interviewed, consisting of 106 agents in Nigeria and 80 in Cotonou. The stakeholders included importers, dock workers, clearing and forwarding agents, employees of stevedoring firms and officials of relevant ministries (finance and transport in particular). It was not possible to get customs to respond to the questionnaires owing to bureaucratic requirements.

It seems a number of importers in Nigeria prefer to use Cotonou port, which is nearby but in another country. Anecdotal evidence seems to point to the fact that this is not just on account of the significantly lower tariffs, but also because other charges and associated costs borne by importers were much smaller than in Lagos. In addition, processes and procedures in Cotonou were considered more predictable. Interestingly, as the markets in the Republic of Benin are small, many of such imports are thereafter moved by land through the Seme border to Lagos and sold in the Nigerian market. In addition, most of the landlocked neighbours of Nigeria are increasingly turning to Cotonou even when it might be farther and less accessible than Lagos.

The survey aimed to generate views of port users on the major obstacles to port efficiency in Nigeria as well as means of attending to these. The questionnaires were administered in two ports – Lagos and Cotonou. A number of key results emerged.

First, and most striking, were the preferences of port users for each of the ports as well as the reasons for such choice. Not one of the importers (whether in Nigeria or in Benin) indicated a preference for the Lagos port for his business. Only five clearing and forwarding agents preferred to use Lagos port. On the other hand, while all 23 Beninoise that show a preference for any port at all were willing to use Cotonou ports, 15 Nigerians would want to use Cotonou port. The study proceeded to find out whether these results were in any way indicative of the sorts of business these men are in and requested information on the extent to which their choice of ports reflected pressures from their businesses. Interestingly, only one respondent who preferred Lagos port indicated that this was on account of the nature of his business. The rest of the respondents who answered this question made it clear that it had little or nothing to do with the nature of their businesses but more with the nature of the ports themselves.

Second, asked to make a direct comparison, all respondents suggested that Lagos port compared poorly with Cotonou by a large and significant margin. This was the unanimous view of importers, but was also present to a substantial degree amongst other respondents. 75 per cent of dock workers, 78 per cent of clearing and forwarding agents, 54 per cent of government officials and 97 per cent of all others concurred with the view that Cotonou was significantly better than Lagos. Only amongst government officials (most of whom were Nigerians) does one see support for structures in Nigeria. This is consistent as the government officials are often not direct victims of inconsistencies in port policies and operations in the same way as are importers. All the same, more than half of the officials clearly identified the superiority of the Cotonou port in service.

Third, almost half of all importers indicated they would switch trade towards Lagos if tariffs were equalized between Lagos and Cotonou. The remainder (53 per cent and some of which are Beninoise) reflected a preference on using Cotonou port for reasons besides the tariff levied. Correspondingly, 60 per cent of clearing and forwarding agents and 82 per cent of government officials would not mind using Lagos port just on account of equalization of tariff across the two sets of ports. 80 per cent of Nigerians notified that they would use Lagos port if the rates were the same while 64 per cent of Beninoise would use Cotonou port.

Further questions examined the specific factors contributing to or determining the inefficiencies in the ports. Respondents were asked to rank eight factors determining the level of overall inefficiency in the ports. These included: (i) lack of infrastructure/poor technology (cranes, docks); (ii) corruption; (iii) bureaucracy/delays in process of clearing goods; (iv) ownership and organizational structures in the ports; (v) the activities of labour unions; (vi) multiple levies; (vii) poor access to information on ports; and (viii) frequent changes in operational modalities and laws governing the ports.

The results are quite striking. Almost unanimously, there is a consensus that the greatest problem of the ports is corruption. Over 86 per cent of all respondents share this opinion. Most others classified it as the second or third most important of the eight factors. Importers overwhelmingly voted it the most important – with 97.3 per cent of them insisting it is critical in determining ports' efficiency. Clearing and forwarding agents supported this stance with 82.8 per cent of them voting it in the first or second position in contributing to problems in the ports. Government officials consistently deviated from the other sets of respondents in their thoughts on the problem in the ports. Only 16.7 per cent of them voted corruption the most important problem and another 58 per cent of them voted it as the third or fourth most important problem.

Bureaucratic bottlenecks in port operations appear the second most important problem faced by port users, particularly in Lagos port. About 71 per cent of all respondents voted it the second most important problem. Again importers topped the chart with 92 per cent of them voting it the second most important. The position of the importers was strongly supported by all other respondents – including government officials – with 72 per cent of clearing and forwarding agents, 67 per cent of government officials and 52 per cent of 'others'. Port users were also not impressed with the structure of levies and this was identified as the third most important hindrance to port use. Referring to both the level and rate of change of the levies, there seems general dissatisfaction with fees charged and the manner in which they are charged. Government officials again differed slightly with 42 per cent of them thinking it should be the fourth most important problem. The fourth problem fingered by stakeholders is the state of infrastructure followed closely by the structure of ownership of facilities in the ports as well as activities of labour unions. A priori, one imagines that access to information in a port like Lagos would be a problem. But this turned out not to be as much as imagined. It was placed second least important among the eight factors. Obviously it could – and probably does – constitute an important impediment but in the opinion of stakeholders, compared to other human infrastructure affecting ports, such importance pales. Evidence points to the fact that, currently, most users tend to get information on changes as and when required, but face other problems in adapting to such information changes. This poses a significant challenge but also presents an opportunity and strength that could be built upon.

12.4.3 Obstacles to efficiency

Using responses from the instrument outlined in the previous section, this section attempts to estimate some of the key obstacles to efficiency in Lagos ports with intent to track bottlenecks to port efficiency. Port efficiency is proxied by the time (number of days) it takes to clear goods from the ports. Explanatory variables considered include documentation, delays in customs service, poor rail systems, insecurity, number of agencies in the ports and corruption. Inadequacy of infrastructure is captured by 'inefficient port services', which is further broken down to specific activities that require the employment of such infrastructure. These are container stacking, delays in inspection procedures, unclear or cumbersome clearance procedures, lack of automated transaction-processing system, container parking space and hypo scan X-ray equipment. So the specification could be represented as:

$$\text{Clearance days } j = b_1\text{ExDoc}_{ij} + b_2\text{Customs}_{ij} + b_3\text{Porail}_{ij} + b_4\text{Levies}_{ij} + b_5\text{Insec}_{ij} + b_6\text{Agency}_{ij} + b_7\text{Corpt}_{ij} + b_8\text{ConStack}_{ij} + b_9\text{Delays}_{ij} + b_{10}\text{Proc}_{ij} + b_{11}\text{Auto}_{ij} + b_{12}\text{ParkSp}_{ij} \tag{12.1}$$

where ExDoc is excessive documentation, Customs is delays in customs clearance, Porail is the rail service, Levies depict undefined and multiple levies, Insec is insecurity, Agency is multiplicity of agencies operating in the ports, Corpt is corruption of customs officials, ConStack is container stacking, Delays represent delay in inspection procedures, Proc is clearance procedures, Auto is the automated transactions procedures and ParkSp is availability of parking space, i is the respondent agent, and j is the country of operation (Nigeria).

To ease interpretation and ensure consistency in the estimation, the original data obtained via likert scale responses were converted to continuous variables. The dependent variable becomes continuous: 24 hours will be 1, two months will be 60, and so on. Explanatory variables will be converted to dummies. Initial graphing of some of the explanatory variables indicates some form of clustering of responses around '"very strong" and "moderately strong" obstacles'. As such, there will be two dichotomous classifications where only 'very strong obstacles' will have the value 1. Every other response will be pooled into the 'nil' response with a value 0 and classified as not being strong enough to merit policy attention. A linear regression is then used to estimate the relative impact of the different variables on efficiency. To track the data generating process, a general-to-specific estimation is adopted. We present the equation on Nigeria (Table 12.5).

Overall, the estimates from the equations corroborate earlier data on the specific areas of difficulty in doing business in Nigerian ports. There seems to be some consistency in the number and character of variables that were significant. For example, corruption, excessive documentation, large number of agencies, container stacking and lack of transaction processing system were significant in determining port efficiency. A number of other variables which a priori were believed to impact on port efficiency, like poor rail service, undefined levies, lack of hypo scan equipment and inadequate parking space, did not show up as significant at all. These had to be dropped at one point or other in the course of estimation, indicating that they were not really very relevant in determining port efficiency. In the stakeholders' view, the two most significant bottlenecks to port efficiency are excessive documentation and the attendant corruption. These impact and are impacted upon by the large number of agencies in the ports and also show up in container stacking and poor transaction system. Interestingly, the results show that such complementary infrastructure elements as poor rail service, lack of hypo scanning system, inadequate container parking space and undefined levies do not really hurt port services in Lagos as much as corruption and excessive documentation. While rail service, for example, is important for effective movement of goods to and from the ports and therefore coordination of port activities with the rest of the economy, Nigerians think it is less of a problem than corruption. Facilities at the ports are getting outdated and increasingly less capable of rendering service in tandem with demands. Yet they are not considered as important as the 'invisible hand' of corruption in hindering efficiency of the ports. Likewise stakeholders do not consider the flow of communication between

Table 12.5 Regression estimates (Nigerian responses)

Variable	Coefficient	Standard error	Beta	*t*-Statistic
(Constant)	15.808	2.097		7.539
Excessive documentation	5.537	.997	.588	5.552
Corruption	–10.904	2.168	–.587	–5.031
Large number of agencies	3.679	1.263	.342	2.913
Container stacking	–3.662	1.729	–.237	–2.118
Lack of transaction processing system	–2.062	1.120	–.208	–1.842

Dependent variable: cargo clearance time.

port users and the authorities so grossly insufficient as to result in significant loss of output. In effect, the problem with Nigerian ports is more with human (corruption, documentation requirements and attendant delays) infrastructure than physical (cranes, docks) infrastructure. There is no doubt that such human infrastructure deficiency is a bit more difficult to rectify and deal with than physical infrastructure.

12.5 Port and customs reforms in Nigeria

Beginning from 2003, Nigeria engaged in a process of restructuring and deregulation of its ports and customs procedures and other trade facilitation measures. The main objective of the port reform, itself a component of a broad transport sector reform, was to increase efficiency and reduce the size and role of the public sector. The process was also designed to increase competition and improve service delivery. The idea was to reduce the unattractiveness of Nigerian ports to both shippers and importers by reducing turnaround time for cargo and ships, insecurity of cargo, and unproductive labour force in the NPA and other port agencies. It also targeted reducing the multiplicity of agencies in the ports, corruption, and excessive charges on port users. The framework is such that the reforms facilitate adjusting the capacity of sea transport in Nigeria to demand changes, thus encouraging international trade while reducing the fiscal burden of the sector on government.

The main components of the Nigerian port reforms include concessioning of facilities and service delivery in major ports. The reform is expected to cover all major ports in the country. The Bureau of Public Enterprises (BPE) hired CPCS Transcom of Canada as Legal, Restructuring and Concession Advisers. The work assigned for CPCS Transcom is to propose a legal and regulatory framework, formulate the restructuring process, prepare the concession plan, assist in the bidding process and negotiation with the selected bidders and provide technical support to the Presidential Task Force on the Ports Reform.

The two years between 2003 and 2005 witnessed a speedy move towards actualization of the partial privatization project. By April 2004, most due diligence work and a detailed plan for the concessions, including bid documents, were prepared. This was followed in July 2004 with the preparation of the legal and regulatory framework to convert the NPA into the true ports landlord and to establish an independent regulatory commission. By September of the same year, CPCS Transcom also prepared a legal and regulatory report that led to the production of the first draft of Ports and Regulatory Commission Bills. Thereafter, the BPE issued bid documents for the terminals in four rounds, in 2004 and 2005, and immediately afterwards concessioned 13 terminals. Three of the 13 terminals have been handed over to private operators and concession agreements have been signed for another five terminals. Negotiations for two terminals are complete while technical bids have been evaluated for the remaining three. Another 12 terminals were slated for concessioning through direct negotiation. This was on account of the complexity of existing leases (Dangote and Flour Mills Ltd, among others, have existing leases on some of the terminals). Three of the 12 have been handed over, concession agreements for six have been signed, two are in negotiations and the bid documents for one have been issued. The NPA has also commenced dividing itself into two autonomous port authorities, pending enactment of the Port Reforms Act. The government has also earned substantial revenue from the privatization. For example, AP Moller, one of the concessionaires, won the bid for the Apapa container terminal with the amount of $1 billion. In addition, it is estimated that private port operators will invest $500 million in ports development and pay $5 billion to the government as fees over the concessioning period. Even though not all the ports have been concessioned yet, progress made within the last two years presents a sharp departure from historical trends.

The legal hinge upon which current port activities are based is the Cabotage law enacted in 2003, which came into effect in 2004. The Act broadly aims to increase domestic capacity building (human and material) for coastal shipping. It therefore provides for restriction of the use of foreign vessels in domestic coastal trade to promote development of indigenous tonnage and established a Cabotage Financing Fund. But the act has a number of challenges: one of such is the lack of guarantee of availability of cargo. Where cargo cannot be guaranteed or made readily available in an 'open market' environment, indigenous tonnage will not thrive. In particular, there is the possibility of repeating the adverse experiences of the 40:40:20 cargo policy under the now moribund National Shipping Policy Act 1987 which, in part, led to the demise of the Nigerian National Shipping Line Ltd and several indigenous shipping lines. The process of registration on the Cabotage Vessel Register is susceptible to administrative and data bottlenecks. Such issues as beneficial ownership, 'genuine' joint ventures and Nigerians fronting for foreigners in a manner reminiscent of the old Indigenization Policy under the 1977 Nigerian Enterprise Promotion Council Act are serious challenges. Equally, the criteria for licences under Sections 9–15 of the Act have been identified as rather elastic and capable of abuse since it may prove strenuous to determine, for example, that 'there is no wholly Nigerian owned vessel that is suitable and available to provide the services or perform the activity described in the application'. The Cabotage Vessel Financing Fund, which is expected to be derived essentially from a 2 per cent surcharge on coastal trade cargo, is yet to become operational.

A port reforms bill has been sent to the National Assembly. The bill is expected to provide the anchor for increased private sector involvement in and reduced government control of ports. Owing to the critical position of the ports sector, there are a number of pressures for and against the bill. Different groups are lobbying to align the contents of the bill to their interests. This has led to undue delays in passing the bill. The bill which went to the National Assembly since 2004 is yet to be passed. In effect, the legal framework for the reforms, ongoing and proposed, is still not set. The lingering of the bill continues to pose a challenge not only to the undone work in the sector but equally to the recorded improvements in the sector.

Besides the legal framework, there are a number of outstanding issues necessary to properly situate the port reforms and significantly increase its overall success. Some of these could be seen from an examination of a few of the provisions of the customs reform toolkit. Table 12.6 below summarizes some of the issues in the toolkit and some comments on the extent of Nigeria's compliance with each provision.

12.6 The human factor in port reforms

Interestingly, a number of the items still outstanding as captured in Table 12.1 relate to human bottlenecks. These include full implementation of the Automated Systems for Customs Data (ASYCUDA) project to all area commands and reducing the number of agencies at the ports as well as customs reforms and reform of the Nigeria Ports Authority. Excessive documentation as a problem is a fallout of some of these unresolved human factors. Findings from both the field survey and available secondary evidence point to this set of problems as the most crucial for the ports. Though there have been preliminary improvements in the state of the ports, there remain innumerable rent-generating regulations, bureaucratic locks and sector privileges. These reflect in low quality of services, high tariffs, scarce investment and progressive deterioration of the infrastructure as well as port equipment. The superabundance of rules and regulations still discourages private investment. Centralization of port administration with the attendant lack of flexibility is also still a problem.

Table 12.6 Port reforms toolkit and progress in reforms in Nigeria, 2003 to date

Serial number	Provisions of port reform toolkit	Comments on compliance
1.	Outsourcing of services to specialized private sector service providers	Some services in Lagos ports are presently outsourced
2.	Designation of public ports for general cargo imports, where the basic infrastructure is owned by the state but operations are private	Currently obtainable in some ports
3.	Designation of specialized ports that are completely private and serve large export sectors	Yet to be undertaken
4.	Concessions of up to 30 years aimed at promoting the modernization of port facilities and services	Currently ongoing for a number of terminals
5.	Extending the ASYCUDA project to all customs area commands and operational units	Yet to be undertaken
6.	Reducing the number of agencies involved with physical examination of goods	Yet to be undertaken
7.	Legal structure	Yet to be undertaken
8.	Customs reforms	Yet to be undertaken

Despite being a critical aspect of reducing the human bottlenecks, customs reforms have been painfully slow. An assessment of Nigeria's private sector (World Bank, 2002) noted that customs procedures and their enforcement are some of the most contentious and inefficient aspects of government regulation in Nigeria. In the estimation of many shipping and logistic firms, Nigeria Customs Service is perhaps one of the most uncertain customs environments in the world. False invoicing, counterfeit documentation, extortion, fraud, unclear security arrangements and other hazards increase the costs of imports by an estimated 45 per cent. Nigeria's customs clearance system is widely criticized for its complexity and unpredictability, as well as widespread corruption. Clearance procedures are open to multiple interpretations by officials and other government agents, and disagreements about the classification of goods and their tariff rate are very frequent. The service is considered considerably overstaffed with 18 comptrollers and over 17,000 officials. With multiple rules, waivers and high level of discretion in determining payable tariffs in customs, revenue losses on account of corruption and associated malpractices have been very high, ranging between 17 per cent and 47 per cent for the decade 1995–2005. A few challenges like high and complex tariff system, poor training of officials and low wages have helped to complicate the problems in the ports. In addition, there is a wrong emphasis of the service on revenue generation, which seems to work against a couple of other macroeconomic policies.

The Nigerian Ports Authority is also a heavy employer. It boasts 33 general managers and assistant general managers, 24 of which were declared 'redundant' by the Minister of Transport in 2003. This unwieldy management structure naturally translates to incompetence and high debt. In its attempt to impose sanity on the ports authority, the federal government had to step in several times to revoke contracts awarded by the authority. As at December 2003, the authority owed about $34 million. Entrenched interests in both employment and rents in the authority have been strengthened over the years so that reforms in the sector are considered a near impossibility. Cronyism in employment resulted in strong unions as individuals and groups worked to consolidate won grounds. This has meant that reaching an agreement with labour unions on severance packages and preventing widespread strike have formed some of the most critical issues in the efforts to reform the Nigeria Ports Authority (see Box A12.1 in the Appendix, www.csae.ox.ac.uk/books).

Dealing with the human factor in reforms could be daunting. It is about people. It is about jobs, employment and livelihoods; it is about relationships, rents and rewards. As such, even though it must be handled, this has to be done with a great deal of care. So far, attempts at injecting a new lease of life into customs service and the NPA have been weak and grossly inadequate. As a preliminary step, the number of comptrollers in the customs service has been reduced from 18 to 13 and deputy comptrollers from six to three. The government established a special unit within the Economic and Financial Crimes Commission to check practices of the customs service, but this needs to be strengthened. The bill for the empowerment of relevant government agencies to reform the ports needs to be seriously worked on and facilitated, keeping in mind the need to maintain balance between the human capacity and efficiency needs of the ports.

12.7 Some case studies

Beginning with the United Kingdom and going on to several other countries in Asia, Latin America and Africa, a number of countries have undertaken massive port reforms. In fact, it may not be entirely out of order to argue that the massive increases in world trade in the last two decades are owed not only to containerization but also to the extensive reforms to increase the capacities of ports to contain the growing trends. We just examine two of such cases – Argentina (highly successful in Latin America) and Malaysia (a foremost story in Asia).

12.7.1 Argentina

The Argentine port system is spread among 12 provinces, along a 4600 km coast, and consists of both public and private ports. There are 40 public ports in activity and only one of these – Port of Buenos Aires – is administrated by the national government; the rest are managed by provinces, in some cases, with private sector participation and municipal administrations. There are also 30 private ports, dealing mostly in grain or industrial products. During the 1990s Argentina engaged in a process of restructuring and deregulation of its ports. Faced with a port sector that constituted a barrier to trade and hindered the fulfilment of productivity gains, the Argentine government designed and implemented a strategy based on a combination of privatization, deregulation and decentralization (to provinces). The reform aimed to increase efficiency and reduce public sector involvement in the ports, increase competition and improve service quality.

Before the reforms (at the end of the 1980s) the Argentine port sector was characterized by a weak and corrupt institutional framework, declining traffic and high tariffs. There were also insufficient investment and undue 'subsidies' of private operations, and institutional organization was poor. Port administration was highly centralized and five public entities shared port administration with overlapping responsibilities. Naturally, coordination, particularly of investment, was poor and facilities deteriorated so much so that, at one point, La Plata dock in the ports of Rosario, Buenos Aires, collapsed into the water. As a result, some private groups started investing in private handling terminals. While international trade cargo grew phenomenally between 1970 and 1989, total cargo in Argentina was moving in the opposite direction and fell 10 per cent from 83 million to 75.1 million tons and cabotage traffic fell from 58.2 million to 40.8 million tons over the same period. This was followed by a strong modal shift towards road transport and an increase in the transport of oil through pipelines. Tariffs and charges increased steadily and, just before the reforms, Argentina had some of the highest port charges in the world. Between 1980 and 1991 stevedoring fees increased 250 per cent in real terms and public elevators were by far more expensive than private ones as a result of tariff regulations.

The legal framework for the Argentine reforms is Decree 817 of 1992. The Decree liberalized contractual arrangements with stevedoring companies, deregulated pilotage and towage services, provided for free and independent establishment of tariffs, and abolished previous labour agreements and norms hampering productivity. Operators were free to enter, build, manage and operate a port for commercial, industrial or recreational use. The only condition is compliance with the standard supporting services requirements such as customs, safety and environmental regulation. Management and decision-making power were decentralized and devolved to provinces, but major ports (Buenos Aires, Bahia Blanca, Quequén, Rosario and Santa Fe) were subject to the newly created Port Administration Societies (SAP). The provinces responded by adapting management of ports under them to their specific constraints and preferences. There was a labour reform aimed at eliminating restrictive practices, promoting a stable labour relation between port workers and the private operators and minimizing the social impact of lay-offs (Sgut, 2000). The outcome was greater competition within and between ports.

The effects of the reforms were near-instantaneous and far-reaching – the Puerto Nuevo de Buenos Aires was transformed from the most expensive port in Latin America into one of the cheapest. There was also a reduction in fiscal burden on the part of the central government, improving resource allocation, and some loss-making, inefficient ports were closed by the provinces. Investment rose and was better managed. Between 1991 and 2000, capacity in Buenos Aires ports increased sixfold from 400,000 to 2.5 million TEU/year; the number of cranes increased from three to 22; and operational surface rose to 157 hectares from 65.

12.7.2 Malaysia

Malaysia shares a number of sociopolitical and economic characteristics with Nigeria, being ethno-socially diversified. For a number of years, the country was also largely dependent on natural (particularly agricultural and mineral) resources. Commercial exportation of oil started at about the same time in both Nigeria and Malaysia. The two countries also pursued import-substitution industrialization as national economic development policy particularly in the late 1960s and early 1970s (Soludo *et al.*, 2003). The two countries at one point had huge public sector outlay and afterwards started programmes of privatization.

The Kelang Container Terminal (KCT) was a flagship divestiture of the government of Malaysia shortly after inception of the privatization programme (Jomo, 1995). It remained, therefore, a reference point for the government on the potentials of the proposed policy objective of a 'Malaysia Incorporated'. For workers, on the other hand, employee welfare for the privatized KCT became a benchmark for negotiations on options for welfare in many other public enterprises slated for privatization. Indeed, for a long time the KCT privatization was celebrated as a proof of the success of Malaysia's privatization policy. It has consequently generated a number of studies, each one demonstrating a lot of efficiency and welfare gains arising from the privatization (Nankani, 1988; Leeds, 1989; Jones and Fadil, 1992;

Adam and Cavendish, 1995). At the outset of the privatization programme in Malaysia, the government was in dire need of public support for the programme. Thus it became incumbent for the first set of public enterprises to be privatized to find one that was politically not too sensitive but, at the same time, had potential for profitability (or a track record of profitability). The Kelang Container Terminal fitted the bill and had the added attractiveness of being run below international standards of efficiency even though it was not outright unprofitable.

Post-privatization performance of KCT has been quite impressive. Within two years of its privatization, TEUs handled in the terminal shot up from 244,120 to 273,335; turnaround time dropped from an average of 13.4 hours to 11.3 hours while container dwell time in the port fell from 8 days to 3.8 days (Goh and Jomo, 1995). Jones and Fadil (1992) conducted an extensive study on the efficiency and welfare gains of the privatization noting that output growth of the terminal grew along with GDP for the years prior to divestiture but thereafter grew much faster than GDP, indicating that the growth in output of the terminal was not as a result of exogenous shifts in demand. Throughput also grew consistently by about 20 per cent per annum for the first six years after the privatization. The government seems to have been one of the top gainers in the exercise, gaining RM683 million in tax and RM52 million in privatization proceeds (less transaction costs). This is in return for giving up RM378 million in profit flow from the terminal prior to the privatization.

Dealing with the workforce in the privately run KCT was as usual one of the knottiest issues in the privatization of the terminal. Three options were generally given to workers in the new KCT. The first was to retire with a generous lump sum severance package and entitlement to early pension benefits. The second was to decide not to join a private-sector-run KCT, in which case the Kelang Port Authority (the parent body) would be obliged to absorb them on the same conditions as obtained in their previous employment. The third option was to terminate their contract with the government and join the new KCT on terms no less favourable than previously given to them. In the last case, they were granted job security for the first five years except in cases of gross indiscipline. Many chose to stay with the new KCT. The new administrators of the terminal chose to adopt a programme of incentive-based reward system and additional welfare packages based on improved output. On the whole, there was an estimated RM66 million gains in higher wages. But it seems as though this was 'bought' at increased work hours from the workers, probably lowering the overall welfare gains that accrued to workers on account of the change in ownership. However, consumers also had some gains both in incentives and reduced transaction costs as well as overall reduction in time-related costs.

But this has not always been so. At inception of the privatization, just as in many other countries and cases, there was mass resistance of the privatization by the workers' union of the Kelang Port Authority and, in particular, the Kelang Container Terminal (Adam and Cavendish, 1995). However, a number of points seem to have worked against sustaining such resistance. Widespread dissatisfaction with the waste, inefficiency and corruption usually associated with public enterprises led to indifference to, and in many cases outright support for, the privatization policy. As such, it was a direct conflict between the protection of personal interests for the apparently threatened workers and widespread indifference by those who felt that the privatization might at least be a relief from the gross public inefficiency and monopoly. The labour unions worked hard to protect the interest of their workers and did get a fair bargain after all. But eventually, after the first five years, the privatized KCT was free to hire and fire. But beyond the micro-management of the employees of the KCT, the government went further to amend its pensions act to ensure that workers in privatized firms do not lose accumulated pension entitlements on account of such changes. Employee share participation was also used, even though with limited success, to sustain incentives for performance. But this went more to management than to employees in the case of KCT.

12.8 Conclusion

This chapter is about policy options. Primary and secondary data point to the need for structural reforms of Nigerian ports. The country case studies also show that successful port reforms are possibilities. Specifically, there are challenges in the Nigerian port reforms that need to be attended to. Given the many similarities between Nigeria and, say, Malaysia, there is the temptation to conclude by urging Nigeria to 'go and do likewise'. But in every case, reforms have to be context-specific. So there is a need to keep an eye on the macroeconomic and social contexts of the present reforms to increase their overall impact and sustainability.

Over the past decade many ports have introduced private participation in port operations through different forms of concession or lease agreements. A central objective of port privatization and deregulation policies is stimulating greater efficiency by engendering a more competitive market and commercial approach to management. Indeed, evidence of deregulation of port services elsewhere suggests that (i) the degree of private sector involvement in sample container terminals is positively related to efficiency of ports and (ii) improved productive efficiency has followed the implementation of privatization and deregulation policies within the transport sector (Trujillo and Serebrisky, 2005). It also generates funds for investment, increases efficiencies and ensures cost-effective services. To avoid monopolistic behaviour in such cases, a sound regulatory framework is necessary, but has to be such as does not hamper commercial entrepreneurship. But privatization is just one of the options and in many cases may mean no more of a solution to the problems of public enterprises than the public enterprises themselves have come to mean to the problems they were established in the first place to solve. Ultimately, the aims are to increase efficiency and minimize rent-seeking behaviour of agents. This means that privatization itself has to be properly managed for effectiveness (Jomo, 1995).

A major challenge in managing private entry into areas that may be natural monopolies is the regulatory framework. A recurrent problem found in many reforms is that attention may be paid to obtaining the necessary legal framework for private participation (often given the history of government dominance) at the expense of attention to regulation and increase in competition, which could be requisites for effective performance of such enterprises. Malaysia's initial efforts at reforms suffered from this in as much as employee and other policies attendant upon the reforms were ad hoc for nearly a decade before attempts were made to institutionalize them. In the Nigerian case, the fact that the enabling bill for the port reforms has spent close to two years in preparation and passage (and is not yet out!) has the tendency of reducing attention to the institutionalization of other regulatory roles expected of government to make the whole process both credible and sustainable.

Owing to poor investments in the sector, Nigerian ports are characterized by poor infrastructure. This could have been partly responsible for the long history of declining throughput and cargo share in Africa. But the survey of stakeholders in the ports shows that human restructuring to deal with issues of corruption and documentation delays is more important. In effect, while it will be important to upgrade facilities in the ports and make them compliant with the provisions of Kyoto 1999, this will be with the intent to depersonalize services at the ports. Port competition is fast becoming a reality of the twenty-first century and agencies that are associated with this cannot afford to impede it any more. Fortunately, Cotonou is always likely to be there to remind the country of any policy failure in this direction. Given this, it seems that the option of online service provision for most port facilities can be delayed only at the risk of huge economic losses to the country.

Presently, Lagos is a must call port. This is hardly necessary. Meaningful improvement in efficiency can result from increased competition – both within and between ports. Currently the competition is between Lagos and Cotonou; but the government can speed up action to redirect the competition. In effect, there will still be competition to Lagos, but this would come from other ports in Nigeria. A number of concessions are now ongoing for Port Harcourt owing to the potential for returns there. There is a need to do the same for other ports – notably Warri and Calabar. But more importantly, it has to be understood that, for the alternative ports, initial investments to improve facilities may have to come from mainly the government with complementation from the private sector concessionaires. The aim will then be to upgrade operating facilities in all the ports to international standards so that importers can have a choice. In addition, it may not be an entirely unworthy idea to think towards decentralization of control of the ports to sub-national governments as in the Argentine case, even if only to break the monopoly of the Nigeria Ports Authority. This could be complemented with initial incentives like reduced charges for users of ports outside Lagos to increase cargo to these ports. Over time such incentives could be withdrawn. So far, the licensing of private operators in the ports has been with the aim of fostering competition among operators. This has to be strengthened to give options to port users and encourage within-port competition.

The necessity of executive support cannot be overemphasized. Even though we were unable to look critically into it in this chapter, the Tanzanian port reform experience (reputed to be one of the most successful in sub-Saharan Africa) comes in handy here. The success of the Tanzanian reform has been attributed to strong executive support for the programme. Prior to the early 1990s, Tanzanian ports had some of the highest costs and other ports in East Africa thrived on the inefficiency of the Dar-es-Salaam ports. When the country embarked on its reform in the late 1990s, there was much opposition from some interest groups. But the country was able to push through the reforms, concessioning some of its ports and partially privatizing operations in other cases. It has been reported by various sources that the success of the Tanzanian port reforms was owed mainly to the president, who took it upon himself to ensure that he delivered on it.

Finally, there is a need for a reminder here that change everywhere entails winners and losers. In many cases, losers are those with a long history of entrenched interests – from rents, employment and access. Many of the interests are not harmful to growth, but a number of others are. Effective reforms often target reducing harmful interests and promoting profitable ones. But history seems to point to the fact that the losers are often more vocal and seem to shout loudly about their losses, often identifying such losses with majority losses. On the other hand, each set of reforms is expected to yield winners. But often too, the winners simply smile at their gains and keep quiet. Successful reforms therefore entail a great deal of effort at communicating the gains and potential threats to all stakeholders. A helpful way of doing this is to empower the gainers and increase their access to communication channels. This single item could make or mar a reform, and may not be very sensitive to the weight of gains or losses accruable to the reform.

References

Adam, Christopher and William Cavendish, 1995, 'Early Privatizations', in K.S. Jomo (ed.), *Privatizing Malaysia: Rents, Rhetoric, Realities*, Boulder, CO: Westview Press.

Cameron, Steve, 2003, 'The Scramble for Africa: Accelerating Move towards the Commercialization of Africa's Ports', *Portstrategy*, June, 22.

Clark, Ximena, David Dollar and Alejandro Micco, 2004, 'Port Efficiency, Maritime Transport Costs and Bilateral Trade', Working Paper 10353, National Bureau of Economic Research (NBER).

Goh, Winnie and K.S. Jomo, 1995, 'Efficiency and Consumer Welfare', in K.S. Jomo (ed.), *Privatizing Malaysia: Rents, Rhetoric, Realities*, Boulder, CO: Westview Press.

González, María Manuela and Lourdes Trujillo, 2005, 'Reforms And Infrastructure Efficiency in Spain's Container Ports', World Bank Policy Research Working Paper 3515, February.

Jomo, K.S., 1995, 'Overview', in K.S. Jomo (ed.), *Privatizing Malaysia: Rents, Rhetoric, Realities*, Boulder, CO: Westview Press.

Jones, Leroy and Azim Abbas Fadil, 1992, 'Kelang Container Terminal', paper presented at World Bank Conference on the Welfare Consequences of Selling Public Enterprise: Case Studies from Chile, Malaysia, Mexico and the U.K., Washington, DC, 11–12 June.

Leeds, Roger, 1989, 'Malaysia: Genesis of a Privatization Transaction', *World Development*, 17 (5), 741–56.

Levinson, Marc, 2006, 'Container Shipping and the Decline of New York, 1955–1975', *Business History Review*, 80 (1).

Limao, N. and A.J. Venables, 2001, 'Infrastructure, Geographical Disadvantage and Transport Costs', *World Bank Economic Review*, 15 (3), 451–79.

Nankani, H., 1988, *Techniques of Privatization of State-owned Enterprises, Volume II: Selected Country Case Studies*, World Bank Technical Paper 89, Washington, DC.

Oji, Okey George, 2005, 'ECOWAS Common External Tariff and Differential Efficiency of Lagos and Cotonou Ports: Implications for the Competitiveness of Nigerian Ports', final report submitted to the African Economic Research Consortium, 2005.

Rajhi, Taoufik and Jean Michel Marchat, 2003, 'The Short Term Impact of a CET on the Manufacturing Sector in Nigeria: Preliminary Results from a Firm Level Analysis', World Bank Regional Program on Enterprise Development.

Sgut, M., 2000, 'Informe sobre reestructuración portuaria. Impacto social del Puerto de Buenos Aires', paper presented at XX Reunión del Comité Técnico Permanente de Puertos de la Organización de los Estados Americanos, Oficina Internacional del Trabajo, Cali, Colombia.

Soludo, Charles C., Okey George Oji and Chukwuma Agu, 2003, 'Potential Impacts of Extension of UEMOA Tariffs to all ECOWAS Member States: A Case Study of Impacts on Revenue and Trade Balance in Nigeria', paper written for ECOWAS as part of its survey of the impact of CET on the regional economy of West African states.

Tovar, Beatriz, Sergio Jara-Diaz and Lourdes Trujillo, 2003, 'Production and Cost Functions and their Application to the Port Sector: A Literature Review', World Bank Policy Research Working Paper 3123, August.

Trujillo, Lourdes and Tomás Serebrisky, 2005, 'An Assessment of Port Reform in Argentina: Outcomes and Challenges Ahead', *Maritime Policy & Management*, 32 (3), 187–9.

World Bank, 2001, *The World Bank Port Reform Toolkit*, Washington, DC: The World Bank.

World Bank, 2002, *Globalization, Growth, and Poverty: Building an Inclusive World Economy*, Washington, DC: Oxford University Press.

World Bank, 2006, 'Doing Business, Economy Rankings', International Finance Corporation, The World Bank Group (available at www.doingbusiness.org/EconomyRankings/).

13
Nigeria's Power Sector: Opportunities and Challenges

Prasad V.S.N. Tallapragada and B.S. Adebusuyi[1]

13.1 Introduction

Nigeria's power sector has been a reflection of the economic growth strategy of the country. Power is a strategic infrastructure and represents the most important requirement for moving the economy forward. In post-independence Nigeria, the need for large scale investments in power infrastructure resulted in government dominance in the sector's activities. The National Electric Power Authority (NEPA) was the government-owned utility company responsible for generation, transmission and distribution of electricity throughout Nigeria. It is estimated that about 40 per cent of Nigerians have access to electricity. Of the 6113 MW of installed generating capacity, only about 3300 MW is available, whereas demand is estimated to be in excess of 10,000 MW. The transmission and distribution infrastructures are in a dilapidated and deplorable state because of lack of maintenance and inadequate funding, making it difficult to evacuate power from generation sites to consumption points. Electricity tariffs are below the cost of service and there is poor revenue collection performance as about 30–40 per cent of power supplied is never billed. This has resulted in the dismal performance of the utility, financial losses and its consequent inability to invest for expansion and improvement.

The magnitude of the losses is best illustrated by the fact that the power sector is incurring a cash loss of around $2 million per month. The annual subsidy support from the Federal Government of Nigeria (FGN) to cover losses and investments amounts to nearly $400 million annually, higher than the country's federal budget for health. Also, poor quality of supply led to widespread customer dissatisfaction. As the federal government's decision to reduce subsidy support for the sector takes shape, there is a striking opportunity for improvements in almost every aspect of electricity sector management. In the process Nigeria has the potential to make significant gains by reducing losses, introducing commercial practices and eventual privatization to sustain the recovery.

The general problems of the power sector, and the factors that spur countries in the developing world to embark on its reform, have been succinctly identified (Turkson, 2005) to include: poor management and performance of state-run electricity companies, resulting in higher cost and inadequate expansion of electricity services; inability of the state to finance expenditure for new investment and maintenance; economic crises and the need to remove subsidies for the sector in view of limited resources available for other pressing public expenditure needs. Others are: the desire to raise immediate revenue for the government through the sale of assets from the sector; and pressure on governments from donor agencies to reform their power sectors along globalization lines and the need to decrease the size of government. Efforts to reform Nigeria's electricity sector to enhance efficiency and investment growth are on these lines. Incessant supply shortages in power services in the form of outages and blackouts have debilitating effects with attendant costs on the economy. Generally, secure and low-cost supplies of electricity and other forms of modern energy are crucial for economic development and social progress. The prospects of the reforms in the sector for improved growth in investment and efficiency are the main consideration of this chapter. The rest of the chapter is structured as follows: Section 13.2 reviews the Nigerian electric power sector before the reforms; Section 13.3 analyses recent developments in the sector; institutional reforms in the sector are discussed in Section 13.4; Section 13.5 treats the issues of efficiency and investment growth; Section 13.6 discusses some country experiences; and Section 13.7 highlights the way forward and concludes the chapter.

13.2 Nigeria's electric power sector before the reforms

Traditionally, the power sector in most African countries including Nigeria has been under monopoly and is dominated by the public sector. The Federal Ministry of Power and Steel is the apex government organ responsible for formulating policies on the power sector. The main executing agency of the government in the power sector was the National Electric Power Authority before the current reforms. The organization until recently had the sole mandate to develop and maintain the electric power system for all parts of Nigeria. NEPA had nine power stations with a combined installed capacity of 6113 MW. The total generating capacity is made up of hydro (1938 MW) and thermal plants (4160 MW). The thermal plants include Egbin, Sapele, Afam, Delta, Oji and Ijora, while the hydro stations include Kanji, Jebba and Shiroro. There are also other smaller installations which include coal-fired power stations at Oji River in Enugu State and isolated stations at Calabar, Kaduna, Markurdi, Mubi, Maiduguri, Minna and Suleja. The aggregate electricity generated in Nigeria, which in 1970 stood at 1547 million kWh, rose to 7140.4 million kWh in 1980. By 1995, it stood at 15,856 million kWh, and then it rose by 1997 to 16,116.9 million kWh (Figure 13.1). However, between 1990 and 1999, no new capacity was added to the entire sector. This was in spite of increasing demand as the economy continued to expand. Similarly, there was no major overhaul carried out on any of the existing plants. Consequently, available capacity declined continuously as only 19 out of a total of 79 generating units installed were in operation. Of the 5996 MW of installed capacity in the 1990s, therefore,

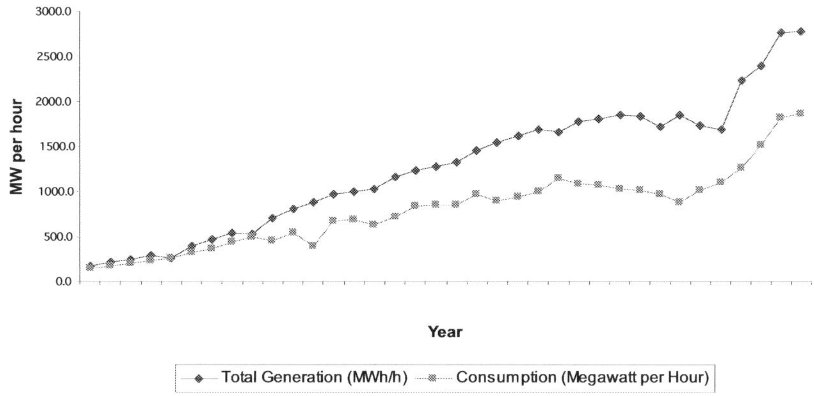

Figure 13.1 Electricity generation and consumption in Nigeria 1970–2000.

less than 3000 MW was available as against daily requirement of 6000 MW; consequently, load shedding became inevitable.

The national grid was characterized by radial lines that were vulnerable and old and did not cover most parts of the country. The last transmission line built by NEPA, before the inception of the present administration, was in 1987. Total NEPA transmission infrastructure included 5000 km of 330 kV lines, 6000 km of 132 kV, 23 substations of 330/132 kV and 91 substations of 132/330 kV. It also includes the National Control Centre, Oshogbo and the Supplementary National Control Centre at Shiroro.

Power distribution infrastructures included 23,753 km of 33 kV lines, 19,226 km of 11 kV lines, 697 substations of 33/11 kV and 20,543 substations of 33/0.415 kV. There were also 1790 distribution transformers and 680 injection substations across the country. The power transformers and circuit breakers were inadequately maintained, overloaded, insufficient and tended to break down regularly. Consequently, there were high system losses in the range of 30–40 per cent, compared with the international target of about 10–12 per cent (Figure 13.2). The inefficiency in the sector thus manifested in unreliability of power supply, low capacity utilization and availability factor, and a deficient maintenance culture. The activities of the marketing unit of NEPA were characterized by irregular billing with erroneous or arbitrarily estimated bills, while illegal connections were rampant.

In terms of efficiency and performance, Nigeria's electric power sector had been rated by the UNDP/World Bank Report, 1993, as having one of the highest rates of losses (33 per cent), the lowest generation capacity factor (20 per cent), the lowest revenue at 1.56 c/kWh, the lowest rate of return (–8 per cent) and the longest average accounts receivable period (15 months) (Table 13.1).

It is also relevant to note that the methodology used for measurement of system losses is itself not scientific. While system losses have been rightly defined as units received (in kWh) less the units billed (in kWh), it is difficult to use this

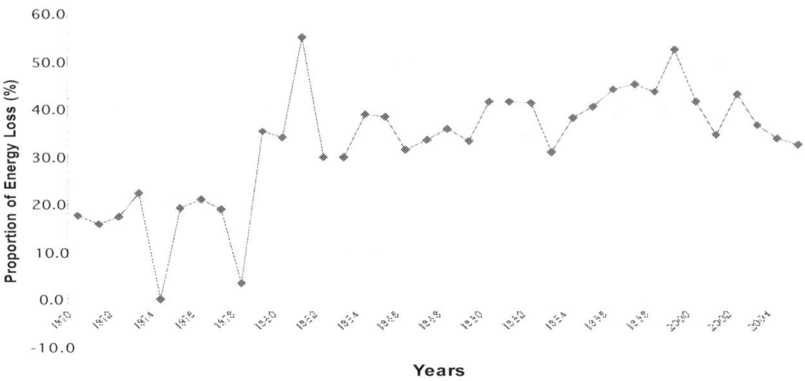

Figure 13.2 Proportion of electricity loss 1970–2005.

simple formula for determining the actual losses for the following reasons. (a) The number of units billed cannot be ascertained till there is 100 per cent metering of all consumption points. (b) There is typically a lag between reading the injection point meters and the consumption point meters. Meters at the injection points are all read once at the start of the month. Meters at the consumption points are read at different times in the month. Generally, different categories of consumption have different billing cycles. If the above formula is to be applied, all the injection point meters and all the consumption point meters have to be read at the same time point in time. (c) It is also essential that all the injection points at different voltage levels are metered, and that all grid interfaces are metered to get a reliable figure of units received into the system.

A more reliable measurement of the system performance with respect to system losses as well as collection efficiency is the measure of revenue recovered per kWh injected into the system (Box 13.1).

Based on the performance comparison of NEPA with the Nigerian Electricity Supply Corporation (NESCO), which was a private electricity supply company located in Jos, Plateau State, with seven hydro power stations and energy capability of about 170 million kWh per annum, Sule and Anyanwu (1994) noted that NESCO performed well compared with NEPA. For example, as at end of 1991, its unit price of energy was 0.094 naira while NEPA's was 0.32 naira. Futhermore, NESCO made estimated profits of 318,000 naira and 954,000 naira in 1990 and 1991, respectively. Finally, NESCO's system losses were also considerably lower than NEPA's (Tables 13.2 and 13.3).

The dismal performance of the sector was further corroborated by a 1989 World Bank Study which showed that 25 per cent of electricity consumed by industrialists was self-generated and only about 8 per cent did not have standby power generation facilities. Low morale, indiscipline and corruption pervaded the entire sector. In addition to high technical loss there was a poor payment pattern of the customers in the system, and collections were less than 50 per cent

Table 13.1 Power sector performance of some developing countries

Country	GDP per capita (US$)	System losses (%)	Generation cap. ftr. (%)	Average rev. (c/ kwh)	Rate of return (%)	Accts. receivable (months)
Low-income countries						
China	340	17	54	2.10	5	1
Côte d'Ivoire	683	14	28	15.8	2	4
Ghana	374	22	48	1.69	9	6
India	292	22	43	5.77	6	6
Indonesia	476	17	32	5.10	0	1
Kenya	329	15	56	6.15	5	–
Nigeria	267	33	20	1.56	(8)	15
Pakistan	320	25	61	3.84	14	3
Sri Lanka	386	15	26	5.40	8	5
Sudan	472	20	27	8.87	9	–
Zimbabwe	608	10	47	3.68	21	–
High-income countries						
Algeria	2181	13	41	5.64	(1)	8
Argentina	2640	21	37	4.49	7	2
Brazil	2241	17	49	5.37	6	–
Korea	4079	6	46	7.61	8	–
Malaysia	2052	16	37	7.10	12	1
Mexico	2111	14	45	3.67	1	2
Portugal	4049	8	37	8.23	8	11
Venezuela	3391	19	33	2.32	–	1
Yugoslavia	2615	13	48	2.92	–	3

Source: UNDP/World Bank (1993: 81, Annex 9) cited in Sule and Anyanwu (1994).

of power generated. Sule and Anyanwu further found that NEPA's total revenue fell short of total operating expenses by wide margins of 49.2 and 48.8 per cent in 1987 and 1988, respectively, but narrowed to 2.5 per cent in 1989. However, the financial situation improved after 1990 following a 59.2 per cent increase in tariff (from naira 0.201 to naira 0.32). Generally, until mid-1989, NEPA's tariff was low and hardly changed. According to the study, although the required break-even tariff was 0.41 naira, 0.43 naira and 0.78 naira in 1990, 1991 and 1992, the actual tariff was lower; thus the level of subsidy was 28.1, 34.4 and 143.8 per cent in 1990, 1991 and 1992, respectively. Following the commercialization of the utility in 1991, the enterprise was expected to operate without subventions from

Box 13.1 NEPA status as of September 2003 (before unbundling into successor companies)

Key facts
Annual generation plus power purchase = 21,914 GWh (average)
Value of power generated/purchased annually* = 129 billion naira
Value of power billed to customers annually = 72 billion naira
Funds lost due to technical and non-technical losses = 57 billion naira
Funds collected against above billing = 50 billion naira
Funds lost annually including non-collection losses** = 79 billion naira
Result: nearly 55 per cent of power and revenues are lost principally at the distribution end of the business.
*At average retail tariff of 5.9 naira/kWh.
**Pertaining to the billing year.

the budget, and to fix rates, prices and charges. Unfortunately the utility viewed commercialization merely in terms of raising its tariffs while the power supply situation worsened.

According to Ugwuh (2005), the dismal performance in the sector was painted by a survey which revealed that manufacturers in Nigeria generate about 72 per cent of the total power required to run their factories and, in some extreme cases, some companies operate independent of NEPA. The discernible unsatisfactory financial performance by NEPA made it unable to mobilize sufficient investment capital outside the budget for power development. Moreover, numerous customers of the parastatal, particularly the government and its parastatals, account for a large share of the huge debt owed to the power utility. For example, over 30 billion naira was owed to the power utility as at 2001.

Table 13.2 Unit selling price of electricity (kobo)

	1987	**1988**	**1989**	**1990**	**1991**
NEPA	7.1	7.5	20.1	33.8	32.8
NESCO	2.9	4.1	4.1	8.5	9.4

Source: Sule and Anyanwu (1994).

Table 13.3 System losses (%)

	1987	**1988**	**1989**	**1990**	**1991**
NEPA	32.8	35.0	31.2	39.7	43.2
NESCO	9.1	8.4	9.5	10.2	10.7

Source: Sule and Anyanwu (1994).

This underperformance culminated in the drive for the reform of the power sector. In the realization of this objective, the federal government passed a law to reform the energy sector and create an electricity sector in the country that would be competitive and market driven. Other objectives of the law are: to create, promote and preserve an efficient electricity sector; to maximize access to electricity (both urban and rural); to ensure that prices are fair to both consumers and regulated companies; and to ensure the safety, security, reliability and quality of service.

The new electricity law, which is a trendsetter for the sub-Saharan Africa region, is very progressive and also provides for open access to the grid along with bilateral contracts between generators and consumers.

13.3 Recent developments in the power sector

A set of comprehensive efforts has been undertaken since 1999 in order to boost the performance of the sector. This is based on the declining performance of NEPA in providing quality power for consumers in the country over the years. Such efforts include massive rehabilitation of power infrastructure, construction of emergency power plants and promotion of the development of independent power plants.

13.3.1 Generation

The sector has experienced a boost in the generating capacity, which was achieved following the concerted efforts by the government to bridge the generation, transmission and distribution gap that had existed in the power sector. The strategy employed involved obtaining private sector participation through a combination of rehabilitation of old plants, installation of new plants, and construction of emergency power plants.

Emergency power project (EPP)

In order to alleviate the electricity supply problems in some parts of the country, a total of 50 MW of diesel-fired emergency power project (EPP) was contracted for the Federal Capital.This was executed through Geometric (35 MW) and Geometric/Renatec (15 MW) until the completion of the 330 kV line and associated substations being constructed to bring additional power from Shiroro to Abuja. The Abuja EPP was terminated after the completion of the substations in 2004.

Rehabilitate-operate-and-transfer (ROT)

Given the huge cost associated with the rehabilitation of generating plants, the federal government decided to attract private sector capital and technical expertise by approving the implementation of rehabilitate-operate-and-transfer (ROT) programmes at NEPA's power stations in Afam and Sapele. Shell and AES were to rehabilitate the Afam and Sapele power stations, respectively, from which an additional 1150 MW (Afam 450 MW, Sapele 700 MW) was expected when completed. Table 13.4 lists the existing generating facilities in the country. The government further approved various sums of money for the rehabilitation of some of the plants like Egbin, Kainji and Shiroro power plants. Also, in 2004 the federal government started the construction of four new independent power plants at Papalanto in Ogun State, Alaoji in Delta State, Omotosho in Ondo State and Geregu in Kogi State to generate 1234 MW as well as seven new gas-fired plants in the Niger Delta region following a presidential committee recommendation.

Independent power plants (IPPs)

With demand outstripping supply, independent power projects are becoming a major source of new power generation capacity and have thus opened the way for private sector participation. In pursuance of the drive towards attracting private sector capital and efficiency into the generation sector, NEPA (now Power Holding Company of Nigeria) officials and consultants had discussions and negotiations with several potential independent power producers with the view to engaging them in satisfying the supply gap in the electricity sector in the country. Furthermore, the federal government launched the National Integrated Power Project (NIPP) to build independent power plants (IPPs) with a generating capacity of 4500 MW. The federal government also invited all oil Joint Venture Companies

Table 13.4 Status of existing power generating stations on national grid (as of 1 January 2007)

Station	Type	Installed capability (MW)	Present capability (MW)
EGBIN	ST 6×220	1320	1045
AES	GT 9×33.5	300	234.
SAPELE	ST 6×120	720	158
SAPELE	GT 4×75	300	0
IJORA	GT 3×20	60	0
DELTA	GT 20 units	1205	520
AFAM	GT 20 units	990	200.
CALABAR	Diesel 6 units	11	1
KAINJI	Hydro 8 units	760	320
JEBBA	Hydro 6 units	578	180
SHIRORO	Hydro 4 units	600	300
OKPAI	GT 8 units	480	140
Trans Amadi, Rivers	GT 4 units	100	36
		7424	3134

ST, steam turbine; GT, gas turbine; MW, megawatts.

(JVC) partners to assist in the development of the power sector by investing in IPPs. In response to the federal government's call for more investments by the private sector in the electric power sector, many state governments and oil-producing companies, and two companies from China and Korea, embarked on various power projects throughout the country. For instance, the Lagos State government built a 270 MW capacity plant, which was commissioned in April 2002 and run by AES and designed mainly to feed the Lagos metropolis. The Rivers State government also completed a 36 MW power plant at Trans Amadi in Port Harcourt, which was commissioned in October 2002. Other states, including Akwa Ibom, Kwara, Jigawa, Nassarawa and Imo, similarly embarked on the construction of independent power plants. Power purchase agreements (PPAs) have already been signed with some of the independent power producers.

Consequently, total generation (MWh) rose from 1689.9 in 2001 to 2237.3 in 2002, 2398.5 in 2003 and 2763.6 in 2004. It was 2779.3 MWh in 2005.

Table 13.5 provides a matrix of the PHCN power generation projects under implementation, while Table 13.6 shows the power generation projects that are under implementation under the National Integrated Power Project.

The government of Nigeria has thus embarked on an ambitious programme of increasing its generation capacity to around 15,000 MW from the current level of 3300 MW. These capacity additions are required in view of the severe power generation capacity crunch the country is experiencing, and so the government should make all efforts to go ahead in this direction. At the same time, the government will have to carefully review several aspects related to these projects in order to ensure that these projects do not impose a burden that the sector cannot sustain.

There can be different perceptions and views on the issue of power purchase agreements as well as the securitization packages. It is critical to ensure that the process attains the principal objective of ensuring that Nigeria optimizes the benefits from these capacity additions with proper resolution of relevant issues associated with these initiatives.

The proposed IPPs have several implications for the power sector in view of their long-term impact. In view of the proposed securatization packages being contemplated, these agreements could prove to be a major burden on the financial

Table 13.5 PHCN power generation projects under implementation (January 2007)

Name of Plant	Generation type	Capacity (name plate, MW)
Gerego Thermal Power Station, Kogi State	Gas turbine	414
Omotosho Thermal Power Station, Ondo State	Gas turbine	335
Papalanto Thermal Power Station, Ogun State	Gas turbine	335
Aloiji Therrmal Power Station, Abia State	Gas turbine	504
Total, on-going PHCN projects		*1588*

Table 13.6 NIPP power generation projects under implementation (January 2007)

Name of plant	Generation type	Capacity (name plate, MW)
Calabar Thermal Power Station, River State	Gas Turbine	564
Egbema Thermal Power Station, Imo State	Gas Turbine	338
Eyaen Thermal Power Station, Edo State	Gas Turbine	451
Gbarain/Ube Thermal Power Station, Bayelsa State	Gas Turbine	225
Ibom Power, Thermal Power Station	Gas Turbine, Combined Cycle Ext	188
Ikot Abasi Thermal Power Station, Delta State	Gas Turbine	300
Sapele Thermal Power Station, Delta State	Gas Turbine	451
Omoku Thermal Power Station, River State	Gas Turbine	225
Total, On-going NIPP projects		*2742*

NIPP, National Integrated Power Project

resources of the government as a whole. Table 13.7 lists the status of proposed major power projects, and Table 13.8 lists planned independent power projects.

- The proposed power purchase agreements have a contracted 'dispatch' capacity of 20 years with take or pay features, whereas the project investments in the case of the joint venture IPPs are proposed to be recovered over a lesser period of time. Since the capacity prices are indexed to OECD Consumer Price Index (CPI) and wage indices, these projects could prove to be a major drain on the sector.
- The Engineering, Procurement and Construction (EPC) contracts need to be transparent and competitively bid. Otherwise it would be difficult to conduct proper diligence on the costs. Similarly, non-disclosure of the cost of financing, and in particular resorting to the use of affiliate companies, also renders the costs involved non-transparent. Another cause for concern is the full recourse of project liabilities and guarantees to power purchasers. In this scenario, the issue of liquidated damages and deemed capacity, as opposed to actual generation, and metering will pose difficult challenges ahead.
- Inclusion of gas development costs within the IPP power tariffs involves guarantee of the direct exploration risks of the major gas producers. These gas development costs which are in the PPA agreements cover exploration risks, capacity and North American CPI, all of which are locked in for 20 years, even though cost recovery is guaranteed within five years. Hence, it is preferable that the gas pricing issues are segregated through an independent gas supply agreement.
- Another implication could be that the international credit rating agencies will require Nigeria to capitalize the PPA capacity prices, which are denominated

Table 13.7 Status of planned major power projects

Location of power plant	Capacity (MW)	Status	Remarks
Egbema, Rivers	338	Proposed	
Lagos	540	Proposed	
Omoku, Rivers	230	Being test-run	Transmission infrastructure under construction
Calabar, Cross Rivers	561	Proposed	
Eyaen, Edo	451	Proposed	
Imo, Oguta	540	Proposed (MOU signed with a US-based company)	
Ikot Abasi, Akwa Ibom	300	Proposed (MOU signed with Eskom SA)	
Ibom, Akwa Ibom	188	Proposed	
Sapele Delta	450	Proposed	
Gbarain, Bayelsa	225	Proposed	
Ilorin, Kwara	105	Proposed (MOU signed with Alliance Energy Ltd)	
Kolo Creek/Nun River, Bayelsa	60	Working but being rehabilitated	The only source of electric power in the state
Mambilla	2600	Proposed	Hydro facility
Zungero	950	Proposed	Hydro facility
Gerego, Papalanto, Omotosho, Aloji	2300	Proposed combined cycle extensions	
Afam VI – Shell	500	Proposed gas turbine	
Exxon Mobil – Bonny Island	388	Proposed gas turbine	
Farm Electric Ltd	150	Proposed gas turbine	
Ethiope Energy Ltd	2800	Proposed gas turbine	
ICS Power Ltd	624	Proposed gas turbine	
Supertek Nigeria Ltd	1000	Proposed gas turbine	
Enugu Power Plant	2000	Coal plant – under discussion with Eskom SA	
ABB Power Plant – Abuja	450		

MOU, memorandum of understanding.

Table 13.8 Independent power projects by indigenous and foreign companies under implementation

State	Company	Location of IPP	Capacity (MW)	Remarks
Lagos	ENCON	Ikorodu	100	Financed by IFC
Lagos	Shell/Agbara Estates Ltd	Agbara	40	
Ogun	ENCON	Ota	200	
Rivers	ROCSON, USA	Okoloma	700	Connected to the national grid
Rivers	TotalFinaElf		400	
Rivers	Shell	Afam	700	
Rivers	Exxon Mobil	Bonny	388	
Abia	Geometrics	Aba	120	Financed by IFC
Kogi	Dangote	Obajana	350	
Total			*3448*	

in foreign exchange, and locked in for 20 years, as part of the country's international debt profile.

- The Ministry of Finance is being called upon to securitize these PPA capacity prices, when it does not have full information to assess their value over time. It is difficult to determine the costs involved as sufficient information (such as due diligence of EPC contracts) is not available for deploying the rate base or the return on rate base methodologies.
- Prospects for privatization of sector entities, particularly the distribution companies, are bound to be affected given that the proposed securatization package provides the IPPs a first call over the revenues and the special purpose entity.

Ideally instead, each party should guarantee their own risks, and full cost recovery should be provided through an appropriate fiscal regime. The IPP could charge the fuel cost as a pass through in its tariff. A solution could be to create a capacity formula, which can be reset, after cost recovery of the fixed assets, assuming financing costs will also have been amortized. The alternative is to limit the term of the PPA, in the first instance to five years, and to renegotiate the terms after cost recovery. Once the capacity pricing formula is reset to reflect the return of rate base, power costs will face considerable reduction. Also, the proposed agreements seek to extend various upstream fiscal incentives such as those associated with oil and gas exploration to these IPP investments apart from others such as import duty exemption. These should be monetized and factored into the PPA. The significant savings that could be achieved in this fashion would potentially enable the current power sector tariff revenue, and any tariff increases, to adequately meet all payment obligations.

Appropriate resolution of these issues along with an appropriate domestic gas pricing regime (which has recently been announced) will render the tariffs economic and sustainable. The private sector is also exposed to considerable risk due to unsustainable agreements. Hence, in order to avoid undue burden and potential adverse consequences to both parties, the PPAs and the securitization packages should incorporate these features after careful review.

13.3.2 Transmission

Under the National Integrated Power Project (NIPP) being implemented with government funding, the Transmission Development Project (TDP) and the National Energy Development Project (NEDP) being implemented with World Bank assistance, considerable efforts are being made to enhance the transmission infrastructure. These include: Markurdi–Jos 286 km DC 330 kV substations; New Heaven–Markurdi 245 km DC 330 kV substations; Ikot Ekpene–New Heaven 249 km 2*DC 330 kV substations; Afam–Ikot Ekpene 150 km DC 330 substations; Ikot Abassi–Eket–Uyo–Itu 117 km DC 132 kV substations; and Omoku–Egbema–Owerri–Onitsha 195 km DC 330 kV substations. Others include: Ikorodu–Erukan–Alausa 75 km DC 132 kV substations; Benin North–Asaba 132 km DC 132 kV substations; Idofian–Ganmo 14 km DC 132 kV substations; and substation extensions at Ikeja West, Oworonsoki, Agbara and Ojo.

While these transmission infrastructure improvements are critical to ensure that transmission bottlenecks and constraints are removed to evacuate the significant power injection that will take place as a result of capacity additions, it is also important to put in place the necessary infrastructure, legal and institutional frameworks to optimize the benefits from the transmission improvements as well as to sustain them with adequate revenue streams. Development of an efficient wholesale market is essential for this to happen.

Development of an efficient wholesale electricity market

Nigeria has undertaken the following steps for establishing a wholesale electricity market: (1) the legal framework for open access has already been unveiled through the Electric Power Sector Reform Act; (2) the Regulatory Commission has already been established and has been functioning; (3) the institution of market operator has been established and is operational; (4) the required infrastructure for the Energy Management System/Supervisory Control and Data Acquisition System (EMS/SCADA) is being constructed. While achieving a liberalized wholesale market seems far-fetched in the short run, it is expected that the market will mature with multiple and significant players as well as infrastructure and operational improvements in generation, transmission and distribution sectors in the long run. It should, however, be recognized that, given the structure of the Nigerian power market today, and the severe power shortages, a wholesale market cannot be envisioned in the near future. However, significant planned capacity additions could move the sector in that direction.

Market operator and an independent system operator

As the unbundled entities of the former NEPA are now fully corporatized, the market operator has assumed responsibility to channel revenue streams from the distribution companies to the transmission and generation companies. The average bulk tariff levied on the distribution companies is 4 naira/kWh. It is evident that this tariff level is only sustainable for the strongest distribution companies and substantial subsidies are still needed to fill the revenue gaps to assure adequate maintenance of the existing grid and payment to independent generators. Given the large constraints on generation capacity and the general shortage of available electricity, the bulk power supply is divided between the distribution companies based on their respective share of past consumption through so-called 'vesting contracts'. As the power supply increases, the share of supply will increase proportionally until the constraints are fully relieved as projected in 2010.

13.3.3 Distribution

By 1999, the distribution sub-sector was in dire need of upgrading because many of its 22,000 distribution transformers and 680 injection substations were overloaded. To enhance the capacity to distribute the quantum of additional power being generated, the government has invested huge sums of money in this sector since 1999. Under the NIPP, the World Bank-assisted NEDP and the TDP, there is an ongoing capacity expansion of distribution infrastructure to 2666 km of 11 kV lines, 1701 km of 33 kV lines, 3540 MVA additional injection capacity and 22,598 distribution transformers. It is expected that this effort would help reduce the system average interruption index and annual average total duration of power interruption to consumers. In terms of funding, NEPA has received improved funding from the government since 1999. Although total receipts have fallen short of both proposed and allocated funds under the budgets, in 2004 NEPA received full funding from the 2004 federal government budgetary allocation as actual receipts in 2004 amounted to 46.476 billion naira.

In addition, net grants received by NEPA from the federal government, which the authority applies to the rehabilitation of generation, transmission and distribution infrastructure, had remained substantial, and were 82.9 billion naira in 2002, 91.8 billion naira in 2003 and 126.4 billion naira in 2004 (Figure 13.3). NEPA's metered customers rose from 3.3 million in 2001 to 4,656,000 and 4,805,000 in 2002 and 2003, respectively. Customer population, however, dropped to 4.56 million in 2004 as a result of a data sanitation exercise. By 2007, NEPA's distribution business was unbundled and the aggregate revenues of the successor distribution companies averaged 7.75 billion naira per month.

In the electricity distribution sector, as in other infrastructure areas, it is important to produce efficient results on commercial principles, provide good customer service, sustain the assets and scale them up. Since 2003, the Nigerian power utility, with the assistance of the World Bank, has developed a methodology called CREST (Commercial Reorientation of Electricity Sector Toolkit) to introduce and foster the mechanisms that put the sector on this path of efficiency. CREST is a

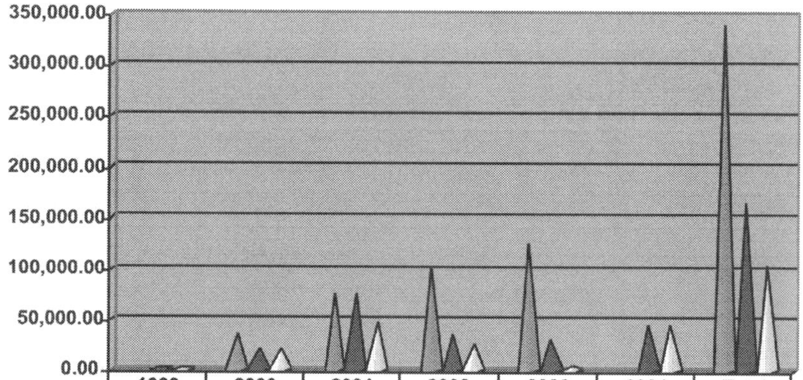

	1999	2000	2001	2002	2003	2004	Total
Proposed	-	36,036.00	75,151.00	102,303.0	125,313.0	-	338,803.0
Allocatio	2,206.00	23,014.00	75,000.00	35,000.00	31,000.00	46,476.00	166,220.0
Receipt	2,206.00	23,014.00	47,905.00	27,040.00	5,207.00	46,476.00	105,374.0

Figure 13.3 Federal government expenditure on the power sector.

way of making the electricity infrastructure work more efficiently and deliver better results.

The CREST programme is based on global best practice, particularly from distribution operations in India, the US and Europe. The programme seeks to introduce efficiencies into electricity distribution management through a best practice framework that is anchored on the following principles:

- *right incentives* for distribution business to be a net cash generator for (i) reduced tariffs in the long run and for supply of quality power, and (ii) gradually eliminating the need for government support;
- *operational philosophy* to change from that of a service provider to that of retail trade in electricity;
- *re-engineering business processes* with innovative technology adaptations, leveraging information technology for efficiency, energy balancing, performance monitoring, and new HR practices;
- *reorienting the market* with introduction of competition, well established regulation, standards of service, retail outsourcing and developing technical and human skills within the local market, for sustainable private sector participation.

13.4 Institutional reforms in the power sector

Power sector reform involves management or ownership changes in the structure of the sector and introduction of a stable and credible sector regulation (Turkson, 2005). Management or ownership changes involve the reform of the public monopolies to operate as commercial entities with varying degrees of private sector involvement such as management contract, selling out non-core activities of the industry, partial privatization, and full privatization of the core activities of the industry. Structural changes on the other hand involve partial or complete unbundling of the generation, transmission and distribution activities of the industry into separate business units, and introduction of competition and an incentive-based regulatory system in the industry. Following government's renewed focus on the electric power sector the Electric Power Sector Reform (EPSR) Act was enacted.

13.4.1 Key features of the EPSR Act

- The NEPA Initial Holding Company (IHC) formed within six months, with the shares to be held jointly by the Bureau of Public Enterprises (BPE) and Ministry of Finance. Assets and liabilities of NEPA to be transferred to the IHC.
- Staff of NEPA to be transferred to IHC or the Regulatory Commission.
- All rights and obligations (such as pensions) to be properly maintained and allocated.
- Incorporation of NEPA successor companies within eight months of initial transfer date with shares in successor companies to be held jointly by Ministry of Finance and BPE, and assets, liabilities and employees of IHC to be transferred to successor companies within one year.
- The Act provides for National Electricity Regulatory Commission to be set up as a formal, independent regulatory agency and governs the appointment and tenure of its six commissioners.
- NERC and Licensee(s) shall develop:
  - customer service standards;
  - customer complaint handling standards and procedures;
  - codes of practice for the needs of special customers;
  - procedures for dealing with customers who have difficulty paying bills;
  - procedures for applying for electricity service;
  - procedures for disconnecting non-paying customers;
  - information to be made available to consumers, and the manner of its dissemination.
- A Rural Electrification Agency to be established and operate under the close supervision of the Minister of Power and Steel.
- A Rural Electrification Fund will be established to promote access of electricity to rural areas.

13.4.2 Sector regulation

Major initiatives of the Nigeria Electricity Regulatory Commission (NERC), since its formation, include development and issuance of a Multi Year Tariff Order (MYTO), development of a grid code, customer satisfaction, metering and efficiency standards. NERC also proposes to benchmark technical and commercial quality of service at the distribution level that would be a natural outgrowth of the performance code that will be drafted by the end of the year. Apart from this, the NERC has initiated an exercise to benchmark power purchase agreements, through the proposed rule-making exercise with assistance from the World Bank. The rule would require that generation licensees that operate certain generation facilities (above 100 MW and selling to purchasers who resell to captive customers) would be required to complete a series of questionnaires and tables. The questionnaires and tables would allow the Commission to review and benchmark the price terms and risk allocation provisions of proposed PPAs. The motivation for the proposed rule is that it would allow NERC to fulfil its statutory obligation to ensure that purchases are economical and tariffs are fair and balanced for both consumers and investors. By providing a systematic checklist of key features and observed values, NERC's review of individual PPAs and benchmarking across PPAs is likely to lead to better PPAs and fewer disputes in the future. It is also anticipated that the proposed rule could later lead to future NERC actions on developing a model PPA and guidance on future competitive bidding rules. This exercise requires extensive consultations with key industry stakeholders.

13.4.3 Rural Electrification Strategy and development of renewable energy

The federal government has set a target of achieving 75 per cent rural electrification from the current low level of 40 per cent. In this connection, a Rural Electrification Strategy and Plan have been developed to include (i) the expansion of the main grid, (ii) the development of isolated and mini-grid systems, (iii) creating an enabling environment to provoke investment in renewable energy power generation, and (iv) fostering public–private partnerships in the supply of electricity to the rural populace. The policy seeks to achieve the following targets against which the performance would be measured: (a) ensuring that 75 per cent of rural population have reliable electricity by 2020; (b) providing electricity to all local government headquarters and other strategic towns and villages by 2010; (c) reducing cost per connection of rural electricity schemes on a sustainable basis. These policy goals and objectives would be coordinated by the Rural Electrification Agency (REA). The strategy being contemplated by the REA for rural access expansion comprises two elements: (a) activities related to pilot projects aimed at testing innovative approaches to electricity access expansion in rural and peri-urban areas; (b) activities related to implementation support for the National Renewable Energy Master Plan.

A National Renewable Energy Master Plan (REMP) has been prepared by the Energy Commission, and the Ministry of Energy is in the process of launching its implementation. By the end of 2007 the REMP envisages an aggregate electricity demand of 7000 MW, with new renewable energy (excluding large-scale hydro) playing a marginal role. In 2015 Nigeria will probably achieve a doubling of electricity demand to about 14,000 MW of which new renewables will constitute about 5 per cent (701 MW). In 2025, aggregate electricity demand will increase to 29,000 MW with new renewable energy making up 10 per cent of the overall energy demand of the country. Small hydro plants will represent over 66 per cent of the entire new renewable energy contribution, solar photovoltaic (PV)

17 per cent, biomass 14 per cent, wind 1.3 per cent and solar thermal 0.7 per cent. The total cost of REMP implementation up to 2025 is projected at 610 billion naira or about $4.8 billion.

13.4.4 Privatization of the power sector entities

The earlier legal and regulatory framework in Nigeria's power sector was mainly designed for regulated power utility with little or no provision for private sector participation. The passage of the EPSR Act therefore introduced important regulatory changes which involve dismantling the monopoly of NEPA. This is aimed at encouraging competition and efficiency through private participation, specifically in generation and distribution of electricity.

The Initial Holding Company

As part of the provision of bill, the National Council on Privatisation (NCP) in 2005 formed the Power Holding Company of Nigeria (PHCN), which took over the assets and liabilities of NEPA. The shares of the company are held by the Ministry of Finance and BPE on behalf of the federal government, while the process of transferring the employees of NEPA to the service of either the NERC or the PHCN is in progress.

The Successor Companies

In order to prepare the PHCN for eventual privatization, the company's activities were unbundled into smaller units based on their essential functions: generation, transmission and distribution. The aim was to make each of the units a fully business-oriented outfit. The exercise resulted in the formation of 18 business units made up of six generating units (GENCOs), one transmission unit (TRANSYSCO) and 11 distribution units (DISCOs). The GENCOs were made up of the existing power generating stations at Egbin, Kainji, Shiroro, Jebba, Afam, Sapele, Ughelli Ijora and Calabar. Each of the GENCOs was saddled with the responsibility of generating power and supplying to the DISCOs via the TRANSYSCO, at an agreed rate. On account of the structure of the Nigerian electric transmission lines (radial), only one transmitting business unit was formed to sell electric power to the DISCOs, thus making it a single buyer model for the present. The 11 distribution units were therefore charged with the responsibility of getting electric power supply down to the final consumers, collecting the bills, paying the GENCOs and the TRANSYSCO, and then carrying out necessary activities that would boost the performance of the authority. Each of the DISCOs was further divided into business districts for ease of administration. Eventually, it is expected that the single buyer model will transit into a multi-buyer model in which the distribution companies and other consumers will be able to have bilateral contracts with the generating companies and the TRANSYSCO will then essentially perform a wheeling and load dispatching function. Once that transition takes place, the need for an independent System Operator to manage the load dispatching function in conjunction with the market operator may arise.

Nigeria Electricity Liquidation Management Agency

As a transition measure, all long-term assets, liabilities and residual items (pension and other unfunded liabilities) have been parked in this Agency, so that these can be liquidated in an orderly manner over the long term. While this is an appropriate mechanism, consistent with international practices, the only important consideration is that the mandate of the agency, along with relevant rules and regulations for liquidation, needs to be clearly spelt out.

Service entity for successor companies

Upon the completion of the unbundling and corporatization process, the need for an entity (especially for six generation and 11 distribution companies) is being felt. The major needs are in the areas of corporate planning (least-cost generation expansion, load-flow analysis, system protection, investment analysis, project preparation and evaluation), financial management (financing of investments, evaluation of options, financial instruments), commercial operations (pricing and tariff analysis, customer service options) and procurement function (bidding processes, contracts). There are instances of formation of such a 'service entity' created for meeting the above needs of the successor companies on a commercial basis in other countries that have embarked on similar reform programmes. This entity could build on capacity already generated in the sector for implementing large projects and can evolve into a corporate planning and strategic entity that can provide these services, not only to the successor entities in the Nigerian power sector, but also to entities in other sectors in Nigeria and in the region.

Rightsizing and pension issues

As the BPE embarks on the privatization of these successor entities it is critical to consider the staff rightsizing and pension issues. The liaison unit, which has replaced the PHCN, and the successor companies are still in the process of developing a rightsizing and redeployment plan. The power utilities are now contemplating joining the new pension scheme in accordance with the provisions of the Pension Reform Act of 2004. Commencing the new scheme will enhance the enabling environment, provide comfort to employees and potential private operators, and facilitate faster privatization.

13.5 Efficiency and investment issues in Nigeria's power sector reforms

The need for large-scale investments in power infrastructure have prompted the actions of successive governments in Nigeria in financing the sector's capital and operational needs. This had tended to crowd out the private sector as well as issues of efficiency. For example, issues such as efficient pricing of infrastructural services like electricity have not received adequate attention, while prices had been kept artificially low to ensure that input prices into other sectors remain low. It is therefore expected that the reforms in the electric power sector meant to attract domestic and foreign private investment will also ensure efficiency in service delivery. This section therefore explores some of the expected efficiency and investments issues that would spur growth in the sector.

13.5.1 Efficiency issues

Improved management of utilities

The record of unsatisfactory technical and financial performance of NEPA has been observed to be associated with the quality of management. The reform programme is therefore expected to address this issue. For example, the unwieldy staff strength of NEPA (which was 30,428 in 2001, 29,994 in 2002, 30,269 in 2003 and 31,668 in 2004, see Figure 13.4) needs to be rightsized, as a bloated labour force contributes to higher operational costs. This is important, as it has been recognized that the cost of poor utility management in the past has been transferred to the population at large in the form of higher prices. The ratio of customers per employee appears to be ridiculously low and reflects inefficient utilization of resources.

It is expected that private participation and increased competitiveness in the sector will radically improve this. For example, as a result of the reform and in line with the objective of unbundling NEPA into 18 new business units to ensure efficiency in generation, transmission and distribution, key performance indicators which would guide efficiency were developed.

The CREST approach described in the earlier section is an effort by the distribution successor entities to improve efficiency. Nigeria has large investment requirements. In view of this, any investment influx will not demonstrate the desired impact unless it is directed to achieve specific outcomes in identified areas. In order to address this concern, the distribution entities are adopting a cluster approach. Clusters are a group of customers that are served by an electrically demarcated distribution and sub-transmission network. The CREST programme and

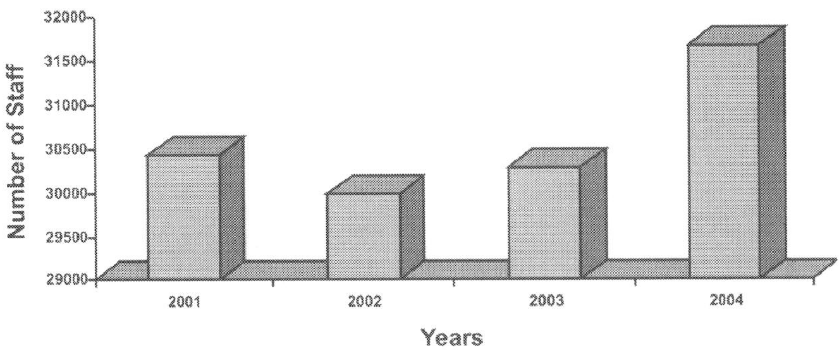

Figure 13.4 NEPA staff strength.

related investments would be implemented in these clusters to create 'islands of excellence'. Efforts would be made to develop these clusters in such a way that measurable and tangible improvements would be targeted in these clusters in terms of improved distribution sector performance that would lead to improved revenues, reduced losses and enhanced customer satisfaction in terms of quality of supply, reduced fault redressal times and reduced billing complaints. These investments will strengthen the distribution infrastructure, improve quality of supply and customer satisfaction, and facilitate realization of potential in the sector to be a net cash generator instead of being the burden that it is currently on the economy. Some of the areas where this approach is being followed include Karu, Kubwa, Luth, Ogba, Agege, Idi Araba, and Challenge (Ibadan). The first CREST pilot in the Wuse area has been completed at a cost of $5 million and has yielded very good results in terms of improved quality of supply, customer satisfaction and better commercial performance from the utility. Encouraged by the results of the pilot, the government of Nigeria has decided to scale up this programme, particularly its main component – the High Voltage Distribution System – throughout the country. The World Bank projects are also following this up with about $100 million. Two points worth mentioning are that (i) the Nigerian government is adopting the project governance framework, including specifications, bidding packages, standards and processes designed under the CREST programme and (ii) the CREST involves carrying out small-scale works with mostly private local enterprises, which contributes to promotion of local capacity and services.

Since the initiation of the reform programme in 2003 along with efficiency initiatives such as the CREST programme, the revenues of the sector have gone up from 4 billion naira a month to 7.5 billion naira. The system losses have also been reported to have come down by 9 per cent.

13.5.2 Tariff

The establishment of NERC is expected to facilitate the emergence of an appropriate tariff which would take into account the interest of all stakeholders. Hitherto, the government has adhered to the belief that low-priced electricity is critical to achieving economic and social development. Therefore, the tariff was hardly changed, the average end-user retail tariff remaining at 5.9 naira per kWh, among the lowest in the continent. Given that it does not cover costs, the regulator is now expected to move towards a cost-reflective tariff regime. The current thinking is to move to tariffs that will allow a reasonable return on investments while providing incentives to maintain and expand deliveries to the people. For example, between 2001 and 2004, NEPA's average unit prices of electricity were 3.38 naira, 3.39 naira, 2.77 naira and 4.20 naira, while the average unit costs of electricity were 4.06 naira, 4.72 naira, 6.50 naira and 6.32 naira, respectively (Figure 13.5). Thus the gap between unit cost and unit price of electricity remains reasonably wide; this cannot be covered by efficiency improvements alone. After unbundling of NEPA in 2004, the prices have remained stagnant while the successor company-wise costs, which have risen, are as yet unclear with apportioning of assets and liabilities still under way.

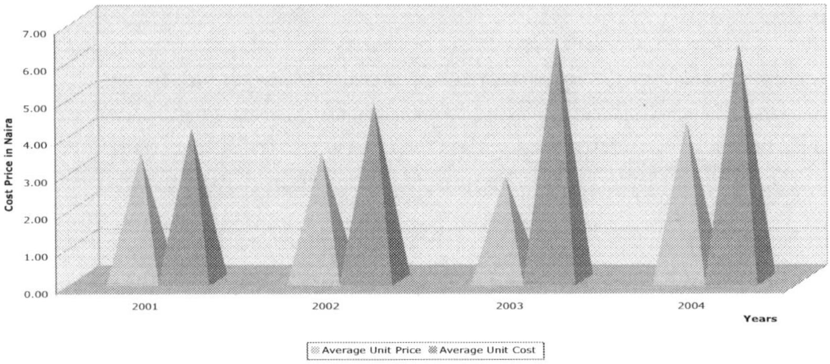

Figure 13.5 NEPA's cost and price of electricity.

Under existing practice, NEPA appeared to operate a baseline tariff strategy in which there were lower prices up to a certain level of consumption (Table 13.7).

13.5.3 Reducing energy loss and power theft

Overall, the issue of efficiency also has implications on the level of energy loss in the system. This is because energy loss represents loss of revenue to energy providers. Some of these losses cannot be explained from a technical point of view and are a reflection of management inefficiency. Such losses have been traceable to metering problems such as meter bypassing and tampering, or rent-seeking behaviour among meter readers, illegal connections to the grid, revenue collection problems and non-payment of bills. The reform programme is expected to address these issues. It is expected that the management of the new entities in the sector would deploy adequate resources and expertise to ensure accurate billing and steady regular income collection. For example, collection efficiency is expected to increase from 70 per cent to 95 per cent while distribution capacity would increase from 8425 MVA to 15,165 MVA. Moreover, the distribution companies are expected to be commercially oriented with marked efficiency in operations. Energy losses through transmission and distribution networks are also expected to be minimized as the companies in this sector would be able to properly manage the system. It is therefore expected that transmission and distribution losses will be reduced from 44.5 per cent to 15 per cent while transmission capacity will increase from 5838 MVA to 9340 MVA in due course. The CREST approach described earlier will be an important tool for the sector in achieving loss reduction, particularly in the distribution sector. Recognizing this fact, the government of Nigeria has allocated around $1 billion under NIPP for distribution programmes which follow CREST principles.

13.5.4 Carbon finance opportunities in the power sector

There is an opportunity for the Nigerian power sector to leverage carbon finance from the energy loss reduction and efficiency programmes embarked upon by it. Some initiatives have been identified in this context. The Nigerian power sector entities have been developing the related methodologies to access carbon finance for these initiatives.

Sulphur hexafluoride (SF_6) gas is released during repair and replacement of switchgear material in the electricity grid. SF_6 is a highly potent gas covered under the Kyoto Protocol. By following certain best practice processes, such SF_6 releases can be reduced. The methodology proposed by the World Bank, based on SF_6 emission reductions in the Nigerian transmission grid, was recently approved by the United Nations Framework for Climate Change (UNFCC) methodology panel. This was the first SF_6 methodology to be approved under the Kyoto Protocol and represents a major breakthrough on emission trading of SF_6. The Transmission Corporation of Nigeria (TRANSYSCO or TCN) project is expected to generate approximately $5 million worth of carbon credit revenues in exchange for reduced greenhouse gas emissions over the years from 2008 to 2012. The TCN is currently finalizing the Emission Reduction Purchase Agreement in this context. This represents the first step by the Nigerian power sector entities in accessing the benefits of the Clean Development Mechanism under the Kyoto Protocol.

The conversion to High Voltage Distribution Systems as part of the CREST programme leads to significant technical loss reductions and therefore substantial reduction of carbon emissions due to avoided generation. Since a cluster-based approach is being adopted for the CREST interventions, application of small-scale methodology is being considered. The relevant data are being developed for the Karu CREST cluster in the Abuja Distribution Company area. It is hoped that that this will lead to an Emission Reduction Purchase Agreement in due course.

13.5.5 Investment issues

The target of increasing electric power generation in the country to 10,000 MW by 2007 has been set under the National Economic Empowerment and Development Strategy (NEEDS). In an effort to achieve this target, government has invested huge sums of money in the sector since 1999, but this has been inadequate. This has prompted the need for the attraction of huge private sector investment into the sector, especially in power generation and transmission. According to NEPA (2004), about $1.54 billion is required for the development of the Nigerian transmission grid to cope with the effective evacuation of 6500 MW. The investment requirement for achieving 50 per cent access to electricity by 2020 is about $300 million a year. An estimated $2.5 billion spread over seven years is the minimum budgetary support needed. Also, over the same period an estimated $3.5 billion of private investments are expected to flow into the sector. Currently, the oil companies operating in the country have made some efforts to complement the government's effort in power generation by embarking on the construction of independent power plants. Moreover, unbundling of transmission into TCN is expected to result in source funding from bilateral and multilateral institutions for the development of additional transmission capacity. Furthermore, since one of the main objectives of sector regulation is to attract private sector investment into the industry, it is expected that the NERC will make rules that will guarantee a business-friendly environment through cost-reflective tariff and cost recovery.

Also, the provision of stable and predictable regulatory systems would assure investment protection.

13.5.6 Increasing the sector's access to finance

High debt profile and the loss-making business of the state-owned utility monopolies are major impediments to ready access to finance from financial institutions. The World Bank is already assisting the power sector entities with $272 million in various projects. The NIPP has allocated $9.1 billion for power sector investments. With the ongoing reforms, which are expected to usher in improved efficiency, this problem will perhaps be addressed. Moreover, it is expected that, as the power sector reform progresses, the federal government will consider converting to equity all deferred and overdue debt service and loans to the sector, and would absorb the burden of unfunded liabilities such as pension costs. This will undoubtedly improve the financial leverage of the business units. Access to finance has been identified as a major obstacle to private sector participation in businesses in Nigeria. The reform in the banking sector, particularly the consolidation programme, however, is expected to provide the needed financial elixir. This would task the locally recapitalized banks with developing special financing packages for investors. Also, the capital market is expected to respond adequately to the challenges of providing capital for operators in the power sector. The World Bank group is also actively exploring providing support with risk-mitigation instruments to attract private sector participation and capital in the sector.

13.6 Lessons from other countries

A review of the experiences of other countries carried out by Newbery (2002) provides a useful insight into power sector reforms which could guide policy actions in Nigeria.

13.6.1 Chile

Following the passage of the electricity law in 1982, Chile's two state-owned integrated companies, ENDESA and Chilectra, were divided into separate generation and local distribution companies. ENDESA was divided into five separate generating companies and eight distribution companies. The interconnected transmission system, however, was placed under ENDESA, giving it potentially preferential access and storing up problems for the future. The restructured companies were subsequently privatized and by 1991 there were 11 power generating companies, 21 electricity distribution companies and two integrated transmission companies. Chilegener, one of the competing generating companies, increased its profit, investment and productivity after divestiture. The increase in profit was due to a move to marginal cost pricing and increased capacity utilization, thanks to improved regulation. The sequencing of reform in Chile is instructive in that the reform of the regulatory system and the restructuring of state enterprises occurred first, to ensure that the new enterprises had some experience of the regulatory regime before privatization. Privatization proceeded slowly, avoiding some risks of underpricing with attendant large transfers to shareholders, while wide share ownership created political support for the new system.

13.6.2 Argentina

Argentina started its reforms in 1992 and applied most of the lessons it learned from Chile's experience. The reform started by transforming the structure, ownership and regulation of its electricity supply industry. The generating companies were split into smaller units such that no generator had more than 10 per cent of capacity initially, whereas distribution was regulated as a natural monopoly. This led to 70 firms trading in the bulk supply market by the end of 1993. The number of generating companies in 1997 stood at 40 and were mostly private, while there were over 20 distribution companies, many of them provincial. The national grid and the three federal distribution companies were privatized, as were about half the provincial distribution companies.

The reforms had a very positive effect on plant availability (which increased from 45 per cent to 72 per cent) and power outages, while the pool prices were giving market signals not only for investment in generation but also in transmission. Additional net capacity of 4927 MW was added to the system, while available capacity increased from 5930 MW in 1992 to 13,530 MW in December 1997.

13.7 Recommendations and conclusion

13.7.1 Recommendations

The reforms in the power sector have started to register some encouraging results. The advent of the IPPs has certainly improved the availability of power by boosting national installed capacity. However, there are still a number of challenges that are yet to be addressed. The first is the need to diversify the sources of power generation in the country. Currently about 69 per cent of total contribution to the national grid is thermal and gas based. Also, most of the proposed power plants are gas based. With the issues of communal crisis and youth restiveness in the regions where the gas is sourced, the security of this vital resource would be of paramount interest to investors. The concern about the preponderance of thermal-based generation facilities is also very important because of the issues related to global climate change. There is therefore need for appropriate incentives for investors to diversify into other sources of producing electric power. Studies have identified several sites in Nigeria for small and medium hydro power plants which can be profitably developed. Similarly, the development of biomass, wind and solar energy generating capacity needs to be encouraged.

Another important issue is the need to place increased emphasis on transmission and distribution. Special incentives can be given to investors at the distribution end of the industry. In particular, cognizance should be taken of the fact that the high initial cost of connecting small households to the network and the high cost of monitoring and implementing the customer service system (metering, billing and so on) have the potential to adversely affect the profitability of distribution companies.

There is also a need to address the issue of increasing access to electricity. This will entail dealing with the issue of tariffs for the poor. Whatever the case is, the full cost of energy according to category ought to be known and revealed, while every energy consumer should be educated to pay for what they consume. In this regard, consideration should be given to the encouragement of the formation of small community electrification cooperatives. Under this approach power would be sold to local cooperatives for distribution to the population. The cooperatives would be responsible for collection of payments and minimizing non-technical losses.

Equally important is the need to encourage small-scale IPP development which can easily be locally managed. Currently, most of the IPPs (proposed or under construction) are capital-intensive in nature, which may dissuade local investors. However, the capital requirements for small IPPs are modest and can be sourced with relative ease. Furthermore, small IPPs will lend themselves to replication in many communities thereby further strengthening the level of local participation and deepening private sector involvement. In this regard, local agro-processing concerns and heavy industrial consumers such as cement companies and chemical companies should be encouraged.

There is need to strengthen regulatory skills in NERC in order to ensure adequacy of expertise to set equipment standards for operators, thoroughly evaluate relevant costing, evaluate power purchase agreements (PPAs), protect consumers' interests, establish and monitor performance standards and also continually disseminate information to relevant stakeholders. It is also important to ensure that the sector's payment obligations arising out of the PPAs keep in step with revenue streams that are bolstered by cost-reflective tariffs and reasonable efficiency levels.

The ambitious privatization programme could be successful if solutions to unresolved issues such as the unfunded pension liabilities provide reasonable comfort to both the private sector and the employees in order to attract adequate capital to the sector and to improve service delivery. The CREST, which is a good example of leveraging best practice for innovation and a demonstration of achieving scale-up of investment and enhancing developmental impact, should be scaled up to harness optimum efficiency gains. Full benefits of restructuring will be achieved after the unbundled entities are privatized and competition is introduced through use of a multi-buyer model. Success of privatization also depends on rightsizing of staff and the entities joining the new pension scheme. Performance of 'unbundled' companies will be improved after the unbundled units develop business plans and sign performance contracts with the government. An effectively functioning service company, Nigeria Electricity Liquidation Management Agency, and an independent system operator are key to improved performance of the power sector.

There is need for careful consideration of how to allocate access to the most profitable commercial and industrial customers who are today generating their own power at high cost. Such customers are likely to remain outside the public sector framework for some time to come, but they may be willing to participate in purely market-based solutions that would accelerate improvements in their power supply, while also increasing their efficiency and productivity, with positive impacts on economic growth.

13.7.2 Conclusion

In conclusion, reforming Nigeria's power sector for growth in efficiency and investment is essential, but it requires commitment by the government to sustain it. It also requires continual dissemination of information by the regulators to the various stakeholders and will benefit from the reforms in the banking sector in terms of provision of capital. The power sector's growth and efficiency will catalyse the growth process in the economy.

Reform initiatives, such as the new electricity law, the regulatory mechanism, the restructuring of the monopoly company into smaller functionally focused entities, staff rightsizing and the planned privatization with private sector risk-mitigating instruments, will hopefully put the sector on a path of recovery. The new electricity law provides for open access to the grid along with bilateral contracts between generators and consumers. The Rural Electricity Agency should be adequately strengthened to scale up rural access, and renewable energy programmes should be implemented as per the master plan. The government should establish a set of performance benchmarks to monitor improvements in commercial performance of power companies until they are privatized.

Note

1 The views expressed in this chapter are those of the authors and do not represent those of the World Bank or the Central Bank of Nigeria.

References

Central Bank of Nigeria, 2000, The Changing Structure of the Nigerian Economy and Implications for Development: Annual Reports and Accounts (various issues).

Central Bank of Nigeria, 2001, Macroeconomic Issues in the Nigerian Economy.

National Electric Power Authority (NEPA): Annual Report and Accounts, 2001–2004.

Newbery, David, 2002, 'Issues and Options for Restructuring Electricity Supply Industries', University of Cambridge, Department of Applied Economics, Working Paper 0210.

Sule, E.I.K. and C.M. Anyanwu, 1994, 'An Appraisal of Electricity Supply in Nigeria and the Privatisation Option', CBN Occasional Paper, 30 August.

Turkson, J., 2005, 'The Electricity Utility Industry: Path to Restructuring in Sub-Saharan Africa' (available at www.worldenergy.org).

Ugwuh, C., 2005, 'Private Sector/Consumer Perspective in the Power/Energy Sector', a paper presented by the President, Manufacturers' Association of Nigeria at the National Workshop on Electric Power Sector Reform (EPSR) Act.

UNDP/World Bank Energy Sector Management Assistance Programme (ESMAP), 1993, *Energy Mission Aides Memoire (2003–2007)*, World Bank Energy Sector Team.

Section IV

The Well-being of Households: Income and Education

14
Poverty in Nigeria

Simon Appleton, Andrew McKay and Babatunde Adewumi Alayande[1]

14.1 Introduction

Nigeria has a reputation in popular discussion as being fantastically unequal. Sala-i-Martin (2006: 364) reviews the world distribution of income and finds Nigeria 'perhaps the most interesting case'. His estimates, based on national accounts together with survey estimates of income distribution, imply that mean income per capita has fallen since 1970 while inequality has 'exploded'. He surmises that the proportion of people living below one dollar a day has increased (to 70 per cent), but that the income of the more affluent has also increased. He posits that the distribution of income in Nigeria has become bimodal, with a few non-poor separating from the mass of the poor (see Figure 2 of Subramanian and Sala-i-Martin, 2003). An in-depth Oxfam study of poverty in Nigeria cites the UNDP *Nigeria 2000/2001 Human Development Report* as explaining that Nigeria has a Gini coefficient 'close to one' (Oxfam, 2003: 7). Such perceptions of extreme inequality are supported by the contrast between the large oil revenues Nigeria earns and the fragile livelihoods most of its citizens eke out in smallholder agriculture and non-farm self-employment. Oil money has allowed the creation of a large public sector, whose workers are seen as relatively privileged. Moreover, oil is widely seen as having fostered corruption and capital flight, contributing to the creation of an affluent, internationally mobile elite.

Despite this widespread view of Nigeria as an exceptionally unequal place, there have been relatively few in-depth studies of poverty and inequality using primary micro-data.

The salient academic studies are somewhat dated – Canagarajah and Thomas (2001) compared the evolution of poverty between 1985 and 1992, and Anyanwu (2005) analysed the determinants of rural poverty in 1996. Official poverty profiles for 1980–96 and for 2003/2004 are provided by Federal Office of Statistics (1999, 2005). This chapter analyses the 2003/2004 Nigeria Living Standards Survey in depth. This was a large scale government survey conceived by Chukwuma C. Soludo, former Economic Advisor to the President of the Federal Republic of Nigeria, now Governor of the Central Bank of Nigeria, with one of its principal aims being the creation of a stand-alone Poverty Profile. The present chapter builds upon the official Poverty Profile for Nigeria 2004 (Federal Office of Statistics, 2005), following its 'objective' method of setting the poverty line and providing multivariate analysis of the determinants of poverty, as well as providing further analysis of wages and employment.

The chapter is largely exploratory – we do not approach the survey wishing to test specific hypotheses. Rather we seek to address three broad issues. First, how poor and unequal is Nigeria? How accurate are the popular conceptions of Nigeria as having high levels of absolute poverty and extreme inequality? To anticipate our findings, we argue that, while absolute poverty is indeed high, the extent of inequality in Nigeria has been over-emphasized. Second, we wish to investigate what explains poverty and inequality in Nigeria. Stated like this, the research question is too broad to be satisfactorily answered by simply analysing one household survey. The causes of poverty and inequality could be viewed on many levels – macroeconomic, historical, sociological, cultural, geographical, intra-household, perhaps even psychological and genetic – that a fairly conventional cross-sectional household living standards survey could not hope to comprehensively address. More prosaically, we wish to investigate the household level socio-economic factors that are associated with poverty – the determinants (or arguably just correlates) of poverty. The third question we address is a key issue in Nigerian political economy – who benefits from the large state funded by oil revenues? In particular, we approach this from the production side, looking at the rents received by government employees.

This chapter has three main substantive parts. Section 14.2 explains the data and the conceptualization of household welfare, before moving on to present basic statistics on poverty and inequality. Section 14.3 presents various multivariate models of welfare and poverty. Section 14.4 provides an analysis of the data on household labour, focusing on access to employment and on earnings. We end by considering the implications of our key findings for the policy debate in Nigeria.

14.2 Poverty and inequality statistics

14.2.1 Data and methods

The main data source for this chapter is the Nigeria Living Standards Survey (NLSS) of 2003/2004, an integrated household survey collected by the National Bureau of Statistics (formerly, Federal Office of Statistics) of Nigeria. The survey ran from September 2003 to August 2004. It covered the entire country and was designed to be nationally representative after the application of population weights. In the analysis that follows, descriptive statistics will be obtained after weighting, but econometric modelling will be done on the unweighted data except where noted otherwise.

The NLSS used multi-stage cluster sampling. The first stage was the enumeration area (EA) – ten EAs were surveyed each month in each of Nigeria's 36 states (five EAs in Abuja). The second stage was the household, with five households being sampled from each EA. It should be noted that essentially the same sampling design has been adopted by all four National Consumer Surveys (1980, 1985, 1992 and 1996), although the overall sample size has risen with the increase in the number of states in Nigeria (Anyanwu, 2005). With the NLSS, the sampling conventions led to an intended sample size of 21,900 households, from 4380 clusters. The large number of clusters in the NLSS is a strength of the survey, as is the all year round coverage of each state. The sampling design was intended to provide robust estimates at the state level (Federal Office of Statistics, 2005).

The survey collected a wide range of information, covering household composition, health, education, employment, housing, social capital, agriculture, consumption, non-farm enterprises, financial assets and income. The coverage of consumption was a particular focus, with seven interviewer visits to each household within a 30-day period (with a minimum four-day interval), designed to capture consumption of everyday items between visits. This seems a good method of collecting consumption data, from the point of view of minimizing recall errors. A simple schedule of income between visits was also used, which seems less than ideal (the questions were at a household, rather than individual level; only cash income was inquired about; and the 30-day recall period seems too short). Usable income on wage earnings can be obtained from the employment section, but we have not been able to obtain good data on self-employment earnings from the survey.

These specific issues with the design of the NLSS are one reason why we choose to use consumption, rather than income, as the basis of our welfare measure. In addition, there are general reasons to expect income to be under-reported; inherent problems in measuring income from self-employment in a developing country; and a presumption (from the Permanent Income Hypothesis) that consumption may be a better measure of long-run income than current income. Our consumption variable includes the value of home consumption of food. It is essentially private consumption – there is no valuation of goods and services received by the household paid for by the state.

Our consumption aggregates differ from those used in the official poverty profile (Federal Office of Statistics, 2005) in two respects. Firstly, we use the measure of health spending derived from the consumption section of the questionnaire rather than the health section. This issue is discussed in detail in the Supplementary material (www.csae.ox.ac.uk/books) and has a dramatic effect on the results, lowering health spending from 14 per cent of consumption to 1.5 per cent. Secondly, we impute some food spending for the 285 households (1.5 per cent of total) who report zero food spending (see Supplementary material in the Appendix, www.csae.ox.ac.uk/books, for details).

We deflate nominal consumption using the food and non-food cost of living indices derived for the official poverty profile. This was a Laspeyres index based mainly on CPI prices and constructed for each of the six main regions (South South and so on) on a monthly basis. We also follow the official poverty profile in deflating real consumption by the number of adult equivalents in the household, applying a scale devised by the FAO (see Supplementary material in the Appendix, www.csae.ox.ac.uk/books, for details). This scale is based on WHO calorific estimates of requirements by age and sex. It may be appropriate given that the poverty line is anchored to estimates of calorie requirements. However, it implicitly assumes that non-food needs are proportional to food needs, which may be a strong assumption – particularly, the implication that women need only 73 per cent as much as men. No adjustment is made for possible economies of consumption, so the poverty of large households may be overstated.

For the poverty line, we use the 'objective' line derived in the official poverty profile, adjusted for our lower estimate of health spending. The profile describes this as a 'Food Energy Intake' poverty line, since it estimates the cost of obtaining 2900 calories per day. The figure of 2900 calories appears to have been somewhat arbitrarily chosen by the National Bureau of Statistics on the grounds that it 'approximated the level of poverty obtained using the relative measure' (Federal Office of Statistics, 2005: 35). However, the figure of 2900 is wholly defensible; this is the calorie intake that the WHO (1985) recommends for a man doing work of 'medium' intensity (such as subsistence agriculture). The food poverty line is the cost of obtaining these calories, based on the consumption patterns of the poorest 40 per cent of the population. Note that the 'objective' poverty line would be described by Ravallion (1998) as using the 'Cost of Basic Needs' (CBN) approach to setting a poverty line, not the 'Food Energy Intake' method. This is because it costs a given food basket and does not simply read off the poverty line from observed relation(s) between energy intake and consumption. Since we compare the consumption per adult equivalent with this poverty line, we have implicitly allowed for the lower calorie requirements of children. The official profile then adds to the food poverty line an allowance for non-food requirements based on those 200 households whose consumption per adult equivalent was around the food poverty line. Note that Ravallion terms this the 'lower bound' estimate of non-food requirements – the higher bound estimate would be non-food spending when *food* consumption equalled the food poverty line. We retained the food poverty line used in the official poverty profile, but recalculated the non-food requirements using our lower estimate of health spending. This generated a poverty line of 28,084 naira per adult equivalent per month, 98 per cent of the value of the official profile's line of 28,758.

Several other poverty lines have been used in the literature on Nigeria. The official poverty profile also estimates a 'dollar a day' poverty line, at 21,608 naira per person per month. It estimates that 51.6 per cent of Nigerians have consumption per capita below this level. Thus it appears that the 'dollar a day' line is roughly comparable to the 'objective' CBN line, which the official profile finds gives a poverty incidence of 53.8 per cent. While the dollar a day line is useful for international comparisons, it seems inferior to a domestically determined absolute poverty line. This is because the conversion of domestic currency values into PPP dollar terms is unnecessary for domestic purposes. Moreover, such conversions are difficult and imprecise, with conversion factors not being regularly updated and potentially subject to large revisions. It is preferable to rely on a poverty line in domestic currency and to use domestic price indices to keep it in real terms.

However, the official poverty profile – and indeed official discussion of poverty – focuses on a 'relative' poverty line in order to get results that are comparable with poverty estimates in previous surveys. The use of the term 'relative' poverty line is potentially confusing; unfortunately, official reports on poverty in Nigeria provide a good example of this confusion.[2] One could conceive of two alternative definitions of a relative poverty line. A weak definition would be a relative poverty line that is a line derived not from some estimate of households' absolute 'needs' but relative to living standards in a country. A strong definition would be a relative poverty line that is not fixed over time, but changes as the living standards of the country change. In FOS (1999), the poverty line is defined as two thirds of mean consumption per capita in 1985 and then held constant in real terms when computing poverty in other years.[3] It thus meets the weak definition of a relative poverty line, but not the strong definition. However, in FOS (2005), the poverty is defined as two thirds of mean consumption per capita in 2003/2004, not 1985. It thus meets the strong definition of a relative poverty line. What this means is that the poverty counts in FOS (2005), although intended to be comparable with those in FOS (1999), are not, because the poverty lines are different.

14.2.2 Existing evidence on poverty and inequality trends

In this chapter, we do not focus on trends in poverty and inequality, since we have analysed only the NLSS 2003/2004. However, reviewing the literature on poverty and inequality in Nigeria, it is hard not to comment on the evidence on trends. Table 14.1 presents some key statistics from the literature, as well as the implications of the national accounts for the level of real private consumption per capita.[4] It should be said at the outset that there are problems of data quality or comparability with the relevant statistics, creating potential measurement errors that affect the reliability of estimates of trends over time. Population figures for Nigeria are controversial: we use a figure of 127 million for 2004 whereas the World Development Indicators report 139 million. Where possible, we use the CPI data provided by the Central Bank of Nigeria but this differs from the series provided by the IMF. Private consumption is calculated as a residual in the national accounts and thus will be affected by all the measurement errors from other components of expenditure. Survey estimates of private consumption are more direct, and the surveys do seem to have followed comparable sampling procedures. However, we have not had access to the questionnaires from earlier surveys and thus cannot verify the extent to which the questions on consumption are comparable over time.

Simply looking at the national accounts estimates of real private consumption per capita for the survey years in Table 14.1 would suggest that average living standards fell sharply between 1980 and 1985, then stabilized before dropping again after 1996. However, plotting the entire series during this period in Figure 14.1 shows that such a reading would be misleading. Although there was a precipitous fall in living standards during the first half of the 1980s, thereafter consumption has been so volatile that it is hard to discern a trend and the pattern

Table 14.1 Evidence on poverty and inequality trends

	Per capita consumption, (PCC) 1985 prices pa		Inequality	Poverty (% poor)
	National accounts	Survey	Gini	<2/3 1985 PCC
1980	1477	1008		28.1
1985	915	591	0.387	46.3
1992	905	749	0.450	42.7
1996	861	441	0.465	65.6
2003/2004	663	675	0.488	54.4
Memo item: current paper estimates (based on adjusted PCC)				
2003/2004	N.A.	595	0.413	63.6

Population takes 1991 census figure and assumes 2.83 per cent growth.
Other data for 1980–1996 are from FOS (1999). For survey PCC, we convert 1996 prices to 1985 by deflating by the raising factor 28.56 used by FOS (1999).
Other data for 2003/2004 are from FOS (2005). Jan 2004 prices are deflated to 1996 prices using the ratio of the CPIs as provided by the IMF.
Sources: National accounts consumption and CPI provided by Central Bank of Nigeria.

might best be described as one of oscillation. This implies that we should be cautious in inferring long-term trends from periodic surveys – if the survey happens to occur in a peak or a trough, it may give a misleading impression.

Figure 14.1 also plots the survey estimates of private consumption per capita. These are always less than the national accounts estimates, sometimes dramatically so. The national accounts estimates exceed the survey ones by around 50 per cent in 1980 and 1985, and by nearly 100 per cent in 1996. However, the discrepancy is much less (11 per cent) for 2004. This is despite us plotting our adjusted figure for per capita consumption, which is 12 per cent lower than the one

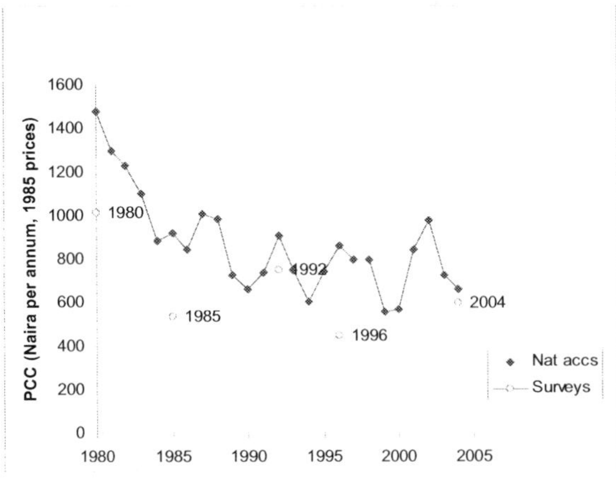

Figure 14.1 Real private consumption per capita.

reported in FOS (2005). These large and variable discrepancies lead the surveys to a rather different story about changes in living standards from that implied by the macro-data. While both series agree on the precipitous decline in the first half of the 1980s, the surveys imply a marked rally by 1992 and then a further fall. Unlike the national accounts, the 2003/2004 survey implies that mean living standards in Nigeria are higher than in 1996. In fact, after adjusting the consumption aggregate, per capita consumption in 2003/2004 is close to its 1985 value – although still substantially less than the estimates for 1980 and 1992. Since they provide direct estimates, rather than being a potentially error-prone residual, one is inclined to put more faith in the surveys, although, as has been said, we have been unable to check for full comparability over time.

The main advantage of the surveys, aside from providing a direct estimate, is that they provide information on the distribution of living standards. The measures of inequality – such as the Gini coefficients reported in Table 14.1 – imply continual rises in inequality from 1985 to 1996. However, the official report that inequality had increased even further by 2003/2004 is based on a computational error. When correctly calculated, even using NBS's own unadjusted consumption aggregates, the Gini coefficient for 2003/2004 is 0.425, not 0.488. Using the adjusted aggregates, it is 0.413. This is much lower than the values for the 1990s surveys and closer to the 1985 figure of 0.387. This implies that most of the rise of inequality since 1985 has been reversed.

A key interest of the surveys is in monitoring poverty. Owing to lack of access to the data, we have not been able to verify the poverty series published by FOS (1999).[5] However, it is clear that the entry for 2003/2004 that has been reported by FOS (2005) is problematic. We have already noted the confusion over the 'relative' nature of the poverty line. The poverty line for 2003/2004 is defined as two thirds of that year's mean per capita consumption whereas those for the earlier years are defined as two thirds of the mean per capita consumption in 1985. In addition, the reported poverty headcount of 54.4 per cent was obtained by comparing nominal expenditure with a poverty line of two thirds of per capita consumption in constant January 2004 prices. It is more appropriate to compare constant (January 2004) price expenditure per capita with such a poverty line but, if we do that, we obtain a headcount of 56.7 per cent, rather than the official 54.4 per cent. For consistency with the FOS (1999) poverty estimates from earlier surveys, however, we need to use the poverty line of 395.4 naira per annum in 1985 prices, equivalent to 24,467 naira in January 2004 prices.[6] Using this line implies a poverty headcount of 58.1 per cent. All these figures so far use the NBS consumption aggregates. If we make the adjustments mentioned in the previous section, the final poverty headcount (on a per capita basis) rises to 63.6 per cent. This is still below the 1996 figure of 65.6, but only just. Moreover, it is higher than the headcounts for any of the other surveys. Ideally, more work should be done to verify this conclusion – for example, by examining the comparability of the various questionnaires (the sampling procedures appear to have been largely comparable). However, it appears that the official reports of the fall in poverty in Nigeria have been overstated.

14.2.3 Poverty indicators

We now return to focus on the 2003/2004 NLSS, working with our preferred welfare measure of private consumption per adult equivalent and an absolute poverty line of 28,084 naira. We present three indices of poverty in the general class of Foster–Greer–Thorbecke (1984) poverty measures. One is the head count index, which measures the proportion of the population whose expenditure levels fall below the poverty line. A second measure of poverty known as the poverty gap index takes into consideration variation in how far poor households' expenditure levels fall below the poverty line. The poverty gap measures the average shortfall between the poor households' expenditure levels and the poverty line. A third measure is the poverty severity index, which takes into account the distribution of living standards among the poor. The severity index is sensitive to inequality among poor households, indicating more poverty when the average poverty gap is more unequally distributed among the poor.

The Foster–Greer–Thorbecke (FGT) class of poverty measures is defined as:

$$P\alpha = \frac{1}{N}\sum_{i=1}^{N}\left(1 - x_i^* / z\right)^{\alpha} \qquad (14.1)$$

where $x^*_i = x_i$ if $x_i \leq z$

$= z$ if $x_i > z$

Here, x_i is the expenditure level of the individual, z is the poverty line and N is the number of individuals in the population. For particular values of α it gives the three poverty indexes. Thus, if α equals zero the FGT index becomes the head count index. If α equals one, the FGT index is the poverty gap. This is the average gap between individuals' expenditure levels and poverty line where non-poor persons are assigned a gap of zero. If α is greater than one, the FGT index becomes sensitive to distribution among the poor.

The national incidence of poverty as shown in Table 14.2 shows a headcount index of 57.8 per cent, poverty gap of 24.4 per cent and severity index of 13.5 per cent. Figure 14.2 plots the headcount for various multiples of our preferred poverty line. Also included for comparison are the poverty incidence curves for Ghana and Uganda estimated for 1999 and 2003 respectively, showing that – regardless of where the poverty line is set – Nigeria is estimated to have a higher level of absolute poverty than either Ghana or Uganda. (We should note that the curves might not be strictly comparable, since they use different food baskets. However, it is interesting that, in each case, the poverty lines drawn up are close to the 'dollar a day' benchmark lines used for international comparisons.)

Analysis of poverty incidence by urban/rural residence of the household head shows a higher prevalence of poverty among rural dwellers than among urban residents. The headcount index shows a poverty incidence of 45.6 per cent among urban residents whereas it is 67.4 per cent for rural dwellers. A regional comparison shows that the North East has the highest incidence of poverty of 70.3 per cent, followed by the North Central region with a headcount index of 66.5 per cent. Table 14.2 further shows the South East region has the lowest incidence of poverty with a headcount index of 39.8 per cent. The federal capital territory (FCT) also has an intermediate incidence of poverty with a headcount index of 50.8 per cent.

The sex comparison of poverty reveals a higher incidence of poverty in male-headed households across the three indices of poverty. The headcount index shows a poverty incidence of 59.5 per cent for male-headed households against 42.8 per cent for female-headed households.

Analysis of poverty by employment status of household head shows that household heads that engage in agricultural activities are the worst hit by poverty with a headcount index of 68.4 per cent. Household heads that are not working come second with a headcount index of 53.3 per cent. However, those in government employment have the lowest incidence of poverty with a headcount index of 39.8 per cent.

A decomposition analysis of poverty into various skill classifications as presented in Table 14.2 shows that the unskilled household head category suffers the highest incidence of poverty in Nigeria with a headcount index of 66.9 per cent. The skilled labour category has the lowest incidence of poverty of 38.9 per cent.

14.2.4 Inequality

Table 14.3 reports population shares; mean welfare levels for each case and four different measures of inequality. These measures are: the Gini, the GE(0) and GE(1) generalized entropy indices (Theil mean log deviation measure and Theil entropy indices respectively); and the Atkinson inequality index for a value of the ε parameter equal to 1. The classification of states into regions and so on is reported in Table A14.A2 in the Supplementary material in the Appendix (www.csae.ox.ac.uk/books). Figure 14.3 presents an estimate of the density of the log of our welfare variable (private consumption per adult equivalent). It can be seen that it appears fairly normally distributed, with no sign of the bimodal property identified by Sala-i-Martin (2006).

The overall Gini coefficient is 0.405. Note that this Gini coefficient is lower than the 0.488 figure published in the Nigeria poverty profile study (Federal Office of Statistics, 2005); but there was an error in the latter due to weighting. Nigeria's level of inequality is slightly above average by international standards. Milanovic (2003) uses WIDER data on inequality to estimate that the average Gini coefficient for non-African countries in the 1990s was 0.38. However, Nigeria is not exceptional compared to several other African countries. For example, comparable Gini coefficients are 0.38 for Ghana in 1998/99 and 0.43 for Uganda in 2002/3. Indeed, Nigeria may even be somewhat more equal than most African countries. Milanovic uses 20 observations on African countries around 1998 and finds an average Gini coefficient of 0.47. (Note, for Asia the comparable mean is 0.356 and for Latin America it is 0.505.)

Table 14.2 Poverty indicators

	Headcount index		Poverty gap index		Severity index	
	Index	Contribution to total (%)	Index	Contribution to total (%)	Index	Contribution to total (%)
National	57.8	100	24.4	100	13.5	100
Urban	45.6	34.8	18.8	34.0	10.6	34.4
Rural	67.4	65.2	28.8	66.0	15.9	65.6
By administrative region						
North West	65.4	29.0	27.2	28.6	14.5	27.5
North East	70.3	16.2	30.3	16.6	16.5	16.3
North Central	66.5	15.7	31.9	17.8	19.7	19.9
South South	55.8	14.5	21.7	13.3	11.0	12.2
South West	46.1	15.6	21.1	16.8	12.8	18.4
South East	39.8	8	12.7	6.2	6	5.2
FCT	50.8	1	20.0	0.6	10.3	0.5
By sex of household head						
Male Headed	59.5	92.3	25.2	92.4	13.9	92.3
Female Headed	42.8	7.7	18.0	7.6	10.1	7.7

By sector of employment of household head:						
Agriculture	68.4	57.5	29.2	58.0	16.0	57.5
Government	39.8	8.6	16.5	8.4	9.1	8.3
Private wage	48.1	3.6	20.7	3.7	11.9	3.8
Non-farm self-employment	50.2	26.1	21.0	25.8	11.9	26.4
Nonworking	53.3	4.3	21.6	4.1	11.6	3.9
By occupational skill class of household head:						
Unskilled	66.9	66.8	28.5	67.4	15.8	67.2
Semi-skilled	46.5	21.5	19.2	21.5	10.7	21.7
Skilled	38.9	6.9	16.5	7.0	9.4	7.2
Not Applicable	53.3	4.3	21.6	4.1	11.6	3.9

Source: Authors' computation from the NLSS data.

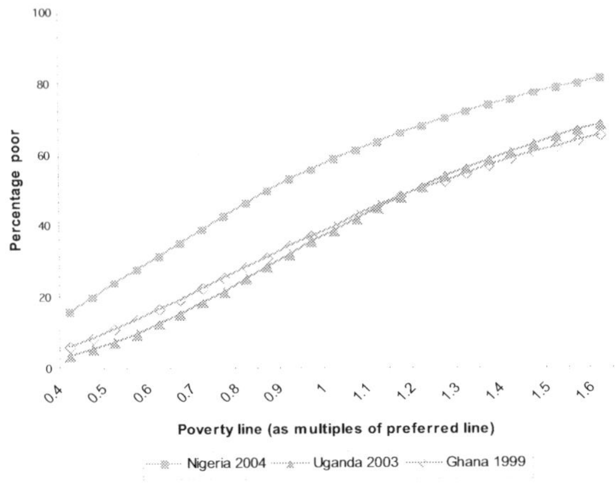

Figure 14.2 Poverty incidence curves.

Average urban consumption levels are more than 50 per cent higher than average rural levels, even after taking account of price differences. According to all indices, inequality within urban areas is higher than within rural areas.

By region, average consumption levels are highest in the South East followed by the Federal Capital Territory and the South West. Average consumption levels are lowest in the North Central region. The average consumption level in the

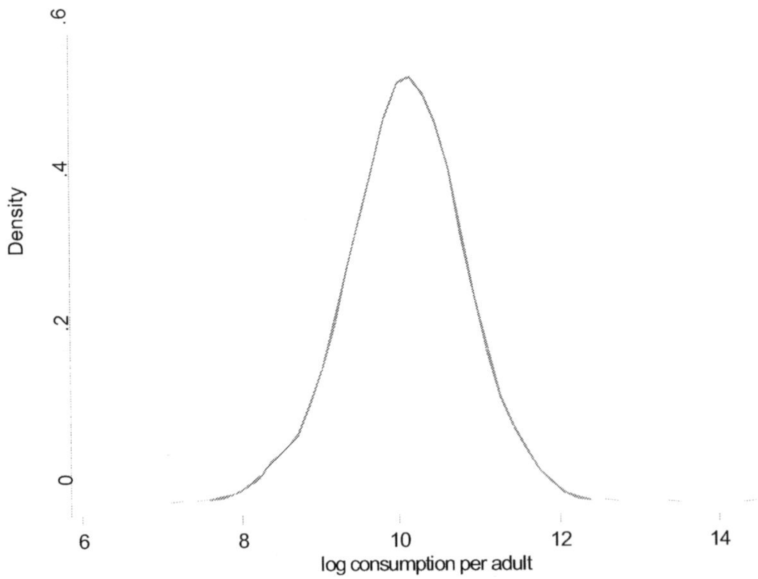

Figure 14.3 Kernel estimate of the density of log consumption per adult equivalent.

Table 14.3 Inequality indicators

	Population share (%)	Mean	Gini	GE(0)	GE(1)	A(1)
National	100.0	34,678	0.405	0.291	0.322	0.252
By sector						
Urban	44.1	39,510	0.417	0.320	0.361	0.274
Rural	55.9	26,041	0.363	0.229	0.228	0.204
By region						
North West	25.7	28,497	0.387	0.252	0.273	0.222
North East	13.4	28,614	0.441	0.350	0.643	0.295
North Central	13.7	26,295	0.416	0.313	0.296	0.269
South South	15.0	32,356	0.371	0.233	0.233	0.208
South West	19.6	37,829	0.419	0.338	0.314	0.286
South East	12.1	39,228	0.332	0.190	0.192	0.173
FCT	0.7	38,415	0.406	0.283	0.278	0.246
By north/south						
South	46.6	36,432	0.385	0.269	0.260	0.236
North	53.4	28,094	0.410	0.294	0.374	0.254
By oil/nonoil states						
Nonoil states	79.1	31,354	0.416	0.307	0.349	0.265
Oil states	20.9	34,360	0.361	0.224	0.224	0.200
By employment status of household head						
Agriculture	48.6	25,554	0.358	0.222	0.221	0.199
Government	12.5	44,889	0.437	0.358	0.489	0.301
Private wage	4.4	36,954	0.414	0.315	0.313	0.270
Non-farm self-employment	30.0	35,560	0.403	0.295	0.290	0.256
Nonworking	4.6	36,806	0.416	0.301	0.302	0.260
Decompostion analysis: share of between group inequality (%)						
By urban/rural				7.4	6.7	5.1
By region				3.7	3.3	5.3
By north/south				2.9	2.6	4.0
By state				16.4	13.2	21.6
By oil/nonoil state				0.2	0.2	1.0
By employment status				7.6	6.9	5.0

Source: Authors' computation from the NLSS data.

south of the country is nearly 30 per cent higher than the average consumption level in the north (including FCT).

However, inequality is higher within the north of the country than within the south according to all inequality measures reported here. The highest inequality levels are in the North East according to all measures; other relatively high inequality regions are North Central and South West. Inequality levels are lowest in the South East.

Mean consumption in oil-producing states is nearly 10 per cent above the country average; but note that this is less than the average north–south differential. All measures of inequality in oil-producing states are *lower* than those in non-oil-producing states.

Households whose head works in agriculture have the lowest average consumption level, only 73 per cent of the national average. Households whose head works for the government have the highest average consumption levels, about 30 per cent above the national average. This is also the household category showing the highest level of inequality; those where the head works in agriculture have the lowest levels of inequality. The other categories – including the case where the household head is not working – are intermediate between these two extremes in all respects.

Decompositions of the GE and Atkinson inequality indices are performed to identify the within and between group components of overall inequality. They show relatively large urban/rural between group inequality (taking account of the fact that there are only two categories); as well as quite a large between employment category effect; and a large between state effect (though the last partly reflects the number of states). The between group component of inequality accounted for by the north–south distinction, or especially the distinction between oil-producing and non-oil-producing states, is very small. In these latter cases inequality within the categories is a very large proportion of the total.

14.3 Determinants of poverty and consumption

14.3.1 Modelling poverty and welfare

We explore a variety of ways of modelling our preferred welfare measure (private consumption per adult equivalent) and whether it falls below the poverty line. Table 14.4 includes a simple regression for the log of the welfare measure as well as a logit model for whether a household is poor. Also included is a tobit model for the log welfare measure, censored at the (log) poverty line. The regression provides information about the determinants of welfare at the mean, but the logit and tobit may be informative if the determinants are different for poorer households – for example, if they have lower returns to assets (Appleton, 2001a).

In a similar vein, Table 14.5 presents quantile regression for the log of the welfare measure (see Nguyen *et al.*, forthcoming, for another illustration of applying quantile analysis). The Q50 regression provides the results for the median household, conditional on the observed explanatory variables. The Q25 regression shows the results for the lower conditional quartile and the Q75 shows the results for the higher conditional quartile. Interpreting differences between the quartiles is difficult because they differ in the unobserved determinants of welfare and these are, by their nature, hard to pin down. The unobservables may include time-invariant factors – such as 'ability' – as well as time-variant ones – such as poor weather. They will also include any measurement error. We estimate the three quantile regressions simultaneously and use bootstrapped standard errors, using the *STATA* command *sqreg*.

In all the above models, we use a common set of explanatory variables. These can be grouped into the following conventional categories: *human capital* – the education levels of household members; *assets* – household land and capital; *demographics* – the size, age and sex composition of the household; together with controls for unobserved *regional* and *monthly* factors. What is rather unconventional is that we are able to include a variety of measures of *social capital*, based on various household responses to questions on that topic. As is common with cross-sectional results, there are problems with potentially endogenous regressors. We attempt to limit those problems by excluding variables that clearly reflect contemporaneous choices by the household or are direct measures of economic status (for example, housing quality or consumer durables). Our education measures are only for adults who have completed their education. For the social capital variables, we do not take the household's own responses but rather the average responses of other households in the cluster. Unfortunately, the survey surveyed only five households per cluster, so these measures suffer from the problem of small numbers. Nonetheless, as will be discussed, in preliminary work we generally found a close correspondence between these measures and corresponding measures based only on the household's own responses.

In what follows, we focus our discussion on the simple regression results in Table 14.4, referring to the other models only when there is an interesting difference. All results discussed are significant at the 5 per cent level, unless stated otherwise.

14.3.2 Human capital

The human capital variables are all measured as averages for household members aged 15–64 who have completed their education. For example, the regression implies that increasing the primary education of all such members in a household would raise welfare by 2 per cent *ceteris paribus*. Surprisingly, secondary schooling has the same effect. This is somewhat unusual, given that most studies find secondary education to have larger monetary returns (Appleton, 1999a). Since the Nigerian education system consists of six years of primary and secondary education, our results imply that a household where all members complete their schooling would have welfare about a quarter (24 per cent) higher than that of a comparable household where the members are all unschooled. However, these effects are rather low by international standards, where the benchmark is typically that one year of schooling raises wages by 10 per cent (Psacharopoulos, 1994).

Table 14.4 Modelling welfare and poverty

	OLS			Tobit			Logit		
Constant	10.867	(146.35)	***	10.807	(124.07)	***	0.452	(7.03)	***
Primary	0.021	(8.07)	***	0.021	(6.59)	***	0.018	(7.41)	***
Secondary	0.020	(6.03)	***	0.017	(4.10)	***	0.013	(4.19)	***
Teacher training	0.186	(3.1)	***	0.166	(2.42)	**	0.152	(3.07)	***
Koranic education	0.109	(5.13)	***	0.133	(4.90)	***	0.062	(2.85)	***
University	0.624	(10.71)	***	0.552	(8.06)	***	0.415	(7.91)	***
Polytechnic	0.389	(8.49)	***	0.438	(7.62)	***	0.354	(8.16)	***
Age	–0.017	(–10.1)	***	–0.015	(–7.50)	***	–0.010	(–7.26)	***
Age squared	2.43E-04	(10.07)	***	2.00E-04	(7.84)	***	1.55E-04	(7.30)	***
Log l nd pae	0.025	(14.46)	***	0.031	(14.67)	***	0.009	(5.79)	***
Log non-farm capital pae	0.042	(20.44)	***	0.055	(16.52)	***	0.033	(14.65)	***
Log adult equivalents	–0.435	(–41.7)	***	–0.452	(–36.13)	***	–0.320	(–32.09)	***
Proportion under 5	0.063	(1.87)	*	0.130	(3.22)	***	0.036	(1.17)	
Proportion 5–14	–0.075	(–2.53)	**	–0.059	(–1.67)	*	–0.044	(–1.62)	
Proportion female 15–64	0.098	(3.49)	***	0.151	(3.98)	***	0.123	(4.41)	***
Proportion over 65	–0.229	(–6.85)	***	–0.174	(–3.79)	***	–0.133	(–4.09)	***
Female household head	–0.086	(–5.32)	***	–0.076	(–3.79)	***	–0.046	(–3.15)	***
Urban	0.245	(17.92)	***	0.247	(15.35)	***	0.159	(13.31)	***
North West	–0.118	(–3.04)	***	–0.152	(–3.07)	***	–0.092	(–2.45)	**
North East	–0.177	(–4.61)	***	–0.184	(–3.70)	***	–0.116	(–3.09)	***
North Central	–0.325	(–8.25)	***	–0.376	(–7.62)	***	–0.163	(–4.37)	***

South South	–0.051	(–1.31)		–0.045	(–0.89)		–0.033	(–0.87)	
South West	–0.068	(–1.72)	*	–0.073	(–1.45)		–0.019	(–0.51)	
South East	0.142	(3.67)	***	0.197	(3.89)	***	0.136	(3.59)	***
Community programme	0.066	(5.44)	***	0.080	(5.42)	***	0.053	(4.64)	***
Conflict	0.181	(5.34)	***	0.217	(4.85)	***	0.134	(4.03)	***
Crime	0.185	(3.97)	***	0.143	(2.41)	**	0.146	(3.31)	***
Loan1	0.101	(3.33)	***	0.116	(3.22)	***	0.087	(3.13)	***
Loan2	0.087	(2.86)	***	0.087	(2.40)	**	0.069	(2.47)	**
Loan3	0.017	(0.48)		0.040	(0.94)		0.067	(2.05)	**
Loan4	–0.031	(–0.78)		–0.023	(–0.48)		0.003	(0.07)	
Trust2	–0.057	(–3.36)	***	–0.058	(–2.76)	***	–0.021	(–1.30)	
Trust3	–0.024	(–1.44)		–0.009	(–0.43)		–0.015	(–0.92)	
Trust4	–0.059	(–2.65)	***	–0.030	(–1.06)		–0.031	(–1.39)	
Trust5	0.013	(0.41)		0.040	(1.01)		0.018	(0.59)	
Coop1	0.072	(1.9)	*	0.069	(1.57)		0.026	(0.78)	
Coop2	0.053	(1.32)		0.057	(1.21)		0.026	(0.74)	
Coop3	0.054	(1.2)		0.033	(0.63)		–0.002	(–0.06)	
Coop4	–0.037	(–0.68)		–0.031	(–0.47)		–0.073	(–1.44)	
Help1	–0.177	(–3.62)	***	–0.159	(–2.84)	***	–0.140	(–3.42)	***
Help2	–0.089	(–1.82)	*	–0.069	(–1.24)		–0.072	(–1.77)	*
Help3	–0.105	(–2.1)	**	–0.081	(–1.40)		–0.092	(–2.15)	**
Help4	–0.194	(–3.08)	***	–0.152	(–2.02)	**	–0.130	(–2.33)	**

Also included but not reported for brevity: month dummies and controls for missing values. The variables Loan#, Trust#, Coop# and Help# are the cluster averages of dummy variables for different responses on a Likert scale to questions about loan availability, trust, cooperation and altruism. The averaging is only done over other households in the community. For example if 'Trust5' was equal to 0.2 that would imply 20% of other households in the community reported very high levels of trust (chose response number 5 on the Likert scale). See text for detail on the wording of the questions.
Source: Authors' computation from the NLSS data.

Table 14.5 Simultaneous quantile regression for log welfare

	Q25			Q50			Q75		
Constant	10.454	(119.93)	***	10.975	(117.94)	***	11.313	(105.44)	***
Primary	0.020	(8.81)	***	0.023	(10.48)	***	0.024	(6.92)	***
Secondary	0.016	(2.99)	***	0.022	(5.66)	***	0.026	(4.91)	***
Teacher training	0.194	(2.05)	**	0.284	(2.64)	***	0.258	(3.43)	***
Koranic education	0.147	(6.6)	***	0.099	(4.71)	***	0.056	(2.56)	***
University	0.472	(5.87)	***	0.621	(10.04)	***	0.723	(12.21)	***
Polytechnic	0.426	(12.76)	***	0.380	(7.57)	***	0.389	(6.65)	***
Age	–0.014	(–5.91)	***	–0.016	(–8.36)	***	–0.017	(–8.3)	***
Age squared	2.01E–04	(5.51)	***	2.32E-04	(8.52)	***	2.53E-04	(8.36)	***
Log land pae	0.033	(11.48)	***	0.018	(9.01)	***	0.004	(1.9)	*
Log non–farm capital pae	0.045	(17.9)	***	0.037	(17.32)	***	0.033	(13.96)	***
Log adult equivalents	–0.471	(–36.93)	***	–0.460	(–38.64)	***	–0.435	(–42.28)	***
Proportion under 5	0.152	(3.03)	***	0.068	(1.96)	**	–0.058	(–1.3)	
Proportion 5–14	–0.038	(–0.98)		–0.055	(–2.16)	**	–0.128	(–4.9)	***
Proportion female 15–64	0.126	(3.06)	***	0.119	(3.8)	***	0.038	(1.27)	
Proportion over 65	–0.169	(–3.16)	***	–0.230	(–5.34)	***	–0.288	(–5.82)	***
Female household head	–0.077	(–3.34)	***	–0.095	(–4.29)	***	–0.074	(–5.88)	***
Urban	0.251	(13.86)	***	0.239	(16.28)	***	0.232	(11.24)	***
North West	–0.103	(–1.85)	*	–0.098	(–1.56)		–0.061	(–0.9)	
North East	–0.140	(–2.39)	**	–0.147	(–2.33)	**	–0.132	(–1.88)	*
North Central	–0.475	(–7.58)	***	–0.190	(–2.83)	***	–0.064	(–0.96)	

South South	–0.040	(–0.68)		–0.067	(–1.04)		–0.011	(–0.18)	
South West	–0.009	(–0.14)		–0.001	(–0.02)		0.012	(0.18)	
South East	0.174	(3.01)	***	0.171	(2.87)	***	0.186	(2.85)	***
Community programme	0.072	(3.72)	***	0.076	(6.88)	***	0.077	(7.27)	***
Conflict	0.186	(3.51)	***	0.179	(6.74)	***	0.149	(4.59)	***
Crime	0.130	(2.91)	***	0.204	(3.99)	***	0.262	(4.91)	***
Loan1	0.108	(2.8)	***	0.098	(2.95)	***	0.069	(2.22)	**
Loan2	0.112	(2.72)	***	0.099	(3.01)	***	0.075	(2)	**
Loan3	0.026	(0.49)		0.026	(0.68)		0.030	(0.84)	
Loan4	0.004	(0.09)		–0.053	(–1.37)		–0.040	(–0.88)	
Trust2	–0.083	(–3.64)	***	–0.068	(–3.54)	***	–0.031	(–1.28)	
Trust3	–0.016	(–0.44)		–0.047	(–2.09)	**	–0.015	(–0.57)	
Trust4	–0.018	(–0.71)		–0.050	(–1.93)	*	–0.063	(–1.98)	**
Trust5	0.009	(0.32)		0.016	(0.47)		0.024	(0.56)	
Coop1	0.090	(1.73)	*	0.070	(2.28)	**	0.032	(0.77)	
Coop2	0.051	(0.83)		0.062	(1.59)		0.036	(0.9)	
Coop3	0.055	(0.76)		0.044	(0.98)		0.035	(0.65)	
Coop4	–0.036	(–0.47)		–0.004	(–0.08)		–0.037	(–0.67)	
Help1	–0.226	(–2.93)	***	–0.254	(–5.84)	***	–0.144	(–2.83)	***
Help2	–0.159	(–2.02)	**	–0.181	(–4.14)	***	–0.106	(–2.28)	**
Help3	–0.134	(–1.63)		–0.186	(–3.64)	***	–0.145	(–2.62)	***
Help4	–0.260	(–3.35)	***	–0.287	(–4.85)	***	–0.167	(–2.3)	**

Source: Authors' computation from the NLSS data.

This comparison may be thought invalid because we are comparing wage effects with overall effects on consumption, only a relatively small part of which in Nigeria is paid for out of wages. It may be that education is not particularly rewarded in African agriculture or indeed non-farm self-employment. Nonetheless, a study of Uganda implies education may be valuable in getting people out of low-return agriculture into higher-return activities, such as non-farm self-employment and wage employment (Appleton, 2001b). As a consequence, the returns to schooling in Uganda in 1999/2000 were not far from the 10 per cent benchmark.

The relatively low returns to schooling we find do not have direct implications for education policy. Schooling may be regarded as intrinsically valuable or as having other benefits besides pecuniary ones. However, it does caution against predicting dramatic economic effects from educational expansion – as might be expected given claims that the social return to primary education in Africa is 24 per cent (Psacharopoulos, 1994). Our estimate of the effect of education looks directly only at the monetary benefits of education. Following the Mincerian short-cut method, we could regard the coefficient on years of schooling in a semi-log income function as a rate of return if it is assumed that the only cost of a year of education is sacrificing a year of consumption (income). For primary schooling, this would be to overestimate the costs – primary school students are typically too young to make much of a contribution to household income and the pecuniary costs of their education are often modest (roughly the cost of a teacher divided by the average class size). Work done on Kenya implies that, if the opportunity cost of primary school students' time is zero, a 2 per cent 'Mincerian' return may imply a social return of around 24 per cent (Appleton, 1999b). For post-primary schooling, the short-hand rate of return calculation probably overstates returns: the assumption about opportunity cost is reasonable, but significant pecuniary costs are neglected.

Our estimates condition on various variables that may in fact be routes through which education affects welfare – for example, assets, household size and location. Further work will explore the robustness of our findings.

Various other educational attainments were included in the model, although data was not available on the years spent acquiring them. People who reported Koranic schooling as the highest education attained were assumed not to have formal schooling. Overall, the effect on welfare of reporting such schooling was comparable to five years of formal schooling. University education had a large effect on welfare. If all adults had attended university, welfare would be 87 per cent higher *ceteris paribus*.[7] Polytechnic and teacher training education had somewhat smaller effects, at 48 per cent and 20 per cent respectively.

The coefficients on the human capital variables in the tobit models were broadly comparable to those in the regression – it does not seem that education pays any differently for the poor and the non-poor. All the variables also played a significant role in the logit models for poverty too. However, in the quantile regressions, there was some tendency for the coefficients on formal education to rise in size when moving from the first quartile to the median and then the third quartile.

For example, averaging six years of secondary schooling would raise welfare by 9.6 per cent for the lower quartile, 13.2 per cent for the median and 15.6 per cent for the upper quartile. If we make a leap and interpret the unobservables as reflecting 'ability', this implies higher returns to education for the more able. However, it is also marked that the reverse is true for Koranic education: its impact on the welfare falls as we consider higher quartiles. The result of this is that, for the lower quartile, Koranic education is equivalent to over seven years of primary schooling, while for the upper quartile it is worth just over two.

As well as the average of education of adults (aged 15–64) not in full-time study, we also included their average age and that average age squared. This may capture an aspect of human capital, as older workers learn more from their experience. Ultimately, there may also be negative effect of age, as older people may reduce their labour supply and/or become less productive as they age. This would imply an inverse U-relation between age and welfare, when in fact the models imply the reverse – a U-shaped relation. The turning point of the U-shaped effect is 35 years of age.

14.3.3 Demographics

The number of adult equivalents in the household is the most statistically significant determinant of welfare in the models. The simple regression implies an elasticity of –0.44. Note that this effect may be exaggerated to the extent that there are economies of consumption within the household (Lanjouw and Ravallion, 1995).

Increased proportions of people aged over 65 have a strong negative effect on welfare, as does the proportion of children aged 5–15 years of age. Both of these effects are stronger in the tobit than the regression, and in the quantile regression become more negative as the quartile rises. High dependency ratios appear less harmful to welfare for the poor or those with unfavourable unobservable characteristics than for the mean or median household. One may speculate that poor households use dependants more productively, for example by working on household enterprises. An increased proportion of children under five in the household is associated with higher welfare – perhaps reflecting reverse causality (prosperous households can afford more children).

There are subtle relations between welfare and gender. Female-headed households are associated with lower welfare, *ceteris paribus* – 9 per cent lower in the regression. However, there is a positive effect of an increased proportion of women among the adults aged 15–64 and not in full-time education (compared to the default category of equivalent men). In the regression, the coefficient on this proportion implies that the change from an all-men household to an all-women one would raise household welfare by 10 per cent. It may be that women as heads of household face a variety of disadvantages but that more prosperous households tend to have a higher proportion of women in them (for example if a rich man is able to support more than one wife). The favourable effect of women on the household is stronger in the tobit than the regression, and stronger in the lower quartile regression than the upper one (where the variable in fact is not statistically significant).

14.3.4 Location variables

Living in urban areas raised welfare by around 28 per cent in the simple regression. Generally speaking, the Federal Capital Territory (the default), the South West or South South were the most favourable areas to reside in, *ceteris paribus*, and did not differ significantly from each other at the 5 per cent level. Other areas were disadvantaged, although the rankings were somewhat different from the order one would expect from the raw differentials in poverty rates. For example, the coefficient on residing in North Central is the most negative of the regional dummies despite the region only being ranked fifth out of seven on the descriptive statistics. The estimated effects do not markedly differ across models, with the exception of North Central. This has a very large negative effect on the lower quartile regression but has less than half that effect on the median and only an insignificant effect on the upper quartile regression.

14.3.5 Social capital

Several explanatory variables were created from the NLSS questions on social capital. To limit possible problems of endogeneity and reverse causation, the variables were created as averages of the responses of *other* households in the cluster.

The participation of other households in community programmes was positively associated with welfare. The size of the coefficient implied that, if all neighbouring households were involved in such programmes, welfare would rise by 7 per cent. Other variables to capture the cooperative nature of a community were constructed from a hypothetical question about the perceived willingness of the community to work together to resolve a water supply problem. The coefficients on these variables implied that welfare was higher in more cooperative communities, *ceteris paribus*, but the effects were statistically insignificant at the 10 per cent level.

Variables for the incidence of conflict and crime had perversely positive effects. In preliminary work, similar results were obtained when we used the households' *own* experience of conflict and crime. One possible interpretation of this perverse result is that more affluent communities tend to experience more crime – perhaps because they have more goods to steal. Interestingly, the crime variable had twice as strong an effect on the upper quartile as the lower one.

One question asked whether households had people that they could borrow a small amount of money from, beyond their immediate household and close relatives. The models show a monotonic relation between welfare and the likelihood with which neighbouring households could expect to receive loans. If all neighbours said there were definitely such people who would loan money, then welfare was 10 per cent higher than if they said there were definitely not such people. (Similar results were obtained using the households' own expectations, rather than those of their neighbours.) In the quantile regressions, these effects were somewhat smaller for the upper quartile than the median or lower quartile.

Contrary results were obtained from responses to a question about whether most people in the neighbourhood were ready to help if needed. Disagreeing strongly with this question was associated with the highest welfare, *ceteris paribus*. One interpretation of these seemingly conflicting results is that access to credit, rather than charity, is economically useful. Alternatively, it may be that, in affluent communities, credit becomes more easily available but households become more self-reliant.

Finally, one question asked about whether respondents agreed with the statement: 'In this neighbourhood one has to be alert or someone is likely to take advantage of you.' Neighbours' responses to this question had a non-monotonic relation with household welfare, with the most favourable effects coming from when there was either strong agreement or strong disagreement with this. Responses to these questions on trust had no effect on the logit for being poor, however.

14.3.6 Employment

In our core models, we did not include variables for employment status, as they could be regarded as choice variables. They may also be routes by which some of the other variables – notably education – affect welfare and poverty. However, for descriptive purposes, it is interesting to see the impact of adding employment to the list of explanatory variables discussed above. We classified adults of working age (15–64 years) into five categories, based on their main employment: agricultural; non-agricultural self-employed; private waged; public waged; and not working (for example retired). We then augmented the models in Tables 14.4 and 14.5 with variables for the proportion of working members in non-farm self-employment, private wage employment and public wage employment. Agriculture was kept as the default category and variables added for the log of working adults (plus one, to avoid zeros) together with a dummy for there being no working adults in the household. Table 14.6 reports the resulting coefficients on these employment variables; for brevity, the other coefficients are not reported.

The results in Table 14.6 suggest a public sector wage premium. If all household members were employed in the public sector, welfare would be 22 per cent higher, *ceteris paribus*. This holds both on average (in the simple regression) and for the poor (in the tobit). Public sector employment also has a significant effect in reducing the probability of being poor. As an approximation, a household with all workers in the public sector would have a probability of being poor that was 16.8 percentage points below that of a household with no government employees. The quantile regressions for log welfare also show strong positive effects of public wage employment.

The other findings in Table 14.6 are somewhat unexpected. We anticipated that agriculture would be the form of employment least favourable to household welfare and also that there would be clear benefits to private wage employment. However, these predictions were not supported. Private sector wage employment is not associated with higher welfare than agriculture in any of the models, *ceteris paribus*. Non-farm self-employment always has a negative coefficient, implying it is less favourable than farming, although it is not always significant. These

Table 14.6 Effect of employment sector on welfare and poverty

	Non-farm self-employment	Private wage employment	Public wage employment
Simple regression (log welfare)	–0.025 * (–1.73)	–0.039 (–1.00)	0.197 *** (7.75)
Tobit	–0.025 * (–1.81)	–0.039 (–1.19)	0.197 *** (8.84)
Logit (scaled coefficient)	–0.029 ** (–2.22)	–0.028 (–0.91)	0.168 *** (7.82)
Median regression	–0.053 *** (–3.54)	–0.051 (–1.47)	0.220 *** (9.16)
Lower quartile	–0.023 (–1.32)	–0.008 (–0.02)	0.242 *** (8.89)
Upper quartile	–0.041 ** (–2.61)	0.020 (0.55)	0.212 *** (8.30)

Coefficients on variables for proportion of household workers engaged in different kinds of employment (agriculture is the default). T-ratios in brackets.
Source: Authors' computation from the NLSS data.

results would seem to suggest that there is not a large gap in the returns to labour between agriculture and other forms of employment outside the public sector. There is thus no evidence of 'dualism' between 'backward' agriculture and 'modern' non-agricultural employment in the sense envisaged by Lewis. However, the existence of the public sector wage premium does suggest the possibility of a type of dualism in the form of 'Lewis through the looking glass' (Gelb *et al.*, 1991).

14.4 Labour market outcomes – wages and employment

Both the econometric analysis of consumption and the poverty analysis in Section 14.2 above strongly highlight the substantial benefit of working for the public sector in Nigeria. Households having one or more member working in the public sector have significantly higher levels of consumption, other things being equal; and it is among households whose head works in the public sector that poverty levels are lowest, by some margin. Such a public sector premium exists in many countries (see Terrell, 1993, for Haiti; Skyt-Neilsen and Rosholm, 2001, for Zambia; Hyder and Reilly, 2005, for Pakistan), but the magnitude is particularly striking in this case – including, surprisingly, relative to private sector wage employment.

The NLSS questionnaire collects information on the economic activities that household members are engaged in, including data on earnings for those in wage employment as well as an attempt, based on a direct question, to estimate earnings for those in self-employment activities (including agriculture). Only 18.6 per cent of working Nigerians are engaged in wage employment for their main activity, and three quarters of these work in the public sector. Median earnings are highest for public sector employees (16,000 naira per month; Table 14.7), followed by private sector employees and the non-farm self-employed, with average agricultural earnings lagging far behind.[8] Mean values are much higher than median values, reflecting a high degree of inequality in estimated earnings from the main job (though not necessarily such a high degree of inequality of wage rates, or of incomes across households that may comprise several individuals and different income sources). Further, the mean value of earnings from private sector employment is in fact higher than that for public sector employment, in contrast to the pattern for the median. This highlights a higher degree of inequality among private sector earnings, but in fact this higher mean value is just the result of one very high estimate[9] without which it would in fact be lower.

The self-employment earnings data estimated in this way may be of questionable reliability but the data on earnings from wage employment should be more reliable. Note that it is data on earnings that are available; the questionnaire did not collect sufficient data on time worked in the main job, and so does not allow separate analysis of hours worked and wage rates, presumably because its main focus was on income estimation. The earnings data used in this chapter include estimates of earnings in kind received by workers in various forms: including payment in the form of food, subsidized housing and transport, and other in-kind payments. Focusing on earnings (rather than, say, wage rates) is appropriate for the present analysis, the focus of which is to understand whether and why households with a member working in the public sector appear to be better off than those without. It also helps in understanding the factors that enable individuals to enjoy higher earnings.

14.4.1 The public–private sector earnings differential

Focusing attention now on employees only, the distribution of the logarithm of monthly earnings of employees in the public and private sector is plotted as kernel density functions in Figure 14.4. These graphs also indicate that public sector workers are better paid on average than those in the private sector; but also that at the top of the distribution private sector employees may be better off.

A simple but straightforward way of analysing the public–private wage differential further is by regressing the logarithm of the estimated monthly wage on a dummy variable indicating whether or not the work was conducted in the public sector (government or parastatal), in a regression in which population weights are applied. The coefficient gives an estimate of the magnitude of the earnings differential. Subsequently by adding in turn to the regression a series of further dummy variables capturing other factors that might influence the public–private wage differential, it is possible to make a simple estimate of how much of the public–private sector earnings differential remains after taking these other factors into account.[10] The estimated results for the public sector coefficients in the different regressions are presented in Table 14.8.[11] The pure public sector earnings premium is a very large 33.8 per cent; this is reduced to 21.9 per cent after age and gender are also controlled for (public sector workers are older on average than

Table 14.7 Summary characteristics of earnings, disaggregated by employment status

Employment status	Mean earnings (000s of naira per month)	Median earnings (000s of naira per month)	Standard deviation (000s of naira per month)	Number of observations
Agriculture	28.9	4.0	394.0	7,276
Government employment	49.5	16.0	319.3	2,227
Private wage employment	99.0	10.4	994.6	754
Non-farm self-employment	68.1	8.0	529.2	5,794
Total	54.6	8.0	508.8	16,051

Source: Authors' computations from NLSS data.

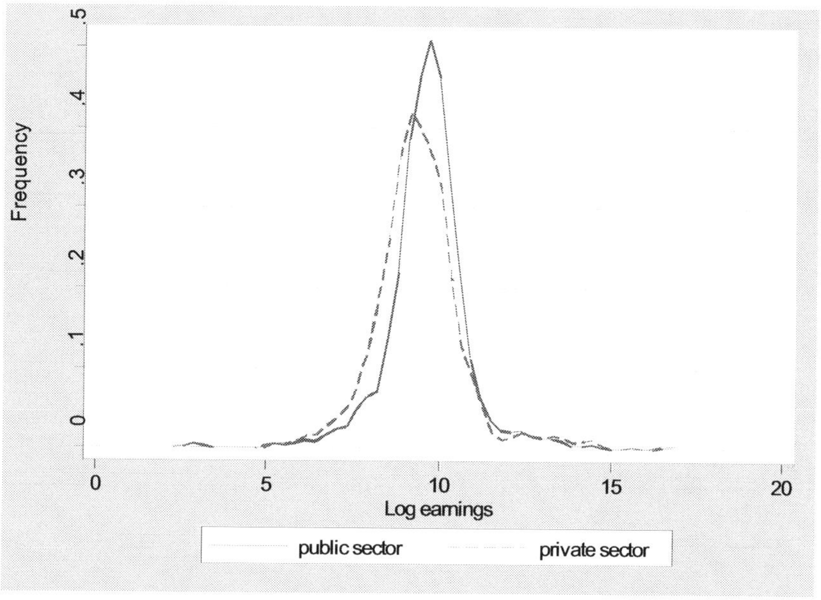

Figure 14.4 Kernel density plots of the logarithm values of public and private sector earnings.
Source: Computed by authors from NLSS data. The horizontal axis reports values of the logarithm of annual earnings.

their private sector counterparts – though also more likely to be female which operates in the opposite reduction because females are paid less on average). Once education factors are taken into account, however, the public sector premium reduces substantially to 9.7 per cent, though the corresponding coefficient is still highly statistically significant. In other words, an important part of the public sector premium reflects the significantly higher levels of education of public sector workers compared to private sector workers; for example, 19.5 per cent of public sector employees have degrees compared to 9.6 per cent in the private sector (with similar large differentials at senior secondary level). The public sector attracts workers that have higher education levels to begin with; but even after controlling for this, a public sector premium remains.

OLS regressions, though, may be significantly affected by extreme values, which it has already been noted are present in the earnings data. Moreover, the earnings differential is likely to vary across the earnings distribution, as suggested by Figure 14.4 above. A more promising approach, therefore, may be to use a quantile regression equivalent to estimate the public–private gap at different quantiles, again allowing for some of the other control factors. This data is also reported in Table 14.8, based on quantile regressions at the following percentiles: 10, 25, 50, 75 and 90. The coefficients now should be interpreted as the impact of having a public sector job on the conditional wage distribution in the corresponding quantile.

Table 14.8 Estimates of the public–private sector wage premium, allowing for different worker characteristics, in percentage points

		Quantile regressions				
	OLS	**Q10**	**Q25**	**Q50**	**Q75**	**Q90**
Public sector wage premium (no conditioning variables)	33.8***	69.3***	51.1***	41.5***	26.2***	6.9
After taking account of age and gender	21.9***	59.1***	43.9***	32.3***	19.0***	–3.0
Also taking account of education level	9.7***	52.4***	31.3***	15.4***	4.8	–29.4**
Also taking account of region	8.1*	50.6***	26.6***	15.4***	3.0	–22.7***
Also taking account of sector	11.9**	38.6***	28.1***	13.0***	7.6	–13.9*

The values in this table report the coefficients on a dummy variable for being employed in the public sector, in a regression for the logarithm of earnings. Other factors are introduced as explanatory variables as noted in the first column. *** denotes significance of the coefficient of the public sector at the 1 per cent level; ** at the 5 per cent level and * at the 10 per cent level.
Source: Authors' computations from NLSS data.

The differentials vary substantially by quantile. In all cases (with or without controls) the public sector premia are very large at low quantiles of the conditional distribution, but fall moving up to high quantiles, with the public sector premium being replaced by a discount in some cases at the ninetieth percentile. In other words, at the lower end of the distribution there is a substantial public sector premium; and this remains statistically significant in many cases even after taking account of the fact that public sector workers have characteristics which make them likely to earn more (such as higher levels of education). The public sector premium remains throughout most of the conditional distribution, though at the seventy-fifth percentile and above it is predominantly accounted for by education differentials. Only at the ninetieth percentile is there some evidence for a significant public sector discount, with public sector workers receiving lower earnings relative to the private sector given their educational characteristics. But whether this reflects differences in wage rates or in hours worked unfortunately cannot be identified from this data.

In short, it is very beneficial for those at the lower end and middle of the earnings distribution to work in the public sector in terms of the average earnings they can command, to add to any possible additional benefits in terms of employment security and the like. This is a very important factor enabling households that can access such jobs the opportunity to improve their living conditions and potentially move out of poverty. But this extra earnings benefit of working in the public sector appears to disappear at the extreme upper end of the distribution.

14.4.2 Disaggregating the public–private sector differential

While the preceding analysis just distinguished workers according to whether they are employed in the public or private sectors, there is in fact significant heterogeneity within and between these sectors. The public and private sectors are engaged in different economic sectors to different extents; and within the public and private sectors there are important differences in types of employers (for example parastatals versus government).

In the public sector 75 per cent of workers are employed in professional and technical activities (among the best-paid sectors) or clerical work (a relatively low-paid activity), with many of the rest employed in services. The private sector by contrast is more dispersed, including higher proportions of people working in relatively low-paid sectors such as services, sales, agricultural labour and production. But still more than a quarter of private sector employees work in professional and technical activities. In this sector the mean earnings in the private sector are higher compared to the public (Table 14.9); but the median earnings of professional and technical workers are higher in the public sector. And, in fact, the mean value in the private sector is higher only because of the one extreme value identified above. In most of the other (generally lower-paid) sectors both the mean and median earnings of private sector workers are lower than those of their public sector counterparts. This provides one important explanation of the distributional pattern of the public–private differential identified above: many private sector employees are in low-paying sectors, and often receive lower payment in these sectors compared to their public sector counterparts. At the top end, though, the best-qualified employees may receive as good or higher earnings in the private sector.

The public sector in the above classification groups together those working in parastatals as well as regular government employees. Median and mean wages are higher among those working for parastatals, and this is certainly the case for the largest economic sector categories: professional and technical workers, and clerical and related staff. But at the same time, higher proportions of those working for parastatals are employed in lower average pay sectors such as sales, agriculture/forestry, manufacturing and production. So there is not a systematic pattern of advantage for parastatal workers.

14.4.3 A preliminary assessment of factors influencing public and private sector wage earnings

In most countries there is often a substantial benefit to an individual being able to access waged employment, rather than relying on more insecure and uncertain self-employment activities; and in Nigeria as in many countries this benefit appears to be greatest for those able to access public sector jobs. Estimation of a multinomial logit model distinguishing public sector wage employment, private sector wage employment and self-employment (the omitted case) highlights strongly the importance of education.[12] Individuals that possess high levels of education (here chiefly senior secondary, degree-level or technical and vocational training) are significantly more likely to be engaged in wage work in general, and in the public sector in particular. Education is clearly an important factor enabling access to these more secure and better-paid jobs relative to the other alternatives most individuals have open to them. The other significant factor is age, in that the likelihood of working in the public sector (relative to the self-employment base case) increases with age up to a maximum of around 49 years, after which it declines with age.

Of greater interest, though, are the factors that influence levels of earnings in the jobs they hold. A preliminary investigation of this, again by means of quantile regressions, is reported in Tables 14.10a and 14.10b for public and private sector workers respectively. What these results highlight is again the importance of education and age factors. In all quantile regressions, the impact of age on earnings is in line with classic earnings function pattern – earnings increasing with age, though to a decreasing extent. But the most potentially policy-relevant finding apparent from these regression results is the very strong impact of education.

Education factors have large quantitative impacts on earnings in all six regressions, but there are some important differences between the public and private sector, and at different parts of the distribution within each. Looking first at the public sector, having completed primary education has a large, statistically significant impact of similar magnitude (around 44 per cent) on earnings in the lower quartile and median regressions, but not at all in the upper quartile. The same general point applies to completed senior secondary education and to technical

Table 14.9 Summary earnings from public and private sector wage employment, by sector of employment and skill level

	Median earnings (000s of naira per month)		**Mean earnings (000s of naira per month)**		**Number of observations**	
	Public	**Private**	**Public**	**Private**	**Public**	**Private**
By sector:						
Professional and technical	18.9	15.0	51.3	282.0	957	193
Administration	20.8	25.0	55.8	88.2	35	6
Clerical and related	14.5	12.0	33.6	15.9	724	123
Sales workers	10.0	6.5	22.2	22.3	42	59
Service industry	12.0	7.0	90.6	9.1	279	98
Agriculture and forestry	10.0	8.0	30.9	16.1	96	70
Production and transport	15.6	9.1	99.7	81.6	18	55
Manufacturing and ...	14.5	15.0	20.8	15.6	16	21
Others	15.0	12.0	29.9	25.9	60	129
By skill level:						
Unskilled	12.0	9.0	25.5	19.8	343	248
Semi-skilled	12.5	10.0	59.9	28.7	736	304
Skilled	18.9	15.0	46.7	270.2	1148	202
Total	15.5	10.0	48.3	94.4	2227	754

Source: Authors' computations from NLSS data.

Table 14.10a Quantile regression results for correlates of log earnings: public sector workers

	First quartile (Q25)			Median (Q50)			Upper quartile (Q75)		
	Coefficient	Z score		Coefficient	Z score		Coefficient	Z score	
Constant	7.138	29.61	***	7.434	28.40	***	8.089	26.22	***
Age	0.077	7.63	***	0.070	6.16	***	0.058	4.56	***
Age squared	–0.001	–7.58	***	–0.001	–5.44	***	–0.001	–3.88	***
Some education	0.094	0.80		0.194	1.55		0.542	3.56	***
Primary	0.445	4.34	***	0.444	4.08	***	0.048	0.37	
Junior secondary	–0.391	–3.56	***	–0.444	–3.81	***	–0.407	–2.89	***
Senior secondary	0.324	2.90	***	0.337	2.84	***	0.277	1.93	*
Technical/vocational	0.480	2.87	***	0.486	2.74	***	0.103	0.48	
Degree	0.629	11.84	***	0.603	10.73	***	0.628	9.21	***
Hhsize	–0.011	–1.73	*	–0.004	–0.55		–0.004	–0.56	
Female	0.047	1.16		–0.007	–0.16		–0.060	–1.15	
Married – monogamous	0.024	0.36		–0.002	–0.04		0.088	1.08	

Married – polygamous	–0.072	–0.83		–0.064	–0.71		0.042	0.39	
Cohabiting	–0.073	–0.26		–0.204	–0.71		0.478	1.32	
Divorced	–0.036	–0.21		–0.145	–0.83		–0.094	–0.45	
Separated	–0.313	–2.78	***	–0.287	–2.39	**	–0.160	–1.12	
Widowed	0.010	0.08		0.013	0.10		–0.013	–0.09	
North West	–0.090	–0.81		–0.132	–1.12		–0.180	–1.27	
North East	–0.136	–1.29		–0.109	–0.97		–0.062	–0.46	
North Central	–0.109	–1.04		–0.079	–0.72		–0.212	–1.59	
South South	–0.081	–0.78		–0.056	–0.51		–0.039	–0.29	
South West	–0.127	–1.21		–0.129	–1.16		–0.221	–1.64	
South East	–0.206	–1.92	*	–0.176	–1.55		–0.231	–1.69	*
Pseudo R squared	0.0874			0.0969			0.0842		
No. of observations	2254			2254			2254		

Dependent variable: log of earnings per month.
*** Denotes statistical significance at the 1 per cent level, ** at the 5 per cent level and * at the 10* level.
Source: Authors' estimation based on NLSS data.

Table 14.10b Quantile regression results for correlates of log earnings: private sector workers

	First quartile (Q25)			Median (Q50)			Upper quartile (Q75)		
	Coefficient	Z score		Coefficient	Z score		Coefficient	Z score	
Constant	6.771	11.66	***	7.941	17.30	***	7.496	20.71	***
Age	0.067	2.74	***	0.056	3.08	***	0.088	6.34	***
Age squared	–0.001	–2.31	**	–0.001	–3.08	***	–0.001	–6.19	***
Some education	–0.036	–0.17		0.075	0.43		0.248	1.73	*
Primary	0.377	1.99	**	0.243	1.59		0.271	2.13	**
Junior secondary	0.080	0.40		–0.044	–0.27		–0.052	–0.40	
Senior secondary	0.103	0.52		–0.027	–0.16		–0.137	–1.03	
Technical/vocational	0.318	1.00		0.416	1.54		0.641	2.77	***
Degree	0.948	4.60	***	0.994	5.70	***	1.448	10.04	***
Hhsize	0.008	0.49		–0.001	–0.06		–0.010	–0.90	
Female	–0.352	–3.08	***	–0.433	–4.63	***	–0.332	–4.43	***
Married – monogamous	0.068	0.46		0.103	0.85		–0.025	–0.25	
Married – polygamous	0.245	1.04		0.301	1.56		0.167	1.12	

Cohabiting	0.179	0.43		−0.664	−1.24		−1.268	−9.04	***
Divorced	−0.622	−1.47		−0.389	−1.01		−0.723	−2.54	**
Separated	−0.209	−0.73		−0.362	−1.54		−0.319	−1.68	*
Widowed	−0.481	−1.66	*	−0.029	−0.12		−0.283	−1.39	
North West	0.000	0.00		−0.265	−0.90		0.111	0.47	
North East	0.091	0.25		−0.068	−0.22		0.113	0.46	
North Central	−0.375	−1.10		−0.375	−1.30		−0.148	−0.64	
South South	−0.132	−0.40		−0.088	−0.32		0.056	0.26	
South West	−0.037	−0.11		−0.122	−0.44		−0.027	−0.12	
South East	−0.283	−0.85		−0.410	−1.45		−0.092	−0.41	
Pseudo R squared	0.1071			0.1125			0.1245		
No. of observations	754			754			754		

Dependent variable: log of earnings per month.
*** Denotes statistical significance at the 1 per cent level, ** at the 5 per cent level and * at the 10* level.
Source: Authors' estimation based on NLSS data.

and vocational training. In the upper quartile regression it is only degree-level education that has a significant impact on earnings. In fact, having a degree has an impact of similar (more than 60 per cent) magnitude and statistical significance across the three regressions; interestingly, it has a large impact at the lower end too. In the private sector regression the education variables are generally much less likely to be statistically significant, except in the case of degree-level education, the impact of which is very large in magnitude (more so than in the public sector) and highly statistically significant in all three quantile regressions. In contrast to the public sector, here the magnitude is much higher in the upper quartile regression compared to the median and lower quartile. Technical and vocational education also has a large, statistically significant impact on earnings in the upper quartile regression, but not in the other two.

Among the other factors which are statistically significant in these regressions, the gender factor is of particular interest. In the private sector, females are systematically paid substantially less than males (other things being equal) throughout the entire distribution. And fewer females work as private wage employees. In the public sector, though, no statistically significant gender differential is apparent in any of the regressions.

It is clear from these results that education is a very important factor enabling individuals to get access to wage jobs, and obtain often substantially higher earnings within these jobs. In many cases this appears to apply even at the lower end of the distribution. In particular there seems to be a substantial private return to having degree-level qualification, and this latter point applies in the private sector even more than its substantial impact in the public sector. However, and importantly for policy purposes, this does not generally translate into an equivalent social return. And it is expected to be much greater than the impact on household consumption, given that household incomes come from many other sources besides wage earnings. So this is not in conflict with the results of Section 14.3; and the education variables are measured differently in any case.

In summary, and consistently with the preceding sections of this chapter, there are substantial benefits to working as a wage employee in the public sector in Nigeria. Public sector employees generally have higher levels of human capital than their private sector counterparts; but even controlling for this a significant earnings premium exists for public sector employment – except at the very top of the earnings distribution where the private sector may fare better. In reality, large numbers of those working in the private sector are working in low-pay sectors; and even most of those in the better-paid sectors are paid less than in the public sector. In both sectors, though, there is a very strong message about the importance of education in raising earnings, with degree-level qualifications generally having the biggest private impacts.

14.5 Conclusions

Our preliminary results imply several broad issues for policy-makers and raise a number of options for policy. We group our discussion in three, centring on our findings in three areas: (1) the level of poverty; (2) the level of inequality; (3) the determinants of welfare and poverty.

On the level of poverty, there appears to be some confusion in the official estimates of poverty, particularly for the 2003/2004 survey, due to the adoption of a 'relative' poverty line. The poverty line used for earlier surveys was derived relative to living standards in 1985 but then held constant in real terms over time. However, there appears to have been some institutional memory loss with the most recent official poverty line survey defining the line relative to living standards in 2003/2004. We would argue strongly that Nigeria's official practice of using a relative poverty line – in the strict sense of one that rises with general living standards – is misguided.[13] It may well be true that poverty is ultimately relative. As countries become more affluent, the minimum living standards they regard as acceptable inevitably rise. For example, one of the authors of this chapter has argued that urban China is now sufficiently prosperous that the absolute 'dollar a day' measure of poverty is irrelevant – a survey of Beijing identified no household living below that line (Appleton *et al.*, 2006). However, in order that the poverty indicators track material living standards over time, it is necessary to hold the poverty line constant in absolute terms. A purely relative approach, where the poverty line is two thirds of mean consumption, means that poverty will fall if all living standards collapse, so long as those of the rich collapse faster (one could term this a 'Pol Pot' scenario). By contrast, if everyone's living standards rise, but those of the rich rise faster, poverty will appear to get worse (one is reminded of Deng Xiao Peng's dictum 'let some get rich first'). Indeed, one could argue that working with a strictly relative concept of poverty risks conceptualizing anti-poverty strategy as a zero sum game and focusing on redistribution. Overall economic growth will not reduce relative poverty, unless the growth happens to be progressively redistributed. The National Bureau of Statistics appears to accept the argument for an absolute poverty line, noting that it is 'preferred for evaluating effectiveness of poverty reduction policy' (Federal Office of Statistics, 2005: 115). It also suggests (34) that 'It may be an opportune moment to transition to the objective method'. Presumably the moment is opportune because the objective (absolute) and relative poverty measures for 2003/2004 are very similar in magnitude. A switch in the series may not cause much adverse comment from policy-makers and the public, if the numbers for the base year (2003/2004) are essentially the same. We note here that the setting of the poverty line should be a matter of public consultation and debate. Since it concerns what minimum standard of living is considered acceptable, it embodies value judgements and is not something that should be set by technocrats or outside experts. For monitoring purposes, the precise location of the poverty line may not be important – one can use dominance analysis to seek out results that are robust. However, if the poverty line is used to determine access to services or to target subsidies, then its precise location becomes a matter of considerable public interest.

On the level of inequality and absolute poverty, analysis of the NLSS 2003/2004 suggests that the common perceptions are only half right. It is true that absolute poverty is high – covering nearly six out of ten Nigerians. This is true whether the precise poverty line is the 'objective' measure of the NBS – anchored on calorie requirements – or the 'dollar a day' line (the two alternative absolute measures being in close agreement). However, the view that Nigeria is exceptionally unequal does not seem supported. It is not more unequal than most other African countries. Moreover, inequality is down on the 1990s figures. Linked to this, our models of welfare revealed a surprising absence of a pure gap between the welfare of those in farming and in private non-farm employment or self-employment. This suggests an absence of a 'dualistic' economy, at least within the private sector. Taken together, these findings imply that poverty in Nigeria should be construed as a mass phenomenon and some of the earlier descriptions in the literature might be misleading. For example, the Canagarajah and Thomas paper is entitled 'Poverty in a Wealthy Economy', which implies that the problem is one of distribution. However, this does not seem to square with the evidence of pervasive poverty in almost all sectors and parts of the country. This is not to deny significant inequalities exist – rural–urban, north–south, by state and so on. Some of these inequalities could conceivably be used to target the poor. But one must be wary of the likely errors of targeting – both including the non-poor and excluding some of the poor. A project that benefited all the residents of a particularly poor state might have only a small 'leakage' to the non-poor, as almost all the residents might well be poor. This may be useful for an international NGO, whose funds are limited and so must be selective. However, it is not clear how much leverage it provides the federal government – since targeting only one state would inevitably mean omitting the vast majority of Nigeria's poor. More generally, the Nigerian public faces a choice over how equal a society it desires and how much redistribution it is prepared to sanction. The level of inequality of aversion, like the setting of the poverty line, is a value judgement and not one that should be left to 'experts'. In practice, it may be hard to obtain a meaningful public consensus when the issue is presented in such abstract terms. Here the work of the economist Amartya Sen may be useful, when he poses the question 'inequality of what?' and effectively answers 'of basic capabilities' (Sen, 1997). This approach chimes with the emphasis of the World Development Report 2006 on inequality (World Bank, 2006), which argues for equalities of opportunities (Sen's 'capabilities' are ultimately best interpreted as 'opportunities'). In practical terms, this approach may imply a focus on absolute poverty – so that people are able to consume essential marketed commodities – together with an emphasis on making sure people all have access to key public services, like education, health, water and sanitation.

Finally, we turn to the issue of what particular anti-poverty programmes are likely to be most suitable for Nigeria. At a very general level, our portrayal of Nigeria as being characterized by mass absolute poverty and unexceptional inequality would seem to imply that the emphasis perhaps should be on overall economic growth rather than redistribution. The problem is not that there is poverty in a wealthy economy, but that the economy is not wealthy enough. The primary emphasis, therefore, should perhaps be on policies to promote strong and sustained economic growth, or at least avoid a repetition of the mismanagement that has stalled Nigeria's growth in the past. Our models of welfare, poverty and earnings do provide some insights into the likely success of more specific policies. Schooling may have strong effects on raising the earnings of those lucky enough to be employed in waged jobs. But this is only a small part of the population; and the relatively small effects on household consumption and poverty suggest that education is unlikely to be a 'magic bullet' to fight poverty. If each extra average year of schooling raises welfare by only 2 per cent, then even a major educational expansion is unlikely to transform the Nigerian economy (even assuming that such an expansion does not further depress returns). However, it is important to warn that this does not negate the fact that education is likely to be regarded as intrinsically valuable (literacy and numeracy are likely to be included by most people among the basic capabilities that should be available to all). Nor do our results bear on the returns to investments in the quality of education. Conversely, the large negative effects of household size on welfare suggest that policies to limit population growth may bring benefits. Another area for further investigation is the apparent premium to working in the public sector, which appears to be a rather inequitably distributed rent. Indeed, the simple poverty decompositions by sector suggest that the government should focus on the self-employed – whether in agriculture or non-agricultural enterprises. These are the main income-generating activities of most Nigerians and interventions to promote growth here are likely to have the biggest effect on overall poverty.

Notes

1 Alayande is at the Department of Economics, Olabisi Onabanjo University Ago-Iwoye; Appleton is at the School of Economics, University of Nottingham; McKay is at the Department of Economics, University of Sussex. We are very grateful to Geoffrey Greenwell for his advice on many aspects relating to the data. Very helpful comments, suggestions and advice were received in the project workshop, and from Barry Reilly and Leticia Veruete-McKay.

2 A corresponding ambiguity arises with the concept of an absolute poverty line. Is it merely one that is fixed in real terms over time (a weak definition)? Or one derived from some objective estimate of needs (a strong definition)? The poverty statistics in FOS (1999) measure absolute poverty in the weak sense, although the line used was not an absolute poverty line under the strong definition.

3 FOS (1999) used a poverty line of 395.4 naira per annum in 1985 prices and adjusted it according to the CPI for estimating poverty in other years. The line was originally derived as two thirds of the mean per capita expenditure in the 1985 survey, although the line was maintained for consistency with earlier reports despite revisions that put two thirds of mean per capita expenditure at 355 naira.

4 The national accounts estimates of private consumption may be subject to considerable errors, as they are estimated as a residual, although the National Bureau of Statistics does try to calibrate them to survey estimates. We deflate the current value of private consumption by the CPI. Both the CPI and national accounts data were provided by the Central Bank of Nigeria. For consumption, we start with the 1991 census estimate of 88,992,220 and apply a growth rate of 2.83 per cent (the procedure used by Federal Office of Statistics, 2005).

5 Canagarajah and Thomas (2001) published estimates of 43 per cent poor in 1985, falling to 34 per cent in 1992. However, it is clear from FOS (1999: 6) that these are erroneous early official estimates, affected by 'an error in data dictionary, affecting both

the 1985 and 1992 datasets' and should be revised upwards to be the values given in Table 14.1.

6 The rise in prices between 1985 and 2003/4 was so large that updating the poverty line is problematic. We take the January 2004 CPI value of 119 (with a May 2003 = 100 base) and splice it to the earlier CPI series (base = 1985) by multiplying by 52. Using the IMF CPI numbers gives a lower conversion factor, 53.42 rather than 61.88.

7 The effect is calculated as $\exp(\beta)-1$ where β is the relevant coefficient.

8 These earnings estimates have not been corrected for regional price differences; but these are small relative to the magnitude of difference in the earnings figures.

9 The highest annual private sector earning translates to about $120,000 per annum, compared to a median earning of less than $100! The high value is exceptional compared to all other observations of private sector wage earnings.

10 This of course involves various strong assumptions, including that the coefficients of the additional terms added are not allowed to differ between the public and private sectors.

11 For the sake of brevity the full econometric results for these regressions are not presented here, but they can be supplied on request.

12 Results are not presented here, but are available on request.

13 Here, we would also reiterate the point made earlier, that the apparent volatility of private consumption in the national accounts implies that surveys to monitor poverty should be more frequent.

References

Anyanwu, John C., 2005, 'Rural Poverty in Nigeria: Profile, Determinants and Exit Paths', *African Development Review*, 18 (1), 435–460.

Appleton, Simon, 1999a, 'Education and Health at the Household Level in Sub-Saharan Africa', Centre for International Development Working Paper No. 33, Harvard University.

Appleton, Simon, 1999b, 'Have Returns to Education Changed over Time? Evidence from Kenya, 1978–1995', CSAE Working Paper 99.6, with Arne Bigsten and Damiano Kulundu Manda, CSAE, Oxford.

Appleton, Simon, 2001a, 'The Rich are Just Like Us, Only Richer: Poverty Functions or Consumption Functions? Evidence from Uganda', *Journal of African Economies*, 10 (4), 433–469.

Appleton, Simon, 2001b, 'Education, Incomes and Poverty in Uganda', CREDIT Research Paper 01/22, University of Nottingham.

Appleton, Simon, Lina Song and Qingjie Xia, 2006, 'Growing Out of Poverty: Trends and Patterns in Urban Poverty in China 1988–2002', paper presented at the Beijing Forum, 27–29 October.

Canagarajah, S. and S. Thomas, 2001, 'Poverty in a Wealthy Economy: The Case of Nigeria', *Journal of African Economies*, 10, 143–173.

Federal Office of Statistics, 1999, *Poverty Profile for Nigeria 1980–1996*, Lagos: Federal Office of Statistics.

Federal Office of Statistics, 2005, *Poverty Profiles 2004*, Lagos: Census and Survey Department, Federal Office of Statistics.

Foster, J., J. Greer and E. Thorbecke, 1984, 'A Class of Decomposable Poverty Indices', *Econometrica*, 52, 761–765.

Gelb, Alan, John B. Knight and Richard Sabot, 1991, 'Public sector employment, rent seeking and economic growth', *Economic Journal*, 101, 1186–1199.

Hyder, A. and B. Reilly, 2005, 'The Public–Private Sector Pay Gap in Pakistan: A Quantile Regression Analysis', *Pakistan Development Review*, 44 (3), 271–306.

Lanjouw, P. and M. Ravallion, 1995, 'Poverty and Household Size', *Economic Journal*, 105 (433), 1415–1434.

Milanovic, Branco, 2003, 'Is Inequality in Africa Really Different?', Policy Research Working Paper 3169, World Bank, Washington, DC.

Nguyen, B.T., J.W. Albrecht, S.B. Vroman and M.D. Westbrook, forthcoming 2007, 'A Quantile Decomposition of Urban–Rural Inequality in Vietnam', *Journal of Development Economics.*

Oxfam, 2003, *Poverty in Nigeria*, Oxford: Oxfam.

Psacharopoulos, G., 1994, 'Returns to Investment in Education: A Global Update', *World Development*, 22 (9), 1325–1344.

Ravallion, Martin, 1998, 'Poverty Lines in Theory and Practice', Living Standards Measurement Study, Working Paper No. 133, World Bank, Washington, DC.

Sala-i-Martin, Xavier, 2006, 'The World Distribution of Income: Falling Poverty and ... Convergence, Period', *Quarterly Journal of Economics*, 121 (2), 351–397.

Sen, A.K., 1997, *On Economic Inequality*: with a substantial annexe *On Economic Inequality After a Quarter Century*, by J. Foster and A. Sen, 2nd edition, Oxford: Clarendon Press.

Skyt-Nielsen, H. and M. Rosholm, 2001, 'The Public–Private Sector Wage Gap in Zambia in the 1990s: A Quantile Regression Approach', *Empirical Economics*, 26, 169–182.

Subramanian, Arvind and Xavier Sala-i-Martin, 2003, 'Addressing the Natural Resource Curse: An Illustration from Nigeria', IMF Working Paper 03/139, IMF, Washington, DC.

Terrell, K., 1993, 'Public–Private Wage Differentials in Haiti: Do Public Servants Earn a Rent?', *Journal of Development Economics*, 42, 293–314.

WHO, 1985, 'Energy and Protein Requirements', WHO Technical Report Series 724, Geneva: WHO.

World Bank, 2006, *World Development Report 2006: Bridging the Gulfs of Inequality in Developing Countries*, New York: Oxford University Press.

15

The Impact of Universal Primary Education on Socio-economic Outcomes: A Nigerian Experiment

Una Okonkwo Osili[1]

15.1 Introduction

Universal education is widely viewed as critical to poverty reduction and economic growth. However, more than 100 million children in developing countries do not have access to primary school education. According to recent UNICEF statistics, 7.3 million Nigerian children, of which number 67 per cent are girls, are not enrolled in school. Over the past four decades, successive Nigerian governments have set targets and policies towards achieving universal primary education. Achieving universal primary education – and gender equality in education – remains an important policy objective for Nigeria and many other developing countries.

The goal of this chapter is to examine the impact of Nigeria's universal education policies on socio-economic outcomes. In particular, we focus on one of Nigeria's most far-reaching educational initiatives to date – the Universal Primary Education programme (UPE). The UPE was a nationwide programme that was introduced in September 1976, and has been characterized as 'one of the most ambitious education projects in African history' on account of the magnitude of the programme in terms of government resources and the number of children who benefited (Bray, 1981: 1). Spurred by oil revenues, the government allocated funds to provide free tuition in primary schools, to construct new primary school classrooms, and to train new teachers. Macro-level evidence from Nigeria suggests a striking expansion in primary schooling outcomes in the years of the UPE programme (1976–81). Nigeria's gross primary enrolment rate increased from 50.3 in 1975 to 120.7 in 1981 (World Bank, 2002).[2] However, the programme ended in 1981, after which schools were returned to regional governments and school fees were introduced in many states.

The Nigerian government has recently launched the Universal Basic Education (UBE), joining other developing countries in seeking to achieve targets based on internationally agreed Millennium Development Goals (MDGs). Important and timely insights can be gleaned from the accomplishments and challenges associated with the UBE's predecessor, the UPE programme. Between 1974 and 1979, the total cost of the UPE programme in Nigeria (including capital and recurrent expenditures) was about 2.2 billion naira (in nominal terms) – on average, about 2–3 per cent of annual real GDP during this period. Policy-makers in Nigeria and other developing countries often have to weigh the costs and the private and social returns associated with universal education programmes. One key concern is the appropriate level of public sector investment in education – how much should be invested at various levels of education as well as the socio-economic benefits associated with these investments.

In this chapter, we use data from the Nigerian Demographic Health Surveys (NDHS) to investigate the long-term impact of the UPE programme. Specifically, we exploit state-level variation in programme intensity to study the causal impact of schooling on labour market and non-labour market outcomes. Data from the Nigerian experience with UPE provide a unique opportunity to study the impact of exogenous variation in exposure to universal schooling on labour and non-labour market outcomes. In this way, this chapter joins a growing number of studies in which researchers have sought to identify the causal impact of education policies and programmes in developing countries.[3] An important advantage of this approach is that we can deal with self-selection issues, in that education may be associated with better labour and non-labour market outcomes, not because of its causal impact, but mainly because of omitted individual, household and community variables.

Our empirical analysis focuses mainly on the impact of the UPE programme on women. This approach has some distinct advantages. First, although women account for over half of the population in Nigeria and many other African countries, they are under-represented in the formal private sector, the public sector and the political sphere. While there has been progess in many states, a persistent gender gap in access to education results in fewer girls and young women attending and completing primary and secondary schooling. Second, a large number of studies have documented that (1) educated women tend to have fewer and healthier children and lower infant mortality and (2) their children are more likely to acquire schooling and participate fully in productive activities in the economy. In future work, we plan to extend the analysis to study the impact of the UPE programme on both men and women.

Evidence from Nigeria suggests that investments in primary school education associated with the UPE programme had a significant impact on schooling and labour and non-labour market outcomes. Controlling for age and other socio-economic variables, cohorts with the highest rates of exposure to the programme (based on their year of birth and state of education) completed more years of schooling and tended to have higher rates of formal labour force participation. However, the most significant benefits of the programme extended to non-labour market outcomes. Women with the highest rates of UPE exposure were more likely to delay their first marriage, had fewer children, and experienced lower rates of infant mortality than cohorts of women born earlier or later. Our empirical analysis includes state fixed effects, and we also attempt to control for sources of time-varying heterogeneity at the state level. Finally, we use programme exposure (based on year of birth and state of schooling) as an instrument for years of schooling in order to identify the causal impact of schooling on labour and non-labour market outcomes.

This chapter is organized as follows: Section 15.2 provides some background on the UPE programme in Nigeria. Section 15.3 presents data sources and the empirical framework. In Section 15.4, we discuss our results. Section 15.5 presents conclusions.

15.2 Background

15.2.1 Why was the UPE programme initiated?

The UPE programme was formally announced on 1 October 1974 by the military head of state, General Yakubu Gowon. The formal announcement was made in Sokoto State in northern Nigeria. An important goal of the nationwide UPE programme was the reduction of regional imbalances between the northern and southern regions of Nigeria (Bray, 1981).

Regional inequalities between the northern states and southern states of Nigeria were particularly evident in access to schooling. In 1974, there were only 4225 primary schools in northern Nigeria compared to 10,313 in southern Nigeria (Annual Abstract of Statistics, 1981). Primary school enrolment levels in the northern states were only 25 per cent of those in southern states (854,666 primary school students in the northern states compared to 3,356,731 in southern states). The need to reduce regional disparities was brought into even sharper focus during the reconstruction efforts that followed the Nigerian Civil War (1967–70). During the tenure of the then military head of state, General Olusegun Obasanjo, the UPE programme was implemented. Primary education was free, funded at the federal level, and universally available throughout the country starting in September 1976. Fuelled by the oil boom revenues, the government also provided grants to states to construct new primary schools and teacher training institutions, and for the payment of teachers' salaries. The Third National Development Plan (Federal Republic of Nigeria, 1978) made provision for the expansion in primary school classrooms. The plan allowed for 107,505 primary school classrooms in the northern states compared to 35,045 primary school classrooms in the southern states.

15.2.2 Education policy in Nigeria prior to the UPE

The UPE programme of the 1970s was built upon earlier efforts to improve education in Nigeria.

Early regional universal education programmes were generally limited in their overall impact. Table 15.1 summarizes the important dates. The first universal education scheme in Nigeria was launched in January 1955 in the Western Region of Nigeria. Figure 15.1 provides a map of Nigeria. In 1955, tuition fees were abolished for all levels of primary schooling in the Western Region. According to S.O. Awokoya (1952), then Education Minister for Western Region, education was seen as 'imperative' and 'urgent'. The priority afforded to education was reflected

Table 15.1 Landmark events and universal primary education in Nigeria

1842	First English-speaking missionaries arrive in Nigeria; marks beginning of formal schooling
1955	Western Region launches free schooling programme in January 1955
1957	Eastern Region launches 'Education without payment of fees' in January 1957
1957	Lagos (federal territory) launches its free schooling programme
1958	Reintroduction of school fees in Eastern Region in January 1958 (only the first two years of primary schooling remained free)
1976	Nationwide UPE launched throughout the country on 6 September 1976
1981	End of UPE programme
1999	UBE programme commences (includes first three years of secondary school)

Source: Bray (1981).

in the Western Region's budget, with primary education consuming nearly 40 per cent of the government's recurrent budget (Nwachukwu, 1985: 141). Although schooling was not compulsory, the student population increased significantly in the Western Region. In 1954, there were 457,000 primary school students in the Western Region and by 1955 this number had increased to 800,000, outpacing projections (Nwachukwu, 1985: 144).[4] Female enrolments rose during this period even though there was no explicit targeting of girls. Although girls constituted less than 20 per cent of primary school students in 1954, their proportion increased to nearly 40 per cent by 1966 (Nwachukwu, 1985: 145).

Following the Western Region model, the Eastern Region launched a universal primary school programme in January 1957 that provided education without fees. However, the Eastern Region's programme was less successful owing to insufficient planning. In the face of financial difficulties, the programme was scaled back to provide free schooling only in the first two years of primary schooling. Although the educational system had experienced initial expansion, primary school enrolments in Eastern Nigeria declined following the reintroduction of school fees in 1958. Lagos, the former capital of Nigeria, also introduced a universal primary education programme in January 1957. Unlike the other programmes, it also expanded teacher training colleges at the same time. By 1964, nearly 90 per cent of primary-age students were enrolled in primary school in Lagos (Nwachukwu, 1985: 172).

Although there had been some limited efforts in northern states to increase adult literacy during the 1950s, access to formal schooling remained low throughout much of the North (Bray, 1981). Many northern states faced geographical and cultural barriers to expansion in formal schooling. The distance from the Atlantic coast hindered earlier efforts by Christian missionaries to establish schools. In

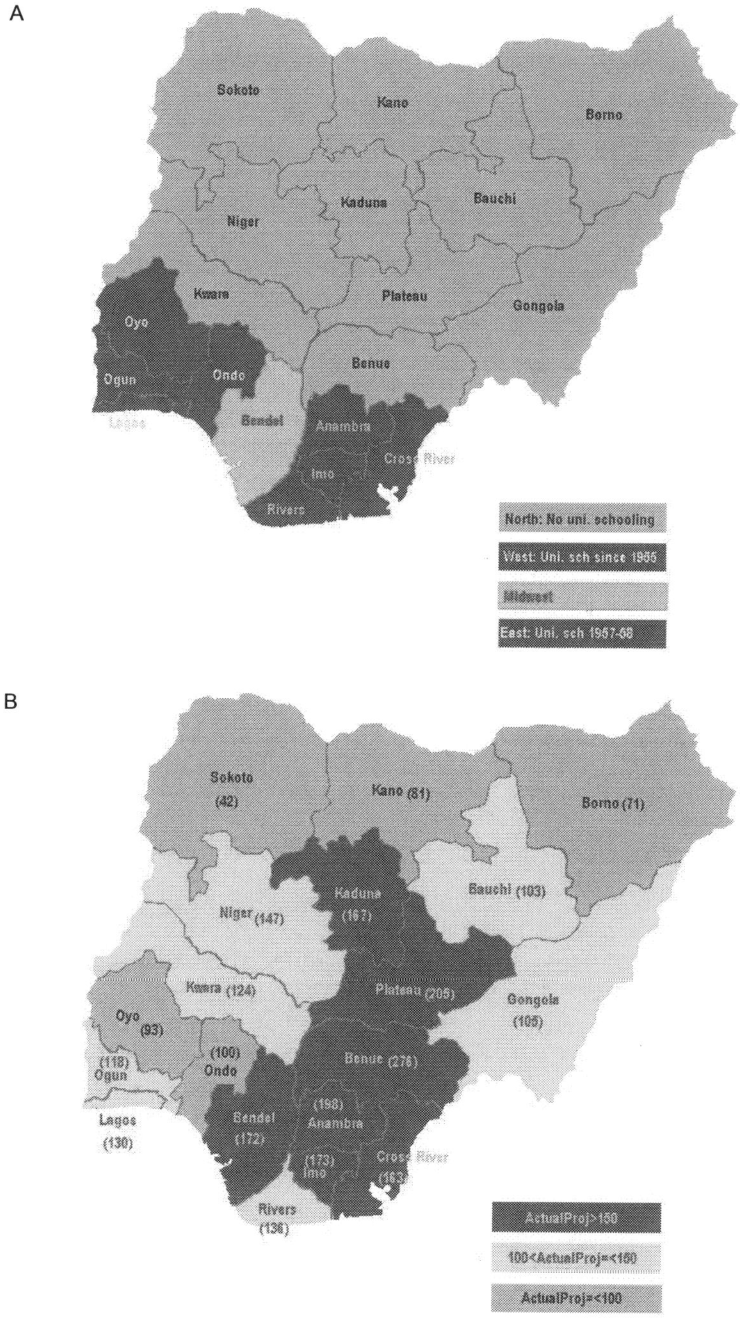

Figure 15.1 (A) The states of Nigeria in 1976 and their experience with universal primary education. (B) Universal primary education in Nigeria: actual versus projected enrolment ratios in the first year of the programme (for Grade 1).

addition, British indirect rule and colonial policy of non-interference in Islamic religious practices meant that primary school enrolment rates, particularly for women, were extremely low in the North. By 1970, less than 10 per cent of the primary school age population was enrolled in school in several northern states (UNESCO, 1971).

15.2.3 The introduction of nationwide universal primary education

The UPE scheme was formally launched in September 1976. In the years that followed, primary school enrolments doubled from 6 million students in 1976 to 12 million students by 1980 (Francis, 1998). By 1982, Nigeria had 14.5 million primary school students (Francis, 1998). The number of primary schools also expanded significantly during this period. Table 15.1 summarizes the trends in the number of students and primary schools before and during UPE with information from various years of the *Annual Abstract of Statistics* and *Social Statistics in Nigeria*.[5] The introduction of the nationwide UPE had a major impact on schooling inputs and student participation in primary school education.

A key component of the UPE policy in Nigeria involved the introduction of free tuition primary schooling throughout the country. Although the free tuition component of the programme was viewed as central to its success, policy-makers also recognized that a significant expansion in schooling inputs would be required to achieve the goal of universal primary education in Nigeria. To this end, the government emphasized the construction of new classrooms in primary schools and teacher training institutions. Many states also focused on recruitment of students into primary schools and teacher training institutions by using local administrative officials and mass media at the community level.

The Nigerian government faced some challenges in implementing the UPE programme. Bray (1981: 84–5) provides evidence that states with low school enrolments (prior to the UPE programme) faced tremendous obstacles in implementing the UPE programme – these obstacles included teacher shortages, lack of administrative capacity to handle student and teacher recruitment, falling education standards, and delays in school construction. In addition to the well-known challenges, there were some less recognized problems. At the time of the programme's announcement, Nigeria's four administrative regions had been split into 12 states. But by 1976, when the UPE programme commenced, additional states were created and Nigeria had 19 states.[6] Furthermore, the programme commenced during a period of significant institutional change as Nigeria made the transition to civilian rule in 1979, after more than a decade of military rule. Table 15.2 displays the disbursed federal capital expenditures on primary school classroom construction by state in 1976.[7] The states that received the highest levels of federal capital funds for classroom construction per capita were located mainly outside the former Western Region of Nigeria. This fact is not surprising given that these states had relatively low primary school enrolment rates (proportions of children enrolled) and levels (total numbers of children enrolled) and other educational inputs prior to the UPE programme.

Table 15.2 Federal capital funds allocated for primary school construction in 1976 (in naira)

			Using 1953 census population estimates for towns		Using state population estimates based on 1963 census	
State	**Region**	**Funds allocated**	**Population**	**Funds/ capita**	**Population**	**Funds/ capita**
Low-intensity areas						
Oyo	Western	1,744,305	1,243,090	1.40	7,330,400	0.24
Ogun	Western	321,524	166,274	1.93	2,182,600	0.15
Ondo	Western	717,838	219,741	3.27	3,841,400	0.19
Lagos (Capital Region)	Western	13,890,626	267,407	51.95	2,244,500	6.19
High-intensity areas						
Ana bra	Eastern	8,342,532	213,561	39.06	5,061,500	1.64
Borno	Northern	2,601,302	77,730	33.47	3,415,500	0.76
Kaduna	Northern	11,116,441	145,440	76.43	5,168,500	2.15
Rivers	Eastern	5,821,876	71,634	81.27	2,420,400	2.41
Imo	Eastern	8,271,194	93,633	88.34	3,666,300	2.26
Kano	Northern	12,131,038	130,173	93.19	8,126,800	1.49
Sokoto	Northern	8,369,744	87,845	95.28	6,387,300	1.31
Kwara	Northern	9,538,412	94,264	101.19	2,412,800	3.95
Bauchi	Northern	2,973,215	29,075	102.26	3,421,500	0.87
Gongola	Northern	5,005,510	47,643	105.06	4,894,700	1.02
Bendel	Midwestern	10,062,666	76,092	132.24	3,462,300	2.91
Niger	Northern	2,025,000	12,810	158.08	1,681,000	1.20
Plateau	Northern	6,287,450	38,527	163.20	2,852,100	2.20
Benue	Northern	3,175,804	16,713	190.02	3,463,300	0.92
Cross-River	Eastern	10,256,206	46,705	219.60	4,218,300	2.43

The region refers to one of the four administrative areas defined in 1965 shortly after independence. The population estimates derive from the 1953 population census, the last census conducted by the British Colonial Administration, which is considered the most accurate given controversies surrounding the 1963 and 1973 censuses. However, when mapping the 1953 town population numbers to the state boundaries of 1976, only towns with more than 15,000 people were included. As shown in the final columns, the ranking and relative amounts by region are similar when using 1976 projected population estimates from the 1963 census.

Source: Social Statistics of Nigeria (1979: 30). Information is not available on actual expenditures on classroom construction. Population figures are from national censuses.

Another challenge that the government faced during the implementation of the UPE programme was the lack of accurate population data for the newly formed states. Stolper (1966) emphasizes the need for accurate data in formulating and implementing development policy in Nigeria. Because census figures form the basis for political representation and revenue allocation, Nigeria's dominant ethnic groups competed for an advantage in the head counts.[8] Past census efforts in Nigeria yielded highly controversial results and this made it challenging to estimate the number of children that would be eligible to benefit from the programme. During the first year of UPE, the number of students enrolled in Grade 1 increased by 82 per cent to 3 million students. This exceeded predictions that only 2.3 million would enrol (Federal Republic of Nigeria, 1978–79). Projected enrolments were based on the 1963 census, and it was assumed that all six-year-olds in the state would be enrolled. Actual enrolments were based on state-level data provided by the state ministries of education (Federal Government of Nigeria, 1978–79: 52). The results of Nigeria's 1973 census were widely contested, and these results were never publicly released. The implementation of the UPE programme would have benefited from accurate, updated population statistics.[9]

The Nigerian UPE ended in September 1981 when the federal government handed over the financing of primary schools to states and regional governments. As a result of reduced funding for primary schools, the reintroduction of school fees in many states, and declining oil revenues in the 1980s, primary enrolments fell or stagnated in many states after the programme ended (Francis, 1998).

15.2.4 Conceptual issues

Nigeria's UPE programme provides an opportunity to investigate how policy changes affect a household's decision to invest in schooling. In particular, the parental decision to enrol a child in primary school or higher levels of schooling can be modelled as a human capital investment decision. Within this framework, households choose to enrol in schooling if the present discounted benefits outweigh the costs associated with primary education. These costs include: (1) direct costs, such as tuition, books and maintenance costs; (2) the opportunity costs or forgone earnings opportunities associated with primary schooling; and (3) the 'psychic' costs of schooling which provide a role for non-cognitive skills, such as motivation and ability, some of which may be difficult to measure. From the onset, it is important to emphasize that the indirect costs of primary schooling may differ across regions.

In the standard model of human capital investment, the returns to schooling are derived from market production. However, female educational investments may also yield returns in non-market production including improvements in child mortality, nutrition, and lower fertility. Economic theory suggests that a nationwide expansion in free primary schooling should lower the direct cost of parental investments in education, and thus should have a direct effect on female enrolments, labour market outcomes and non-labour market outcomes.

There are two potential interpretations for impact of schooling on labour and non-labour market outcomes. One explanation is a human-capital based model in which schooling directly imparts skills and knowledge, which then have a productive effect on labour market and non-labour market outcomes. An alternative explanation is that self-selection in the educational attainment process may be useful in clarifying why education leads to higher rates of labour force participation and higher wages as well as lower fertility and improved child health and nutrition outcomes. For the primary schooling decision, families may choose different levels of education for their children based on tastes, abilities and/or resources. For example, individuals who complete only a few years of primary schooling could be drawn from a different segment of the ability distribution from individuals who complete more than six years of schooling. Furthermore, individuals who complete secondary school (particularly in regions with low levels of schooling) are likely to be a highly selective group. The potential importance of self-selection in the schooling investment decision means that estimates of schooling that do not take the endogeneity of the schooling decision may lead to biased estimates. To deal with the issue, we adopt an instrumental variable approach in our empirical analysis.

15.3 Data and empirical framework

15.3.1 The data: The Nigerian Demographic Health Survey

To study the impact of the UPE programme, we rely mainly on the 1999 Nigerian Demographic Health Survey (NDHS). This dataset is a nationally representative sample containing rich information on socio-economic and demographic variables for 9810 Nigerian women, ages 15 to 49. The NDHS survey is ideal for this study because by design it provides reliable information on levels and trends in education, labour market outcomes, fertility and child mortality for a large number of women.

The NDHS contains some retrospective information that allows us to link information about educational policies in the administrative region of an individual's birth to each woman in our sample. We have assembled a time series on various education indicators in the administrative region of birth including the number of primary schools, primary school students, teacher training institutions, and students in teacher training institutions. These data were obtained from various years of the *Annual Abstract of Statistics* and *Social Statistics in Nigeria*, which are compiled by the Federal Office of Statistics in Nigeria. Table 15.3 presents summary statistics.

Table 15.4 provides summary statistics for the household variables that we use in the empirical analysis. To study the impact of the UPE on education and socio-economic outcomes, we use information from the NDHS on a respondent's region of birth to link individuals to educational policies and institutions. Table 15.4 also includes summary statistics on the 12 states that existed in Nigeria when

Table 15.3 Changes in schooling inputs (state means with standard deviations in parentheses)

	Mean before UPE (1970–75)	Mean after UPE (1976–81)
Number of primary schools	1439 (1177)	3244 (1477)
Number of pupils	408,728 (366,558)	1,025,155 (534,654)
Number of teacher training institutions	15.9 (8.1)	27.8 (11.0)
Number of students in teacher training	423[illegible] (1686)	20,834 (8246)

The unit of analysis is 1970 state. There were 12 states in Nigeria in 1970.
Sources: Federal Office of Statistics, 1981, *Annual Abstract of Statistics*, Lagos, Nigeria. Federal Office of Statistics, 1986, *Annual Abstract of Statistics*, Lagos, Nigeria.

the UPE programme was announced in 1974. Although the NDHS surveys have many important advantages, the data also have several shortcomings. First, they fail to provide good information on wages or income at the household or individual level. Second, they provide only limited information on the migration status of an individual. Therefore, we use an individual's state of education to study the impact of the programme.[10] Our sample consists of both migrants and non-migrants.[11] Ideally, we would also like to know precisely when an individual started and completed primary school, but the NDHS survey does not provide this information. Finally, because the cohorts born after the initiation of the UPE programme (1976–81) were just reaching their mid-twenties by 1999, we cannot fully exploit them to study the impact of education on socio-economic outcomes.

15.3.2 Estimating the impact of UPE

Empirical strategy no. 1: differences-in-differences (DD)

We use the differences-in-differences technique to evaluate the impact of the UPE programme on schooling, labour and non-labour market outcomes. By noting that the UPE occurred between 1976 and 1981 and had a larger impact on certain states (namely, the high-intensity states), we examine whether the introduction of universal primary education caused discontinuities in educational attainment, participation in the formal labour market, and other non-labour market outcomes. This approach has been used in recent studies, including Duflo (2001).

The first difference we use is the age at the beginning of the UPE programme. Given the timing of UPE, the programme should have had an important effect on individuals born between 1970 and 1975. We assume that most individuals start school at age six.[12] In general, primary school lasts for six years in Nigeria. However, data from Nigeria show a high prevalence of underage and overage

Table 15.4 Summary statistics of the 1999 NDHS data

	Mean	Standard deviation
A. 1999 Nigerian demographic and health surveys		
Currently working	0.41	
Work outside home (conditional on working)	0.65	
Wage earner (conditional on working)	0.86	
Number of children born (at the time of the survey)	2.16	(2.78)
Number of births before age 25	2.35	(1.81)
First birth before age 16	0.14	
First birth before age 18	0.25	
Years of education: female	5.00	(4.71)
Completed more than six years of education: female	0.34	(0.47)
Year of birth		
Born 1982–89	0.26	
Born 1976–81	0.22	
Born 1970–75	0.18	
Born 1964–69	0.15	
Born 1958–63	0.12	
Born 1952–57	0.07	
Born 1946–51	0.02	
Religion and ethnicity		
Muslim	0.44	
Christian	0.54	
Other religion	0.02	
Hausa	0.24	
Yoruba	0.22	
Ibo	0.14	
Other ethnicity	0.40	
Residency characteristics		
Low-intensity state (Western Region – 1965 definition)	0.18	
High-intensity state (non-western region)	0.82	
Number of observations	9810	

Table 15.4 continued

	Mean	Standard deviation
B. State characteristics		
1970 state characteristics ($n=12$)		
State female share in primary school enrolment in 1970	33.74	(6.69)
Official gross primary school enrolment rates in 1970	53.70	(49.91)
Projected number of primary school classrooms	12,583	(9195)
Projected number of classrooms: teacher training institutes	514	(367)
1976 state characteristics ($n=19$)		
Federal capital funds allocated to the 1976 state for UPE programme (primary school construction) in 1976 (in naira)	6,455,404	(4,145,556)
Average population (1953 census estimates)	160,465	(272,468)
Population (1963 census estimates)	2,843,827	(1,269,354)
Projected population in 1976 (based on 1963 census)	4,013,221	(1,773,927)
Projected enrolments in Grade 1 – 1976 (in thousands)	120.94	(53.06)
Actual enrolments in Grade 1 – 1976 (in thousands)	157.48	(79.53)
Area in square miles	18,035	(14,477)
State female civil service employment	1312	(3993)

Sources: Annual Abstract of Statistics (various years), *Social Statistics in Nigeria* (various years). There were 12 states in Nigeria in 1974 when the UPE programme was first announced (see the 1970 state characteristics). In 1976, seven additional states were created bringing the total number of states in Nigeria to 19 states. Number of births before age 25 is calculated for women who are 25 and older.

enrolments in first grade in Nigeria. This suggests that the programme may have also affected individuals other than the main target group. Therefore, the cohort we use for the control group were ages 15 to 20 when the UPE was initiated (they were born between 1956 and 1961) and therefore were less susceptible to overage enrolment.

The second difference we use is by state of residence. The introduction of the UPE programme to Nigeria had varying effects on the states within the country. One measure of programme intensity is federal capital funds disbursed to each state in 1976, the first year of the programme. As noted earlier, the federal capital funds were disbursed for primary classroom construction and provision was made for 150,995 new classrooms at the primary school level, and 6699 new classrooms in teacher training institutions.[13] We exploit the variation in state-level UPE programme intensity using the federal funds disbursed for classroom construction to each state. Beyond capturing state-level variation in the intensity of the programme, the federal funds disbursed for classroom construction measure has some significant advantages in the Nigerian context. First, information on the federal capital funds disbursed for classroom construction is available for all 19 states that existed when the UPE programme commenced in 1976. In contrast, data on planned classroom construction which have been used in some studies is only available for the administrative units (12 states) that existed when the programme was first announced in 1974. Second, the federal capital funds variable represents actual funds disbursed to the states rather than the planned allocation of resources, allowing us to track more closely changes in schooling inputs that took place during the course of the programme.

Our DD estimation can be described as follows:

$$S_{ijk} = \alpha_i + BX_{ijk} + \delta(\text{programme intensity}_k \times \text{young}_{jk}) + \alpha_1\text{programme intensity}_k + \alpha_2\,\text{young}_{jk} + \varepsilon_{ijk} \quad (15.1)$$

where *i* indexes individuals, *j* indexes cohorts, and *k* indexes states. S_{ijk} captures the schooling decision of an individual *i* of cohort *j* in state *k*. X_{ijk} includes controls for year of birth dummies, religion dummies, ethnic origin dummies and 1970 state dummies. The variable 'programme intensity' is measured as the federal per capita disbursed funds per capita for the primary school construction in the state where an individual was educated. 'Young' is a dummy variable that captures whether an individual was born between 1970 and 1975, just before the UPE programme was implemented. Otherwise, these variables are equal to 0. The parameter δ is the reduced-form estimate of universal primary education – it measures whether individuals in high programme intensity states that experienced large changes due to the UPE programme also experienced rapid growth in schooling differently from individuals in the low programme intensity states that did not experience much change due to the programme.

Empirical strategy no. 2: instrumental variable approach

To estimate the impact of education, we use a reduced-form model of the labour and non-labour market outcomes for women. As noted earlier, an important issue within the existing literature concerns the causal interpretation of the effect of education on labour and non-labour market outcomes. If education has a causal effect on formal labour force participation, then an expansion in schooling will induce higher formal labour force participation rates, holding other variables constant. However, unmeasured individual, household and community-level resources may affect both education and labour market decisions. For example, an increase in the level of economic development in the community may lead to higher educational attainment and increased labour force participation. Furthermore, education may serve as a proxy for less measurable factors, such as ability, cognitive skills, motivation and parental background, and these factors may be important determinants of a woman's decision to participate in the labour market (Thomas, 1999). Ignoring these factors would lead to biased estimates of the impact of education on fertility within the context of Ordinary Least Square (OLS) estimation.

The standard response to this identification problem is the instrumental variable approach. Valid instruments are variables that affect the level of educational attainment but have no direct impact on labour and non-labour market outcomes. The key measure of programme intensity in the state of schooling is federal disbursed funds per capita for primary school construction in the state where an individual was educated. If we assume that the UPE programme had no direct effect on labour market outcomes, other than through its effect on educational attainment, then we can use exposure to the UPE programme as an instrument for schooling. The age and state of schooling determines an individual's exposure to the UPE programme. The key dependent variable is whether an individual participates in the formal labour force.

The instrumental variable approach is described as follows:

$$L_{ijk} = \alpha_i + BX_{ijk} + S_{ijk} + \varepsilon_{ijk} \tag{15.2}$$

In the equation (15.2) above, L_{ijk} represents the labour force participation of individual *i* of cohort *j* living in state *k*. More formally, OLS estimates may lead to biased estimates if ε_{ijk} is correlated with schooling because of unmeasured ability and other factors, such as family background, social norms or community wealth. Two assumptions are required for exposure to the UPE programme (which is based on age and region of residence) to be a valid instrument. The first assumption is that exposure to the programme is correlated with schooling outcomes (after other explanatory variables are controlled for). Equations (15.1) and (15.2) above form the basis for the first-stage regression. The second assumption required is that the UPE programme had no direct impact on labour or non-labour market outcomes – but only through its impact on schooling.

15.4 Results

15.4.1 Descriptive analysis – measuring the impact of UPE by using the NDHS

In the empirical analysis, we first demonstrate the impact of the UPE programme on female schooling. These results allow us to consider closely whether the change in education policy led to higher investments in female schooling. The results also form the basis for our first-stage regression when we investigate the effect of female schooling on labour and non-labour market outcomes. To identify the impact of the UPE programme, we limit our sample to women of two cohorts: those born between 1956 and 1961 (ages 15 to 20 when the programme started) and those born between 1970 and 1975. Individuals born between 1970 and 1975 were ages one to six when the programme started and are likely to have been the primary beneficiaries of the programme. (We also refer to this cohort as the 'UPE cohort'.) In contrast, individuals who were born between 1956 and 1961 may have been too old to benefit from the UPE programme.

Ordinary Least Squares (OLS) estimation may lead to biased estimates of the impact of the UPE programme in the presence of unobserved state-level heterogeneity. This concern deserves close attention because the high-intensity states that experienced large changes in enrolments and schooling inputs during the UPE programme also had significantly lower educational and social indicators prior to the introduction of the UPE. For example, school availability and teacher quality tended to be lower in the high-intensity states, particularly in the northern states of Nigeria. Therefore, our main specification includes 1970 state fixed effects to deal with time-invariant, unobserved heterogeneity at the state level. The fixed-effects regression allows us to 'sweep out' time-invariant, unobserved state characteristics, such as pre-UPE school availability and teacher quality, as well as initial differences in the level of economic development in the state, which may affect schooling investments. The state fixed effects that we include refer to an individual's state of education.

Table 15.5 reports the effect of UPE on several measures of educational attainment. We exploit state-level variation in UPE programme intensity by using the federal capital funds per capita allocated for classroom construction in the state of education interacted with the UPE cohort dummy. From these results, we find that, at the mean, a 100 naira increase in disbursed per capita construction funds associated with the UPE programme increased the probability of primary school and secondary school attainment by 1 and 0.5 percentage points, respectively. Similarly, we find that a 100 naira increase in disbursed funds for primary school construction per capita increased the number of schooling years completed by 0.8 and the probability of being literate by 1 percentage point.[14] All specifications include year of birth dummies, state fixed effects, ethnic origin, and religion dummies and time-varying controls for female civil service employment. We report robust standard errors that are clustered at the 1970 state level and year of birth.

In interpreting our DD analysis, we have to be concerned that our results may reflect the combined effect of a 'true' programme effect as well as spurious mean reversion. In particular, schooling in high-intensity states might have risen over time even in the absence of the programme mainly because initial schooling outcomes were lower in these states in the pre-programme period. To account for mean reversion, the estimates include the interaction of the female share of primary-school enrolment in the 1970 state and the UPE cohort dummy.

Another concern that arises in interpreting the results in the baseline model is that our estimates do not account for the impact of time-varying, state-level heterogeneity. The UPE programme was implemented during the oil boom era in Nigeria. We also have to be concerned that schooling may have increased faster in high programme-intensity regions not only because of the UPE programme but also on account of omitted variables, including time-varying changes in government programmes and policies that took place during this period. During this period in Nigeria, public-sector employment, as well as the wages of civil servants,

Table 15.5 The impact of the UPE programme on socio-economic outcomes: programme intensity measured by 1976 per capita federal funds disbursed for primary school construction. Treatment group: born 1970–75 (age 1–6 in 1976); control group: born 1956–61 (age 15–20 in 1976)

	Schooling				**Market and non-market outcomes**			
Dependent variable	**Primary school completion**	**Secondary school completion**	**Years of schooling**	**Literate**	**Wage earner**	**No of children before age 25**	**Age at first marriage**	**Child mortality (before age 25)**
	(1)	(2)	(3)	(4)	(5)	(6)	(7)	(8)
Born 1970–75[a] Federal capital funds	0.001	0.0005	0.008	0.001	0.0007	–0.003	0.006	–0.00003
	(0.0003)	(0.002)	(0.003)	(0.0003)	(0.0002)	(0.001)	(0.003)	(0.0001)
Observations	2655	2655	2655	2655	1532	2655	2655	2655

a Baseline model: year dummies, dummy variables for religion and ethnicity (and any other background characteristics), year of birth dummy variables, state fixed effects (to deal with state-level heterogeneity) and young dummy interacted with the female share of enrolment in the state in 1970.

grew. The expansion in the federal civil-service labour force may be correlated with the timing of the UPE programme. To account for this factor, we control for state-level growth in the civil service by interacting the time-varying female civil service employment rates in state of education. Our results are robust to the inclusion of this additional control variable.

15.4.2 DD analysis: the impact on labour and non-labour market outcomes

Table 15.5 also focuses on the impact of UPE on labour and non-labour market outcomes. Because the UPE cohort was a relatively young group at the time of the 1999 NDHS survey, we limit the analysis of non-labour market outcomes to child mortality, early marriage and early fertility indicators. A key labour market variable of interest is the indicator of formal labour force participation. (All estimates include year of birth dummies, religion dummies and 1970 state fixed effects). Robust standard errors are clustered at the 1970 state and year of birth levels.

We find that the UPE programme had a positive impact on the likelihood that an individual participated in the formal labour force. However, this effect is relatively small. In contrast, we find that the UPE programme appeared to have a robust, negative and statistically significant effect on early fertility and a positive and significant effect on a woman's age at first marriage. In addition, estimates in column 8 show that the UPE programme had a negative impact on child mortality. We interpret these results as initial evidence that the UPE programme had an impact on the number of labour and non-labour market outcomes primarily through its effect on female schooling.[15]

15.4.3 The impact of universal schooling on socio-economic outcomes

The instrumental variable strategy

A critical issue that emerges is whether the increases in female schooling induced by the UPE programme had a direct impact on socio-economic development in Nigeria. In the first part of the analysis, we have shown that an individual's year of birth interacted with the state classroom construction funds per capita had a positive and significant impact on both primary and secondary school completion, particularly in the high-intensity states. The next step is to investigate whether these gains in female schooling had an impact on socio-economic outcomes. We adopt the instrumental variable approach, in order to discern the causal impact of schooling on socio-economic outcomes. The ideal candidate instrument would affect schooling outcomes but have no direct impact on labour and non-labour market outcomes. The key instrumental variable in the analysis is year of birth interacted with federal capital funds on primary classroom construction per capita (measured at the 1976 state level).

We begin with presenting results from an Ordinary Least Squares (OLS) regression. These results ignore the endogeneity of the schooling decision. Schooling may be correlated with observed and unobserved individual and community attributes, which would lead to biased estimates of the impact of schooling on

Table 15.6 The impact of primary schooling on socio-economic outcomes – an instrumental variables approach: treatment group born 1970–75 (age 1–6 in 1976); control group born 1956–61 (age 15–20 in 1976)

	Specification			
Dependent variable	**N**	**OLS**	**ILS**	**IV**
		(1)	(2)	(3)
Wage earner	1532	0.047 (0.0201)	1.052 (0.6022)	0.474 (0.243)
Work outside home	1307	0.106 (0.028)	0.715 (0.7219)	0.885 (0.530)
No of children before age 25	2660	–1.093 (0.083)	–3.047 (1.254)	–2.433 (0.8822)
Age at first marriage	2354	2.764 (0.2269)	10.254 (4.7245)	6.316 (2.899)
Birth before age 16	2660	–0.138 (0.016)	–0.398 (0.0241)	–0.309 (0.160)
Child mortality before age 25	2651	–0.005 (0.0009)	–0.003 (0.013)	–0.004 (0.010)

Baseline model: year dummies, dummy variables for religion and ethnicity (and any other background characteristics), year of birth dummy variables, state fixed effects (to deal with state-level heterogeneity) and young dummy interacted with the female share of enrolment in the state in 1970.

labour and non-labour market outcomes. For example, individuals educated in more developed communities may have better access to schooling, and also more favourable labour market opportunities. Table 15.6 (column 1) reports OLS estimates of the effect of education on labour and non-labour market outcomes.

The results from the OLS estimation (column 1) suggest that completing primary schooling has a positive and significant effect of the probability of participating in the formal labour force. We should note that the effects of schooling on non-labour market outcomes appear to be larger in magnitude. From the results, while primary school completion is associated with a 4 percentage point increase in the probability of formal employment, it is associated with a 14 percentage point decrease in the likelihood of early parenthood (before age 16). In addition, primary school completion is associated with a significant reduction in the number of children born before age 25.

We also present results that address the endogeneity bias that may be present in the OLS estimates. Column 2 presents the indirect least squares estimates. Here, we use a single instrument – the primary classroom construction funds per capita in the state of education (measured in per capita terms) interacted with the 'young' cohort dummy. From column 2, we find that primary school completion induces greater labour force participation, reduced early fertility and births before age 16, and lowered child mortality. In general, the estimates in column 2 that correct for the endogeneity of schooling lead to larger estimates of the impact of female schooling on socio-economic outcomes.[16]

Our preferred estimates are shown in column 3. Here, we use several instruments (such as primary classroom construction funds per capita in the state of education (measured in per capita terms) interacted with year of birth indicators) to estimate the causal impact of female schooling on socio-economic outcomes. The results from column 3 provide additional evidence that, when we instrument for schooling, we find that the impact of schooling on socio-economic outcomes becomes larger. Our estimates from column 3 suggest that an additional year of schooling increases formal labour force participation by 47 percentage points. However, this effect is less precisely estimated than our OLS estimates (shown in column 1). This indicates that the OLS estimates may underestimate the magnitude of the effect of schooling on labour and non-labour market outcomes. However, not all the differences between our OLS and Two Stage Least Squares estimates are statistically significant.

These results are consistent with the existing literature on the impact of schooling on both labour and non-labour market outcomes. These studies indicate that female education has a robust negative effect on fertility and population growth, while family planning and other variables do not appear to have a consistent, negative effect. We should note that early fertility may be less indicative of final fertility outcomes for women. To examine this outcome, we examine the 2003 NDHS which allows us to examine fertility outcomes nearly four years later for the UPE cohort and find that number of births before age 30 is still significantly lower for the UPE cohort compared to unaffected cohorts.

In the tables above, we have presented evidence on the effect of education on child mortality as well as other socio-economic outcomes. Finally, we include 1970 state fixed effects and state-level time-varying controls in all specifications. The inclusion of state fixed effects allows us to account for the role of time-invariant observed and unobserved community determinants of fertility and child mortality. For example, social and cultural norms towards conception, and the presence of family-planning programmes and health facilities, as well as other contextual factors, may influence early fertility decisions and child mortality. The result on the impact of female schooling on early fertility and child mortality also appears robust to the inclusion of time-varying changes in employment opportunities for women.

Why did the UPE programme end? The political economy of policy reversal

In the analysis above, we have documented that Nigeria's nationwide experiment with universal education yielded significant gains. A central question is why the UPE programme lasted only five years and ended abruptly, given the significant gains associated with the programme. Economic factors contributed to the Shehu Shagari government's decision to abandon the programme. By the late 1970s, real oil revenues, which accounted for nearly 80 per cent of the Nigerian government revenues and close to 90 per cent of export earnings, had fallen. Projections for oil prices were less optimistic, and the government attempted to reduce spending in order to adjust to anticipated future declines in real oil revenues. Moreover, the costs of implementing the UPE programme had proved to be much higher than

Table 15.7 Federal government recurrent grants and capital funds released to the states for the UPE scheme (in naira): 1974–79

	1974–75	**1975–76**	**1976–77**	**1977–78**	**1978–79**[a]
Recurrent grants (in naira)	39,155,000	117,010,475	386,311,443	456,641,489	501,084,000
Capital grants (in naira)	56,198,858	181,310,279	223,212,634	155,199,993	59,755,391
Total	95,353,858	298,320,754	609,524,077	611,841,482	560,839,391
Recurrent grants as fraction of total	0.41	0.39	0.63	0.75	0.89

a In 1978–79, only the allocation rather than actual expenditure is available.
Source: Social Statistics in Nigeria (1979: 31). Nominal rather than real expenditures are presented.

initial estimates. Of particular importance were the recurrent costs associated with the programme (see Table 15.7). In 1974–75, recurrent costs were only 41 per cent of total programme costs. By 1978–79, recurrent costs increased significantly on an annual basis to account for nearly 90 per cent of total programme costs. The federal government's budget picture was further complicated by the rise in inflation and public corruption, along with a mounting external debt burden during this period (Bienen, 1985).

Notwithstanding the economic climate in the early 1980s, political factors may have contributed to the demise of the UPE programme. The UPE programme was announced during a transition from military rule (the Gowon and Obasanjo governments) to a civilian government headed by President Shehu Shagari. Interestingly, although the UPE programme was nationwide, the rising recurrent costs associated with it may have disproportionately benefited states with pre-existing high levels of primary school enrolment – and many of these states were located outside the North.[17] Insights from the Nigerian case suggest that the favourable effects of democratic regimes on education and other public goods may not be guaranteed. While stable, inclusive, representative democracies can improve access to education, fledgling democracies may have difficulty balancing short-term political interests with long-term commitments to socio-economic development. Nigeria's ethnic fractionalization can help explain why the UPE programme became less politically sustainable even under a democratically elected government.

15.5 Conclusions

In this chapter, we investigate the impact of a large-scale policy experiment in Nigeria on education and socio-economic outcomes. Results from Nigeria suggest that the UPE programme (1976–81) had a significant impact on both schooling and socio-economic outcomes, and the returns to universal primary education programmes over the long term may be substantial. Under the assumption that exposure to the UPE programme is a valid instrument for schooling, we can construct instrumental variable estimates of the impact of female education on labour and non-labour market outcomes. The instrumental variable estimates are generally higher than OLS estimates. Interestingly, the higher levels of educational attainment associated with the programme had considerable implications for non-labour market outcomes, such as fertility, age at first marriage and child mortality, with smaller effects on labour market outcomes. One possible explanation for these results is that the completion of primary schooling may have greater significance for non-labour market outcomes. We find that the UPE programme is also associated with lower fertility and a reduction in child mortality.

An important lesson from Nigeria's experiment with universal education is the need to evaluate the impact of current and future educational spending within a cost–benefit framework. Nigeria can benefit from strong institutions that can evaluate the efficacy of government spending and provide this information to the public. The presence of such institutions will improve the ability of democratically elected governments to deliver on the promise of improved public goods, particularly in education and health. Because Nigeria faces significant challenges in implementing the new nine-year universal basic education (UBE) programme and realizing Millennium Development Goals (MDGs), it is critical that policymakers recognize the need to evaluate the costs and benefits of public expenditure on education.

Notes

1 The author would like to acknowledge the contributions of Bridget Terry Long and Ngozi Egbuna who collaborated on this research project. I would also like to thank Rina, Paul and Aneto Okonkwo for assistance with data collection. This chapter also benefited greatly from discussions with Ifeanyi Osili, Izevbuwa Osayimwese, Peter Rangaza and Anne Royalty. Yuling Han, Xia Jie and Yuan Liu provided excellent research assistance.

2 The number of primary school children in Nigeria increased from 4.4 million in 1974 to 13.8 million by 1981. In the five years before the UPE programme commenced (1970–75), gross enrolment rates increased by only seven percentage points, from 43.7 in 1970 to 50.3 in 1975 (World Bank, 2002).

3 For example, Case and Deaton (1999) use data from South Africa to study the impact of increased resources on schooling outcomes. Duflo (2001) relies on an individual's date of birth and region of schooling to identify the impact of a large-scale school construction programme in Indonesia on educational attainment and wages. Angrist *et al.* (2002) study the impact of school vouchers in Columbia.

4 There is some concern that educational expansion in the Western Region resulted in a trade-off with educational quality. Although 71 per cent of students passed the school exit exam in 1961, this number had fallen to 44 per cent in 1964 mainly because of lower teacher quality (Nwachukwu, 1985: 146).

5 Although the ideal trend to display is gross enrolment rates, we do not have accurate population estimates for this time period because the 1973 population census in Nigeria was widely disputed and not publicly released.

6 Currently, Nigeria has 36 states and one Federal Capital Territory. The number of states has changed over time to improve equity in the revenue-sharing system at the federal level. Federal government revenue allocations to states and local governments are governed by a formula based on population, need and, to a lesser extent, derivation. In order to examine the impact of the programme, we map each individual's region of education to match the 19 states that existed when the UPE programme commenced in 1976.

7 State population estimates are based on the 1953 Population Census in Nigeria. Both the 1963 and 1973 population censuses yielded highly controversial results. The 1953 census was the last one conducted by the British Colonial Administration, and we use the population of towns with more than 15,000 residents to maintain consistency in administrative boundaries.

8 Added to the political controversies, the process of collecting accurate census data within developing countries has some well-documented challenges (see Deaton, 1997). In the Nigerian case, regions with low literacy rates found it difficult to recruit enumerators who could record accurate counts. Seasonal migration and religious practices such as purdah also posed challenges for census workers, particularly in the North (Prothero, 1956). In the southern states, census workers faced resistance because respondents feared that data collection would be linked to taxation or military recruitment.

9 Aluko (1965) provides a review of the political challenges that accompanied the 1963 census and earlier census efforts in Nigeria since the 1900s, including claims that headcounts in northern Nigeria in the 1963 census may have been inflated. To reduce political controversy, the 1991 Nigerian census eliminated questions on religion and ethnicity.

10 Specifically, we can identify where an individual was educated if she moved to her current place of residence before the age of six. We do not have information about moves after age six. However, about two thirds of our sample has never moved. Data from the 1991 census suggest that most moves take place within a state or region. The only state in Nigeria with a large share of migrants from other states is Lagos State.

11 We compare the characteristics of individuals by migration status. We do not find any significant differences between movers and non-movers in average years of schooling completed or primary-school completion. However, non-migrants do tend to be younger and have fewer children than movers.

12 One concern with this approach is the possible prevalence of underage and overage enrolments in Nigeria. According to a recent Multiple Indicator Cluster Survey (MICS) conducted by UNICEF in 1999, underage enrolments, overage enrolments and grade repetitions are likely to be of importance in Nigeria. For example, of the sample of 977 female students enrolled in first grade (Primary 1), 19 per cent were age five, 31 per cent were six, and 21 per cent were seven. About 4 per cent of the sample were four and about 15 per cent were above seven. The high prevalence of underage and overage enrolments in first grade suggests that the programme may have affected individuals other than the main target group.

13 Our measure of UPE programme intensity is also highly correlated with the projected expansion in classrooms at teacher training institutions. We have also found that projected classroom constructions detailed in Nigeria's Third National Development Plan are highly correlated with actual changes reported in the number of classrooms in each state based on the Federal Office of Statistics, *Annual Abstract of Statistics*.

14 In our empirical work, we define primary school completion as the completion of more than six years of schooling.

15 Other cohorts also may have benefited from UPE thanks to underage and overage enrolments. In a working paper version of this chapter, we investigate the extent to which these additional cohorts may have benefited from the programme.

16 The one exception here is the result on the proportion of children born to mothers under age 25 that did not survive. However, the OLS and Indirect Least Squares (ILS) estimates are not significantly different as the ILS estimates are less precisely estimated.

17 Several authors have studied the role of ethnic fragmentation on economic outcomes (see Alesina and LaFerrara, 2005 for a review of the literature). Young (1976: 470–471) argues that General Yakubu Gowon, who initiated the UPE programme, came from a minority ethnic group so could act as a 'balancer' and could implement policies that benefited the nation rather than specific ethnic interest groups.

Selected references

Acemoglu, D. and J.A. Robinson, 2006, *Economic Origins of Dictatorship and Democracy*, New York: Cambridge University Press.

Aluko, S.A., 1965, 'How Many Nigerians? An Analysis of Nigeria's Census Problems, 1901–63', *Journal of Modern African Studies* 3 (3), 371–92.

Angrist, J.D., E. Bettinger, E. Bloom, E. King and M. Kremer, 2002, 'Vouchers for Private Schooling in Colombia: Evidence from a Randomized Natural Experiment', *American Economic Review*, 92 (5), 1535–58.

Annual Abstract of Statistics/Federal Government of Nigeria, various years, Lagos: Federal Office of Statistics.

Awokoya, S.O., 1952, 'Proposals for an Educational Policy for the Western Region of Nigeria', *Western Regional Gazette*, 13 (10), 463–70.

Becker, G.S., 1981, *Treatise on the Family*, Cambridge, MA: Harvard University Press.

Bienen, H., 1985, *Political Conflict and Economic Change in Nigeria*, London: F. Cass.

Bray, M., 1981, *Universal Primary Education in Nigeria: A Study of Kano State*, London: Routledge and Kegan Paul.

Caldwell, J.C., I.O. Orubuloye and P. Caldwell, 1992, 'Fertility Decline in Africa: A New Type of Transition?', *Population and Development Review*, 18 (2), 211–42.

Case, A. and A. Deaton, 1999, 'Schooling Inputs and Educational Outcomes in South Africa', *Quarterly Journal of Economics*, 114 (3), 1047–84.

Deaton, A., 1997, *The Analysis of Household Surveys: A Microeconometric Approach to Development Policy*, Baltimore, MD: Johns Hopkins University Press.

Duflo, E., 2001, 'Schooling and Labor Market Consequences of School Construction in Indonesia: Evidence from an Unusual Policy Experiment', *American Economic Review*, 91 (4), 795–813.

Fafunwa, B.A., 1974, *History of Education in Nigeria*, London: Allen and Unwin.

Federal Government of Nigeria, 1978–79, *Blueprint/Implementation Committee for the National Policy on Education*, Lagos: Federal Government of Nigeria.

Federal Republic of Nigeria, 1978, *Third National Development Plan, 1975–1980*, Lagos: Central Planning Office, Federal Ministry of Economic Development and Reconstruction.

Francis, Paul A., 1998, 'Hard Lessons: Primary Schools, Community and Social Capital in Nigeria', World Bank Technical Paper No. 420, Africa Region Series, World Bank, Washington, DC.

Knowles, S., P. Lorgelly and P. Owen, 2002, 'Are Educational Gender Gaps a Brake on Economic Development? Some Cross-Country Empirical Evidence', *Oxford Economic Papers*, 54 (1), 118–49.

Nwachukwu, A.E., 1985, 'An Historical Analysis of the Roots of Universal Public Primary Education in Nigeria (1900–1980)', PhD dissertation, University of Kansas.

Prothero, R.M., 1956, 'The Population Census of Northern Nigeria 1952: Problems and Results', *Population Studies*, 10 (20), 166–83.

Schultz, T. Paul, 1984, 'Studying the Impact of Household Economic and Community Variables on Child Mortality', *Population and Development Review*, 10 (Supplement: Child Survival: Strategies for Research), 215–35.

Schultz, T.P. (ed.), 1995, *Investment in Women's Human Capital*, Chicago: University of Chicago Press.

Schultz, T.P., 1998, 'Demand for Children in Low Income Countries', in Mark Rosenzweig and Oded Stark (eds), *Handbook of Population and Family Economics*, Vol. 1A, Amsterdam: Elsevier.

Social Statistics in Nigeria, various years, Lagos: Federal Office of Statistics.
Stasavage, D., 2005, 'Democracy and Education Spending in Africa', *American. Journal of Political Science*, 49 (2), 343–58.
Stolper, W.F., 1966, *Planning without Facts: Lessons in Resource Allocation from Nigeria's Development*, Cambridge, MA: Harvard University Press.
Thomas, D., 1999, 'Fertility, Education and Resources in South Africa', in C.H. Bledsoe, J.B. Casterline, J.A. Johnson-Kuhn and J.G. Haaga (eds), *Critical Perspectives on Schooling and Fertility in the Developing World*, Washington, DC: National Academy Press
UNESCO, 1971, 'Education in Nigeria', *Educational Projects for External Aid* Vol. 1, Report 560, Paris: UNESCO.
World Bank, 2002, *African Development Indicators*, Washington, DC: World Bank.
Young, C., 1976, *The Politics of Cultural Pluralism*, Madison, WI: University of Wisconsin Press.

16

Female Schooling and Women's Labour Market Participation in Nigeria

Adebayo B. Aromolaran[1]

16.1 Introduction

Currently there are pressures on African governments by international development organizations to pursue education policies which emphasize gender balance because contemporary economic development literature strongly associates economic growth and poverty reduction with increasing investment in female education. Schultz (2002) presents a detailed argument on why governments should invest more to educate girls. Specifically, increased female schooling is believed to be associated with decline in population growth rate due to reduced fertility rate, growth in per capita income due to increased income earning opportunities for women, increase in women empowerment due to increased control over economic resources, increase in child quality/welfare due to increased bargaining power for women in the household, and increase in available public resources for development due to increased tax base.

A substantial part of these effects of female schooling is thought to derive indirectly from the direct effect of schooling on labour market supply behaviour of women. For example, Willis (1973) argues that increases in women's education would affect demand for children only if the woman engages in market work. Thus, a good reason why it might be useful to investigate the strength of relationship between female schooling and labour market participation derives from this argument that the strength of the linkage between female education and economic growth/poverty reduction depends substantially on the strength of the relationship between female schooling and labour market participation decisions of women.

Even though statistics on the trend in labour force participation in Nigeria have not been consistent, there are indications that the labour force participation of women aged between 25 and 64 years increased substantially across age groups between 1970 and 1992 (see Table 16.1). Female labour force participation increased by as much as 20–30 percentage points for women in the age-cohort 40–59 years and between 4 and 8 percentage points for others. Since we observe these increases in female labour force participation in a period when GDP per capita,[2] real wages, and male labour market participation rates declined, while unemployment

Table 16.1 Nigeria: economically active population as a proportion of total population by sex and age

	Female		Male	
Age group (years)	1970	1992	1970	1992
0–14		1.8		4.0
15–19	19.2	13.8	56.1	31.5
20–24	25.5	27.0	85.7	62.0
25–29	29.2	33.3	96.2	92.0
30–34	31.4	36.5	97.3	97.8
35–39	31.4	47.5	97.3	98.9
40–44	31.4	52.2	97.3	98.7
45–49	31.4	62.2	97.3	99.2
50–54	35.0	64.1	97.9	97.5
55–59	34.2	58.4	96.6	97.9
60–64	34.2	42.0	90.6	79.4
65+	30.1	30.6	90.2	50.0

Source: ILO (1970, 1992)

rates increased,[3] it is possible that the observed increases resulted from changes in supply-side factors, such as rising average levels of female schooling.

Table 16.2 shows that female primary school enrolment in Nigeria increased from 32 per cent in 1970 to 87 per cent in 1994. Furthermore, Table 16.3 shows that between 1990 and 1999, primary schooling attainment rates increased by 5–10 percentage points for women in the age cohort 15–29 years and 15–25 percentage points for women in the age cohort 30–49 years. Attainment rates in the first three years of secondary education increased by 15–20 percentage points for women aged 15–29 years and 8–18 percentage points for women aged 30–49 years. We also observe from Table 16.3 that attainment rates at the level of 'primary school completed' is about 40 percentage points higher for the younger age cohort 15–19 than for the older age cohort 40–49 years in both 1990 and 1999, implying that school attainment is higher among the younger generation. This observed increasing trend in female schooling is consistent with the trend shown in Figure 16.1, which depicts the trend in average years of schooling across age groupings as obtained from the Nigerian labour force survey data used for the analysis reported in this chapter.

Thus, in spite of consistent decline in measures of macroeconomic performance over the past three decades, female labour force participation in Nigeria has increased. This study will provide an insight into how increasing exposure of women to different levels of formal education may have contributed to these observed increases in female labour force participation.

Table 16.2 Gross school enrolment rates in Nigeria (1970–94)

	1970			1975			1985			1994		
	Female	**Male**	**Gap****	**Female**	**Male**	**Gap**	**Female**	**Male**	**Gap**	**Female**	**Male**	**Gap**
Primary	32.2	55.3	23.1	40.3	60.3	20.0	91.8	115.4	23.6	86.6	109.4	23.2
Secondary	3.1	7.2	4.1	5.6	10.4	4.8	27.9	40.1	12.2	30.3	36.2	5.9
Post-secondary	0.1	0.9	0.8	0.3	1.7	1.4	1.9	5.2	3.3	2.3*	6.0*	3.7

*1990 figures; **Gap is male–female percentage point difference.
Source: UNESCO (2001).

Table 16.3 Schooling attainment of women in Nigeria by age and grade

	15–19 years		20–29 years		30–39 years		40–49 years	
Grades	**1990**	**1999**	**1990**	**1999**	**1990**	**1999**	**1990**	**1999**
1	0.651	0.731	0.517	0.641	0.288	0.507	0.184	0.353
2	0.654	0.725	0.515	0.640	0.282	0.501	0.177	0.342
3	0.628	0.716	0.503	0.633	0.266	0.493	0.163	0.322
4	0.602	0.70	0.492	0.624	0.241	0.477	0.138	0.292
5	0.576	0.673	0.471	0.609	0.220	0.464	0.123	0.278
6	0.533	0.64	0.452	0.598	0.207	0.452	0.110	0.264
7	0.307	0.482	0.24	0.428	0.09	0.287	0.043	0.118
8	0.268	0.418	0.226	0.416	0.084	0.276	0.036	0.116
9	0.208	0.339	0.202	0.390	0.078	0.261	0.031	0.111

Source: Filmer (2000).

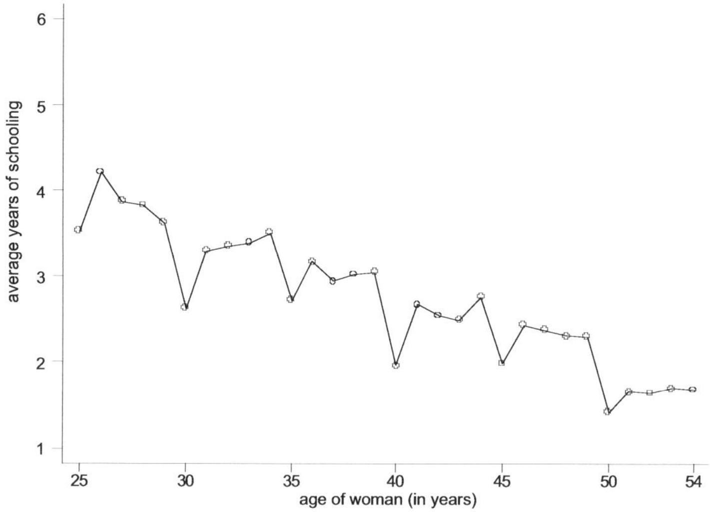

Figure 16.1 Average years of schooling – age profile (for women aged 25–54 years).

Furthermore, the result of this investigation will help to assess the potential effect of the universal basic education (UBE) programme on female labour supply behaviour. The UBE bill was signed into law by the Nigerian government in 2004 and provides for a mandatory nine years of schooling for every Nigerian child. The programme is expected to be funded with not less than 2 per cent of Nigeria's consolidated national revenue fund. A major goal of this programme is gender balance in educational attainment.

The study uses the static family labour supply framework to address a number of important empirical questions. First, how responsive is the probability of a woman working for income outside the home to the number of years of her schooling? Second, how does the responsiveness vary within and across different levels of education? Third, what implications does the result hold for education policy in Nigeria, as well as other developing countries with similar political, social and economic institutions?

This investigation is important for a number of reasons. First, studies that examine the effect of female schooling on the decisions of married women in Nigeria to work or not outside the home are rare. Secondly, for a country such as Nigeria where the annual percentage population growth rate has remained above 2.65 in the past three decades, a substantial response of women's labour supply to increased schooling would identify increased investment in women's education as a potential policy strategy for reducing the national population growth rate through reductions in fertility. Finally, most analyses on returns to schooling have examined the relationship between schooling on one hand and either wage rates or labour market earnings on the other hand (see Aromolaran, 2006), yet individuals obtain returns to human capital investment not only by achieving increased prices for the rental of their labour/human capital services, but also by increasing productivity in home or non-market work. The results of this study will give some insights into the effects of female schooling on non-market productivity of married women.

The remaining part of this chapter is organized as follows: the second and third sections of the chapter examine the empirical literature and set up the theoretical framework of analysis, while the fourth section explores the data. The empirical models to be estimated and hypotheses to be tested are outlined and discussed in Section 16.5, while Section 16.6 presents and discusses the results of data analysis. Section 16.7 summarizes the findings of the study and concludes the chapter.

16.2 Literature review

Even though the decision of married women to seek employment outside the home is a function of a variety of factors such as economic considerations, family composition and personal factors,[4] education is regarded as the cornerstone of women's empowerment. It is widely thought that education enables women to respond to opportunities, to challenge their traditional roles and to change their lives (UNDP, 1997). A more educated woman finds more attractive employment opportunities available to her, particularly since higher wage offers come with more schooling. Since education level may indicate a woman's earning potential, an increase in education level conditional on market wage rate can increase the probability of her participation in producing cash income on the grounds of higher opportunity cost for not producing cash income (Khandker, 1987). Thus economic theory of the household postulates a positive causal relationship between the level of formal education attained by married women and the probability of engaging in market work. This hypothesis has been supported by results from numerous empirical investigations using different methodologies and datasets from different countries (Mahoney, 1961; Mincer, 1963; Spencer, 1973; Bloch and Smith, 1977; Jones and Long, 1979; Smith, 1980; Killingsworth, 1983; Killingsworth and Heckman, 1986; Khandker, 1987; Schultz, 1990a, 1991, 2002; Lam and Duryea, 1999). Presently, studies of this kind using data from Nigeria are rare.

Of particular relevance to this study are the papers by Bloch and Smith (1977), Jones and Long (1979), Rosenzweig and Schultz (1989), Schultz (1990a, 1991) and Lam and Duryea (1999).

Bloch and Smith (1977) analysed the May 1973 current population survey (CPS) and found the relationship between education and women's labour force participation to be positive for both white and black females in the United States. Their estimates show that the marginal effect of an additional year of schooling on the probability of market employment is 6.56 per cent for white females and 3.00 per cent for black females. However, the inclusion of marital status in the set of explanatory variables may have biased the estimates of the schooling effects since marital status is endogenous to the labour market participation model.

Using the national longitudinal survey (NLS), Jones and Long (1979) extended the Bloch and Smith model to include correlates of educations such as certification in a trade or profession, health and migration. They found a 50 per cent reduction in the linear positive marginal effect of education on employment probability of women. However, the inclusion of possibly endogenous variables such as health, migration, and presence of a child of under six years in the household may have been responsible for the downward bias of the estimated education coefficient.

Furthermore, evidence from a group of 61 countries, analysed by Schultz (1990b), suggests that the share of women in wage employment is positively associated with increase in per capita income across countries, and with literacy for both males and females within countries; but that the effect of literacy on the fraction of female wage earners was independent of per capita income effect.

Schultz's (1991) cross-country regressions show that increasing women's education (schooling was used as proxy for women's wage market opportunities) will increase women's participation in wage employment and that this positive effect is substantially larger than the estimated negative cross-effect of husband's schooling on wife's labour force participation.

Findings from a number of empirical investigations in developing countries suggest that the marginal effect of schooling on women's labour force participation is very low at the primary education level and rises very sharply at post-secondary education level (Schultz, 1990a; Lam and Duryea, 1999). The estimated female participation equation from the Thailand data in Schultz (1990a) showed that an additional year of primary, secondary and higher education raises the probability of wage employment by 0.41 per cent, 9.81 per cent and 16.5 per cent respectively for females and 5.98 per cent, –3.75 per cent and 5.21 per cent for males.

Lam and Duryea (1999) explained these observed small responses of female labour force participation to increases in schooling at low levels of education as evidence that market wage offers and home/reservation wages are equalized at low levels of schooling. They argued that at higher levels of education market wage offers rise faster than reservation wages with additional years of schooling.

Rosenzweig and Schultz (1989) examined the association between schooling and productivity in household activities. They found that more educated couples have increased abilities to seek out information on household inputs about which information is relatively scarce and which require careful use, suggesting that increased non-market efficiency/productivity is associated with increased schooling. Consequently, female labour market participation might not respond substantially to increased investment in female education, particularly at the primary level, if the market benefits of education do not sufficiently outweigh the non-market benefits.[5]

16.3 Theoretical framework

The theoretical construct upon which the analysis in this chapter is based is the time allocation theory formalized in Becker (1965). He postulated that the married woman allocates her time resources between home and market production in such a way as to maximize her preference function, given the market wage offer and the shadow price of home production time (home wage). That is, women acting rationally will allocate more time away from home production into market production as their market earning capacities relative to shadow price of home production increase, or as the opportunity cost of time spent in home production increases.[6]

Conceptually, a woman will only supply labour to the market if the market wage offer, w^m, is at least as high as a particular reservation wage, w^r. Otherwise she does not participate in the labour market. A reservation wage is the wage level below which a married woman will not enter the labour market. It is the value which the household assigns to a marginal unit of the woman's time in home production and consumption. Reservation wage, w^r, varies from individual to individual based on her other lifetime choices and is therefore not exogenous to the labour supply model. It is determined by such factors as unearned income of household, number of children below six years, education of the family members, wage of husband, and state of household technology (see Heckman, 1974). Whenever $w^r > w^m$, no labour is supplied to the market by the particular individual.

Within the family labour supply model framework in which the family maximizes the joint household utility function which includes the additively separable utilities of the husband and the wife (who are assumed to be the major decision-makers in the household), maximizing utility subject to full income constraint implies a reduced form expression for labour supply or leisure demand given by expression (16.1):

$$L_f = L_f\,(W_f, W_h, V_h, Z, \gamma) \tag{16.1}$$

That is, female labour supply, L_f, is a function of market wage offers for wife (W_f) and husband (W_h), non-earned income of household (V_h), observable household characteristics (Z) and non-observable household characteristics (γ). L_f can take either of two forms. It can represent the exact number of labour hours supplied by the women or can be defined as a dichotomous variable taking the value of 1 when a woman is working in the market and the value of 0 when she is not working in the market. In the latter case, L_f is simply interpreted as labour market participation. This chapter will adopt this latter form of the simple static labour supply model. According to Schultz (1991), most of the labour market response of married women occurs in their participation rate and not in the hours worked among participants.

Female schooling can affect labour market participation through a number of channels. First is the direct effect that is obtained by conditioning the effect of schooling on market wages. Since education level indicates a woman's earnings/market productivity potential, an increase conditional on market wages can increase the probability of her participation in producing cash. Second is the indirect effect when education affects labour market participation indirectly through its direct effect on market wages, especially since higher wage offers come with higher schooling. Third, women's education affects reservation wages by generating non-market benefits through increased efficiency in home production.

A more educated woman is likely to have a taste for higher levels of child quality outcomes such as improvements in childbirth, child nutrition, child health, child education and child survival outcomes.

In the model adopted in this chapter, the market wage offer, w^m, received by the woman, as well as the reservation wage, w^r, depends on own schooling, S, and potential post-schooling experience, A. Consequently, expression (16.1) can be written as expression (16.2):

$$L_f = L_f\,(S_f, A_f, W_h, V_h, Z, \gamma) \tag{16.2}$$

Thus, increased schooling is expected to increase the market wage rate and thus influence the allocation of women's time away from home production into market production. However, because more schooling, especially at lower levels of education, can also increase reservation wages, the response of women's participation rates to schooling is diminished. This response will approach zero as the effect of schooling on reservation wages approaches the effect on market wage rate or, in other words, as the productivity of schooling in non-market work approaches the productivity of schooling in market work.

Thus, labour market participation will respond positively to increasing years of schooling if the inequality condition in expression (16.3) is satisfied; that is, when the marginal productivity of schooling in market work is greater than the marginal productivity of schooling in non-market work.

$$\partial w^m/\partial S > \partial w^r/\partial S, \text{ evaluated at } L_s = 0 \tag{16.3}$$

where $\partial w^m/\partial S$ represents marginal productivity of schooling in market work and $\partial w^r/\partial S$ represents marginal productivity of schooling in home work.

Thus, the coefficient of schooling in the estimated labour market participation function is not different from zero if the marginal productivity of schooling in non-market work is equal to the marginal productivity of schooling in market work.

16.4 Data

16.4.1 Description of sample

This study draws its sample from the sub-sample of the Nigerian General Household Survey (GHS) data[7] comprising 50,204 work-age adult females who are aged between 30 and 54 years. The reason for restricting the sample is that a sizeable proportion of women below the age of 30 years are unmarried,[8] while a substantial proportion of those over 54 years may have retired from waged employment. The data show that 89 per cent of women aged between 30 and 54 years are married; 28,982 (57.7 per cent) of the sub-sample are married and had information on their husbands; 15,502 (30.9 per cent) are married but provided no information on their husbands; 5720 (11.4 per cent) are single. Only women for whom information on a male spouse is reported are regarded as married for the purpose of this study. This adds up to 28,982 individuals. After further cleaning of data, 28,691 married women between the ages of 30 and 54 years made up the sample used for this analysis of labour market participation of married women.

16.4.2 Occupation characteristics of married women in Nigeria

Tables 16.4 and 16.5 describe the work characteristics of the married women in Nigeria. 4.17 per cent of the married women are in wage employment, 26 per cent in self-employment and 14 per cent in cooperative work, while 55.7 per cent are not employed. The corresponding figures for all women are 4.36 per cent, 34 per cent, 13.4 per cent and 47.8 per cent respectively.[9] Only about 1.4 per cent of the sample of married women is accounted as unpaid family workers.[10]

Cooperative workers were not adequately described in the survey. However, their characteristics as gleaned from the data suggest that they could pass for unpaid family labour. 90 per cent of them work in the agricultural sector, 63 per cent are female, 58 per cent are married and 38 per cent are single. 51 per cent are spouses of the head of household, 32 per cent are sons, 9 per cent are daughters, and 8 per cent are sons-in-law. Furthermore, no cooperative worker is head of household, 99 per cent earn no income, 61 per cent never attended school, 3.5 per cent are currently in school and 35 per cent have completed schooling. Average age is 30 years.

Further investigation showed that 96 per cent of the married women who are not employed are homemakers who are not actively looking for a job, while 3.4 per cent are retired and are not looking for a job. Also, the proportion of non-employed married women is higher in the Northern region than the southern part of Nigeria. The proportions are 79 per cent and 97 per cent for the North East and North West zones of Nigeria respectively. The figures for the South East, South West and South South zones are 23 per cent, 12 per cent and 24 per cent respectively. The proportion of non-employed in the sample of married women in the north central zone is 54 per cent. This observed difference in labour market patterns between the core north and the southern parts of Nigeria may necessitate a further investigation into the possible differences in the responses of married women in the north compared with married women in the south. This issue may be addressed in another paper.

Table 16.5 sheds some light on the occupational structure of the sample of married women who work. 66 per cent of the self-employed are engaged in trading, while 28 per cent are engaged in farming. Most women in wage employment are either teachers or clerks (66 per cent). Only about 10 per cent of female wage workers are professional/technical workers, while about 2 per cent are administrative workers. Most of the female cooperative workers (92 per cent) are involved in farm production.

16.4.3 Descriptive analysis of the relationship between female schooling and women's labour market participation

Table 16.6 summarizes the nature of association between the likelihood of labour market participation of married women and the level of education attained. We

Table 16.4 Percentage distribution of women by marital status and employment type

Employment type	All women	Married women with information on spouse*	Married women without information on spouse	Single women**	Male spouses
Employer	0.239	0.262	0.187	0.280	0.964
Wage worker	4.36	4.17	3.55	7.55	13.3
Self-employed	34.14	25.7	32.49	81.1	85.1
Cooperative worker	13.44	14.1	15.78	3.36	0.168
Unpaid family worker	0.0339	0.014	0.0129	0.140	0.0349
Not employed	47.8	55.7	48.0	7.53	0.446
Mean age (years)	38.7 (6.7)	35.7 (5.1)	42.6 (6.5)	42.4 (7.1)	44.7 (5.6)
Mean years of schooling	2.74 (4.1)	2.74 (4.2)	1.92 (3.7)	3.47 (4.5)	3.7 (4.9)
Number of observations	50,198	28,691	15,502	5,720	28,691

* This is the sub-sample used for the main analysis in this chapter.
** This includes those that are widowed, divorced, and separated, and never married.
Figures in parentheses are standard deviations.

Table 16.5 Occupational distribution for women living with spouse only (percentage)

Title of job	Wage worker	Self-employed	Cooperative worker	Employer	Unpaid family worker
Teacher	34.7			27.4	
Clerk	31.9			26.0	
Trader	2.91	66.2	6.37	28.8	28.6
Farmer	7.44	28.3	92.5	8.22	57.1
Professional/technical	10.01				
Tailor		1.76			14.3
Mechanic				1.37	
Admin/managerial	1.71			2.74	
Agricultural				1.37	
Admin/managerial				1.37	
Others	11.33	3.7	1.22	2.73	
Total percentage	100	100	100	100	100

observe that overall participation in market work increases with level of education, even after controlling for age.

Figure 16.2 presents graphical representations of the relationship between female schooling and women's labour market participation. We observe that participation rate in self-employment rises sharply in the first year of schooling and stays high up to 12 years of schooling, after which it declines sharply. The implication of this is that the first year of schooling seems to be very critical in influencing labour market participation of married women. This may be an indication that the basic reading, writing and numerical skills sufficient to motivate women into self-employment are learnt in this first year of schooling. After this first year of schooling, the marginal effect of the five remaining years of primary education on labour market behaviour appears to be minimal.

On the other hand, participation rate in wage employment is close to zero below two years of schooling, after which it increases slightly and stabilizes at a low level between two and six years of schooling. The rate rises sharply at seven years of schooling (first year in secondary school), but is still dominated by participation rate in self-employment up till 13 years of schooling (first year in post-secondary school). From the first year of post-secondary education, participation rate in wage employment rises sharply to above 70 per cent and dominates participation rate in self-employment, which declines sharply to below 10 per cent. As shown in Figure 16.3 (see also Figures A16.1–A16.4 in the Appendix, www.csae.ox.ac.uk/books), the observed pattern is fairly consistent across age groupings.

Thus, the relationship between female schooling and the participation rate in self-employment is approximated by an inverted U-shaped curve, with kinks at 1 and 12 years of schooling, while that of the wage sector is approximated by a 'three-step function' with upward jumps at 7 and 13 years of schooling.

There are a number of ways in which we can explain the observed low response of wage-market participation to increasing years of schooling at primary school level. First is that this low response is the result of the equalization of the marginal productivities of schooling in both wage and non-wage work. That is, the marginal productivity of primary schooling in non-wage work is at least as high as the marginal productivity of schooling in wage employment at levels of schooling below seven years. Furthermore, as the level of education increases beyond the first six years, the marginal productivity of schooling in wage employment appears to exceed the marginal productivity of schooling in non-wage work.

Figure 16.2 also shows a trade-off in the response of participation rates to marginal changes in years of schooling as education level increases. For example, self-employment accounts for a larger share of overall labour supply response of married women with less than 12 years of schooling, while wage work accounts for a larger share when the woman has attended at least one year of post-secondary education (that is, the thirteenth year of schooling).

Another possible explanation for the observed pattern is the existence of labour market segmentation. This could be the case if the labour market is so structured that the only waged jobs available to women are those which require high levels of schooling, or if low-paying wage jobs such as in the manufacturing sector

Table 16.6 Relationship between level of education and married women's labour market participation rates by age group

Age group (years)	Education levels	Wage employment (A)	Self-employment (B)	Employers (C)	Total employment (A+B+C)	Cooperative workers	Not employed	No. of observations
30–34	No formal education	0.00263	0.0859	0.000	0.0885	0.131	0.780	7984
	Primary	0.0193	0.479	0.00131	0.500	0.162	0.337	2282
	Secondary	0.129	0.483	0.00912	0.621	0.083	0.296	1535
	Post-secondary*	0.689	0.139	0.0383	0.866	0.0144	0.119	209
35–39	No formal education	0.00361	0.154	0.000172	0.157	0.151	0.691	5813
	Primary	0.0251	0.544	0.00359	0.573	0.164	0.263	1950
	Secondary	0.167	0.492	0.00585	0.665	0.070	0.265	1026
	Post-secondary	0.713	0.140	0.0394	0.892	0.00716	0.100358	279
40–44	No formal education	0.00630	0.187	0.000574	0.194	0.179	0.626	3487
	Primary	0.0196	0.569	0.0000	0.589	0.161	0.250	1017

	Secondary	0.165	0.563	0.00652	0.735	0.0739	0.191	460
	Post-secondary	0.757	0.0786	0.0571	0.893	0.000	0.107	140
45–49	No formal education	0.00372	0.271	0.00297	0.278	0.202	0.519	1344
	Primary	0.0308	0.600	0.00473	0.635	0.154	0.211	422
	Secondary	0.224	0.444	0.160	0.684	0.0963	0.219	187
	Post-secondary	0.711	0.184	0.000	0.868	0.0263	0.0789	38
50–54	No formal education	0.0119	0.212	0.000	0.224	0.184	0.592	419
	Primary	0.0178	0.553	0.000	0.571	0.0893	0.339	56
	Secondary	0.050	0.450	0.000	0.500	0.100	0.400	20
	Post-secondary	1.00	0.000	0.000	1.000	0.000	0.000	10

*Figures in this row show that 86.6% of married women aged between 30 and 34 years who have some secondary education are employed in market work, 1.44% are cooperative workers and 11.9% are not employed. Furthermore, the figures show that 68.9% of married women are wage earners, 13.9% are self-employed and 3.83% are employers.

Figure 16.2 Labour market participation rate and years of schooling of married women (ages 30–54 years).

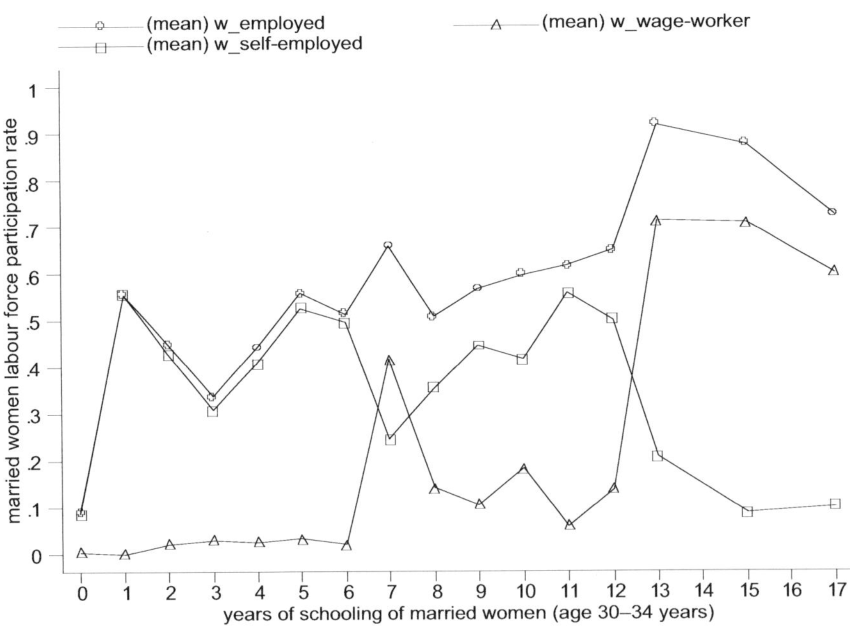

Figure 16.3 Labour market participation rate and years of schooling of married women (ages 30–34 years).

discriminate against women. Table 16.5 shows that only 47 per cent of wage workers are professionals, administrative workers and teachers. Since these are the jobs that clearly require a level of education, that is above the first six years, labour market segmentation may not be a good explanation for the observed low response of wage market participation to schooling at the primary level of education.

In summary, the observed pattern suggests that primary education plays a vital role in getting women to substitute time in self-employment for home time, while post-secondary education motivates the substitution of both time in self-employment and time in home work with wage employment. Thus, the preliminary examination of the Nigeria labour force data shows that better educated women tend to participate more in the labour market, after controlling for age. The observed patterns are an indication that female labour supply behaviour is guided by considerations of relative productivity of time in home and market work. The strength of the relationship between female schooling and labour market participation will, however, need to be established by a formalized model of female labour supply which controls also for the husband's wage opportunities as approximated by his schooling.

16.5 Empirical model specification and estimation

16.5.1 Model specification and description

The following specifications of the female labour supply function are estimated:

Model 1

$$L_j = \alpha_0 + \alpha_1 S_f + \alpha_2 S_m + \gamma_1 E_f + \gamma_2 E_f^2 + \lambda_1 D97 + \lambda_2 D98 + \mu \qquad (16.4)$$

Model 2

$$L_j = \beta_0 + \beta_1 S_{fp} + \beta_2 S_{fs} + \beta_3 S_{fps} + \beta_7 S_m + \gamma_1 E_f + \gamma_2 E_f^2 + \lambda_1 D97 + \lambda_2 D98 + \mu \qquad (16.5)$$

where

- $j = 1,2,3$
- L_1 is total, overall or aggregate labour market participation (wage employment or self-employment) indicator variable (1 for labour market participation and 0 for non-employed/home workers)
- L_2 is wage market participation indicator variable (1 for wage market participation and 0 for non-wage market workers (i.e. self-employed + home workers))
- L_3 is self-employment participation indicator variable (1 for participation in self-employment and 0 for others (wage workers + home workers))
- S_f is the total years of schooling of woman, undifferentiated by levels (0–17)
- E_f is the number of years of working experience of woman (potential)[11]

- E_f^2 is the quadratic term of years of working experience multiplied by 10^{-2}
- S_{fp} is the number of years of primary schooling of woman (0–6)
- S_{fs} is the number of years of secondary schooling of woman (0–6)
- S_{fps} is the number of years of post-secondary schooling of woman (0–5)
- S_m is the total years of schooling of husband, undifferentiated by levels (0–17)
- $D97$ is the indicator variable for period 1997/98
- $D98$ is the indicator variable for period 1998/99
- μ captures the effect of excluded explanatory variables and is assumed to be independent and identically distributed.

The empirical model will take the form of a probability model (PM), since the dependent variable is a one–zero dummy for participation in market work. The estimated coefficients of schooling will provide estimates of the likelihood of a woman with one additional year of total, primary, secondary or post-secondary education engaging in market work.

The first model (expression 16.4) investigates the effect of total years of schooling of women on market work decision. It assumes that both the average and marginal effects of years of schooling on the likelihood of market work participation does not differ across levels of education (primary, secondary, post-secondary). The model also assumes a linear relationship between schooling and labour market participation. Theoretically, we expect that α_1 is positive.

The second specification (expression 16.5) assumes that differences exist in the marginal effects of increasing years of schooling across education levels (primary, secondary and post-secondary), but retains the restriction of linearity of the effect of schooling within each level of education. α_1 is split into three component parts, β_1, β_2 and β_3. The expected sign for β_1, β_2 and β_3 is positive for wage market and overall labour market participation. In self-employment β_1 is expected to be positive while β_2 and β_3 are expected to carry a negative sign (see Figure 16.2).

Factors such as non-labour income of family, family background, husband's premarital assets, woman's landholding, schooling distance, market distance, were excluded from the estimated model for labour market participation because of data limitations. Other factors such as location (rural/urban), religion, health, family size and family structure were excluded primarily to avoid simultaneous equation bias, since their values are the result of past or current decisions of the family and their observed correlation with labour force participation may not be causal or behavioural.

However, we introduce the husband's years of schooling (S_m) for two purposes. First, to control for husband's potential market wage opportunities and, second, to capture the effects of some of the excluded exogenous right hand side variables, such as family background. We expect husband's education to be a fair proxy for family background, because women whose parents are more educated and more market-work-oriented are likely to marry men with more education.

Both the linear and non-linear probability models are estimated to judge the robustness of the schooling coefficient estimates. Both techniques are expected to give similar results except in cases where the distribution of the categorical dependent variable is highly skewed.[12]

16.5.2 Test of hypotheses

The following hypotheses are tested with the empirical models estimated in this study. The first test is the test of non-linearity from model 2 in expression 16.5. The null hypothesis states that the marginal effect of female schooling on labour supply behaviour is equal across levels of education (i.e. H_0: $\beta_1=\beta_2=\beta_3$). If this null hypothesis of equality in the linear coefficients of schooling at the three different levels of education is rejected, the relative magnitudes of β_1, β_2 and β_3 will indicate the relative importance of each level of education to the labour supply behaviour of married women.

The second test is the test of significance of the coefficients of female schooling from models 1 and 2 in expressions 16.4 and 16.5. The null hypothesis states that the marginal effect of total, primary, secondary and post-secondary schooling on labour market participation of married women is significantly different from zero (i.e. H_0: $\alpha_1\neq0$; $\beta_1\neq0$; $\beta_2\neq0$; $\beta_3\neq0$). For example, if this null hypothesis is rejected at the primary level of education for wage employment, it would imply that the marginal productivity of primary schooling in wage employment is not different from marginal productivity of schooling in non-wage employment. Furthermore, an inability to reject the null hypothesis at primary level of education for overall labour market employment (wage+self-employment) would imply that marginal productivity of primary schooling in market work is greater than marginal productivity of primary schooling in home or non-market work.

16.5.3 Econometric challenges in the estimation of the coefficient of female schooling

The first estimation problem that may impose some limitation on the results of this study is the possibility of sample selection bias. Even though the static family labour supply framework adopted for this investigation necessitates the use of only women who report information on their spouse, restricting the sample to this subset of the total sample of women may subject my estimate of the effect of schooling on the probability of labour market participation to selection bias. This problem may arise if the married women are systematically more likely to stay out of the labour market because of the market wealth and productive capacity of their husbands. Table 16.4 for example, shows that participation rate in market work is substantially lower among married women (44 per cent) than single women (92 per cent), implying that marital status rightfully belongs to the labour market participation equation. This is likely to result in a biased estimate of the effect of schooling on labour market participation of all women, if schooling is correlated with marital status. Specifically, if the probability of living with a spouse declines with schooling, we are faced with an upward selection bias, and our estimated schooling coefficient will overstate the true population parameter. If, on the other hand, probability of getting married increases with schooling, there will be a downward selection bias and an underestimation of the population parameter by the sample estimate of schooling effect.

Table 16.7 shows that the probability of living with a spouse varies systematically with schooling conditional on age.[13] It is surprising, though, to observe that, rather than an expected negative correlation between schooling and marital status, the data show a positive association for a larger proportion of the observation.[14]

Since schooling is positively correlated with the probability of being married in this population, as shown for most age groups in Table 16.7, we expect the estimate of schooling coefficients in the labour market participation equation to be biased downwards, if marital status is a true source of selectivity bias in this model.

To adequately address this problem we would need to model the marriage market and use the selection-bias correction technique of Heckman (1979) to correct for selectivity bias in the estimate of the schooling coefficient. This approach will, however, not be adopted in this chapter because of the difficulty of finding a suitable identifier for the decision to live with a spouse which will not be correlated with the error term in the labour force participation equation as done in Schultz (1990a). In other words, data limitation does not offer a reasonable basis for identifying this structural model. However, to gain some insight into the extent of the bias we may be confronted with, I estimate the schooling effects for our restricted sample and compare the estimates with that of the sub-sample of single women.

A comparison of the estimated marginal effects of schooling for married women and single women (see Tables A16.1 and A16.2 in the Appendix, www.csae.ox.ac.uk/books) does not provide conclusive evidence of the presence of a significant downward selection bias in the estimates for the sample of married women, especially for the overall labour market estimates. Thus, our estimate of marginal effects of schooling on labour supply behaviour of married women is not likely to be substantially different from the effect for the entire population of women.

A second reason why the results of this study should be interpreted with caution is the possibility that schooling is endogenous to the labour market participation model. The estimates of the coefficient on female schooling would be biased if there exist certain characteristics, different from their educational attainment, that make women who have more schooling to be more likely to engage in market work (for example, ability bias). This factor must be such that, even without schooling, such a woman would still be more likely to engage in market work. Duflo (2001) presents a case where exogenous variations in schooling were generated through the use of a nationwide school construction programme in Indonesia as an identifying instrument for schooling. Even though we note the possibility of endogenous schooling, the unavailability of data to effectively endogenize schooling in this model is a limitation of this study. In any case, this limitation does not diminish the importance of these results in giving us a first indication of the effect of education on labour market participation in Nigeria using the labour force survey data due to the following reasons. First, it has been argued that, since schooling itself may be measured with a certain degree of classical measurement error, the resulting attenuation bias of classical measurement error may offset the upward ability bias that leads to the possible upward bias of the coefficient of education. Second, since the expected underestimation of the schooling coefficient

Table 16.7 Proportion of women who are married or single by age group and level of education

Age	Education level	Married with information on spouse	Married with no information on spouse	Single women	No. of observations
30–34	No education	0.843	0.130	0.0272	9472
	Primary education	0.792	0.110	0.0988	2883
	Secondary education	0.760	0.104	0.137	2021
	Post-secondary education	0.647	0.102	0.251	323
35–39	No education	0.731	0.214	0.0544	7951
	Primary education	0.732	0.159	0.108	2662
	Secondary education	0.698	0.163	0.138	1469
	Post-secondary education	0.738	0.127	0.134	378
40–44	No education	0.480	0.440	0.080	7262
	Primary education	0.509	0.319	0.173	2000
	Secondary education	0.568	0.305	0.127	810
	Post-secondary education	0.660	0.236	0.104	212
45–49	No education	0.281	0.558	0.161	4785
	Primary education	0.288	0.447	0.265	1467
	Secondary education	0.371	0.441	0.187	503
	Post-secondary education	0.342	0.486	0.171	111
50–54	No education	0.0989	0.639	0.262	4233
	Primary education	0.0734	0.659	0.267	763
	Secondary education	0.0803	0.719	0.201	249
	Post-secondary education	0.146	0.687	0.164	67

due to downward selection bias is likely to offset the expected overestimation of the schooling coefficient due to endogeneity, the net effect of these biases may approach zero. Third, the introduction of the years of schooling of the husband into the model is likely to correct for some of the potential effect of ability bias in this model.

16.6 Results and discussion

16.6.1 Description of some key model variables

The average married woman has 2.62 years of schooling (see Table A16.3 in the Appendix, www.csae.ox.ac.uk/books). This is made up of 1.91, 0.63 and 0.06 years of primary, secondary and post-secondary schooling respectively. Furthermore, while women engaged in market work (wage or self-employment) have an average of 5.7 years of schooling, the average non-employed woman (mainly homemakers) has attended school for only about 1.22 years. The average female wage worker has 11 years of schooling, while the average self-employed worker has had 4.82 years of schooling.

Thus, among married women in Nigeria, average total years of schooling are highest for wage earners and lowest for the non-employed, implying that, on average, wage workers are more educated than non-wage workers and market workers are more educated than home/non-market workers. Specifically, the average wage worker has 6.2 more years of schooling than the average self-employed worker and 9.8 more years of schooling than the average home/non-market worker.

For comparison, on average, husbands have 3.67 years of schooling. While husbands who are wage workers have an average of 11.3 years of schooling, self-employed and non-employed husbands have an average of 6.2 and 2.07 years of schooling respectively. Thus, on average, husbands have 1.05 more years of schooling than wives. Male wage workers have just 0.3 more years of education than wives who are wage workers, while male self-employed workers have 1.22 more years of schooling than self-employed wives.

About 30 per cent of married women are engaged in market work. 4 per cent are engaged in wage work and 26 per cent in non-wage market work (self-employment). 56 per cent are full-time home workers while 14 per cent are unpaid family workers (called cooperative workers).

16.6.2 Non-linearity in the effect of schooling on women's labour market participation

The results show that the relationship between the labour market participation and schooling of women is non-linear. The evidence of non-linearity is the different marginal effects estimated for different levels of education in all three equations (aggregate market, wage market and self-employment equations). I estimate that one additional year of primary, secondary and post-secondary education will increase the likelihood of aggregate labour market participation of women by

5.5 per cent, 1.7 per cent and 5.2 per cent respectively (see Table 16.8). For wage employment, the numbers are –0.001 per cent, 2.9 per cent and 15.2 per cent (see Table 16.9) and, for self-employment, 5.4 per cent, –1.2 per cent and –10.8 per cent respectively (see Table 16.10). Thus, while the marginal effects of schooling on women's labour market participation increase from primary to post-secondary education in wage employment, they decline in the self-employment sector. This is evidence of a trade-off between the two sectors.[15] The results from the estimation of this model fairly approximate the bivariate graphical relationship between labour market participation rate and years of schooling as depicted in Figures 16.2 and 16.3 (see also Figures A16.1–A16.4 in the Appendix, www.csae.ox.ac.uk/books) discussed in Section 16.4.

16.6.3 Effect of total years schooling on aggregate labour market participation of married women

The results presented in Table 16.8 show that an additional year of total schooling could increase the aggregate labour market participation (wage employment plus self-employment) rate of married women by as much as 4 per cent. Thus an additional year of female schooling on the average would increase labour market participation by 4 percentage points, from its current level of 30 per cent to 34 per cent.

Furthermore, Table 16.8 shows that one additional year of primary, secondary and post-secondary education will increase the likelihood of aggregate labour market participation of women by 5.5 per cent, 1.7 per cent and 5.2 per cent respectively, suggesting that the marginal productivity of schooling is higher in market work (wage employment plus self-employment) than in home/non-market work at all levels of education. However, it is important to note that secondary school education has the smallest marginal effect on married women's decision to engage in market work. This may be interpreted as indicating that the marginal productivities of schooling in home and market work are closest at the secondary school level of education. The result is a V-shaped curve of relative productivity of schooling in market and home work, implying that investment in primary and post-secondary education has the greatest potential for increasing aggregate labour market participation of married women in Nigeria.

Another way of interpreting this result has to do with the quality of secondary school education in Nigeria. The result may be evidence that secondary education in Nigeria does not prepare female students adequately for the labour market. This may be a consequence of the low funding of secondary education relative to primary and tertiary education. Participants at the first regional conference on secondary education in Africa held in Kampala, 2003, stressed the neglect of secondary education by both African governments and donor agencies and argued that increased funding of secondary education is compulsory for the educational development of Africa. It was suggested that every child should be given the opportunity to complete a high-quality and relevant lower secondary school education.

Table 16.8 Probability model regression results for total market employment

Explanatory variables	**LPM**	**Probit**	**LPM**	**Probit**
Wife's total years of schooling	0.0404 (46.2)	0.0395 (39.99)		
Wife's years of primary schooling			0.0550 (42.9)	0.0527 (37.21)
Wife's years of secondary schooling			0.0171 (9.66)	0.0155 (8.00)
Wife's years of post-secondary schooling			0.0519 (8.96)	0.0675 (8.50)
Wife's years of potential work experience	0.0326 (10.72)	0.0416 (11.58)	0.0251 (8.15)	0.0332 (9.06)
Quadratic of wife's work experience $\times 10^{-2}$	–0.0484 (–7.26)	–0.0629 (–8.08)	–0.0336 (–4.99)	–0.0463 (–5.84)
Husband's total years of schooling	0.0160 (21.45)	0.017 (20.67)	0.0147 (19.7)	0.0159 (19.2)
1997/98 year dummy	–0.0127 (–2.29)	–0.0153 (–2.29)	–0.125 (–2.26)	–0.152 (–2.28)
1998/9 year dummy	–0.00668 (–1.13)	–0.0082 (–1.16)	–0.00585 (–1.00)	–0.0074 (–1.04)
Constant	–0.311 (–9.29)		–0.232 (–6.82)	
Adjusted R^2	0.255		0.262	
Pseudo-R^2		0.210		0.216

Number of observations is 28,691.
Reported parameter estimates are marginal effects.
Figures in parentheses are *t*-values.

Table 16.9 Probability model regression results for wage employment[a]

Explanatory variables	**LPM**	**Probit**	**LPM**	**Probit**
Wife's total years of schooling	0.0181 (45.33)	0.00358 (28.1)		
Wife's years of primary schooling			–0.000911 (–1.67)	0.00248 (8.22)
Wife's years of secondary schooling			0.0286 (37.98)	0.00512 (18.67)
Wife's years of post-secondary schooling			0.152 (61.34)	0.0127 (19.15)
Wife's potential years of work experience	–0.00656 (–4.72)	0.000144 (0.33)	0.00893 (6.80)	0.00233 (3.72)
Quadratic of wife's years of work experience × 10^{-2}	0.0139 (4.57)	0.00397 (0.39)	–0.0177 (–6.14)	–0.00403 (–2.81)
Husband's total years of schooling	0.00102 (3.00)	0.00873 (7.59)	0.00273 (8.62)	0.00132 (8.61)
1997/98 year dummy	0.0120 (0.47)	0.000415 (0.43)	0.00181 (0.77)	0.000853 (0.66)
1998/99 year dummy	0.00329 (1.22)	0.000975 (0.96)	0.00172 (0.69)	0.00126 (0.92)
Constant	0.0597 (3.89)		–0.0105 (–7.2)	
Adjusted R^2	0.168		0.284	
Pseudo-R^2		0.362		0.386

a A notable problem with the reported estimates of probability of wage employment is that the estimated coefficients differ substantially between the linear probability model and the probit model approaches. Since this divergence was not observed for self-employed and total workforce in Tables 16.7 and 16.5 respectively, a possible explanation may be the very small proportion of the population that is engaged in wage jobs. The proportion is below 4 per cent in this dataset. Given the very limited amount of observations on women in wage employment, it is understandable that the probit model which utilizes that MLE estimation procedure will return a coefficient biased towards zero. In such a case, the probability model estimate through OLS estimation procedure would be more reliable.
Number of observations is 28,691.
Reported parameter estimates are marginal effects.
Figures in parentheses are *t*-values.

Table 16.10 Probability model regression results for self-employment (women living with spouse and aged between 30 and 54 years)

Explanatory variables	**LPM**	**Probit**	**LPM**	**Probit**
Wife's total years of schooling	0.0215 (23.8)	0.0200 (22.5)		
Wife's years of primary schooling			0.0540 (41.72)	0.0480 (37.2)
Wife's years of secondary schooling			–0.0123 (–6.91)	–0.0091 (–5.24)
Wife's years of post-secondary schooling			–0.108 (–18.4)	–0.113 (–14.5)
Wife's potential years of work experience	0.0402 (12.8)	0.0429 (13.2)	0.0165 (5.30)	0.0209 (6.22)
Quadratic of wife's years of work experience × 10^{-2}	–0.0647 (–9.38)	–0.0685 (–9.67)	–0.0168 (–2.47)	–0.0238 (–3.28)
Husband's total years of schooling	0.0147 (19.05)	0.0144 (18.8)	0.0116 (15.4)	0.0120 (15.6)
1997/98 year dummy	–0.0141 (–2.47)	–0.0150 (–2.47)	–0.146 (–2.62)	–0.01605 (–2.63)
1998/9 year dummy	–0.0111 (–1.83)	–0.0122 (–1.89)	–0.00866 (–1.46)	–0.00966 (–1.49)
Constant	–0.380 (–10.9)		–0.130 (–3.78)	
Adjusted R^2	0.124		0.1712	
Pseudo-R^2		0.109		0.148

Number of observations is 28,691.
Reported parameter estimates are marginal effects.
Figures in parentheses are *t*-values.

16.6.4 Effect of female schooling on wage and non-wage market participation rates

According to Tables 16.9 and 16.10, a marginal increase in total years of schooling would raise labour market participation rate among married women by 6 per cent in the wage sector and 2.9 per cent in the self-employment sector. However, a decomposition of total years of schooling into primary, secondary and post-secondary school effects shows that the observed positive effect of total years of schooling on labour market participation derives substantially from the marginal effect of post-secondary schooling in the wage sector and primary schooling in the self-employment sector.

We also observe a trade-off between the schooling effect in the wage and self-employment sectors. Specifically, an additional year of primary education decreases participation of married women in wage employment insignificantly by 0.001 per cent and increases participation probability in self-employment by 5.4 per cent. In contrast, an additional year of post-secondary education increases labour market participation probability by 15.2 per cent in the wage sector and decreases participation probability in self-employment by 10.8 per cent. With an additional year of secondary education, the likelihood of participation in the wage market increases by a modest 2.86 per cent and likelihood of participation in self-employment declines by 1.23 per cent. This trade-off fairly approximates the results of the graphical analysis in Section 16.4.

Thus, increasing participation in self-employment is motivated more by increasing years of primary education, while increase in wage market participation is enhanced more by increasing years of post-secondary education.

In terms of marginal productivity of schooling, the estimates of schooling coefficients for the wage sector would imply that, at the primary level of education, additional years of female schooling are associated with a greater rise in productivity of married women in non-wage work than in wage employment. However, at the post-secondary level of education, the result suggests that additional years of schooling raise productivity in wage work relative to productivity in non-wage work, resulting in a substantially positive marginal effect of schooling on wage market participation. Thus, increasing primary schooling for women in Nigeria would tend to raise productivity in non-wage market work (self-employment) more than productivity in wage work, while increasing post-secondary education would probably raise wage productivity more than productivity in non-wage work. The results also suggest that the marginal productivity of primary schooling in self-employment is higher than in both home work and wage work.

16.6.5 Implications of results for Nigerian education policy

The most recent education policy in Nigeria is the Universal Basic Education (UBE) programme, which was signed into law in 2004. The policy provides for federal government assisted compulsory schooling up to the first three years of secondary school, by which time a student would have accumulated nine years of schooling. A major thrust of the policy is to address the problem of low girl enrolment in schools.

Given the results of this study, any education policy that would bring about a rise in the average years of schooling among married women, from the current average of 2.62 years to 6 years (that is, primary education completed) would imply a 13 percentage point rise in labour market participation (wage or self-employment) from the current level of 30 per cent to 43 per cent. Furthermore, the attainment of an average of nine years of female schooling (junior secondary school completed), would imply a 25 percentage points rise in participation rate to 55 per cent.

Thus, raising the average years of female schooling from the present 2.6 years to 9 years (that is, junior high school or middle school completed) could double labour market participation rates among married women in Nigeria.

Education policy could also change the composition of the female work force through the observed trade-off between wage employment and self-employment as education level increases from primary to post-secondary level. From the results of the study, a rise in the average level of education from the present 2.62 to 6 years would have no effect on the wage market participation rate, which currently stands at 4 per cent. A further rise in average education to nine years would increase wage market participation rate from 4 to 11 per cent, while achieving 14 years of schooling (or two years of post-secondary schooling: Ordinary National Diploma, National Certificate of Education, Registered Nursing Certificate and so on) would raise the participation rate in the wage sector by 30 percentage points from 11 to 41 per cent. On the other hand, an increase in years of schooling to six years would imply a rise in the rate of participation in non-wage market work (or self-employment) to 48 per cent from the current 26 per cent. A further rise in schooling to an average of nine years would decrease the participation rate in self-employment by three percentage points from 48 per cent to 45 per cent. Achieving two years of post-secondary education (or 14 years of schooling) would further diminish the participation rate in self-employment to 21 per cent.

Thus, increasing the average years of schooling of girls to nine, as envisioned under the UBE programme, would only slightly increase the ratio of participation rates in wage employment relative to aggregate market participation to 0.20 (11/5) from the current 0.140 (4.17/26). To significantly change the sectoral composition of female labour market participation, education policy would need to encourage increased post-secondary school attainments among women. For example, the results of this study suggest that, if average years of post-secondary schooling increase from the current 0.06 years (or two weeks) to about two years, the ratio of wage market participation rates to aggregate market participation rate would approach 0.66 (41/62).

16.7 Conclusion

This study investigates the strength of relationship between female schooling and labour market participation using a sample of married women between the ages of 30 and 54 years from Nigeria. The importance of the investigation derives first from the argument that the effect of female education on economic growth and poverty reduction depends substantially on the strength of the linkage between female schooling and labour market participation decisions of women. Specifically, I analysed the contributions of primary, secondary and post-secondary schooling of women to cross-sectional variations in female participation probabilities in overall market, wage and self-employment, and drew implications for the underlying relationship between market and non-market productivity of schooling. The major findings of the study are summarized as follows.

First, I find that the pattern shown by the estimated reduced form labour market participation model reasonably approximates the graphical analysis of the relationship between female schooling and labour market participation rates. Specifically, I find that the relationship between women's labour market participation and years of schooling is significantly positive and non-linear across levels of education. In addition, I find that the relationship involves a substantial amount of trade-off between wage and self-employment sectors as education level increases from primary to post-secondary. Participation rate in self-employment is enhanced more by increases in years of primary schooling, while participation rate in wage employment responds more to increases in years of post-secondary schooling among married women.

Secondary schooling was found to exert the least influence on the decision of a woman to substitute time in market work for time in home work, suggesting that the existing low-quality and inadequately funded secondary education does not sufficiently equip married women to gain employment in the wage sector. Given the results of this study, the observed increase in female labour force participation rates over the past three decades could be explained in part by increases in average years of primary, secondary and post-secondary schooling.

The results also suggest that any education policy that would increase the average years of schooling among married women in Nigeria from the current 2.6 years to 9 years (junior high school or middle school completed) would almost double labour market participation rates by achieving an increase from 30 per cent to 55 per cent. A sector decomposition of these effects shows that wage work participation rates would increase from 4 per cent to 11 per cent and self-employment participation rates would rise from 26 per cent to 44 per cent as years of female schooling increase from the current 2.6 years to 9 years (junior high school completed).

Thus a substantial increase in female enrolment and completion of six years of primary schooling and the first three years of secondary education, as outlined in the new Nigerian universal basic education policy, would potentially double labour market participation rates among married women in Nigeria. However, the participation rates in wage employment relative to self-employment are not likely to increase significantly unless the average level of post-secondary education is significantly increased from its present level of less than one month to about two years.

Notes

1 I thank the Economic Growth Center, Yale University, USA and the Rockefeller Foundation Grant for Postdoctoral Research on the Economics of the Family in Low Income Countries for providing the financial support for this study. I am especially grateful to T. Paul Schultz for his comments on previous drafts of this chapter. I also appreciate the useful comments I received from participants at the Economic Growth Center Development Lunch Seminar series and participants at the Conference on Growth, Poverty Reduction and Human Development in Africa, organized by the Centre for Study of African Economies (CSAE), Oxford University, UK, 2004.

Finally I wish to acknowledge the Federal Office of Statistics (FOS), Lagos, Nigeria, who provided me with the Nigerian labour force survey data used for the analysis in this chapter. I am responsible for any errors that remain.

2 GDP per capita declined from $264 to $253 during the period (World Bank, 2001)

3 All these are indications that labour market demand would have been on the decline during the period.

4 Factors that have been found in empirical studies to be correlated with the probability of a woman's entering into the labour market include observed family income net of earnings of wife, variance of family income net of wife's, potential market wage indicator (education level or realized market wages of wife), home wage of wife, taste (or a shift variable indicating influence of socio-affiliation), family background, and religion (Spencer, 1973); woman's age, woman's education, husband's education, husband's premarital asset, landholding, schooling distance, market distance, community male wage, community female wage, community child wage (Khandker, 1987); marital status, income other than own earnings, and presence of children under six (Killingsworth and Heckman, 1986); family size, presence of children under six, and family income (Mahoney, 1961). However, Schultz (1980) argues that including many of these variables will introduce simultaneous equation bias into the estimate of schooling effect. Since the values of many of these variables are as a result of past or current decisions of the family, their observed correlation with labour force participation may not be causal or behavioural.

5 Aromolaran (2002) estimates private wage returns to an additional year of primary education for females to be as low as 2 per cent.

6 In contrast, Cain *et al.* (1979) argue that the low level of labour market participation by married women in many developing countries is attributable more to the powerful norms of female seclusion due to patriarchy, which severely restricts women from working outside the family, than a utility maximization-based choice process which is dependent on relative price movements as argued by economists.

7 The GHS is a national household data collection project carried out by the Federal Office of Statistics (FOS). The overall sample includes 24,889 households in 1996/97, 32,024 in 1997/98 and 27,649 in 1998/99, for a total of 375,399 individuals, of whom 54.8 per cent are of age 15 to 64 and considered of labour force age. To my knowledge this dataset has not been widely analysed. The number of females between the ages of 15 and 64 is 104,864.

8 The data show that only 60 per cent of women aged below 30 years claim to be married, while 92 per cent of those between 30 and 40 years are married. This percentage decreases to 70 per cent for those aged 50–54 years, most of whom are unmarried because of the deaths of their husbands.

9 In this study, wage workers are individuals who worked for wage income in the week preceding the survey; self-employed workers are those who worked for income in own-businesses in the week preceding the survey; while the not-employed consist mainly of home-makers who are not looking for work. The 48 per cent reported as the proportion of all women that are not-employed is similar to that estimated from the Nigerian Demographic and Health Survey (DHS) for 1999. The DHS data showed that 50.3 per cent of women in Nigeria did not work in the last 12 months.

10 An International Labour Organization report shows that 10 per cent of the female work force are unpaid family workers, making the 1.4 per cent in this data look more like an understatement. However, if we recategorize cooperative workers as unpaid family labour, the new figures for unpaid family labour would be closer to the ILO figure.

11 Potential work experience was calculated as (age–years of schooling–6) for those with nine or more years of schooling and (age–15) for those with less than nine years of schooling.

12 The LPM estimate is the preferred choice here because of the underlying assumption that the marginal effect of schooling on probability of labour market participation is constant within education levels. Secondly, the estimates of the probit model may become imprecise or biased if the distribution of the values of the categorical dependent variable is heavily skewed. For example, the wage employment equation may face this problem since workers in waged employment are just about 4 per cent of the sample. The result is that 96 per cent of the observations carry a value of 0 while only 4 per cent carry a value of 1 for the dependent variable. With this kind of wage employment data, the probit estimate through maximum likelihood estimation procedure would give a less accurate estimate of the true population parameter compared to the LPM. However, there are two major disadvantages of the LPM. The first is that its predicted outcomes may sometimes fall outside the permissible range of 0 and 1. This becomes a serious problem when we are interested in the predicted probabilities for values of the independent variables that lie towards the tails of the distribution. Secondly, the standard errors of the LPM estimates are not consistent (owing to the heteroskedastic characteristics of the error term). The result is that the LPM model is a less preferred model for testing hypothesis than the probit model. Consequently, we estimate the probit version of these labour market participation models to provide a more robust test of hypothesis for the estimates of schooling effects obtained from the LPM as well as examine the stability of the estimates themselves given different empirical estimation approaches.

13 The increasing likelihood of living with a spouse as schooling increases among older women may be an indication that marital unions are more stable the higher the level of education of the spouses. The stability of conjugal unions of more educated couples may arise from a more efficient process of sorting and matching than for couples with lower levels of education. A second possible explanation for this observed pattern among older women is that life expectancy is likely to be higher for more educated couples. As a result, a lower proportion of unions are broken before the age 54 years among more educated couples than less educated couples.

14 Ages 30–34, 35–39 and 40–54 constitute 29.6 per cent, 25.1 per cent and 45.3 per cent respectively of the sample of married women.

15 Empirically, it is observed that the estimates are fairly robust to difference in specification. That is, estimates from the linear probability model are virtually the same magnitude and direction as estimates from the probit model.

References

Aromolaran, Adebayo B., 2002, 'Private Wage Returns to Schooling in Nigeria (1996–1999)', Economic Growth Center Discussion Paper No 849, Yale University.

Aromolaran, Adebayo B., 2006, 'Estimates of Mincerian Returns to Schooling in Nigeria', *Oxford Development Studies*, 34 (2), 265–292.

Becker, G.S., 1965, 'A Theory of the Allocation of Time', *Economic Journal*, 75 (299), 493–517.

Bloch, Farrell E. and Sharon P. Smith, 1977, 'Human Capital and Labor Market Employment', *Journal of Human Resources*, 12 (4), 550–60.

Cain, Mead, Syeda R. Khanam and Shamasun Nahar, 1979, 'Class Patriarchy and Women's Work in Bangladesh', *Population and Development Review*, 5 (3), 405–38.

Duflo, E., 2001, 'Schooling and Labor Market Consequences of School Construction in Indonesia: Evidence from an Unusual Policy Experiment', *American Economic Review*, 91 (4), 795–813.

Filmer, Deon, 2000, 'Educational Attainment and Enrollment Profiles: A Resource Book Based on an Analysis of Demographic and Health Survey Data', mimeo, Development Research Group, The World Bank.

Heckman, James, 1974, 'Shadow Prices, Market Wages, and Labor Supply', *Econometrica*, 42 (4), 679–94.

Heckman, J.J., 1979, 'Sample Selection Bias as a Specification Error', *Econometrica*, 47 (1), 153–62.

ILO, 1970, *International Labor Organization Year Book of Labor Statistics, 1970*, Geneva: ILO.

ILO, 1992, *International Labor Organization Year Book of Labor Statistics, 1992*, Geneva: ILO.

Khandker, Shahidur R., 1987, 'Labor Market Participation of Married Women in Bangladesh', *Review of Economics and Statistics*, 69 (3), 536–41.

Killingsworth, M., 1983, *Labor Supply*, Cambridge: Cambridge University Press.

Killingsworth, Mark R. and James J. Heckman, 1986, 'Female Labor Supply: A Survey', in O. Ashenfelter and R. Layard (eds), *Handbook of Labor Economics*, Vol. 1, Amsterdam: Elsevier Science Publishers.

Jones, Ethel B. and James E. Long, 1979, 'Human Capital and Labor Market Employment: Additional Evidence for Women', *Journal of Human Resources*, 14 (2), 270–79.

Lam, David and Suzanne Duryea, 1999, 'Effects of Schooling on Fertility, Labor Supply, and Investment in Children, with Evidence from Brazil', *Journal of Human Resources*, 34 (1), 160–92.

Mahoney, Thomas A., 1961, 'Factors Determining Labor Force Participation of Married Women', *Industrial and Labor Review*, 14 (4), 563–77.

Mincer, Jacob, 1963, 'Labor Force Participation of Married Women', in H.G. Lewis (ed.), *Aspects of Labor Economics*, National Bureau of Economic Research, Princeton, NJ: Princeton University Press.

Rosenzweig, Mark R. and T. Paul Schultz, 1989, 'Schooling, Information and Non-Market Productivity: Contraceptive Use and Effectiveness', *American Economic Review*, 72 (4), 803–15.

Schultz, T. Paul, 1980, 'Estimating Labor Supply Functions of Married Women', in James P. Smith (ed.), *Female Labor Supply: Theory and Estimation*, Princeton, NJ: Princeton University Press.

Schultz, T. Paul, 1990a, 'Testing the Neoclassical Model of Family Labor Supply and Fertility', *Journal of Human Resources*, 25 (4), 599–634.

Schultz, T. Paul, 1990b, 'Women's Changing Participation in the Labor Force: A World Perspective', *Economic Development and Cultural Change*, 38 (3), 456–88.

Schultz, T. Paul, 1991, 'International Differences in Labor Force Participation in Families and Firms', Economic Growth Center Discussion Paper 634, Yale University.

Schultz, T. Paul, 2002, 'Why Governments Should Invest More to Educate Girls', *World Development*, 30 (2), 207–25.

Smith, James P., 1980, *Female Labor Supply: Theory and Estimation*, Princeton, NJ: Princeton University Press.

Spencer, Byron G., 1973, 'Determinants of Labor Force Participation of Married Women: A Micro-study of Toronto Households', *Canadian Journal of Economics*, 6 (2), 222–38.

UNDP, 1997, *Human Development Report 2000/2001: Attacking Poverty*, Washington, DC: World Bank.

UNESCO, 2001, 'Statistics on Country Gross School Enrollment Ratios, 1965–1999' (available at www.unesco.org).

Willis, Robert J., 1973, 'A New Approach to the Economic Theory of Fertility Behavior', *Journal of Political Economy*, 81 (2), S14–S64.

World Bank, 2001, *2001 World Bank Development Indicator CD*, Washington, DC: World Bank.

Index

Information in tables is indicated by *table*; information in figures is indicated by *fig*

Made in the USA
Las Vegas, NV
29 November 2025

35369577R00254